ASSER International Sports Law Series

For further volumes:
http://www.springer.com/series/8858

Ian S. Blackshaw

# Sports Marketing Agreements: Legal, Fiscal and Practical Aspects

T·M·C·ASSER PRESS

Springer

Prof. Ian S. Blackshaw
80 rue Principale
62310 Sains-les-Fressin
France
e-mail: ian.blackshaw@orange.fr

ISSN 1874-6926
ISBN 978-90-6704-792-0 e-ISBN 978-90-6704-793-7
DOI 10.1007/978-90-6704-793-7

Library of Congress Control Number: 2011938391



Published by T.M.C. ASSER PRESS, The Hague, The Netherlands www.asserpress.nl

Produced and distributed for T.M.C. ASSER PRESS by Springer-Verlag Berlin Heidelberg



*Cover design:* eStudio Calamar, Berlin/Figueres

Printed on acid-free paper

Springer is part of Springer Science+Business Media (www.springer.com)

## Series Information

Books in the *ASSER International Sports Law Series* chart and comment upon the legal and policy developments in European and international sports law. The books contain materials on interstate organisations and the international sports governing bodies, and will serve as comprehensive and relevant reference tools for all those involved in the area on a professional basis.

The Series is developed, edited and published by the ASSER International Sports Law Centre in The Hague. The Centre's mission is to provide a centre of excellence in particular by providing high-quality research, services and products to the sporting world at large (sports ministries, international—intergovernmental—organisations, sports associations and federations, the professional sports industry, etc.) on both a national and an international basis. The Centre is the co-founder and coordinator of the Hague International Sports Law Academy (HISLA), the purpose of which is the organisation of academic conferences and workshops of international excellence which are held in various parts of the world. Apart from the Series, the Centre edits and publishes *The International Sports Law Journal.*

*Series Editors*
Dr. Robert C. R. Siekmann, Director Asser International Sports Centre
e-mail: r.siekmann@asser.nl

Dr. Janwillem Soek
e-mail: j.soek@asser.nl

M. A. van der Harst LL.M.
e-mail: m.van.der.harst@asser.nl

**Editorial Office**
ASSER International Sports Law Centre
T.M.C. Asser Instituut
P.O. Box 30461
2500 GL, The Hague
The Netherlands
www.sportslaw.nl

ASSER International Sports Law Centre

# Foreword

I am pleased to write the Foreword to Professor Ian Blackshaw's book on the Legal, Fiscal and Practical Aspects of Sports Marketing Agreements, particularly as various sports marketing methods and principles, as he points out in this book, in many ways originated and developed in the United States. Sports marketing has now taken root in the rest of the world as well, and, despite the economic downturn and recession, it continues to flourish.

In his book, Professor Blackshaw adopts an efficient and useful approach to this subject by combining theory with practice. As shown in the Table of Contents, a wide range of sports marketing agreements are covered, including: Sports Broadcasting Agreements, often the life blood of a major sporting event; and New Media Rights Agreements, which often provide sports marketers with an extra dimension for commercializing sports events particularly through online media such as "webcasting."

Of particular importance, the book covers the impact of the European Union (EU) on the commercialization of sports events, particularly the Competition Rules of the EU, which apply whenever sport constitutes an economic activity. As sport becomes a bigger and bigger business around the world it is difficult to conceive of any situation in which the necessary economic activity could be absent. As a result, the EU aspects of sports marketing are very important in practice and must be taken into account when negotiating and drafting sports marketing agreements with a European dimension.

This book also tackles the important impact of tax law and rules on sports marketing. It specifically covers the fiscal aspects of Sports Image Rights Agreements and the need to shelter the considerable revenues that sports personalities, such as David Beckham, may earn from the commercial exploitation of their image in a wide range of consumer goods and services on an international scale.

Professor Blackshaw is a leading authority on the use of Alternative Dispute Resolution (ADR) for the extra-judicial settlement of sports disputes of various kinds, particularly commercial ones that transcend national boundaries. Demonstrating this expertise he includes a comprehensive chapter on ADR and extols its merits for dealing with sports disputes that are bound to arise under a wide range of sports marketing agreements due to the large amounts of money involved and put at risk. Coupled with this focus on ADR, throughout the book he reinforces the need to draft clear and unambiguous agreements as another method to avoid disputes.

Overall, Professor Blackshaw's book contains many useful insights and important information regarding a variety of sports marketing agreements that will be of interest to readers from every aspect of the sports industry, including; sports administrators, rights holders, marketers, advertisers, broadcasters and their professional advisers, and others who are involved in the organization, promotion and commercialization of sports events and personalities. This book will also become a useful resource for academics, researchers, scholars and students in sports marketing and law.

Congratulations to Professor Blackshaw on this important and highly practical book. I recommend this book to individuals involved in sports marketing and sports law around the world. I look forward to relying on it in my own sports law research and courses in the future.

Milwaukee, Spring 2011

Prof. Paul Anderson
Associate Director
National Sports Law Institute
Marquette University Law School
Milwaukee, WI
USA

# Author's Preface

Sport is now big business—worth more than 3% of world trade and 3.7% of the combined GNP of the 27 Member States of the European Union with a population of some 500 million—and a whole new body of law and practice has grown up in the field of the commercialisation of sports events and the exploitation of the image and personality rights of elite athletes, all of which is commonly referred to—in the jargon—as Sports Marketing.

Indeed, without the considerable revenues derived from various forms of Sports Marketing, especially Sponsorship and Sports Broadcasting and New Media Rights—many major sporting events, such as the Olympic Games and the FIFA World Cup, could not be organised and staged; and likewise many athletes could not afford to train and participate in them—much to the disappointment of sports fans around the world.

The aim of this book, therefore, is to provide sports administrators and their professional advisers, especially their lawyers, marketers, media advisers, advertising, PR and sports agents, sports law students and researchers, as well as others involved in the commercialisation, marketing and promotion of major sporting events and sports personalities, with an overview of the legal, fiscal and practical aspects of drafting and enforcing a wide range of standard Sports Marketing Agreements and also particular sports-specific clauses, including so-called 'Morality Clauses' in Sports Image Rights and Endorsement Agreements, particularly relevant to the recent fall from grace of Tiger Woods and, indeed, of other sports personalities.

The book also includes many samples of these Agreements, whose structures and contents are discussed, analysed and explained in the text of the relevant chapters. This special feature of the book will be of particular interest to legal practitioners, sports administrators, agents and managers.

The book includes

- many samples of these Agreements, whose structures and contents are discussed, analysed and explained in the text of the relevant chapters. This special feature of the book will be of particular interest to legal practitioners, sports administrators, agents and managers.

- a chapter on Stadia Naming Rights Agreements, a unique and lucrative form of sports sponsorship, which, like Sports Marketing itself, originated in the States, but is proving to be popular elsewhere.[1] A General Precedent of such an Agreement is also included.
- the important aspect of dispute resolution, especially the various forms of alternative dispute resolution (ADR) methods and mechanisms, especially commercial Mediation, that particularly lend themselves to the *extra judicial* settlement of sports-related disputes, which, not surprisingly, with all the money sloshing around in world sport, are on the increase. Samples of 'Dispute Resolution Clauses' are included and discussed in the chapter devoted to this subject.
- the European Union (EU) aspects of the subject, especially the application of the EU Competition Rules to restrictive provisions, such as territorial restrictions in Sports Licensing and Merchandising Agreements.
- a chapter on some of the tax aspects of the subject, particularly in relation to the possibilities of the tax sheltering off-shore of the substantial financial benefits of the licensing of sports image and personality rights of leading sports persons.

This is a fascinating and money-spinning field of sports law and it is the author's further aim that this book will quickly establish itself as the leading work of its kind, combining as it uniquely does the theory and the practice.

The Law is stated as of 1 January, 2011 according to the sources available at that date.

The Hague, Spring 2011

Prof. Ian Blackshaw
Honorary Fellow
ASSER International Sports Law Centre
The Hague
The Netherlands

[1] For example, the Arsenal Football Club's new 'Emirates' Stadium in London.

# Acknowledgments

The author of this book wishes to thank Professor Robert Siekmann, the director of the TMC Asser Instituut International Sports Law Centre, The Hague, The Netherlands, and Dr. Janwillem Soek, the Centre's senior researcher, for all their interest, encouragement and support for this book and its final editing; Mr. Philip van Tongeren, the director of TMC Asser Publishing, for publishing the book in the Asser International Sports Law Series; and my good friend and learned colleague, Keith McGarry, for locating several of the precedents included in the book; and last, but, by no means least, my wife Christine for all her patience and understanding whilst I was writing the book.

Of course, in the time-honoured phrase, the responsibility for the book as a whole, including any errors that may have crept into the final text, rests with the author alone.

# Contents

# Abbreviations

| | |
|---|---|
| ABTA | Association of British Travel Agents |
| ADR | Alternative Dispute Resolution |
| ATMs | Automated Teller Machines |
| CAS | Court of Arbitration for Sport |
| CJEU | Court of Justice of the European Union |
| CO | Swiss Code of Obligations |
| EBU | European Broadcasting Union |
| ECHR | European Convention on Human Rights |
| EEA | European Economic Area |
| EU | European Union |
| FCPA | US Foreign Corrupt Practices Act |
| FIFA | International Federation of Association Football |
| HMRC | Her Majesty's Revenue and Customs |
| ICANN | Internet Corporation for Assigned Names |
| ICC | Incorporated Cell Company |
| IMG | International Management Group |
| IOC | International Olympic Committee |
| IP | Intellectual Property |
| IPRs | Intellectual Property Rights |
| IR | Image Rights |
| IRRA | Image Rights Representation Agreement |
| ISL | International Sport Leisure and Culture |
| KNVB | Royal Netherlands Football Association |
| LOCOG | Organising Committee of the London 2012 Summer Olympics |
| NBC | National Broadcasting Company |
| NFF | Norwegian Football Federation |
| NIC | National Insurance Contributions |
| OECD | Organisation for Economic Co-operation and Development |
| PAYE | Pay-As-You-Earn |
| PCC | Protected Cell Company |
| PCT | Patent Cooperation Treaty |

| | |
|---|---|
| PLT | Patent Law Treaty |
| SFCs | Specialist Financial Centres |
| SOPARFI | Société de Participations Financières |
| TRIPS | Trade Related Aspects of Intellectual Property Rights |
| UDRP | Uniform Domain Name Dispute Resolution Policy |
| UEFA | Union of European Football Associations |
| VIK | Value in Kind |
| WIPO | World Intellectual Property Organization |

# Chapter 1
# Introductory Remarks

## 1.1 Introductory Remarks

Sport is now big business accounting for more than 3% of world trade. In the European Union, sport has developed into a discrete business worth more than 2% of the combined GNP of the 27 Member States comprising some 500 million citizens.

Indeed, according to Sepp Blatter, the President of FIFA, the World Governing Body of Football—and the Author of this Book would entirely agree with him—sport is now a 'product' in its own right, and there is much to play for not only on but also off the field of play. Whether this is a good thing as far as the integrity and so-called 'Corinthian Values' of sport is concerned is, of course, another matter—and, perhaps, a subject for another Book!

For example, licensing and merchandising rights in relation to major sports events, such as the FIFA World Cup and the Olympic Games, are 'hot properties', commanding high returns for the rights owners ('licensors') and concessionaires ('licensees') alike.[1]

Again, the commercial exploitation of the image rights of famous sports persons, such as David Beckham and Tiger Woods, is also big business.[2]

Likewise, sports broadcasting and new media rights are also money-spinners. For example, the English FA Premier League sold its broadcasting rights for the 2010–2013 seasons for another record sum of £1.782 billion!

The commercialisation and marketing of sport, sports events, sports teams and sports personalities has developed over the last 30 years or so into a discrete sports marketing industry with its own peculiarities and characteristics.

---

[1] See Chaps. 10 and 11 by Ian Blackshaw in '*Sports Law*' by Gardiner et al., 2006, Third Edition, Cavendish Publishing, London.

[2] See '*Sports Image Rights in Europe*', Ian S. Blackshaw & Robert C. R. Siekmann (Eds.), 2005 TMC Asser Press, The Hague, The Netherlands.

I. S. Blackshaw, *Sports Marketing Agreements: Legal, Fiscal and Practical Aspects*,
ASSER International Sports Law Series, DOI: 10.1007/978-90-6704-793-7_1,

Much of the pioneering work in the field of sports marketing was done by the late Horst Dassler of the sports goods and clothing manufacturer, ADIDAS, through the Swiss-based sports marketing company, International Sport Leisure and Culture (ISL), which he founded.[3] He revolutionised the marketing of the Olympic Games, by introducing a unified and global approach, and other major international sporting events, including basketball, football and track and field, through the development of sponsorship, merchandising and other commercial and promotional techniques. Another pioneer in sports marketing was the late Mark McCormack, who founded International Management Group (IMG), which is still going strong today. His particular *forte* was the promotion and marketing of major sports personalities, such as the legendary golfer, Arnold Palmer, who was his first client; and IMG was also Tiger Woods' first Agency.

[3] In the summer of 2001, ISL was declared Bankrupt by a Swiss Court with debts of reputedly £350 million. The insolvency of ISL was largely due to ever increasing guarantees given by the Company in connection with the marketing of major international sports events, which it could not fulfil.

# Chapter 2
# Negotiating Drafting and Interpreting Sports Marketing Agreements: Some General Legal and Practical Points and Considerations

## 2.1 Introductory Remarks

It has been generally well said, that if a commercial deal makes business sense, it also makes legal sense and it is relatively easy, therefore, to draw up the corresponding legal agreement—and, where necessary, enforce it. And this is certainly true of Sports Marketing Agreements, which come in all shapes and sizes. All the commercial and financial arrangements that have been negotiated need to be covered by clearly drafted provisions to avoid any legal challenges to the validity of the Sports Marketing Agreement concerned on the grounds of its uncertainty. Otherwise, the parties may find themselves with a void Agreement, which they cannot rely on or legally enforce. Clarity is the name of the game!

Before dealing with the subjects of drafting and interpreting Sports Marketing Agreements, which, as will be seen, go hand in hand, a word or two on the general principles of negotiating contracts generally would not be inappropriate.

## 2.2 Negotiating Sports Marketing Agreements

When negotiating Commercial Agreements generally and Sports Marketing Agreements, in particular, especially those with an international dimension, attention should be paid to the following general principles of negotiating.

Negotiating is an art—not a science—and there are a number of useful guidelines to be followed in order to achieve a successful outcome.

In basic terms negotiating is 'getting to yes'. Like any other form of advocacy—persuading another person to accept your point of view—a negotiation needs to be carefully *planned*. Before you start, you need to know clearly what your objectives are and how you are going to achieve them. Make sure, however, that your objectives are *realistic* and *reasonably achievable*.

I. S. Blackshaw, *Sports Marketing Agreements: Legal, Fiscal and Practical Aspects*,
ASSER International Sports Law Series, DOI: 10.1007/978-90-6704-793-7_2,

An important part of the planning process is to gather as much *intelligence* about the other side in the negotiation as possible. You will need to know, amongst other things, the kind of people you are dealing with; their strengths and weaknesses; and their aims and objectives. Be prepared generally!

Again, as part of the planning process, the negotiation needs to be *structured* into distinct phases. The first phase should identify any points of agreement and get those out of the way; the next, any points of disagreement and the reasons for them. The following phases should be to evaluate, from your own point of view and that of the other side, the importance of these differences and the possibilities for any compromises. Try to identify the matters that are negotiable and the ones that are not negotiable. The points that can be conceded and '*given away*' and the ones that cannot—the ones that are *deal breakers* if not agreed!

Watch out for and try to interpret any *body language*—that is, non-verbal communications and gestures. This is very important in multi-cultural negotiations.

Negotiation also needs *time* and *patience* and should not, therefore, be rushed to avoid bad deals.

Every negotiation should be conducted in a courteous and conciliatory manner. When tempers and blood pressures begin to rise, it is time to take a break!

The use of *role play*—the *hard* person and the *soft* one—should be handled carefully. You should decide, in advance, on the particular roles to be played by each of the members of your negotiating team. And, having done so, you should stick to them! In particular, you should appoint one of the members of the team to lead the negotiations and someone else to take notes and keep a record of everything that is said and 'agreed' during them. As to the composition of your negotiating team, if the issues raised involve technical, legal and/or financial matters, make sure that there is someone who is qualified and, therefore, can deal with them.

Likewise the imposition of any *deadlines*, which are designed to move the negotiation along and reach a conclusion more speedily, should also be carefully managed. As in litigation, so also in good negotiation, you should never issue a threat that you are not able and have no intention whatever of carrying out!

*Timing* is also very important. Choose your moment carefully to press home a particular point. Always know when and how to retreat.

In international negotiations, be aware of and allow for *cultural differences* and the need, where necessary, for the other side to *save face*. This is especially important in negotiations with the Chinese and Japanese and also with parties from the Middle East, where pride may be at the heart of the matter or dispute.

Always remember that negotiating is *getting to yes*, and so always try to make it easy for the other side to say *yes*.

You should be aware of all these negotiating techniques, not only to use them effectively in your own interests, but also be aware of any of them when they are being used against you!

In addition to all the other points that I have mentioned, there is one vital or *golden rule* that should always apply to any negotiations and it is this:

*Do not insist on getting the last penny*!

And always remember: *in a successful negotiation, everybody wins something*!

Many Books and Articles have been written and many Seminars and Courses are offered on the subject of Successful Negotiating, particularly on Negotiating Strategies and Tactics. A general article on this important aspect of Negotiating, intended to whet the appetite of the reader of this Book to investigate the subject of Negotiating in more detail, is reproduced in the first appendix of this Chapter (2.5.1), for general information and interest purposes. Likewise, in the second appendix of this Chapter (2.5.2), the reader will find some general tips on How to Negotiate Successfully.

## 2.3 General Principles of Drafting and Interpreting Sports Marketing Agreements

As regards effective drafting, the following general principles should be borne in mind:

- Before starting to draft an agreement, the whole design of the document should be worked out (remember, the agreement will be looked at and interpreted as a whole);
- Nothing should be omitted or included at random;
- The order of the agreement should be strictly logical;
- The ordinary and usual technical language should be followed; and
- Legal language, should, as far as possible, be precise and accurate.

Sir Ernest Gowers of *Plain Words* fame[1] gave the following advice (in rather quaint terms) on making the meaning clear in a legal document:

> "The inevitable peculiarities of the legal English are caused by the necessity of being unambiguous. That is by no means the same as being readily intelligible; on the contrary, the nearer you get to the one the further you are likely to get from the other...... it is accordingly the duty of the draftsman.... To try to imagine every possible combination of circumstances to which his words might apply and every conceivable misinterpretation that might be put on them, and to take precautions accordingly. He must avoid all graces, not be afraid of repetitions, or even of identifying them by aforesaids, he must limit by definition words with a penumbra dangerously large, and amplify with a string of near-synonyms words with a penumbra dangerously small; he must eschew all pronouns when their antecedents might possibly be open to dispute, and generally avoid every potential grammatical ambiguity....... All the time he must keep his eye on the rules of legal interpretation and the case-law on the meaning of particular words, and choose his phraseology to fit them."

[1] 'The Complete Plain Words' by Sir Ernest Gowers, first published in 1954 and never out of print since!

To avoid ambiguities and, therefore, disputes on the meaning, interpretation, scope and application of legal documents, keep sentences short and avoid convoluted ones with lots of relative clauses. Also, use simple and clear language and make sure that the document follows a logical and chronological order and, is therefore, easy to read and follow.

For further practical guidance on the art of effective drafting of legal documents, see the very useful little handbook entitled, *The Elements of Drafting*.[2]

It should be added that, under the rules of interpretation (technical term: *construction*) according to English Law, the aim is to discover the intention of the parties from the language they have used in their written agreement, and, in that process, giving the words used their ordinary and natural meaning.[3] Only on an exceptional basis, where there is ambiguity or contradiction on the face of the document, may the Court call upon *parol* evidence (that is, oral external evidence) in order to discover the real intention and meaning of the parties to the particular Agreement.[4]

In this connection, take care with the use of *Recitals* (the so-called *Whereas* clauses). These should be very carefully drafted, stating the background to and the reason(s) for the Agreement. For example, Recitals are important in the case of a Trademark Licence Agreement (which is what a Sports Merchandising Agreement essentially is), where there has been a previous dispute regarding the mark. If the *operative part* of the Agreement is ambiguous or in conflict with the Recitals, the Recitals will prevail when it comes to determining the meaning of the Agreement. Lord Esher, MR, well expressed the legal position in the English case of *Ex p Dawes Re Moon* as follows:

> "If the recitals are clear and the operative part is ambiguous, the recitals govern the construction. If the recitals are ambiguous, and the operative part is clear, the operative part must prevail. If both the recitals and the operative part are clear, but they are inconsistent with each other, the operative part is to be preferred."[5]

So watch out and avoid such ambiguities inconsistencies!

Whilst on the subject of ambiguities, mention should be made of the *contra proferentem* rule of construction of contracts. This rule derives from the Latin maxim: *verba chartarum fortius accipiuntur contra proferentem—the words of written documents are construed more forcibly against the party offering them.*

This rule provides that any ambiguous term will be construed against the interests of the party that imposed it in the Agreement. Thus, the interpretation of

---

[2] E. L. Piesse & J. Gilchrist Smith, Stevens and Sons Ltd, London, 2nd edition 1954.

[3] Often called the 'objective' method of interpretation.

[4] See *Street v Mountfort* [1985] AC 809. On the contrary, under Civil Law in Continental Europe, it is much easier to introduce and rely on parol evidence to clarify and explain any ambiguity in an Agreement. This approach is often called the 'subjective' method of interpretation. In other words, what did the parties intend to say?

[5] *(1886) 17 QBD 275, at p. 286, CA.*

the term concerned will be construed in favour of the party against whom it was unilaterally included. In other words, there was no negotiation—it was 'a take it or leave it' situation. Again, the rule only applies where a Court determines that the term is ambiguous. This often forms the basis of a contractual dispute.[6]

The *rationale* for the rule is to encourage the person who drafted the contract to be as clear and explicit as possible and to take into account as many foreseeable situations as possible.

Again, the rule reflects the Courts' inherent dislike of standard form take-it-or-leave-it contracts, known as 'contracts of adhesion'—in other words, these are terms and conditions of business, take them or leave them! The Courts take the view that such contracts are the result of unequal or unfair bargaining positions of the parties. To mitigate these effects, the doctrine of *contra proferentem* gives the benefit of any doubt to the party upon whom the contract was imposed.

This rule applies in numerous States of the US. For example, §1654 of the California Civil Code, enacted in 1872, provides as follows:

> "In cases of uncertainty… the language of a contract should be interpreted most strongly against the party who caused the uncertainty to exist."

The rule particularly applies to clauses in Agreements that impose on one party restrictions that are not clearly drafted and are, therefore, ambiguous, where the party claiming the restrictions contends that they apply in a particular situation, which is not expressly covered by the wording of the clause, is met with the counter argument that such party could have made the position clear by expressly providing for that situation but has failed to do so.

Again, there is a need for clear and precise drafting of Agreements.

A further point in the interests of clarity: the draftsman should use a *definition/interpretation clause*, especially to define *terms of art*; and also use *Annexes/Appendices* for technical information, which is particularly useful in Sports Licensing and Merchandising Agreements (e.g. to define and calculate complex royalties arrangements).

Drafting and interpretation of Agreements should always go hand in hand; they are two sides of the same coin!

Also, it is advisable to include a *dispute resolution clause*, especially if the parties wish to refer any disputes arising under, out of, or in relation to their Sports Marketing Agreement to the Court of Arbitration for Sport (CAS), based in Lausanne, Switzerland, in relation to which there are standard clauses provided by the CAS for such purposes (see Chap. 17).

Another point: use so-called *boiler-plate* clauses carefully and only where, according to the particular circumstances of the case, they are appropriate and add something to the meaning and effect of the agreement.

---

[6] See the English Court of Appeal case of *Peak Construction (Liverpool) Ltd v McKinney Foundation Ltd* [1970] 1 BLR 111 and, in particular, the following remarks of Lord Justice Salmon in his judgement at p. 121: "*The liquidated damages and extension of time clauses in printed forms of contract must be construed strictly contra proferentem.*"

For example, the so-called *Entire Agreement* clause, which expressly excludes from the agreement, *inter alia*, any and all representations or warranties (both oral and written) given before the agreement was signed and which may have induced one of the parties to enter into the agreement in the first place. In this connection, the High Court decision in the case of *White v. Bristol Rugby Club*[7] is instructive. White, a professional rugby player, signed a three-year contract to move from his previous club to Bristol. The contract expressly stipulated that it was subject to an 'entire agreement' clause, so that no oral representations made in the course of negotiations applied in respect of its express terms and conditions. White subsequently decided not to join Bristol and asserted that he had been told during the pre-contract negotiations that he could opt out of the contract on the repayment of the advance made to him by Bristol. The Court held that the entire agreement clause precluded White from relying on an oral opt-out term.[8]

Furthermore, take care of express warranties and conditions—distinguishing between the two of them for legal purposes—especially when acting for the grantor of the rights being licensed. A warranty, if breached, gives rise to a claim in damages only, whereas a condition *goes to the root of the contract*—in other words, is a fundamental term of the contract—and, if breached, entitles the other party to terminate the contract and also claim damages.[9] Expect to find in a Sports Licensing and Merchandising Agreement, the following mutual warranties:

- both parties are free to enter into the Agreement and have all the necessary rights and title to do so;
- neither party has entered into any conflicting/competing arrangements;
- neither party shall hold itself out as representing the other or binding the other;
- neither party will do or omit to do or allow anything to be done to impair the rights; and
- the use of the rights granted in accordance with the terms of the Agreement shall not cause the infringement of any intellectual property rights of any third party.

The so-called *severance* clause is particularly useful in the case of a Sports Merchandising Agreement containing territorial restrictions on the exploitation of the rights granted (especially when part of a wider geographical licensing programme), in order to avoid the whole of the Agreement being held to be void on National or European Competition Law grounds. The standard *severance* clause runs as follows:

> "If any provision or term of this Agreement shall be become or be declared in conflict with Law or Public Policy or otherwise illegal invalid or unenforceable for any reason

---

7 [2002] IRLR 204.

8 For further comment on this case, see Blackshaw, Ian (2002) 5(1) Sports Law Bulletin, p. 3.

9 See, respectively, the English cases of *Bettini v Gye* (1876) 1 QBD 183 and *Poussard v Spiers* (1876) 1 QBD 410.

whatsoever such term or provision shall be divisible from this Agreement and shall be deemed to be deleted from this Agreement provide always that if such deletion substantially affects or alters the commercial basis of this Agreement the parties shall negotiate in good faith to amend and modify the provisions and terms of this Agreement as may be necessary or desirable in the circumstances and the validity of the remainder shall not in any event be affected by any severance taking effect pursuant to the terms of this clause."

Likewise, the so-called *waiver* clause, which usually runs as follows:

"No failure or delay by either party to enforce at any time any one or more of the terms of this Agreement shall be a waiver by the said party of the term or right therein or prevent that party at any time subsequently from enforcing all the terms of this Agreement."

A general point: be careful of using the phrase *best endeavours* in relation to obligations undertaken in the agreement. This phrase has been interpreted by the Courts quite onerously as: *leaving no stone unturned*! This, according to the particular circumstances, could turn out to be quite a heavy financial burden to discharge. In view of its importance and also the variations on theme—'best endeavours', 'reasonable endeavours' and 'all reasonable endeavours'—and the need to avoid sloppy and traditional drafting, the legal meaning of these expressions are summarised in Chap. 18 of this Book.

Another important and sport-specific provision to be included in Sports Licensing and Merchandising Agreements—and, indeed, in all events-related Sports Marketing Agreements (for example, Sports Sponsorship Agreements)—is the one making the Agreement subject to the general and commercial/marketing rules and regulations of the Sports Governing Body concerned.

For example, in the case of the Olympics, the Olympic Charter (the latest version of which dates from July 2007) includes a number of articles dealing with the question of the marketing of the Games. See, for example, the provisions of Rule 7 of the Charter, which deals with the rights over the Olympic Games and the so-called 'Olympic Properties' and their commercialisation. Paragraphs 1 & 2 of this Rule provide as follows:

" 1. The Olympic Games are the exclusive property of the IOC which owns all rights and data relating thereto, in particular, and without limitation, all rights relating to their organisation, exploitation, broadcasting, recording, representation, reproduction, access and dissemination in any form and by any means or mechanism whatsoever, whether now existing or developed in the future. The IOC shall determine the conditions of access to and the conditions of any use of data relating to the Olympic Games and to the competitions and sports performances of the Olympic Games.
2. The Olympic symbol, flag, motto, anthem, identifications (including but not limited to "Olympic Games" and "Games of the Olympiad"), designations, emblems, flame and torches, as defined in Rules 8–14 below, shall be collectively or individually referred to as "Olympic properties". All rights to any and all Olympic properties, as well as all rights to the use thereof, belong exclusively to the IOC, including but not limited to the use for any profit-making, commercial or advertising purposes. The IOC may license all or part of its rights on terms and conditions set forth by the IOC Executive Board."

Note, in particular, the inclusion of data rights in paragraph 1 of Rule 7.
A standard Sports Governing Body compliance clause runs as follows:

> "This Agreement is expressly subject to the rules and regulations of [the Governing Body] wherever relevant and for the avoidance of doubt in the event that any of the said rules and regulations in any way conflicts with any obligation arising pursuant to this Agreement that rule and/or regulation shall prevail over the conflicting obligation arising pursuant to this Agreement and such obligation shall be suspended during any period such conflict exists."

Two other 'boiler-plate' clauses that may usefully be included in a Sports Marketing Agreement are the following:

### *'Good Faith' Clause*

> "The Parties hereto hereby mutually agree and declare that both during and after the termination of this Agreement for whatever cause they will act at all times and for all purposes towards one another in the utmost good faith with a view to giving full legal and practical effect to the terms and conditions whether express or implied of this Agreement and any amendment or amendments thereto."

### *'Covenant for Further Assurance' Clause*

> "The Parties hereto hereby mutually agree and declare that both during and after the termination of this Agreement for whatever cause they will at their own expense and in a timely manner sign and execute any and all such further documents and deeds and do any and all such further acts and things as may be required to give full legal and practical effect to the terms and conditions whether express or implied of this Agreement and any amendment or amendments thereto."

These two clauses are discussed in more detail in Chap. 19 on 'Boiler Plate' Clauses.

Also, having drafted your Agreement, do not forget to read it through as a whole to make sure that it makes sense and there are no contradictions, inconsistencies or conflicts in the document. In other words, that it all hangs together and makes sense. Self-editing of legal documents is absolutely essential in all cases. In any case, the basic canon of interpretation of contracts is that "the contract must be read and construed as a whole".[10]

The other canons of construction, which should always be borne in mind when drafting Agreements, are as follows:

> "Secondly, a contract must be construed objectively, according to the standards of a reasonable third party who is aware of the commercial context in which the contract occurs. Thirdly, a commercial contract must be given a commercially sensible construction; a construction which produces a sensible result should be preferred over one which does not. This means that when a court is faced with competing constructions, it should consider

---

[10] Per Lord Drummond Young in *Emcor Drake and Scull* v *Edinburgh Royal Joint Venture* 2005 SLT 1233, who set out seven canons of construction as follows:
"[13] First, a contractual provision must be construed in the context of the contract in which it is found. The contract is construed as a whole and, if possible, all the provisions of the contract should be given effect."

which meaning is more likely to have been intended by reasonable businessmen. Fourthly, ... in construing a formal commercial contract, which lawyers have drafted on behalf of each of the parties, the court would normally expect the parties to have chosen their words with care and to have intended to convey the meaning which the words they chose would convey to a reasonable person. Fifthly, ... the Court must be alive to the position of both parties and to the possibilities (a) that the provision may represent a compromise and (b) that one party may have made a bad bargain. ... Sixthly ... the parties must give effect to the parties bargain and must not substitute a different bargain from that which the parties have made. Seventhly, it is permissible ... to have regard to the circumstances in which the contract came to be concluded for the purpose of discovering the facts to which the contract refers and its commercial purposes, objectively considered...".[11]

One final point: be careful when, as is often the case, of including a general clause in Sports Marketing Agreements, usually insisted upon by Sports Governing Bodies, especially in Sports Sponsorship and Sports Licensing and Merchandising Agreements, making the Agreement subject to the general prohibition of not doing anything which *may bring the Sport of......... into disrepute*. This is a difficult provision to interpret and apply, in practice, as it is essentially subjective in nature. It is rather like including a general provision on 'public policy', which has been described by one English Judge, namely Mr. Justice Burrough, as: "a very unruly horse, and when once you get astride it you never know where it will carry you. It may lead you from the sound law. It is never argued at all but when other points fail."[12]

## 2.4 Concluding Remarks

Included throughout the Book are a number of Precedents—general/standard forms—for a wide range of Sports Marketing Agreements that will need to be negotiated and drafted.

But beware! Precedents should be used only as a general guide or checklist and should not be blindly and slavishly followed.

All Sports Marketing Agreements are the result of a particular commercial deal that has been negotiated between the parties to them and need, therefore, to be individually tailored and customised to fit and reflect the particular facts and circumstances of each case. In other words, when drafting Sports Marketing Agreements it is not a case of *one size fits all.* Drafting, to be legally and practically effective, needs to be contextual in all cases and should never be carried out in a vacuum. Furthermore, drafting and interpretation go hand in hand and should always be considered as two sides of the same coin.

You have been warned!

[11] Para [13] Ibid.

[12] *Richardson v Mellish* (1824), 2 Bing. 229, 252, 130 Eng. Rep. 294, at p. 303.

## 2.5 Appendices

### *2.5.1 Appendix 1*

**Best Practice Negotiation Skills: How to Determine the Best Negotiation Strategy**

By Jan Potgieter*

One of the most overlooked negotiation skills is the skill of selecting the most appropriate negotiation strategy for your negotiation.

Are you approaching all your commercial negotiations with a standard approach?

Should you only use a win/win approach to negotiations?

Traditionally, negotiated outcomes can be classified into one of the following categories:

- Lose/Lose (all parties lose)
- Win/Lose (I win and you lose)
- Lose/Win (I lose and you win)
- Win/Win (we both win—could also be described as compromise)
- Win More/Win More (we unlock synergies—could also be described as being collaborative)

Whilst I agree with the notion that a win/win approach is the only sustainable way to gain competitive advantage, it is well worth considering how you would practically apply this approach in today's global marketplace.

It would be short sighted to conclude that all negotiations are made equally and should therefore be approached in the same way. It would be similar to say that one nation's culture & beliefs are the appropriate culture and therefore the standards that apply to that culture should be applied in interacting with people across the world, irrespective of their background.

There is another dimension within the context of commercial negotiations that should be considered—the old economic dilemma of 'guns or butter'.

The 'guns or butter' story illustrates that with limited resources, organisations and individuals are forced to make choices. In order to have more butter, one must sacrifice guns and vice versa. In a practical sense this means that resources can only be allocated in relation to the relative strategic importance of the activity at issue.

In the case of negotiations that are considered strategic in importance to the organisation, we are more likely to pursue a collaborative or compromising approach. Conversely, when we deem the outcome of certain negotiations to have a limited impact or no impact at all on the achievement of strategic organisational

* Jan Potgieter is the Founder & CEO of Business Negotiation Solutions Limited. Reproduced with the kind permission of the author.

objectives we could decide to be competitive in our approach or even to avoid negotiation completely.

We would not be responsible stewards of corporate resources if we were to approach all negotiations in a similar fashion. There is also a philosophical dimension to the approach to negotiation pursued by many organisations. Some organisations are renowned for their collaborative approach to doing business whilst others have a reputation for a mercenary approach to conducting business.

Some players in the retail sector have reputations of dealing ruthlessly with suppliers—they rationalise their approach by arguing that it is in the interest of the consumer. Whilst I agree that this approach is short sighted and probably not sustainable in the long run, it would be naïve not to recognise the fact that, at least commercially speaking, a lot of organisations have little interest in collaborative or compromising type negotiations within certain departments.

It is interesting to note that whilst most organisations pride themselves on providing 'solutions' to the issues confronting their clients, a significant proportion of their so called negotiations actually revolve around haggling about price.

I have no doubt that there is a sincere intention to engage on a solution based principle it just seems that this is much easier said than done where the rubber hits the road. A lot of the time companies' stated intentions to engage on a win/win based principle is similar to the new year's resolutions so many of us make every year. There is scant chance of us achieving our resolutions without putting in place a supporting plan and taking action to achieve our goals.

Many organisations lack a clear organisational negotiation strategy & process which exposes them to the risks associated with a huge variance in the results of their negotiated agreements.

Organisations and individuals should recognise that collaborative negotiation demands the investment of significant resources. In order for us to be truly collaborative, we have to spend much time getting to know each other. In a commercial context, this plainly does not make sense in some cases. Consider the purchase of a pure commodity such as paper for a small or medium sized organisation—if there are no value added services presented or required, it would be sub optimal to pursue a collaborative relationship with the provider of such a commodity.

It would make more sense to pursue a competitive approach to the procurement of paper than a collaborative or even compromising approach. In practise, many organisations would approach the purchase of paper or stationery in a way where they would request multiple quotations and award the business to the lowest bidder. As a matter of fact, in some cases no negotiation at all would take place.

An interesting note here is that this does not mean that the paper supplier has lost as a result of this transaction—they have won the order, but the telling thing is that we were not really interested in their interests at all; we were only focused on our desired objectives.

So pursuing a win/lose strategy in this example has not really resulted in a loss for the supplier, but it does mean that we were not really interested in their desired outcomes.

The flip side of this example is that if you are selling commodity type products, you have to realise that before you will be in a position to negotiate, you must create for yourself a base to do this from—hence the move towards providing solutions.

How then do we decide which negotiation strategy to follow? Within a commercial context, the following negotiation strategy options are available to us:

1. Avoiding negotiation altogether.
2. Engaging in a competitive negotiation where we seek to achieve our goals aggressively.
3. Engaging in an accommodating negotiation where we seek to satisfy only the needs of our counterparty to the exclusion of our own needs.
4. Using a compromising approach where we seek to satisfy some of our needs and interests and some of the needs and interests of our counterparty.
5. Deploying a collaborative negotiation approach where we seek to satisfy all our needs and interests in addition to satisfying all the needs and interests of our counterparty.

The negotiation strategy that is appropriate will be determined by your answers to the following three questions:

1. How strong are my alternatives to this particular negotiation?
2. How important is a long term relationship in the context of this negotiation?
3. How much time do you have available for negotiation?

It follows that in many cases, buyers would be pursuing an approach where they are avoiding negotiation or being competitive and sellers would like to be compromising or collaborative.

How then to deal with this situation?

A key part of the negotiation preparation process should be focused on trying to understand your counterparties needs, interests and objectives. This will assist you in identifying the likely negotiation strategy that they will be pursuing.

If your counterparty is avoiding a negotiation, you can be sure that your organisation is not being viewed as a contributor of competitive advantage to your counterparty's organisation. Your challenge would in the first instance be to reconsider the way that your products and services are packaged.

The aim should be to add to the achievement of the strategic business objectives of your counterparty by identifying the components of your offering that matches their strategic needs. If you find yourself at the wrong end of a competitive negotiation, it would serve you well to be familiar with the most often used negotiation tactics as you will most certainly be confronted with a tactical approach.

Unless you are well versed in negotiation tactics, it will be difficult for you to maximise the value that you will be able to extract from the negotiation as there is no sincere interest on the part of your counterparty to satisfy any of your needs or interests.

### 2.5.2 Appendix 2

**Fifteen Rules Every Negotiator Should Know***

1. ***Remember, everything is negotiable.*** Don't narrow a negotiation down to just one issue. Develop as many issues or negotiable deal points as you can and then juggle in additional deal points if you and the other party lock onto one issue.
2. ***Crystallize your vision of the outcome.*** The counterpart who can visualize the end result will most likely be the one who guides the negotiation.
3. ***Prepare in advance.*** Information is power. Obtain as much information as possible beforehand to make sure you understand the value of what you are negotiating. Remember, very few negotiations begin when the counterparts arrive at the table.
4. ***Ask questions.*** Clarify information you do not understand. Determine both the implicit and explicit needs of your counterpart.
5. ***Listen.*** When you do a good job listening, you not only gain new ideas for creating win/win outcomes but also make your counterpart feel cared for and valued. This also allows you to find out what the other party wants. If you assume that his or her wants and needs are the same as yours, you will have the attitude that only one of you can "win" the negotiation.
6. ***Set a goal for each deal point.*** Define your minimum level of acceptance for each goal. If you aren't clear on your goals, you will end up reacting to the propositions of your counterpart.
7. ***Aim your aspirations high.*** Your aspirations will likely be the single most important factor in determining the outcome of the negotiation. You can aim high just as easily as you can aim low.
8. ***Develop options and strategies.*** Successful people are those who have the greatest number of viable alternatives. Similarly, successful negotiators are those who have the most strategies they can use to turn their options into reality.
9. ***Think like a dolphin.*** The dolphin is the only mammal who can swim in a sea of sharks or in a sea of carp. Dolphins are able to adapt their strategies and behaviors to their counterparts. Remember, even when negotiating with a shark, you have an option—you can walk away!
10. ***Be honest and fair.*** In life, what goes around comes around. The goal in creating win/win outcomes is to have both counterparts feel that their needs and goals have been met, so that they will be willing to come back to the table and negotiate again. An atmosphere of trust reduces the time required to create win/win outcomes.

---

* January 22nd, 2007. Reproduced with permission of Sales Renaissance, www.SalesRenaissance.com.

11. ***Never accept the first offer.*** Often, the other party will make an offer that he or she thinks you will refuse just to see how firm you are on key issues. Chances are, if you don't have to fight a little for what you want, you won't get the best deal.
12. ***Deal from strength if you can.*** If that's not possible, at least create the appearance of strength. If the other party thinks you have no reason to compromise in your demands, he or she is less likely to ask you to.
13. ***Find out what the other party wants.*** *Concede slowly, and call a concession a concession.* Giving in too easily tells the other party that you will probably be open to accepting even more concessions.
14. ***Be cooperative and friendly.*** Avoid being abrasive or combative, which often breaks down negotiations.
15. ***Use the power of competition.*** Someone who thinks it's necessary to compete for your business may be willing to give away more than he or she originally intended. Sometimes just the threat of competition is enough to encourage concessions.

# Chapter 3
# The Importance of Intellectual Property Rights in Sports Event Marketing

## 3.1 Introductory Remarks

In this chapter, we will explain the important part played by Intellectual Property Rights (IPRs) in Sports Events Marketing. Indeed, without IPRs, it would be impossible to market sports events, sports persons and sports teams, because sports bodies and individuals would have nothing to commercialise or sell. No one is going to pay for the grant of any rights to be associated with sports events or to sponsor sports personalities and teams without those rights being recognised by law and, as such, being legally enforceable against others that I have not been granted those rights and—even more importantly—have not paid anything at all for the privilege of exploiting them commercially.

Not only do IPRs play an important role in Sports Events Marketing, but their creative use is also crucial for the protection and commercialisation of the valuable Image Rights of Sports Personalities. This is an important and complex topic in its own right and is, therefore, dealt with separately in Chap. 12 on Sports Image Rights Agreements.

Sport is big business and has become an industry in its own right worth more than 3% of world trade and 2% of the combined GNP of the 27 Member States of the European Union. So, there is much to play for both on and off the field of play.

As mentioned above, we will now see just how important IPRs are, especially trademarks and copyright,[1] and in what ways they can be used creatively for the successful commercial exploitation of sports events, especially international ones. For a broader and more extensive treatment of the subject of IPRs and their

[1] Other IPRs, such as Patents, for example, are of limited application and importance in sports law, although they do figure—to a certain extent—for example; in connection with the commercialisation of sports equipment and so-called 'sports movements' such as the '*Fosbury flop*'.

I. S. Blackshaw, *Sports Marketing Agreements: Legal, Fiscal and Practical Aspects*,
ASSER International Sports Law Series, DOI: 10.1007/978-90-6704-793-7_3,

importance in sport generally, see Paper on *The Importance of IP Rights in Sport* presented by Ian Blackshaw at the 2008 Global IP and Patents Meeting in London.[2]

## 3.2 Sports Events Marketing

The basic problem Sports Events Marketers face under English Law lies in the fact that there is no legally recognised right in a sporting event *per se*. See *Victoria Park Racing and Recreation Grounds Co Ltd v Taylor and Others* [1937] 58 CLR 479. In that case, Latham CJ held that:

> "A spectacle cannot be 'owned' in any ordinary sense of that word."

In other words, a Sports Event as such is not a species of property that can be protected in its own right. So, Sports Event Marketers need to rely on other rights that are legally recognised and protected.

Firstly, we will consider trademark protection, and then copyright protection.

### *3.2.1 Trademark Protection*

Perhaps the most distinctive and recognised sports event mark in the world are the five interconnected rings in blue, yellow, black, green and red symbolising the world-wide reach of the Olympic Movement and the Olympic Games—often referred to as the 'greatest sporting show on Earth!'.

The Olympic Rings enjoy special legal protection at the international and national levels around the world. At the international level, they are protected by the so-called 'Nairobi Agreement'—the Agreement on the Protection of the Olympic Symbol of 1981.

At the national level in the UK and in connection with the staging of the Summer Olympic Games in London in 2012, the Rings—as a bid pre-condition—are protected under the provisions of the London Olympic Games and Paralympic Games Act of 2006. This Act also protects the use of the Olympic Motto and the use of such expressions as *the Games*, *Olympians*, and *Olympiad*, as well as *strap lines* in advertisements, such as *Come to London in 2012* and *Watch the games here this Summer*. All these measures are designed to provide Olympic brand protection and combat various forms of so-called *Ambush Marketing* for the benefit of the Official Sponsors of the Games, who pay mega bucks for a package of 'top line' sponsorship rights, against those who, in the advertising and

---

[2] Reproduced in The International Sports Law Journal, ISLJ 2008/3–4, at pp. 146–150 (both inclusive).

promotion of their products and services, falsely and unfairly claim an association or affiliation with the Games. However, these statutory measures have been described by the UK Advertising Industry as "draconian" and threatening the right of free speech, which includes commercial speech, that is, advertising!

As regards trademark protection, which is probably, in practice, the most important form of legal protection of sports events, sports bodies and organisations and also sports persons (particularly in relation to their image rights), the UK Trade Marks Act of 1994 defines a trademark in section 1(1) as:

> "... any sign capable of being represented graphically which is capable of distinguishing goods or services of one undertaking from those of other undertakings. A trade mark may, in particular, consist of words—including personal names—designs, letters, numerals or the shape of goods or their packaging."

This is a wide definition[3] and so a trade mark may be granted in respect of, for example; distinctive sounds, as in the case of the Australian Football League, which has registered the sound of a football siren for football and associated services.[4]

Thus, provided the basic legal requirement of distinctiveness is satisfied, it is possible to register the names and associated *logos* of sports events as trademarks. However, the name 'Euro 2000' failed the distinctiveness requirement and could not be registered as a trademark *per se*. But, *prima facie*, combined with a distinctive *logo*, this event name could be registrable as a trademark. Likewise, an attempt in 1998 to register the name 'World Cup' also failed through lack of distinctiveness. Again, combined with a distinctive and original logo, such a mark can be protected as a trademark and also enjoys copyright protection as an 'artistic work'.[5] Under section 4 (1)(a) of the UK Copyright Designs and Patents Act of 1988, "a graphic work, ... irrespective of artistic quality" qualifies for legal protection as an 'artistic work' under the Act.

Sports event 'mascots' may also qualify, in principle, for registration as trademarks, again subject to their being distinctive. And also as registered designs.

Although not an event mark, it would perhaps be remiss not to mention the ADIDAS 'three stripes' trademark case, in which the long-awaited Preliminary Ruling by the Court of First Instance of the European Court of Justice (ECJ) (C-102/07) was rendered on 10 April, 2008. This case, which well illustrates the need for trademark protection in the sporting arena generally, concerned the extent of the legal protection under Trademark Law within the European Union afforded

---

3 Notice that the list of examples is illustrative and not exhaustive.

4 For further information on trademarks generally and, in particular, their territorial nature and, therefore, the need, in the case of Sports Events that are going to be commercially exploited internationally, to register them widely around the world and also in the relevant use classes under the Nice Classification of Goods and Services for Trademarks, see Chap. 10 entitled, '*Intellectual Property Rights and Sport*', by Ian Blackshaw in '*Sports Law*' by Gardiner et al., Third Edition, 2006 Cavendish Publishing, London.

5 See later.

to the three vertical stripes on sports and leisure goods produced and sold by Adidas. The facts of this case were as follows:

The Parent Company of the Adidas Group, Adidas AG, is the proprietor of a figurative trademark composed of three vertical, parallel stripes of equal width that feature on the sides of sports and leisure garments in a colour which contrasts with the basic colour of those garments. Its Subsidiary Company, Adidas Benelux BV, holds an exclusive licence, granted by Adidas AG, to use this mark on garments marketed in the Benelux countries.

Marca Mode, C&A, H&M and Vendex are competitors of Adidas, who also market sports garments featuring two parallel stripes, the colour of which contrasts with the basic colour of those garments.

Adidas took the competitors to Court in The Netherlands claiming the right to prohibit the use by any third party of an identical or similar sign which would cause confusion in the market place. Marca Mode and the other defendants to these proceedings, however, claimed that they are free to place two stripes on their sports and leisure garments for decorative purposes. Their defence was based on the so-called requirement of availability, namely that stripes and simple stripe motifs are signs which must remain available to all and, therefore, they did not need the consent of Adidas to use the two-stripe motif on their garments.

Adidas won at first instance; were overruled on appeal; and the case finally came, on a point of law, before The Supreme Court of The Netherlands (*Hoge Raad der Nederlanden*), which sought clarification from the ECJ on the main point at issue, namely, whether the requirement of availability is an assessment criterion for the purposes of defining the scope of the exclusive rights enjoyed by the owner of a particular trademark.

The ECJ ruled, first, that the requirement of availability of certain signs is not one of the relevant factors to be taken into account in the assessment of the likelihood of confusion. The answer to the question as to whether there is that likelihood must be based on the public's perception of the goods covered by the mark of the proprietor on the one hand and the goods covered by the sign used by the third party on the other. The national court must determine whether the average consumer may be mistaken as to the origin of sports and leisure garments featuring stripe motifs in the same places and with the same characteristics as the stripes motif of Adidas, except for the fact that the competitors' motif consists of two rather than three stripes.

Secondly, the ECJ turned its attention to the specific protection granted to trademarks with a reputation. It noted that the implementation of that protection does not require the existence of a likelihood of confusion between the sign and the mark. The mere fact that the relevant section of the public establishes a link between the two is sufficient. Since the requirement of availability is extraneous both to the assessment of the degree of similarity between the mark with a reputation and the sign used by the third party and to the link which may be made by the relevant public between that mark and the sign, it cannot constitute a relevant factor for determining whether the use of the sign takes unfair advantage.[6]

Protection of a registered trademark lasts for an initial period of 10 years and, provided the mark is used commercially and the renewal fees are paid, the registration can be renewed for further periods of 10 years *ad infinitum.*

It is advisable, for trademark protection reasons, to use the device R in a circle (®) after the trademark wherever and whenever it is used; or the legend: 'X is registered trademark of ABC'.

### *3.2.2 Copyright Protection*

The difference between trademark protection and copyright protection lies in the fact that in order to obtain the former, it is necessary to register the trademark concerned in a public registry, whereas in the case of copyright in a protected 'work', no such registration is generally required: copyright exists by operation of law once the work is created and published.

As mentioned above, copyright protection exists and can be claimed in respect of a composite event mark, which combines the name of the event incorporated in a distinctive and original logo by the use, for example, of distinctive lettering and colours. Such a logo is regarded for copyright purposes as an 'artistic work' irrespective of artistic merit, pursuant to the provisions of section 4 (1)(a) of the UK Copyright Designs and Patents Act of 1988. The 'work' need not, for example, be a Picasso!

Copyright in an artistic work lasts for the life of the author plus 70 years (see section 12 of the 1988 Act).

Wherever and whenever the logo appears, it is advisable to claim copyright in it by using the international copyright notice, consisting of a C in a circle (©), the name of the copyright owner and the year of publication. For those countries (and there are not that many of them) in the world that are not members of the Berne Convention for the Protection of Literary and Artistic Works, the words 'all rights reserved' should be added.

Another point to note: generally speaking, there is no copyright in a slogan, as a literary work. See the decision in *Exxon Corporation v. Exxon Insurance Consultants International Ltd.*[7] However, a slogan is registrable as a Trademark.

One final point worth mentioning is that there is some legal protection that can be afforded to a sports event by registering the name of that event as a 'domain

---

[6] For the full text of the ECJ Preliminary Ruling in the ADIDAS 'three stripes' trademark case, see: http://www.curia.europa.eu/jurisp/cgibin/form.pl?lang=EN&Submit=rechercher&numaff=C-102/07.

[7] [1982] RPC 69.

name'. 'Cyber Squatters'[8] can be ordered to cancel the registration of the offending 'domain name' or be ordered to transfer it to the complainant. This is so under the Internet Corporation for Assigned Names and Numbers (ICANN) Uniform Domain Name Dispute Resolution Policy (UDRP) even though the name is not registered as a trademark—in other words, so-called 'Common Law' trademarks are protected. This could be useful in the hypothetical case study mentioned below. Most domain name disputes are handled through the World Intellectual Property Organization (WIPO) Arbitration and Mediation Center, which is based in Geneva, Switzerland.[9] See further on the subject of settling sports domain name and other disputes through WIPO in Part Three of the Book '*Sport, Mediation and Arbitration*'.[10]

## 3.3 Hypothetical New Sports Event Case Study

To illustrate the legal importance and practical application of IPRs in sport as well as the general principles explained above, let us consider the following hypothetical case study.

The International Volleyball Federation wishes to introduce a new event into their calendar of events, entitled: "European Beach Volleyball Grand Prix Series".

As will be seen from the above summary of the legal requirements for obtaining trademark protection, the mark concerned must be distinctive and not generic. Clearly the words *Beach Volleyball*, *Grand Prix* and *Series* are descriptive and not inherently distinctive. Likewise, the word *European* is geographical and also, again, descriptive of the event. Descriptive and geographical marks are expressly excluded from registration as trademarks according to the provisions of section 3(1)(c) of the UK Trade Marks Act 1994. The legal position elsewhere is the same. Trademark protection of the name *per se* is not, therefore, legally possible.

So what can be done? There is, in fact, a way round these legal obstacles and that is by incorporating the event name in a distinctive logo and thereby creating, what is known in the jargon, as a 'composite mark'. The logo may be rendered distinctive by the use of distinctive lettering or script and also colours.

Also, as mentioned, the logo qualifies for copyright protection as an 'artistic work' under the provisions of section 4 (1)(a) of the UK Copyright Designs and Patents Act, 1988.

Thus, by turning the event name into a distinctive and original logo, trademark and copyright protection has been secured. *Quod erat demonstrandum*!

---

8 'Cybersquatting' is the abusive registration and bad faith use of an Internet 'domain name' (an Internet address—often described as an 'electronic trademark').

9 www.wipo.int

10 By Ian S. Blackshaw, 2009, TMC Asser Press, The Hague, The Netherlands, at pp. 193–235.

It should be stressed that, without these specific legal protections, the event name and the event itself cannot be commercialized as, for example, sponsors and merchandisers cannot be granted any IPRs that they can use against infringers and counterfeiters, including so-called 'Ambush Marketing'. Major sports events are very attractive to those companies and business organisations who wish to be associated with them without having to pay the mega sums for the privilege of doing so!

Of course, someone needs to design the event logo and this raises some copyright issues too, depending upon whether the logo is created in-house or by an outside graphic artist. Many International Sports Governing Bodies have their own in-house dedicated marketing departments, which include 'creative staff' who can do this work. In that case, the copyright belongs to the Sports Body concerned.

Under the provisions of section 11(2) of the 1988 Copyright Act, where a literary, dramatic, musical or artistic work, or, indeed a film is made by an employee in the course of his/her employment—in other words, it is part of the employee's job description/specification—the employee is the first owner of any copyright in the work. It should be noted that, for this result to apply, it is not sufficient that the work (or the film) is made by an employee; it must be made in the course of that employee's employment. Thus, if by agreement with the employer, an employee produces the logo in his/her spare time and outside the terms and scope of his/her employment, the first copyright owner of the 'work' is the employee. The legal distinction between an employee and an outside contractor is that, in the former case, the employee is employed under the terms of a contract of service and, in the latter, the person concerned is acting under a contract for services. This is not a matter of semantics: it is a substantive matter of fact in each case! It is, therefore, incumbent on the employer to make the copyright position crystal clear in writing, to avoid any litigation. See the case of *Ray v. Classic FM* [1998], unreported.

Thus, where the sports event logo is produced outside by an independent contractor—a graphic artist or design studio—section 11(2) (above) does not apply and the first copyright owner is the outside contractor.

Of course, in the latter case where the logo is commissioned, there not only needs to be a Commissioning Agreement, but also a Copyright Assignment from the outside party to the Sports Body concerned.

## 3.4 Copyright Assignment

Let us now take a brief look at the legal requirements that need to be met where the logo is commissioned from and produced by someone outside the Sports Body concerned.

Clearly, in such a case, the copyright needs to be transferred to the Sports Body from the outside body. Under the provisions of section 90(3) of the Copyright Designs and Patents Act, 1988, the Assignment must be made in writing in order to transfer the legal and beneficial title to the copyright in the work concerned. However, the 1988 Act does not prescribe any other formalities or any particular form of words. Thus, the document may be quite simple, but, in order to be legally effective, a clear and express intention to assign/transfer the copyright in the work concerned must be evidenced from the words used in the Assignment.

Thus, a copyright licence or authorisation will not, generally, be implied purely on the basis that, in the particular circumstances of the case, it may be reasonable to do so: there must be a clear intention of the parties. See *Blair v. Osborne & Tomkins.*[11]

In practice, a fairly detailed document needs to be drawn up along the lines of the basic general precedent of a Copyright Assignment which is set out in the Appendix to this article.

As will be seen, it is advisable, *inter alia*, to include in the Assignment some warranties of title on the part of the 'Author' who is assigning the copyright in the sports event logo; to define the rights in the logo that are being assigned (this is where a Definitions Clause comes in very useful) and also to include an Indemnity Clause in relation to any breaches on the part of the 'Author' of any of the provisions of the Assignment Agreement, particularly obligations.

Precision in drafting, as mentioned above, is the name of the game, from a legal point of view.

## 3.5 Concluding Remarks

The importance of IPRs in providing the necessary legal protection to major international sports events cannot be over emphasised. In fact, it is fair to say that, without the creative use and application of IPRs, major sports event organisers have nothing to commercialise or to sell to sponsors, merchandisers, broadcasters and many others who wish to be commercially—and I would add—officially associated with these events.

Getting it right and drawing up the corresponding formal Agreements is crucial to the successful exploitation of the sports events concerned. For these purposes, event organisers and managers need to employ the legal experts.

Not to do so, I would submit, is not only false economy but sheer commercial and financial folly!

[11] [1971] 2 WLR 503.

## 3.6 Appendix

### Copyright Assignment*

THIS ASSIGNMENT is made the ........ day of ............................ 20[....]

**Between**

(1) ........................................................................................................................
whose registered office is at
("Author")

(2) ........................................................................................................................
whose registered office is at
("Company")

## Recitals

A. The Author is author of and copyright owner in the Work

B. The Company wishes to take an assignment of the copyright in the Work upon the terms set out herein

### Operative Provisions

**1. Definitions**

1.1 The following definitions shall apply in this Agreement:

**"Act"** means the Copyright Designs and Patents Act 1988 as amended from time to time

**"Fee"** means £[ ]

**"Right"** means any and all vested, contingent and/or future copyrights, any and all accrued rights of action and any and all other rights of intellectual property including but not limited to database rights, design rights, rights in respect of registered designs, rights in respect of trade marks (including but not limited to make application for registration of any of the same) and any other applicable rights of whatever nature in and in relation to the Work whether now known or created in the future to which the Author is entitled by virtue of any of the laws in force in any part of the Territory for the entire duration of any such rights (including any renewal or extension thereof)

**"Term"** means the full period of copyright in the Work including all renewals, reversions and extensions of copyright in the Work arising under the laws in force in each part of the Territory

* By I.S. Blackshaw.

**"Territory"** means the world
**"Work"** means the artistic work a copy of which is annexed as Exhibit 1

**2. Assignment**

2.1 In consideration of the Fee the Author assigns the Rights to the Company with full title guarantee in the Territory for the Term in respect of which the Company shall pay the Author the Fee on signing this Agreement

2.2 at any time after the date of this Agreement each of the parties shall at the request and cost of the party execute or procure the execution of any document and do or procure the doing of any act as the party requires so that the party receives the full benefit of all the provisions of this Agreement

**3. Warranties**

3.1 The Author represents and warrants to the Company that

3.1.1 the Author is sole author of the Work and was throughout the creation of the Work a "qualifying person" within the meaning of the Act

3.1.2 the Author is the absolute and unencumbered legal and beneficial owner of the Right in the Work throughout the Territory and has not assigned or licensed any rights in the Work to any person

3.1.3 there is no present or prospective claim in respect of any rights in the Work which may infringe any of the Rights

3.1.4 the Work is original to the Author and does not infringe any right of copyright right in respect of databases right in respect of designs registered designs trade marks or other intellectual property right moral right or right of privacy or right of publicity or personality or any other third party right

3.1.5 copyright in the Work is valid and subsisting pursuant to the laws of the United Kingdom and the United States of America and the provisions of the Berne Convention and Universal Copyright Convention

3.1.6 the Work contains nothing which is obscene blasphemous libellous or otherwise unlawful and the exploitation of the Work will not infringe the rights of whatever nature of any third party in any part of the world

**4. Indemnity**

4.1 The Author hereby agrees to indemnify and keep indemnified the Company from any loss expenses damages cots or prejudice including without prejudice to the generality of this provision the Company's legal costs on a solicitor and own client basis arising directly or indirectly as a result of any breach or non-performance by the Author of any of the Author's obligations or warranties in this Agreement

4.2 The Author irrevocably and unconditionally waives all rights in respect of the Work to which he is now or may be entitled under the Copyright Design and Patents Act 1988 ss77 and 78 and any similar rights in force during the Term in any part of the Territory

**5. Alterations to the Work**

5.1 The Author irrevocably and unconditionally waives all moral rights in the Work to which he is entitled under section 80 of the Act and any similar rights to which he is entitled in any part of the Territory

5.2 The Company reserves the right to alter the Work as in its discretion it sees fit and the Author consents to any and all such alterations

[Boilerplate Clauses]

[Execution Clauses]

Exhibit 1

# Chapter 4
# Letters of Intent, Heads of Agreement and Preliminary Agreements

## 4.1 Introductory Remarks

Sport marketing is a fast-moving business, involving as it does the competitive acquisition of very valuable and lucrative rights, which allow companies and firms to associate and promote themselves and their products and services with prestigious international sporting events, such as the Olympic Games and the FIFA World Cup. In other words, sports marketing rights involve the transfer of very valuable goodwill, which has been built up in the sporting events concerned over a long period of time, to a corporate or commercial entity for the benefit of its business. This gives the companies and firms, so the commercial and financial arguments run a marketing advantage over their competitors and an additional platform on which to enhance the attraction and saleability of their products and services to a wide range of consumers, many of whom are sports fans, around theworld.

There is often, therefore, a pressing need for the parties to Sports Marketing arrangements to have something in writing to 'tie up' and 'secure' the deal, especially in those cases of opportunistic marketing. Thus, Letters of Intent, Heads of Agreement and Preliminary Agreements are frequently signed—often religiously so—by the parties concerned in Sports Marketing transactions.

One can see the commercial rationale and advantages of signing these kinds of documents in anticipation of and before full-blown and lengthy Agreements reflecting the deal, including so-called 'boiler plate' clauses, are formalised, but the real issue, in practice, is to what extent are these documents legally binding and enforceable on the parties to them. In other words, do they in a legal sense 'secure' the deal?

I. S. Blackshaw, *Sports Marketing Agreements: Legal, Fiscal and Practical Aspects*,
ASSER International Sports Law Series, DOI: 10.1007/978-90-6704-793-7_4,

## 4.2 Legal Nature and Validity

### *4.2.1 The Position in England*

All these kinds of Preliminary Agreements, as far as their legal nature and validity are concerned, are, of course, subject to the general principles of the Law of Contract. One difficulty, under the English Common Law of Contract, is the principle that an agreement to agree is not a legally binding contract[1] and this principle may catch Letters of Intent, especially clauses in them that provide that the parties will agree something in the future. For example, clauses that require the parties to negotiate and agree the detailed terms to be included in a formal Sports Marketing Agreement governing and formalising their commercial and financial arrangements may not be legally binding and, therefore, unenforceable.

Another problem under the English Law of Contract, is the requirement for the terms and conditions of the parties' agreement to be clear, unambiguous and settled, particularly the main terms and conditions such as price. Such vague terms may be held by a Court to be void for uncertainty and, therefore, unenforceable. It is essential, therefore, in the case of Heads of Agreement that they will contain—at the very least—details of the rights granted, whether they are exclusive or non-exclusive, the term for which they and the territory in which they are granted, and, of course, the price to be paid for them.

A further problem is the need, under the English Law of Contract, if an agreement is to be legally valid and enforceable, for there to be a clear intention by the parties to create legal relations between them. Did the parties wish and manifest that wish for the obligations to be legally binding on them, or are we dealing only with a simple 'wish list'? This point is particularly relevant to Letters of Intent. Clearly, any Letters of Intent which are expressly made 'subject to contract' will not be legally binding until the contemplated contract is entered into by the parties. However, even without such a pre-condition, it may not be entirely clear whether the Letter of Intent is legally binding or not. They are, generally speaking, from this particular legal point of view, quite problematic in practice.

[1] See *R&D Construction Group Ltd v Hallam Land Management Ltd* [2009] CSOH 128 and the leading English cases on 'agreements to agree' referred to therein. In para [34] of his judgement, Lord Hodge expressed the matter thus: "*Where terms which the law treats as essential or which the parties have agreed are essential for their bargain have not been agreed and cannot be objectively ascertained, the contract is unenforceable.*"
See also the remarks of Millet LJ in the English case of *Little v Courage Ltd* [1994] 70 P&CR, 469, at p. 476:
"*An undertaking to use one's best endeavours to obtain planning permission or an export licence is sufficiently certain and capable of being enforced: an undertaking to use one's best endeavours to agree, however, is no different from an undertaking to agree, to try to agree, or to negotiate with a view to reaching agreement; all are equally uncertain and incapable of giving rise to an enforceable legal obligation.*"

It has been well said judicially in the English High Court case of *British Steel Corporation v Cleveland Bridge and Engineering Co Ltd*[2] that:

> ".... There can be no hard and fast answer to the question in whether a letter of intent is a binding agreement: everything must depend upon the circumstances of the particular case."

In other words, each case must be construed and judged on its own particular facts and circumstances. In view of the importance of this decision, the full text of the Judgement of Mr Justice Goff (as he then was) is set out in Appendix 1 (4.4.1) to this Chapter.

Again, the intention to exclude legal relations must be clear and express if the document is not to be legally binding on the parties and, therefore, unenforceable. A so-called 'backhanded' attempt to include wording in an agreement in order to avoid legal relations being created will not succeed. See the English case of *Edwards's v Skyways Ltd.*[3] Again, in view of its importance, the text of the Judgement of Mr Justice Megaw (as he then was) is set out in Appendix 2 (4.4.2) to this Chapter.

A short form and a long form of a general precedent of a Letter of Intent is set out, for illustrative purposes only, in Appendices 3–5 (4.4.3–4.4.5) to this Chapter.

Preliminary Agreements create their own particular legal problems. Whilst there is usually a clear intention for the parties to create legal relations between them, whether or not a Preliminary Agreement is otherwise legally enforceable will depend upon the detailed terms and conditions included in them.

The legal situation elsewhere in Europe, under Civil Law principles of contract, may well be different.

### *4.2.2 The Position in Switzerland*

For instance, the position in Switzerland, where a number of Sports Marketing Agreements are entered into, for example by US and UK companies and firms, with International Sports Governing Bodies, that are based in Switzerland and thus governed by Swiss Law, is as follows:

First of all, it should be noted that, under Swiss Law, there are no special rules for Letters of Intent and Preliminary Agreements in relation to sporting matters. Thus, only the 'normal' rules apply.

The Swiss Code of Obligations (CO) does not contain any explicit rules regarding Letters of Intent. However, applying the general rules of Swiss Contract Law, a Letter of Intent has usually no binding nature for the parties involved,

2 [1984] 1 All ER 504.

3 [1964]1 All ER 494.

except where the parties agree explicitly on such effect (which would make it a regular contract regarding the issue of its legal binding nature).

Nevertheless, a Letter of Intent may lead to civil liability under the principle of *culpa in contrahendo*[4] if certain conditions are met. Such special circumstances are, for example, if the negotiations on a future contract are initiated but the initiator of the contract negotiations had, in fact, never the intention to conclude such a contract. In general, the *culpa in contrahendo* liability covers all the unlawful behaviour in connection with the contract negotiations.

Article 22 of CO sets forth the legal effects of Preliminary Agreements and the legal requirements for such agreements. Under Swiss Law, such an Agreement may be binding either for one or for all parties involved in the agreement and may also be concluded in favour of a third party. Article 22 para 2 CO states that in cases where the Law, for the protection of the contracting parties, requires a certain form for the validity of the future contract, this form requirement also applies to the preliminary contract. Apart from these special rules, the general rules of Swiss Contract Law apply to preliminary agreements. Therefore, such agreements may not be of an illegal or have an excessive binding nature.

Article 22 of CO provides (in English translation) as follows:

> "E. Contents of the contract
>
> ...
>
> IV. Preliminary Contract
>
> Art. 22
>
> By contract, the parties may validly agree to conclude a contract in the future. Where the law, for the protection of the contracting parties, requires a certain form for the validity of the future contract, the form requirement also applies to the preliminary contract."

Thus, in the case of Preliminary Agreements under Swiss Law, the parties must negotiate in good faith and, if the Preliminary Agreement, lacks certain provisions to make it complete, the parties can be required to continue and complete the negotiations—again, in good faith—in order to finalise and conclude a legally binding Agreement.

[4] This Doctrine holds that damages should be recoverable against a party whose blameworthy conduct during negotiations for a contract brought about its invalidity or prevented its perfection. In other words, the party concerned did not negotiate in good faith with the intention of finalising the contract.

## 4.3 Appendices

In the Appendices of this Chapter, the reader will find the Judgements of two important and relevant English Cases, as well as some General Precedents, for comparative and illustrative purposes.

### *4.3.1 Concluding Remarks*

Irrespective of their legal validity and enforceability, all these kinds of preliminary documents, therefore, may be useful and valuable as a kind of '*aide memoire*' to guide any future negotiations and the drafting of what I might call the real Agreement—that is, the one that will fully represent the deal that the parties have made and, therefore, the one that will be legally binding on them. In other words, Heads of Agreement, Letters of Intent and Preliminary Agreements will be binding in honour only and, as one English Judge once reputedly remarked when faced with moral arguments in a case: 'this is a Court of Law, not morals!'

Against that strict legal background, under English Law at least, these kinds of preliminary agreements do serve a practical and useful commercial purpose to a certain extent, and, presumably, that is why they seem to be popular, especially in connection with Sports Marketing Agreements of various kinds, and are entered into by the parties in the first place.

## 4.4 Appendices

### *4.4.1 Appendix 1*

All England Law Reports/1984/Volume 1/British Steel Corp v Cleveland Bridge and Engineering Co Ltd—[1984] 1 All ER 504; reproduced with permission Nexis Lexis (UK Law Reports)

**[1984] 1 All ER 504**

**British Steel Corp v Cleveland Bridge and Engineering Co Ltd**

**Queen's Bench Division (Commercial Court)**

**Robert Goff J**

**6, 9, 10, 11, 12, 13, 16, 17, 18 November, 21 December 1981**

*Contract—Quantum meruit—Work done in anticipation of contract—No contract concluded—Steel manufacturer negotiating with contractor to make and supply cast-steel products for construction work—Contractor requesting manufacturer to commence production in anticipation of contract being entered into—Manufacturer making and supplying cast-steel products—Parties unable to agree on contractual terms—Whether contractor entitled to value of products on a quantum meruit.*

The defendants successfully tendered for the fabrication of steel work in the construction of a building. The design required steel beams to be joined to a steel frame by means of steel nodes. The plaintiffs, who were iron and steel manufacturers, were approached by the defendants to produce a variety of cast-steel nodes for the project. The plaintiffs prepared an estimated price based on incomplete information and sent it to the defendants by telex on 9 February 1979. After further discussions as to the appropriate specifications and technical requirements the defendants sent a letter of intent to the plaintiffs on 21 February which (i) recorded the defendants' intention to enter into a contract with the plaintiffs for the supply of cast-steel nodes at the prices itemised in the telex of 9 February, (ii) proposed that the contract be on the defendants' standard form, which provided for unlimited liability on the part of the plaintiffs in the event of consequential loss due to late delivery, and (iii) requested the plaintiffs to commence work immediately 'pending the preparation and issuing to you of the official form of sub-contract'. The plaintiffs would not have agreed to the defendants' standard form of contract and intended to submit a formal quotation once they had the requisite information. The plaintiffs did not reply to the letter of intent since they expected a formal order to follow shortly and instead they went ahead with the manufacture of the nodes. The defendants then indicated for the first time that they required delivery in a particular sequence.

There were further discussions as to the proper specifications to be met in the manufacture but no final agreement was reached. The specifications were then changed extensively by the defendants after the first castings proved to be unsatisfactory. On 16 May the plaintiffs sent the defendants a formal quotation on their standard form, quoting a significantly higher price with delivery dates to be agreed. The defendants rejected the quotation and again changed the specifications. The plaintiffs went ahead with the manufacture and delivery of the nodes and eventually, at a meeting between the parties on 1 August, the parties reached provisional agreement on the basis of the quotation given on 16 May but they were unable to agree on other contract terms such as progress payments and liability for loss arising from late delivery. By 28 December all but one of the nodes had been delivered, delivery of the remaining node being held up until 11 April 1980 due to an industrial dispute at the plaintiffs' plant. The defendants refused to make any interim or final payment for the nodes and instead sent a written claim to the plaintiffs for damages for late delivery or delivery of the nodes out of sequence. The amount claimed far exceeded the quoted price. The plaintiffs thereupon sued for the value of the nodes on a quantum meruit, contending, inter alia, that no binding contract had been entered into. The defendants counterclaimed for damages for breach of contract for late delivery and delivery out of sequence and claimed a right of set-off, contending, inter alia, that a binding contract had been created by the various documents, especially the letter of intent, and by the plaintiffs' conduct in proceeding with the manufacture of the nodes.

**Held**—A contract could come into existence following a letter of intent, either by the letter forming the basis of an ordinary executory contract under which each party assumed reciprocal obligations to the other, or under a unilateral contract (i.e an 'if' contract) whereby the letter amounted to a standing offer which would result in a binding contract if acted on by the offeree before it lapsed or was validly withdrawn. On the facts, an executory contract had not been created by the plaintiffs acceding to the defendants' request in the letter of intent that they begin work on the nodes pending the issue of a formal sub-contract, since at that stage the parties were still negotiating over material contractual terms such as price and delivery dates and it was therefore impossible to say what those terms were. Furthermore, in all the circumstances an 'if' contract had not been created by the plaintiffs carrying out the work, since that work was at that stage being done pending a formal sub-contract, the terms of which were still in a state of negotiation, in particular with regard to the plaintiffs' liability for consequential loss and delay, so that it was impossible to determine the extent of the liability. Instead, the parties had confidently expected a formal contract to be concluded and the letter of intent had requested the plaintiffs to commence work, which they had done in order to expedite performance under the anticipated contract. Since the parties had ultimately been unable to reach final agreement on the price or other essential terms, the contract was eventually not entered into and therefore the work performed in anticipation of it was not referable to any contractual terms as to payment or performance. In those circumstances, the defendants were obliged to pay a reasonable sum for the work done pursuant to their request. In any event, assuming an 'if' contract had been concluded, the plaintiffs would not have been under a contractual obligation to complete the contract work and a fortiori would not have been under any obligation to complete within a reasonable time. Moreover, even if the plaintiffs had been under a contractual obligation to complete the work within a reasonable time, on the facts, they would not have been in breach of that obligation. Accordingly, the plaintiffs were entitled to succeed on their claim and the defendants failed in their counterclaim and set-off (see p. 509 *j* to p. 510 *f* and *j* to p. 511 *f* and *j* to p. 512 *a* and *e f*, post).

*Hick v Raymond & Reid* [1891–4] All ER Rep 491 applied.

**Notes**

For quantum meruit claims, see 9 *Halsbury's Laws* (4th edn) paras 692–696, and for cases on the subject, see 12 *Digest* (Reissue) 145–148, *836–850.*

For rights to set-off and counterclaim for breach of contract, see 9 *Halsbury's Laws* (4th edn) para 608.

For unilateral contracts, see ibid paras 206, 239, 248, 252.

**Cases referred to in judgment**

*Courtney & Fairbairn Ltd v Tolaini Bros (Hotels) Ltd* [1975] 1 All ER 716, [1975] 1 WLR 297.
*Foley v Classique Coaches Ltd* [1934] 2 KB 1, [1934] All ER Rep 88, CA.
*Hillas (W N) & Co Ltd v Arcos Ltd* (1932) 147 LT 503, [1932] All ER Rep 494, HL.
*Lacey (William) (Hounslow) Ltd v Davis* [1957] 2 All ER 712, [1957] 1 WLR 932.
*May & Butcher Ltd v R* (1929) [1934] 2 KB 17, [1929] All ER Rep 679, HL.
*OTM Ltd v Hydranautics* [1981] 2 Lloyd's Rep 211.
*Pantland Hick v Raymond & Reid* [1893] AC 22, sub nom *Hick v Raymond & Reid* [1891–4] All ER Rep 491, HL.
*Sanders & Forster Ltd v A Monk & Co Ltd* [1980] CA Transcript 35.
*Turriff Construction Ltd v Regalia Knitting Mills Ltd* (1971) 222 EG 169.

**Action**

By a writ issued on 11 July 1980 the plaintiffs, British Steel Corp (BSC), sued the defendants, Cleveland Bridge and Engineering Co Ltd (CBE) for £229,832·4370 being the total price outstanding for 137 cast steel nodes manufactured, sold and delivered to CBE between 12 July 1979 and 11 April 1980. By their points of defence and counterclaim, CBE admitted liability in the sum of £200,853 but claimed a right of set-off in respect of the sum of £867,735.68 which they counterclaimed against BSC as damages for breach of contract. The facts are set out in the judgment.

*Philip Naughton and John Grace for BSC.*

*Richard Seymour for CBE.*

*Cur adv vult*

**21 December 1981. The following judgments were delivered.**

**Robert Goff J.**

In this action the plaintiffs, British Steel Corp (whom I shall refer to as BSC), are claiming from the defendants, Cleveland Bridge and Engineering Co Ltd (whom I shall refer to as CBE), the sum of £229,832·4370 as the price of 137 cast-steel nodes and other related goods sold and delivered to CBE, or alternatively are claiming the like sum on a quantum meruit. In their defence and counterclaim, CBE admit that the goods were sold and delivered to them, and further admit liability in a sum of £200,853; but that admission is subject to a plea of set-off against the sum of £867,735·4368 counterclaimed by them on the ground that BSC had, in breach of contract, delivered the nodes too late and out of sequence. Accordingly CBE's net counterclaim is for the difference between these two sums, viz £666,882·4368.

An order was made limiting the hearing before this court to certain specified issues. However, after a short discussion at the beginning of the hearing, it was agreed that the hearing would only be extended by a short time if I dealt with the whole question of liability; and since I felt that it was desirable that I should do so, to avoid a possibly unsatisfactory division of the trial into various issues to be tried by different tribunals, I acceded to a joint application to try the whole issue of liability, leaving only quantum to be decided later if necessary, probably by an official referee. In point of fact, by the end of the trial on liability, the quantum of BSC's claim had been agreed by the parties to be the sum claimed by them in their statement of claim, viz £229,832·4370.

I turn then to the facts of the case. This is a case in which there is no doubt that BSC did in fact manufacture the 137 cast-steel nodes in question at the request of CBE, and did deliver them to CBE. But, despite protracted negotiations between the parties, no formal contract was ever entered into between them. CBE complained that BSC were late in delivering the nodes, and that the causes of delay were (with one minor exception) all within the control of BSC; they also complained that BSC failed to deliver the nodes in the sequence requested by CBE. In these circumstances, two main areas of dispute developed between the parties. First, was there any binding contract between the parties at all, under which the nodes were delivered? CBE contended that there was such a contract, which was to be found in certain documents (including a letter of intent issued by CBE dated 21 February 1979) and the conduct of BSC in proceeding with the manufacture of the nodes. BSC's primary contention was that no binding contract was ever entered into, and that they were entitled to be paid a reasonable sum for the nodes on a quantum meruit, a claim sounding not in contract but in quasi contract. The motives of the parties in putting their cases in these different ways lay primarily in the fact that, unless there was a binding contract between the parties there was no legal basis for CBE's counterclaim for damages in respect of late delivery or delivery out of sequence. So far as delivery was concerned, CBE's submission was that BSC's obligations, under the contract alleged by them to have come into existence, was to deliver the goods in the requested sequence and within a reasonable time.

The first issue is concerned therefore with an analysis of the legal relationship between the parties. The second issue is whether, if CBE are right in their submission that there was a binding contract as alleged by them, BSC were in breach of that contract in delivering the goods late and out of sequence. This latter issue is concerned primarily with consideration of the various events and difficulties which occurred in production of the nodes by BSC, and deciding whether, in the light of these events, BSC failed to deliver the goods within a reasonable time as alleged by CBE.

It is right that I should record at this stage that, on the arguments as finally developed before me, BSC abandoned an argument that a binding contract was concluded between the parties, on BSC's standard terms, at a meeting held on 1 August 1979 and also that CBE did not press an argument that there was a contract contained in or evidenced by certain documents. I have no doubt that both parties were right in deciding not to pursue these respective arguments.

Having outlined the issues before the court, I shall now proceed to set out the background facts of the case.

The plaintiffs are, as I have said, BSC; but in this case I am concerned with a profit-making division of BSC, the Forges, Foundries and Engineering Group (FFE). The head office of FFE is at their River Don works at Sheffield; in or near Sheffield they have not only offices, but also a large foundry and a laboratory. Another medium-sized foundry within FFE is at their Craigneuk works at Motherwell, in Scotland; it is with this foundry that I am chiefly concerned in this case. Craigneuk (as I shall call it), although forming part of FFE, has its own general manager and sales manager, and enters into contracts without reference to the head office of the group in Sheffield.

CBE are a company concerned with steel fabrication. Their works are at Darlington and at Port Clarence on Teesside. They form part of the Trafalgar House group of companies.

A company associated with CBE, Cementation (Saudi Arabia) Ltd, in which Trafalgar House hold a substantial shareholding, was concerned in the construction of a bank (known as the Sama Bank) at Dammam in Saudi Arabia. It was intended that CBE should be subcontractors for the fabrication of steel work for the bank. The bank was to be of an unusual construction. The main body of the building was to be suspended from four columns, and was to have a steel lattice-work frame. There was a requirement for nodes for use at the centres of the lattice work, providing the points at which diagonal steel beams would join the lattice work on the surface of the building.

[His Lordship then made the following findings of fact. CBE discovered that BSC had been working on the development of cast steel nodes and accordingly contacted BSC. Thereafter discussions took place between the parties with a view to a contract being entered into for the manufacture of the cast steel nodes for CBE by BSC. BSC prepared an estimated price based on the incomplete information which was then available to it and on 9 February 1979 sent the following telex to CBE:

> 'STEEL CASTINGS FOR NODES NODE PLATE DRG 773/73 £1225 EACH NODES DRG 773/41 £941 EACH PROPOSED PRICE FOR REMAINING ITEMS £1300 PER TONNE. PRICES WOULD REMAIN FIXED FOR DURATION OF CONTRACT. CONTRACT WILL BE SUPPLIED IN UNMACHINED CONDITION FINISHED TO NORMAL FOUNDRY STANDARDS. MATERIAL, HEAT TREATMENT AND INSPECTION WOULD BE IN ACCORDANCE WITH INFORMATION CONTAINED IN OUR TELEX DATED 29 JAN 79. PATTERN COSTS £6500 LUMP SUM DELIVERY: COMMENCE DELIVERY IN 10 WEEKS FROM RECEIPT OF ORDER AND FINAL DRAWINGS AT A RATE TO BE AGREED.'

Further discussions on technical aspects and appropriate specifications for the manufacture of the nodes took place between the parties and then on 21 February 1979 CBE sent a letter of intent to BSC which read as follows:

'SAMA BANK—DAMMAM

We are pleased to advise you that it is the intention of Cleveland Bridge & Engineering Co. Ltd. to enter into a Sub-Contract with your company, for the supply and delivery of the steel castings which form the roof nodes on this project. The price will be as quoted in your telex (Mr Dorrance to Mr Roberts) dated 9th February '79 which is as follows: Nodes to drawing No. 773/73 £1225 each Nodes to drawing No. 773/41 £941 each. The price for the remaining items being £1300 per tonne. In addition the pattern costs will be a lump sum of £6500. The form of Sub-Contract to be entered into will be our standard form of sub-contract for use in conjunction with the I.C.E. General Conditions of Contract, a copy of which is enclosed for your consideration. We also enclose a copy of the Client's fabrication Specification in relation to Structural Steelwork (pp. 5A.1 to 5A.37 incl.) which is to be complied with where applicable. However, the specification for the castings will generally be in accordance with the discussions held at the Consultant Engineer's offices on 20th February '79 at which your Mr Dorrance and other representatives of your company were present. We understand that you are already in possession of a complete set of our node detail drawings and we request that you proceed immediately with the works pending the preparation and issuing to you of the official form of sub-contract.'

In fact BSC were not then in possession of a full set of drawings. BSC did not reply to the letter because a formal order was expected to follow shortly thereafter. BSC would not have agreed to the ICE conditions of contract which provided for unlimited liability for consequential loss arising from late delivery. BSC intended to submit a formal quotation for individual prices once they had a full set of documents from which to make their calculations. In the mean time BSC processed the letter as an order and began preparations for manufacture in order not to delay final deliveries. On 27 February 1979 CBE sent a telex to BSC giving details of test plates which would be required, and also the sequence in which delivery of the nodes was required by CBE. That was the first intimation which BSC had that CBE required the nodes to be delivered in a particular sequence. There were further discussions and negotiations between the parties over the specifications to be met in the manufacture of the nodes and, because little had been agreed, Mr Kain, BSC's works manager, sent the following telex to CBE on 4 April:

> 'THERE ARE FAR TOO MANY UNRESOLVED QUERIES... WE ARE VERY CONCERNED THAT THIS COULD RESULT IN INCREASED COST AND DELAYS AT LATER STAGES DURING MANUFACTURE. WE ARE THEREFORE NOT PREPARED TO PROCEED WITH THIS CONTRACT UNTIL WE HAVE AN AGREED SPECIFICATION COVERING ALL THESE POINTS WHICH HAS BEEN RATIFIED BY CLEVELAND BRIDGE.'

Thereafter there were further discussions between the parties and although a number of matters remained unresolved it was agreed that BSC should go ahead with the manufacture of the first cast. The first experimental nodes cast were not satisfactory and CBE required extensive alterations to the patterns and specifications. The parties met on 15 May and apparently agreed on a further revision of the draft specifications. On 16 May BSC sent CBE a formal quotation on their standard form, quoting a price of £212,100 with the date of delivery to be agreed. This was a substantial increase in the prices quoted in BSC's telex of 9 February and CBE decided that the increased price was unacceptable. As a result BSC offered to reduce the price by 9%. Meanwhile BSC did all it could to make up production time lost by the rejection of the first cast, and to expedite delivery of the nodes. CBE continued to query the reasons for the price increase and again raised questions over the specifications (which had been revised by CBE on a further occasion since 15 May). Further problems were experienced by BSC in the production of suitable nodes but these were eventually overcome. On 6 July at a heated meeting between the parties BSC urged CBE to accept the quotation of 16 May and to place a formal order with them. CBE responded by tabling a contract on its standard form based on the prices contained in BSC's telex of 9 February. This contract was rejected by BSC. Despite the failure to agree on a price or other contract conditions BSC went ahead with the casting and delivery of nodes in stages in an effort to comply with CBE's requirements for delivery. At a meeting between the parties on 1 August 1979 provisional agreement was reached on the price contained in BSC's quotation of 16 May but the parties were unable to agree at that stage on the other contract conditions, especially those relating to consequential damages and a proposed performance bond.

BSC agreed to submit a revised delivery schedule and to attempt to speed up delivery of the completed nodes. Further disruption was caused to production by an industrial dispute and by further technical difficulties. Eventually both of these difficulties were overcome. Deliveries continued despite a failure to agree the contract terms, especially the mode of payment, and despite CBE's failure to make any interim payment. By 28 December BSC had delivered all but one of the 137 nodes, the last node being held back by BSC to ensure that payment would be made by CBE. A steelworkers' dispute began on 1 January 1980 which lasted several weeks with the result that the last node was not delivered to CBE until 11 April 1980. In the meantime CBE refused to make any payment to BSC until the nodes were on site in Saudi Arabia, on the basis that CBE would not be paid by the main contractors until that time. That was inconsistent with CBE's earlier assurances about progress payments. After a stormy meeting between the parties on 6 February, BSC heard nothing more from CBE about payment, apart from a self-exculpatory letter from CBE two days later, until in April 1980 CBE submitted a written claim to BSC for damages for late delivery, which claim far surpassed BSC's claim for the price of the goods delivered. CBE's written claim for damages precipitated BSC's own action for damages commenced by writ on 11 July 1980 in which CBE counterclaimed and claimed a right of set-off. His Lordship continued:]

Such are the facts of the case. I now turn to the first issue in the case, which is concerned with the legal basis for BSC's claim for payment, and in particular whether there was any binding contract between BSC and CBE and, if so, what were its terms. As I have already indicated, it is the contention of CBE that there was such a contract; whereas BSC contends that they are entitled to payment in quasi contract.

As I indicated at the beginning of this judgment, CBE alleged two alternative contracts in their points of defence and counterclaim; but the first of these alternatives was not pursued. Their remaining submission was that the agreement between the parties was comprised in the request by CBE to BSC, in their letter dated 21 February 1979, that BSC proceed to manufacture the nodes (viz the request contained in CBE's letter of intent), the notification by CBE to BSC in their telex dated 27 February 1979 as to the sequence in which delivery of the nodes was required, and the conduct of BSC in proceeding with the manufacture of the nodes. As I have also indicated, although BSC allege in their pleadings that an agreement was reached between the parties, on BSC's standard conditions, at the meeting of 1 August 1979, the allegation was rightly abandoned by BSC in the course of the hearing, and they advanced their claim for payment simply on the basis of quasi contract.

Now the question whether in a case such as the present any contract has come into existence must depend on a true construction of the relevant communications which have passed between the parties and the effect (if any) of their actions pursuant to those communications. There can be no hard and fast answer to the question whether a letter of intent will give rise to a binding agreement: everything must depend on the circumstances of the particular case. In most cases, where work is done pursuant to a request contained in a letter of intent, it will not matter whether a contract did or did not come into existence, because, if the party who has acted on the request is simply claiming payment, his claim will usually be based on a quantum meruit, and it will make no difference whether that claim is contractual or quasi-contractual. Of course, a quantum meruit claim (like the old actions for money had and received and for money paid) straddles the boundaries of what we now call contract and restitution, so the mere framing of a claim as a quantum meruit claim, or a claim for a reasonable sum, does not assist in classifying the claim as contractual or quasi contractual. But where, as here, one party is seeking to claim damages for breach of contract, the question whether any contract came into existence is of crucial importance.

As a matter of analysis the contract (if any) which may come into existence following a letter of intent may take one of two forms: either there may be an ordinary executory contract, under which each party assumes reciprocal obligations to the other; or there may be what is sometimes called an 'if' contract, i.e. a contract under which A requests B to carry out a certain performance and promises B that, if he does so, he will receive a certain performance in return, usually remuneration for his performance. The latter transaction is really no more than a standing offer which, if acted on before it lapses or is lawfully withdrawn, will result in a binding contract.

The former type of contract was held to exist by Mr Edgar Fay QC, the official Referee, in *Turriff Construction Ltd v Regalia Knitting Mills Ltd* (1971) 202 EG 169; and it is the type of contract for which counsel for CBE contended in the present case. Of course, as I have already said, everything must depend on the facts of the particular case; but certainly, on the facts of the present case (and, as I imagine, on the facts of most cases), this must be a very difficult submission to maintain. It is only necessary to look at the terms of CBE's letter of intent in the present case to appreciate the difficulties. In that letter, the request to BSC to proceed immediately with the work was stated to be 'pending the preparation and issuing to you of the official form of sub-contract', being a sub-contract which was plainly in a state of negotiation, not least on the issues of price, delivery dates, and the applicable terms and conditions. In these circumstances, it is very difficult to see how BSC, by starting work, bound themselves to any contractual performance. No doubt it was envisaged by CBE at the time they sent the letter that negotiations had reached an advanced stage, and that a formal contract would soon be signed; but, since the parties were still in a state of negotiation, it is impossible to say with any degree of certainty what the material terms of that contract would be. I find myself quite unable to conclude that, by starting work in these circumstances, BSC bound themselves to complete the work. In the course of argument, I put to counsel for CBE the question whether BSC were free at any time, after starting work, to cease work. His submission was that they were not free to do so, even if negotiations on the terms of the formal contract broke down completely. I find this submission to be so repugnant to common sense and the commercial realities that I am unable to accept it. It is perhaps revealing that, on 4 April 1979, BSC did indeed state that they were not prepared to proceed with the contract until they had an agreed specification, a reaction which, in my judgment, reflected not only the commercial, but also the legal, realities of the situation.

I therefore reject CBE's submission that a binding executory contract came into existence in this case. There remains the question whether, by reason of BSC carrying out work pursuant to the request contained in CBE's letter of intent, there came into existence a contract by virtue of which BSC were entitled to claim reasonable remuneration; i.e. whether there was an 'if' contract of the kind I have described. In the course of argument, I was attracted by this alternative (really on the basis that, not only was it analytically possible, but also that it could provide a vehicle for certain contractual obligations of BSC concerning their performance, e.g. implied terms as to the quality of goods supplied by them). But the more I have considered the case, the less attractive I have found this alternative. The real difficulty is to be found in the factual matrix of the transaction, and in particular the fact that the work was being done *pending* a formal sub-contract the terms of which were still in a state of negotiation. It is, of course, a notorious fact that, when a contract is made for the supply of goods on a scale and in circumstances such as the present, it will in all probability be subject to standard terms, usually the standard terms of the supplier. Such standard terms will frequently legislate, not only for the liability of the seller for defects, but also for the damages (if any) for which the seller will be liable in the event not only of defects in the goods but also of late delivery. It is a commonplace that a seller of goods may exclude liability for consequential loss, and may agree liquidated damages for delay. In the present case, an unresolved dispute broke out between the parties on the question whether CBE's or BSC's standard terms were to apply, the former providing no limit to the seller's liability for delay and the latter excluding such liability altogether. Accordingly, when, in a case such as the present, the parties are still in a state of negotiation, it is impossible to predicate what liability (if any) will be assumed by the seller for, e.g. defective goods or late delivery, if a formal contract should be entered into. In these circumstances, if the buyer asks the seller to commence work 'pending' the parties entering into a formal contract, it is difficult to infer from the buyer acting on that request that he is assuming any responsibility for his performance, except such responsibility as will rest on him under the terms of the contract which both parties confidently anticipate they will shortly enter into. It would be an extraordinary result if, by acting on such a request in such circumstances, the buyer were to assume an unlimited liability for his contractual performance, when he would never assume such liability under any contract which he entered into.

For these reasons, I reject the solution of the 'if' contract. In my judgment, the true analysis of the situation is simply this. Both parties confidently expected a formal contract to eventuate. In these circumstances, to expedite performance under that anticipated contract, one requested the other to commence the contract work, and the other complied with that request. If thereafter, as anticipated, a contract was entered into, the work done as requested will be treated as having been performed under that contract; if, contrary to their expectation, no contract was entered into, then the performance of the work is not referable to any contract the terms of which can be ascertained, and the law simply imposes an obligation on the party who made the request to pay a reasonable sum for such work as has been done pursuant to that request, such an obligation sounding in quasi contract or, as we now say, in restitution. Consistently with that solution, the party making the request may find himself liable to pay for work which he would not have had to pay for as such if the anticipated contract had come into existence, e.g. preparatory work which will, if the contract is made, be allowed for in the price of the finished work (cf *William Lacey (Hounslow) Ltd v Davis* [1957] 2 All ER 712, [1957] 1 WLR 932). This solution moreover accords with authority: see the decision in *Lacey v Davis*, the decision of the Court of Appeal in *Sanders & Forster Ltd v A Monk & Co Ltd* [1980] CA Transcript 35, though that decision rested in part on a concession, and the crisp dictum of Parker J in *OTM Ltd v Hydranautics* [1981] 2 Lloyd's Rep 211 at 214, when he said of a letter of intent that 'its only effect would be to enable the defendants to recover on a quantum meruit for work done pursuant to the direction' contained in the letter. I only wish to add to this part of my judgment the footnote that, even if I had concluded that in the circumstances of the present case there was a contract between the parties and that that contract was of the kind I have described as an 'if' contract, then I would still have concluded that there was no obligation under that contract on the part of BSC to continue with or complete the contract work, and therefore no obligation on their part to complete the work within a reasonable time. However, my conclusion in the present case is that the parties never entered into any contract at all.

In the course of his argument counsel for BSC submitted that, in a contract of this kind, the price is always an essential term in the sense that, if it is not agreed, no contract can come into existence. In support of his contention counsel relied on a dictum of Lord Denning MR in *Courtney & Fairbairn Ltd v Tolaini Bros (Hotels) Ltd* [1975] 1 All ER 716 at 719, [1975] 1 WLR 297 at 301 to the effect that the price in a building contract is of fundamental importance. I do not however read Lord Denning MR's dictum as stating that in every building contract the price is invariably an essential term, particularly as he expressly referred to the substantial size of the contract then before the court. No doubt in the vast majority of business transactions, particularly those of substantial size, the price will indeed be an essential term, but in the final analysis it must be a question of construction of the particular transaction whether it is so. This is plain from the familiar trilogy of cases which show that no hard and fast rule can be laid down but that the question in each case is whether, on a true construction of the relevant transaction, it was consistent with the intention of the parties that even though no price had been agreed a reasonable price should be paid (*May & Butcher Ltd v R* (1929) [1934] 2 KB 17, [1929] All ER Rep 679, *W N Hillas & Co Ltd v Arcos Ltd* (1932) 147 LT 503, [1932] All ER Rep 494 and *Foley v Classique Coaches Ltd* [1934] 2 KB 1, [1934] All ER Rep 88). In the present case, however, I have no doubt whatsoever that, consistently with the view expressed by Lord Denning MR in *Courtney & Fairbairn Ltd v Tolaini Bros (Hotels) Ltd*, the price was indeed an essential term, on which (among other essential terms) no final agreement was ever reached.

It follows that BSC are entitled to succeed on their claim and that CBE's set-off and counterclaim must fail. But, in case this matter should go further, I propose, having heard the evidence and the submissions of the parties, to express my opinion on the question whether, if BSC were under any obligation to deliver the goods in a reasonable time, they were in breach of that obligation. In this part of my judgment, I do not propose to consider any question of delivery out of sequence; an obligation to deliver in a certain sequence could only have arisen from an express term in a contract between the parties, and I am satisfied that no such express term can possibly be said to have been agreed in the present case; and if any court should hereafter form a different view, the difference between the actual and contractual order of delivery can be ascertained without difficulty.

I turn to the question of delivery within a reasonable time. It was common ground between the parties that the principles I had to apply in this connection were those stated by the House of Lords in *Pantland Hick v Raymond & Reid* [1893] AC 22, [1891–4] All ER Rep 491, viz that the question of what constituted a reasonable time had to be considered in relation to the circumstances which existed at the time when the contractual services were performed, but excluding circumstances which were under the control of the party performing those services. As I understand it, I have first to consider what would, in ordinary circumstances, be a reasonable time for the performance of the relevant services; and I have then to consider to what extent the time for performance by BSC was in fact extended by extraordinary circumstances outside their control.

[His Lordship then considered the evidence and concluded that a reasonable period for the manufacture of the 137 nodes was 551/2 weeks and that since such a period would have gone well beyond 11 April 1980 when the last node was in fact delivered it followed that if, contrary to his Lordship's previously expressed opinion, BSC had been bound to complete the work within a reasonable time they would not have been in breach of that obligation. His Lordship continued:]

However, as I have already held, there was in my judgment no obligation on BSC to deliver the nodes within a reasonable time. It follows that BSC are entitled to judgment on their claim in the sum of £229,832·4370 and that CBE's set-off and counterclaim must be dismissed.

*Judgment for the plaintiffs.*

*Solicitors: Lovell White & King (for BSC); A Paul Powell, Darlington (for CBE).*

K Mydeen Esq Barrister.

### 4.4.2 Appendix 2

All England Law Reports/1964/Volume 1/Edwards v Skyways Ltd—[1964] 1 All ER 494; reproduced with permission Lexis Nexis (UK Law Reports)

**[1964] 1 All ER 494**

**Edwards v Skyways Ltd**

**Queen's Bench Division**

**Megaw J**

**15, 16, 17, 21 January 1964**

*Contract—Intention to create legal relationship—Agreement to make "ex gratia" payment—Oral negotiations on redundancy of employees—Employing company agreeing to make "ex gratia" payment to redundant employees—Consideration given by employees—Company subsequently rescinding agreement—Whether agreement legally binding. Contract—Uncertainty of terms—"Approximating to"—Whether agreement for payment of sum approximating to total of contributions to pension fund too vague.*

The plaintiff was employed by the defendant company as an aircraft pilot, and as such he was a member of the defendant company's contributory pension fund and entitled under its rules on leaving the defendant company's service in advance of retirement age to a choice between two options, either to withdraw the sum of his own contributions to the fund or to take the right to a paid-up pension payable at retirement age. In January, 1962, the defendant company wrote the plaintiff, among others, informing him that it was necessary to declare a redundancy of approximately fifteen per cent of the defendant company's pilot strength and giving him three months' notice terminating his employment. At a meeting on 8 February 1962, between authorised representatives of the defendant company and Balpa, the plaintiff's trade association, it was agreed (as recorded in the notes of the meeting) that "pilots declared redundant and leaving [the defendant company] would be given an ex gratia payment equivalent to the defendant company's contributions to the pension fund". The representative of the defendant company actually said at the meeting that the defendant company would make ex gratia payments "approximating to" the defendant company's contributions. Having been informed of the recorded agreement, and having found other employment and left the defendant company's employment at the end of March, 1962, the plaintiff elected on 1 May 1962, to withdraw his contributions to the pension fund and to receive the ex gratia payment that the defendant company proposed to make. The defendant company paid to the plaintiff the amount of his contributions, but did not make the ex gratia payment, and rescinded the decision to make ex gratia payments, having regard to the defendant company's financial difficulties and creditors. The plaintiff brought this action to recover a sum equal to the total contributions made by the defendant company in respect of him to the pension fund. The defendant company contended that the recorded agreement was not intended to create legal relations and was too vague, and thus was not legally binding. It was admitted at the hearing that there was consideration moving from the plaintiff and that at the time of the meeting of 8 February 1962, the defendant company tended to carry out the recorded agreement.

**Held**—Where, as here, there was agreement and the subject of agreement related to business affairs, the onus of establishing that the agreement was not intended to create legal relations, which was on the perty setting up that defence, was a heavy onus (see p. 500, letter *a*, post); and the defendant company had failed to discharge it for the following reasons—

(i) the words "ex gratia" were used simply to indicate that the party agreeing did not admit any pre-existing liability on the defendant company's part, and the more use of the phrase "ex gratia" as part of a promise to pay (even if prompted by the purpose of avoiding the incidence of income tax) did not show that the promise, when accepted, should have no binding effect in law (see p. 500, letters *d* and *f*, and p. 501, letter *d*, post), and
(ii) the use of the words "approximating to" on behalf of the defendant company did not render the terms of the agreement too vague to be enforceable, for at most the phrase would connote on the evidence a rounding off of a few pounds downwards to a round figure (see p. 501, letter *f*, post).

Observations of Scrutton LJ and Atkin LJ in *Rose and Frank Co v J R Crompton & Bros Ltd.* ([1924] All ER Rep at pp. 240, 252) considered.

**Notes**

As to the negativing of the intention of the parties to enter into legal relations, see 8 *Halsbury's Laws* (3rd Edn) 54, para 90, note (a) and p. 69, para 118, note (h); as to uncertainty in the terms of an agreement, see ibid, pp. 83, 84, para 144; and for cases on the subject, see 12 *Digest* (Repl) 21–23, *3–12*.

**Cases referred to in judgment**

*Balfour v Balfour*, [1918–19] All ER Rep 860, [1919] 2 KB 571, 88 LJKB 1054, 121 LT 346, 12 *Digest* (Repl) 21, *3*.
*Rose and Frank Co v Crompton (JR) & Bros Ltd* [1924] All ER Rep 245, [1923] 2 KB 261, 92 LJKB 959, 129 LT 610, *revsd* HL, [1924] All ER Rep 245, [1925] AC 445, 94 LJKB 120, 132 LT 641, 12 *Digest* (Repl) 22, *4*.

**Action**

In this action the plaintiff Peter John Edwards, an aircraft pilot, formerly employed by the defendant company, Skyways Ltd claimed payment of a sum equal to the total of the defendant company's contributions on his behalf to the aircrew superannuation fund of which he had been a member. The action was founded on an oral agreement reached at a meeting on 8 February 1962, which had been arranged to negotiate matters arising out of a "redundancy declaration" affecting fifteen per cent of the defendant company's pilot strength. At this meeting the defendant company through their representatives, acting on the authority of a resolution of the board of directors, promised the representatives of the British Air Line Pilots Association, acting for the plaintiff and other redundant pilots concerned, that to each of those pilots who left their service and opted to take a refund of his own contributions to the superannuation fund (rather than take the right to a paid-up pension payable on retirement age) they would make an ex gratia payment approximating to (or equivalent to) the contributions made to the fund by the defendant company in respect of that pilot. On 2 May 1962, the defendant company's board of directors by resolution rescinded their earlier decision to make ex grattia payments to redundant aircrew. The facts appear in the judgment.

The cases noted below* were cited in argument in addition to those referred to in the judgment.

**Thomas v Brown*, (1876), 1 QBD 714, *Central London Property Trust v High Trees House Ltd*, [1956] 1 All ER 256, n, [1947] 1 KB 130, *Robertson v Minister of Pensions*, [1948] 2 All ER 767, [1949] 1 KB 227, *Combe v Combe*, [1951] 1 All ER 767, [1951] 2 KB 215

*[1964] 1 All ER 494 at 496*

*J P Comyn QC and J D F Moylan for the plaintiff.*
*A W Hamilton for the defendant company.*

**21 January 1964. The following judgment was delivered.**

**Megaw J**

read the following judgment. The plaintiff, Captain Peter John Edwards, was employed as an aircraft pilot by the defendant company, Skyways from June, 1955, until 31 March 1962, with the rank of first officer for the first few months, and thereafter as captain. His terms of employment provided for three months' notice of termination. On 26 January 1962, the defendant company, being in financial difficulty and not having sufficient work to continue to employ all its staff, wrote a letter to the plaintiff, at the same time sending similar letters to other persons. The plaintiff was told that it would be "necessary to declare a redundancy of approximately 15% of our pilot strength", and he was given three months' notice. He was offered alternative employment either as a captain based at Lympne Airport with a subsidiary company (which would have involved him in moving his home) or as a first officer on the defendant company's four engined fleet (which would have involved reduction of pay and status).

The question of the threatened redundancy was taken up with the defendant company by the British Air Line Pilots Association, to which the plaintiff belonged. The association took the view that certain procedure which had been agreed in 1948 in the National Joint Council with regard to redundancies had not been observed by the defendant company. A meeting took place between representatives of the association and representatives of the defendant company on 8 February 1962. It is not in dispute that the representatives of the association were the duly authorised agents of the plaintiff, and that the representatives of the defendant company had full authority from that company in respect of all that was done and agreed at that meeting affecting the plaintiff. Two days before the meeting, on 6 February at a meeting of the board of directors of the defendant company, a resolution had been passed in these terms:

> "The board approved that the secretary be empowered in his discussions with the British Air Line Pilots Association to agree should circumstances require to the payment to redundant aircrew members of ex gratia amount approximating to the company's contributions for each member of the Pension and Superannuation Fund."

It appears that the defendant company realised that the association would be seeking to secure some form of compensation for its members who were being declared redundant and that it was accordingly authorising the secretary, in advance, to deal with the question when it arose. The secretary of the defendant company, Mr David John Davies, himself drafted the resolution. It was based on what had been done at the time of an earlier redundancy in the defendant company in 1959, when, after discussions with the association, the defendant company had paid sums to redudant aircrew staff, the sums being at any rate closely related in amount to the total superannuation contributions made by the company in respect of the particular redundant employee.

At the meeting on 8 February 1962, the defendant company's representatives included, amongst others, Mr Davies, the secretary, and Mr Lees, the personnel officer. The association's representatives included, amongst others, Mr Follows, who was then the secretary, and Captain Clink, the chairman of the association's local committee with the defendant company, who was also an employee of the defendant company. The plaintiff himself was not present. As to what happened at the meeting, so far as is relevant to the issues in this action, there is no real dispute on any matter of substance. Each of the witnesses who gave evidence before me was truthful and fair in giving his recollection. Such minor differences as there were in their accounts of the conversations are not on matters of any real significance. I need not recount much of what took place at the meeting. The substance of it is accurately summarised in a document headed "Notes", which was prepared the next morning by Mr Follows with the assistance of Captain Clink, on the basis of manuscript notes made during the meeting. There is no doubt that everyone present at the meeting thought that all major difficulties had been resolved and that various matters of principle had been agreed. I need mention only one of the matters discussed and agreed.

The plaintiff (and there were other pilots in a similar position) would have been entitled under his terms of service, if he left his employment with the defendant company for any reason other than dismissal for misconduct, to take a paid-up pension; that is, a pension which would, without further contribution to be made by anyone, become payable when he reached the normal retiring age stated in the pension scheme. It would be calculated by reference to the total contributions paid, up to date, by himself and by the defendant company on his account. Alternatively, the plaintiff would be entitled to withdraw his own contributions in cash. Mr Follows had in mind what had happened in the 1959 redundancy when the company had agreed to pay, and had paid, redundant pilots sums of money equivalent, at least broadly, to the company's pension contributions in respect of them, in addition to the pilots' own contributions which they were contractually entitled to withdraw. He, therefore, at the meeting, asked that similar financial compensation should be paid by the defendant company, on this occasion. Mr Davies, on behalf of the defendant company, having already in anticipation received his board's authority, quickly and readily agreed.

This agreement is recorded as follows in notes to which I have referred:

> "The following general principles were then accepted in relation to the redundancy and consequential matters";

and then, after certain other matters, this appears:

> "Pilots declared redundant and leaving the company would be given an ex gratia payment equivalent to the company's contribution to the Pension Fund. They would, of course, be entitled to a refund of their own contributions to the fund."

The pilots affected were informed of the various decisions and agreements in a publication called "Newsletter", addressed by the association to its members on 9 February 1962. The agreement as to the defendant company's contributions is there recorded as follows:

> "After considerable discussion, the following points were agreed between the company and the association: … 4. To those pilots who are finally declared redundant, the company will make an ex-gratia payment equivalent to their (the company's) own contributions to the Provident or Pension Scheme."

There is reason to believe that Mr Davies, the secretary, saw this "Newsletter", and did not challenge the accuracy of what was there recorded. Mr Davies' own account of what he said on the point at the meeting is as follows:

> "Having the board's authority, I said we would make ex gratia payments approximating to the company's contributions for those pilots who chose to take their contributions rather than paid-up pension policies."

I think it is probable that Mr Davies's recollection is right when he says that he himself used the words "approximating to". It may well be that both that phrase and "equivalent to" were used during the discussion. No one attached any particular significance to the point, and I do not regard verbal niceties as being of importance. Mr Davies in evidence agreed that "equivalent to" is a reasonable interpretation of what he said. Mr Lees agreed that everyone left the meeting with a clear impression that the defendant company would pay an amount equal to the defendant company's contribution. I am satisfied that that is the substance of what was understood and agreed when the meeting ended.

The issue in this action is whether, as a result of what was agreed at the meeting, the plaintiff when he decided not to accept any of the offered alternatives but to leave the company's service and withdraw his own pension contributions, acquired a legal right, to be paid by the defendant company a sum equal to the contributions which they had paid to the pension fund on his behalf. The plaintiff says that there was a legally binding contractual right. The defendant company say that, while there may have been a moral right, or an obligation binding in honour, there was not a legally enforceable right. Before considering the issue, I should complete my outline of the history of the matter.

The plaintiff, not desiring to accept the defendant company's offer of continuing employment with the various disadvantages involved, sought and obtained other employment to begin on 1 April 1962, and the defendant company agreed that the plaintiff should leave their service on 31 March before the full three months' notice had run. On 15 April 1962, the plaintiff wrote to Mr Roberts, the assistant secretary of the defendant company, asking for information to enable him to make up his mind about the option between, on the one hand, his undoubted legal right to take the paid-up pension, and, on the other hand, the right which it had been agreed (whether or not as an obligation binding in law) that he should have, to withdraw his own contributions and receive what he described (no doubt following the wording of the "Newsletter" which he had seen) as, "the amount of the ex gratia payment which the company proposes to make in the event of my taking the cash refund". Mr Roberts replied on 17 April giving him approximate figures: a paid-up policy of about £180 per annum at the age of 50; his own contributions of approximately £630, less tax of approximately £60; and "The ex gratia payment will be approximately half as much again as your own contributions, but as this is purely ex gratia there is no question of tax." The following day the plaintiff wrote to Mr Roberts telling him how he had decided to exercise what he believed to be his option: "I have decided to take the cash refund of my contributions, with the company's ex gratia payment". The plaintiff, with the complete frankness which was characteristic of his evidence, said that he could not now be sure whether he would have exercised the option the same way, if he had not though that the defendant company were going to pay him that which they had agreed to pay in respect of their own contributions. He would certainly have thought much more deeply about it. He might still have decided to take the immediate cash provided by the refund of his own contributions.

On 1 May 1962, the defendant company sent the plaintiff a cheque for £609 1s, in respect of his own contributions. On 2 May 1962, the very day after that payment had been made to, and accepted by, the plaintiff in the belief that a further sum was to follow—because the defendant company had so promised—the board of directors of the defendant company met and passed another resolution. It was in these terms:

> "It was resolved that the company's previous decision to make ex gratia payments to redundant aircrew be rescinded because of the large number of staff involved and in view of the position that the company's contributions to the scheme which were returnable to the trustees could not, under the rules of the scheme, be utilised directly by the company. Mr Ryland and Mr Davies would draft a letter to the staff concerned explaining the position and Mr Davies would arrange with the insurance company for an extension of the option period to be made for all aircrew members who had already opted for cash so that they could reconsider their decision."

I offer no comment, except to mention the explanation given on behalf of the defendant company. It is said that they found themselves in financial difficulties, with various creditors, secured and unsecured, pressing them. Although at the time when they made the promise they intended to honour it, later they thought that in the existing financial situation they should decline to honour it because they believed that it was not legally binding, and because other creditors, with legal obligations, might have been prejudiced. The defendant company have not gone into liquidation. The plaintiff has not been paid, because the obligation was merely, as I understood the defendant company's view, a moral one, which they repudiated. It is not necessary for me to set out the subsequent history, since it does not affect the issue, namely: Was there a legal obligation on the part of the defendant company?

The defendant company admit, as I understand it, that at the meeting a promise was made on their behalf with their authority, although the actual word "promise" was not used. In the defence it was pleaded that no consideration moved from the plaintiff. That plea was expressly abandoned at the hearing. It was conceded that there was consideration. The defendant company admit that it was their intention to carry out their promise when they made it, and that the plaintiff's representatives, and the plaintiff himself, believed, and acted in the belief, that the promise would be fulfilled. Everyone, at the end of the meeting, believed that there was an agreement which would be carried out. But the defendant company say that the promise and the agreement have no legal effect, because there was no intention to enter into relations in respect of the promised payment.

It is clear from such cases as *Rose and Frank Co v J R Crompton & Bros, Ltd* and *Balfour v Balfour*, that there are cases in which English law recognises that an agreement, in other respects duly made, does not give rise to legal rights, because the parties have not intended that their legal relations should be affected. Where the subject-matter of the agreement is some domestic or social relationship or transaction, as in *Balfour v Balfour*, the law will often deny legal consequences to the agreement, because of the very nature of the subject-matter. Where the subject-matter of the agreement is not domestic or social, but is related to business affairs, the parties may, be using clear words, show that their intention is to make the transaction binding in honour only, and not in law; and the courts will give effect to the expressed intention. Scrutton LJ expressed it thus, in *Rose and Frank Co v J R Crompton & Bros Ltd* ([1924] All ER Rep at pp. 249, 250; [1923] 2 KB at p. 288).

> "It is quite possible for parties to come to an agreement by accepting a proposal with the result that the agreement concluded does not give rise to legal relations. The reason of this

> is that the parties do not intend that their agreement shall give rise to legal relations. This intention may be implied from the subject-matter of the agreement, but it may also be expressed by the parties. In social and family relations such an intention is readily implied, while in business matters the opposite result would ordinarily follow. But I can see no reason why, even in business matters, the parties should not intend to rely on each other's good faith and honour, and to exclude all idea of settling disputes by any outside intervention with the accompanying necessity of expressing themselves so precisely that outsiders may have no difficulty in understanding what they mean. If they clearly express such an intention I can see no reason in public policy why effect should not be given to their intention."

In the same case, Atkin LJ said ([1924] All ER Rep at p. 252; [1923] 2 KB at p. 293):

> "To create a contract there must be a common intention of the parties to enter into legal obligations, mutually communicated expressly or impliedly. Such an intention ordinarily wii be inferred when parties enter into an agreement which in other respects conforms to the rule of law as to the formation of contracts. It may be negatived impliedly by the nature of the agreed promise or promises, as in the case of offer and acceptance of hospitality, or of some agreements made in the course of family life between members of a family as in *Balfour* v. *Balfour*. If the intention may be negatived impliedly it may be negatived expressly."

In the present case, the subject-matter of the agreement is business relations, not social or domestic matters. There was a meeting of minds—an intention to agree. There was, admittedly, consideration for the defendant company's promise. I accept the propositions of counsel for the plaintiff that in a case of this nature the onus is on the party who assets that no legal effect was intended, and the onus in a heavy one. Counsel for the plaintiff also submitted, with the support of the well-known textbooks on the law of contract, (Anson, and Cheshire And Fifoot), that the test of intention to create or not to create legal relations is "objective". I am not sure that I know what that means in this context. I do, however, think that there are grave difficulties in trying to apply a test as to the actual intention or understanding or knowledge of the parties; especially where the alleged agreement is arrived at between a limited liability company and a trade association; and especially where it is arrived at a meeting attended by five or six representatives on each side. Whose knowledge, understanding or intention is relevant? But if it be the "objective" test of the reasonable man, what background knowledge is to be imputed to the reasonable man, when the background knowledge of the 10 or 12 persons who took part in arriving at the decision no doubt varied greatly between one another? However that may be, the defendant company say, first, as I understand it, that the mere use of the phrase "ex gratia" by itself, as a part of the promise to pay, shows that the parties contemplated that the promise, when accepted, should have no binding force in law. They say, secondly, that even if their first proposition is not correct as a general proposition, nevertheless here there was certain background knowledge, present in the minds of everyone, which gave unambiguous significance to "ex gratia" as excluding legal relationship.

As to the first proposition, the words "ex gratia" do not, in my judgment, carry a necessary, or even a probable, implication that the agreement is to be without legal effect. It is, I think, common experience amongst practitioners of the law that litigation or threatened litigation is frequently compromised on the terms that one party shall make to the other a payment described in express terms as "ex gratia" or without admission of liability". The two phrases are, I think, synonymous. No one would imagine that a settlement, so made, is unenforceable at law. The words "ex gratia" or "without admission of liability" are used simply to indicate-it may be as a matter of amour propre, or it may be to avoid a precedent in subsequent cases-that the party agreeing to pay does not admit any pre-existing liability on his part; but he is certainly not seeking to preclude the legal enforceability of the settlement itself by describing the contemplated payment as "ex gratia". So here, there are obvious reasons why the phrase might have been used by the defendant company in just such a way. They might have desired to avoid conceding that any such payment was due under the employers' contract of service. They might have wished-perhaps ironically in the event-to show, by using the phrase, their generosity in making a payment beyond what was required by the contract of service. I see nothing in the mere use of the words "ex gratia", unless in the circumstances some very special meaning has to be given to them, to warrant the conclusion that this promise, duly made and accepted, for valid consideration, was not intended by the parties to be enforceable in law.

The defendant company's second proposition seeks to show that in the circumstances here the words "ex gratia" had a special meaning. What is said is this: When a payment such as this is made by an employer to a dismissed employee the question whether it is subject to income tax in the hands of the recipient is important; it was understood by the defendant company and by the association, and by all their respective representatives at the meeting, that if the company's payment were made as the result of a legally binding obligation, it would be taxable in the hands of the recipient; whereas, if it were to be made without legal obligation on the part of the company, it would not be taxable. (It was not argued before me whether this assertion is right or wrong in law. It was said by the defendant company that that was quite immaterial; what was material was that the parties so believed.) Thus, it is said, the phrase "ex gratia" was used, and was understood by all present to be used, deliberately and advisedly as a formula to achieve that there would be no binding legal obligation on the company to pay, and hence to save the recipient from a tax liability. It is said that the offer was accepted by the association with full knowledge and understanding of these matters. Hence, it is said, the agreement by tacit consent, a consent evidenced by the use of the words "ex gratia" against this background of common understanding, was an agreement from which legal sanction and consequences were excluded. In my judgment, that submission also fails because the evidence falls far short of showing that this supposed background of avoidance of tax liability was present as an important element in the minds of all, or indeed any, of the persons who attended the meeting of 8 February 1962, or, if this be something different, in the minds of the defendant company or of the association; or that they all, or any of them, directed their minds to the significance of the words "ex gratia" which is now suggested on behalf of the defendant company. The question of tax liability, and the possible influence thereon of the use of the words "ex gratia", may indeed have been present in some degree, and as one element, in the minds of some of the persons present at the meeting. That, however, is far from sufficient to establish that the parties—both of them—affirmatively intended not to enter into legal relations in respect of the defendant company's promise to pay.

Lastly, the defendant company say that, even if the agreement were otherwise in all respects a binding agreement, it is not enforceable because its terms are too vague. This is founded on the submission that the precise words used by Mr Davies at the meeting were "approximating to"; that these precise words are a part of the agreement; that they leave a discretion to the defendant company; that therefore there is no enforceable agreement, and they can refuse to pay anything. I have already indicated my conclusion on the evidence as to what was indeed agreed at the end of the meeting. If this be right, there is nothing in this point. Even if it were wrong, I do not think that English law provides that in such circumstances the plaintiff would be entitled to nothing. At most "approximating to", if that were the contractual terms, would on the evidence connote a rounding off of a few pounds downwards to a round figure. If a contract for the sale of goods is valid and binding when it provides for "about 1,000 tons in seller's option", or "1,000 tons, up to ten per cent more or less in buyer's option", it would seem hard to justify treating such a contract as this as a nullity, and I do not think that the law so requires.

I do not have to consider a further issue of alleged failure to mitigate damages, as this was expressly abandoned by the defendant company at the hearing. I shall hear submissions as to the precise form which the order of the court should take.

*Judgment for the plaintiff.*

*Solicitors: Evan Davies & Co (for the plaintiff); McKenna & Co (for the defendant company).*

K Diana Phillips Barrister.

Encyclopaedia of Forms and Precedents/BOILERPLATE AND COMMERCIAL CLAUSES vol 4(3) 2008/(B) Commentary/D: WHICH CONTRACT TERMS APPLY?/25: SUBJECT TO CONTRACT (AND OTHER DENIALS OF LEGALLY-BINDING CONTRACT)/25.2 Heads of agreement

**25.2 Heads of agreement**

The phrase 'subject to contract' is also sometimes found in heads of agreement and other preliminary documents which are designed to summarise the main commercial terms of a proposed contract. This type of document is often called either:

(a) Heads of Agreement; or
(b) Heads of Terms; or
(c) Term Sheet; or
(d) Letter of Intent; or

(e) Comfort Letter; or
(f) Memorandum of Understanding

Documents of this kind do not have any automatic legal status. They may or may not be intended to be legally binding. Rather than just insert the words 'subject to contract' at the head of the document, it may be preferable to state more specifically what the status of the document is, as in the example below.

Where the transaction is wholly within England and Wales (with English parties, performance to take place in England and Wales, etc.), some of the provisions in the example below may be thought unnecessary. In international contracts it should be borne in mind that local laws may provide that a party is liable if it withdraws from negotiations without good reason after a defined stage, e.g. after Heads of Terms have been signed.

The following example states that the Heads of Terms are not legally binding except for paragraph X. The parties might wish, for example, a confidentiality provision or a lock-out clause to be binding but the rest of the Heads to be non-binding.

> 'These Heads of Terms set out the main commercial principles of a proposed agreement between (*parties*) ('the Parties') relating to (*subject matter*). The Parties intend to negotiate and (subject to obtaining approval from their respective Boards of the negotiated terms) execute a full written agreement ('the Agreement'), no later than [90] days from the date on which they sign these Heads of Terms. The parties intend that the Agreement will include provisions based on the principles of these Heads of Terms and other provisions. However, [except for paragraph X below,] these Heads of Terms are not intended to be legally binding, nor to create, evidence or imply any contract, obligation to enter into a contract or obligation to negotiate. Either party may withdraw from the negotiations without incurring any liability to the other party, at any time prior to the execution by both parties of the Agreement.

Encyclopaedia of Forms and Precedents/BOILERPLATE AND COMMERCIAL CLAUSES vol 4(3) 2008/(C) Forms and Precedents/H: ANCILLARY AGREEMENTS/71.3 Letter of intent: simple form

## *4.4.3 Appendix 3*

**71.3**
**Letter of intent: simple form***

(*date*)
(*address*)
Dear Sirs,

Letter of Intent

I refer to the discussions which have been taking place between (*name*) of (*name of company*) ('Company A') and (*name*) of (*name of company*) ('Company B') relating to a proposed strategic alliance between Company A and Company B, and in particular to the document entitled (*title*) and dated (*date*) and prepared by (*name*) (the 'Proposal').

I am pleased to confirm that it is our intention to negotiate the terms of an agreement between Company A and Company B under which, among other matters:

1 Company A would sponsor a [three year] programme of research to be conducted by Company B as outlined in the Proposal [and based on the costs set out in the Proposal]; and
2 Company A would own, and have the exclusive right of commercialisation of, any compounds discovered or developed in the programme of research [on terms to be agreed].

It is our intention to negotiate and execute such an agreement no later than *(number)* months from the date of this letter. If this is also Company B's intention, please would you arrange for the enclosed copy of this letter to be signed by an authorised representative of Company B and returned to us at the above address.

I hope this letter gives you the assurances you need, but please note that this letter should not be construed as creating any legal obligations.

Yours faithfully
(*signature*)
For and on behalf of Company A Limited
Acknowledged and agreed for and on behalf of Company B through its authorised signatory:
(*signature*)

Encyclopaedia of Forms and Precedents/BOILERPLATE AND COMMERCIAL CLAUSES vol 4(3) 2008/(C) Forms and Precedents/H: ANCILLARY AGREEMENTS/71.4 Letter of intent: longer form

* Source: Lexis Nexis; reproduced with permission.

### 4.4.4 *Appendix 4*

**71.4***
**Letter of intent: longer form**

Subject To Contract

(*date*)
From:
To:
Dear (*name*)
Re: (*specify*)

This 'Letter of Intent' for the above referenced matter is intended to outline the general terms which are being discussed between (*name of company*) ('Company A') and (*name of company*) ('Company B') in relation to those services which are attached hereto as Tables 1 and 2. [These tables are extracted from the (*name*) Plan Proposal for (*insert details*) which was presented to Company B in (*insert details*)]. At the present time, Company A and Company B are engaged in discussions and negotiations regarding timelines, budget, management services and contract terms, Company A's initial proposal for which was contained in the aforementioned development plan, with a view to reaching a final agreement between the parties.

It is agreed that the confidentiality of Company B proprietary information regarding the above referenced matter that may be disclosed to Company A during these negotiations will be maintained in accordance with the confidentiality agreement signed between Company B and Company A and subsequently in accordance with the master study agreement when signed. Should Company B and Company A not reach an agreement the documents will be returned and the terms of the aforementioned confidentiality agreement will be honoured. Notwithstanding this confidentiality as part of this letter of intent, the proposed agreement between the parties will contain a detailed section addressing this subject which will include a provision that the ownership of the data generated in this study will remain with Company B.

Company B and Company A will continue discussions and negotiations in good faith to execute an agreement within [90 days] of the execution of this letter of intent. [Company B and Company A recognise that this letter of intent is necessary to expedite this matter due to the desired project timelines. Company B and Company A agree and recognise that a signed agreement is necessary to proceed with the study beyond the initial [90-day] period set forth above.]

Upon execution of this letter of intent, Company B will advance money to Company A in the amount of £… [(plus VAT)[2]] on account of any and all charges Company A shall reasonably determine appropriate and necessary, in consultation with Company B [and in accordance with the schedule of activities (Table 3)

* Source: Lexis Nexis; reproduced with permission.

attached to this letter], in providing the aforementioned services. Payment of this money shall be made to Company A's bank account at (*insert details*). Such amounts shall be applied and deducted from any amount due from the initial payment under the proposed agreement between Company B and Company A regarding this study. Should a final agreement not be reached, any balance remaining in this account will be refunded to Company B (plus any VAT paid thereon)[3] minus expenses properly incurred and committed but not yet paid and less a £... administrative fee. Company B shall have the option to audit the charge and expense documentation at any time following the execution of this letter of intent and up to [3 years] following the completion of this engagement.

In case of early cancellation of the work covered by this letter of intent by written notice from Company B, the provisions of the previous paragraph shall be deemed terminated.

During the term of this letter of intent relating to the Project Proposal:

1 Company B shall indemnify Company A and its directors, officers, employees and agents in respect of all liabilities, costs, claims, loss, damage, demands, actions and expenses (to include any settlements or ex-gratia payments and reasonable legal and expert costs and expenses) arising directly or indirectly from any:

   1.1 material breach of any of the provisions contained in this letter of intent; or
   1.2 negligence; or
   1.3 material act, omission or default however caused

   on the part of company B or its directors, officers, employees, agents and representatives.

2 Company A shall indemnify Company B and its directors, officers, employees and agents in respect of all liabilities, costs, claims, loss, damage, demands, actions and expenses (to include any settlements or ex-gratia payments and reasonable legal and expert costs and expenses) arising directly or indirectly from any:

   2.1 material breach of any of the provisions contained in this letter of intent; or
   2.2 negligence; or
   2.3 material act, omission or default however caused

   on the part of Company A, or its directors, officers, employees, agents and representatives.

We thank you for the confidence you have placed in Company A and we look forward to working with you. Except as provided above, Company B shall not have any financial obligations to Company A or any third party under or in connection with this letter of intent. Either party may terminate this letter of intent

and/or their negotiations at any time without liability except as described under heads 1 and 2 above.
IN WITNESS of which the parties to this letter of intent have signed below through their authorised representatives.

1 This is an example of a letter of intent in which some terms are binding, and some of the envisaged services are to be provided while negotiations are continuing and before a final binding agreement is made.
2 Where an advance payment is made it will normally create a tax point for VAT purposes where it is envisaged that the advance will form part of the total payment: see *Customs and Excise Comrs v Richmond Theatre Management Ltd* [1995] STC 257.
3 Where VAT has been paid on the advance and repayment is due, an amount equal to the VAT charged must be repaid to Company B and a VAT credit note should be issued to Company B. The amount of the VAT credited should not be reduced by virtue of the expenses or administration fee deducted from the advance.

### 4.4.5 *Appendix 5*

**Letter of Intent—Sponsorship**[*]

**[To Be Typed on Headed Notepaper of the Company]**

Dear Sirs,

Proposed sponsorship —[ ] ("the Tournament")

This letter sets out on the basis referred to at clause 10 the principal terms upon which [ ] ("the Company") makes its offer to [ ] ("you"/"your"/"yourself" and corporate expressions) in relation to your proposed sponsorship of the Tournament.

**1. Consideration**

1.1 We propose to offer you the various sponsorship rights set out in clause 2 of this letter ("the Rights") in relation to your proposed sponsorship of the Tournament due to take place during the period commencing on [ ] and concluding on [ ] ("the Term") for a fee of [ ] ("the Fees") exclusive of VAT which will be paid as follows:

| **Payment Date** | **Amount** |
|---|---|

**2. Rights**

During each season of the Term, subject to payment of the Fees, the Company is prepared to offer the sponsorship and ancillary rights in relation to the Tournament set out below.

2.1 Designations

2.1.1 The exclusive right for you to describe yourself as "Official Sponsor of the Tournament;

2.1.2 The non-exclusive right for you to describe yourself as "Official Partner of the Company"; and such other designations as may be agreed;

2.1.3 The exclusive right for you to describe the [service/product] ("the Product") the "Official [Service/Product] of the Tournament" and/or the "Official [Service/Product] of the Company;

2.1.4 The exclusive right for you to describe yourself as the "Official Supplier of [Service/Product] to the Tournament and/or the "Official Supplier of [Services/Product] to the Company"

---

[*] Source: Lexis Nexis; reproduced with permission.

2.2 Use of Marks

2.2.1 The non-exclusive right to use (subject in each case to the Company's prior written approval and terms of use) those logos and trade marks owned or controlled by the Company set out at Schedule 1 hereof in relation to all promotional activity undertaken by you in relation to the promotion of the Product only and your exploitation of the Rights.

2.3 Advertising Rights

2.3.1 You will receive the following advertising rights in respect of matches taking place as part of the Tournament only ("Matches")

2.3.1.1 the right to display the trade mark(s) or logos of or relating to the Products referred to at Schedule 2 ("the Marks") upon six (6) (90 cm × 6 m) TV perimeter advertising sites at each Match;

2.3.1.2 one (1) full page colour programme advertisement for all Matches.

2.4 Tickets

2.4.1 You have the right to receive the following ticket allocations:

2.4.1.1 fifty (50) best available category match tickets at no extra cost for each Match;

2.4.1.2 the right to purchase a reasonable number of additional match tickets (subject to availability and at your additional cost) for all Matches

in each case subject always to any and all conditions of issue and ground regulations applicable to the same from time to time in force.

2.5 Hospitality

2.5.1 (Subject to availability and in each case subject always to any and all conditions of issue and ground regulations applicable to the same from time to time in force) the right to use hospitality facilities at each Match for a maximum number of people as follows:

2.5.1.1 [ ]

2.6 Branding

2.6.1 The non exclusive right to receive branding by way of the display of the Marks as follows:

2.6.1.1 on a total proportion not greater than [ ]% and not less than [ ] of the total visible surface area (evenly distributed with any other marks displayed there) of interview backdrops produced by or on behalf of the Company at all Matches;

2.6.1.2 on all official promotional print activity of the Company in respect of the Tournament; and

2.6.1.3 on all tickets for the Matches.The Company agrees not more than [ ] further trade marks or logos of other partners or sponsors of the Tournament and/or the Company shall be displayed alongside the Marks as referred to above and that the Marks shall be displayed in such manner as in the reasonable opinion of the Company accord with your premier stations as the exclusive sponsor of the Tournament.

2.7 Additional Rights

2.7.1 You will also receive the following rights:

2.7.1.1 the right to place approved amounts of agreed content in respect of the Products on the official website of the Company;

2.7.1.2 agreed branding by way of display of the Marks on the official website of the Company;

2.7.1.3 an "above the fold" hypertext link from your website situated at [insert details] to the official website of the Company;

2.7.1.4 the right to a press conference announcing your sponsorship of the Tournament at a time and location to be mutually agreed;

2.7.1.5 tannoy announcements in a form to be agreed to be made as agreed at each Match;

2.7.1.6 (subject to available space at venues hosting matches and to applicable regulations and to agreement as to the manner in which the same is to take place in each instance) the right to sample and promote the Products at venues hosting each Match;

2.7.1.7 where a giant television screen is placed at venues hosting the Matches the right to agreed advertising and branding opportunities in respect of the Products on such screen; and

2.7.1.8 such additional rights as the Company may make available at its discretion and on such terms as may be agreed from time to time.

**3. Condition**

3.1 This offer is subject to the negotiation and entry into a full long form sponsorship agreement ("the Sponsorship") drafted by the Company in a form satisfactory to all parties containing warranties, indemnities and covenants (and reasonable limitations) appropriate to an arrangement of this nature together with all appropriate third party guarantees of your liabilities pursuant to the Sponsorship.

**4. Timing**

4.1 It is our intention to proceed as quickly as possible with the proposed sponsorship and we aim to sign this letter on or before [ ] and to complete the proposed transaction by [ ] (or as soon as reasonably practicable thereafter).

**5. Other Partners**

5.1 The Company agrees that it shall not during the Term grant to any person:

5.1.1 the rights referred to at clauses 2.1.1, 2.1.3 and 2.1.4; and/or
5.1.2 any right to display any signage referring to that person at any venue hosting any Match during the course of any Match where such rights are to be used by that person in the advertising promotion or marketing of [any product/service defined in the Sponsorship as being competitive with the Products]

5.2 Save as set out expressly in this clause 5 the Company shall be entitled freely to grant such rights in connection with the Tournament as it sees fit to such persons as it sees fit without restriction and nothing herein shall have the effect of placing any constraint on the rights of participants in the Tournament from granting any rights in respect of advertising marketing promotional or sponsorship rights or services to any person provided the same is in accordance with the rules of the Tournament a copy of which has been provided to you.

**6. Television**

6.1 As part of the Sponsorship there will be terms dealing with the anticipated level of television exposure for matches forming part of the Tournament and, in particular, the Company acknowledges that it has agreements in place with broadcasters in respect of the territories where matches forming part of the Tournament take place.

## 7. Confidentiality

7.1 In consideration of the mutual agreement of the parties to the proposed transaction, by countersigning and returning the enclosed copies of this letter, it is agreed that neither party or any of their respective directors, officers, employees or professional advisers shall disclose the contents of this letter or any discussions between the Company and you (and for the fact that this letter or such discussions have taken or are taking place) to any third party apart from their own professional advisers who will be under the same obligation to keep all aspects of the proposed transaction confidential or as required by law or the provisions of any relevant stock exchange.

## 8. Exclusivity

8.1 The Company understands that you will incur substantial costs and expenses in proceeding with due diligence investigations and instructing advisers to draft and negotiate documents, which it would not do if it did not have exclusive negotiating rights for a reasonable period of time. Accordingly, in consideration for such costs and expenses to be incurred by you, the Company agrees by countersignature of this letter:

8.1.1 not to enter into, directly or indirectly, or continue discussions or negotiations or enter into any agreement or arrangement with any person other than you regarding the grant of the rights referred to at clause 2.1.1 and not to invite or solicit any such discussions agreement or arrangement;

8.1.2 not to withdraw from negotiations with you in respect of the subject matter of this letter save where the Company has proper commercial reason for so doing. For the purpose of clarification an without prejudice to the generality of the foregoing the Company shall be deemed to have proper commercial reasons where you have indicated that any of the terms set out herein is no longer acceptable to you or have sought materially to add to the rights to be granted to you pursuant to the Sponsorship over and above the terms referred to herein or by way of substitution for terms set out herein; in each case for a period of [ days] from the date of this letter ("the Exclusivity Period") unless the Company and you agree in writing to the contrary. The Company agrees to supply to you such information as it reasonable requests in connection with the subject matter of this letter.

## 9. Costs

9.1 Subject to paragraph 9.2, each party will pay the costs and expenses incurred by it in connection with the negotiation, entering into and completion of this letter and the Sponsorship and any allied documentation.

9.2 If the Company breaches any of its obligations in this letter, or if during the Exclusivity Period the Company withdraws from the negotiations with you provided for herein, then the Company will pay to you promptly on demand an amount equal to all costs and expenses (including, but not limited to, the fees of your legal, accounting and financial advisers and their out-of-pocket expenses) together with any value added tax incurred by you whether before or after the date of this letter in investigating the affairs of the Company and in the preparation of this letter and the Sponsorship and any other allied documents.]

**10. Status of this Letter**

10.1 Save for clauses 7, 8 and 9 which are intended to and shall create a binding legal agreement upon the terms set out therein governed by the laws of England and Wales (and in respect of which the Courts of England shall have exclusive jurisdiction) the provisions of this letter are not intended to be binding in law and are not intended to nor shall create any binding contractual obligation between the Company and you upon the terms here set out or otherwise nor any representation by either party upon which the other is entitled to rely.

The Company very much looks forward to progressing negotiations with you as quickly as possible, and would be grateful if you could sign and return the enclosed copy of this letter to indicate your agreement with its terms.

Yours faithfully

......................................

**For and on behalf of**

Read and agreed.

......................................

**For and on behalf of**

# Chapter 5
# Confidentiality and Non-Disclosure Agreements

## 5.1 Introductory Remarks

Confidentiality and Non-Disclosure Agreements are frequently used in many industries, including the sports industry, in relation to and in connection with the negotiation, drafting and conclusion of Sports Marketing Agreements of various kinds, especially Sports Sponsorship and Merchandising Agreements.

The sporting world is a very small one in which everyone tends to know one another and would also like to know one another's business. So, there is a tendency to keep things under wrap in—at least—the preliminary stages of discussing and negotiating sports marketing deals. In particular, the fact that the parties are in negotiations at all is usually the subject of a confidentiality/non-disclosure obligation on both sides, apart from the nature, and details of the negotiations, especially the financial terms and arrangements, as well as the outcome of the negotiations, including any breakdown in the negotiations and the resulting failure to reach an agreement. Also, there should be an express agreement for the parties to maintain confidentiality after the negotiations have ended for whatever reason. In other words, for the secrecy obligations to survive expiration/termination of the Agreement. All these matters need to be expressly defined in and covered by the terms of the Confidentiality/Non-Disclosure Agreement.

Before commencing sports marketing negotiations, it is standard practice for the parties to sign a Confidentiality/Non-Disclosure Agreement along the lines of the general precedent set out below.

I. S. Blackshaw, *Sports Marketing Agreements: Legal, Fiscal and Practical Aspects*,
ASSER International Sports Law Series, DOI: 10.1007/978-90-6704-793-7_5,

## 5.2 General Legal Principles on Confidentiality

The general law on confidentiality, especially regarding sensitive commercial and business information, often referred to in the jargon as '*proprietary information*', is well settled and the subject matter (confidential information) and also the extent of the obligations of secrecy to be undertaken and observed by the parties need to be very carefully defined and clearly set out and delineated in the corresponding Confidentiality/Non-Disclosure Agreement.

There are some clearly recognised general legal exceptions to complying with and observing secrecy obligations and these are as follows:

- once the confidential information has entered the public domain and become common knowledge through no fault of the parties bound by the secrecy obligation;
- again, if the confidential information was already known to one of the parties when the secrecy obligation was undertaken by the parties concerned;
- where the confidential information is disclosed to one of the parties by a third party that is not bound by any secrecy obligations;
- where one of the parties is required by Law to disclose the confidential information to a Court or the Stock Exchange or to the parties' legal advisers; and
- where the parties agree to the confidential information being disclosed to a third party.

In each of the above situations, the secrecy obligations cease to be legally binding on the parties or party concerned to the extent and for the purposes applicable.

In the last case above, the purpose and the extent of the disclosure and any specific conditions attached to the agreed disclosure need to be clearly defined and expressed in writing. For example, the parties may mutually agree to disclose the fact and outcome of the negotiations to the Media in a Press Release, the terms of which have to be mutually and prior to disclosure agreed by them, as well as the Media to be informed, for example, print media. Once, however, as it were 'the cat is out of the bag', it is difficult, if not impossible, to control the further dissemination of the confidential information concerned as the so-called 'public interest' may demand.

Again, in the case of negotiations in respect of international Sports Marketing Agreements, it is advisable to include a '*proper law*' clause in the Confidentiality/ Non-Disclosure Agreement expressly indicating the Law that will govern the Agreement generally and also, in particular, in the event of any dispute arising under, out of or in connection with the Agreement. This clause should be combined with a jurisdiction and dispute resolution clause, especially one providing for some form of ADR, such as Arbitration or Mediation or a combination of the two, known in the jargon as '*Med-Arb*'—Mediation to identify the issues, and, if Mediation is unsuccessful, Arbitration to settle them. The parties may wish to expressly confer jurisdiction on the Court of Arbitration for Sport, based in Lausanne, Switzerland.

Finally, of course, the corresponding Sports Marketing Agreement resulting from the successful negotiations should itself include some appropriate confidentiality provisions and, again, the confidential information should be clearly defined and may well, in the case of a Sports Merchandising Agreement, include, for example, details of customers and business plans of the Licensee. Further, the Agreement will need to contain a provision imposing the same obligations of confidentiality and non-disclosure on the part of the parties' employees who have access to the confidential information. There will also need to be included in the Agreement an obligation on the part of the parties to use the confidential information only for the purposes of the Sports Marketing Agreement, as well as a general contractual requirement on the part of the parties to maintain adequate security arrangements for storing and safeguarding the confidential information concerned and preventing it from getting into the hands of third parties, including competitors.

## 5.3 Confidentiality/Non-Disclosure Agreement General Precedent

A General Form of Confidentiality/Non-Disclosure Agreement, which will need to be adapted and customised to the particular situation in which it needs to be used, is set out, for illustrative purposes, in the Appendix of this Chapter (5.5).

Precedents should not be slavishly followed but used as a general guide and kind of drafting 'road map'.

## 5.4 Concluding Remarks

Although pre-contract and post-contract confidentiality/nondisclosure obligations can, according to the nature and complexity of the Sports Marketing Agreement concerned, be quite complicated and convoluted, as will be appreciated, they are very important and should not be overlooked or omitted.

As with any other contractual provisions involving the imposition of legal obligations on the parties, they need to be well defined and clearly expressed to avoid disagreements in the future, especially regarding the scope and extent of them in particular situations. A certain degree of prescience on the part of the draftsman is required!

## 5.5 Appendix

**General Form of Confidentiality/Non-Disclosure Agreement**[1]
**Commencement Date and Parties**
**Whereas:**
The parties have agreed to provide each other with information which they consider to be confidential in nature (the "Confidential Information") to <insert brief details of reason for disclosure, e.g. to enable the Recipient to provide services as a consultant to the company> (the "Purpose").

## Now It Is Agreed between the Parties as Follows:

1. In consideration of each of the parties disclosing to the other Confidential Information for the Purpose the parties hereby undertake that they shall:
   (i) not communicate, disclose or make available all or any part of the Confidential Information to any third party;
   (ii) not directly or indirectly use, or permit others to use, the Confidential Information other than for the Purpose;
   (iii) not make any announcement or disclosure in connection with the Confidential Information or the Purpose without the prior written consent of the other party.
2. The obligations of confidentiality and non-use will not apply with respect to any of the following:
   (i) information which is generally available to the public at the date of this agreement;
   (ii) information already known to the party at the time of disclosure;
   (iii) information which is subsequently disclosed by third parties having no obligations of confidentiality;
   (iv) information which is or becomes generally available to the public in printed publications in general circulation in the United Kingdom through no act or default on the part of the parties or their agents, employees or professional advisers.
3. Without prejudice to the generality of clause 2 information shall not be deemed to be generally available to the public by reason only that it is known to only a few of those people to whom it may be of commercial interest and a combination of two or more parts of the Confidential Information shall not be

[1] By I.S. Blackshaw.

deemed to be generally available to the public by reason only of each separate part being so available.

4. The parties shall each ensure that all measures necessary are taken to secure theconfidentiality of the other party's Confidential Information including but not limited to:

   (i) keeping separate all Confidential Information and all information generated based on the Confidential Information from all other documents and records;
   (ii) keeping all documents and any other material bearing or incorporating any of the Confidential Information at the party's usual place of business in the United Kingdom;
   (iii) not using, reproducing, transforming or storing any of the Confidential Information in an externally accessible computer or electronic information retrieval system, not transmitting it in any form or by any means whatsoever outside the party's usual place of business and not copying all or any part of the Confidential Information without the prior written consent of the Company and then only to the extent that the same is required for the Purpose;
   (iv) allowing access to the Confidential Information only to those employees and/or to the informing each of the said employees and professional advisers of the confidential nature of the Confidential Information and of the obligations in respect of the Confidential Information and ensuring such employees and professional advisers comply with the confidentiality and non-disclosure obligations contained in this agreement;
   (v) obtaining from employees having access to the Confidential Information their undertakings to maintain the same as confidential and taking such steps as may be reasonably desirable to enforce such obligations;
   (vi) delivering all documents and other materials in the possession, custody or control of the party, its agents, employees or professional advisers that bear or incorporate any part of the Confidential Information of the other party.

5. The failure by either party to enforce at any time any one or more of the terms or conditions of this agreement shall not be a waiver of them or of the right at any time subsequently to enforce all terms and conditions of this agreement.
6. The parties agree that damages might not be a sufficient remedy to any breach of the terms of this agreement and that as a result injunctive or other equitable relief may be obtained in respect of any breach or anticipated breach.
7. All rights in the Confidential Information are reserved by the party to which it belongs and no rights or obligations other than those expressly set out in this agreement are granted or to be implied from this agreement. In particular no licence is granted directly or indirectly by this agreement relating to any invention, discovery, patent, copyright or other industrial or intellectual

property right now or in the future held, made, obtained or licensable by either party.

8. The rights, duties and obligations of the parties and the validity, interpretation, performance and legal effect of this agreement shall be governed and determined by the laws of England and the parties hereby submit to the non-exclusive jurisdiction of the English Courts.

AGREED by the parties:
SIGNED by ________________________________
Name (print) ________________________________
Position ________________________________
Authorised signatory
for and on behalf of ________________________________
Date (Day / Month / Year) _____ / _____ / _____
SIGNED by ________________________________
Name (print) ________________________________
Position ________________________________
Authorised signatory
for and on behalf of ________________________________
Date (Day / Month / Year) _____ / _____ / _____

# Chapter 6
# Sports Event Management Agreements

## 6.1 Introductory Remarks

Having organised a sporting event, including having appointed the host country and entered into a corresponding agreement with the Local Organising Committee, it is necessary to manage and stage the sporting event in such a way that the event organisers, managers, sponsors, merchandisers and all other stakeholders associated with it commercially and financially reap the maximum returns from their involvement and investment in it. It can be said, therefore, without contradiction, that, without good management, the sports event concerned will not be able to deliver these benefits. The more successful the event is from a sporting point of view, the more successful it is from a business and financial point of view.

Normally, rather than managing the sporting event itself, the event organiser appoints someone else, usually on an exclusive basis and in a defined geographical territory, to carry out, under its close supervision and direction, the actual management and staging of the event. This is usually a Sports Marketing/Management Agency, with the required expertise and experience, especially in relation to major international sporting events, such as International Management Group (IMG), the pioneering Sports Marketing Agency founded by Mark McCormack, the 'godfather of sports marketing'.

## 6.2 Sports Event Management Agreements

To achieve these desirable and required outcomes, it is necessary to negotiate and draft a clear and comprehensive Sports Event Management Agreement. As will be seen from the contents of the General Precedent of an Event Management Agreement, which is set out in the Appendix (6.4) to this chapter, a lot of planning

I. S. Blackshaw, *Sports Marketing Agreements: Legal, Fiscal and Practical Aspects*,
ASSER International Sports Law Series, DOI: 10.1007/978-90-6704-793-7_6,

and considerable attention to detail goes into the successful management of an event; and all these details and arrangements need to be properly reflected in the corresponding provisions of the Agreement.

As with all Sports Marketing Agreements, the rights granted to and obligations imposed on the event manager need to be spelled out in precise detail. It is usual to define the scope of the work to be undertaken by the event manager in a Schedule to the Agreement (referred to as the 'Services' to be provided by the event manager to the event organiser, that is the rights holder in the event). This, in practice, can serve as a useful checklist for the person(s) responsible for delivering the agreed and defined 'Services' to the event organiser which actually constitute and comprise the event management itself.

As usual, the financial clauses in a Sports Event Management are also key to its successful implementation and, therefore, need to be clearly defined. Note, in particular, the need to include provisions regarding the budget for the management of the sports event as well as the accounting requirements to be fulfilled.

Likewise, the various warranties and obligations given by the rights holder and the event manager to one another are also very important and need to be drafted with care and precision to avoid any ambiguities. On the rights holder's part, particular mention may be made of the warranty of authority to enter into the Sports Event Management Agreement and fulfil its obligations under it; and on the part of the event manager, particular mention may be made of the obligations to provide the 'Services' in a timely and professional manner and not to do anything which, in the reasonable opinion of the rights holder, is or might be prejudicial or defamatory to the name and image of the rights holder, the Governing Bodies, the Event or the particular Sport concerned (a 'not to bring the sport into disrepute' clause, which, without the precise circumstances constituting such disrepute being spelled, may be arguable and, therefore, difficult to enforce in practice).

Note in the General Precedent of the Sports Event Management, which is set out in the Appendix (6.4) to this chapter, the extended definition of the 'Venue' for the sports event, which is useful to combat 'Ambush Marketing' situations that may take place around the 'Venue' as well as within the 'Venue'.

Note also the need to include clauses on the protection and safeguarding of the intellectual property and commercial rights; taking out insurance; and confidentiality requirements; as well as the use of Schedules for various purposes, including providing details of the trademarks involved.

Finally, also take note of the need to include in the termination clause, not only the grounds for terminating the Sports Event Management Agreement, but also the effects and consequences of termination.

## 6.3 Concluding Remarks

As will be seen from the above account, the management of a major sporting event is a complex affair and operation, which requires a great deal of planning and detailed arrangements in order to ensure the success of the event for all the stakeholders concerned.

All these arrangements need to be faithfully and fully reflected in the provisions of the corresponding Sports Event Management Agreement and great care should, therefore, be taken in drafting the Agreement.

As always in Sports Marketing Agreements, attention to detail and precision are the name of the game!

## 6.4 Appendix

**Event Management Agreement***

**This Agreement** is made the day of 2[ ]

**Between**

(1) [ ] [ ] whose registered office is at [ ] ("the Rights Holder")

(2) [ ] [ ] whose registered office is at [ ] ("the Event Manager")

**Recitals**

A. The Rights Holder controls all rights relating to the Event (as defined below)
B. The Rights Holder wishes to appoint the Event Manager to organise and stage the Event

**Operative Provisions**

**1. Definitions**

1.1 In this Agreement the following expressions shall have the following meanings:

**"Budget"** means the budget for the Event set by the Rights Holder and agreed with the Event Manager or as varied in accordance with this Agreement
**"Consideration"** means the sums set out in clause 9
**"Commercial Rights"** [ ]
**"Commercial Affiliate"** [ ]
**"Event"** means [ ] due to take place in years [ ] and any associated or ancillary event or competition taking place at the same time
**"Governing Body"** means [ ]
**"Intellectual Property"** means patents trade marks (whether registered or unregistered) rights in any designs (whether registered or unregistered) and applications for any of the foregoing trade or business names copyright and rights in performances
**"Representatives"** means those third parties engaged by the Rights Holder to carry out services in relation to the Event including without being limited to television production and broadcasting public relations and promotions and all commercial partners sponsors and advertisers appointed by the Rights Holder in relation to the Event
**"Services"** means those services in relation to the Event which are described in Schedule 1
**"Term"** means the period from the date of this Agreement until thirty (30) days after the end of the Event unless terminated earlier in accordance with this Agreement

* Source Lexis nexis; permission obtained.

**"Territory"** means the United Kingdom
**"Trade Marks"** means the marks set out in Schedule 2
**"Venues"** means the venues used for the Event in any year including the immediately surrounding areas from which any material for broadcasting rights could be obtained or which could be used for advertising which would be visible to television cameras within the venue including the city centre areas roads used in the Event areas used for official functions press centres media area information centres and all other areas necessary for the proper organisation of the Event

**2. Appointment**

2.1 The Rights Holder appoints the Event Manager to provide the Services for the Event throughout the Term in the Territory upon the terms and conditions set out in this Agreement and its Schedules
2.2 The Event Manager agrees to perform the Services in the Territory for the Event throughout the Term

**3. Exclusivity**

3.1 The Rights Holder shall not appoint any third party to provide the Services in the Territory during the Term
3.2 The Event Manager shall provide the Services for the Rights Holder in the Territory during the Term on the following basis

3.2.1 (subject to clause 3.2.2) on a non-exclusive basis during the year of the Term and
3.2.2 on an exclusive basis for the period of time commencing at least [ ] days prior to the start of the Event during the Event and for not less than [ ] days after the Event

**4. Finances**

4.1 In consideration of the Event Manager performing the Services and subject to the terms of this Agreement the Rights Holder shall pay to the Event Manager the Consideration in the amounts and on the dates set out in clause 9
4.2 The Event Manager shall perform the Services in accordance with the Budget
4.3 Subject to clause 11 the Rights Holder shall provide such monies and pay all invoices and bills and enter into such contracts as are necessary for the Event Manager to provide the Services as soon as practicable after receipt of such invoices bills and contracts from the Event Manager
4.4 The Event Manager shall forward immediately after receipt all invoices bills and contracts entered in accordance with the Budget relating to the provisions of the Services directly to the Rights Holder for payment
4.5 Subject to clause 4.7 and unless otherwise agreed in writing by the Rights Holder the Event Manager is not entitled to receive or hold any income monies arising or refunds of expenditure ("monies") in providing the

Services for the Event. If the Event Manager does receive or hold such monies it must immediately inform the Rights Holder hold such monies to the Rights Holder's order as bare trustee for the benefit of the Rights Holder and immediately forward such monies to the Rights Holder in accordance with the Rights Holder's instructions

4.6 The Event Manager shall not contract with or invoice for the services of any associated company of the Event Manager (within the meaning of the Income and Corporation Taxes Act 1988 Sections 416 and 417) except as expressly provided in the Budget or otherwise in this Agreement

4.7 The parties shall agree the most practicable method of payment for expenses and costs incurred during the Event

**5. Budget And Accounting**

5.1 The Rights Holder may (in consultation with the Event Manager) vary the Budget the allocation of funds from the categories specified within the Budget and vary the Budget for items of expenditure not anticipated by the Budget. Any such variation may be made by the Rights Holder and may also be made at the reasonable request of and in consultation with the Event Manager but is subject to the final decision of the Rights Holder

5.2 The Event Manager shall remain responsible for the Budget and shall not incur any expenditure in excess of the itemised amount anticipated in the Budget unless the Budget is varied in accordance with clause 5.1

5.3 If the Budget exceeds the total costs actually incurred for the Event then the amount of underspend on any item of the Budget may (in the absolute discretion of the Rights Holder) be utilised for other items in the Budget in accordance with clause 5.1

5.4 The Event Manager shall during the Term submit to the Rights Holder such information regarding the progress of Event organisation an analysis of expenditure to date estimates of any likely variation to the Budget as well as copies of contracts correspondence invoices receipts and any other documentation relating to the Services and/or the Event as the Rights Holder may reasonably request

5.5 The Event Manager shall maintain full accurate and proper records and books of account relating to the Event with all invoices vouchers and other records evidencing all receipts expenses charges and taxes incurred in providing the Services for the Event

5.6 The Rights Holder may inspect audit and take copies of all books and records relating to the Event the Event Manager shall produce all such material to the Rights Holder with reasonable notice of such request provided that the Rights Holder is not entitled to computer programmes and materials relating to systems and controls independently created and wholly owned by the Event Manager

## 6. The Event Manager's Obligations

6.1 The Event Manager shall

6.1.1 provide the Services and organise the Event to the best of its ability in accordance with best commercial practice

6.1.2 at all times comply with the Rights Holder's instructions and provide the Services in a timely and professional manner

6.1.3 not do anything which in the reasonable opinion of the Rights Holder is or might be prejudicial or defamatory to the name and image of the Rights Holder the Governing Bodies the Event or the sport of [ ]

6.1.4 shall not issue any press releases on or relating to the Event or make any comment on the Rights Holder other than as permitted under this Agreement

6.1.5 endeavour to comply with and observe all provisions in the Governing Bodies' rules and regulations from time to time in force

6.1.6 use its reasonable endeavours to comply with all applicable laws and regulations in the provision of the Services and the organisation of the Event

6.1.7 ensure that the sufficient personnel of a suitably senior or junior level are available at all reasonable times to carry out the Services along with such other personnel as the Event Manager may decide (in consultation with the Rights Holder) to use in providing the Services

6.1.8 liaise and co-operate with the Representatives when providing the Services to the best of its ability

6.2 The Event Manager shall procure that its representatives

6.2.1 make themselves available at all reasonable times and upon reasonable notice to the Rights Holder for the purposes of consultation and advice relating to this Agreement and the Event

6.2.2 at the event of the Event Manager attend meetings with representatives of the Rights Holder and such Representatives sponsors or prospective sponsors as may be necessary for the performance of its duties under this Agreement

6.3 The Events Manager shall in relation to its appointment under this Agreement

6.3.1 describe itself as "Events Manager" for the Rights Holder

6.3.2 not hold itself out or permit any person to hold it out as being authorised to bind the Rights Holder in any way and

6.3.3 not do any act which might reasonably create the impression that it is so authorised

**7. The Event Manager's Warranties**

7.1 The Event Manager warrants and represents that

7.1.1 it has the full rights and title to enter this Agreement and to perform the obligations undertaken by it and that it has not entered into any agreement with any third party which might conflict with the terms of this Agreement

7.1.2 neither the signature nor the execution nor the performance by the Event Manager of this Agreement contravenes any law regulation or similar enactment or any judgment injunction or award of any court or authority or any provision of any existing agreement or contract or the Event Manager Memorandum and Articles of Association or any limitation on the powers of the directors or other officers of the Event Manager

7.1.3 as of the date of this Agreement there is no litigation arbitration or administrative proceedings before any court arbitrator or authority presently pending or threatened against the Event Manager

**8. The Rights Holder's Warranties and Obligations**

8.1 The Rights Holder warrants and agrees that it

8.1.1 has full authority to enter into this Agreement and to undertake all of the obligations on its part contained in this Agreement

8.1.2 shall keep the Event Manager fully informed of all relevant matters relating to the Event

8.1.3 shall provide the Event Manager with an adequate statement confirming its appointment under this Agreement

8.1.4 shall take any action which (in its reasonable opinion) is necessary to ensure that the Event Manager can provide its services under this Agreement

**9. The Consideration**

9.1 The Rights Holder shall pay the Event Manager [ ] ("the fee") in [ ] equal monthly instalments of [ ]

9.2 All payments due are exclusive of VAT which may be or become payable. The Rights Holder shall pay any such VAT to the Event Manager upon receipt of an appropriate VAT invoice from the Event Manager

**10. Appointment of Representatives**

10.1 The appointment of Representatives in relation to the Event shall be made on such terms and conditions as the Rights Holder in its absolute discretion may from time to time determine. The Event Manager shall not (unless previously agreed in writing with the Rights Holder) make or give any promises warranties guarantees or representations concerning the Event and shall use all reasonable endeavours to ensure full delivery of the Rights Holder's commitments and obligations to the Representatives and shall inform the Rights Holder of an act omission or breach of contract by any Representative of which it becomes aware during the Term. The Event Manager shall render all reasonable assistance to the Rights Holder at the Rights Holder's expense and request in dealing with any such act omission or breach of contract

**11. Intellectual Property And Commercial Rights**

11.1 The Event Manager shall promptly and fully notify the Rights Holder of any actual threatened or suspected infringement in the Territory of any Intellectual Property of the Rights Holder which comes to the Event Manager's notice and of any claim by any third party so coming to its notice and the Event Manager shall at the request and expense of the Rights Holder do all such things as may be reasonably required to assist the Rights Holder in taking or resisting any proceedings in relation to any such infringement or claim

11.2 Nothing in this Agreement shall give the Event Manager any rights in respect of any Intellectual Property or Trade Marks used by the Rights Holder in relation to the Event or of the goodwill associated therewith and the Event Manager hereby acknowledges that except as expressly provided in this Agreement it shall not acquire any rights in respect thereof and that all such rights and goodwill are and shall remain vested in the Rights Holder

11.3 The Event Manager shall not use any trade marks or trade names so resembling the Trade Marks or trade names of the Rights Holder or of the Event or of the Governing Body as to be likely to cause confusion or deception

11.4 The Event Manager shall not authorise any third party to use the Trade Mark or any Intellectual Property of the Rights Holder or of the Event or of the Governing Body. If any third party requires the use of the Trade Marks or any Intellectual Property of the Rights Holder or of the Event then the Event Manager shall inform the Rights Holder of such requirement. The Rights Holder may (in its absolute discretion) grant such third party the right or licence required

11.5 The Event Manager shall at the expense of the Rights Holder take all such steps as the Rights Holder may reasonably require to assist the Rights Holder in maintaining the validity and enforceability of the Intellectual Property of the Rights Holder during the continuance of this Agreement

11.6 Without prejudice to the right of the Event Manager or any third party to challenge the validity of any Intellectual Property of the Rights Holder the Event Manager shall not do or authorise any third party to do any act which would or might invalidate or be inconsistent with the Intellectual Property of the Rights Holder and shall not omit or authorise any third party to omit to do any act which by its omission would have that effect or character

**12. Confidentiality**

12.1 Confidentiality

12.1.1 Subject to sub-clauses 12.2 and 12.3 each party

12.1.1.1 shall treat as strictly confidential and use solely for the purposes contemplated by this Agreement all documents materials and other information whether technical or commercial obtained or received by it as a result of entering into or performing its obligations under this Agreement and relating to the negotiations relating to or the provisions or subject matter of this Agreement ("confidential information") and

12.1.1.2 shall not except with the prior written consent of the party from whom the confidential information was obtained publish or otherwise disclose to any person any confidential information

12.2 Permitted Disclosures

12.2.1 Each party may disclose confidential information which would otherwise be subject to sub-clause 12.1.1 if but only to the extent that it can demonstrate that

12.2.1.1 such disclosure is required by law or by any securities exchange or regulatory or governmental body having jurisdiction over it wherever situated (and including without limitation the London Stock Exchange the Panel on Takeovers and Mergers and the Serious Fraud Office) and whether or not the requirement has the force of law

12.2.1.2 the confidential information was lawfully in its possession prior to its disclosure by the other party (as evidenced by written records) and had not been obtained from the other party

12.2.1.3 the confidential information has come into the public domain other than through its fault or the fault of any person to whom the confidential information has been disclosed in accordance with sub-clause 12.3

12.2.1.4 information required by the Governing Body provided that any such disclosure shall not be made without prior notice to the party from whom the confidential information was obtained

12.3 Persistence of restrictions

12.3.1 The restrictions contained in this clause shall survive the termination of this Agreement

## 13. Termination

13.1 The Rights Holder may terminate this Agreement in any year during the Term by giving [ ] days notice of such termination to the Event Manager. Upon termination the Event Manager shall send the Rights Holder a final account of all commitments of whatever nature up to the date of receipt of such notice along with all papers relating to the Event and the Rights Holder in its possession custody or power and the provisions of clauses 13.3 and 13.4 shall apply. The Rights Holder shall not be liable to the Event Manager for any further payments or any claims whatsoever

13.2 Either party may terminate this Agreement forthwith upon notice in the event that the other

13.2.1 commits a material breach of any obligation under this Agreement which breach is incapable of remedy or cannot be remedied in time for the Event

13.2.2 commits a material breach of any obligation under this Agreement and if such breach is capable of remedy fails to so remedy such breach within 28 days of receiving notice from the other requiring remedy

13.2.3 enters into a composition or arrangement with its creditors has a receiver or administrator or administrative receiver appointed or becomes insolvent or unable to pay its debts when they fall due

13.3 Consequences of termination

13.3.1 Upon termination in accordance with clause 13

13.3.1.1 the rights and obligations of the parties under this Agreement shall terminate and be of no future effect except that clause 11 and 12 shall remain in full force and effect

13.3.1.2 any rights or obligations to which any of the parties to this Agreement may be entitled or be subject before such termination shall remain in full force and effect

13.3.1.3 termination shall not affect or prejudice any right to damages or other remedy which the terminating party may have in respect of the circumstances which gave rise to the termination or any other right to damages or other remedy which any party may have in respect of any breach of
this Agreement which existed at or before the date of termination

13.4 Upon termination in accordance with clause 16 and upon expiry of the Term the Event Manager shall (at the request of the Rights Holder) return all items (including but not limited to) signage materials premises promotional publication advertising material relating to the Rights Holder and/or the Event to the Rights Holder or such third party as the Rights Holder nominates

**14. Insurance**

14.1 Subject to any exclusions excesses condition and limitations imposed by the insurers and provided insurance can be obtained at reasonable rates the Rights Holder agrees to take out and maintain an insurance policy to cover usual damages claims actions judgments costs and expenses arising out of with the staging of the Event

**15. Co-Operation and Communication**

15.1 Both Parties agree to work in close co-operation to the benefit of the Event

**16. Force Majeure**

16.1 Effect of force majeure

16.1.1 Neither party to this Agreement shall be deemed to be in breach of this Agreement or otherwise liable to the other as a result of any delay or failure in the performance of its obligations under this Agreement if and to the extent that such delay or failure is caused by force majeure (as defined in sub-clause 16.2) and the time for performance of the relevant obligation(s) shall be extended accordingly

16.2 Definition of force majeure

16.2.1 For the purpose of this clause "force majeure" means any circumstances not foreseeable at the date of this Agreement and not within the reasonable control of the party in question including without limitation

16.2.1.1 any strike lockout or other industrial action or any shortage of or difficulty in obtaining labour or raw materials

16.2.1.2 any destruction temporary or permanent breakdown malfunction or damage of or to any premises plant equipment (including computer systems) or materials

16.2.1.3 any breach of contract default or insolvency by or of any third party (including an agent or sub-contractor) other than a company in the same group as the party affected by the force majeure or an employee or officer of that party or company

16.2.1.4 any action taken by a governmental or public authority of any kind including not granting a consent exemption approval or clearance

16.2.1.5 any civil commotion or disorder riot invasion war threat of or preparation for war

16.2.1.6 any fire explosion storm flood earthquake subsidence epidemic or other natural physical disaster

16.3 Obligations of affected party

16.3.1 A party whose performance of its obligations under this Agreement is delayed or prevented by force majeure

16.3.1.1 shall forthwith notify the other party of the nature extent effect and likely duration of the circumstances constituting the force majeure

16.3.1.2 shall use all reasonable endeavours to minimise the effect of the force majeure on its performance of its obligations under this Agreement and

16.3.1.3 shall subject to sub-clause 16.4 forthwith after the cessation of the force majeure notify the other party thereof and resume full performance of its obligations under this Agreement

16.4 Termination for force majeure

16.4.1 If any force majeure delays or prevents the performance of the obligations of either party for a continuous period in excess of one month the party not so affected shall then be entitled to give notice to the affected party to terminate this Agreement specifying the date (which shall not be less than seven days after the date on which the notice is given) on which termination will take effect. Such a termination notice shall be irrevocable except with the consent of both parties and upon termination the provisions of clauses 14.4 and 14.5 apply

**17. Indemnity**

17.1 Each party (a "defaulting party") agrees to indemnify and keep indemnified the other party (a "non-defaulting party") from and against any cost loss liability claim or damage which any non-defaulting party incurs or suffers as a result of any default by the defaulting party in the due and punctual performance of any of its obligations or breach of its warranties under this Agreement

**18. Nature of Agreement**

18.1 The Rights Holder may perform any of the obligations undertaken by it and exercise any of the rights granted to it under this Agreement through any other company which at the relevant time is its holding company or subsidiary (as defined by s 736 of the Companies Act 1985) or the subsidiary of any such holding company and any act or omission of any such company shall for the purposes of this Agreement be deemed to be the act or omission of the Rights Holder

18.2 The Event Manager shall ensure that all dealings with sponsors Representatives and third parties it introduces to the Rights Holder in providing the Services for the Event are on the best arms length commercial terms available and where dealing with any associated company of the Event Manager (as defined by the Income and Corporation Taxes Act s 416–417) shall where practicable procure at least two other quotations for the provision of the Services in quotation which it shall send to the Rights Holder

18.3 The Rights Holder may assign this Agreement and the rights and obligations hereunder

18.4 This Agreement is personal to the Event Manager which may not without the written consent of the Rights Holder assign mortgage charge (otherwise than by floating charge) or dispose of any of its rights hereunder or sub-contract or otherwise delegate any of its obligations hereunder

18.5 The Event Manager shall not without the prior written consent of the Rights Holder employ sub-contractors or agents. If with such consent it does so every act or omission of the sub-agent shall for the purposes of this Agreement be deemed to be the act or omission of the Event Manager

**19. Provisions Relating to this Agreement**

19.1 [Boilerplate Clauses]
[Execution Clauses]

**SCHEDULE 1**
**The Services**

1. The Event Manager will have regard at all times to the Rights Holder's objectives and instructions in relation to the smooth running and organisation of the Event and shall provide the Rights Holder with the following services during the Term including (without limitation) the following

1.1 all matters relating to Event personnel including without being limited to accommodation and travel arrangements
1.2 organisation of prize money
1.3 assisting in the development of all organisational printed materials
1.4 production of signage and advertising boards
1.5 liaison with city authorities and police
1.6 organisation of the transport fleet
1.7 Event infrastructure and all matters connected with equipment
1.8 core press centre and facilities
1.9 liaison with media specialist writers/broadcasters and dealing with enquiries relating to the Event

1.10 Event preparation and planning
1.11 liaison with all necessary local authorities
1.12 liaison with and provision of rights to Representatives
1.13 ticketing arrangements
1.14 assistance for broadcasters outside broadcast units and other Representatives
1.15 liaison with the Governing Bodies

2. Close liaison with the Rights Holder and the Representatives to co-ordinate their respective roles in connection with the Event
3. The parties may agree that the Event Manager shall be responsible for further services which are similar to the Services and shall negotiate an appropriate increase in the Consideration

**SCHEDULE 2**
**The Trade Marks**
(....)

# Chapter 7
# Sports Corporate Hospitality Agreements

## 7.1 Introductory Remarks

Corporate Hospitality is a global industry worth around US$15 billion annually, and is an important component of the sports marketing mix and a significant contributor to the 'bottom line' of many sports event organisers, who offer a wide range of commercial rights and packages.

Corporate Hospitality at major sports events, such as Formula One, the Olympic Games and the FIFA World Cup, is very popular with companies around the world and does not appear to have declined or suffered too much as a result of the recession and economic downturn. Corporate Hospitality is used by companies for a variety of corporate purposes. For example, for entertaining their clients or rewarding their employees—especially sales and marketing executives for reaching their financial and commercial targets.

Companies have realised the value of Corporate Hospitality which enables them to associate themselves with the popularity and power of sport and, in a sense, bask in its reflected glory. As there is a considerable amount of corporate pride—if not 'one-upmanship'—riding on such forms of hospitality, and a considerable amount of goodwill resting on the success of the sporting events concerned, it is very important for the organisers and also users of the hospitality on offer to get things right—not only from an operational and commercial point of view, but also from a legal point of view. A well negotiated and drafted Corporate Hospitality Agreement is, therefore, a *sine qua non*.

I. S. Blackshaw, *Sports Marketing Agreements: Legal, Fiscal and Practical Aspects*,
ASSER International Sports Law Series, DOI: 10.1007/978-90-6704-793-7_7,

## 7.2 Corporate Hospitality Agreements

As with all Sports Marketing Agreements, one of the most important provisions is the *grant of rights* clause.

This defines the extent of the rights granted by the event organiser to the provided of the hospitality and any restrictions on the exercise of those rights. For example, there will be a requirement that the party providing the hospitality must use event-sponsored products, such as drinks and snacks (popular sponsorship product categories), and not those of competitors. Thus, if Coca-Cola is the Title Sponsor of the Sports Event concerned, the hospitality provider will not be allowed to serve Pepsi! Again, there need to be restrictions on 'give-aways' ('premiums'), which themselves need to be defined in the Agreement, so that there is no conflict between these items and those of the event sponsors.

To secure the financial performance of the corporate hospitality provider's obligations, Bank Guarantees and Bonds may be required. Indeed, it has been proposed, following some spectacular bankruptcies in the hospitality and leisure sectors,[1] that corporate hospitality companies should be part of a bonding scheme, rather like ABTA scheme covering travel agents, who organise and sell 'package holidays'.

Also, it could be advisable for the event organiser and the corporate hospitality provider to enter into a joint venture company to deliver the corporate hospitality. Such an arrangement would give both parties better legal control over infringers of their respective rights.

The Corporate Hospitality Agreement will also need to contain appropriate 'warranties': for example, from the sports event organiser that it owns the rights being granted and that the event will be held; and, from the corporate hospitality provider, that the 'event marks' and the 'official designations' will be properly used.

The Agreement will also need to include appropriate '*force majeure*' provisions to cover the legal, financial and practical consequences/effects of the hospitality not being provided, as a result of the corresponding sporting event having to be cancelled or postponed for some unforeseen cause or other. In this connection, claims from suppliers for cancelled contracts and claims for 'disappointment' form invited guests need to be considered and factored into the Agreement. Suitable insurance arrangements also need to be put in place to cover such contingencies and appropriate endorsements of interests on the Policy concerned need to be expressly made. Detailed clauses are needed in the Agreement to cover these arrangements. For example, the amount of insurance; the risks covered; who is responsible for taking out the Policy concerned; and, importantly, who is liable to pay the premiums.

Again, the Agreement will need to contain express provisions regarding the 'applicable law' and the settlement of disputes, especially where foreign elements

---

[1] See some recent examples quoted in '*Hospitality and leisure insolvency*' by Emma Widdowson at www.insolvencylawforum.co.uk/index.php?...hospitality.

are involved. In this connection, the use of Alternative forms of Dispute Resolution (ADR) should be considered. See further on Dispute Resolution Clauses in Sports Marketing Agreements in Chap. 17.

From a practical point of view, to ensure the success of any corporate hospitality programme, the sports event organiser needs to have legal and actual control over the venue, especially in the areas where the hospitality will be provided, in order to prevent and/or deal particularly with 'Conflict' and 'Ambush Marketing' situations. In these respects, the Corporate Hospitality Agreement will need to include obligations on the part of the sports event organiser to prevent and/or deal effectively and in a timely manner with any and all such situations and also on the part of the corporate hospitality provider not only to report such situations to the sports event organiser but also to cooperate fully with the organiser in putting a end to such situations.

One final point: in certain jurisdictions the provision of corporate hospitality—particularly on a lavish scale with expensive corporate mementos/souvenirs—may be regarded as a bribe and, therefore, constitute a criminal offence. For example, under the new UK Bribery Act of 2010. As Tom Beezer of the UK Law Firm Bond Pearce in a Client Briefing Paper of 7 July, 2010[2] has rightly pointed out:

> "We don't want to scaremonger but lavish corporate hospitality could fall foul of the new legislation. That will not be taking someone for lunch down the road but perhaps more excessive hospitality like picking a client up in a private jet, wining and dining them with champagne and caviar en route to a sporting event overseas while spending a week in a six star hotel. Certain industries are more susceptible than others.
>
> Different areas of the world may have a completely different view of how a relationship should be properly constructed and what is acceptable. Your overseas representatives, who may not be as aware of the UK legislation, might be doing something perfectly normal where they are based but the UK mother ship could fall foul of the Act.
>
> Many UK companies with overseas operations are likely to be aware of the US Foreign Corrupt Practices Act (FCPA) but the new UK legislation goes further to cover the bribery, or attempted bribery, individuals and companies as well as public officials and organisations. What is seen as acceptable and part of local custom in many parts of the world may be totally unacceptable under the new law."

## 7.3 Corporate Hospitality Agreement and Terms and Conditions for the Sale and Purchase of Corporate Hospitality Rights Packages

In Appendix 1 (7.5.1) to this chapter a General Precedent of a Corporate Hospitality Agreement will be found; and, in Appendix 2 (7.5.2), some General Terms and Conditions for the Sale and Purchase of Corporate Hospitality Rights Packages.

---

[2] '*Corporate hospitality could fall foul of new Bribery Act*'. Website: www.bondpearce.com.

In both cases, these documents are provided for general guidance and illustrative purposes only.

## 7.4 Concluding Remarks

Corporate Hospitality is a firm feature and fixture of prestigious national sporting events, such as the Wimbledon Tennis Championships and the Henley Royal Regatta, and international ones, such as the Olympic Games and the FIFA World Cup, offering substantial financial and public/client relations benefits for sports event organisers and corporate hospitality providers alike.

To be effective and successful for all concerned, it is absolutely essential to draw up clear and legally watertight Corporate Hospitality Agreements, which reflect the particular commercial, financial and practical arrangements of the deal struck by the parties.

General Precedents should be used and adapted accordingly to suit the particular circumstances of each case.

# 7.5 Appendices

## *7.5.1 Appendix 1*

**Corporate Hospitality Agreement** *
**Lease Agreement Made and Entered into by and Between:**

[...]
(hereinafter referred to as the Lessor)

and LESSEE: ______________________________

ID/REG NO: ______________________________

1. Lease of Premises
The Lessor hereby lets and the Lessee hereby rents the Premises as set out below:
(a) Town : [...]
(b) Street name : [...]
(c) Name of building : **Ellis Park Stadium**
(d) Private Suite No : ______________
(e) Maximum seating : ______________
(hereinafter referred to as "the Premises")

2. Lease Period
2.1 Commencement date : ______________
2.2 Expiry date : ______________
2.3 Lease duration ______________
2.4 The Lessee shall have the right to renew this Lease subject to the provisions of Clause 3, Annexure "A".

3. Rental
The Lessee shall pay to the Lessor in respect of the Premises the following rental:

Option 1 (An annual payment)*

| | | | | | Cost per Seat | Net Rental R + | VAT @ 14% R | TOTAL Rental R |
|---|---|---|---|---|---|---|---|---|
| Year 1 | From | | To | | | | | |
| Year 2 | From | | To | | | | | |
| Year 3 | From | | To | | | | | |
| Year 4 | From | | To | | | | | |
| Year 5 | From | | To | | | | | |

As from Year 6 and onwards, the Rental will escalate by 10% (ten percen) or CPI whichever is the greater.

* Reproduced with the permission of Prof. S.J. Cornelius, University of Pretoria, in consultation with Van Gaalen Attorneys, South Africa.

Or:

Option 2 (A single payment for the Rental period)*

| | | | | | Cost per Seat | Net Rental<br>R + | VAT @ 14%<br>R | TOTAL Rental<br>R |
|---|---|---|---|---|---|---|---|---|
| | From | | To | | | | | |

*Delete whichever is not applicable

4 Services

The Lessee shall pay the Lessor in respect of the Premises the following service levy, inclusive of water and electricity:

| | **NET LEVY** | **VAT @ 14%** | **TOTAL LEVY** |
|---|---|---|---|
| **YEAR 1** | | | |

The service levy is subject to a reasonable annual increase taking into account the Consumer Price Index and any increases in rates and tariffs by the relevant local authorities.

5. Use of Leased Premises

The Premises shall be used only for the purposes of attending at the Stadium sports and other events approved by the Lessor and for no other purpose whatsoever, unless the prior written consent of the Lessor has been obtained and subject to such conditions as the Lessor may in its sole discretion prescribe in respect of use for such other purpose.

6. Deposits

The following deposits will be payable by the Lessee to the Lessor prior to the Lessee taking occupation of the Premises, which is subject to clause 5 of the Standard Terms of Lease.

6.1 Rental:R_______________

6.2 Key :R_______________

7. Place of Payment

Payment of amounts due by the Lessee shall be made to the Lessor as follows:

7.1 at the Lessor's *domicilium* address; or

7.2 electronically into the bank account of the Lessor, wherefore the Lessee must fax confirmation of the deposit to the Lessor. The Banking details:

[...] BANK

[...]

8. Lessor's Domicilium

The Lessor's domicilium citandi et executandi for all purposes hereunder, arising from and applicable to the Lease Agreement, is:

[...]

**Ellis Park Stadium**
[...]
or such other address as the Lessor may from time to time appoint in writing.

9. LESSOR'S POSTAL ADDRESS & CONTACT NUMBERS
**Postal:** [...]

10. Lessee's Domicilium
The Lessee's domicilium citandi et executandi for all purposes hereunder, arising from and applicable to the Lease Agreement, is:
________________________________
________________________________
________________________________
________________________________
________________________________
or such other address as the Lessee may from time to time appoint in writing.

11. Lessee's Postal Address & Contact Numbers
**Postal:**______________________
______________________
______________________
**Tel:** ______________________
**Fax:** ______________________
**Cell:** ______________________
**Person' Name:**______________________

12. Costs
The costs of:
11.1 the administration fee for the drafting and completion of this Lease Agreement to the amount of R [...] (VAT inclusive), and;
11.2 the stamp duties;
shall be paid by the Lessee to the Lessor upon demand.

13. Standard Conditions
13.1 The parties agree that the Standard Conditions annexed hereto and initialed by them for identification purposes, forms part of this Lease Agreement and must be read as if duly incorporated herein.

Signed At ______________on this______ day of________________20____ .

As Witnesses:
1. ________________________________
For the Lessee
2. ________________________________
Full names – Who warrants
that he/she is duly authorized hereto.

________________

Designation
As Witnesses:
1. ________________________________
For the Lessor
2. ________________________________
Full names

________________
Designation

Annexure "A"

## Standard Terms of Lease*

### 1. Definitions

In this Lease Agreement, unless the context indicates otherwise:

1.1 **"Main Agreement"** means the Lease Agreement, to which these Standard Terms of Lease is attached.

1.2 **"Premises"** means the Premises indicated in clause 1 of the Main Agreement and all the Lessor's fixtures, fittings, appliances, equipment and electrical and sanitary installations thereon and pertaining thereto, which is subject to clause 1 of the Main Agreement.

1.3 **"Property"** means all the buildings and other structures and all facilities erected on the erven on which the Stadium is.

1.4 **"Event"** means any promotional entertainment, sporting, cultural event or any other event, staged under the auspices of or sanctioned by [...] and/or [...], at the Stadium.

1.5 **"Event days"** means any day or days on which an event takes place.

1.6 **"Event Security Services"** means the security services involved in the event security at any sports or other organised events which falls under the direct control of [...] and/or [...], which includes, but are not limited to the following institutions:

- The South African Police Service;
- Johannesburg Metropolitan Police Service;
- Knights Event Management;
- Court Security; and
- Diligence Security.

1.7 [...]

1.8 [...]

1.9 **"the Stadium"** means the Ellis Park Stadium.

### 2. Interpretation

2.1 Words in the singular include the plural and vice versa.

2.2 Words referring to the male gender shall include the female gender and vice versa.

2.3 The impersonal pronoun shall include the masculine and feminine pronouns.

2.4 Words referring to persons shall include firms, associations, companies, partnerships and corporate bodies, juristic persons and vice versa.

* Reproduced with the permission of Prof. S.J. Cornelius, University of Pretoria, in consultation with Van Gaalen Attorneys, South Africa

2.5 Any reference to the period, currency, unexpired period, termination or date of termination of this Lease Agreement, shall include any renewal or extension thereof.

2.6 Any reference to the Lessor shall, where applicable, include the Lessor and its successors in title and their respective employees or agents.

2.7 Any reference to the Lessee shall, where applicable, include the Lessee's agents, employees, servants, customers, clients, licensees, contractors, invitees, visitors and guests.

**3. Duration**

3.1 This Lease shall commence on the commencement date and shall continue thereafter until the expiry date as set out in clause 2 of the Main Agreement.

3.2 Upon the termination of this Lease, the Lessee shall have the option to enter into a new Lease on such terms and conditions as may be determined by the Lessor. This option must be exercised in writing at least 60 (sixty) days prior to the expiry date mentioned in clause 2.2 of the Main Agreement.

**4. Purpose For Which The Premises Shall Be Used**

4.1 The Premises shall be used for the purpose described in clause 5 of the Main Agreement and for no other purpose without prior written consent having been obtained from the Lessor.

4.2 The Lessee may not use the Premises or allow the Premises to be used for residential purposes.

**5. Deposit**

5.1 The Lessor shall, on termination of this lease, notwithstanding anything to the contrary herein contained, be entitled to recover any amount which the Lessee may be indebted to the Lessor during the currency or at the expiration of the Lease Period, including but not limited to damage to the Premises, loss of rental and other levies in arrears and rental in arrears, in full from the deposit, provided that, should there be a shortfall, the Lessee shall remain liable for payment of such shortfall to the Lessor.

5.2 The Lessee shall not be entitled at any time during the Lease Period to set off the deposit against any amount due and payable by the Lessee to the Lessor, but should the Lessee attempt or purport to do so, then, the Lessor shall, notwithstanding anything to the contrary contained in the Lease Agreement, be entitled forthwith to terminate this Lease Agreement without prejudice to any and/or all the rights of the Lessor in terms of or arising from the Lease Agreement and/or the Common Law and/or Statute.

**6. Payment Of Amounts Due**

6.1 The Lessee shall pay without any deduction or setoff (for any reason whatsoever), the rental, as well as any increases in the annual rental and any other amounts which may become due and payable in terms of this Lease Agreement, as stipulated in clause 3 of the Main Agreement.

6.2 Payment shall be made during office hours of the Lessor, free of bank exchange and other charges, in South African currency:

6.2.1 at the address of the Lessor stipulated in clause 8 of the Main Agreement or such other address which the Lessor may from time to time notify the Lessee of in writing; or

6.2.2 electronically in the bank account of the Lessor as stipulated in clause 7.2 of the Main Agreement.

6.3 A certificate signed by the Lessor's auditors of the amount due by the Lessee and the date on which it is payable in terms of this lease shall be *prima facie* evidence of the correctness of the contents thereof.

**7. Conditions of Leased Premises**

7.1 The Premises are let 'as is'.

7.2 The Lessee takes the Premises in its present state and condition and the Lessee admits to having acquainted itself with the condition thereof. Should the Lessee require any additional items, the Lessee can, with the written consent of the Lessor, at its own cost and expense furnish and equip the leased premises to the Lessee's requirements.

7.3 The Lessee shall not move or remove or permit the moving or removal of any article or installation of the Lessor in or upon the Premises.

7.4 The Lessee shall, on vacation of the Premises and to the extent necessary, at the Lessee's expense and to the satisfaction of the Lessor, cause the interior of the Premises, including but not limited to all keys, locks, windows and/or electrical and plumbing installations and fittings and appurtenances therein, to be put in a proper state of repair and condition, fair wear and tear excluded.

**8. Default In Payment of Amounts Due**

8.1 If the Lessee fails to pay the rental or any other amounts for which he is liable in terms of this Lease Agreement on the due date, the Lessor may charge interest on the total amount outstanding from time to time at current bank overdraft rates of the Lessor's bankers from time to time. Interest will be calculated monthly from and including the due date for payment thereof until such amount has been paid in full.

8.2 Failure by the Lessor to charge interest on any amount in arrears shall in no way prejudice or affect the right of the Lessor to charge such interest thereon with retroactive effect, at any time thereafter.

## 9. Breach of Lease Agreement

9.1 Should the Lessor commit any material breach of any term of this Lease Agreement and fail to remedy that breach within a period of 10 (ten) days after posted written notice from the Lessee calling on it to do so (provided that should that breach be one which cannot reasonably be remedied within 10 (ten) days then the Lessor shall be allowed such additional time as is reasonably required therefore) then the Lessee shall, in addition to and without prejudice to all other rights available to the Lessee, be entitled to cancel the agreement.

9.2 Should the Lessee:

9.2.1 fail to pay any amount owing by Lessee in terms of this Lease Agreement on the due date thereof; or

9.2.2 commit any other breach of any term of this Lease Agreement and fail to remedy that breach within a period of 10 (ten) days after posted written notice from the Lessor calling on it to do so (provided that should that breach be one which cannot reasonably be remedied within 10 (ten) days then the Lessee shall be allowed such additional time as is reasonably required therefore) or should such other breach occur on 2 (two) separate occasions during the period of this Lease Agreement or any renewal thereof; or

9.2.3 reach or attempt to reach a general compromise with the Lessee's creditors; or

9.2.4 be provisionally or finally wound up or placed under judicial management or should a meeting of the Lessee's shareholders be convened for the purpose of considering a resolution to wind up the Lessee voluntarily or should such a resolution be passed, or should any scheme or offer of compromise under section 311 of the Companies Act relating to the Lessee be submitted in terms of that section, or if the Lessee seeks to make any compromise with the general body of its creditors (whether formally or informally); or

9.2.5 permit any of its goods to be attached pursuant to a court judgment; or

9.2.6 suffer any judgment to be entered against it and fail to satisfy that judgment or apply for the rescission thereof (and unless such application is successful the Lessee shall be deemed not to have applied for rescission at all) within 10 (ten) days of such judgment, then in any of the abovementioned events the Lessor shall in addition to and without prejudice to all other rights available to the Lessor as a result thereof be entitled, but not obliged, notwithstanding any previous waiver or anything to the contrary herein contained, either:

9.3.1 forthwith to cancel this Lease Agreement and to resume possession of the premises, but without prejudice to its claim for arrears of rent and any other amounts owing hereunder or for damages which it may have suffered by reason of the Lessee's breach of the Lease Agreement or of the premature cancellation in which case the Lessee shall pay to the Lessor, over and above any rental and other monies which may be in arrears in terms of the Lease Agreement as at date of cancellation, the following amounts:

9.3.1.1 Rental which the Lessor would otherwise have received from the Lessee in terms of the Lease Agreement for the period reckoned from the date of cancellation to the date upon which the Premises are re-let or the date upon which the Leased Period would have expired in the normal course of events, whichever is the earlier.

9.3.1.2 The difference between the rental and other monies which the Lessor would have received from the Lessee in terms hereof and the rental and other monies which the Lessor receives from the new Lessee, calculated from the date of commencement of the new Lease Agreement to the date upon which the Leased Period would have expired in the normal course of events, should the rental and other monies receivable in terms of the new Lease Agreement be less than the rental and other monies which the Lessee would have had to pay.

9.3.1.3 The costs of repair of any damages to the Premises, including but not limited to the costs of removal of fixtures and fittings and signage.

9.3.1.4 Any other damages which the Lessor may suffer as a result of the premature termination of the Lease Agreement.

9.3.2 to vary the Lease Agreement by making it thereafter terminable by one month's written notice given by the Lessor or in such other way as the Lessor may, in its sole discretion deem appropriate.

## 10. Lessor's Hypothec

For the duration of the Lease Agreement all furniture, fittings and fixtures, equipment, stock, etc. brought onto the Premises shall be subject to the Lessor's hypothec and shall serve as collateral security for the proper fulfillment by the Lessee of all his obligations in terms of the Lease Agreement. The Lessee may not pledge or otherwise encumber or dispose of the aforementioned assets or remove them from the Premises, except in the ordinary course of business.

## 11. Additional Services

It is recorded that a liquor licence or licenses in respect of the Stadium is/are held by a third person, or persons subject to certain conditions and restrictions regarding the consumption of liquor in the Stadium:

11.1 The Lessee shall not commit or allow to be committed by itself and/or its agents, officials, employees, contractors or invitees, any offence, act or omission which could jeopardise any licence or authority contemplated in 11.1, the Lessee indemnifying the third person(s) contemplated in 11.1 against any loss or damage sustained and arising from any such act or omission by the Lessee or its agents, officials, employees, contractors or invitees.

11.2 The Lessee shall not be entitled to provide in the leased premises any alcoholic beverages, non alcoholic beverages, mineral water, cold drinks or any other refreshments to be consumed in or about the leased premises unless such drinks and other refreshments are supplied and/or sold and/or distributed directly by the Lessor, its members, employees or agents for the sole account of the Lessor and upon such terms and conditions as may be agreed between the Lessor and the Lessee.

11.3 The Lessor undertakes that the prices at which such alcoholic and non alcoholic beverages, mineral water, cold drinks or any other refreshments shall be supplied and/or sold and/or distributed to the Lessee by the Lessor shall be at competitive retail prices as determined by the retail market in the area in which the Stadium is situated.

11.4 It shall be the sole responsibility of the Lessee to procure that satisfactory arrangements are made with the Lessor regarding the supply, sale and distribution of such alcoholic or non alcoholic beverages, mineral water, cold drinks or any other refreshments.

11.5 The Lessee shall procure that no such alcoholic and non alcoholic beverages, mineral water, cold drinks and/or any other refreshments not supplied, sold or distributed by the Lessor are consumed in or about the leased premises.

11.6 Neither the Lessor, [...] nor their agents or employees shall be liable for the receipt or non-receipt or the delivery or non-delivery of any goods excluding those services provided in clause 11.3, personal effects or correspondence of the Lessee to the leased premises, nor shall they be liable for anything which the Lessee or any employee, contractor, invitee or agent of the Lessee may have deposited or left in the leased premises or in any part of the Stadium.

11.7 All goods brought onto the leased premises or in any part of the Stadium by the Lessee or its employees, agents, contractors or invitees shall be placed there at their sole risk, and no liability whatsoever therefore is undertaken by the Lessor or its agents or employees.

11.8 The Lessor shall provide telephone and television connection points in the leased premises, provided that the Lessor is not in any way liable for the provision of telephone, telex or any other communication systems and services to the leased premises.

**12. Use of Leased Premises**

12.1 The Lessee shall use and have the use and enjoyment of the leased premises only for the purposes of attending events in the Stadium, and for no other purpose unless the prior consent of the Lessor has been obtained.

12.2 The use of the leased premises by the Lessee shall be restricted to the Lessee and the Lessee's representatives and invitees up to the maximum number of persons as stipulated in clause 1 (e) of the Main Agreement.

12.3 The Lessor shall procure that the Lessee shall receive season admission tickets to seats in the Stadium per event, in the number as stipulated in clause 1 (e) of the Main Agreement. The tickets shall entitle the holders thereof to be admitted to the Stadium and the leased premises and the private seats allocated to the leased premises, and to attend, without additional charge, international and provincial rugby football matches held under the direct control of [...], and such other events of which the Lessor may notify the Lessee in writing from time to time.

12.4 In respect of any event held at the Stadium other than an event contemplated in 12.3, the Lessee shall, in order to be admitted to the Stadium be obliged to purchase admission tickets to seats in the Stadium at the price determined by the person or entity under whose auspices such event is to be held for such admission tickets, provided that the Lessee shall, once admitted to the Stadium in the manner aforesaid, be admitted free of charge to the leased premises provided that the Lessee and the Lessee's representatives and invitees shall not exceed an amount as stipulated in the clause 1 (e) of the Main Agreement.

12.5 The Lessee shall at all times ensure that no nuisance emanates from the leased premises, and shall not cause any nuisance or disturbance on or about the leased premises or cause or allow any interference of the use of any other premises leased by other tenants in the Stadium or by spectators or other persons in the Stadium, and the Lessee indemnifies the Lessor against any claim made by any person against the Lessor by reason of such nuisance or disturbance.

12.6 The Lessee shall further ensure that the leased premises closes and is completely vacated no later than two (2) hours after the Main match or any other event in the Stadium, has officially concluded or finished, unless the prior written consent of the Lessor has been obtained.

12.7 The Lessee acknowledges that [...] shall only provide Event Security Services for a period of two (2) hours after the scheduled conclusion of any event which falls under the direct control of [...] and/or [...]. The Lessor shall, subject to clause 33, not be liable for any loss, damage or injury incurred in/around the leased premises and/or the stadium outside of the said period stipulated in clause 12.6.

12.8 The Lessee shall not use or occupy the leased premises or cause or allow it to be used or occupied in contravention of any law or in any manner which may impair the good reputation of the Lessor.

**13. Defects**

Should the Lessee on taking occupation of the Premises find any of the keys, locks, doors, windows, washbasins, taps, sanitary conveniences, drains or down pipes, electrical or other equipment of the Premises in disrepair, the Lessee shall notify the Lessor in writing of all defects within 7 (seven) days of taking occupation and the Lessor shall take all reasonable steps to repair such defects as soon as possible. Should the Lessee fail to give such notice to the Lessor, the Lessee shall be deemed to have acknowledged that on taking occupation of the Premises the aforesaid items were received in good order and condition.

**14. Maintenance**

14.1 The Lessee shall keep the interior of the Premises in good order and condition and hereby acknowledges, subject to the provisions of clause 13 that, on taking occupation, he received the Premises in a good, clean and satisfactory condition. The Lessee undertakes to leave the Premises in the same good order and condition, fair wear and tear excepted, on expiration or prior termination of this Lease Agreement.

14.2 The Lessee shall not, without the prior written consent of the Lessor, mark, paint, drill or drive nails, screws or fasteners of any nature into or in any way deface the walls, doors, floors, ceilings or partitions of the Premises.

14.3 The Lessee shall at all times during the lease period keep and maintain in proper order and condition all wiring, switches, lamps and fittings for electrical light and power, as well as all pipes and fittings for the supply of water to the Premises.

14.4 For the duration of the Lease Agreement, the Lessor shall not be liable for, whether wholly or in part, the replacement of or repairs to the floor covering in the Premises. The Lessee shall be liable for the costs of replacement of or repairs to the floor covering, power and telephone outlets, defective fluorescent tubes, electric bulbs, starters and choking coils and any other item supplied by the Lessor in or on the Premises.

14.5 The Lessee shall not without the prior written consent of the Lessor, effect any repairs or permit repairs to be effected to the Premises and/or replace any equipment for which he is liable in terms of this clause. The Lessor shall decide whether the Lessor or the Lessee or any other party shall affect the repairs or replacement and shall determine the conditions, which shall apply to the repair work and/or replacements.

The repair work and/or replacements shall be executed to the satisfaction of the Lessor at the expense of the Lessee.

14.6 The Lessee shall not change the colour scheme of the Premises without the prior written consent of the Lessor.

14.7 The Lessee shall forthwith on demand pay to the Lessor all costs incurred or which may have to be incurred, as a result of repairing the damages to the Premises, caused by the Lessee. A certificate signed by an authorised representative of the Lessor stating the amount of the costs aforementioned (or the anticipated costs to be incurred) shall be prima facie proof of the amount due and payable by the Lessee to the Lessor. This provision shall not in any way prejudice the Lessor's rights pursuant to sub clause 14.8 below.

14.8 If the Lessor is prevented from letting the Premises due to the fact that repairs are being done to the Premises in terms of sub clause 14.7, the Lessee shall, notwithstanding termination of the Lease Agreement, pay to the Lessor an amount equal to the rental and other moneys which the Lessee would have had to pay to the Lessor had this Lease Agreement not been terminated, until such time as the said repairs have been completed and the Premises occupied by a new Lessee.

**15. Water Closets, etc.**

The water closets and other water apparatus shall not be used for any purposes other than those for which they are constructed and no sweepings, rubbish, rags, ashes, chemicals or other substances shall be thrown therein. Any damage thereto resulting from misuse shall be borne by the Lessee. The Lessee shall in the use of the communal toilet rooms and lavatories show due consideration for other users thereof and shall be responsible for any damage, breakage or blockage cause by the Lessee or its invitees or employees.

**16. Alterations by Lessee**

16.1 The Lessee shall not effect any alterations and/or additions to the Premises without prior written consent of the Lessor being had and obtained. In the event of alterations and/or additions being effected with or without prior approval of the Lessor, provided that any such alterations, additions or improvements, whether it is a necessary, luxury and/or useful alteration, addition or improvement and/or whether such alteration, addition or improvement is classified as a fixture or a fitting, shall become the property of the Lessor without any obligation on the part of the Lessor to pay compensation therefore, whether during or upon termination of this Lease;

16.2 Should consent be given pursuant to subclause 16.1, the alterations and/or additions or the use thereof shall nevertheless be effected strictly in accordance with the reasonable requirements and conditions imposed by the Lessor and in accordance with all the rules and regulations made from time to time by the suppliers of electricity, by insurance companies and by a local authority or any other competent authority.

16.3 The Lessee may under no circumstances without the prior written consent of the Lessor, install or arrange to be installed any heaters or air conditioning units on the Premises.

## 17. Signs, Nameplates, Advertising Boards etc.

The Lessee may not erect, affix or paint any advertising or other signs on the Premises, without the prior written consent of the Lessor.

## 18. Unlawful Occupation

If occupation of the leased premises by the Lessee becomes unlawful by virtue of any statute, provincial ordinance or by-law of any local authority or any other decree, rule or regulation, this Lease shall be cancelled without affecting any claim that the Lessor may have acquired against the Lessee prior to such cancellation.

## 19. Interruption of Services

19.1 In the event of any interruption in any electric current or water to the leased premises—

19.1.1 the Lessor shall not be liable to the Lessee for any loss or damage sustained by the Lessee as a result thereof;

19.1.2 the Lessee shall have no right against the Lessor for cancellation of this Lease or for any remission of rental, provided that such interruption is not attributable to the Lessor's default in making payment of municipal charges in respect of electric current or water.

## 20. Provision of Services

The Lessor may at any time during the Lease Period install electric wiring, air conditioning equipment, water pipes, telephone cables or any other equipment or wiring through the Premises, should it be necessary for the supply of electricity, air conditioning, water of any other service to any other part of the Building and/or the Property. The Lessor shall endeavour to ensure that as little inconvenience as possible is caused to the Lessee. The Lessee may not reduce the rental, withhold or defer payment of rental or any other amounts, or terminate this Lease Agreement as a result of any such inconvenience or disruption of his business activities.

## 21. Keys and Locks

No duplicate keys of any lock on the Premises or any other lock on the Property shall be made nor shall any additional or replacement lock be fixed to any door of the Premises without the prior written consent of the Lessor. On vacating the Premises, the Lessee shall deliver all keys and duplicate keys in good order to the Lessor. The Lessee shall be liable for any loss of or damage to the keys and locks of the Premises and shall, at the request of the Lessor, either replace the keys and locks or have the lock mechanisms and lock combinations changed and provide new keys.

## 22. Damage to or Destruction of Leased Premises

22.1 Should the Stadium or the leased premises or any part thereof be damaged or destroyed to an extent which renders the leased premises substantially unsuitable for use as contemplated in this Lease Agreement, then—

22.1.1 the Lessee shall have no claim of any nature whatever against the Lessor as a result thereof;

22.1.2 the Lessor shall be entitled to determine within 1 (one) month after such destruction or damage, whether or not to terminate this Lease from the date of that destruction or damage, and shall notify the Lessee of its decision.

22.2 Should the Lessor elect to terminate this Lease, and provided that the Lessee has not caused or contributed to the destruction or damage contemplated in 22.1, then the Lessee shall be entitled to a pro rata remission of any rental prepaid for the unexpired period of this Lease, and apart from such right, neither party shall have any claim of whatsoever nature against the other as a result of such destruction or damage.

22.3 Should the Lessor elect not to terminate this Lease, then—

22.3.1 the Lessor shall reinstate the Stadium or the leased premises at its own cost as soon as possible in the circumstances;

22.3.2 the Lessee shall not be entitled to any remission for rental in respect of any period of reinstatement contemplated in 22.3.1;

22.3.3 the lease period shall be extended for a period equal to the period during which the suite was unsuitable for use as contemplated in this Lease Agreement.

22.4 Should the Stadium or the leased premises or any part thereof not be destroyed or damaged to an extent which renders the leased premises substantially unsuitable for use as contemplated in this Lease Agreement, then—

22.4.1 this Lease shall not terminate;
22.4.2 the Lessor shall repair the damaged part of the Stadium or the leased premises or such part thereof as soon as possible in the circumstances;
22.4.3 the Lessee shall have no claim of any nature against the Lessor;
22.4.4 the lease period shall extend for the period in which the suite was unsuitable for use as contemplated in this Lease Agreement.

## 23. Consent

If there is a dispute between the Lessor and the Lessee as to whether the Lessor has unreasonably withheld its consent or approval in any case where this lease precludes the Lessor from withholding its consent or approval unreasonably, then the onus shall be on the Lessee to prove the Lessor has withheld its consent or approval unreasonably

## 24. Lessor's Right to Extend and/or Alter

Nothing in this Lease Agreement shall be interpreted so as to limit the Lessor's right at any time to make alteration or addition to the Property, the Stadium and/or the Premises.

## 25. Communal Convenience and Services

25.1 The Lessee and its invitees and employees may, together with the other lessees, invitees and employees on the Property, use the toilets and any other convenience allocated by the Lessor for communal use.
25.2 The Lessee shall comply with any rules laid down from time to time by the Lessor for the use of the aforementioned conveniences. Should there be an interruption in any of the communal services or facilities or should any such services and conveniences or equipment become unusable, the Lessee may not reduce the rental, withhold or defer payment of rental, or terminate the Lease Agreement.
25.3 Communal conveniences and facilities are used at the Lessee's risk and the Lessor shall not be liable for any injury, damage or loss, however caused, which the Lessee or his invitees, employees or agents may suffer as the result of the use as aforesaid.

## 26. Parking Facilities

The Lessee and his invitees, agents, and/or employees shall park their vehicles on the parking spaces at his own risk and the Lessor, [...],[...] or their officers or employees or agents shall not be liable for any loss or damage whatsoever, whether due to the Lessor's, [...]'s, [...]'s or their officers or employees or agents negligence or not, to a vehicle, its accessories or contents, while it is parked on the Property. The Lessor, [...] or [...]or their officers or employees or agents shall furthermore not be liable for any personal accident or third party claims, which may arise from the use by the Lessee parking areas.

**27. Inspection, Building Operations and Repairs**

The Lessor may enter, inspect and have repairs effected to the Premises at all reasonable times and when required to do so by any lawful authority.

**28. Cleaning Services**

28.1 The Lessor shall render reasonable cleansing and janitorial services in the leased premises at such intervals in the leased premises and in accordance with such standards as shall be determined by the Lessor from time to time.

28.2 The Lessee shall pay the Lessor a service levy as stipulated in clause 4 of the Main Agreement.

28.3 The Lessee shall procure that the Lessor shall have reasonable access to the leased premises to render such reasonable cleaning and janitorial services.

28.4 The Lessor shall not be responsible for any carpet shampooing and extraordinary cleaning, janitorial or repair services of the leased premises arising from any abuse or abnormal use thereof and any such services rendered shall be extra for the account of the Lessee.

**29. Nuisance**

The Lessee shall at all times ensure that no nuisance emanates from the leased premises, and shall not cause any nuisance or disturbance on or about the leased premises or cause or allow any interference of the use of any other premises leased by other tenants in the Stadium or by spectators or other persons in the Stadium, and the Lessee indemnifies the Lessor against any claim made by any person against the Lessor by reason of such nuisance or disturbance.The Lessee shall also be obliged, at his own expense, to comply with the requirements of all regulations, laws, provisional ordinances and local authority rules and regulations concerning nuisance.

**30. Firefighting, Evacuation Exercises and Security**

30.1 The Lessee shall take part and cooperate with the Lessor in all security activities, firefighting, fire-prevention and evacuation exercises which the Lessor may order from time to time.

30.2 The Lessee shall at all times co-operate with and assist the security personnel of the Lessor, [...] or [...] at the Stadium in maintaining the level of security required by them.

## 31. Value-Added Tax

All amounts due by the Lessee to the Lessor in terms of this Lease Agreement are subject to the payment of value-added tax by the Lessee at the then ruling rate.

## 32. Severance

Should any clause or provisions of this lease be found to be invalid or unenforceable in any way, such clause or provision shall be deemed to be separate and devisable from the remaining portion of this lease and the validity and enforceability of the remaining terms and conditions of this lease shall not be affected.

## 33. Disclaimer

The Lessor, [...], [...] or their officers or employees or agents or invitees shall under no circumstances be liable for any damages, loss or injury to the Lessee or any employees, officers, private contractors, clients or invitees of the Lessee, all arising from any act or omission by the Lessor, [...], [...] or any of their officers, agents, employees or invitees in or about the leased premises or the Stadium, except where the Lessor was grossly negligent, the Lessee indemnifying the Lessor, [...] and [...] against any such claims in respect of the leased premises including the seats allocated to the leased premises

## 34. Insurance

The Lessee shall from the commencement date and throughout the currency of this Lease, at the Lessee's expense, procure that insurance cover to the satisfaction of the Lessor is provided, so as to cover public liability and damage and/or loss to the contents of the leased premises

## 35. Cession And Sub-Letting

35.1 The Lessee shall not, without the prior written consent of the Lessor, transfer, cede or assign its rights or interest in this Lease Agreement or sub-let the Premises or any portion thereof, or to part with possession of, or suffer, permit or allow any other person the use of occupation of the Premises or any portion thereof. The Lessor shall not however, unreasonably withhold its consent.

35.2 In the event of the Lessor allowing the Lessee to cede his rights and obligations to a third party, the Lessee shall sign as surety for the third party's lease, binding himself jointly and severally in respect of moneys owing to the Lessor and for the due fulfillment by such third party of all his obligations under the Lease Agreement, or any cancellation thereof.

## 36. Company, Close Corporation or Trust in the Course of Formation

If this Lease Agreement is signed for the Lessee by a person who professes to act as agent or trustee on behalf of a company, close corporation or trust to be formed, then:

36.1 this signatory in his personal capacity hereby warrants to the Lessor that the entity for which he is acting will within 60 (sixty) days from date of signature of the Lease Agreement by the Lessor:

36.1.1 be duly formed or incorporated; and
36.1.2 pass a resolution adopting this Lease Agreement without modification;

36.2 until the entity is formed or incorporated and has adopted this Lease Agreement, the signatory, in his personal capacity, shall be liable for all the obligations imposed on the Lessee in terms of this Lease Agreement;
36.3 if the entity is not formed or incorporated within the period prescribed in 36.1, if having been so formed or incorporated, it does not within the said period comply with the obligation in terms of 36.1.2, then the signatory in his personal capacity shall be deemed to be the Lessee in terms of this Lease Agreement;
36.4 in the event of the entity being duly formed and incorporated and adopting and ratifying this Lease Agreement in terms of this clause, then the signatory by his signature to this Lease Agreement, hereby binds himself jointly and severally in favour of the Lessor as surety and principal co-debtor with the Lessee, under renunciation of the benefits of excussion, division and cession of action, for all the obligations of the Lease Agreement in terms of this Lease or any cancellation thereof.

## 36. Sureties

36.1 In the event that the Lessee is a private company or a close corporation or a trust, each director, member or trustee of the Lessee, as the case may be, shall sign the Lessor's standard form of Surety.
36.2 In the event that the Lessee is a married person or a minor, the spouse or guardian of the Lessee, as the case may be, shall sign the Lessor's standard form of Surety.
36.3 In the event that the Lessee is a partnership, each partner shall sign the Lessor's standard form of surety.

## 37. Legal Costs

Should the Lessor institute any action against the Lessee for payment of moneys payable in terms of this Lease Agreement, or for any other breach of the Lease Agreement, with or without cancellation of the Lease Agreement, the Lessee shall also be liable to the Lessor for all legal costs, including collection commission, on a scale as between attorney an own client, as well as costs incurred to trace the Lessee.

## 38. Jurisdiction

The Lessee hereby consents that, notwithstanding the provisions of the Magistrate's Court Act, No 32 of 1944, with regard to jurisdiction in connection with course of action and the amount claimed, a competent Magistrate's Court shall have jurisdiction in respect of any legal action which the Lessor may institute against the Lessee arising from this Lease Agreement. The Lessor will, however, have the right, notwithstanding the aforegoing and at his own discretion, to institute any legal action, which exceeds the jurisdiction of the Magistrate's Court against the Lessee in the competent division of the High Court.

## 39. Notice

Any notice, consent or other communication to a party:

39.1 is valid only if it is in writing, except where it is stated in this Lease Agreement that it may also be given verbally;

39.2 if sent to that party by prepaid registered post in a correctly addressed envelope to its chosen address, is to be deemed to have been received by it on the 7th day after posting;

39.3 if delivered by hand at the chosen address of that party between 09:00 and 16:00 on a business day, it is to be deemed to have been received by it upon that delivery.

## 40. Redevelopment

The Lessor may cancel this Lease Agreement without the payment of any compensation to the Lessee with 6 (six) month's written notice to the Lessee, if the Lessor or the registered owner of the Property from time to time wishes to demolish the Building or wishes to rebuild, redevelop, renovate or alter the Building or any part of the Building or to incorporate the Building into any scheme of building or redevelopment involving any adjoining building and/or properties.

**41. Relocation/Rebuilding**

41.1 The Lessor reserves to itself the right to relocate the Lessee from the Premises to another area within the Building. In such an event the Lessor shall be obliged to give to the Lessee not less than 3 (three) month's written notice that it requires the Lessee to relocate to a new location in the Building. Such written notice shall contain the following information:

41.1.1 a description of the new location specifying its approximate size and placement in the Building;

41.1.2 the basic monthly rental for the purposes of and in the place of that stipulated in clause 3 of the Main Agreement;

41.2 All the other terms and conditions of this Lease Agreement shall remain unchanged and shall continue in full force and effect as fully and as though the Premises had not been relocated.

41.3 The Lessor undertakes to use its best endeavours to perform all work reasonably necessary to effect such relocation in a manner so as to cause the least possible inconvenience to the Lessee. All reasonable relocation expenses shall be for the Lessor's account.

41.4 Should the Lessee neglect, fail or omit to consent to relocation within 30 (thirty) days after the notice referred to in clause 41.1, the Lessor shall be entitled to terminate this Lease Agreement and the Lessee shall have no recourse or other relief against the Lessor by reason of termination of this Lease Agreement;

41.5 Notwithstanding any provision in this Lease Agreement, it is agreed that in the event of the Lessor or the registered owner of the Property from time to time, deciding to embark on a rebuilding scheme involving the Premises, the Lessor shall be entitled to cancel this Lease Agreement upon giving 6 (six) month's written notice of termination to this effect. The Lessee shall vacate the Premises upon expiry of the aforementioned notice period and shall have no recourse or other relief against the Lessor. Without derogating in any way from the generality of the aforegoing, it is specifically agreed that renovations, alterations, extensions, additions or replacement may constitute a rebuilding scheme for the purposes of this clause.

**42. Lessee's General Obligations**

42.1 The Lessee shall not:

42.1.1 contravene or permit a contravention of—

42.1.1.1 any of the conditions of title of the property on which the Stadium is situate or in terms of which the Lessor occupies the Stadium or

42.1.1.2 any measure having the force of law with which the Lessor must comply as occupier of the Stadium or

42.1.1.3 any law, by-law or regulation relating to tenants or occupiers of the Stadium or affecting the conduct of any events in the Stadium;

42.1.2 bring or allow to be brought or kept on the leased premises any matter or thing or activity whereby the fire or any other insurance policy held from time to time by the Lessor, [...] and/or [...] in respect of the Stadium may be liable to become void or voidable, or whereby the premium for any such insurance may be increased, and if the premium for such insurance is increased as a result of such thing brought onto or kept on the leased premises, whether with the Lessor's written consent or not, the Lessor, without prejudice to any of its rights hereunder, may recover from the Lessee the amount due in respect of any additional premiums;

42.1.3 have any claim of any nature whatsoever for any loss or damage which the Lessee may suffer in or about the leased premises or the Stadium arising out of—

42.1.3.1 *vis major*; or

42.1.3.2 *casus fortuitus*; or

42.1.3.3 any other cause either wholly or partly outside the Lessor's control

## 43. Whole Agreement

This Agreement constitutes the whole agreement between the parties as to the subject-matter hereof and no agreements, representations or warranties between the parties other than those set out herein are binding on the parties.

## 44. Variation

No addition to or variation, consensual cancellation or novation of this Agreement, including this clause and no waiver of any right arising from this Agreement or its breach or termination shall be of any force or effect unless reduced to writing and signed by both the parties or their duly authorised representatives.

## 45. Relaxation

No latitude, extension of time or other indulgence that may be given or allowed by either party to any other party in respect of the performance of any obligation hereunder or the enforcement of any right arising from this Agreement and no single or partial exercise of any right by any party shall under any circumstances be construed to be an implied consent by such party or operate as a waiver or a novation of, or otherwise affect any of that party's rights in terms of or arising from this Agreement or estop such party from enforcing, at any time and without notice, strict and punctual compliance with each and every provision or term hereof.

### 7.5.2 *Appendix 2*

## General Terms and Conditions for the Sale and Purchase of Corporate Hospitality Rights Packages*

Terms and Conditions, forming the "Agreement"

1. Definitions used in these Conditions

 1.1 "Booking Form" means the booking form signed by the Customer, to which these Conditions are attached and incorporated into the Agreement between the Customer and [x.co.uk].
 1.2 "Conditions" means the terms and conditions set out in this Agreement together with any other terms agreed in writing.
 1.3 "Customer" means the legal entity detailed above with whom [x.co.uk] make this Agreement.
 1.4 "Event" means the event(s) included in the Package, as specified in the Booking Form.
 1.5 "Force Majeure" means an event beyond [x.co.uk]'s control, including (but not limited to) an act of God, civil disorder, war or military operations, terrorism or threat of terrorism, national or local emergency, acts or omissions of government, industrial disputes, fire, flood, weather or natural disaster, any other act or omissions of persons for whom [x.co.uk] is not responsible, or events which are unforeseeable and could not have been reasonably avoided.
 1.6 "Literature" means specifications, itineraries, dates, menus and other such similar information published by [x.co.uk] on the various Packages.
 1.7 "Package" means the hospitality services detailed in the Booking Form, including the Event identified on the Booking Form (if any).
 1.8 "Price" means the Price for the Package plus VAT (where applicable) as set out in the Booking Form.

2. Terms of Sale

 2.1 The Customer wishes to purchase the Package (and entry to any Events contained within the Package) and hereby appoints [x.co.uk] (and [x.co.uk] accepts such appointment) to provide the Package and book entry to any Events contained within the Package on behalf of the Customer, in accordance with this Agreement. The Customer hereby gives its authority to [x.co.uk] to purchase tickets or other goods/services in the name of the Customer (as agreed with the Customer and confirmed on the Booking Form, or as agreed in writing with the

---

* Reproduced with the permission of Hospitality finder Ltd.

Customer) when [x.co.uk] makes such bookings and/or completes such purchases.

2.2 [x.co.uk] agrees to sell and the Customer agrees to buy the Package, subject to these Conditions and it is expressly agreed that these Conditions represent the entire agreement between the parties in respect of the purchase of the Package and may only be varied or amended by the written agreement of both parties.

2.3 [x.co.uk] employees or agents are not authorised to make representations (whether oral or in writing) concerning alterations to the information in the Literature or these Conditions and any such alterations shall only be binding when confirmed in writing by a director of [x.co.uk]. The Customer acknowledges in signing the Booking Form attached to this Agreement that they have not relied on any such representations

2.4 [x.co.uk] may at any time and without liability amend any error or omission in their Literature (including any alterations on Price or description of the Package) or invoice or any other document issued by it.

3. Reservations and Payment

3.1 The Literature constitutes an invitation to treat and no binding agreement for the sale of a Package shall exist until a valid Booking Form is received back from a Customer within the stated deadline duly signed by a person having authority to sign on behalf of the Customer, and such Booking Form has been acknowledged by [x.co.uk], with confirmation of availability of Event(s) contained within the Package, by [x.co.uk] issuing its receipt.

3.2 Payment of a deposit of 50% of the Price is required to be paid to [x.co.uk] by the Customer within 14 days of receipt by [x.co.uk] of a signed Booking Form from a Customer, when [x.co.uk] shall issue its pro-forma invoice for payment. The balance of the Price is payable by the Customer not less than 12 weeks before the Event. The dates for payment are confirmed on the Booking Form. Once [x.co.uk] receives payment from the Customer, it shall issue a full VAT invoice for all sums payable in accordance with this Agreement.

3.3 On requests for bookings placed within 12 weeks of the Event, full payment of the Price is due from the Customer upon receipt of the pro-forma invoice sent by [x.co.uk], which shall be generated upon receipt of the signed Booking Form and provide confirmation of your booking of the Package. A full VAT invoice shall then be issued once full payment of the Price has been received from the Customer by [x.co.uk].

3.4 [x.co.uk] shall be entitled to charge the Customer interest on all overdue balances at the rate of 8% per annum above the base lending rate from time to time of National Westminster Bank Plc (both before and continuing after any Court Judgement) from the date payment became due to the date of payment in full with such interest being applied on a daily basis.

3.5 [x.co.uk] agrees to transfer payment to suppliers, as appropriate, for Events and other parts of a Package, once payment has been received from the Customer in accordance with the Conditions of this Agreement.

4. Additional Services

4.1 From time to time [x.co.uk] may provide additional goods and/or services which do not form part of the Package and [x.co.uk] shall act as agents of the Customer and only on the basis that no liability of any kind shall attach to [x.co.uk] for the provision of such additional goods and/or services.

4.2 [x.co.uk] shall issue a separate invoice for any additional goods and/or services which shall be payable within 5 days of the date of the invoice unless the order is placed within 12 weeks of the Event when payment is due upon receipt of the invoice.

5. Alterations

5.1 Whilst [x.co.uk] will use all reasonable efforts to deliver the Package, it reserves the rights to alter the Package in anyway and for any reason which in its absolute discretion it considers necessary.

5.2 [x.co.uk] shall be entitled to increase the Price at any time and for any reason which in its absolute discretion it considers necessary and payment of the additional sum shall be made by the Customer within 7 days of the invoice.

5.3 The Customer shall be entitled to cancel the Package and (subject to Clause 9.5) receive a refund if [x.co.uk] increase the Price, providing written notice of Cancellation is given by the Customer within 4 days of the date of the invoice notifying the Customer of the increase

5.4 The suppliers of any tickets and/or Events (which may make up part of your Package) reserve the right to alter details of a booking, seat allocations or make other changes to tickets and/or Events booked by Hospitalifyfinder.co.uk on the Customer's behalf, without notice. [x.co.uk] will provide the Customer with notice of any changes or variations tickets and/or Events that it may be notified of by a supplier, although [x.co.uk] shall not be liable for any losses to the Customer if notice is not provided to [x.co.uk] by the supplier of any changes or variations to tickets and/or Events that have been purchased on behalf of the Customer by [x.co.uk] under this Agreement.

6. Exclusive Facilities

6.1 Where a Customer requests an exclusive facility at venue where an Event is being held, this will be subject to an additional exclusivity fee plus VAT where applicable. Such exclusivity fee shall be confirmed to the Customer in writing.

6.2 [x.co.uk] shall issue a separate invoice for the exclusivity fee which shall be payable within 7 days of the date of the invoice unless the request is made within 12 weeks of the Event, when payment is due upon receipt of the invoice

7. Ticketing and documentation

7.1 [x.co.uk] will despatch, where possible, car park and other passes and information to the Customer prior to the Event date, providing the Price and any additional charges have been paid in full and cleared funds. When it is not possible to despatch all relevant documentation relating to the Package to the Customer prior to the Event for any reason (for example, the booking made by the Customer is too close to the Event date for despatch to the Customer of the information), [x.co.uk] reserves the right to make the tickets and all other relevant information available for collection by the Customer at an agreed location on the Event date.

8. Warranties and Liability

8.1 [x.co.uk] cannot guarantee and does not warrant that the Event will take place on the date of dates agreed or at all or the ability of its suppliers to supply (all of which shall be treated as Force Majeure). In the circumstances of an event of Force Majeure, the Customer shall not be entitled to any refund except to the extent that [x.co.uk] is able to obtain a refund from relevant third parties.

8.2 [x.co.uk] shall not be liable for any consequential loss or damage including (but not limited to) loss of business or profits, loss of goodwill or loss of contracts sustained by the Customer in any circumstances.

8.3 Nothing in this Agreement shall exclude or limit the liability of [x.co.uk] for its negligent acts or omissions which cause death or personal injury, or for any fraudulent misrepresentation.

8.4 Except for claims under Clause 8.3, the liability of [x.co.uk] to the Customer for breach of this Agreement or negligence or otherwise shall be limited to a maximum of the Price paid by the Customer to [x.co.uk] under this Agreement.

8.5 Tickets or other entry to events which may form part of the Package booked for the Customer are subject to the ticket provider/supplier/venue owner's own terms and conditions and the Customer acknowledges that they shall be bound by those terms and conditions to the ticket provider/supplier/venue owner, in addition to its responsibilities under this Agreement. The ticket provider/supplier/venue owner reserve the right to remove people from a venue or event, at their discretion, and a Customer's entry to a venue or event will be subject to not only the terms and conditions of the venue owner and rules and regulations of the venue, but also the event organiser and Customers must ensure they read their tickets and any other materials/literature forwarded to them by [x.co.uk] and/or the venue owner/ticket provider/supplier when they receive such materials/literature, to ensure that they familiarise themselves with these terms prior to the event and/or attendance at the venue.

9. Cancellation and Termination

   9.1 The Customer shall be entitled to cancel the Package at any time by giving notice in writing to [x.co.uk], subject to the terms of this Clause 9 and the Conditions of this Agreement.
   9.2 In the event of cancellation for whatever reason, save as prescribed in Clause 8.1, the Customer shall forfeit any payment made under Clause 3.2 above and if not yet paid, shall remain liable for such payment in accordance with this Agreement.
   9.3 In addition to Clause 9.2 above, if cancellation is made 12 weeks or less before the Event date, then the full Price remains due and shall be payable forthwith by the Customer to [x.co.uk].
   9.4 If any payment of the Price is not received by the due date, [x.co.uk] shall be entitled, at its sole discretion, to treat the Package as cancelled by the Customer and in those circumstances, [x.co.uk] shall issue a written notice of cancellation to the Customer and the provisions of Clauses 9.2 and 9.3 apply.
   9.5 Tickets are generally not able to be cancelled and no refunds are offered. However, each Event is different and the Customer will be bound by the supplier/venue owner terms and conditions and [x.co.uk] shall not be responsible to the Customer in the event of any cancellation, refusal of entry or other termination of the Customer's right to enter an event/venue.

10. Confidentiality and Data Protection

   10.1 The parties agree to keep confidential any information disclosed to the other party where such information is specifically highlighted as being confidential information ("Confidential Information"). The obligations of confidentiality shall continue for as long as the Confidential Information remains confidential, unless any disclosure of the Confidential Information is required in order for a party to comply with its obligations under this Agreement, or if the Confidential Information is required to be disclosed as a matter of law.
   10.2 [x.co.uk] collects, stores and processes personal data in accordance with its Privacy Policy.

11. General

   11.1 Any failure or delay by [x.co.uk] in enforcing or exercising any of the terms of rights or powers arising under this Agreement shall not constitute a waiver of those terms or rights or powers and shall not affect [x.co.uk]'s right to enforce or exercise them at some later stage.
   11.2 If for any reason any of the Conditions set out in this Agreement are held to be illegal and/or unenforceable then the remainder of the

Agreement will continue in force but without those particular conditions.

11.3 Any notices to be served in accordance with this Agreement must be served personally or by ordinary First Class mail or facsimile. All invoices and notices served by [x.co.uk] will be sent to the Customer at the address on the Booking Form or such other address that has been notified to [x.co.uk] in writing. All notices to be served by the Customer shall be sent to our registered office address and such notices shall be deemed to take effect only when acknowledged by [x.co.uk] in writing.

11.4 Any legal costs, expenses or charges incurred by [x.co.uk] in recovering any outstanding payments shall be paid by the Customer on a full indemnity basis.

11.5 The parties to this Agreement do not intend that any term of the Agreement shall be enforceable by virtue of the Contracts (Rights of Third Parties) Act 1999 by any person that is not a party to it.

11.6 The Agreement is to be considered in accordance with the Laws of England and Wales and the parties hereby submit to exclusive jurisdiction of the English Courts.

# Chapter 8
# Sports Sponsorship Agreements

## 8.1 Introductory Remarks

Despite the recession and economic climate generally, sports sponsorship, which may be described as the 'bed rock' of all sports marketing arrangements, continues to be a popular marketing tool for companies around the world as the following examples demonstrate.

Usain Bolt, the 24-year old Jamaican triple Olympic gold and world record sprint champion, signed in August 2010 what is believed to be the biggest sponsorship deal in the history of Athletics with PUMA, the Swiss-based sports clothing and shoes manufacturer, with whom he has been associated and financially supported since he was 15 years old. He has extended his current sponsorship contract for three years until 2013 for a sum reputed to be in the region of US$20 million and is due to bring out a new clothing line with his own branding in December 2010!

Bolt, who is currently out of action due to a hamstring injury, wants to be a legend in his sport and make his sporting brand as big as that of the legendary former American professional basketball player Michael Jordan. Puma is reported to have gained the equivalent in advertising exposure of US$105 million from the publicity derived from its association with Bolt! This shows the value of sports sponsorship to a company engaged in the manufacture, promotion and sale of consumer products around the world. As they say in marketing circles: one good brand deserves another and each feeds off each other!

According to Jochen Zeitz, chairman and chief executive of Puma, Bolt could achieve a similar profile to David Beckham who, of course, is a well-established and lucrative brand in his own right:

> "He's the best paid athlete in history and also one of the best paid athletes overall. I would say if you asked about the rareness of Usain Bolt he's up there with some of the best in any sport. He connects to the fans in a unique way, and not just in a stadium—he can connect on the performance side as well as the lifestyle side—and I think that's the difference to many other athletes who do great things but cannot really find that connection to the fans."

I. S. Blackshaw, *Sports Marketing Agreements: Legal, Fiscal and Practical Aspects*,
ASSER International Sports Law Series, DOI: 10.1007/978-90-6704-793-7_8,

And the author of this Book would add that is what successful sports sponsorship is all about: sporting prowess; lifestyle; and connecting with the fans! And, that, incidentally, is where Tiger Woods came unstuck!

The new Usain Bolt sponsorship deal raises the question of how sports sponsorship generally has been faring due to the general economic slowdown, which despite politicians' claims that we are coming out of the global recession, is still reverberating and having adverse economic effects on various business sectors around the world.

On the other hand, it appears that the global sports industry—worth more than 3% of world trade—is, in fact, faring very well under the present economic circumstances, if current major football sponsorship deals, that have recently been announced, are anything to go by!

Here are the top ten football sponsorship deals that have been reported to date and are quite impressive:

***(1) Manchester United and Nike—£302.9 million over 13 years***
The biggest of all club-level football sponsorship deals was agreed in 2002 between Nike and Manchester United. Nike replaced Umbro as United's kit provider, agreeing to pay United a mind-blowing sum of £302.9 million!

***(2) Juventus and Tamoil—£165 million over 10 years***
At the time this sponsorship agreement was signed in 2005, the potential ten-year shirt naming rights deal—worth £75m over the first five years, and £90m if renewed for the next five—between Juventus and the Libyan-owned oil company, Tamoil, was claimed to be the biggest in football history. However, just over a year later, the football corruption scandal erupted in Italy and, not surprisingly, the deal came to an abrupt end! Juventus only received £24 million of the £165 million pledged.

***(3) Barcelona and Nike—£130 million over five years***
In 2006, Barcelona secured a sponsorship deal with their kit manufacturer, Nike, worth over £26m per year.

***(4) Chelsea and Adidas—£100 million over 10 years***
Also, in 2006, Chelsea signed a £10 million per year sponsorship agreement with Adidas for a term of 10 years.

***(5) Arsenal and Fly Emirates—£100 million over 15 years***
So far, the biggest naming rights—as opposed to kit manufacturer—deal has been signed between Arsenal and the Dubai-owned airline Fly Emirates. It is worth £100 million, and includes naming rights on Arsenal's shirts as well as their new state-of-the-art stadium. The deal was signed in 2004 and is for a term of 15 years.

***(6) Liverpool and Standard Chartered Bank—£81 million over four years***
Starting with the 2010-2011 season, Standard Chartered Bank will pay Liverpool over £20 million a year for a 4-year term for pride of place of their name on their jerseys.

***(7) Manchester United and Aon Corporation—£80 million over four years***
Manchester United have secured a shirt sponsorship deal for 4 years starting with the current 2010–2011 season worth £80 million with the American Insurance Group Aon Corp.

***(8) Bayern Munich and Deutsche Telekom—£72 million over three years***
Bayern Munich have signed a shirts sponsorship deal with Deutsche Telekom worth £24 million a year for 3 years starting from the 2010–2011 season.

***(9) Real Madrid and Bwin—£54.9 million over three years***
Real Madrid have extended their sponsorship deal with Austrian betting provider Bwin for £18.3 million per year until 2013.

***(10) AC Milan and Fly Emirates—£52 million over five years***
Fly Emirates, who, incidentally, are fast becoming the biggest name in football sponsorship, has recently signed a new sponsorship deal with AC Milan, which is worth at least £52 million over 5 years, plus performance-related bonuses. According to football blogger Steve Chappell[1]:

> "Sponsorship, especially in the form of logos on jerseys, has become a part of football culture. But football sponsorship, of course, offers much more than sentimental or aesthetic value. In an increasingly dicey financial era for football clubs, precious few can claim to be safe from potential disaster .....Sponsorship deals are a crucial source of income for football clubs, and the clubs that associate themselves with the highest bidders will have a better chance of surviving a tumultuous time in a dangerous business. For sponsors, football can be an extremely effective boost for brand recognition."

The value of football sponsorship, as mentioned above, is borne out by the fact that in 2010, English FA Premier League Clubs have reportedly negotiated a world record level of shirt sponsorships of some £100 million for the new season (2010–2011).

The latest sponsorship deal involving an English FA Premier League Club was announced on 26 November, 2010: a global sponsorship of Manchester United, the world's biggest football club with 333 million fans across the globe, by the well-known Japanese Company Epson, who became, with immediate effect, Official Office Equipment Partner to the Club for a two-season period for a reported sponsorship fee of £3 million. The *rationale* for this particular sponsorship—and, indeed, the value of sports sponsorship in general—was well explained by Epson's Global President, Minoru Usui, in the following terms:

> "The partnership with Manchester United aligns Epson with an exciting and globally recognised brand, bringing us closer to our customers worldwide. Leading the way through constant creativity and innovation both brands share a commitment to achieving the highest standards. Our vision to excite and inspire customers is represented by Manchester United's success on the pitch and the unique printer and projector technologies for which Epson is renowned."[2]

---

[1] www.blog.sport.co.uk/football

[2] Epson Corporate News Release: www.global.epson.com/newsroom/2010/news_20101126.htm.

So, sports sponsorship—at least as far as the 'beautiful game' and athletics are concerned—is very much alive and well despite—or, perhaps, according to some economists who argue to spend your way out of recession, because of—the world economic recession!

In fact, according to Matt Cutler of *SportBusiness International*,[3] citing The World Sponsorship Monitor Annual Review, produced by IFM Sports Marketing Surveys, sponsorship deals in the sports market rose by 15 per cent in 2009, compared with 2008, whilst the number of withdrawals remained stable at 8 per cent.

Sport dominated the sponsorship sector with 88 per cent of all deals in both in terms of number reported and value. According to Nigel Geach, director of IFM Sports Marketing Surveys:

> "Sponsorship as a marketing discipline gives an excellent return on investment. Both rights holders and sponsors are working together more to maximise this return—the figures in the TWSM annual review are very encouraging for the future."

However, the current economic climate was reflected in the fact that there were fewer sports sponsorship deals over $10 million reported in 2009.

It will be interesting to see what the figures for 2010 reveal when they are published and whether the present trends continue. Based on the above examples, it is expected that they will indeed as sport is a very attractive marketing vehicle!

## 8.2 Sports Sponsorship Agreements

### *8.2.1 Generally*

There are a variety of Sports Sponsorship Agreements that may be entered into by Sponsors with the Sponsored party (Rights Holders). Where the Rights Holders are individuals—sports personalities—the agreements they enter into are known as Endorsement Agreements.

Sponsorship is perceived, in many business quarters, as an attractive alternative to other forms of traditional advertising and promotion, particularly in terms of cost-effectiveness, which always high on the corporate financial agenda. This is particularly true in the field of sports sponsorship, in which an ever-increasing range of prestigious national and international sports events are on offer for commercial exploitation. What is sponsorship in general and sports sponsorship in particular?

Sponsorship is a commercial arrangement whereby a sponsor pays a certain sum of money (sponsorship fee) and/or provides certain products, services or other facilities (value in kind (VIK)) to the Rights Holders, in return for which the

---

[3] www.SportBusiness.com

sponsor is granted certain rights of association with the Rights Holders, through which the sponsor can promote its image and sale of its products and/or services.

In the sporting context, the sponsor's association is generally with the Rights Holders' sports event and usually with the emblems, logos and mascots (the event marks), which identify and distinguish the particular sports body and its event. For example, in the case of the Olympic Games, the Olympic Rings belonging to the International Olympic Committee and particular distinctive emblems, incorporating the Rings, of the Organising Committee of the Host Nation and the National Olympic Committees participating in the Olympic Games. Combined with the sponsorship rights are usually '*designations*'—the right of the sponsor to describe itself as 'official sponsor' of the XYZ event—in all advertising and promotional literature and also on all product packaging, labeling and merchandising materials.

### *8.2.2 Commercial Opportunities*

Sports sponsorship offers a wide range of commercial rights and opportunities, including:

- Title Sponsorship
- Event Sponsorship
- Broadcast Sponsorship of the Event
- Team and Individual Sponsorship (including corporate logos on team and individual athletes' clothing
- Official Designations (such as official airline and official credit card to the event)
- Official Supplierships (such as sports goods and equipment for the event)
- Franchise (such as the exclusive sale of the sponsor's soft drink(s) at the event) and display rights (the right to mount displays of the sponsor's goods at the event)
- Official Programme Sponsorship
- Product and Character Merchandising (such as official event and team mascots)
- Commemorative Items (such as official stamps, pins, coins, stickers)
- Premium and other Promotional Items (such as key rings bearing the event marks)
- Corporate Hospitality
- Tickets and Access to VIP Areas (such as 'The Paddock Club' in Formula 1)

The list is almost limitless depending upon the marketing and promotional creativity and ingenuity of the event organizer, the sponsors and their advertising agencies and public relations consultants. With the advent of sponsorship of television and radio programmes on 1 January, 1991 under the UK Broadcasting Act, there is a possibility of confusion arising in the minds of the general public between an event sponsor and the event broadcast sponsor. This happened in the case of the 1991 World Rugby Football Cup, where Sony was perceived to be the sponsor of the event, whereas, in fact, Sony was the sponsor of the television coverage of the event, much to the discomfiture of Heinz, the sponsor of the event, who had paid a substantially larger sum for the privilege! Rival companies have deliberately used such confusion on subsequent occasions in relation to other sporting events as a form of 'Ambush Marketing'.

Likewise, title sponsorship of an event adds a further complicating dimension, which needs careful handling, both commercially and legally, to avoid 'conflict marketing' and thereby diluting the value of the sponsorship rights granted. In view of the wide range of sports events, as well as the variety of the 'rights packages' on offer, a sponsor needs to match very carefully the event, the kind of association and the type of rights acquired with the image of the sponsor company and that of its products/services.

For example, a particular brand of cigarettes may be successfully 'teamed' with an international global sailing event, whereas a particular brand of popular car may 'sit' more comfortably with a football competition. Incidentally, tobacco sponsorship of sporting events in Europe became illegal at the end of 2004 under specific EU legislation. Positioning in marketing, in general, is very important and this is equally true of sponsorship, in particular. Sports sponsorship, to use a sporting metaphor, is, therefore, very much a matter of '*horses for courses*'.

### *8.2.3 Legal Issues*

Apart from the marketing aspects, attention also needs to be paid to the legal aspects of sports sponsorship, especially the content and the drafting of the corresponding Agreement. The Sponsorship Agreement will need to cover, amongst other things, the following matters;

- the rights being granted
- product and/or service category (where there are, as is usually the case, there are multiple concurrent sponsorships)
- territorial issues
- warranties—especially by the event organiser regarding broadcast coverage of the event
- duration, options and renewals of the sponsorship rights
- financial terms and conditions
- obligations of the event organiser
- obligations of the sponsor
- public and product liability
- insurance
- indemnities
- access to the venues and accreditations

- event cancellation and '*force majeure*'
- termination
- post-termination arrangements and restrictions
- options to renew
- applicable law and dispute resolution

Perhaps the most important of the above legal matters is the definition of the rights to be granted to the Sponsor and the obligations to be undertaken by the Rights Holders, especially in relation to the broadcasting of the event. These obligations will include, for example, ensuring 'clean' stadia for the exercise of franchise and advertising rights and 'clean' broadcast' signals for the television coverage of the event. Otherwise, the Sponsor may find that exclusivity is compromised through a competitor also being associated with the event in some other way, for example, one drinks company sponsoring the event, whilst a rival drinks company is the title sponsor of the event.

Likewise, potential conflicts between other classes of Sponsor, within a particular sponsorship hierarchy, also needs to be anticipated and suitable provisions included in the corresponding Agreements. Thus, the rights and obligations of the parties need to be spelled out in the Sports Sponsorship Agreement and nothing left to chance or the to parties' goodwill. In particular, the product or service category granted to the Sponsor needs to be carefully defined. For example, does the 'soft drinks' category include sports and isotonic drinks, and what about mineral waters? If these right are to be granted to some other Sponsor, they need to be expressly excluded from the 'grant of right' clause in the Agreement.

As the value of any sports sponsorship will largely depend upon the extent of the broadcast coverage of the event concerned, it is also advisable to include suitable 'warranties' by the Rights Holders on the minimum television coverage of the event and also, where appropriate, an obligation on that party to procure that any broadcaster of the event refers to the event using the name of the 'title sponsor' (for example, the Coca-Cola such and such sporting event). Failure to reach the minimum television coverage will constitute a ground for termination by the Sponsor of the Sponsorship Agreement.

Likewise, the Rights Holders should also 'warrant' that the event will be held at the agreed venue and on the agreed date(s). In the event of cancellation and '*force majeure*', the circumstances constituting which, in an English Agreement should be spelled out (in Civil Law countries, this is not necessary, as the conditions are implied under the relevant Code), appropriate provisions should be included in the Agreement for a corresponding suspension and/or reduction of the sponsorship fee, if not termination of the Agreement, depending upon the seriousness and length of time the particular contingency lasts.

Again, the Sponsor will want to be protected against 'Ambush Marketers' and will, therefore, require a specific warranty from the Rights Holders to take whatever legal and/or practical measures may be available to prevent, as far as possible,

'Ambush Marketing' occurring—this can be achieved through a comprehensive 'Brand Protection Programme'[4] designed and carried out by the Rights Holders—and, in those cases, where Ambush Marketing does, in fact, occur, to take legal action, wherever and whenever possible, against 'Ambush Marketers' to protect not only the Sponsor, but also the integrity and value of the Sports Event itself. According to the facts and circumstances of the particular case, it may be possible to obtain an injunction and/or damages against 'Ambush Marketers'.

Likewise, the Sponsor will want to be protected against so-called 'Conflict Marketing'. The problem of conflicting Sports Sponsorships and Endorsements can arise in various situations. For example, where a sports personality, who has his own individual clothing sponsor, competes in a sporting event, which is sponsored by a rival clothing manufacturer, whereby, under the terms of the event sponsorship, all competitors are required to wear that rival's sports wear bearing its distinctive logo. Again, the problem also crops up where the individual sports personality, with his own sponsor, is a member of a team and the team sponsor is a competitor of the sponsor of the individual concerned. This is particularly acute in football, which is not only the world's favourite game, but also the most lucrative, because of its wide appeal as a vehicle for brand promotion and exposure. These situations will need to be covered by suitable provisions in the Sports Sponsorship Agreement; once again, requiring the Rights Holder to avoid them, wherever and whenever possible, and also deal with them effectively and in a timely manner whenever they occur. For further information on this important subject, including the measures that can be taken to avoid and/or stop 'Conflict Marketing', see *Co-Branding in Sport: Conflicts and Some Possible Ways of Resolving them in Europe* by Ian Blackshaw,[5] which is reproduced in full in Appendix 1 (8.5.1) to this chapter.

As mentioned earlier, in lieu of or in addition to a sponsorship fee, a Sponsor may provide the Rights Holders with a non-monetary benefit, but nevertheless having value. This is called 'value in kind' (VIK) and needs to be defined for contractual purposes and valued for tax purposes (see Chap. 15). In particular, the

---

[4] For example, an elaborate and wide ranging scheme was put into action and successfully implemented during the 2002 Salt Lake City Winter Olympics. Likewise, strict rules, having the backing of statutory law, have been put into force by the Organising Committee (LOCOG) of the London 2012 Summer Olympics. See the London 2012 official website at www.london2012.com, which summarises the rules and explains the legal *raison d'être* for them.
The International Olympic Committee has introduced a 'Naming and Shaming' procedure in which offenders are exposed in a Press Conference! This seems to have been quite effective on occasions, but must be handled discreetly to avoid any claims of Defamation (Trade Libel/Injurious Falsehood).
For further information on this important topic of 'Ambush Marketing' generally, see Chapter 11 by Ian Blackshaw in *Sports Law* by Gardiner et al., 2006 third edition, Cavendish Publishing, London.

[5] See The International Sports Law Journal, ISLJ 2006/1-2, at pp. 100–102.

extent of the Sponsor's obligations to provide the value in kind concerned need to be spelled out in the Sponsorship Agreement. For example, in an 'official office equipment' sponsorship category, the number and type of computers, photocopiers and other specified items of office equipment to be supplied to the event organizers and their officials and the terms of their maintenance, if appropriate, need to be stated.

Often Sponsors require an option to renew or extend the Sponsorship Agreement on its expiration or a right of first refusal. Such clauses need to be carefully drafted too. In the first case, care must be taken not to use loose wording, which, in effect, grants an option to renew or extend in perpetuity. For example, to avoid this result, the following wording should be used:

> "The Sponsor shall have the right to extend this Agreement for a further period of....... [state the length of time in words and figures] on the same terms and conditions of this Agreement *with the exception of this present clause....* [emphasis added]."

Without these qualifying words, the Agreement may be extendable for, say, one year periods for ever.

As for rights of first refusal, these are usually accompanied by a 'matching option', which also needs to be carefully worded. Also, depending upon the particular circumstances, such a matching option, also known as *the English clause*, may raise competition law issues, if the effect is to exclude competitors of the Sponsor being able to bid for the Sponsorship rights (see Chap. 16).

In view of the international nature of Sports Sponsorship, particular attention also needs to be paid to the legal system which will govern the relationship between the parties, as well as the method and place for resolving any disputes. Alternative Forms of Dispute Resolution, such as Mediation by the Court of Arbitration for Sport, rather than traditional ones through the Courts or Arbitration Tribunals, such as the International Chamber of Commerce in Paris, France or the American Arbitration Association in New York, USA, are proving popular and cost-effective in practice (see Chap. 18).

### *8.2.4 Sports Stadia Naming Rights Agreements*

Another form of sports sponsorship, which originated in the United States and is proving popular around the world, is Corporate Naming Rights of Stadia and Arenas. See, for example, the deal between Arsenal Football Club and Fly Emirates Airline mentioned above.

In view of its importance and cost-effectiveness compared with traditional forms of corporate advertising, we will devote a separate chapter to the subject of Sports Stadia Naming Rights Agreements. See Chap. 9.

## 8.3 General Precedents of a Sports Sponsorship Agreement and a Sports Title Sponsorship Agreement

The reader will find general Precedents of these Agreements in Appendix 2 (8.5.2) and Appendix 3 (8.5.3) respectively of this chapter. Again, for general information purposes.

## 8.4 Concluding Remarks

Sports Sponsorship is the bed rock of Sports Marketing and, in its varied forms, is a significant revenue earner for Sports Bodies and Rights Holders. It is a complex subject and those responsible for designing a Sponsorship Programme, with its hierarchy of rights; negotiating the corresponding Sports Sponsorship deals; and drafting the required Agreements certainly need to have their wits about them—not least, in recognising and dealing with actual and potential so-called 'Conflict Marketing' situations, which, if not handled properly and in a timely manner, can undermine the whole Sponsorship Programme and its profitability.

# 8.5 Appendices

## *8.5.1 Appendix 1*

### Co-Branding in Sport: Conflicts and Some Possible Ways of Resolving Them in Europe

*by* **Ian Blackshaw**[*]

**Introductory Remarks**

Sport is now a global industry worth more than 3% of world trade and almost 2% of the combined GNP of the enlarged European Union comprising 25 Member Sates with a total population of 450 million.[6] It is not surprising, therefore, that the world's major consumer corporations are falling over one another in their rush to sign up sports personalities, like the Beckhams of this world, to promote and endorse their products and services.

As Anne M. Wall has pointed out:

> "Athletes can be ambassadors for the products and services they use. Their endorsement and positive publicity can lift consumer brand awareness, enhance brand image and stimulate sales volume. Upon introduction, licensed products that carry a celebrity's name can establish instant credibility for the brand in the market place."[7]

Indeed, many such personalities are in demand to endorse and promote, through their fame and notoriety in the sporting world, a range of products marketed by a variety of companies.[8]

This is fine and dandy as long as the corporations and their products are not in competition with one another. Exclusive deals are the order of the day. So branding conflicts are not an uncommon phenomenon in sport and need to be resolved.

---

[*] This is an abridged version of a Paper presented by Ian Blackshaw to a Conference on Co-Branding Issues in Various Industries organised by the Benelux Chapter of the Licensing Executives Society International and held in Rotterdam, The Netherlands, in May 2005. Previously published in *The International Sports Law Journal* (2006), pp. 100–101. Reproduced with permission of the author and the ISLJ.

[6] Branding has played a significant role in making sport such big business. This process is often referred to as the 'commodification' of sport. For more on this subject, see 'Sports Law' by Simon Gardiner, Mark James, John O'Leary, Roger Welch, Ian Blackshaw, Simon Boyes and Andrew Caiger Third Edition August 2005 Cavendish Publishing London.

[7] See 'Sports marketing and the law: protecting proprietary interests in sports entertainment events' *Marquette Sports Law Journal* 1996 at p. 154.

[8] Sports 'stars' like David Beckham, Venus and Serena Williams and Tiger Woods earn more off than on the field of play through lucrative sponsorship and endorsement deals.

**The Problem: Conflicting Sports Sponsorships and Endorsements**

The problem of conflicting sports sponsorships and endorsements can arise in various situations. For example, where a sports personality, who has his own individual clothing sponsor, competes in a sporting event which is sponsored by a rival clothing manufacturer, whereby, under the terms of the event sponsorship, all competitors are required to wear that rival's sports wear bearing its distinctive logo.

Again, the problem also crops up where the individual sports personality, with his own sponsor, is a member of a team and the team sponsor is a competitor of the sponsor of the individual concerned. This is particularly acute in football, which is not only the world's favourite game, but also the most lucrative, because of its wide appeal as a vehicle for brand promotion and exposure.

So what happens when a footballer has his own shirt sponsor, whilst the sponsor of the team strip is a competitor? How can such conflicts be resolved?

Generally speaking, with some difficulty, by employing a combination of common sense, pragmatism, and negotiation. But this can be a rather 'hit and miss' way of doing things in practice. Let us take a few specific examples of how such conflicts are dealt with in some major European sporting countries.

**Some European Solutions**

*England*

When it comes to players in the English FA Premier League (FAPL), the world's most financially successful National League, the new players' standard contract, introduced for the 2003–2004 season, contains some important and useful provisions for dealing with the problem in clause 4.[9]

These provisions are quite strict and are legally binding on the player in a "Club Context" which is defined as follows:

> ""Club Context" shall mean in relation to any representation of the Player and/or the Player's Image a representation in connection with the name colours Strip trademarks logos or other identifying characteristics of the Club (including the trademarks and logos relating to the Club and its activities which trademarks and logos are registered in the name of and/or exploited by any Associated Company) or in any manner referring to or taking advantage of any of the same."

In practice, therefore, the exploitation of a player's celebrity status is restricted when it comes to using the player's image in his club kit. However, clause 4.3 of the FAPL contract specifically recognises that the player may have "*commitments … when on international duty in relation to the Player's national football association …*" And clause 4.2.2 of the FAPL contract allows a player to have his own boots sponsorship and a goalkeeper to have his own gloves sponsorship.

[9] The full text of clause 4 of the standard FA Premier League Players' Contract is set out on pp. 341–343 of the Book 'Sports Image Rights in Europe' by Ian S. Blackshaw and Robert C.R.Siekmann (Eds.) 2005 TMC Asser Press, The Hague, The Netherlands.

Furthermore, the player's general freedom to conclude other image rights and promotional/public relations deals outside the FAPL contract is specifically provided for in clause 4.5, which reads as follows:

> "Except to the extent specifically herein provided or otherwise specifically agreed with the Player nothing in this contract shall prevent the Player from undertaking promotional activities or from exploiting the Payer's Image so long as:
>
> 4.5.1 the said promotional activities or exploitation do not interfere or conflict with the Player's obligations under this contract; and
>
> 4.5.2 the Player gives reasonable advance notice to the Club of any intended promotional activities or exploitation."

Also, clause 4 of the FAPL contract is negotiable under the terms of clause 4.11, which provides (in part) as follows:

> "Nothing in this clause 4 shall prevent the Club from entering into other arrangements additional or supplemental hereto or in variance hereof in relation to advertising marketing and/or promotional services with the Player or with or for all or some of the Club's players (including the Player) from time to time."

Obviously, in practice, the possibility of changing the terms of the contract applies to the more established and better known English Premier League players! Commercial negotiation is always a matter of relative bargaining power.

The overall aim and effect of clause 4 of the FAPL contract is to prevent players from endorsing the brands, products and services of the competitors of the League's principal sponsor(s), currently 'Barclaycard'. Otherwise, the value of that sponsorship would be diluted.

*France*

In France, the matter is governed by article 511 of the Charter of Professional Football. When signing the contract of employment, each player agrees in a specific addendum to grant to his club the right to exploit his image and/or name, collectively or individually, provided at least five players' image and/or names are exploited in the same way.

A collective exploitation of those rights can be entrusted, partially or entirely, to the French Football League, to centralise exploitation and control.

Since 1 July, 1998, players are free to use boots and gloves bearing brands or logos of their own choosing.

*Germany*

In Germany, the matter is generally governed by contract and the applicable legal rules.

Thus, in clothing sponsorship contracts, an individual sports person can only assign rights that have not yet been granted to someone else. So, if a footballer agrees in the employment contract with his club to use a specific strip, he cannot sign an outfitter contract for himself with some other manufacturer. He can only exploit any rights that have not been 'exhausted' in his club contract of employment.

However, as such rights are generally granted to the club on an exclusive basis, it is clear that the individual player's room for manoeuvre is very restricted—if not non-existent.

*The Netherlands*
In the Netherlands, such conflicts are often settled through the Courts.

For example, in the case of *Notten cum suis and KNVB* (Royal Netherlands Football Association),[10] after it had been customary for several years for players in the Dutch football team to enter into their own football boots contracts, the KNVB changed over to a contract with Adidas, under which the Dutch team players were obliged to wear Adidas boots. The Utrecht District Court found against the KNVB, because there had been no consultations with the players in advance about the change to the normal procedure and the monies arising from the Adidas sponsorship contract were enjoyed only by the KNVB. So, the principle of prior contractual rights applied.

This same principle was also applied by the Breda District Court in the case of *Ajax-Umbro and Brian Roy-Borsumij*, involving a contract entered into by the player, Brian Roy, with a clothing supplier, Borsumij, prior to his joining Ajax, who had a deal with Umbro but were aware of the player's existing contract.

Under the provisions of section 46, Book 2, of the Dutch Civil Code, sports bodies can, in certain circumstances, impose legally binding obligations on their members in relation to third parties regarding sponsorship and other rights. This statutory provision reads (in translation) as follows:

> "To the extent that the contrary does not follow from the articles, the association may stipulate rights for and on behalf of its members and, in so far as this has been explicitly provided by the articles, enter into obligations for the same and on their behalf. It may take legal action for and on behalf of the members to enforce such stipulated rights, including the right to claim damages."

In this context, the case of *KNVB and Feyenoord*[11] is the leading authority. It was held that, in order to impose obligations on members, the statutes of the sports body must be clear and that it is not sufficient for the sports body to use general and vague language. In this case, the Royal Netherlands Football Association (KNVB) wished to bind all the Dutch Clubs in the Premier Division to certain arrangements made with a third party regarding the right to televise home games. The Amsterdam Court of Appeal held that the statutes were not concrete enough and too generally worded for the claimant Feyenoord to be bound by the obligations owed to the third party concerned. For someone to be legally bound by a stipulation of this kind, the nature of the obligation concerned must be clearly set out in the statutes. Otherwise, the effect of general wording would be tantamount to the Clubs having given the KNVB full discretionary powers, which was not, in fact, the position.

---

[10] Utrecht District Court, 23 February, 1976.

[11] Amsterdam Court of Appeal, 8 November, 1996.

*Norway*
In Norway, the Norwegian Football Federation (Norges Fotballforbund) (NFF) in their agreements with players provide that the players can enter into up to three personal sponsorship agreements, provided that they do not conflict with the federation's sponsorship programme. And, furthermore, that one of the three individual sponsorship agreements must be for charitable purposes!

The rationale of the NFF restrictions is purely a commercial one to protect the value of the exclusive rights of sponsorship sold by the NFF to their own sponsor(s).

Under the arrangements, the NFF must accept the personal sponsor prior to the individual player concluding the corresponding agreement. In practice, the NFF co-signs the agreement. Either way, potential conflicts can be identified and nipped in the bud. And, thus, expensive and lengthy law suits avoided.

**Concluding Remarks**
The problem of sports branding conflicts involving sports personalities and teams/clubs and how to resolve them is a thorny and commonplace one. This is largely the result of the popularity of sports branding in its different forms and the demands made by sponsors for product/service category exclusivity in their sports marketing arrangements.

In some cases, these conflicts are not only foreseen by sports bodies, but are also provided for in their Regulations and/or their standard forms of player contracts. In other cases, the parties may have to rely on legal solutions through the Courts—largely based on the application of general principles of contract law. Because of the need, in many cases, for such conflicts to be resolved quickly, mediation may provide an effective alternative dispute resolution method.

In the majority of cases, potential conflicts are often solved, in practice, by creative marketing solutions and other pragmatic *ad hoc* arrangements, particularly in relation to award ceremonies and the press conferences that inevitably follow them. It has not been unknown for some sports persons to wrap themselves in their national flags, not as a sign of patriotism, but as a means of covering up a conflicting brand or logo on their sports clothing!

One thing, however, is clear, as sports personality branding continues to grow in importance—not least in financial terms—there is much work for sports lawyers, especially in those cases where amicable and pragmatic solutions cannot be achieved in a conflicting situation.

## *8.5.2 Appendix 2*

Encyclopaedia of Forms and Precedents/SPORT AND SPONSORSHIP vol 39(2) 2004/(C) Forms and Precedents/B: SPONSORSHIP/Standard sponsorship agreement

**Standard Sponsorship Agreement***

This Agreement is made the ......... day of ...........
Between:

(*name of rights holder, e.g sporting federation*) [(*company registration number*)] [of (*address*) (or) whose registered office is at (*address*)] ('the Federation') and (*name of sponsor*) [(*company registration number*)] [of (*address*) (or) whose registered office is at (*address*)] ('the Sponsor')

Whereas:
The Federation is the owner of the exclusive rights to and the organiser of a series of annual Events at a number of different Venues throughout the Territory which the Sponsor agrees to sponsor in accordance with the terms of this Agreement.

IT IS AGREED as follows:

**Definitions and interpretation**
In this Agreement the following words or phrases shall, unless the context otherwise requires, have the following meanings:

| | |
|---|---|
| 'Company Liaison Officer' | the liaison officer appointed by the Sponsor in accordance with clause 6; |
| 'Events' | (*insert number*) events specified in Schedule 1 to be held at the Venues during each Year of the Term and to be organised and/or supervised by the Federation which are to be televised or intended to be televised in whole or in part by the Television Company; |
| 'Federation's Database' | the databases set up by the Federation containing information obtained from the marketing and promotion of the Event programme; |
| 'Federation Liaison Officer' | the liaison officer appointed by the Federation in accordance with clause 7.21 of this Agreement; |

* This precedent provides for the sponsorship of a series of events, in this case road running events. It illustrates the rights granted in relation to such events and the obligations which might be entered into by the parties. Source Lexis Nexis; reproduced with permission.
Where VAT is payable under this Agreement the following clause should be inserted:
'All fees, disbursements and expenses payable under this Agreement are subject to the addition of VAT'.

| | |
|---|---|
| 'Intellectual Property Rights' | any and all intellectual property rights including (without limitation) patents, trade marks and designs (whether registered or unregistered) including any applications for the foregoing, copyrights, database rights and rights in performances; |
| 'Product Group' | the goods and services falling within the categories of business specified in Schedule 3; |
| 'Sponsor's Group' | the Sponsor and its subsidiary and associated companies as each such term is defined in the Companies Act 1985 as amended by the Companies Act 1989; |
| 'Sponsor's Group Products' | (*insert product group*); |
| 'Sponsor's Logos' | such of the Sponsor's Group's logos and trade and service marks which the Federation is permitted by the Sponsor to use pursuant to this Agreement; |
| 'Sponsorship Fees' | the fees payable by the Company pursuant to clause 4 of this Agreement for the Sponsorship Rights; |
| 'Sponsorship Rights' | the rights set out in Schedule 2; |
| 'Subsidiary Sponsor' | other non-title sponsors and proposed sponsors of the Events or any part thereof; |
| 'Television Company' | the organisation(s) televising some or all of the Events by terrestrial and/or satellite broadcast; |
| 'Term' | the period set out in clause 2 of this Agreement; |
| 'Territory' | means [the United Kingdom]; |
| 'Venues' | the venues as set out in Schedule 1 or such other venues as may be agreed at which the Events shall be held; and |
| 'Year' | a period commencing on (*date*) and expiring on (*date*) in the following calendar year or the date of termination of this Agreement, if sooner. |

In this Agreement the singular includes the plural and vice versa and any gender includes any other gender.
The clause headings do not form part of this Agreement and shall not be taken into account in its construction or interpretation.
References to clause(s) and schedule(s) are references to clause(s) and schedule(s) of and to this Agreement.

**Term of Agreement**

1.1 This Agreement shall commence on (*date*) and shall remain in force until and including (*date*) unless previously determined as provided in this Agreement.

1.2 The Sponsor shall have the option to extend the period of this Agreement for a further Year, such option to be exercised by giving written notice to the Federation on or before (*date*) of its desire to do so. If the option is exercised by the Sponsor the provisions of this Agreement shall apply during such extended period but excluding any provision for further extension of the Term.

**Grant of rights**

2.1 Subject to the terms of this Agreement:

2.2 the Sponsor agrees to sponsor the Events which shall be known and referred to by the names set out in Schedule 1 or such other name as may be agreed between the parties to this Agreement; and

2.3 the Federation grants to the Sponsor the Sponsorship Rights.

**Consideration**

In consideration of the due and proper performance by the Federation of its obligations under this Agreement and the grant to the Sponsor by the Federation of the Sponsorship Rights the Sponsor shall pay to the Federation during the Term the following amounts:

3.1 in the first Year of this Agreement the sum of £...; and

3.2 in any subsequent Year (including for the avoidance of doubt any extended period) such sum as shall be equal to the Sponsorship Fee payable in the immediately preceding Year increased by the Retail Prices Index.

3.3 If in any Year the whole or a substantial part of any Event does not take place in accordance with this Agreement the Sponsorship Fees in respect of such Year shall be reduced by [...%] per cancelled Event.

3.4 The Sponsorship Fees payable by the Sponsor in each Year of this Agreement shall be paid by the Sponsor to the Federation in four equal instalments together with the VAT thereon on receipt of a valid invoice from the Federation as follows:
- in respect of the first Year of the Term on 1 April (or such later date as shall be agreed by the Sponsor and the Federation), 1 June, 1 August and 1 November; and
- in respect of any subsequent Year on each of 2 March, 1 June, 1 August and 1 November in such Year.

3.5 The Federation shall provide the Sponsor with VAT invoices one week prior to the due date for each of the instalments referred to in clause 3.4 above.

**Responsibility for organisation**

4.1 The Sponsor's Group shall have no responsibility for the organisation or operation of the Events and the Federation shall indemnify the Sponsor and each member of the Sponsor's Group in accordance with clause 7.

**The Sponsor's obligations**

5.1 The Sponsor shall appoint the Company Liaison Officer to liaise with the Federation to facilitate the operation of the Sponsor's Group's sponsorship of the Events under this Agreement.

**Federation's obligations**

6.1 The Federation undertakes and agrees with the Sponsor in respect of each Year during the Term (at its own cost save where expressly stated otherwise) that it shall:

6.2.1 organise or procure the organisation of the Event to a high standard and the best of its ability;
6.2.2 promote each of the Events;
6.2.3 (in consultation with the Sponsor's Group and subject to the approval of the Sponsor's Group) design logos for the Events, which will prominently feature the Sponsor's name and/or Sponsor's Logos;
6.2.4 make every effort to ensure that each of the Events take place upon the dates and at the locations agreed by the Sponsor and the Federation throughout the Territory;
6.2.5 not promote, provide, sell or permit the promotion, provision or sale of products or services falling within the Product Group other than the Sponsor's Group Products within the Venues;
6.2.6 show to the reasonable satisfaction of the Sponsor's Group that it has taken all reasonable steps to comply with the obligations set out in clause 7.2;
6.2.7 give 6 weeks' prior written notice to, and to consult in advance with, the Sponsor's Group, with regard to in each case the dates and Venues of the Events;
6.2.8 use its best endeavours to support the Sponsor's Group in seeking to exercise and exploit the rights granted under this Agreement and in particular (but not exclusively) where requested to do so it shall make representations to the Television Company or such other person or body as may be appropriate with a view to ensuring that the Sponsor's Group gains the maximum advantage from the Sponsorship Rights granted under this Agreement;
6.2.9 assist in developing with the Sponsor's Group ways and means of exploiting its association with the Events;
6.2.10 take all steps necessary to ensure that the Sponsor's Group receives the full benefit of the Sponsorship Rights and any other rights in relation to the Events which may become available in the future and to prevent so called 'ambush marketing';
6.2.11 use its best endeavours to ensure that the Events are televised by the Television Company on the [Sporting] Programme (or a suitable alternative live broadcast) for a minimum of...... minutes throughout the Territory;

6.2.12 obtain and secure compliance with all necessary consents, licences and approvals of all relevant governmental, local or other competent authorities in connection with the organisation and operation of each of the Events;

6.2.13 require (and take all reasonable steps to ensure that) all competitors in the Events do not promote any competitor of the Sponsor or any product other than Sponsor's Group Products whilst competing in the Event or in any associated activities;

6.2.14 use its best endeavours to contract or otherwise arrange or procure for the participation in the Events of leading athletes;

6.2.15 provide competent announcers of good reputation and standing for the Events;

6.2.16 use its best endeavours to help host the VIP guests of the Sponsor's Group and to provide the opportunity for executives of the Sponsor's Group or their spouses to present prizes and to participate at the Events;

6.2.17 ensure that the Sponsor's Group receives a sponsor's credit on all promotional materials used at or in relation to the Events;

6.2.18 not do or omit to do anything which is prejudicial to the good image of the Sponsor's Group;

6.2.19 provide Venues which shall in all respects be suitable and safe for the staging of Events;

6.2.20 in the event of any circumstances occurring in respect of any or all of the Events which seriously damage or are likely to seriously damage the image and good standing of the Sponsor take such steps as may be reasonably required by the Sponsor including, but not limited to, ceasing to use and removing all reference to the Sponsor's Logos in conjunction with the Events;

6.2.21 and/or liaise and fully co-operate with the Sponsor's Group in the handling of all publicity arising out of such circumstances so as to minimise the likelihood of any damage arising to the image and good standing of the Sponsor's Group;

6.2.22 appoint the Federation Liaison Officer to liaise with the Company's Liaison Officer to facilitate the operation of the Sponsor's sponsorship of the Events under this Agreement;

6.2.23 ensure that any promotions carried out by Subsidiary Sponsors in relation to any or all of the Events carry the Event logo;

6.2.24 compile and make available to the Sponsor's Group free of charge at such times and in such manner as the Sponsor's Group requires the Federation's Database;

6.2.25 promote and publicise on a regional and national basis the Events by all reasonable means and in consultation with the Sponsor's Group; and

6.2.26 without prejudice and in addition to any other provision of this Agreement fulfil the further obligations set out in schedule 5.

**Indemnity and insurance**

7.1 The Federation shall indemnify the Sponsor's Group against and at its own expense effect and maintain adequate insurance in respect of any third party or public liability arising out of the organisation or operation of the Events and shall procure that the interest of the Sponsor's Group is noted on any insurance policy taken out in respect of the Events.

7.2 The Federation shall at its own expense effect and maintain adequate insurance against cancellation of all or any part of the Events and without prejudice to the generality of the foregoing against all and any liability it may have to the Sponsor's Group however arising as a result of any such cancellation.

**Warranties and undertakings**

8.1 The Federation warrants and undertakes:

8.1.1 that it has the exclusive right to grant the Sponsorship Rights and undertakes not to grant in relation to the Events, rights and licences the same as or similar to the Sponsorship Rights to any third party wishing to advertise or promote any similar product or service to the Product Group;

8.1.2 that it shall not without the prior approval of the Sponsor's Group, which shall not be unreasonably withheld in the case of a non-competing person or company, grant Subsidiary Sponsor status to any person or company and that it shall submit for prior approval by the Sponsor's Group the rights proposed to be granted to any such potential Subsidiary Sponsor [provided always that no person who actually has or could be perceived by the general public as having a connection with products or services involving tobacco or alcohol shall be a Subsidiary Sponsor]; and

8.1.3 that it shall not appoint more than (*number*) Subsidiary Sponsors in aggregate in respect of the Events.

**Termination**

8.1 Without prejudice to clause 10.2 below either party to this Agreement may by 14 days' notice in writing to the other party determine this Agreement if the other party is in material breach of any of the terms and conditions of this Agreement and fails to remedy such material breach (if capable of remedy) within 30 days of being requested to do so.

8.2 The Sponsor may terminate this Agreement by notice in writing to the Federation at any time with immediate effect if:

8.2.1 the Sponsor's Group believes it has suffered or is likely to suffer significant and damaging adverse publicity as a result directly or indirectly of its connection with the whole or any part of the Events or any other matter arising from this Agreement;

8.2.2 in any Year (*number*) of the Events are cancelled; or

8.2.3 in any Year the Events shall not be televised for at least (*number*) minutes on national network television.

8.3 Any termination of this Agreement shall be without prejudice to any accrued rights and remedies of the parties at the date of termination. Further, without prejudice to any claim for damages which may be maintained by the Sponsor in relation to any breach of this Agreement by the Federation upon any termination of this Agreement by the Sponsor pursuant to clauses 8.1 or 8.2 above the Sponsor shall immediately be released from any further or continuing obligation to pay any Sponsorship Fees and the Federation shall promptly repay to the Sponsor such amount of the total Sponsorship Fees due in respect of the Year during which such termination occurs as shall have been paid to the Federation after deduction by the Federation of the reasonable costs and expenses properly incurred by the Federation in the performance of its obligations arising under this Agreement up to the date of such termination.

**Rights of third parties**

9.1 A person who is not a party to this Agreement may not rely upon or enforce any rights pursuant to the Contracts (Rights of Third Parties) Act 1999.

AS WITNESS etc.

SCHEDULE 1

The Events

(*list events and venues*)

The Events will take place at dates to be arranged after consultation between the parties as provided for in the body of this Agreement which will take into account the calendar and the scheduling requirements of the Television Company.

SCHEDULE 2

The Sponsorship Rights

The Sponsor shall have the following rights in respect of the Events:

The right for the Sponsor's Group free of charge to the branding of the Events by the inclusion of the Sponsor's Group's name '(*insert name*)' and its '(*insert logo*)' logo:

- in the title of the Events;
- on every competitor's number;
- on the cover of the official programme to the Events;
- on all print materials and, without prejudice to the generality of the foregoing, on all:

- mile/kilometre marker posts;
- winning line tapes;
- posters;
- tickets;
- agreed advertising of each Event and mail outs and leaflets;
- banners and perimeter boards (up to [20] in aggregate per Event);
- entry forms;
- directional signage;
- public relations materials initiated by the Federation;
- identification badges;
- photographers' bibs and officials' uniforms;
- the lead car at each Event;
- the winner's podium; and
- the start and finish gantries at the Events; and
- on all official souvenir merchandise and premiums including, without prejudice to the generality of the foregoing, T-shirts and carrier bags available whether for sale or otherwise at the Events.

The right for the Sponsor's Group free of charge to use its connection with the Events, the Events' name, and logo to promote and advertise the Sponsor's Group and the Sponsor's Group Products in any form or media, provided that the costs of any such promotion or advertising shall be borne by the Sponsor's Group.

The right for the Sponsor's Group free of charge to have access to and the right to use information from the Federation's Database at any time subject to giving reasonable notice to the Federation and subject to the Data Protection Act 1998.

The right for the Sponsor's Group free of charge to have the Sponsor's Group's promotional and other literature distributed with tickets to the Events in the pre-Events ticket mailing and post-Events mailing provided that the Sponsor will meet any additional postage costs thereby incurred.

The right for the Sponsor's Group free of charge to hold a press conference to be given at a venue to be chosen by the Sponsor's Group after consultation with the Federation to launch the Events.

The right of the Sponsor's Group free of charge to prime exhibition space at each Event with minimum dimensions of (*number*) metres by (*number*) metres provided that the costs of any such exhibition shall be met by the Sponsor.

The right of the Sponsor's Group free of charge to a marquee to be placed in a centrally located space at each Event of sufficient size within which to stage promotional activities holding an audience of (*specify*) under cover with room for a further audience of (*specify*) outside provided that the costs of any promotional activity shall be borne solely by the Sponsor.

The right for the Sponsor's Group at its own cost to erect additional promotional banners and signage at each Event in prominent locations, provided that the Sponsor's Group shall comply in full with all applicable regulations and byelaws relating to the same, such locations to be subject to the requirements (if any) of the Television Company.

The right for the Sponsor's Group to have a colour back page advertisement (for which all artwork and colour separation costs will be borne by the Sponsor's Group) and one full prominent inside page for editorial (supplied by the Sponsor and agreed in advance with the Federation) in the official brochure and each official Event programme.

## SCHEDULE 3

### The Product Group

(*insert details of goods and services falling within the applicable product categories*)

## SCHEDULE 4

### The Company Logo

| Mark/Logo | Class in which Registered | Number |
|---|---|---|
| (*insert details*) | (*specify*) | (*insert details*) |

## SCHEDULE 5

### Further obligations of the Federation

In respect of each Event the Federation shall at its own cost secure or cause to be secured the following services and facilities:

- a mailing address;
- all necessary administrative support including but not limited to office equipment (to include computer equipment) and accommodation;
- the staffing of and carrying out of all necessary administrative functions to include mail outs, information and the processing of entry forms, fees, numbering and results monitoring;
- all necessary manpower for the conduct of the Event including officials, marshals, stewards, persons to erect gantries, route barriers, boards and route markers, dispensers of refreshments, race numbers (and T-shirts, medals, certificates) and collectors of results data;
- the provision of accommodation for competitors and other personnel connected with each Event;
- adequate security arrangements for all aspects of each Event;
- all necessary approvals and consents to the planning of routes;
- power generation and use of lighting;
- use of route barriers;
- adequate toilet facilities (as per the recommendation of environmental health officers);
- all necessary public address systems;
- use of local transport facilities;

- [race] permits;
- use of finishing funnels and recording systems including videos;
- adequate medical facilities including first aid equipment;
- organisation of communications and protocol;
- VIP seating area[s] at the Venues; and
- clean up operations immediately after the Event.

In respect of each Event the Federation shall further be responsible for and organise at its sole cost as many of each of the following items as is specified or otherwise as shall be required:

- tickets;
- advertising and mail outs;
- leaflets;
- banners and perimeter advertising boards;
- directional signage;
- public relations materials;
- identification badges;
- photographers' bibs and officials' uniforms (at least one per photographer/ official);
- [the lead car] at each Event;
- the winners' podium;
- the start and finish gantries relating to the Event; and
- the marquee (including catering, such catering to be paid for by the Sponsor to be located at the finish of each Event for guests invited by the Sponsor's Group, VIPs [and leading middle distance athletes].

In respect of each Event the Federation shall keep the Sponsor's Group properly advised of all appropriate and/or desirable advertising opportunities including, but not limited to, those in regional television broadcasting, specialist magazines, newspapers and radio (in each case both national and local) and shall liaise with the Sponsor's Group and its agent with regard to maximising and taking full advantage of such opportunities, provided that the decision whether or not to advertise and the responsibility (and the cost) of placing any such advertisement shall be that of the Sponsor's Group.

(*signatures of* (*or on behalf of*) *of the parties*)

## *8.5.3 Appendix 3*

Encyclopaedia of Forms and Precedents/SPORT AND SPONSORSHIP (Volume 39(2)) (2004 Reissue)/(C) Forms and Precedents/B: SPONSORSHIP/Title sponsorship agreement

**Title Sponsorship Agreement**[*, 1]

This Agreement is made the ......... day of ......

Between:

(*name of governing body*) of (*address*) ('the Governing Body') and
(*name of company*)[(*company registration number*)] whose registered office is at (*address*) ('the Company')

Whereas:

The Governing Body is the governing body for the sport of (*specify*) in the Territory and (inter alia) organises and administers the Event.
The Company manufactures (*insert details*) and wishes to sponsor the Event.
The Governing Body is the owner of all commercial rights in and has agreed to grant to the Company various rights in connection with the Event on the terms of this Agreement.

It Is Agreed as follows:

**Definitions and interpretation**

In this Agreement the following words or phrases shall, unless the context otherwise requires, have the following meanings:

| | |
|---|---|
| 'Ancillary Rights' | the ancillary rights set out in Schedule 1; |
| 'Broadcast' | any form of broadcast or transmission by whatever means; |
| 'Broadcast Substitution' | the ability to superimpose an image (by whatever means) onto any surface whether it is real or artificially created or the ability to alter any such surface or image by any means; |
| 'Broadcaster' | any person who Broadcasts the Event (or any Match forming part of the Event) in the Territory; |
| 'Clubs' | the clubs who are members of the Governing Body; |
| 'Commencement Date' | (*date*); |
| 'Commercial Partner' | any third party to whom the Governing Body has granted or may grant during the Term commercial |

[*] Source: Lexis Nexis; reproduced with permission.

| | |
|---|---|
| | rights including (but not limited to) existing sponsors, any Broadcaster, sponsor, supplier, agent or associate; |
| 'Company Marks' | the marks of the Company set out in Schedule 4; |
| 'Company Products' | any Product manufactured, sold or distributed by the Company; |
| 'Competitor' | any person (other than the Company) manufacturing, selling or distributing a Product; |
| 'Designations' | the designations which the Company is entitled to use pursuant to clause 6; |
| 'Event' | the Governing Body competition which is organised [annually] by the Governing Body more particularly described in Schedule 3; |
| 'Fee' | all amounts payable under clause 8; |
| 'Governing Body Marks' | the marks set out in Schedule 2; |
| 'Grounds' | each ground at which Matches are played; |
| 'Internet Rights' | the right to create and maintain a website (as that phrase is commonly understood) and to provide links to other websites relating to or including material relevant to the Event and the exploitation of the Rights; |
| 'IPR' | any and all intellectual property rights including (without limitation) patents, trade marks and designs (whether registered or unregistered) including any applications for the foregoing, copyrights, database rights and rights in performances; |
| 'Match' | any and all matches in the Event; |
| 'Perimeter Boards' | any advertising boards situated at the perimeter of the pitch at each Ground together with fascia boards at such Grounds; |
| 'Premiums' | any article issued for free or nominal consideration used to promote the Company and/or the sale of or advertising of Company Products; |
| 'Product' | (*insert details*); |
| 'Rights' | the rights granted to the Company by this Agreement including (but not limited to) the Ancillary Rights and the Designations; |
| 'Season' | any season during the Term; |
| 'Sponsored Logo' | the official logo or logos used in connection with the Rights; |
| 'Sponsored Title' | the title by which the Event will be known during the term under the terms of this Agreement; |
| 'Term' | the period of this Agreement specified in clause 12; |

| | |
|---|---|
| 'Territory' | means the world; |
| 'TV Perimeter Boards' | perimeter boards which are or may be in view of fixed or hand held television cameras; and |
| 'Venue' | the geographical area surrounding the Grounds |

In this Agreement where the context admits:

- References to statutory provisions shall be construed as references to those provisions as amended or re-enacted or as their application is modified by other provisions from time to time and shall include references to any provisions of which they are re-enactments (whether with or without modification);
- references to 'this Agreement' or to any other agreement or documents referred to in this Agreement means this Agreement or such other agreement or document as amended, varied, supplemented, modified or novated from time to time and include the schedules;
- references to clause(s) and schedule(s) are references to clause(s) and schedule(s) of and to this Agreement and references to paragraph(s) are unless otherwise stated references to paragraph(s) in which the reference appears; and
- references to a 'person' include any individual, company, body corporate, corporation sole or aggregate, government state or agency of a state, firm, partnership, joint venture association, organisation, or trust (in each case whether or not having separate legal personality and irrespective of the jurisdiction in or under the law of which it was incorporated or exists) and a reference to any of them shall include a reference to the others.
  The headings and sub-headings are inserted for convenience only and shall not affect the construction of this Agreement.

Each of the schedules shall have effect as if set out in this Agreement. Where the context requires the singular includes the plural and vice versa.

**Grant of the Rights**[2]

2.1 In consideration of the payment of the Fee the Governing Body grants to the Company the Rights during the Term in the Territory

**Title sponsorship rights**[3]

3.1 The Company shall have the right to be described as the official title sponsor of the Governing Body using the Sponsored Title.

3.2 The Governing Body shall refer to the Event using the Sponsored Title during the Term.

3.3 The Governing Body shall use [all reasonable] endeavours to ensure that each of the Clubs, any Broadcaster and any other third party (including the Commercial Partners) referring to the Event do so using the Sponsored Title.

3.4 The Governing Body shall ensure that the Sponsored Title and/or the Sponsored Logo appears on all official Governing Body publications and printed material (including tickets to each Match) produced by or for the Governing Body and/or the Club and on such press releases and stationery as is provided by the Company concerning the Event, the front cover of the programme for each Match as well as the backdrop during press conferences organised by the Governing Body regarding the Event and (where practicable) the Sponsored Title and/or the Sponsored Logo shall appear on the backdrop for any studio discussion or interview regarding the Event transmitted by a Broadcaster. The Governing Body shall further ensure that all material relating to the Event produced by the Commercial Partners and the Clubs incorporates the Sponsored Title and/or the Sponsored Logo.

**Sponsored Title and Sponsored Logo**[4]

4.1 The Governing Body grants the Company the non-exclusive right during the Term to use or authorise the use of the Governing Body Marks and/or the Sponsored Title and/or the Sponsored Logo on the packaging of Company Products and in all printed, promotional and publicity materials, on merchandise and/or in radio and television commercials for Company Products which may be issued or produced by the Company in the Territory, without being liable to the Governing Body for any royalties, fees or other type of payment, save as set out in this Agreement.

4.2 The Company may register the Sponsored Logo at its own cost as a trade mark in any part of the Territory and may require the Governing Body to execute and register a registered user agreement in relation to the use by the Company of the Governing Body Marks in connection with this Agreement or such registration.

**Television coverage**[5]

5.1 In each Season during the Term the Governing Body shall procure that on terrestrial television at least (*number*) Matches are Broadcast either live, 'as live', or as highlights. The Governing Body shall use its reasonable endeavours to ensure that all Matches are Broadcast (whether on cable, satellite or terrestrial television) as often as is reasonably practicable.

5.2 In relation to all Broadcast coverage of the Event by any Broadcaster the Governing Body shall procure that each Broadcaster and any other person with whom the Governing Body enters into an arrangement for Broadcast of the Event shall ensure that:

5.2.1 the Sponsored Logo and Sponsored Title appear with appropriate prominence in the opening and closing titles of all Broadcasts of Matches, in all trailers, previews and other promotional material or on any screen clock or official timer, and (in the case of commercial broadcasters only) in all pre-advertising breaks which are Broadcast by a Broadcaster in any part of the Territory;

5.2.2 the Sponsored Logo appears in any service provided by a Broadcaster in relation to the results of Matches and in excerpts from any fixtures list relating to the Event; and

5.2.3 during Broadcasts of Matches by a Broadcaster in any part of the Territory the Sponsored Title is always referred to when reference is made in the course of the commentary to, or any studio discussions of, the Event.

5.3 In relation to all Broadcast coverage of the Event by any Broadcaster the Governing Body shall procure that during the Broadcast of Matches by a Broadcaster such Broadcaster makes no attempt to exclude, restrict or alter coverage on screen of Perimeter Boards bearing the Sponsored Logo or the Sponsored Title or any other signage or promotional material of the Company relating to the exercise of the Rights at any of the Grounds or the Venues.

5.4 The Governing Body, the Broadcaster and any other person with whom the Governing Body enters into an arrangement for the Broadcast of Matches shall not be required to perform any of their obligations under the provisions of clause 5 to the extent that performance of any such obligation would cause the Governing Body, such Broadcaster, or any third party to contravene the requirements of any law or binding code of practice.

5.5 The Governing Body shall procure that any Commercial Partner with whom it has an arrangement in relation to the commercial exploitation of the Event or any Match by means of any audio or audio–visual medium whether by Broadcast, online or otherwise (including but not limited to video, transmission to mobile telephone or other hand-held devices or otherwise, Internet usage or any online service) shall use the Sponsored Logo and the Sponsored Title and shall comply with all relevant restrictions in this Agreement.

5.6 The Governing Body shall not and it shall procure that the Broadcaster shall not enter into any Broadcast sponsorship agreement or otherwise enter into any agreement involving Broadcasting in relation to the Event where one of the other parties to such an agreement is a Competitor or is already a party to an arrangement or intends to enter into any arrangement with a Competitor in relation to the Broadcast of the Event or any Match.

5.7 The Governing Body shall ensure that any Broadcaster which is or will be appointed as a licensed broadcaster of the Event will not be authorised to interfere with the television feed or programmes derived therefrom to delete, alter or add to any of the Rights granted to the Company featured therein whether by Broadcast Substitution or otherwise. The Governing Body shall procure that such Broadcasters include a similar provision in any sub-licence or programme sales agreement relating to the Event.

5.8 The Governing Body shall procure the grant to the Company of the first and exclusive right to acquire exclusive Broadcast sponsorship rights in any part of the Territory for all Matches and shall ensure that the following procedure applies:

5.8.1 The Broadcaster shall grant to the Company the right of first and exclusive negotiation with respect to the purchase of any broadcast sponsorship opportunity in relation to its Broadcasts of the Matches on an exclusive basis. In this clause, 'first and exclusive negotiation' means that, before offering any broadcast sponsorship to any third party the Broadcaster shall:

5.8.1.1 first propose to the Company in writing the terms and conditions of acquisition thereof; and

5.8.1.2 second, negotiate exclusively with the Company (unless and until the Company agrees to purchase such broadcast sponsorship) in good faith from the date such proposal is received for 30 days;
whereupon if the Company and Broadcaster fail to reach an agreement by the end of the period specified above the Broadcaster shall be free following (*insert details*) to contract with any third party whose product categories do not conflict with the product categories pertaining to the Company or who is not a competitor of the Company.

5.8.2 In addition, the Governing Body shall ensure that each Broadcaster grants to the Company the right of first negotiation with respect to the purchase of commercial airtime. For the purposes of this clause, 'first negotiation' means that, before offering any commercial airtime to any third party in the Company's product category or to any competitor of the Company the Broadcaster shall:

5.8.2.1 first propose to the Company in writing the terms and conditions of acquisition thereof; and

5.8.2.2 second negotiate exclusively with the Company (unless and until the Company agrees to purchase all such commercial airtime) in good faith from the date such proposal is received for a period of 10 days; whereupon if the Company and the Broadcaster fail to reach an agreement by the end of the period specified above the Broadcaster shall be free to contract with any third parties with respect to such commercial airtime offered to the Company.

**Designations**

6.1 The Company may use the following designations or such other designation (or designations) as the Company notifies to the Governing Body, to associate the Company Products with the Event, as follows:

6.1.1 'Official Sponsor of (governing body)';

6.1.2 'Official Supplier of (governing body)'; and

6.1.3 (subject to the actual supply of Company Products to the Governing Body) 'Official (name of product) of (governing body)'.

6.2 The Company undertakes that it shall not in exercising the Rights use any designations referring to the Event other than the Designations or the Sponsored Title.

6.3 The Company may use the Designations on the packaging of Company Products, in printed promotional and publicity materials, on merchandise and/or all advertising media (including without limitation television and radio commercials) for the Company or Company Products which may be issued or produced by or on behalf of the Company and in exercising any of the Rights.

6.4 Notwithstanding the foregoing terms of this clause the Company is not obliged to use the Designations when exploiting the Rights under this Agreement.

**Exclusivity**

7.1 Subject to the provisions of this clause 7 the Governing Body shall:

7.1.1 not grant to any third party the right during the Term to use any of the Designations, to use any designations which are substantially similar to the Designations, to use the Sponsored Title, to use any title similar to the Sponsored Title or any part thereof (except in so far as is necessary to comply with its obligations under this Agreement) or to describe itself as the title sponsor of any of the Events;

7.1.2 not appoint any person that manufactures Products to be a sponsor of the Event or otherwise to be associated with the Event during the Term;

7.1.3 not appoint any Competitor or renew any agreement with a Commercial Partner who is a Competitor to the Company;

7.1.4 procure that no Competitor has access to advertising on Perimeter Boards at any of the Matches; and

7.1.5 procure that no Competitor is allowed to advertise or distribute promotional material in any way at the Grounds and Venues of any of the Matches.

7.2 Notwithstanding the provisions of clause 7.1 the Company acknowledges and agrees that the Governing Body is not able to prevent Clubs from entering into contracts with Competitors in general and the Governing Body will use its reasonable endeavours to ensure that no such rights the same as or similar to the Rights are granted by any Club to a Competitor and the Club will not by any act or omission or arrangement with their own commercial partners (whether a Competitor or not) devalue or derogate from the Rights.

7.3 The Governing Body shall not during the Term or any renewal thereof enter into any arrangement in connection with any competition or tournament or otherwise under the auspices of the Governing Body where another party to such an arrangement is a Competitor.

## Fees

8.1 In consideration of the grant of the Rights made to it by the Governing Body under this Agreement the Company shall pay the Governing Body the following amounts:

8.1.1 £... in respect of the......... Season;
8.1.2 £... in respect of the......... Season;
8.1.3 £... in respect of the......... Season;
8.1.4 £... in respect of the......... Season; and
8.1.5 £... in respect of the......... Season.

8.2 Each payment in clause 8.1 above includes £... in respect of the cost of admission tickets which the Company has a right to receive under para 8 of Schedule 1 to this Agreement.

8.3 The Company shall pay the amounts due under clause 8.1 not later than 30 days following receipt by the Company of correct invoices from the Governing Body provided that the Governing Body shall not invoice the Company prior to (date) in any Season during the Term.

8.4 The Fees are exclusive of any VAT which may be or become payable and the Company shall pay any such VAT to the Governing Body upon receipt of an appropriate VAT invoice.

## Mutual warranties and indemnities

Each party warrants to the other that:

9.1 it is free and entitled to enter into this Agreement and to perform the obligations undertaken by it under this Agreement and that it has not entered into and will not enter into any agreement with any third party which might conflict with the terms of this Agreement;

9.2 it will not disclose to any third party other than to its professional advisers or as required by law or (in the case of the Governing Body) to the Clubs or as agreed between the parties any information relating to the business or affairs of the other nor any of the contents or provisions of this Agreement; and

9.3 it will indemnify and keep indemnified the other against all actions, proceedings, claims, costs and expenses (including without limitation legal fees) and any other damage or liability suffered by the other as a direct or reasonably foreseeable result of a breach of any of the warranties, undertakings or agreements on its part contained or made in this Agreement.

**The Governing Body's warranties and undertakings**

The Governing Body represents, warrants to and undertakes with the Company that:

10.1 it shall organise the Event to the best of its ability and in accordance with sound business practices and all applicable laws and regulations including legislation governing the safety of sports grounds;

10.2 it shall procure that the Rights shall be made available to the Company for exercise by it in accordance with this Agreement;

10.3 it shall not during the Term knowingly do any act or fail to do any act which causes the value of the Rights to the Company to be materially undermined or diminished;

10.4 it shall not enter into negotiations with or conclude any agreement with a third party relating to sponsorship of the Event after the expiry of the Term before the last Season of the Term without the prior written consent of the Company;

10.5 it shall not knowingly do or fail to do any act during the Term which in the reasonable opinion of the Company is prejudicial to the name or image of the Company or Company Products;

10.6 it shall not during the Term alter the structure or organisation of the Event without the prior agreement of the Company; and

10.7 it shall not during the Term organise any alternative competition the same as or similar to the Event involving the Club or any players eligible to play in any Match in addition to the Event without the prior written consent of the Company.

**Company's warranties and undertakings**

The Company undertakes with the Governing Body that it shall:

11.1 not exercise the Rights in any way or manner which is prejudicial to the image of the Governing Body or the Event;

11.2 supply to the Governing Body samples of any proposed usage by the Company of the Governing Body Marks for the purpose of exercising the Rights for the prior approval of the Governing Body (which shall not be unreasonably withheld or delayed) provided that if the Governing Body has not expressly withheld its approval of any such sample in writing within 5 business days after receipt thereof its approval shall be deemed to have been given; and

11.3 not knowingly do or omit to do anything which might undermine the validity of the Governing Body Marks as registered trade marks.

**Term**

12.1 The Term is deemed to commence on the Commencement Date and continues until 3 months after the last Match of the Event in the (insert details) Season unless terminated earlier in accordance with the terms of this Agreement.

12.2 If at any time during the Term or in the Season immediately after the termination of this Agreement by effluxion of time the Governing Body proposes to enter into any agreements with a third party in relation to some or all of the Rights the following terms apply:

12.2.1 the Governing Body shall notify the Company in writing of the terms of any proposed agreement with a third party which terms shall include but shall not be limited to rights to be granted to and by the Governing Body ('the Proposed Sponsorship Terms'). Such notice must contain full disclosure of the Proposed Sponsorship Terms and include any change made in the Proposed Sponsorship Terms during the option period in clause 12.2.2;

12.2.2 the Governing Body shall grant the Company an option to enter an agreement with the Governing Body on terms equivalent to or better than the Proposed Sponsorship Terms, such option to be valid for 30 days from the date of notice to the Company of the Proposed Sponsorship Terms;

12.2.3 it is agreed that the Company shall be deemed to have matched the Proposed Sponsorship Terms if the financial terms of the deal proposed by the Company are the same as or better than the Proposed Sponsorship Terms.

**Termination**

13.1 Either party may terminate this Agreement immediately upon notice in the event that the other:

13.1.1 commits a material breach of any obligation under this Agreement which breach is incapable of remedy or cannot be remedied in time for the Event;

13.1.2 commits a material breach of any obligation under this Agreement and, if such breach is capable of remedy, fails to so remedy such breach within 28 days of receiving notice from the other requiring remedy; or

13.1.3 enters into a composition or arrangement with its creditors, has a receiver or administrator or administrative receiver appointed or becomes insolvent or unable to pay its debts when they fall due.

13.2 In addition to its rights of termination under clause 13.1 the Company may terminate this Agreement forthwith by giving written notice to the Governing Body if:

13.2.1 the constitution or organisation of the Governing Body has undergone any change which could have a material adverse effect on the value of the Rights to the Company;

13.2.2 the Governing Body breaches its obligations under clause 5;

13.2.3 (specify sport) is brought into disrepute through the actions of the Governing Body or the Clubs or any of them; or

13.2.4 the Broadcast coverage of the Event in any Season falls below the level of coverage achieved for the Event in the (insert details) Season.

**Effect of termination**

14.1 Subject to clause 14.2 upon termination in accordance with clause 13:

14.1.1 the rights and obligations of the parties under this Agreement shall terminate and be of no future effect except that clauses 9.2, 9.3 and 15 shall remain in full force and effect;

14.1.2 any rights or obligations to which any of the parties to this Agreement may be entitled or be subject before such termination shall remain in full force and effect;

14.1.3 such termination shall not affect or prejudice any right to damages or other remedy which the terminating party may have in respect of the circumstances which gave rise to the termination or any other right to damages or other remedy which any party may have in respect of any breach of this Agreement which existed at or before the date of termination.

14.2 Notwithstanding clause 14.1, if this Agreement is terminated by either party or expires due to effluxion of time the Company may sell off or cause to be sold off Company Products and any merchandise or Premiums bearing the Sponsored Title and/or the Sponsored Logo provided that such rights do not extend beyond 180 days after the date of any such termination.

**Limitation of liability**

15.1 Notwithstanding anything to the contrary in this Agreement neither the Governing Body nor the Company shall be liable in any circumstances for any indirect or consequential loss (which expression shall include but not be limited to loss of anticipated profits, loss of anticipated savings and all other economic loss) resulting from any breach of this Agreement.

**Intellectual property**

16.1 Each party shall promptly and fully notify the other of any actual, threatened or suspected infringement in the Territory of any IPR of the other party which comes to the other's notice and of any claim by any third party coming to its notice. Each party shall, at the request and expense of the other, do all such things as may be reasonably required to assist in taking or resisting any proceedings in relation to any such infringement or claim.

16.2 Unless otherwise set out in this Agreement nothing in this Agreement shall give either party any rights in respect of any IPR used by the other or of the goodwill associated therewith and the parties acknowledge that, except as expressly provided in this Agreement, neither party shall acquire any such rights and that all such rights and goodwill are and shall remain vested in the other.

16.3 The Company shall not use any trade marks or trade names so resembling the Governing Body Marks or trade names of the Governing Body as to be likely to cause confusion or deception.

16.4 The Governing Body shall not authorise any third party to use the Company Marks or any IPR of the Company. If any third party requires the use of the Company Marks or any other IPR of the Company then the Governing Body shall inform the Company of such requirement. The Company may (in its absolute discretion) grant such third party the right or licence required.

16.5 Each party shall, at the request and expense of the other, take all such steps as the requesting party may reasonably require to assist it in maintaining the validity and enforceability of the IPR of the other during the Term.

16.6 Neither party shall do or authorise any third party to do any act which would or might invalidate or be inconsistent with the IPR of the other and shall not omit or authorise any third party to omit to do any act which by its omission would have that effect or character.

**Assignment**

17. Neither party may assign any of its rights or obligations under this Agreement without the previous written consent of the other. The Company may appoint agents or sub-licensees to exploit the Rights or manufacture Company Products and undertake obligations on its behalf as it sees fit, provided that the Company remains liable to the Governing Body in respect of such appointments.

**Entire agreement**

18. This Agreement (including the Schedules) constitutes the entire agreement between the parties with regard to the Event and may only be amended in writing signed by the duly authorised representatives of both parties.

**Waiver**

19. No waiver by either party of any breach by the other party of any of the terms of the Agreement shall be deemed to be a waiver of any preceding or succeeding breach of this Agreement.

**Notices**

20. Any notice to be served under this Agreement shall be in writing and served upon the recipient at its address set out above (or such other address as may be notified for this purpose) either by hand, by first class mail, or by facsimile or comparable means of communication and shall be deemed served 72 hours after if sent by mail, on delivery if delivered by hand, and on confirmation of transmission if sent by facsimile or comparable means of communication. All facsimile or comparable means of communication will be followed by postal copies.

**Governing law**

21. This Agreement shall be governed by and construed in all respects in accordance with the laws of England and each party hereby submits to the exclusive jurisdiction of the English courts.

**No partnership or joint venture**

22. Nothing in this Agreement shall constitute or be construed as constituting a partnership or joint venture between the Governing Body and the Company or shall authorise one party to enter into contractual relationships or incur obligations on behalf of the other party.

**Rights of third parties**

23. A person who is not a party to this Agreement may not rely upon or enforce any rights pursuant to the Contracts (Rights of Third Parties) Act 1999.

**Competition law**

24. The parties shall co-operate fully in the preparation and submission of any necessary application/notification to the Commission of the European Communities and/or the relevant United Kingdom competition authorities in respect of this Agreement with a view to securing any negative clearance or exemption as may be required. Each party shall bear its own costs of preparing and submitting such application/notification. The parties agree to effect such application/notification if necessary as soon as may be reasonably practicable after commencement of the Term.

**Execution of further documents**

25. At any time after the date of this Agreement each of the parties shall at the request and cost of the other party execute or procure the execution of such documents and do or procure the doing of such acts and things as the party so requiring may reasonably require for the purpose of giving to the party so requiring the full benefit of all the provisions of this Agreement.

**Force majeure**

26.1 Neither party to this Agreement shall be deemed to be in breach of this Agreement or otherwise liable to the other as a result of any delay or failure in the performance of its obligations under this Agreement if and to the extent that such delay or failure is caused by force majeure (as defined in clause 26.2) and the time for performance of the relevant obligation(s) shall be extended accordingly.

26.2 For the purpose of this clause 'force majeure' means any circumstances (other than those specifically dealt with in clause 13) not foreseeable at the date of this Agreement and not within the reasonable control of the party in question including without limitation:

26.2.1 any strike, lockout or other industrial action or any shortage of or difficulty in obtaining labour or raw materials;

26.2.2 any destruction, temporary or permanent breakdown, malfunction or damage of or to any premises, plant, equipment (including computer systems) or materials;

26.2.3 any breach of contract, default or insolvency by or of any third party (including an agent or sub-contractor) other than a company in the same group as the party affected by the force majeure or an employee or officer of that party or company;

26.2.4 any action taken by a governmental or public authority of any kind including not granting a consent, exemption, approval or clearance;

26.2.5 any civil commotion or disorder, riot, invasion, war, terrorist act, threat of or preparation for war or terrorist act; and

26.2.6 any fire, explosion, storm, flood, earthquake, subsidence, epidemic, disease or other natural physical disaster.

26.3 A party whose performance of its obligations under this Agreement is delayed or prevented by force majeure:

26.3.1 shall forthwith notify the other party of the nature, extent, effect and likely duration of the circumstances constituting the force majeure;

26.3.2 shall use all reasonable endeavours to minimise the effect of the force majeure on its performance of its obligations under this Agreement; and

26.3.3 shall, subject to clause 26.4, immediately after the cessation of the force majeure notify the other party thereof and resume full performance of its obligations under this Agreement.

26.4 If any force majeure delays or prevents the performance of the obligations of either party for a continuous period in excess of one month, the party not so affected may give notice to the affected party to terminate this Agreement, specifying the date (which shall not be less than 7 days after the date on which the notice is given) on which termination will take effect. Such a termination notice shall be irrevocable except with the consent of both parties and upon termination the provisions of clause 14 apply.

**Nature of agreement**

27.1 The Company may perform any of the obligations undertaken by it and exercise any of the rights granted to it under this Agreement through any other company which at the relevant time is its holding company or subsidiary (as defined by the Companies Act 1985 Section 736) or the subsidiary of any such holding company and any act or omission of any such company shall, for the purposes of this Agreement, be deemed to be the act or omission of the Company.

27.2 If any provision of this Agreement is held by any court or other competent authority to be void or unenforceable in whole or in part this Agreement shall continue to be valid as to the other provisions thereof and the remainder of the affected provisions.

27.3 Each party to this Agreement shall pay its own costs of and incidental to the negotiation, preparation, execution and carrying into effect of this Agreement.

AS WITNESS etc.

## SCHEDULE 1

### The Ancillary Rights

**Television extracts**

1. The Company shall have the non-exclusive right to use extracts from footage of Matches Broadcast and/or films or videos made by or on behalf of the Governing Body in promotional and advertising material and in exploitation of the Internet Rights for the purpose of exploiting the Rights in the Territory during the Term. Notwithstanding the generality of the foregoing, the Company shall ensure that any such extracts are not used in any manner which implies that any individual player, any Club or any official of the Governing Body is endorsing or is connected with the Company Products or the Company, unless the Company has obtained the consent of such individual player, Club or official which permits the Company to use any such extracts in such manner.

**Rights relating to the Event and to the trophy**

2.1 The Governing Body shall name the trophy associated with the Event to properly reflect the Sponsored Title.

2.2 A duly authorised officer of the Company shall have the right to jointly present with the President or other representative of the Governing Body the trophy, along with any winners? medals, to the winners, at the appropriate time.

2.3 The Company shall have the right to display the trophy at a location and at a time to be agreed with the Governing Body for an agreed period during each Season (such agreement not to be unreasonably withheld or delayed) subject to the Company complying with the security conditions of any insurance policy arranged by the Governing Body in respect of the trophy. The Governing Body agrees that the policy relating to such insurance will name the Company as an additional insured party. The Company agrees not to change the appearance of the trophy in any way whilst in the Company's possession.

2.4 The Company may attach a set of branded ribbons, provided by the Company and approved by the Governing Body, to the trophy.

**Rights regarding match programmes, tickets and official publications**

3.1 The Sponsored Logo and/or Sponsored Title shall appear on the front cover of the programme of all Matches at a minimum size of (specify) and in the official colours as determined by the Company.

3.2 The Company will receive, free of charge, [2] full pages of advertising in all publications containing any reference to the Event produced by or on behalf of the Governing Body.

3.3 The Company is entitled free of charge to [2] pages of advertising in the Club programme for each Match.

3.4 The Company may purchase such programmes or publications from the Governing Body or the relevant Club at cost price.

**Advertising rights at each Ground**

4.1 During each Season of the Term the Company will receive the following advertising and promotional rights at each Match in each Ground:

4.1.1 subject to para 4.1.2 below the right to display [4] Perimeter Boards at each Ground hosting a Match; and

4.1.2 in the case of each Match which is Broadcast at least [2] of such Perimeter Boards as TV Perimeter Boards.

4.2 Subject to para 4.4 below the Governing Body shall ensure that all perimeter advertising is in the form of fixed advertising Perimeter Boards.

4.3 If any of the Perimeter Boards are not in the form of fixed Perimeter Boards the Governing Body shall ensure that the Company receives an equivalent amount of exposure and of the total time available for such Perimeter Boards as it would otherwise receive under para. 4.2 above.

4.4 All Perimeter Boards and other signage and advertising material to be used in connection with Matches by the Company shall be manufactured, produced and maintained by the Company at its own expense and the appearance of each Perimeter Board shall be subject to the prevailing Governing Body, television and other appropriate regulations.

4.5 All Company Perimeter Boards shall:

4.5.1 be of a size not less than (specify) up to a maximum permissible size according to current regulations; and

4.5.2 so far as possible (and whether or not a Match is Broadcast) occupy a prominent position and be in view of any television cameras present at such Matches.

4.6 All Perimeter Boards shall remain the property of the Company.

4.7 The Governing Body shall ensure that during the Matches:

4.7.1 no Ground carries an amount of perimeter advertising from a single person greater than that of the Company;

4.7.2 no single person is afforded greater promotional opportunities during any Match at a Ground or Venue greater than that afforded to the Company; and

4.7.3 no Competitor is allowed any TV Perimeter Boards.

4.8 The Governing Body shall ensure that during and in the period leading up to the Matches the Perimeter Boards of the Company are not (whether in whole or in part) obscured, altered or moved by any person.

**Pitch activity**

5. The Governing Body shall (so far as regulations allow) provide the Company with the following exclusive rights to display or make reference to the Sponsored Logo:

5.1 on Pitch corner flags;
5.2 on scoreboard messages at all Matches;
5.3 on pitch or field of play markings;
5.4 on player substitute boards at all Matches;
5.5 on dug outs at all Matches Broadcast;
5.6 on centre circle mats at all Matches Broadcast;
5.7 during tannoy or public address announcements at all Matches; and
5.8 at such other display or reference opportunities as may arise during the Term.

**Access**

6. The Governing Body shall use its best endeavours to procure full access on an all area basis (apart from dressing rooms, player tunnels and private functions) for the Company's nominated representatives at all Matches, Grounds and Venues in accordance with a procedure to be agreed with the Governing Body, such agreement not to be unreasonably withheld or delayed.

**Merchandising and promotional rights**

7.1 The Governing Body shall procure that the Company may use the crest of any Club competing in the Event in conjunction with the Sponsored Logo and/or the Sponsored Title for promotional purposes only.
7.2 The Governing Body shall ensure that:

7.2.1 all official match balls used in the Event carry the Sponsored Logo; and
7.2.2 all official replica match balls produced by the Governing Body or any Commercial Partner carry the Sponsored Logo.

7.3 The Company has the exclusive right to exploit such other competition, promotional activity and other sponsorship packages as relate to the Rights that become available during the Term.

**Tickets**

The Governing Body shall procure that the Company receives the following:

8.1 (number) directors' box seats at all Matches;
8.2 (number) complimentary tickets per Match; and
8.3 the right to purchase a further (number) tickets for each Match at cost price for use by the Company, its staff and employees and for use as prizes in promotions run by the Company as part of the exercise of its rights under this Agreement but otherwise in accordance with the terms and conditions of issue of such tickets and (in any event) not for sale or resale by the Company or by any person receiving such tickets from the Company or any person on

its behalf. In addition, the Company acknowledges and agrees that ownership of all tickets remains with the Governing Body.

**Awards**

9.1 The Company has the exclusive right to make or create the following awards in relation to the Rights:

9.1.1 a man of the match award at each Match;
9.1.2 a manager of the month award;
9.1.3 a player of the month award;
9.1.4 a Club of the month award;
9.1.5 a player of the Event award;
9.1.6 a manager of the Event award;
9.1.7 an outstanding achievement of the Event award; and
9.1.8 a score of the Event award.

9.2 The Company may make or create such additional awards as it sees fit, provided always that it is under no obligation to exercise any of the awards listed or which may be created under this para 9.

**Hospitality**

10. The Governing Body shall procure that (at the Company's expense) there are sufficient hospitality facilities available for all of the Company's guests holding tickets for the relevant Match.

**Internet Rights**

11. The Company has the exclusive right without payment of fees (other than as provided for in this Agreement) to exercise the Internet Rights as it sees fit.

**SCHEDULE 2**

**Governing Body Marks**
(***insert details***)

**SCHEDULE 3**

**The Event**
(***insert details***)

**SCHEDULE 4**

**Company Marks**
(***insert details***)

(*signatures of* (*or on behalf of*) *the parties*)

## Notes

1 This Form provides for title sponsorship of a league or cup competition where the sponsor is granted the right to be the title sponsor of the competition. Apart from the other subsidiary sponsors, the member clubs and many of the players taking part in the event are likely to have their own sponsors. In addition, the broadcast of the competition may also be sponsored. As far as possible, the parties need to consider carefully the various areas where conflict with the rights of the other persons, or organisations involved in the competition, may occur, and frame the grant of rights and the obligations of the parties accordingly.

2 As a long-established competition, there may be existing obligations which need to be taken into account when defining the rights to be granted to the sponsor. The sponsor will want to ensure that any existing rights which conflict with the rights being offered are brought to an end as soon as possible.

3 The extent of the obligations on the part of the governing body to require participants to use the sponsored title when referring to the competition, or to ensure that the sponsored title is used in participants' printed material, will depend on the level of control that it has over the participants.

4 Where possible, it is desirable that any logo of the governing body is registered as a trade mark to give better protection to the parties.

5 The obligations on the part of the governing body regarding television coverage of the governing body should reflect the terms of the agreement with the broadcaster. For broadcasting agreements see Form 76 [1617] et seq post.

6 The exclusivity provisions have to be considered carefully in the light of the Competition Act 1998 (47 Halsbury's Statutes (4th Edn) TRADE AND INDUSTRY), and where appropriate, guidance should be sought from the Office of Fair Trading.

7 The parties should consider whether the advertising boards rights should be separated out to save VAT. Specialist tax advice should be sought.

# Chapter 9
# Sports Stadia Naming Rights Agreements

## 9.1 Introductory Remarks

Originating in the States, Sports Sponsorship has spread across the world and grown into a multi billion US$ global business, as companies and firms have come to realise the value of associating themselves and their products and services with prestigious sports events.

As the former leading International Sports Marketing Agency (ISL) once observed in its Corporate Brochure:

> "sports sponsorship has evolved to form an integral part of brand marketing, mature enough for even the most conservative companies to recognize it as a natural, indispensable ingredient in their marketing mix".

In fact, sports sponsorship is now widely perceived as a more attractive alternative to other forms of traditional advertising and promotion, particularly in terms of cost effectiveness, which in these highly competitive times is a crucial consideration.

Similar to sports sponsorship, another kind of marketing phenomenon, delivering equally attractive benefits at considerably less cost than traditional advertising, has grown up in the States and is also being followed in Europe. This is corporate naming of sports stadia and arenas—and even stands. It has been described by one of its users as:

> "the new wave in sponsorship...[which] benefits everybody".

In this chapter, we will take a look at the reasons for the rise in popularity of attaching corporate names to stadia and arenas, and also at some of the contractual legal and drafting issues that the granting and exploitation of the corresponding corporate naming rights can give rise to in practice.

I. S. Blackshaw, *Sports Marketing Agreements: Legal, Fiscal and Practical Aspects*,

ASSER International Sports Law Series, DOI: 10.1007/978-90-6704-793-7_9,

## 9.2 Corporate Naming of Stadia and Arenas

The modern practice of unconnected corporations buying naming rights of stadia and arenas seems to originate in the purchase by the Great Western Bank of the naming rights to the Los Angeles Forum in 1987. Previously, a number of stadia had been named after their corporate founders, for example, the 'Busch Stadium' in St. Louis.

The practice of naming stadia and arenas after corporations has grown over the years, not only in the States, but also in Canada, and not only in relation to new stadia and arenas, but also to refurbished ones.

The practice not only provides income to the stadia and arenas concerned, but also provides the corporations, who hold the naming rights, with very valuable advertising, promotional and public relations benefits. Indeed, without the revenues from the sale of corporate naming rights, many stadia and arenas, without any financial support from the public sector, would never be built and local communities would suffer by being deprived of modern sports facilities.

The sale of corporate naming rights also benefits publicly owned sports facilities by providing additional income that can be used for enhancing them.

So, what are the benefits to corporations in holding naming rights of sports facilities?

## 9.3 Corporate Naming Rights Benefits

Corporations benefit from naming rights in a number of ways.

The use of a corporate name on a sports stadium or an arena receives exposures and impressions, which are difficult, if not impossible, to quantify. Television, radio and the print media all refer to the corporation's name when reporting on events held at that facility.

The name of the stadium also appears on tickets, programmes and other consumer items. Also, people can see the name on the external signage when attending, walking, driving, or even flying past the facility (for example, the Arsenal Emirates Stadium).

All of this adds up to a cost-effective form of advertising for corporations and their products and services. For example, in 1991, America West Airlines purchased the naming rights to a new arena being built for the 'Phoenix Suns' at a cost of US$550,000 for the first year, with an annual uplift of 3%. During the 1993 NBA Finals, when the 'Suns' hosted the 'Chicago Bulls', a single 30-second commercial spot on NBC cost US$300,000. America West's name and logo were seen countless times at a cost of US$583,495, less than the cost of a one-minute television commercial, namely US$600,000.

Corporate naming rights also confer a unique and exclusive kind of benefit on those who hold them, in that they are attached to a relatively limited number of major sports facilities. They enjoy, therefore, a certain *cachet*.

They also create goodwill for corporations by allowing them to project a positive image in the community in which the sports stadia and arenas are located. However, one warning note should be sounded. Naming rights can also present a cultural/social challenge in that, in the case of football stadia and grounds, the local community may take time to adapt to a new corporate name attached to their stadium or ground and continue to refer to the previous—perhaps long-established and traditional—name associated with the sports facility concerned.

Naming rights can also be the vehicle for raising public awareness of corporations and their products and services in regions where they are starting up or expanding their business operations.

Naming rights also allow for cross-promotion through "product tie-ins" at the sports facilities. For example, in the case of a bank owning the naming rights, they will have the right to have ATMs placed in the stadium or arena concerned.

Naming rights often bring with them the right for the corporation to receive, or purchase, a box or a suite at the stadium or arena for corporate hospitality purposes.

Finally, and perhaps most important of all, the costs of purchasing the naming rights can be used by the corporation as tax deductible advertising expenses, under the relevant provisions of the US Internal Revenue Code. These costs are tax deductible in many other countries too.

In order to enjoy the benefits of corporate naming arrangements, the rights themselves need to be well defined and incorporated in, as far as legally possible, water-tight Agreements.

We will now take a look at some of the contractual legal and drafting issues that need to be addressed in order to achieve these results and gain the full benefits of the naming rights concerned.

## 9.4 Contractual Legal and Drafting Issues

As with any kind of Rights Agreement, perhaps the most important provision of all is the "grant of rights" clause.

This defines the nature and scope of the rights granted, and needs to be drafted very carefully and precisely, to avoid any ambiguities and uncertainties, which can lead to misunderstandings and differences, which, in turn, can lead to disputes, which can be time consuming and costly.

For example, are the rights exclusive or non-exclusive? And what is included in the rights package?

As part of a growing trend, in addition to the naming rights granted, other commercial opportunities are included as part of a sports marketing package. These additional rights could include rights to boxes or suites for corporate entertaining, franchise rights, including so-called 'pouring rights', particularly important in the case where a soft drinks company is concerned, team sponsorship rights, and even facility financing rights, where a bank or other financial institution is involved.

Such *tying* arrangements may, however, give rise to Anti-Trust problems in certain circumstances. For example, in 1995, Pepsi acquired quite a comprehensive package of marketing and promotional rights, as part of its naming deal in relation to a new sports facility for the 'Denver Nuggets' and the 'Rocky Mountain Extreme'. For an undisclosed sum, believed to be between 35 and 68 million US dollars, Pepsi acquired the exclusive naming and distribution rights for the facility; plus sponsorship rights for the 'Nuggets' and the 'Extreme'; joint marketing opportunities on television and radio; as well as exclusive marketing rights at other tourist attractions within the entertainment complex surrounding the arena. Quite a stitch up! Similar *tying* arrangements can also present legal problems under European and National Competition Rules.

Allied to the "grant of rights" clause, is the "duration" clause, which is equally important. Naming rights can be granted for any length of time ("term"). The longer the term, the greater the value and, of course, the greater the price. In general, however, the rights tend to be granted on an annual renewable basis. If they are granted for a fixed term, an option to renew is often included in the Naming Rights Agreement. Rights granted in perpetuity, however, can cause legal problems—interminable agreements are generally frowned upon by the Courts and also—not least—by Competition Authorities.

Naming Rights packages need to be accompanied by certain "warranties" by the owner of the stadium or arena, to ensure that they are worth the vast sums paid for them.

For example, these rights are not worth very much if the stadium or arena does not stage many events in the course of a year. The presence of a professional or collegiate team playing its home games at the facility is normally a contractual requirement in naming rights deals, because it guarantees a minimum number of dates that a facility is in operation. This is covered by warranties on the part of the owner of the facility, who warrants its active use during the term of the Naming Rights Agreement.

Of course, in the case of multi-use facilities, that is, those that stage sports and other events, such as concerts, the need for such warranties is not so important. The legal effects and practical consequences of any breaches of such warranties need to be spelled out in the Naming Rights Agreement.

Another important clause in any commercial agreement is the "consideration" clause. This defines the *quid pro quo* for the rights granted. This need not always be money, but can in sponsorship type deals, such as Naming Rights arrangements, be in non-monetary form, that is, value in kind (VIK). This could, for example, in the case of a soft drinks company, be the supply of free product to a sponsored team.

In any case, the amount of the monetary consideration and the value of the benefit in kind need, in each case, to be clearly defined for contractual and also tax reasons.

So also do the payment arrangements—when and where they are to be made. Often, in naming rights deals, instead of a lump sum fee, an annual rights fee is payable, subject to a yearly uplift to cover inflation. This also needs to be spelled out in the Naming Rights

Agreement, especially if the uplift is linked to some cost of living Index, which itself needs to be clearly defined. The payment of interest for late payments, the rate of interest and when it accrues also need to be covered in the Agreement.

The "termination" clause is also an key contractual provision. The grounds for termination, who may terminate and the effects of termination need to be precisely stated in the Agreement. A provision is often included, and it is sensible and practical to do so, whereby non-material breaches can be remedied by the party in default within a specified period of time, say, 15/30 days, failing which the other party may terminate the Agreement. What is material and what is not material needs to be defined and also whether "days" are natural days or working days.

On expiration of the Naming Rights Agreement, the naming rights automatically come to an end by effluxion of time. So, what happens then? In theory, the owner of the stadium or arena can grant the rights to someone else. But this may prove costly to the owner, who would have to incur the expense of repainting or replacing signs, reprinting tickets, producing new seat tags and other items, such as plastic cups and paper napkins, and so on, depending upon the extent of the 'branding'. It is more likely that, in practice, the owner will seek to do a new deal with the former holder of the Naming Rights.

From the point of view of the rights holder, it is prudent and advisable to include in the Naming Rights Agreement an option to renew the Agreement, or, at the very least, a right of first refusal to be granted to the Naming Rights. Any such pre-emptive right should be accompanied by a 'matching option' in favour of the former holder of the naming rights. In other words, if the conditions for granting the rights for a new term are refused by the former holder of them, because they are financially unacceptable, then the rights owner cannot offer a third party better terms than those refused by the former holder of the rights, without first offering the same deal to the latter.

It will be appreciated that options to renew, rights of first refusal and matching options need to be very carefully drafted. In particular, the periods of time and the manner in which they are to be exercised need to be precisely defined. Options and pre-emptive rights, especially matching options, can also raise Competition Law issues. See further on this aspect in Chap. 16.

Another important contractual provision to include in a Naming Rights Agreement is a "confidentiality" clause. For business reasons, the parties to the Agreement will wish to keep the terms confidential, especially the financial ones. They will also wish to control releases of information to the media, as well as the holding and conduct of any Press Conferences. Any secrecy obligations will be subject to any requirements imposed by Law to disclose any confidential material to certain third parties, for example, in Court Proceedings. Furthermore, any information of a confidential character that is already in or subsequently enters the public domain, through no fault of the parties to the Agreement, is not subject to the secrecy obligations undertaken by them. See further on confidentiality clauses in Chap. 5.

Lastly, and by no means least, the parties to a Naming Rights Agreement need to include a "Dispute Resolution Clause". In other words, they need to decide, in advance, how any dispute arising between them under out of or in relation to the Agreement is to be resolved. Nowadays, there are a number of options for the parties to choose from for settling their disputes. They can be traditional and go to Court. They can be more adventurous and choose arbitration. Or they can be thoroughly modern and opt for some alternative form of dispute resolution ("ADR"). ADR comes in several different forms:

- Conciliation;
- Mediation;
- Mini Trials;
- Expert Determination;
- Good Faith Determination.

ADR is flexible, informal, confidential, speedy and inexpensive; whereas, Court and Arbitration Proceedings are, in comparison, generally complex, formal, slow and expensive. See further on Dispute Resolution Clauses in Chap. 17.

## 9.5 The European Scene

Although Naming Rights of Stadia and Arenas, like other aspects of Sports Marketing, originated in the United States probably in 1926, when William Wrigley, the chewing gum magnate and owner of the Chicago Clubs named his team's stadium 'Wrigley Field', as with many things, sports ideas and developments in the States have had a habit, in time, of spreading to the rest of the world—and not least to Europe. New sports stadiums and arenas, similar to the sports and entertainment complexes, which have grown up and been developed in the States, have also begun to be appear in Europe in the last 20 or 30 years or so.

For example, the "Hartwall Areena" in Helsinki, Finland, which was completed in 1997 and is named after its biggest sponsor, Hartwall, the beverage company that is also based in Helsinki. This seats up to 14,000 people and features 78 suites. It is a multi-purpose facility, and has established itself as the country's top location for sport, music and corporate events. It incorporates many media facilities, including 'state of the art' broadcast production and editing suites.

In the UK, 'Bolton Wanderers' Football Club play at the 'Reebok' Stadium and 'Stoke City' Football Club play at the 'Britannia' Stadium. And the famous Oval cricket ground in London has been re-named 'The AMP Oval' after the Australian Financial Services

Company 'AMP', which paid £2 million for a five years' exclusive naming rights deal.

Incidentally, it should be noted that the use of such naming rights has an impact on the traditional sports marketing model of a 'clean stadium' from a branding and promotional point of view.

Generally speaking, however, Europe tends to be soccer mad and tends to build only soccer stadia. However, the promoters of new soccer stadiums being planned and built are beginning to realise that, to rely only on gate receipts, is not enough. These stadia need to generate revenues from other activities, such as the sale of corporate naming rights. Another solution to this financial problem is to incorporate arenas into new stadia to attract other sports, such as track and field, and other events, such as pop concerts.

As part of the funding process of providing new stadia, additional revenues can also be generated, following the practice in the United States of granting naming rights to lending institutions that finance private sports facilities. In these cases, the bank or finance house arranging the finance acquires the naming rights to the new facility and uses the naming rights fees to reduce the debt repayments on the loan. It also acquires valuable promotional and marketing rights as part of the rights package as well.

Furthermore, new and existing stadiums and arenas in Europe also need to learn from the States who are wiring up their facilities to allow spectators to take full advantage of the digital and interactive age directly from their seats! Such developments also offer further marketing opportunities for creative sports marketers.

A General Precedent of a US Corporate Naming Rights Agreement will be found, for illustrative purposes and general guidance, in the Appendix to this Chapter (9.7).

## 9.6 Concluding Remarks

The use of Corporate Naming Rights as an innovative form of sports sponsorship is a continuing marketing phenomenon in the States and is also spreading elsewhere, including many parts of Europe.

Corporate Naming Rights offer a wide range of benefits to stadium and arena owners and corporations wanting to associate themselves and their products and services with major sports and sports events.

They also provide, in many cases, a cheaper and more effective form of advertising and promotion of a companies products and services.

As further investment in new sports facilities in Europe grows, to meet the increasing demands of event organisers, sports players and spectators alike, Corporate Naming Rights Packages are likely to figure in the equation and grow too in Europe, as they continue to do in the States, particularly those which are linked to the financing arrangements of new stadia and arenas.

Like other kinds of commercial and financial arrangements, they need to be well defined and incorporated in well-drafted Agreements. And, where disputes do arise, these need to be settled by the most appropriate and effective means, not forgetting the new forms of alternative dispute resolution, which are available and eminently fit for purpose, especially mediation or a combination of mediation and arbitration—'Med-Arb'.

## 9.7 Appendix

### Arena Naming Rights Agreement*

THIS NAMING RIGHTS AGREEMENT ("Agreement") is entered into as of the 17th day of August, 2000, by and among KIEL CENTER PARTNERS, L.P. a Missouri Limited partnership ("KCP") with offices at 1401 Clark Avenue, St. Louis, Missouri 63103, SAVVIS COMMUNICATIONS CORPORATION, a Delaware corporation ("Savvis") with offices at 717 Office Parkway, St. Louis, Missouri 63141, and BRIDGE INFORMATION SYSTEMS, INC., a Missouri corporation ("Bridge") with offices at 717 Office Parkway, St. Louis, Missouri 63141. SAVVIS COMMUNICATIONS CORPORATION, a Missouri corporation, is the owner of certain intellectual property covered by this Agreement and is signing this Agreement to acknowledge certain obligations with respect to such intellectual property hereunder.

**Recitals**

A. KCP owns and operates the Arena (as defined below). The Arena is currently the venue for home games played by the St. Louis Blues and other sports and entertainment events. Savvis is a publicly-traded company, which as of the date of this Agreement specializes in providing business-to-business Internet service, global data networking services and co-location/hosting provider services.
B. Savvis desires to license from KCP the naming rights to the Arena, as well as other ancillary benefits related thereto. KCP desires to license to Savvis certain naming rights to the Arena, and provide other ancillary benefits related thereto, subject to the terms and conditions set forth herein and subject to certain rights to require Bridge to assume all rights, duties and obligations of Savvis, as provided herein.

**Now, Therefore**, in consideration of the mutual promises, duties and obligations set forth herein, the sufficiency of which is hereby acknowledged, the parties agree as follows:

**Agreement**

1. Definitions.
    a. "Arena" refers to the arena currently known as Kiel Center, including those areas immediately surrounding the Arena which are owned by or under the control of KCP, but specifically excludes the Kiel Opera House.

---

* Reproduced with the permission of Kiel Center Partners, LP Saint Louis, Missouri, United States of America.

b. “Arena Advertising Inventory” refers collectively to the Naming Rights Holder Advertising, Naming Rights Holder Amenities and Naming Rights Inventory as more particularly detailed in Exhibit A, together with all substitutions, additions and enhancements thereto which may subsequently be agreed to by the parties.
c. “Arena Event” refers to a sporting activity, exhibition or game, musical concert, theater event, convention, trade show, charitable event, political event, religious gathering and any such other event which takes place in or at the Arena and which is open to the general public.
d. “Arena Graphic Logo” refers to the trademark incorporating the Arena Mark and an artist’s graphic design, which is to be created pursuant to Section 9 and which is subject to modification pursuant to Section 8 hereof.
e. “Arena Mark” refers to the “words only” trademark comprising all or a portion of one or more Naming Rights Holder House Marks and which is to be created pursuant to Section 9 and which is subject to modification pursuant to Section 8 hereof. As of the Naming Rights Effective Date, the Arena Mark shall consist only of the words “Savvis Center”.
f. “Bridge Business” means the business of being a (i) provider of financial information and/or financial news services, (ii) provider of web design, web hosting and network services, and/or (iii) provider of brokerage and electronic trading services.
g. “Bridge Direct Competitor” means any person or entity which operates primarily as a (a) provider of financial information and/or financial news services; or (b) provider of web design, web hosting and network services; or (c) provider of brokerage and electronic trading services.
h. “KCP Control” means that (i) KCP, (ii) Bill Laurie, (iii) Nancy Laurie, (iv) EPL, LLC, (v) EPL II, LLC (Paige Sports), (vi) EPL III, LLC, (vii) EPL IV, LLC, and/or (viii) any other entity in which a controlling interest is owned by one or any combination of the persons or entities in the foregoing clauses (i)—(vii), directly or indirectly controls a matter, entity, decision and/or action.
i. “Major Dispute” means any dispute between the parties involving (i) the failure by Naming Rights Holder to pay any portion of the Naming Fee on or before the date due and to cure such deficiency within the applicable grace period; (ii) any assertion by Naming Rights Holder that it is not receiving adequate Arena Advertising Inventory benefits pursuant to this Agreement by virtue of the fact that neither an NHL nor an NBA franchise plays its home games in the Arena; (iii) failure of KCP to provide the signage substantially as set forth in Sections 1 and 2 of Exhibit A, subject to the limitations set forth herein; or (iv) a default claimed pursuant to Section 15(c)(ii), 15(c)(iii), 15(c) (iv) or 15(c)(v).
j. “Minor Dispute” means any dispute between the parties which is not a Major Dispute.
k. “Naming Fees” has the meaning set forth in Section 6 hereof.

l. "Naming Rights" means the exclusive right and license during the Term to name the Arena.

m. "Naming Rights Effective Date" means August 31, 2000.

n. "Naming Rights Holder" means the party which, pursuant to this Agreement, has the right to exercise the Naming Rights. As of the Naming Rights Effective Date (as defined herein) Savvis shall be considered the Naming Rights Holder, subject at all times to the provisions of Section 8 hereof.

o. "Naming Rights Holder Advertising" means any and all advertising, promotions and/or sponsorships which are or are intended to advertise, promote or otherwise publicize the name and/or identity and/or business of the Naming Rights Holder as set forth on Exhibit A, together with all substitutions, additions and enhancements thereto which may subsequently be agreed to by the parties.

p. "Naming Rights Holder Amenities" means all benefits and/or amenities provided or to be approved for the use and/or benefit of the Naming Rights Holder other than the Naming Rights Holder Advertising and the Naming Rights Holder Inventory as set forth on Exhibit A, together with all substitutions, additions and enhancements thereto which may subsequently be agreed to by the parties.

q. "Naming Rights Holder Business" means the business of being a (i) business-to-business Internet service provider; (ii) a global data networking provider and/or (iii) a co-location/hosting provider, subject, however, to the provisions of Sections 5 and 8 hereof.

r. "Naming Rights Holder House Marks" means the trademarks of the Naming Rights Holder specifically identified in Exhibit B, subject to the provisions of Sections 8 and 9.

s. "Naming Rights Inventory" means any and all manner of advertising, promotions and/or sponsorships as set forth in Exhibit A hereto, together with all substitutions, additions and enhancements thereto which may subsequently be agreed to by the parties, which are or are intended to incorporate or otherwise utilize the Arena Graphic Logo and/or the Arena Mark.

t. "NBA" refers to the National Basketball Association, or its successor league.

u. "NHL" refers to the National Hockey League, or its successor league.

v. "St. Louis Blues" refers to the St. Louis Blues NHL club or its successor.

w. "Savvis Direct Competitor" means (i) any person or entity which operates primarily as a (a) business-to-business Internet service provider, or (b) global data networking provider, or (c) co-location/hosting provider; or (ii) any person or entity, at least 50.1% of whose business, as determined based on gross revenues if such gross revenues are publicly and readily available at no cost to Naming Rights Holder or, if not so available, then as determined by such other commercially reasonable methods, consists of providing business-to-business Internet service, global data networking services, or co-location/hosting services, or any combination thereof; or (iii) Reuters, Bloomberg or Thomson Companies (including ILX whether or not one of or affiliated with the Thomson Companies); provided, however, that none of the following shall be considered to be a Savvis Direct Competitor: (A) providers of telecommunications equipment and services, such as AT&T, Sprint, MCI, Lucent, Nortel, Qwest, etc., provided that any sponsorship or other arrangements with providers of telecommunications equipment or services shall be specific to local, long distance or wireless telephone service and/or equipment (i.e. AT&T could not advertise as "AT&T" on a dasher board, but could advertise as "AT&T Wireless"); (B) residential and consumer Internet service providers, such as America Online, EarthLink, etc.; (C) providers of Internet search engines or other Internet searching tools, such as Yahoo, Alta Vista, etc.; (D) Dow Jones Companies; and (E) web site design companies. A list of Savvis Direct Competitors as of the Naming Rights Effective Date is set forth in Exhibit C.

x. "Term" means the period from the Naming Rights Effective Date through and including July 31, 2020 (the "Term"), unless earlier terminated pursuant to the terms of this Agreement.

**2. Grant of Rights. Subject to the contingency set forth in Section 26.i below, KCP hereby grants the following rights to Naming Rights Holder:**

a. Naming Rights. During the Term of this Agreement, KCP hereby licenses the Naming Rights to Naming Rights Holder. As of the Naming Rights Effective Date, the Arena shall be known as the "Savvis Center" and all references in this Agreement to the Arena shall then refer to "Savvis Center," subject to the provisions of Section 8 hereof. Subject to the provisions of Section 8 hereof, KCP shall use commercially reasonable efforts during the Term to (i) cause any and all announcements relating to the Arena or an Arena Event in print or broadcast media advertising for the Arena or an Arena Event to refer to the Arena as "Savvis Center"; (ii) identify the Arena as "Savvis Center" in all official documents, press releases, and Naming Rights Inventory; (iii) cause others (including, without limitation, news media, sports teams, service providers, advertisers promotors and sponsors) to identify the Arena as "Savvis Center" (provided that any failure of such parties to refer to the Arena as the Savvis Center shall not be considered a breach of this Agreement); and (iv) use the Arena Graphic Logo and Arena Mark consistent with the provisions of this Agreement. KCP shall use commercially reasonable efforts to include in all contracts (including leases and use agreements) involving the use of the Arena for any Arena Event open to the public or for the provision of services in connection with an Arena Event open to the public, which is entered into after the Naming Rights Effective Date, a requirement to refer to and identify the Arena as "Savvis Center" in all promotional, advertising and other material disseminated to the public by or on their behalf.

b. Arena Advertising Inventory. During the Term of this Agreement, KCP hereby grants to Naming Rights Holder the exclusive right and license to have the Arena Mark or the Arena Graphic Logo prominently displayed on all Naming Rights Inventory and to enjoy the Naming Rights Holder Advertising rights and benefits. KCP agrees to use commercially reasonable efforts to affect all changes necessary to cause the Arena Mark and/or the Arena Graphic Logo, as the case may be, to be displayed on the Naming Rights Inventory as soon as practicable. Provided that Savvis and KCP are able to agree on the design for the Arena Graphic Logo by August 23, 2000, KCP agrees to effect all changes prior to the first home game of the St. Louis Blues for the 2000-01 NHL regular season (the "First Home Game"), with the exception of those items listed in Exhibit A, Sections 1.b, 1.c, 1.e, 4.b, 4.c, 4.e, 4.f, 4.g, 4.h, 6.a, 6.c, 8.a, 9.e, 9.f, 9.g and 12, which will be completed at some time after the First Home Game (subject to the limitations on the items set forth in Section 12 of Exhibit A). KCP shall not permit any person or entity to have a sign or display in the Arena or on the property of the Arena which is larger than signage or a display in the same category and type of signage/display utilized for the Arena Mark, Arena Graphic Logo and/or the Naming Rights Holder House Marks. In the event KCP proposes to grant or permit another person or entity the use of advertising, promotional or sponsorship media of a type which is not included in the Arena Advertising Inventory and which media is not of a type then being utilized by such person or entity or any other person or entity relative to the Arena or an Arena Event, then KCP agrees to discuss with Naming Rights Holder whether such media may be included in the Arena Advertising Inventory for the benefit of the Naming Rights Holder in a manner comparable, but no smaller, less frequent, or less visible to that which KCP proposes to offer to a third party, provided that (i) Naming Rights Holder shall pay for additional inventory at the same rate at which such other person or entity is paying for comparable inventory, and (ii) Naming Rights Holder acknowledges that certain types of advertising benefits may be of such a nature that they cannot become part of the Arena Advertising Inventory (i.e. logos on seats where there is room for only one advertiser), and KCP shall not be required to offer such inventory to Naming Rights Holder pursuant to this Agreement.

c. Advertising Exclusivity. Subject to the restrictions and limitations set forth in Section 3 and 4 below and the provisions on the possible change in the business of the Naming Rights Holder set forth in Section 5, KCP hereby grants "advertising exclusivity" to Naming Rights Holder during the Term. For purposes of this Agreement, "advertising exclusivity" means that no Savvis Direct Competitor (or Bridge Direct Competitor if

Bridge is the Naming Rights Holder) shall be permitted, in connection with the Arena, its operations, or any Arena Event, to advertise itself in media of any type under KCP Control (including without limitation, program advertising in sports team or other programs and/or any of the media identified in Exhibit A hereto) or to promote, sponsor (or co-sponsor) or be advertised or promoted in any manner or in any media of any type under KCP Control (including, without limitation, program advertising in sports team or other programs and/or any of the media identified in Exhibit A hereto).

i. Exclusivity of Advertising for Teams Which Play in the Arena. The parties acknowledge that this Agreement does not grant exclusive advertising rights for those teams or leagues which may play one or more games in the Arena during the Term (except as otherwise provided herein in connection with the St. Louis Blues and in connection with any NBA franchise, subject, however, to the provisions of Section 6.c of this Agreement with respect to an NBA franchise). KCP agrees that, with respect to any team under KCP Control, KCP shall give Naming Rights Holder the first option to negotiate, and shall negotiate in good faith with Naming Rights Holder, to provide Naming Rights Holder with advertising exclusivity within the appropriate category of goods and services (e.g., Naming Rights Holder Business for the Naming Rights Holder in effect as the time), for such team or league during the Term. The parties agree that such exclusivity will require the payment of an additional fee, which KCP agrees shall be commercially reasonable and shall correspond with the applicable market for exclusive advertising rights for the corresponding team.

d. New Teams or Leagues. As described above, in the event that an NBA franchise agrees to play its home games in the Arena, then KCP shall cause the Arena Advertising Inventory to include substantially those items described in Exhibit D. Naming Rights Holder acknowledges and agrees that, in the event that any team or league other than the St. Louis Blues or an NBA Franchise agrees to play its home games in the Arena, Naming Rights Holder shall not be entitled to any specific advertising benefits related to such team or league, except that KCP agrees to cause such team or league (i) to recognize and abide by Naming Rights Holder's Advertising Exclusivity as described herein, and (ii) to refer to the Arena as the "Savvis Center" in all promotions for that team or league which include references to the Arena.

**3. Limitations on Rights in Favor of Naming Rights Holder.**

a. Non-Application of Advertising Exclusivity. The advertising exclusivity granted under this Agreement shall not apply to (i) advertising rights granted separately by the NHL or NBA in connection with their league-mandated national broadcast arrangements (or any other NHL or NBA-mandated advertising); and (ii) shall not preclude KCP or its principals, employees or agents from contracting to host bona fide events at the Arena for which a Savvis Direct Competitor has contracted for sponsorship rights. By way of example, if a Savvis Direct Competitor sponsors a national tour, KCP shall not be prohibited from contracting with that promoter to host such tour in the Arena even if this involves a Savvis Direct Competitor advertising and promoting itself in the Arena and in the marketplace.

b. Likeness. Naming Rights Holder acknowledges and agrees that the rights granted pursuant to this Agreement do not include: (i) the right to use the names, likenesses, voices or images of any NHL players or coaches (including without limitation St. Louis Blues players or coaches) or NBA players or coaches on or in connection with the promotion or advertising of Naming Rights Holder or its services; (ii) except for the player appearances specified in Exhibit A, the right to require players or coaches from any NHL team (including without limitation the St. Louis Blues) or any NBA franchise which may play its games in the Arena to appear on behalf of or endorse Naming Rights Holder or its services; or (iii) the right to use any property owned or controlled by the NHL, the National Hockey League Players Association, any National Hockey League coaches association, the NBA, the NBA Players Association, any NBA coaches association which may at any time be formed.

c. NHL Rights. Notwithstanding any other provision of this Agreement to the contrary, this Agreement shall in all respects be subject to and subordinate to: (i) the NHL Constitution; (ii) the NHL By-Laws; (iii) all other rules, regulations and policies of the NHL and the resolutions of its Board of Governors; (iv) any Collective Bargaining Agreement between the NHL and/or its member clubs and other parties; (v) all consent decrees and settlement agreements entered into, between or among the NHL and its member clubs or the NHL, NHL member clubs and/or other persons in the furtherance of NHL business or interests or as otherwise authorized directly or indirectly by the NHL Board of Governors, the NHL Commissioner, or the NHL Constitution; (vi) any national network agreements between the NHL and third parties; and (vii) any national corporate marketing, licensing, sponsorship or similar agreements between the NHL (or NHL affiliates) and third parties, all as the same may now exist or hereafter be amended or enacted or as they may be interpreted by the Commissioner.

   Notwithstanding any other provision herein to the contrary, Naming Rights Holder agrees that KCP and the St. Louis Blues may allow or authorize any League Sponsor (as defined below) to engage in advertising and promotional activities in the St. Louis market (including, without limitation, in the Arena), or otherwise provide benefits to such League Sponsor, if such League Sponsor is entitled to engage in such activities or receive such benefits pursuant to any sponsorship or promotional licensing arrangement now or hereafter entered into between such League Sponsor and the NHL or any of its affiliates (including, without limitation, NHL Enterprises, L.P. and NHL Enterprises Canada, L.P.). “League Sponsor” means any person or entity which currently is, or at any time becomes, a sponsor or promotional licensee of or with respect to any NHL event or program now or hereafter in existence. By way of illustration only and without limiting the generality of the foregoing, League Sponsors may place advertising and promotional materials (including displays) in the Arena, or conduct sweepstakes or in-store promotions in the St. Louis market in connection with a League event, such as the NHL All-Star Game, or in support of a League program, such as NHL All-Star Fan Balloting, NHL Freeze Play or NHL Breakout. Naming Rights Holder acknowledges and agrees that KCP is not obligated to compensate Naming Rights Holder via credits, make-goods or any other means for any preemptions made pursuant to this Section.

Naming Rights Holder acknowledges and agrees that, in the event an NBA franchise decides to play its home games in the Arena, then this Agreement shall be modified to incorporate a comparable provision regarding NBA rights, rules and regulations.

**4. Restrictions and Limitations on Rights on Exploitation of Arena Advertising Inventory; Restrictions on Exclusivity.**

a. Permitted Restrictions. Naming Rights Holder agrees that KCP shall not be in default under this Agreement if Naming Rights Holder is prohibited or otherwise prevented from receiving the benefit of and/or rights to certain aspects of the Arena Advertising Inventory or if one or more Savvis Direct Competitors is able to promote their goods or services under limited circumstances in connection with one or more Arena Events in a manner which would otherwise be in violation of the advertising exclusivity as a result, in either case, of rules, regulations, restrictions, limitations, agreements, laws, ordinances or requirements to the extent that either (i) the existence or the adoption of such rules, regulations, restrictions, limitations, agreements, laws, ordinances or requirements was not the result of the acts or omissions of KCP or its affiliates, partners, members, shareholders, directors or principals; (ii) the avoidance of implementation or the application of rules, regulations, restrictions, limitations, laws, ordinances, agreements or requirements satisfying the requirements of (i) above is beyond the “commercially reasonable control” of KCP and/or its affiliates, partners, members, shareholders, directors or principals; or (iii) the existence or adoption of such rules, regulations, restrictions, limitations, agreements, laws, ordinances or requirements resulted from the affirmative actions of KCP or its affiliates, partners, members, shareholders, directors or principals, but such affirmative actions were not within the commercially reasonable control of KCP or its affiliates, partners, members, shareholders, directors or principals, to avoid taking (rules, regulations, restrictions, limitations, agreements and/or requirements that satisfy (i) or (ii) above are individually a "Permitted Restriction" and are collectively "Permitted Restrictions"). For purpose of this Agreement, the term "commercially reasonable control" shall mean the level of control exercised in the normal course of business by a similar party in a similar situation. Without limiting the scope of what may constitute Permitted Restrictions, the rights and benefits granted by KCP to Naming Rights Holder are subject to each of the following to the extent such matter is a Permitted Restriction:

i. League, Conference, Governing Body, etc. Rules. Rules and regulations restricting the Arena Advertising Inventory benefits imposed by (i) leagues (i.e. NBA, NHL) or conferences (i.e. NCAA, CUSA) whose teams participate in Arena Events, or (ii) such other governing bodies (i.e. U.S. Figure Skating Association) for certain events (i.e. ice shows). KCP agrees that Naming Rights Holder shall receive the benefit of any NBA, NHL, NCAA or other rule or regulation changes during or prior to the Term of this Agreement to the extent such changes either eliminate, alleviate, reduce or diminish Permitted Restrictions.
ii. National or Regional Television or Radio Limitations. Rules and regulations imposed on KCP by a national or regional television network or radio station with the right to broadcast one or more of the Arena Events.
iii. Local Television or Radio. Limitations imposed by local television or radio broadcasters (not under KCP Control) with the right to broadcast one or more of the Arena Events on local television or radio.
iv. Blackout Rights. Blackout rights or other prevention of public display required by a league, conference or other governing body, or which are otherwise required by an owner, promoter or agent of an Arena Event, provided that KCP shall use reasonable commercially efforts to avoid such rights and requirements.
v. Arena Events Not Under Control of KCP. Restrictions or limitations imposed by owner, promoter or producer of Arena Events not under KCP Control, provided that KCP shall use commercially reasonable efforts to avoid such restrictions or limitations.
vi. City Ordinances, Government Approval, etc. Applicable governmental laws, ordinances, agreements, rules or regulations.
vii. Arena Advertising Inventory Under the Discretion of KCP. KCP may, in its reasonable business judgment, choose to alter or eliminate those Naming Rights Inventory benefits which involve an advertising or promotional campaign by KCP or one of its

affiliates (i.e. Sections 5, 6 and 7 as listed in Exhibit A), provided that KCP will undertake an advertising or promotional campaign which is reasonably comparable to that described in Sections 5, 6 and 7 of Exhibit A.

b. Costs to Implement Permitted Restrictions. In the event that Naming Rights Holder is required to make direct expenditures to comply with the Permitted Restrictions (for example, to bring its web site or the web site of the St. Louis Blues into compliance with the Permitted Restrictions), KCP shall reimburse Naming Rights Holder for such direct expenditures, provided that KCP shall not be required to reimburse Naming Rights Holder for any lost profits or other indirect costs or expenditures, and provided that prior to the implementation of any web site to be established, hosted and maintained by Savvis pursuant to Section 8 of Exhibit A, Savvis shall first submit the plan pursuant to which Savvis will establish and host such web site and KCP shall advise Savvis as to whether such plan or any portions thereof are inconsistent or not permitted under any then-existing Permitted Restrictions.
c. Consultation on Permitted Restrictions. If requested by Naming Rights Holder, KCP agrees to consult with Naming Rights Holder annually with respect to the Permitted Restrictions.

**5. Changes in Business of Naming Rights Holder; Changes in Savvis Direct Competitors.**

a. Naming Right Holder Business Changes. At the option of the Naming Rights Holder, at any one time during the period 45–60 days prior to an anniversary of the Naming Rights Effective Date, Naming Rights Holder may notify KCP of proposed changes to the Naming Rights Holder Business and corresponding proposed changes to the Savvis Direct Competitors to be effective as of the immediately forthcoming anniversary, along with all information reasonably requested by KCP to evaluate such proposed changes. Within 30 days after such notice and receipt of such information, KCP shall advise Naming Rights Holders as to the extent to which such proposed changes would be acceptable and the modifications, if any, to the Naming Fees and the extent of any other fees and charges payable by Naming Rights Holder as a condition to the effectiveness of such changes. Naming Rights Holder shall have 15 days after notice of such proposal to notify KCP that Naming Rights Holder has accepted or rejected such proposal. Failure by Naming Rights Holder to accept or reject such proposal shall be deemed a rejection of it for the forthcoming year only (Naming Rights Holder shall not be deemed to have waived any right to reissue such proposal or any portions of it in subsequent years). If Naming Rights Holder timely accepts such proposal from KCP, the parties shall take those actions necessary to effect such proposal, and the proposed changes shall become effective beginning on the forthcoming anniversary.

b. Notice of Savvis Direct Competitors. KCP and Naming Rights Holder acknowledge and agree that the marketplace in which Naming Rights Holder operates is continually changing, and certain entities which Naming Rights Holder agrees are not currently Savvis Direct Competitors could become Savvis Direct Competitors in the future. At the option of the Naming Rights Holder, at any one time during the period 45–60 days prior to an anniversary of the Naming Rights Effective Date, Naming Rights Holder may notify KCP of persons and/or entities who Naming Rights Holder has a reasonable basis to believe is/are Savvis Direct Competitors (the "Direct Competitor Notice"). KCP shall have 30 days after receipt of such Direct Competitor Notice to notify the Naming Rights Holder that all or any such persons or entities are or are not Savvis Direct Competitors, as the case may be, with reasons stated therefor (an "Objection Notice"). Failure by KCP to send an Objection Notice in a timely manner shall be deemed an approval of all parties listed in the Direct Competitor Notice as Savvis Direct Competitors. If KCP accepts the designation of one or more persons/entities as Savvis Direct Competitors, then those persons/entities shall be considered Savvis Direct Competitors effective as of the forthcoming anniversary date of the Naming Rights Effective Date. For those person(s)/entity(ies) rejected by KCP, Naming Rights Holder shall have the option to protest KCP's determination pursuant to the Dispute Resolution Procedure for Minor Disputes set forth in Section 21, provided that Naming Rights Holder shall have the burden of proof to demonstrate that a person/entity is a Savvis Direct Competitor. In the event that KCP has an existing contract with a newly-determined Savvis Direct Competitor in the ordinary course of business which would impact Naming Rights Holder's advertising exclusivity hereunder, KCP shall have the right to complete the initial term of such contract without defaulting under this Agreement.
c. Changes in Businesses of Existing KCP Sponsors. Provided that the Southwestern Bell Agreement is terminated in accordance with Section 26.i, KCP warrants that, as of the Naming Rights Effective Date, none of its existing agreements involving sponsorship rights interfere with the grant of exclusivity made to Naming Rights Holder as specified in Section 2.c. Subject to the limitation set forth below in this Section 5.c, KCP agrees that, with respect to sponsorships or other agreements involving sponsorship rights which are entered into after the Naming Rights Effective Date, in the event that a sponsor of KCP either changes the nature of its business or acquires another entity such that the sponsor becomes a Savvis Direct Competitor, and Naming Rights Holder and KCP agree that the sponsor is a Savvis Direct Competitor pursuant to the process set forth in Section 5.b, KCP agrees to terminate the sponsorship agreement with that sponsor effective fifteen (15) days after receipt of notice from Naming Rights Holder that a sponsor is a Savvis Direct Competitor, or fifteen (15) days after the completion of any process to determine whether a sponsor is a Savvis Direct Competitor, whichever is later.

This provision shall not apply to, and KCP shall not be required to terminate, agreements involving sponsorship rights which are in effect as of the Naming Rights Effective Date during the existing term of such agreements, the existing term being the term in effect as of the Naming Rights Effective Date, provided that KCP agrees that the requirement for termination set forth in this Section 5.c shall apply in any future renewals or extensions of said existing sponsorship agreements.

**6. Naming Fees.**

a. Fees. In consideration of the benefits provided pursuant to this Agreement, Naming Rights Holder agrees to pay to KCP the following Naming Fees (consisting of the items under both Section 6.a.i and 6.a.ii below):

i. Provided that this Agreement is not terminated pursuant to Section 26.i, upon receipt by Savvis of notice from KCP that the SWB Agreement has been terminated, Savvis shall issue to KCP an aggregate of 750,000 shares of common stock in Savvis, $.01 par value. On such date, Savvis shall deliver certificates representing such common stock in such names and such designations as shall be requested by KCP in writing not less than three business days prior to such delivery.

ii. For the fiscal period of [**], Savvis agrees to pay to KCP the sum of [ **]. For each one year period thereafter, with each period beginning August 1 and continuing through July 31 (the "Fiscal Period"), Naming Rights Holder agrees to pay to KCP an amount equal to 105% of the amount paid during the previous Fiscal Period. Subject to the potential increase set forth in Section 6.c, the Naming Fees due shall be as follows:

| Fiscal Period | Amount Due |
|---|---|
| [ ** ] | [ ** ]; |
| [ ** ] | [ ** ]; |
| [ ** ] | [ ** ]; |
| [ ** ] | [ ** ]; |
| [ ** ] | [ ** ]; |
| [ ** ] | [ ** ]; |
| [ ** ] | [ ** ]; |
| [ ** ] | [ ** ]; |
| [ ** ] | [ ** ]; |
| [ ** ] | [ ** ]; |
| [ ** ] | [ ** ]; |
| [ ** ] | [ ** ]; |
| [ ** ] | [ ** ]; |
| [ ** ] | [ ** ]; |

b. Timing of Payments. For each Fiscal Period beginning with the period of [ ** ], Naming Rights Holder shall pay an amount equal to one-fourth of the amount due for that Fiscal Period on or before each of August 1, November 1, February 1 and May 1;

c. Addition of NBA Franchise. Naming Rights Holder agrees that, in the event that an NBA franchise agrees to play its home games in the Arena, then KCP shall cause the Arena Advertising Inventory to include substantially those items described in Exhibit D. The Naming Fees due for the year in which such home games commence to be played shall increase by the escalating "NBA Sum," which shall be calculated as described below, unless an NBA franchise agrees to begin playing its games in the Arena in the middle of the NBA season, in which case the pro-rata portion of the NBA Sum shall be due for that year. The NBA Sum shall be the sum of [**] for the first year covered by this Agreement (Naming Rights Effective Date through July 31, 2001) and shall increase by the sum of five percent (5%) cumulative for each year thereafter. By way of example, if an NBA franchise decides to play its home games in the Arena beginning in the fifth year of this Agreement (August 1, 2004 through July 31, 2005), then the Naming Fees for that year shall increase by the sum of [**]. Naming Rights Holder acknowledges and agrees that if an NBA franchise begins to play its home games in the Arena prior to August 1, 2006, then the corresponding NBA Sum shall be due for that Fiscal Period and all subsequent Fiscal Periods, in addition to the stock transfer provided for in Section 6.a. Naming Rights Holder further acknowledges and agrees that if an NBA franchise begins to play its home games in the Arena on or after July 1, 2006, then the NBA Sum due for that Fiscal Period and all subsequent Fiscal Periods shall be in addition to the Naming Fees due under Section 6.a. The additional payments shall be made in equal installments on the dates other payments are due as provided in Section 6.b. In the event that the St. Louis NBA franchise or the St. Louis Blues play their home games in a location other than the Arena (excluding exhibitions or one-time appearances in other locations), then the Naming Fees shall decrease by the then-current annual NBA Sum. In the event that both the St. Louis NBA franchise and the St. Louis Blues play their home games in a location other than the Arena, the Naming Rights Holder shall have those termination rights set forth in Section 15.

d. Amounts Are in Addition to Current Sponsorship Fees. Naming Rights Holder agrees that the amounts due hereunder are in addition to any and all sponsorship and suite fees which may be due from Naming Rights
[**] Confidential treatment requested
Holder or Bridge under separate sponsorship and/or suite agreements in effect as of Naming Rights Effective Date.

e. Production Expenses. KCP agrees that all expenses related to the initial modification of the Arena and/or Arena Advertising Inventory and to the printing, manufacturing and installation of the Arena Advertising Inventory to reflect the change in the name of the Arena as provided for in this

Agreement shall be paid by KCP unless otherwise noted in Exhibit A. Naming Rights Holder agrees that any expenses related to any other modification of the Arena Advertising Inventory, whether required as a result of the application of Section 8 or otherwise, shall be the sole responsibility of Naming Rights Holder.

**7. Renewal—Right of First Negotiation.**

Provided that this Agreement has not otherwise been terminated, KCP agrees, beginning on the date three (3) years prior to the expiration of this Agreement, to negotiate exclusively and in good faith for a period of eighteen (18) months with Naming Rights Holder regarding an extension or renewal of this Agreement (the "Exclusive Negotiating Period"). Naming Rights Holder agrees that, in the event no agreement is reached to renew or extend this Agreement during the Exclusive Negotiating Period, KCP shall be free to negotiate with other parties regarding the terms set forth in this Agreement upon the expiration of the Exclusive Negotiating Period.

**8. Name Changes; Bridge's Duty to Assume Obligations of Naming Rights Holder.**

a. Change in Control of Savvis. In the event that a single entity, person or group (the "Acquiror") acquires or otherwise owns more than fifty percent (50%) of the voting shares of Savvis on a non-diluted basis and elects to change the name of Savvis, then Acquiror may request a name change (the "Proposed Name Change"), provided that the Proposed Name Change must be a name related to the actual or proposed corporate name or identity of the Acquiror, and provided that there is no Event of Default by Naming Rights Holder or Acquiror on the date on which the Proposed Name Change is submitted by Acquiror. KCP may, within sixty days after receipt of notice that Acquiror has requested the Proposed Name Change, either accept or reject such Proposed Name Change in KCP's solediscretion. If the Proposed Name Change is accepted by KCP, then Acquiror shall become the Naming Rights Holder and shall pay all expenses and costs incurred by KCP in modifying the Arena Advertising Inventory, Arena Graphic Logo and Arena Mark and any other reasonable actual expenses and costs incurred by KCP to effect such renaming.

   i. Assumption by Bridge in Case of Rejection. If KCP rejects the Proposed Name Change, then Bridge shall replace Savvis as the Naming Rights Holder and shall become and be deemed the Naming Rights Holder, and Bridge shall be deemed to have assumed all rights and obligations applicable to the Naming Rights Holder under this Agreement and may rename the Arena, at Bridge's sole expense, in a manner consistent with its own Naming Rights Holder House

Marks; provided, however, that if KCP determines that if Bridge's financial condition is such that it is not highly probable that Bridge will be able to perform all of its duties and obligations hereunder throughout the Term (hereinafter referred to as an "Acceptable Party"), KCP may disapprove of the assumption by Bridge. In the event that Bridge disputes KCP's determination that Bridge is not an Acceptable Party, then Bridge may elect to resolve that dispute pursuant to the Minor Dispute Resolution procedure set forth in Section 2(a) of this Agreement.

ii. Disapproval of Bridge. In the event that an arbitrator determines that Bridge is not an Acceptable Party, or in the event that Bridge does not dispute KCP's determination that Bridge is not an Acceptable Party, then the duties and obligations of the Naming Rights Holder shall revert back to Savvis and/or Acquiror, as constituted after the Change in Control, and Savvis and Acquiror shall also be responsible for any and all payments due and owing by Savvis and/or Naming Rights Holder at the time of the Change in Control. The parties agree that, in the event that Bridge is not accepted as the Naming Rights Holder pursuant to this Section 8.b(ii), then the Arena shall continue to be named the Savvis Center.

iii. Approval or Acceptance of Bridge. In the event KCP accepts Bridge's assumption of this Agreement pursuant to Section 8.a.i, or if Bridge is determined to be acceptable pursuant to the Minor Dispute Resolution process, and provided that Bridge satisfies all outstanding obligations of the Naming Rights Holder as of the date of assumption, then KCP agrees that Savvis and Acquiror shall, as of the date of assumption, no longer be liable for any duties or obligations set forth in this Agreement.

iv. Bridge Direct Competitor. In the event that Bridge becomes the Naming Rights Holder pursuant to this Section 8, KCP agrees that the term "Bridge Direct Competitor" shall be substituted for the term "Savvis Direct Competitor" and "Bridge Business" shall be substituted for "Naming Rights Holder Business" throughout this Agreement, and Bridge shall be entitled to the benefits afforded thereby, provided, however, that KCP shall be entitled to fulfill any and all contractual obligations pursuant to agreements entered into with Bridge Direct Competitors prior to the date on which Bridge becomes the Naming Rights Holder. Bridge further agrees that it shall not be entitled to seek an amendment to the definitions of Bridge Business and Bridge Direct Competitor, nor shall it be entitled to seek any additions to the list of Bridge Direct Competitors until the first allowed change of such items, as specified in Section 5.a and 5.b, immediately after the date of assumption of this Agreement by Bridge.

b. Limit of One Name Change. The parties hereto acknowledge and agree that a total of only one name change shall be allowed during the Term.

**9. Arena Mark and Arena Graphics Logo.**

a. Development of Arena Mark and Arena Graphic Logo.
The parties agree that KCP shall develop, at KCP's expense, the Arena Mark and the Arena Graphic Logo, provided that the final design of the Arena Mark and Arena Graphic Logo shall be subject to the approval of Naming Rights Holder, which approval shall not be unreasonably withheld, delayed or conditioned. Naming Rights Holder agrees that KCP shall own all right, title and interest, including without limitation the copyright, in and to the Arena Mark and the Arena Graphic Logo, subject to Naming Rights Holder's ownership of all intellectual property rights in and to the Naming Rights Holder House Marks. KCP shall license or acquire from the creator of the Arena Graphic Logo's "artist's design" sufficient rights, including but not limited to rights in any copyright, to permit unrestricted use of the Arena Graphic Logo trademark.

b. License to Use Naming Rights Holder House Marks.
The Missouri Corporation (as defined in Section 17.a) hereby grants to KCP a non-exclusive, royalty-free license to use Naming Rights Holder House Marks during the Term of this Agreement for the purpose of (i) using the Naming Rights Holder House Marks to advertise the Arena and Arena Events subject to the conditions herein and (ii) for the purpose of allowing KCP to create, use, and own the Arena Mark and Arena Graphic Logo. Naming Rights Holder shall have prior approval rights with respect to any form of advertising of the Naming Rights Holder House Marks (excluding advertising containing Arena Mark or Arena Graphic Logo), provided that (1) such approval will not be unreasonably withheld or delayed, (2) the parties shall reasonably agree upon a mutually convenient process for such approvals to be requested and obtained, and (3) KCP shall not be obligated to resubmit a request for approval for proposed advertising similar to that which has already been approved. KCP agrees that it will cause to appear on or within all advertising, promotional or display material bearing the Naming Rights Holder House Marks, below and to the right of said marks or logos, the identification "(R) or "TM" or "SM" as will be designated by Naming Rights Holder. Each of Naming Rights Holder and the Missouri Corporation, if applicable, agrees that it will not, during the Term of this Agreement, attack the title or any rights of KCP in and to the Arena Mark or Arena Graphic or attack the validity of the license granted under this Section 9(b). KCP hereby agrees that its every use of Naming Rights Holder House Marks shall inure to the benefit of Naming Rights Holder and that KCP shall not at any time acquire any rights in Naming Rights Holder House Marks by virtue of any use KCP may make of them. The non-exclusive

license to use the Naming Rights Holder House Marks shall not prevent Naming Rights Holder or, if applicable, the Missouri Corporation, from using the Naming Rights Holder House Marks in any manner whatsoever.

c. License to Use Arena Mark and Arena Graphic Logo.
KCP hereby grants Naming Rights Holder a non-exclusive, royalty-free license during the Term of this Agreement to use the Arena Mark and the Arena Graphic Logo in conjunction with the Naming Rights Inventory, the Naming Rights Holder Amenities and Naming Rights Holder's promotions and advertising. KCP shall have prior approval rights with respect to any form of advertising of the Arena Mark or the Arena Graphic Logo, provided that (1) such approval will not be unreasonably withheld, delayed or conditioned, (2) the parties shall reasonably agree upon a mutually convenient process for such approvals to be requested and obtained, and (3) Naming Rights Holder shall not be obligated to resubmit a request for approval for proposed advertising similar to that which has already been approved. Naming Rights Holder agrees that it will cause to appear on or within all advertising, promotional or display material bearing the Arena Mark or the Arena Graphic Logo, below and to the right of said Arena Mark or Arena Graphic Logos, the identification "(R)" or "TM" or "SM" as will be designated by KCP. KCP agrees that it will not, during the Term of this Agreement or thereafter, attack the title or any rights of Naming Rights Holder in and to Naming Rights Holder House Marks or attack the validity of the license granted under this Section 9(c). Naming Rights Holder hereby agrees that its every use of such Arena Mark or Arena Graphic Logo shall inure to the benefit of KCP and that Naming Rights Holder shall not, during the Term of this Agreement, acquire any ownership rights in the Arena Mark or the Arena Graphic Logo by virtue of any use Naming Rights Holder may make of them.
Upon the termination of this Agreement or expiration of the Term, KCP agrees to cease any and all uses of the Naming Rights Holder House Marks, and all parties agree to cease any and all uses of the Arena Mark and the Arena Graphic Logo, provided that KCP shall have the right to distribute any materials in its inventory bearing one or more of the Naming Rights Holder House Marks, the Arena Mark or the Arena Graphic Logo for a period of six months from the date of termination of this Agreement or expiration of the Term. In the event that a substitution of the Naming Rights Holder occurs during the Term of this Agreement, the Naming Rights Holder House Marks of the substituted Naming Rights Holder shall be licensed according to the provisions of this Section 9 and the license to use the Naming Rights Holder House Marks of the Missouri Corporation and/or the former Naming Rights Holder shall terminate, subject to KCP's right to distribute materials in its inventory for a period of six months from the effective date of such substitution.

d. Proper Use of Arena Mark and Arena Graphic Logo.
Naming Rights Holder recognizes that KCP and the St. Louis Blues will establish a great deal of goodwill through their reputation and the representation of the Arena Mark and/or Arena Graphic Logo. Therefore, Naming Rights Holder shall not use, commercially exploit, permit the use of or permit the commercial exploitation of Arena Mark and/or Arena Graphic Logo in negative advertising, nor in any manner that is contrary to public morals or which has been found to be deceptive or misleading, or which reflects unfavorably on the good name, goodwill, reputation or image of KCP or the St. Louis Blues.

e. Proper Use of Naming Rights Holder' Name, Logo and Marks.
KCP recognizes the great value of the reputation and goodwill associated with the Naming Rights Holder House Marks. Therefore, KCP shall not use, commercially exploit, permit the use of or permit the commercial exploitation of the Arena Mark and/or Arena Graphic Logo or Naming Rights Holder House Marks in negative advertising, nor in any manner that is contrary to public morals or which has been found to be deceptive or misleading or which reflects unfavorably on the good name, goodwill, reputation or image of Naming Rights Holder.
KCP acknowledges the importance of maintaining the high, uniform standards of quality in the products and services sold under the Naming Rights Holder House Marks and the interest Naming Rights Holder has in equally high, uniform standards of quality in the products and services sold under the Arena Mark and the Arena Graphic Logo. Therefore, KCP agrees to maintain and follow standards of quality which are comparable within the industry with respect to the type, nature or quality of the products or services sold under the Arena Mark and the Arena Graphic Logo and products or services advertised under the Naming Rights Holder House Marks. For the Arena Mark and the Arena Graphic Logo, KCP shall require its licensees to maintain and follow standards of quality as may be set by KCP from time to time, but in no circumstance shall the standards of quality be less than the standards which are comparable within the industry.

f. Protection of Arena Mark and Arena Graphic Logo.
Naming Rights Holder shall notify KCP immediately in writing of any infringements of the Arena Graphic Logo or Arena Mark which may come to Naming Rights Holder's attention. KCP shall have the sole right to determine, in good faith and in consultation with legal counsel, whether or not an infringement has occurred. If KCP determines that an infringement has occurred, KCP agrees, at its expense, to use commercially reasonable efforts to cause the infringer to cease and desist from the infringing actions, which efforts may include litigation. Each of Naming Rights Holder and, if applicable, the Missouri Corporation, agrees to cooperate fully with KCP in the event such enforcement actions are necessary. Each of Naming Rights Holder and, if applicable, the Missouri Corporation,

retains the right, at its sole expense, to take any such action as necessary to protect the applicable Naming Rights Holder House Marks from infringement and other unlawful use, including any infringement that may be alleged in the field of goods and services that are now, and in the future, customarily provided at or related to the Arena or Arena Events.

**10. Warranties and Representations.**

a. By KCP. KCP warrants and represents to Naming Rights Holder the following as of the date this Agreement is entered into:

   i. The execution, delivery and performance of this Agreement have been authorized by all necessary corporate action and that it has requisite right, power and authority to enter into and perform this Agreement and to grant the rights and licenses granted to Naming Rights Holder pursuant to this Agreement. KCP agrees to deliver to Savvis, upon execution of this Agreement, certified copies of all corporate resolutions authorizing the execution, delivery and performance of this Agreement;

   ii. KCP is a Missouri limited liability company duly organized under the laws of the State of Missouri and is in good standing in the State of Missouri;

   iii. Subject to the consents required in Section 10.a.i above, no consent of any other person or entity is required for execution by KCP of this Agreement and/or performance under this Agreement;

   iv. Neither KCP nor the St. Louis Blues nor any affiliate of either of them has granted any rights pertaining to the subject matter of this Agreement to any party in a manner which would cause KCP to be in default under any such agreement or which prevents KCP from granting the rights and licenses to Naming Rights Holder under this Agreement;

   v. There is no litigation pending nor is any litigation threatened against KCP relative to any of the matters which are the subject of this Agreement;

   vi. KCP is the owner of the Arena and has a valid and existing ground lease pursuant to that certain Amended and Restated Sublease Agreement dated as of November 24, 1992, by and between KCP and Kiel Center Redevelopment Corporation (a copy of which has been delivered to Savvis) (the "Lease"), which Lease is in full force and effect as of the Naming Rights Effective Date and the term of which is scheduled to run throughout the Term of this Agreement, provided that the Lease is not otherwise terminated or otherwise cancelled;

vii. To the best of KCP's knowledge, there is no existing rule of the NHL, NBA or any league currently utilizing the Arena, nor are there any provisions in existing sponsorship contracts of KCP, which would prevent the Naming Rights Holder from enjoying substantially all of the benefits listed in Exhibit;

viii. Subject to the pending termination of the SWB Agreement as described in Section 26.i, neither KCP nor the St. Louis Blues nor any affiliate of either of them has granted any rights to any person or entity that are or could be inconsistent with or are or could be in conflict with the terms and conditions of this Agreement and/or the rights and benefits granted to Naming Rights Holder hereunder;

ix. This Agreement is made with KCP in reliance upon KCP's representations to Savvis, which by its execution hereof KCP hereby confirms, that Savvis Common Stock issued pursuant to Section 6.a.i (all such securities are referred to as the "Securities" for purposes of this Section 10) to be received by KCP will be acquired for investment for its own account, not as a nominee or agent, and not with a view to the sale or distribution of any part thereof, and that KCP has no present intention of selling, granting participation in, or otherwise distributing the same. By executing this Agreement, KCP further represents that it does not have any contract, undertaking, agreement or arrangement with any person to sell, transfer, or grant participations to such person or to any third person, with respect to any of the Securities;

x. KCP understands that the Securities are not registered under the Securities Act of 1933, as amended (the "1933 Act,") on the ground that the sale provided for in this Agreement and the issuance of Securities hereunder should be exempt from registration under the 1933 Act and that Savvis' reliance on such exemption is predicated on KCP's representations set forth herein;

xi. KCP represents that it is an "accredited investor" within the meaning of Rule 501 under the 1933 Act and that it is experienced in evaluating and investing in companies such as Savvis, is able to fend for itself in the transactions contemplated by this Agreement, has such knowledge and experience in financial and business matters as to be capable of evaluating the merits and risks of his investment and has the ability to bear the economic risks of its investment. KCP further represents that it has had access, during the course of the transaction and prior to its purchase of the Securities, to the information filed by Savvis with the Securities and Exchange Commission and that it has had, during the course of the transaction and prior to its execution hereof, the opportunity to ask questions of, and to receive answers from, Savvis concerning the terms and conditions of the offering of the

Securities and to obtain additional information necessary to verify the accuracy of any information furnished to it or to which it has had access. KCP acknowledges that it has had the opportunity to obtain additional information as desired in order to evaluate the merits and risks inherent in purchasing and holding the Securities;

xii. KCP understands that the Securities may not be sold, transferred or otherwise disposed of without registration under the 1933 Act or an exemption therefrom, and that in the absence of an effective registration statement covering the Securities or an available exemption from registration under the 1933 Act, the Securities must be held indefinitely. In particular, KCP is aware that the Securities may not be sold pursuant to Rule 144 promulgated under the 1933 Act unless all of the conditions of that Rule are met. KCP represents that, in the absence of an effective registration statement covering the Securities, KCP will sell, transfer or otherwise dispose of the Securities only in a manner consistent with their representations set forth herein and then only in accordance with the provisions of Section (xiii) hereof;

xiii. KCP agrees that in no event will it make a transfer or disposition of any of the Securities (other than pursuant to an effective registration statement under the 1933 Act), unless and until (i) KCP shall have notified Savvis of the proposed disposition and shall have furnished Savvis with a statement of the circumstances surrounding the disposition and assurance that the proposed disposition is in compliance with all applicable laws and (ii) if reasonably requested by Savvis, at the expense of KCP or the transferee, she shall have furnished to Savvis an opinion of counsel, reasonably satisfactory to Savvis, to the effect that such transfer may be made without registration under the 1933 Act;

xiv. Legends; Stop Transfer

a. All certificates for the Securities may bear the following or a substantially similar legend:

THE SECURITIES REPRESENTED BY THIS CERTIFICATE MAY NOT BE SOLD, TRANSFERRED, HYPOTHECATED OR OTHERWISE ASSIGNED EXCEPT PURSUANT TO (I) A REGISTRATION STATEMENT RELATING TO THE SECURITIES WHICH IS EFFECTIVE UNDER THE SECURITIES ACT OF 1933, (II) RULE 144 UNDER SUCH ACT, OR (III) AN OPINION OF COUNSEL OR OTHER EVIDENCE SATISFACTORY TO SAVVIS, THAT ANOTHER EXEMPTION FROM THE REGISTRATION REQUIREMENTS OF SUCH ACT IS AVAILABLE.

b. By Savvis. Savvis represents and warrants the following to KCP as of the date this Agreement is entered into:

i. That the execution, delivery and performance of this Agreement have been authorized by all necessary corporate action and that it has requisite right, power and authority to perform this Agreement and to fulfill its duties and obligations to KCP pursuant to this Agreement. Savvis agrees to deliver to KCP, upon execution of this Agreement, certified copies of all corporate resolutions authorizing the execution, delivery and performance of this Agreement;
ii. Savvis is a Delaware corporation duly organized under the laws of the State of Delaware and is in good standing in the State of Delaware;
iii. No consent of any other person or entity is required for execution by Savvis of this Agreement and/or performance under this Agreement;
iv. Neither Savvis nor any of its affiliates have granted any rights pertaining to the subject matter of this Agreement to any party in a manner which would cause Savvis to be in default under any such agreement or which prevents Savvis from honoring its duties and obligations under this Agreement;
v. Neither Savvis nor any of its affiliates is a party or obligor to any agreement that is or could be inconsistent with or is or could be in conflict with the terms and conditions of this Agreement or the duties and obligations due to KCP hereunder;
vi. The Missouri Corporation (as defined in Section 17.a) is the owner of the entire right, title and interest in and to the Savvis House Marks it licenses under this Agreement, and that it has the sole right to grant the license herein;
vii. Savvis's counsel and general counsel shall provide to KCP, on the Naming Rights Effective Date, a legal opinion substantially in the form set forth in Exhibit F;
viii. The authorized capital stock of Savvis consists solely of (i) 250,000,000 shares of Common Stock, $.01 par value per share, of which 92,961,326 shares (as of August 8, 2000) are issued and outstanding on the date hereof, and (ii) 50,000,000 shares of Preferred Stock, par value $.01 per share, of which no shares are issued and outstanding. Except for 11,070,454 shares of Savvis Common Stock (as of August 15, 2000) reserved for issuance pursuant to options currently held by employees of Savvis, there are no outstanding preemptive, conversion or other rights, options, warrants or agreements granted or issued by or binding upon Savvis for the purchase or acquisition of any shares of its capital stock. The Company holds no shares of its capital stock in its treasury;
ix. As of the time such document was filed, all of the most recent documents which Savvis was required to file under the Securities Exchange Act of 1934, including without limitation Form 10-K and Form 10-Qs (the "Disclosure Documents"), all as filed with

the Securities and Exchange Commission ("SEC"): (i) did not contain a misstatement of a material fact or an omission of a material fact required to be stated therein or necessary to make the statements therein not misleading; and (ii) complied in all material respects with the requirements of the 1933 Act or the Securities Exchange Act of 1934, as amended, as the case may be, and the rules and regulations of the SEC promulgated thereunder applicable to such documents. Since the filing of the most recent Form 10-Q, no other document has been required to be filed by Savvis with the SEC which has not been filed;

x. Except as disclosed in the Disclosure Documents, there is no litigation pending or, to the knowledge of Savvis, threatened against Savvis which would have a material adverse effect on its properties, assets or business or which would prevent or hinder the consummation of the transactions contemplated by this Agreement or its obligations thereunder;

xi. All of the shares of Savvis Common Stock to be issued to KCP pursuant to the terms of this Agreement, when issued pursuant to the terms of this Agreement, shall be duly and validly issued, fully paid and non-assessable, without violation of any pre-emptive or dissenters' or similar rights and in full compliance with all applicable securities laws.

c. By Bridge. Bridge represents and warrants the following to KCP as of the date this Agreement is entered into:

i. That the execution, delivery and performance of this Agreement have been authorized by all necessary corporate action and that it has requisite right, power and authority to perform this Agreement and to fulfill its duties and obligations to KCP pursuant to this Agreement;

ii. Bridge is a Missouri corporation duly organized under the laws of the State of Missouri and is in good standing in the State of Missouri;

iii. No consent of any other person or entity is required for execution by Bridge of this Agreement and/or performance under this Agreement;

iv. Neither Bridge nor any of its affiliates has granted any rights pertaining to the subject matter of this Agreement to any party in a manner which would cause Bridge to be in default under any such agreement or which prevents Bridge from honoring its duties and obligations under this Agreement;

v. There is no litigation pending nor is any litigation threatened against Bridge relative to any of the matters which are the subject of this Agreement; and

vi. Neither Bridge nor any of its affiliates has granted any rights to any person or entity that are or could be inconsistent with or are or could be in conflict with the terms and conditions of this Agreement or the duties and obligations due to KCP hereunder.

**11. Not a Lease or License of the Arena.**

This Agreement will not constitute a lease or license of any part of the Arena; rather, it will represent a contractual obligation of KCP to provide to Naming Rights Holder certain advertising benefits.

**12. Force Majeure.**

a. Fire or Other Damage to Arena. If the Arena is damaged by fire, earthquake, act of God, the elements or other casualty or is condemned by an authority exercising the powers of eminent domain or the Arena is transferred in lieu of the exercise of such power so as to render the Arena unusable for its intended purpose at any time during the Term, and KCP reasonably determines that repairs and restoration of the Arena to the size, capacity and permitted use existing prior to the casualty cannot be completed within one year after the damage, then KCP shall have the option, but not the obligation, to repair the damage or loss. In such event, KCP shall notify Naming Rights Holder as to whether KCP shall effect such repair and restoration within thirty (30) days after the casualty. If KCP notifies Naming Rights Holder that KCP is electing not to effect such repairs and restoration, then Naming Rights Holder may elect, upon notice to KCP given within ninety (90) days after the date on of the event, that Naming Rights Holder will effect such repair and restoration provided the terms and conditions respecting such restoration are acceptable to Naming Rights Holder in its sole discretion, in which event this Agreement shall continue in full force and effect. If Naming Rights Holder does not elect to make such repairs and does not, in fact, make such repairs, this Agreement and all licenses granted hereunder shall terminate as of the date of such fire or other casualty and all prepaid license fees and other amounts shall be returned to Naming Rights Holder. If KCP reasonably determines that repairs and restoration of the Arena to the size, capacity and permitted use existing prior to the casualty can be completed within one year after the damage, then KCP shall effect such repairs and restoration and shall complete same within one year from the event. Naming Rights Holder may terminate this Agreement if such repairs or restoration is not completed by the end of such year. All prepaid Naming Fees and other prepaid charges relative to the period from and after termination of this Agreement promptly shall be reimbursed to Naming Rights Holder. The Term of this Agreement shall be extended by the period from the date of the event until such repairs and restoration are complete. In the event this Agreement terminates pursuant to this Section 12.a., then for a period of two years following the termination of this Agreement KCP agrees to afford the Naming Rights Holder at the time of such termination a right of first negotiation with respect to the Naming Rights and Naming Rights

Inventory. KCP agrees to enter into exclusive negotiations with the Naming Rights Holder at the time of termination for a period of thirty days prior to entering into negotiations with any third party regarding the Naming Rights and Naming Rights Inventory. If the parties are unable to reach an agreement prior to the expiration of the 30-day exclusive negotiating period, then KCP shall be free to negotiate with other parties regarding the Naming Rights and Naming Rights Inventory.

b. Other. Except for those circumstances described in Section 12(a) hereof, neither party shall be liable or responsible for any failure to perform its obligations hereunder, which failure is caused or brought about in any manner beyond the control of such party including but not limited to strike, lockout, shutdown, act of God or other work stoppage, NBA, NHL or federal, state, or local government action or inaction (with respect to required approvals), the breakdown or failure of apparatus, equipment, or machinery employed in its supply of said services, any temporary stoppage for the repair, improvement, or enlargement thereof, or any other act or condition beyond its reasonable control, other than such party's inability to perform payment obligations. Subject to Section 12(a) hereof, upon any such event, the affected party's obligations hereunder shall be suspended and the other party shall have no right to terminate this Agreement or to seek damages, provided the affected party acts diligently to effect timely performance of its obligations.

c. Abatement. In the event the Arena is not usable for a period of at least 30 days as a result of the events described under Section 12(a) or Section 12(b), the Term shall be extended for that period of time which the Arena was not usable.

d. Reduction in Naming Fees. If the NHL players strike or the NHL owners lockout the players so that less than 40 regular season home games are played by the St. Louis Blues in the Arena during an NHL season, the Naming Fees due for the Fiscal Period covering that NHL Season shall be reduced by a percentage calculated using the number of regular season games lost (calculated by subtracting the number of regular season games played from 40) divided by the total number of events held during the full Fiscal Period prior to the season in which the games were lost (by way of example, if a strike occurs in the 2001–2002 Fiscal Period, the denominator shall be based on the number of Arena Events held during 2000–2001 Fiscal Period). In the event an NHL players' strike or owners' lockout prior to August 1, 2006, KCP agrees to credit Naming Rights Holder the corresponding amount as calculated pursuant to this paragraph in the Fiscal Period of August 1, 2006—July 31, 2007. In the event that the credit owed to Naming Rights Holder exceeds the Naming Fees due for that Fiscal Period, the credit shall be applied in subsequent Fiscal Periods until credited in full.

If an NBA Franchise elects to play its home games in the Arena during the Term, and if the NBA players strike or if the NBA owners lockout the players so that less than 41 regular season home games are played by that NBA Franchise in the Arena during an NBA season, then the NBA Sum due for the Fiscal Period covering that NBA season shall be reduced by a percentage calculated using the number of regular season games lost (calculated by subtracting the number of regular season games played from 41) divided by the total number of events held during the full year prior to the season in which the games were lost.

**13. Use; Upkeep and Maintenance.**

a. Maintenance. KCP agrees to cause the Arena to be maintained and operated in a good, clean, tenantable and sale repair, order and condition in a manner consistent with that generally applicable at other first-class arenas constructed substantially concurrently with the construction of the Arena.
b. Compliance. KCP shall manage and operate the Arena in compliance with (i) all applicable and material federal, state and local laws, rules, ordinances and regulations (including, without limitation, building and fire codes); and (ii) any other material agreements or obligations imposed by any state or governmental authority with respect to the Arena, its operations, and/or Arena Events.

**14. Indemnification and Reimbursement.**

a. Indemnification By KCP. KCP hereby agrees to protect, defend and indemnify Naming Rights Holder and its respective officers, directors, shareholders, members, partners, agents and employees ("Naming Rights Indemnitees") harmless from and against (i) any and all claims, demands, causes of action, suits and judgments by third parties against the Naming Rights Indemnitees or any of them and (ii) losses, liabilities costs or expenses of any nature whatsoever, including reasonable attorneys' fees and the costs of discovery and expert witness fees incurred by Naming Rights Indemnitees or any of them, as a result of damage, loss or liability suffered by a third party arising directly or indirectly from or out of any acts or omissions by KCP, its officers, directors, agents, partners, subcontractors or employees relating to or arising out of the operation, maintenance and management of the Arena, or acts, omission or any breach of this Agreement by KCP except to the extent attributable to the negligence or willful misconduct of Naming Rights Holder or its respective officers, directors, shareholders, partners, members, agents and employees.
b. Indemnification by Naming Rights Holder. Naming Rights Holder hereby agrees to protect, defend and indemnify KCP and its officers, directors, shareholders, members, partners, agents and employees ("KCP Indemnitees") harmless from and against (i) any and all claims, demands, causes of action, suits and judgments by third parties against

the KCP Indemnitees or any of them and (ii) losses, liabilities costs or expenses of any nature whatsoever, including reasonable attorneys' fees and the costs of discovery and expert witness fees incurred by KCP Indemnitees or any of them, as a result of damage, loss or liability suffered by a third party arising directly or indirectly, from or out of any acts or omissions by Naming Rights Holder, its respective officers, directors, agents, partners, subcontractors or employees relating to the breach by Naming Rights Holder of its obligations hereunder or exercise or utilization by Naming Rights Holder of the rights granted hereunder, except to the extent attributable to the negligence or willful misconduct of KCP or its officers, directors, shareholders, partners, members, agents or employees.

**15. Termination/Remedies.**

a. Failure of Naming Rights Holder to Pay Amounts Due. In the event Naming Rights Holder fails to pay to KCP when due any sum required by this Agreement to be paid and Naming Rights Holder shall fail, for a period of fifteen (15) days following receipt of written notice from KCP specifying such default, to cure such default by payment of the amount due plus interest, compounded daily, at the annual rate of 15% or, if less, the highest rate permitted by law from the date due, then KCP shall have the right to (i) terminate this Agreement upon the expiration of the cure period, (ii) remove immediately the Arena Mark and Arena Graphic Logo from the Naming Rights Inventory, and (iii) assert any and all other remedies which KCP may have pursuant to law or equity, notwithstanding Naming Rights Holder's option to avail itself of the Dispute Resolution procedure set forth in Section 21. KCP acknowledges and agrees that, in order to avoid termination, Naming Rights Holder may notify KCP that it is paying any amounts due "under protest," and Naming Rights Holder shall not waive its right to use the Dispute Resolution procedure in connection with the amounts paid.

b. Failure of NHL or NBA Franchise to Play Home Games in the Arena. In the event that (i) the St. Louis Blues cease to play home games at the Arena for any reason other than a player or officials strike or owner lockout, (ii) no other NHL franchise plays its home games at the Arena, and (iii) no NBA franchise plays its home games at the Arena, then, subject to KCP's right to use the Dispute Resolution Process set forth in Section 21, Naming Rights Holder shall have a period of thirty (30) days, beginning on the date when the last remaining franchise plays its last home game in the Arena or announces that it will no longer play its home games in the Arena, whichever is later, in which to terminate this Agreement. Termination shall be effective upon delivery of notice of termination. If Naming Rights Holder elects to terminate the Agreement pursuant to this Section 15.b, neither party shall have further rights or remedies except for any remedies for a default prior to the date of termination.

c. Default. A party shall be in default hereunder if any of the following events shall occur (each being an "Event of Default"), provided that nothing in this Section 15.c shall limit the termination rights set forth in Sections 15.a, 15.b or 6.c:

   i. Such party fails to perform timely any of its other material obligations hereunder and such default shall continue for a period of thirty (30) days following receipt of written notice from the other party specifying such default. If the default specified in such notice is curable but of a nature such that it cannot be cured through the exercise of reasonable diligence within the thirty (30) day cure period, then such thirty (30) day cure period shall be extended to a period as is reasonable (but in no event more than 180 days subject to delay due to force majeure) to cure such default, provided the non-performing party has proceeded at all times and is continuing to proceed in a diligent and reasonable manner to cure;
   ii. Such party becomes insolvent, or takes the benefit of any present or future insolvency or bankruptcy statue, or makes a general assignment for the benefit of creditors, or files a voluntary petition in bankruptcy or a petition or answer seeking an arrangement, reorganization or readjustment of its indebtedness under the Federal bankruptcy laws or under any other law or statute of the United States or of any State thereof, or consents to the appointment of a receiver, trustee, or liquidator of all or substantially all of its property;
   iii. By court order or decree such party is adjudged bankrupt or an order is made approving a petition filed by any of its creditors or by any of its stockholders or partners, seeking its reorganization or the readjustment of its indebtedness under the Federal bankruptcy laws or under any law or statute of the United States or any state thereof;
   iv. An involuntary petition under any bankruptcy or insolvency law, or an action under present or future insolvency law or statute, is filed against such party and is not dismissed or stayed within 60 days after the filing thereof; or
   v. Such party sells, conveys, assigns or otherwise transfers all or substantially all of its assets.

d. Remedies in the Event of a Default. If either party is in default under Section 15(c) beyond applicable grace or cure periods for an event which constitutes a Major Dispute, then the other party shall be entitled to terminate the Agreement or seek specific performance, and in any event may sue for damages or exercise any remedy available to it in equity including, without limitation, injunctive relief. If either party is in default under Section 15(c) beyond applicable grace or cure periods for an event which constitutes a Minor Dispute, then the other party shall be entitled only to seek monetary relief. The Defaulting Party shall remain subject to the indemnification provisions set forth in Section 14. In any action under this Agreement, neither party shall be liable or responsible under any circumstances for any consequential or punitive damages.

e. Surviving Provisions. In the event of a termination of this Agreement for any reason, the parties agree that all representations and warranties made under this Agreement and the indemnification provisions set forth in Section 14 for any claims, demands, causes of action, suits or judgments by third parties or losses, liabilities, costs or expenses which may arise on or before the effective date of termination.

**16. Entire Agreement.**

This Agreement together with the Exhibits hereto constitutes the entire agreement between the parties and shall become a binding and enforceable Agreement among the parties hereto and their respective successors (including successors and to transferees of the Arena) and permitted assigns upon the Naming Rights Effective Date. No prior verbal or written agreement shall survive the execution of this Agreement. In the event of an alteration of this Agreement, the alteration shall be in writing and shall be signed by both parties in order for the same to be binding upon the parties.

**17. Assignments.**

a. By Naming Rights Holder. Subject to Section 8, this Agreement and the rights and obligations of Naming Rights Holder hereunder may not be assigned without the prior written approval of KCP, which approval may be withheld in the sole discretion of KCP; provided, however, that Savvis may, without the prior written approval of KCP, assign all or any portion of its rights and obligations hereunder to Savvis Communications Corporation, a Missouri corporation which is a wholly-owned subsidiary of Savvis (the "Missouri Corporation"), provided that, in the event of such an assignment, both Savvis and the Missouri Corporation shall be liable for all duties and obligations of Savvis/Naming Rights Holder hereunder.

b. By KCP.

   i. Sale of Arena. In the event KCP proposes to sell the Arena or any interest therein, KCP shall give Naming Rights Holder notice of the name, address phone and telefax numbers and e-mail address of the proposed purchaser, and the proposed closing date reasonably prior to the closing thereof but no less than sixty (60) days' prior to the closing date. KCP shall provide, as a condition to the consummation of such sale, that the purchaser shall expressly assume all obligations of KCP under this Agreement; provided, however, such purchaser shall be deemed to have acquired the Arena subject to this Agreement and to have assumed the obligations of KCP hereunder, provided that no prior approval of Naming Rights Holder or Bridge shall be necessary. All advertising, sponsorship and promotion arrangements and agreements to which such purchaser is a party shall be subordinate to this Agreement and KCP shall ensure that the purchase and sale agreement for the sale of the Arena or any interest therein shall provide for such subordination.

ii. To Affiliated Entity. KCP may assign its rights and obligations under this Agreement or its interest in the restricted stock transferred to KCP pursuant to Section 6.a to any of (i) EPL, LLC; (ii) EPL II, LLC (Paige Sports); (iii) EPL III, LLC; (iv) EPL IV, LLC; (v) Bill Laurie; (vi) Nancy Laurie; (vii) Paige Laurie; (viii) any entity 100% owned or controlled by Bill Laurie, Nancy Laurie or Paige Laurie; or (ix) any other entity whose ownership is identical to that of EPL II, LLC/Paige Sports. Such assignment shall be effective upon giving of notice to the Naming Rights Holder. In no event shall Naming Rights Holder be deprived of the benefits to be provided herein, and Naming Rights Holder shall be in all events be entitled to full credit for the stock delivered under Section 6.c. of this Agreement and all other Fees prepaid under this Agreement.

**18. Notices.**

All notices and other communications hereunder will be in writing and will be deemed given if delivered personally, telecopied (receipt of which is confirmed by the person to whom sent) or mailed by registered or certified mail (return receipt requested) to the parties at the following addresses (or at such other address for a party as will be specified by like notice, or to a substitute party at the address(es) for such substitute party as will be specified by a like notice):

a. If to KCP:

Mark Sauer
President and Chief Executive Officer
St. Louis Blues/Kiel Center
1401 Clark Avenue
St. Louis, Missouri 63103

Richard C. Thomas, President and CEO
Brent P. Karasiuk, COO and General Counsel
Paige Sports Entertainment
609 E. Broadway
Columbia, Missouri 65201

Richard R. Young, Esq.
Holme, Roberts & Owen, LLP
90 S. Cascade Avenue, Suite 1300
Colorado Springs, Colorado 80903-1615

b. If to Naming Rights Holder:

Robert A. McCormick
Chairman and CEO
Savvis Communications Corporation
717 Office Parkway
St. Louis, Missouri 63141

Savvis Communications Corporation
717 Office Parkway
St. Louis, Missouri 63141
Attn: Steven M. Gallant, Esq.
General Counsel

c. If to Bridge:

Bridge Information Systems, Inc.
Attn: CEO
717 Office Parkway
St. Louis, Missouri 63141

Bridge Information Systems, Inc.
Attn: General Counsel
3 World Financial Center
New York, New York 10281

**19. Governing Law:**

This Agreement will be governed by the laws of the State of Missouri without reference to principles of conflicts of laws. Where applicable, this Agreement shall be governed by United States federal trademark and copyright laws.

**20. Confidentiality.**

Each party shall retain in confidence the existence and terms and conditions of this Agreement. No public disclosure of the existence of this Agreement or its terms and conditions shall be made unless such disclosure is approved in advance by KCP and Naming Rights Holder, provided, however, that either party shall have the right to disclose information about this Agreement if required by law. Upon the Naming Rights Effective Date, KCP and Savvis mutually agree that either party or both parties may publicly announce, through press releases or otherwise, that the parties have agreed to rename the Arena the Savvis Center; the terms and conditions of this Agreement shall not be made at such an announcement unless specifically approved in advance by KCP and Savvis.

## 21. Dispute Resolution.

a. Minor Dispute. All Minor Disputes (as defined above) shall be resolved by means of binding arbitration. The parties agree to use reasonable efforts to hold the arbitration within 10 business days of the declaration of a Minor Dispute, but in any event agree to seek to proceed to arbitration as expeditiously as possible. Arbitration shall be conducted in accordance with the Commercial Arbitration Rules of the American Arbitration Association.

   i. A Minor Dispute shall be deemed "declared" when the party declaring such dispute gives Notice (as defined hereinafter) to the other.
   ii. Arbitration shall be held in the City of St. Louis. The arbitrator(s) shall be selected according to the Commerical Arbitration Rules of the American Arbitration Association, it being understood that the parties' preference is to utilize arbitrators knowledgeable in sports business matters.
   iii. The parties shall share the arbitrator(s)' fees, regardless of the outcome of the arbitration.
   iv. Except as may be required by law, neither party nor any arbitrator may disclose the existence, content or results of any arbitration hereunder without the prior written consent of both parties.
   v. Rule R-36 of the January 1, 1999 Commercial Arbitration Rules of the American Arbitration Association shall at all times apply to the provisions of this Agreement.

b. Major Dispute. All Major Disputes (as defined above) shall be mediated by the parties. In the event the parties are unable to resolve the dispute or concern amicably within 60 days of Declaration of a Major Dispute, the parties agree that the matter shall not be subject to arbitration or mediation, and the appropriate remedy, whether at law or in equity, if any, shall be through the courts. The parties agree that jurisdiction and venue for any action to resolve disputes arising under or based upon this Agreement shall be initiated and exclusively prosecuted in the Circuit Court of City of St. Louis, Missouri, except where federal jurisdiction is appropriate, in which case the action shall be initiated exclusively in U.S. District Court in St. Louis, Missouri.
c. Attorneys' Fees and Expenses. In the event of a dispute between the parties, the non-prevailing party in any ensuing litigation shall pay the reasonable attorneys' fees and expenses of the prevailing party (including costs of discovery and expert witness fees.)
d. Major and Minor Disputes Prior to August 1, 2006. The parties acknowledge that Naming Rights Holder shall be entitled to the following remedies in the event that Naming Rights Holder prevails in a Major or Minor Dispute prior to August 1, 2006 and it is determined that Naming Rights Holder is entitled to monetary damages or compensation:

i. Major Dispute. In the event that Naming Rights Holder is awarded monetary damages or compensation in connection with a Major Dispute prior to August 1, 2006, KCP agrees to pay to Naming Rights Holder the amount of monetary damages/compensation awarded. In the event that Naming Rights Holder also elects to terminate this Agreement in connection with such Major Dispute, KCP agrees to pay to Naming Rights Holder the sum of $5,500 for each day from the date of termination through and including July 31, 2006. Naming Rights Holder acknowledges and agrees that, in connection with any payment to be made pursuant to this paragraph, (i) KCP shall not be obligated to return any of the Savvis stock transferred pursuant to Section 6.a; (ii) KCP may repay the amounts due, if KCP so elects in its sole discretion, by transferring shares of Savvis Common Stock issued pursuant to this Agreement to the Naming Rights Holder, in which case KCP shall be credited for the transfer at the closing price of the Savvis stock on the date of the transfer; and (iii) no damages shall be due from KCP to the Naming Rights Holder for any lost profits or lost benefits by virtue of the Agreement being terminated prior to the expiration date.

ii. Minor Dispute. In the event that Naming Rights Holder is awarded monetary damages or compensation in connection with a Minor Dispute prior to August 1, 2006, KCP agrees to credit Naming Rights Holder the amount of the monetary damages/compensation awarded against the amounts owed for the Fiscal Period of August 1, 2006—July 31, 2007, plus interest calculated at eight percent (8%) per annum credited through the date the damages/compensation are/is credited. In the event that the credit owed to Naming Rights Holder exceeds the Naming Fees due for the August 1, 2006—July 31, 2007 Fiscal Period, the credit shall be applied in subsequent Fiscal Periods until credited in full.

**22. Counterparts.**

This Agreement may be executed in counterparts, with signature of each such counterpart being deemed signature to all such counterparts, each of which shall be an original, but all of which together shall constitute one and the same instrument.

**23. No Obligation to Sign Any Players.**

Naming Rights Holder acknowledges and agrees that neither KCP nor the St. Louis Blues can make any representations or warranties as to the success or competitive level of the St. Louis Blues or any other team which may play in the Arena during the Term. Therefore, Naming Rights Holder agrees that the consideration paid pursuant to this Agreement shall in no way be based on, or subject to, the performance of the St. Louis Blues or any other team which may play in the Arena during the Term, nor shall the consideration be based on, or subject to, the St. Louis Blues or any other team which may play in the Arena signing or engaging of any player, coach or general manager, or any other employee or independent contractor.

**24. Number of Events.**

Subject to Naming Rights Holder's rights under Sections 12.d and 15.b, Naming Rights Holder acknowledges and agrees that KCP cannot make any representations or warranties as to the specific number or nature of the Arena Events during the Term, especially as such applies to touring events and concerts. Therefore, Naming Rights Holder agrees that the consideration paid pursuant to this Agreement shall in no way be based on, or subject to, the number and/or nature of the events that may play at the Arena during the Term.

**25. Insurance.**

a. By KCP. KCP shall maintain such insurance as is customarily maintained by owners of comparable facilities. Naming Rights Holder shall be named as an additional insured on such policies, where appropriate.
b. By Naming Rights Holder. Naming Rights Holder agrees to maintain insurance as it deems appropriate. KCP shall be named as an additional insured on such policies, where appropriate.

**26. Miscellaneous.**

a. The term "herein" or "hereunder" mean and shall be deemed to mean "in this Agreement" or "under this Agreement," respectively.
b. No action other than a notice by one party to the other specifically stating that such notice has the effect of waiver, shall constitute a waiver of any particular breach or default of such other party. No such waiver notice from either party shall waive the other party's failure to fully comply with any other term, condition, or provision of this Agreement, irrespective of any knowledge any KCP or Naming Rights Holder officer, employee, or agent may have of any breach or default of, or non-compliance with, such other term, condition, or provision. No waiver of full performance by either party shall be construed, or operate, as a waiver of any subsequent default of any of the terms, covenants and conditions of this Agreement. The payment or acceptance of fees or charges for any period after a default shall not be deemed a waiver of any right or acceptance of defective performance.

c. All remedies available at law or in equity to either party for breach of this Agreement are cumulative and may be exercised concurrently or separately, and the exercise of any one remedy shall not be deemed an election of such remedy to the exclusion of other remedies.
d. If any term or provision of this Agreement, or the application thereof to any person or circumstances, shall to any extent be invalid or unenforceable, the same shall be reduced in scope and coverage to the extent necessary to render the same valid, and, if that is not possible, the remainder of this Agreement, or the application of such term or provision to persons or circumstances other than those as to which it is held invalid or unenforceable, shall not be affected thereby, and each term and provision of this Agreement shall be valid, and be enforced to the fullest extent permitted by law.
e. KCP shall pay all entertainment taxes, personal property taxes, use taxes, and any other taxes or impositions on the rights granted to Naming Rights Holder under this Agreement, provided, however, that nothing in this paragraph shall relieve Naming Rights Holder, Savvis or Bridge from any obligations to pay suiteholder taxes which may be due on a suite rental which is the subject of a separate agreement.
f. Naming Rights Holder will execute, and KCP shall cause its future lenders to execute, a consent and attornment agreement pursuant to which Naming Rights Holder will consent to the assignment of KCP's rights under this Agreement to KCP's future lenders subject to the agreement by such future lenders and their assigns to recognize the rights of Naming Rights Holder hereunder.
g. This Agreement is intended only for the benefit of the parties hereto, the St. Louis Blues and any assigns or substitutes as expressly provided for in this Agreement. No other person or entity is intended to be benefited in any way by this Agreement, nor shall this Agreement be enforceable by any other person or entity.
h. KCP will not modify or terminate nor will KCP permit the modification or termination of the agreement between KCP and the St. Louis Blues attached hereto as Exhibit E.
i. The parties acknowledge that this Agreement and the rights and obligations set forth herein are contingent upon KCP's termination of its existing sponsorship agreement with Southwestern Bell (the "SWB Agreement"). In the event that KCP is unable to procure the termination of the SWB Agreement on or before September 5, 2000, then KCP shall so notify Savvis, and this Agreement shall immediately be null and void. Failure by KCP to provide such notice of termination on or before September 5, 2000 shall be deemed a failure to procure the termination of the SWB Agreement.
j. The paragraph headings in this Agreement are for convenience only and shall not be used in the interpretation nor considered part of this Agreement.

**In Witness Whereof**, the undersigned have caused this Agreement to be duly executed as of the date first above written.

THIS AGREEMENT CONTAINS A BINDING ARBITRATION PROVISION WHICH MAY BE ENFORCED BY THE PARTIES.

KIEL CENTER PARTNERS, L.P.

By: NWL, LLC, General Partner

By:/s/Richard C. Thomas

- - - - - - - - - - - - - - - - - -

Name: Richard C. Thomas
Title: President and Manager

SAVVIS COMMUNICATIONS CORPORATION

By:/s/Robert A. McCormick

- - - - - - - - - - - - - - - - - -

Name: Robert A. McCormick
Title: Chairman and CEO

For purposes of acknowledging any and all of its rights, obligations and agreements under the foregoing Agreement:

BRIDGE INFORMATION SYSTEMS, INC.

By:/s/Thomas M. Wendel

- - - - - - - - - - - - - - - - - -

Name: Thomas M. Wendel
Title: CEO

For purposes of acknowledging any and all of its rights, obligations and agreements under the foregoing Agreement:

SAVVIS COMMUNICATIONS CORPORATION, a Missouri Corporation

By:/s/Steven M. Gallant

- - - - - - - - - - - - - - - - - -

Name: Steven M. Gallant
Title: Vice President and General Counsel

# Chapter 10
# Sports Stadia Concession Agreements

## 10.1 Introductory Remarks

In addition to granting Naming Rights in respect of a sports stadium or arena (venue), sports clubs often grant various 'concessions', also known as 'franchises' (not to be confused with the American meaning and usage of the term to indicate ownership of sports teams), to third parties to provide various products and services at the venue. These arrangements also bring in a welcome income stream and have the further advantage, in the case, for example, of the provision of food and beverages (known as Pouring/Pourage Rights) of being more cost-effective and providing on top a profit for the club concerned, which would otherwise have to operate the concession/ franchise itself, possibly at a loss.

Clearly the commercial and financial arrangements need to be negotiated and agreed between the club and the concessionaire/franchisee and reflected in a well-drafted corresponding Pourage/Concession Agreement.

In this chapter, we will look at the main provisions that need to be included in Sports Pourage and Concession Agreements and in the Appendices we will provide a General Precedent of each of these Agreements.

## 10.2 Sports Pourage and Concession Agreements

As usual, perhaps the most important clause is the 'grant of rights' clause in which the rights granted need to be clearly defined, including the products, the duration of the rights granted (term) and whether the rights are exclusive or non-exclusive. Notice, in particular, the provisions of the Exclusions Clause (4). This provision is designed to deal with any instances of 'conflict marketing' that may arise at the venue as a result of the rights granted under the particular Agreement and under other Pourage and Concession Agreements entered into by the sports club concerned.

I. S. Blackshaw, *Sports Marketing Agreements: Legal, Fiscal and Practical Aspects*, ASSER International Sports Law Series, DOI: 10.1007/978-90-6704-793-7_10,

Again, where the stadium or arena is used for various sporting—and, indeed, other—events, the events for which the pourage rights are granted need to be clearly stated in the Agreement. In those cases, where the stadium or arena is a multi-purpose one and where pourage rights are granted to different parties, even competitors of one another, for different events, each concessionaire will require a so-called ‘clean’ stadium or arena, that is, one that does not contain any competitors’ advertising and signage when being used for the event in respect of which the concessionaire concerned has been granted the pourage rights, which, as will be seen from the Precedent, also include advertising and signage rights. In connection with the advertising and signage rights granted, as usual, the Agreement will contain the standard warranty that the signage will not be obscene blasphemous or defamatory of any third party and shall not infringe their intellectual property rights of any kind. This warranty clause is supplemented by an indemnity clause in which the concessionaire undertakes to indemnify and keep indemnified the sports club concerned against any and all breaches by the concessionaire of any and all of its warranties.

Of course, pourage rights are a form of sports sponsorship and, as such, care needs to be taken in the drafting of the Pourage Agreements where multiple pourage rights are involved, to avoid any and all possibilities of ‘conflict marketing’ so that all the concessionaires are kept happy! In other words, the Agreements need to reflect the various sports marketing arrangements that have been entered into by the sports club concerned in respect of the sports stadium or arena and need to hang together and interconnect.

Notice, finally, that the Sports Pourage Agreement contains a ‘right of first refusal’ clause (called in the Precedent a ‘Rights of First Negotiation’ clause) in favour of the concessionaire to renew the Agreement on certain specified terms and conditions. Notice also that the sports club will not enter into negotiations with, make an offer to nor conclude any agreement with anyone else until the expiration of the ‘negotiation period’ as defined in the clause.

As far as the Concession Agreement is concerned, the example given in the General Precedent grants rights at the sports stadium to supply ‘takeaway’ meals to the spectators and also includes the necessary rights of access to and egress from the stadium, as well as the right to bring and maintain equipment into the stadium for the purposes of exercising the rights granted by the Agreement. As a result of these latter rights, corresponding obligations are also included in the Agreement.

## 10.3 General Precedents of Sports Pourage and Concession Agreements

General Precedents of Sports Pourage and Concession Agreements are included in Appendices 1 and 2 (10.5.1 and 10.5.2) to this chapter. As always, these Precedents are for general information and guidance purposes only and should be adapted to suit the particular facts and circumstances of each case.

## 10.4 Concluding Remarks

Once again, these particular kinds of Sports Marketing Agreements need to be carefully and clearly drafted and, where multiple parties are involved, potential 'conflict marketing' situations need to be avoided by inclusion in the Agreements concerned of appropriate provisions.

The General Precedents provided need to be used as a checklist of the kinds of matters and provisions that may need to be included in the Agreements, depending, of course, upon the particular facts and circumstances of each case.

## 10.5 Appendices

### *10.5.1 Appendix 1*

**Sports Pourage Agreement**

**This Agreement** is made the day of 2[ ]

**Between**

(1) [ ] (CRN [ ] whose registered office is at
[ ] ["the Club"] and
(2) [ ](CRN [ ] whose registered office is at
[ ] ["the Advertiser"]

**Recital**

A. The Club is the operator of the Venue
B. The Advertiser wishes to supply to the Club the Advertisers' Products at the Venue upon the terms of this Agreement

**Operative Provisions**

1. **Definitions**

1.1 In this Agreement the following expressions shall have the following meanings "Advertiser's Products" [the products being promoted e.g. "Fizzy Diet Fizzy caffeine free Fizzy etc."]
"Events" [the Events in respect of which sponsorship rights are granted]
"Products" [the generic products e.g. "soft drinks whether in canned or bottled form or in the form of syrups or powders etc."]
"Venue" means the sports stadium known as [ ] at [ ]

2. **Payments**

2.1 In consideration of the rights and benefits granted to the Advertiser by the Club as set out in this Agreement the Advertiser shall pay to the Club the sum of £[ ] plus VAT per annum for the duration of this agreement payable upon presentation of an appropriate VAT invoice by the Club as follows

2.1.1 £[ ] plus VAT on the date hereof and
2.1.2 £[ ] plus VAT on the date one (1) calendar year following the date hereof and
2.1.3 £[ ] plus VAT on the date two (2) calendar years following the date hereof

## 3. Club's Obligations

3.1 The Club

3.1.1 will purchase solely from the Advertiser such of the Advertiser's Products as the Club sees fit such that the Advertiser's Products are served (on a non-exclusive basis) in any and all food and beverage locations from time to time situated by the Club at its absolute discretion in and around the Venue where Events are held

3.1.2 grants to the Advertiser those pourage rights product marketing (excluding sales) advertising and promotional rights at all Events set out in and upon the terms of this Agreement

## 4. Exclusions

4.1 Nothing in this Agreement shall prevent or restrict the Club from

4.1.1 observing and complying with the rules and regulations of any of [ ] and any other governing body of [the sport] having power to issue regulations or directives with which the Club must comply for any reason and/or abiding by the terms of entry and/or sponsorship of any tournament league or competition in which the Club at any time may participate whilst this Agreement is in force (a "Club Competition") and/or any contractual arrangements pursuant to which the Venue is used by any person firm or company for any purpose not being that of a Club Competition AND FOR THE AVOIDANCE OF DOUBT in the event that any such condition or term of entry and/or sponsorship and/or any such regulation or directive of any governing body and/or any such contractual arrangements shall conflict with any obligation arising hereunder then that condition or term of sponsorship and/or regulation or directive and/or contractual arrangements shall prevail over the conflicting obligation arising hereunder and no failure by the Club to comply with such an obligation arising hereunder shall be construed as or have the effect of being any breach of this Agreement but rather the effect of the conflicting obligation arising pursuant to this Agreement shall be deemed to be suspended throughout any period for which such conflict exists

4.1.2 from serving or offering for sale [any potentially rival product having sponsorship rights granted by the Club or incumbent upon the Club] or

4.1.3 from continuing the operation of any vending machines or other equipment belonging to or operated by or on behalf of any other Product manufacturer PROVIDED ALWAYS that advertising for any other Product shall be displayed at the site of such vending machine only

## 5. Signage

5.1 The Advertiser shall be entitled to erect signage of a nature and quality acceptable to the Club at its own expense (both of construction and erection) such signs to be of a number to be mutually agreed from time to time between the parties and to be displayed at each and all of those outlets at which the Advertiser's Products are exposed for sale from time to time at the Venue

5.2 The Advertiser's said signage shall not be physically or electronically removed replaced or covered up by any means save where the Venue is being used for functions or purposes other than the Events

5.3 In the event that the Club reasonably objects to the nature of any signage erected by the Advertiser pursuant to its rights granted in this Agreement the Advertiser shall forthwith at its own expense remove the said signage and (if it so wishes) replace the same with such signage as is reasonably acceptable to the Club

## 6. Display Of Products

6.1 The Advertiser's Products shall be prominently displayed at each and all of those outlets of the Venue at which the Advertiser's Products are exposed for sale from time to time in a manner and to an extent to be mutually agreed from time to time between the parties

## 7. Maintenance

7.1 Those signs and panels advertising or promoting the Advertiser's Products at the Venue which are constructed in a manner enabling them to be illuminated shall be illuminated at all Events. The Advertiser shall have the right of access to the Venue at reasonable times by prior arrangement with the Club to its permanent signage for the purpose of such replacement modification or removal of such signage as may be mutually agreed from time to time between the parties. The Advertiser will be solely responsible for the insurance and general maintenance (in each case to the reasonable satisfaction of the Club and in relation to insurance such insurance to include insurance against all reasonable third party risks and consequential damages as may prudently be insured against by any reasonable business) of the said signs and panels throughout the duration of this Agreement. The Club shall pay all electrical and other normal operation costs of the said signs and panels throughout the duration of this Agreement save where expressly agreed otherwise

## 8. Containers

8.1 All cups and containers dispensed at any outlets in the Venue at which the Advertiser's Products are exposed for sale from time to time which are to be used to hold the Advertiser's Products shall be trade mark cups and containers approved by the Advertiser and which prominently bear the exclusive trade marks of the Advertiser (the "Advertiser's Containers"). The price paid for the Advertiser's Containers shall be mutually agreed from time to time between the Advertiser and the Club

**9. Promotion Rights**

9.1 Subject to the Club's reasonable prior written approval the Advertiser shall have the right throughout the duration of this Agreement to conduct consumer promotions related to the Products at the Venue during not more than ten (10) Events. All fees and expenses related to such promotions shall be paid by the Advertiser. The nature of such promotions their duration content and scheduled dates and times for commencement and conclusion shall be consistent with usual promotions permitted by the Club and shall be agreed in advance of any such promotion in writing between the Advertiser and the Club. The Club shall extend its reasonable and agreed cooperation to the Advertiser in the conduct and staging of such promotions

**10. Duration**

10.1 This Agreement shall commence upon the date hereof and shall terminate on the date [ ] calendar years thereafter unless otherwise terminated pursuant to clause 10 hereof

**11. Termination**

11.1 Either party may terminate this Agreement upon [ ] business days' notice by service upon the other at the other's principal place of business of notice in writing either by facsimile or by first class post in the event that

11.1.1 the other party has committed any persistent material or fundamental breach of any of its obligations hereunder provided that if the breach is capable of remedy such notice shall only be given if the party in breach shall not have remedied the said breach within two (2) weeks of receipt of notice in writing specifying the breach and requiring it to be remedied or

11.1.2 the other ceases to carry on business has a receiver or administrator appointed over all or any part of its assets or undertaking enters into any composition or arrangement with its creditors or enters into liquidation (other than for the purposes of amalgamation or reconstruction)

11.2 No failure to terminate this Agreement or to exercise any rights hereunder shall operate or be construed as a waiver of such rights and any such termination shall be entirely without prejudice to any and all rights having accrued to either party hereunder

**12. Advertiser's Warranty**

12.1 The Advertiser hereby warrants that any and all signage erected by the Advertiser pursuant to its rights granted by this Agreement shall not be obscene blasphemous or defamatory of any person firm or company and shall not infringe any rights of intellectual property of any nature belonging to any person firm or company

12.2 The Advertiser hereby covenants that it will fully and effectively indemnify and keep indemnified the Club against any claims damage or loss howsoever arising (including but not limited to any indirect or consequential damage) howsoever arising to the Club as a result of breach by the Advertiser of the warranties set out at clause 12.1

**13. Rights Of First Negotiation**

13.1 For a period of [ ] weeks commencing [ ] weeks and concluding [ ] weeks prior to the expiration of this Agreement ("the Negotiation Period") the Advertiser will have the exclusive right to enter into negotiations with the Club with a view to renew this Agreement for a further three (3) year period upon such terms as may be negotiated always provided that nothing in this clause shall be construed as or have the effect of obliging the parties so to renew this Agreement

13.2 The Club shall not enter into any negotiations or make any offer or agreement to or with any person firm or company in relation to the grant of rights to sell or provide Products at the Venue by way of substitution for the Advertiser until expiry of the Negotiation Period

**14. Miscellaneous**

14.1 Boilerplate Clauses]

As witness the hands of the duly authorised representatives of the parties

[Execution Clauses]

## *10.5.2 Appendix 2*

**Sports Pourage Agreement**

**This Agreement** is made the day of 2[ ]

**Between**

(1) [ ] [ ] whose registered office is at [ ] ["the Club"] and
(2) [ ] [ ] whose registered office is at [ ] ["the Licensee"]

**Recitals**

A. The Club is the operator of the Venue of which the Licensed Area forms part
B. The Licensee wishes to sell hot takeaway foods from the Licensed Area upon the terms of this Agreement

**Operative Provisions**

1. **Definitions**

1.1 In this Agreement the following expressions shall have the following meanings

"Access Ways" means the entrance hall corridors lobbies staircases access ways passages lifts and escalators of the Venue or over which the Venue enjoys rights of access the use of which is necessary for obtaining access to and egress from the Licensed Area or such of them as afford reasonable access and egress both for goods and for personnel as above as the Club may from time to time in its absolute discretion designate by the service of not less than twenty-eight (28) days' written notice to the Licensee

"Designated Hours" means [am] to [pm] on Mondays to Fridays [ am] to [ pm] on Saturdays inclusive (Bank or other Public Holidays excepted) or such other hours including time on Sundays as the Club may from time to time in its absolute discretion determine by service of not less than twenty-eight (28) days' written notice to the Licensee together with that period (if not included in the above) commencing two (2) hours before the commencement of and ending two (2) hours following the end of any and all Events

"Equipment" means those items of equipment set out at the Schedule annexed hereto

"Events" means any and all competitive first team matches taking place at the Venue (in any competition of whatever nature) in which the Club participates throughout the duration of this Agreement

"Licensed Area" means the area shown for the purposes of identification only edged and hatched yellow on the plan annexed or such other single continuous area of appropriate space for the Licensee's Business of the same or greater total area within the Venue as the Club may from time to time in its absolute discretion designate by the service of not less than twenty-eight (28) days' written notice to the Licensee

"Licence Fee" means One pound per annum payable on the date hereof and thereafter annually upon each anniversary of the date hereof

"Office" means that office area with secure locking door and cupboard space for the purpose of identification only edged blue on the plan annexed hereto

"Venue" means the sports stadium known as [ ] at [ ]

**2. Licence**

2.1 Subject to clauses 3 and 5 and in consideration of the Licence Fee the Club hereby grants to the Licensee the right (in common with the Club and all others authorised by the Club so far as is not inconsistent with the rights granted hereunder to the Licensee) to use for the duration of this Agreement during the Designated Hours:

2.1.1 for the purpose of the sale to all invitees to the Venue of the Licensee's hot takeaway foods the Licensed Area

2.1.2 for the purpose of ordinary clerical and accounts work solely connected with the Licensee's business at the Venue the Office

2.1.3 for the purposes of access to and egress from the Licensed Area the Access Ways

2.1.4 reasonable access in common with the employees of the Club to such of the amenity and toilet areas provided at the Venue for the employees of the Club as the Club may from time to time reasonably designate by the service of not less than twenty-eight (28) days' written notice to the Licensee

2.2 The Licensee shall be entitled to erect signage of a nature and quality acceptable to the Club at its own expense (both of construction and erection) such signs to be of a number to be mutually agreed from time to time between the parties and to be displayed at those places in the Licensed Area as the parties may from time to time agree

2.3 Subject to the Club's reasonable prior written approval the Licensee shall have the right throughout the duration of this Agreement to conduct consumer promotions related to the Licensee's Goods at the Venue during not more than ten (10) Events. All fees and expenses related to such promotions shall be paid by the Licensee. The nature of such promotions their duration content and scheduled dates and times for commencement and conclusion shall be consistent with usual promotions permitted by the Club and shall be agreed between the Licensee and the Club. The Club shall extend its reasonable cooperation to the Licensee in the conduct and staging of such promotions

## 3. Licensee's Undertakings

3.1 The Licensee agrees and undertakes

3.1.1 to pay to the Club:

3.1.1.1 the Licence Fee (together with any VAT) in advance at the date provided therefor

3.1.1.2 a sum equal to [ ]% of the gross turnover in the Licensee's trading in the Licensed Area such payments to be made in respect of each calendar month's trading in the Licensed Area within [ ] days of the end of the said calendar month together with any VAT payable thereon

3.1.1.3 those sums required to be paid by the Licensee pursuant to the provisions of clause 4

3.1.2 not to bring any furniture equipment goods or chattels into the Venue without the consent of the Club save as may be strictly necessary for the proper exercise of the rights given in clause 2 or in order to carry out the Licensee's obligations hereunder

3.1.3 to keep the Licensed Area and the Office clean and tidy and clear of rubbish at all times and to leave the same in a clean and tidy condition and in good serviceable and decorative repair and free of the Licensee's furniture equipment goods and chattels upon termination of this Agreement for any reason

3.1.4 to maintain at the Licensed Area an attractive display of goods in keeping with the standards maintained elsewhere in the Venue

3.1.5 not to obstruct the Access Ways or cause the same to become dirty or untidy nor to leave any rubbish on them

3.1.6 not to display any signs notices or promotional materials at the Licensed Area save those specifically authorised in this Agreement without the prior consent of a properly authorised employee of the Club and for the purposes of this clause the Catering Manager from time to time of the Venue employed by the Club shall be deemed properly authorised

3.1.7 not to use the Licensed Area the Office or Access Ways in such a way as to cause a nuisance damage disturbance annoyance inconvenience or interference of any nature (including but not limited to noise and smell) to the Club or Venue or any other Licensee or occupant or user of the Venue or adjoining or neighbouring property or to the owners occupiers or users of such adjoining or neighbouring property

3.1.8 to comply with any and all instructions given by the Club in relation to hygiene and food safety and in any event to operate the highest standards of cleanliness and hygiene at all times in the Licensed Area

3.1.9 not to commit any act omission matter or thing which would or might constitute a breach of any statutory requirement affecting the Licensed Area and/or the Office and/or the Venue or which would or might vitiate in whole or in part any insurance effected in respect of the Venue from time to time

3.1.10 to observe any and all reasonable rules and regulations as the Club may make and of which the Club shall notify the Licensee from time to time in writing governing the Licensee's use of the Licensed Area and/or the Office and/or the Access Ways

3.1.11 not to impede in any way the Club or its officers servants or agents in the exercise of the Club's rights of possession and control of the Venue and every part of the Venue

3.1.12 to keep the Licensed Area fully and properly staffed during the Designated Hours

3.1.13 to keep full and adequate records of all business conducted within the Licensed Area and upon reasonable notice to afford the Club suitable facilities and information (including but not limited to the right to inspect the said records on reasonable notice) to assess the Licensee's turnover for the purpose of calculating the payment referred to in clause 3.1.2 of this Agreement

3.1.14 to indemnify the Club and keep the Club fully and effectively indemnified against any and all losses claims demands actions proceedings damages costs or expenses or other liability arising in any way from this Licence any breach of the Licensee's undertakings contained in this clause or the exercise or purported exercise of any of the rights given in clause 2 by the Licensee and or invitee or customer of the Licensee

3.1.15 to use the Equipment only for the purpose for which it is designed and in accordance with any instructions issued by the Club from time to time and to indemnify the Club against any loss or damage to the Equipment

## 4. Club's Undertakings

4.1 The Club agrees and undertakes

4.1.1 to provide reasonable space at the Club's discretion:

4.1.1.1 within the storeroom which forms part of the Venue for storage of the Licensee's goods and

4.1.1.2 at the entrance to the Venue for such of the Licensee's advertisements and signage as the Club may from time to time agree with the Licensee

4.1.2 to provide all services of power reasonably required for the Licensee's business at the Licensed Area and fax and telephone lines for use by the Licensee only at the Licensed Area always provided that the Licensee shall be responsible for any and all charges in relation to the use of any facilities provided pursuant to this sub-clause 4.2

4.1.3 not to permit any of the Licensee's goods to be sold within the Venue save by the Licensee's personnel at the Licensee's cash register at the Licensed Area

4.1.4 to instruct the Club's cleaners to clean the Licensed Area to the same standard as the remainder of the Venue as part of the Club's cleaning schedule and at no cost to the Licensee

4.1.5 to provide and maintain in full and effective working order in the Licensed Area the Equipment for the Licensee's exclusive use always provided that the Licensee shall pay the Club's reasonable charges in connection with all such maintenance and the full costs of any repair or replacements (fair wear and tear excepted) to the said Equipment required as a result of the Licensee's use thereof

4.1.6 not to grant any rights of a similar nature to those granted to the Licensee hereunder to any person firm or company which in the reasonable opinion of the Licensee operates any business directly competing with the business of the Licensee to be operated from the Licensed Area

## 5. General

5.1 The rights granted in clause 2 shall determine (without prejudice to the Club's other rights in respect of any breach of the undertakings contained in clause 3)

5.1.1 immediately on written notice given by the Club at any time following any breach by the Licensee of its undertakings contained in clause 3 provided that if the breach is capable of remedy such notice shall only be given if the Licensee shall not have remedied the said breach within two (2) weeks of receipt of notice in writing specifying the breach and requiring it to be remedied

5.1.2 on not less than six (6) months written notice given either by the Club or the Licensee to the other to expire at any time

5.2 Forthwith upon termination of this Agreement for any reason the Licensee shall vacate the Licensed Area the Office and the Venue and shall remove any and all signage advertising and promotional materials furniture equipment goods and chattels belonging to the Licensee from the Licensed Area the Office and the Venue

5.3 The benefit of this License is personal to the Licensee and not assignable and the rights given in clause 2 may only be exercised by the Licensee and its employees duly authorised independent contractors and customers

5.4 The Club gives no warranty that the Venue is legally or physically fit for the purposes specified in clause 2

5.5 The Club shall not be liable for the death of or injury to any employees independent contractors or customers of the Licensee save only such as may be caused solely by the Club's negligence or for damage to any property of the Licensee or for any losses claims demands actions proceedings damages costs or expenses or other liability howsoever incurred by the Licensee or any person referred to in clause 5.3 in the exercise or purported exercise of the rights granted by clause 2

5.6 [Boilerplate Clauses]

[Execution Clauses]

SCHEDULE 1

Equipment: [list]

# Chapter 11
# Sports Licensing and Merchandising Agreements

## 11.1 Introductory Remarks

Sports Licensing and Merchandising Agreements are an important part of the sports marketing mix and command high returns for the rights owners (licensors) and concessionaires (licensees) alike.

But licensing in general is a specialised business and sports licensing presents its own particular challenges and traps for the unwary. Getting it right brings attractive financial rewards—getting it wrong can result in financial losses and ruin.[1]

Sports Licensing and Merchandising Programmes offer a wide range of commercial opportunities including:

- Sports event and team logos and emblems ('logo licensing');
- Sports event and team 'mascots' ('character licensing');
- Sports stars licensing ('personality licensing'); and
- Sports clothing and footwear licensing ('product licensing')

We will now summarise the main legal, commercial and practical issues involved in concluding Sports Licensing and Merchandising Agreements.

### *11.1.1 Contractual Issues*

The terms and conditions of the licensing deal need to be well defined and incorporated into a clear and unambiguous Licence Agreement. A 'back of the envelope' approach will not do! Even worse are oral agreements, which Sam

[1] See 'Licence to thrill' by I. Blackshaw in 5 *Sports and Character Licensing* 2000 at pp. 6–8.

I. S. Blackshaw, *Sports Marketing Agreements: Legal, Fiscal and Practical Aspects*, ASSER International Sports Law Series, DOI: 10.1007/978-90-6704-793-7_11,

Goldwyn, of Metro Goldwyn Mayer fame, once said are "not worth the paper they are written on!" Badly drafted Agreements lead to uncertainties and misunderstandings, which, in turn, lead to disputes, which can and often do prove costly in terms of time and money for all parties concerned.

The need for a well-drafted Agreement cannot be overstated and repays all the effort, time and money involved in producing one.

So, let us take a look at the main provisions that need to be included in a Sports Licensing and Merchandising Agreement.

Perhaps the most important one is the so-called 'grant of rights' clause. This clause defines the nature and the scope of the rights granted by the licensor to the licensee in relation to the particular sports event. This clause will specify whether the licence granted is an *exclusive* or *non-exclusive* one. It will also define the 'licensed products' to be included in the licence, as well as the 'distribution channels' through which they may be sold. We will return to this subject, which has important commercial and financial consequences later.

The 'grant of rights' clause will also specify the territories in which the products may be sold, as well as the *term* during which the licence will operate. It will often include other restrictions on the use of the *licensed products*, for example, as *premiums*, give-aways or other sales promotional items. It should be noted, *en passant*, that restrictive clauses, such as these and, indeed, any others, could give rise to competition law issues, especially at the EU level under Articles 101 and 102 of the Treaty on the Functioning of the European Union (FEU). This is a complex subject and needs a specific presentation, or even an entire Conference, to do justice to it. However, to underline its importance, suffice to say that Licensing Agreements have received a great deal of attention from the EU Competition Authorities over many years and that breaches of the EU Competition Rules can result in substantial fines—up to 10% of the world-wide group turnover of the offending party!

In defining the rights to be granted by the licensor to the licensee, particular attention needs to be paid to the legal nature and status of those rights. In other words, what 'intellectual property rights' are involved? Also, the Licence Agreement needs to deal specifically with internet and other electronic rights whether or not they are included. We will also return to both these important matters later.

As the rights being granted relate to a particular sports event, there will also be a specific prohibition against using or permitting the rights from being used in any manner contrary to public morals, or which compromise or reflect unfavourably on the good name, good will and reputation of the sports body concerned, its event or its sport. Likewise, the grant or rights will be made subject to the rules of the sports body concerned, for example, in the case of an Olympics Merchandising Programme, the Olympic Charter. If the Licence Agreement is an exclusive one—in other words, only the licensee (not even the licensor) may exploit the licence products in a particular geographical territory during the term of the Agreement—it is usual to impose a minimum annual sales performance on the licensee, in order to maximise the financial returns from the licence. If the sales of the licensed products do not reach the specified minimum, it is open to the licensor to terminate the Licence Agreement.

Combined with such a performance clause is an express undertaking by the licensee to "actively stimulate the demand for and promote the sale of the licensed products within the territory during the term".

In settling the precise terms of the performance requirement, the licensor and licensee should agree on realistic targets. Otherwise, there will be problems of enforcement and viability of the Licence.

A 'performance clause' also has intellectual property implications; likewise do quality control provisions in the Agreement, both of which I shall go into in more detail later. An equally important provision in any Licence Agreement is the 'consideration clause'—the financial *quid pro quo* for the licence. We will deal with this particular matter in more detail later, as well as payment terms and special financial considerations that need to be taken into account in the case of cross-border Licence Agreements.

Sports Licensing and Merchandising Agreements, like other Licence Agreements, are often entered into on a personal basis—in the sense of the personal characteristics, for example, technical competence and financial standing of the licensee (a so-called contract '*intuitu personae*'). Accordingly, the Agreement should be expressly stated to be a contract that can be terminated in the event that such personal characteristics cease to exist. For example, this can occur on a change of ownership or control of the licensee, rendering perhaps the new owner of the licence unsuitable.

It is also usual not to allow any assignment or sub-licence of the licence outside the licensee's corporate group, which needs to be defined, without prior written approval. In such cases, licensees will often require the inclusion of wording, where not legally implied, to the effect that such consent is not to be unreasonably withheld or delayed.

Furthermore, it is also usual to include a general clause to the effect that the Agreement does not constitute or create a partnership, joint venture or franchise; that no party is the agent, employee or servant of the other party; and that the parties act towards one another at all times under and for all purposes of the Agreement as independent contractors.

*Termination* provisions should also be included in the Sports Licensing Agreement. The grounds for termination, by either party, and the practical consequences should be clearly stated. It is usual to make a distinction between a 'minor' breach and a 'major' one. In the case of the former, the party in breach is usually given an opportunity of remedying the breach within a specified period of time (e.g. 15 days); whereas, in the latter case, the Licence Agreement can be terminated forthwith, that is, without notice. Where notice periods are specified in 'days', the Agreement should define whether 'days' are 'natural days' or 'working' ones. Likewise, in the case of 'months', these should be defined as 'lunar' or 'calendar'.

The legal and practical consequences of termination or expiration of the licence should be particularly spelled out.in the Agreement in the case of Sports Licences.

Sports events are often cyclical—the World Cup, for example, takes place every four years—and the circulation of out-of-date merchandise can cause commercial confusion and loss of value. It is usual, therefore, to include a provision in the Licence Agreement requiring the licensee to clear the market of licensed products within, say, six months of termination/expiration, after which any remaining stocks should be destroyed.

Related to termination and for other relevant purposes, the Agreement should also include a *Notice Clause*, under which there is a requirement for all Notices to be given in writing and, in this latter respect, whether Notices can be validly given by fax and e-mail and, if so, when Notice is deemed to have been given and received.

*Rights of first refusal and option clauses* are characteristically found in Sports Marketing Agreements, including Sports Licensing and Merchandising Agreements. Options to renew need to be drafted carefully, otherwise they could become perpetual options, if worded loosely (for example: "The Licensee may renew this Agreement for a further period of [two years] on the same terms and conditions…."). To avoid this outcome, include the words: "with the exception of this present clause." Again, in Sports Marketing Agreements, options to renew are often accompanied by so-called 'matching option' clauses. Likewise these clauses need to be precisely worded to avoid ambiguity and uncertainty rendering them legally void. Also, options to renew and matching options may also raise National and EU Competition Law issues, where they are granted for long periods of time and restrict access of other possible licensees from entering the 'relevant market' for sports licensing and merchandising in relation to a particular sports event. See further on this topic in Chap. 16.

Another important and sensitive area is *confidentiality*. Sports Bodies, as with other kinds of organisations and businesses, like to control the dissemination of confidential information relating to their activities, especially their financial and commercial ones. Accordingly, it is usual to include appropriate provisions on keeping the terms of the Licence Agreement strictly confidential, especially financial details, and also controlling the issue and contents of press releases concerning the licensing deal. See further on this topic in Chap. 5.

### *11.1.2 Intellectual Property Issues*

Before granting or taking a Sports Licensing and Merchandising Agreement, the legal nature and status of the rights being granted need to be considered. Are the rights concerned intellectual property rights and, therefore, protected by Law? Perhaps the most important one in relation to sports marketing is trademarks. The UK Trade Marks Act of 1994 defines a trademark in section 1(1) in very wide terms as follows:

> "… any sign capable of being represented graphically which is capable of distinguishing goods or services of one undertaking from those of other undertakings. A trade mark may,

> in particular, consist of words (including personal names), designs, letters, numerals or the shape of goods or their packaging."

Thus, a trademark could be granted in respect of a particular colour, style of packaging and 'get up' of goods (also known as 'trade dress'). The basic requirement in all cases is distinctiveness.[2]

Perhaps the most distinctive and recognized sports event mark in the world are the five interconnected rings in blue, yellow, black, green and red symbolizing the world-wide reach of the Olympic Movement and the Olympic Games—often referred to as the 'greatest sporting show on Earth!'. The Olympic Rings enjoy special legal protection at the international and national levels around the world. At the international level, they are protected by the so-called 'Nairobi Agreement'—the Agreement on the Protection of the Olympic Symbol of 1981. At the national level in the UK, the Rings are protected under the provisions of the London Olympic Games and Paralympic Games Act of 2006.

Most Sports Licence Agreements are related to particular sports events and involve the use of the particular 'logos' for those events. Essentially, sports logos are designs used for identifying and promoting particular sports and sports events. They often incorporate the name of the particular sports event in distinctive lettering as part of the design.

Insofar as they are original and distinctive, they are registrable as 'device marks' under Trade Mark Law. A prospective licensee will need to check, therefore, whether the sports logo has been registered as a trade mark, or if not, whether an application for registration has been filed at the Trade Marks Registry—or indeed whether the logo is legally registrable at all. If the logo has been registered as a Trade Mark, any unauthorised (i.e. unlicensed) use can be legally prevented. This will affect the value of the Licence.

Sports logos can also benefit from protection as an 'artistic work' under Copyright Law—irrespective of artisitic merit! See section 4(1) (a) of the UK Copyright Designs and Patents Act of 1988. Again, the legal status needs to be checked, because, if the logo does not enjoy trade mark or copyright protection, generally speaking, anybody can use it and the Licence is worthless.

The prospective licensee will need to check in which countries trade mark protection has been obtained - trade mark rights are territorial in nature—and also

[2] On the subject of trade mark registration and protection generally, see the article, entitled '*Trademark protection issues—why register*?' 1999 1 Sports and Character Licensing at p. 26. As to the value of the goodwill in a trade mark, trade name or initials and the extent that it can be legally protected, see the important case of the *World Wide Fund for Nature v World Wrestling Federation Entertainment Inc.* involving the commercial use of the initials 'WWF' decided by Mr. Justice Jacob in the Chancery Division of the High Court on 10 See Form 88 note 13 [3715]. August, 2001. A summary and a comment on this case appears in the September/October 2001 issue of the Sports Law Bulletin vol 4 no 5 at page 5. Subsequently, the World Wrestling Federation changed its name to World Wrestling Entertainment and now uses the intials WWE. This, I think, tends to show that sport is clearly a branch of the world- wide entertainment industry!

for which classes of goods they have been registered. For example, if the Licence is to cover clothing, the sports logo will need to be registered in Class 25 of the Nice Classification of Trademark Goods and Services, which covers clothing, footwear and headgear. If the logo is to be used on sports bags, it will need to be registered in Class 18. For the latest version of the Nice Classification (9th Edition), log on to www.wipo.int/classifications/nice/en/classifications.html

In certain jurisdictions, including the UK, the parties will need to enter into a separate *Registered User Agreement*, which will need to be registered at the local Trade Mark Office.

For trade mark protection purposes, as well as commercial reasons, the Licence Agreement will need to contain 'quality control' provisions. The licensor will need to exercise control over the quality of the licensed products and over the advertising and promotional material for them. Samples of the products will need to be approved by the licensor before being put on the market. In this connection, the Licence Agreement should include a provision requiring the licensee to mark the licensed products and their packaging with trade mark and copyright legends, the wording of which will need to be previously approved by the licensor.

In practice, to avoid bureaucratic delays in obtaining the necessary approvals, which should always be provided in writing, provision is often made in the Licence Agreement for approval to be 'deemed' where, after a certain period of time, there has been no express disapproval, merely silence. Provision should also be made for approval in one format to be 'deemed' to cover approval in a similar format, provided the context remains essentially the same. Without any of these approvals, the value of the sports logo may suffer.

Likewise, the validity of a registered Trade Mark in the UK and elsewhere depends upon its commercial use. For this reason, as well as commercial ones, 'minimum performance obligations' are imposed on licensees, especially where the Licence is an exclusive one.

It is also advisable to include a clause in the Licence Agreement that any use by the licensee of the registered trade mark(s) shall 'enure' for the benefit of the licensor. This includes any additional 'goodwill' created by the licensee in using the mark. For legal protection reasons also, it is necessary to include appropriate provisions in the Licence Agreement for protecting and defending intellectual property rights against infringements by third parties. 'Counterfeiting' is particularly rife as far as consumer goods bearing prestigious sports logos, such as the Olympic Rings, are concerned. The Far East is often the source of these illicit products, but counterfeiting also occurs nearer home.

It is necessary, therefore, to include clear provisions in the Licence Agreement for reporting and dealing with such infringements. These provisions will call for a close liaison and collaboration between the licensor and licensee, particularly as to who is responsible for taking what kind of action, including legal proceedings, and within what time scale. There will also need to be indemnities covering legal costs and other expenses where action is required to be taken by the licensee on behalf of the licensor.

### *11.1.3 Branding and Distribution Channels*

Not only can sports events and products associated with them be branded with a distinctive logo, but so also can sports leagues and players. For example, the popular and highly successful UEFA 'Champions League' has registered the name and a distinctive logo as a 'composite' trade mark.[3]

The same contractual and intellectual property law considerations mentioned above apply in such cases.

Many famous sports persons have registered their names and '*nick names*' as trade marks [e.g. 'Gazza' (Paul Gascoigne)] and 'images' (e.g. the eyes of Damon Hill looking out from the visor of his racing helmet) and have entered into Licence Agreements with Companies and Firms to promote their products and services. These arrangements have proved to be lucrative for both parties.

In all licensing cases, the licensor also needs to control the distribution channels through which the 'licensed products' may be sold, for commercial and legal reasons. See the judgement of Mr. Justice Pumfrey in the Chancery Division of the High Court delivered on 24 July, 2001 in the case of *South Core Inc v Besant and Others (t/a Reef)*.[4] In that case, the Judge held that, in assessing the likelihood of public confusion between two trade marks, the Court has to consider both the likely users of the goods concerned and the distribution channels through which the goods are sold. Although the case concerned a Pop group ('Reef') and the use of their name on T- shirts, the decision has important ramifications for sports logo licensing and sports personality merchandising.

The sales channels affect the public's perception of the product, its quality and price. In marketing terms, it is a matter of 'positioning'. For example, a product sold through '*mail order*' has a lesser image, compared with one sold through a 'luxury retail outlet', such as Harrods. It is in the interests of the licensor and the licensee to project the best image for the licensed product and get the best financial results from the licensing relationship.

The perception of the licensed product as a 'cheap' or 'high quality' item is largely determined by its distribution channels and this affects the value of the brand as an asset in the hands of the brand owner. 'Snob value' helps to raise the price and also the sales of the 'licensed products'. Branding, including sports brands, nowadays is very important and has been likened to a kind of new religion by Peter York, the style guru, as follows:

> "The fastest-growing, most profitable, cleverest global corporations are organised around a new philosophy, a new religion and a new way of working. For these companies their brand is their central asset—physical products are secondary—and most of their quality time is spent making and reworking the brand—its meaning, attitude and social role, its

---

[3] For an interesting article, entitled '*Being distinctive—he problem of creating composite logos*', on the registration and use of 'composite logos' in connection with major sporting events, see the January/February 2002 issue of the '*Sports Law Bulletin*' (vol 5 no 1) at p. 5.

[4] The Times Law Report of 9 October, 2001.

values—because it's the brand that people buy, not the products. Products, so the thinking goes, are generic, copyable, discountable, vulnerable, but brands are unique magic."[5]

This philosophy has been successfully transferred and applied by clever marketers to sport, sports events and sports persons as products competing for consumer attention.

Again, according to York:

> "Nike isn't a maker of high- ; priced trainers but a world voice for sport as an agency of personal growth and achievement ... The Nike swoosh logo means precisely what the crucifix meant to an earlier generation in ghettos—it promises redemption, vindication and a way out."[6]

However, it should be noted that restrictions on the marketing of 'designer' products can raise competition law issues at the EU and national levels (see the Perfume and Levi Straus/Tesco Stores cases).

In the Levi Strauss case, Tesco lost its four-year landmark legal fight for the right to sell designer goods at low prices. Levi Strauss disapproved of its jeans being sold alongside groceries.

The High Court on 31 July, 2002 has upheld a ruling in November, 2001 handed down by the European Court of Justice, which supported Levi's argument that retailers could not sell branded goods from outside Europe without the consent of the trademark owner.

Tesco had sold jeans at about half the price recommended by Levi Strauss, obtaining them from wholesalers in European countries where they were sold more cheaply. But Levi Strauss complained over the effects on its brand of the cost cuts, and of the sale of its clothes in supermarkets.

Levi Strauss said that the High Court ruling would protect a brand that represented the firm's 'most valuable asset', and added that "[f]or 130 years the Levi's name has been a promise of outstanding quality and value. This decision allows us to carry on keeping that promise."

### *11.1.4 Sports Licensing and the Net*

Another important distribution channel nowadays is the internet: 'e-commerce' or 'e-tailing'.

The 'on-line' sale of sports products is gaining ground and the licensor and licensee should consider whether the licensed products are suitable for sale in this manner. For example, clothing products may not be suitable for sale in this way, as the spectacular failure in May 2000 (only six months after its launch) of the clothing e-tailer "www.boo.com" has demonstrated. Purchasers need to see and

[5] Article entitled "*Branded*", *The Times*, February 10 See Form 88 note 13 [3715]. , 2001.

[6] Ibid.

touch clothes before buying, especially highly priced ones. One is reminded here of the seasoned salesman's cry: "never mind the price, feel the quality!"

If products are suitable for sale on the net, appropriate terms should be agreed and incorporated in the Licence Agreement. If these selling rights are not to be included in the Licence, this should also be expressly stated in the Agreement, to avoid any misunderstandings.

### *11.1.5 International Considerations*

Where Sports Licensing Agreements transcend national boundaries, special provisions need to be included in the Agreements, for example, 'force majeure', 'proper law' and 'dispute resolution' clauses.

A 'force majeure' clause can be particularly useful and relevant where the Licence Agreement covers developing countries. The clause will range from a full-blown one in UK and US Agreements, where everything—including the 'kitchen sink' as they say—needs to be covered, to short form clauses in the case of Licences for Civil Law countries, under whose Civil or Commercial Codes, full-blown 'force majeure' provisions are implied and, therefore, automatically included. A well-drafted 'force majeure' clause should:

- set out in general terms what the parties understand by the term 'force majeure';
- oblige the affected party to inform the other party to the contract of the event of 'force majeure', in particular, the nature, extent, effect and likely duration of the event; it may also oblige the affected party to take reasonable steps to mitigate the disruption or any loss caused;
- state that if 'force majeure' applies, the affected party is not in breach of contract and that the contract is suspended until the event ends; and
- either resume performance once the event has ended; or
- provide that where the event continues for a given continuous period of time, the parties are entitled to give notice terminating the contract.

Rather than leave the matter to chance under the Rules of Private International Law, it is advisable for parties to agree in advance in the Spirts Licence/Merchandising Agreement on the Law, which will apply in the event of a dispute. English and Swiss Law are popular choices in International Sports Licence/Merchandise Agreements. Likewise, the parties need to include an express provision in the Licence Agreement on the manner in which any disputes will be settled—by the courts, arbitration or other alternative forms of dispute resolution ("ADR"). In relation to sports matters, the parties could, for example, decide to refer their disputes under the Licence Agreement to the Court of Arbitration for Sport ("CAS"), which is based in Lausanne, Switzerland. The CAS was set up by the IOC in 1983, specifically to deal with a wide range of disputes "arising from the practice of sport". The CAS has proved to be a popular and effective forum for the settlement of sports disputes, including commercial ones.

Alternatively, the parties may decide to use ADR for the settlement of their disputes. Mediation, one of the forms of ADR, is proving to be very successful generally and, in particular, in sports cases. It is interesting to note that the CAS has a Mediation Division.

If the parties in dispute prefer to settle their differences by mediation—and many do because of the special characteristics and dynamics of sport[7]—the CAS model mediation clause is as follows:

> "Any dispute, any controversy or claim arising under, out of or relating to this contract and any subsequent of or in relation to this contract, including, but not limited to, its formation, validity, binding effect, interpretation, breach or termination, as well as non-contractual claims shall be submitted to mediation in accordance with the CAS Mediation Rules."

If mediation proves to be unsuccessful, although mediation providers usually claim a success rate of around 85%, the CAS recommends the following additional clause to be inserted in a contract to cover the above contingency:

> "If, and to the extent that, any such dispute has not been settled within 90 days of the commencement of the mediation, or if, before the expiration of the said period, either party fails to participate or continue to participate in the mediation, the dispute shall, upon the filing of a Request for Arbitration by either party, be referred to and finally settled by CAS arbitration pursuant to the Code of Sports-related Arbitration. When the circumstances so require, the mediator may, at his own discretion or at the request of a party, seek an extension of the time limit from the CAS President."

Thus, the CAS offers disputing parties the possibility of a 'Med-Arb' dispute resolution process: mediation to identify the issues; and arbitration to settle them.

It may be noted, *en passant*, that in a landmark ruling in the English Courts in the case of *Cable & Wireless PLC v IBM United Kingdom,*[8] Mr Justice Colman held that an agreement to refer disputes to mediation is contractually binding. In this case, IBM called on Cable and Wireless to mediate a dispute that had arisen under a contract in which the parties had agreed to mediate future disputes. Cable and Wireless refused to do so, claiming that the reference to mediation in the contract was legally unenforceable because it lacked certainty and was like an unenforceable agreement to negotiate—an agreement to agree is not legally binding under English Law. The judge rejected this argument, holding that the agreement to try to resolve a dispute, with identification of the procedure to be used, was sufficient to give certainty and, therefore, legal effect to the clause.

---

[7] See the case of Richie Woodhall and Frank Warren involving a time-critical dispute under certain management and promotion agreements entered into between them, which was settled within 72 hours by mediation, discussed at page 182 in „Mediating Sports Disputes—National and International Perspectives by Ian S. Blackshaw 2002 TMC Asser Press The Hague, The Netherlands (ISBN 90-6704-146-7).

[8] [2002] 2 All ER (Comm) 1041.

It may be added that, in England too, parties, who, under Court rules, refuse to try—or even *consider* the possibility of mediating—to settle their disputes by mediation at an early stage in the litigation process, may run the risk of being denied their legal costs if ultimately successful, contrary to the normal rule that 'costs follow the event'.[9]

Another form of ADR that may be appropriate—and also cost-effective—for settling disputes under Sports Licensing and Merchandising Agreements is 'expert determination', especially for resolving disputes of a technical, quality control and financial nature. The expert's decision is final and binding on the parties. Of course, the success of this form of dispute resolution depends upon the parties finding and agreeing on a suitably qualified and independent expert, who is also experienced in these matters. In the appointment clause, it should be expressly stated that the person appointed is acting as an expert and not as an arbitrator, to ensure that the expert's decision is final and not subject to any kind of appeal or legal challenge.

Before agreeing to such a provision, however, the parties need to appreciate the legal nature of this dispute resolution procedure, and, in particular, the limited rights of appeal against the expert's findings. In three recent cases, the English Courts have looked at several aspects of expert determination, and, in summary, their findings are as follows:

- once agreed expert determination clauses are binding and the parties have no recourse to the courts;
- where the expert determination clause provides that the expert shall give reasons for a decision the Court will order that they be given; and
- where a defendant refused to take part in an expert determination the claimant may recover damages if it has to issue legal proceedings.

In *Douglas Harper v Interchange Group Ltd,*[10] there has been a clear reiteration that the Courts will enforce an expert determination provision in an Agreement and that a party will be prohibited from bringing Court proceedings where the dispute falls within an expert determination provision and that provision is ignored. In this case, the Agreement contained a comprehensive expert determination procedure. The High Court found that the parties were contractually bound by this procedure, so the plaintiff was barred from issuing Court proceedings claiming commission due. He had not complied with the requirements set out in the expert determination provision.

---

[9] See *Susan Dunnett v Railtrack PLC* [2002] EWCA Civ 302; and *Leicester Circuits Limited v Coats* [2003] EWCA Civ 333. But see also *Halsey v Milton Keynes General NHS Trust* and *Steel v Joy and Halliday* [2004] EWCA Civ 576; [2004] 4 All ER 920, collectively known as the 'Halsey' case and described by Lord Phillips of Worth Maltravers as "the most important English judgement about ADR".

[10] [2007] EWHC 1834.

In *Halifax Life Ltd v The Equitable Life Assurance Society*,[11] the Court provided further confirmation that expert determination procedures are binding on the parties, and although the Court may intervene to resolve issues, such as whether the expert should provide a reasoned decision or not, the actual decision of the expert will not be disturbed. Halifax had agreed to reinsure Equitable Life's unit-linked and non-profit business. This required an assessment of an initial premium for the reinsurance, which was referred to an expert to determine. Crucially the parties agreed that the expert would provide reasons for his decision. The expert made his determination, but failed to give reasons. Halifax challenged the decision claiming that it was non-binding on the ground of manifest error. The High Court said that:

> "In litigation justice will not be done if it is not apparent to the parties why one has won and the other has lost."

And, therefore, held that the appropriate course was to adjourn the hearing of Halifax's claim and to remit the matter back to the expert in order that he could state the reasons for his decision. This allowed Halifax the opportunity to understand the reasons for the decision and to decide whether to continue with its legal challenge. The Judge referred by analogy to the provisions in the Arbitration Act 1996 [Section 70(4) which allows the Court to order an arbitral tribunal to provide reasons or sufficient reasons for its decision] and was able to require the expert to give reasons either by way of remedy in respect of the provisions of the contract, under the court's inherent jurisdiction or under its case management powers contained in the Civil Procedure Rules. This case is a reminder that the Courts can still intervene in an expert determination, although a 'hands off' approach is generally favoured. Parties can take comfort from the fact that they can now expect a properly reasoned decision, if they have expressly agreed that reasons are to be given and they should certainly so provide in their expert determination clause.

*In Sunrock Aircraft Corporation v Scandinavian Airlines System Denmark–Norway–Sweden*,[12] the Court of Appeal upheld the validity of an expert determination clause. It considered the measure of damages to be awarded where a party had refused to participate in the expert determination, but the other party had asked the Court to award damages rather than asking for a mandatory order for expert determination. In this particular case, the Court held that nominal damages were the correct measure of the claimant's loss.

These cases indicate that an increasing number of parties are agreeing to such dispute resolution procedures in their Agreements, whether out of a desire to minimise their legal costs or implement a quicker dispute resolution procedure. They also underline the need for the parties to carefully consider and think through the suitability of such clauses, and also to appreciate that, once agreed, the

---

[11] [2007] EWHC 503.

[12] [2007] EWHC Civ 882.

procedure is compulsory and the expert's findings may only be legally challenged on the narrowest of grounds. The Courts will uphold these clauses.

Certain financial provisions also need to be included in International Sports Licence/Merchandising Agreements and these are dealt with later.

Finally, in view of the 'strict' (i.e. no fault) product liability rules, which apply in the EU under Council Directive 85/374/EEC of 25 July 1985 on the approximation of the laws, regulations and administrative provisions of the Member States concerning liability for defective products,[13] provisions dealing with product liability issues need to be included in the Licence Agreement. The main provisions of this important Directive may be summarised as follows:

> ***Scope***:
> the Directive applies to movables which have been industrially produced, whether or not incorporated into another movable or into an immovable.
> ***Principle of liability without fault***:
> the Directive establishes the principle of objective liability or liability without fault of the producer in cases of damage caused by a defective product. If more than one person is liable for the same damage, it is joint liability.
> ***Producer*** is taken to mean:
> any participant in the production process;
> the importer of the defective product;
> any person putting their name, trade mark or other distinguishing feature on the product;
> any person supplying a product whose producer cannot be identified.
> ***Burden of proof***: the injured person must prove:
> the actual damage;
> the defect in the product; the defect in the product;
> the causal relationship between damage and defect
> ***Limitation Period***: The injured party must bring a claim within three years.

As mentioned above, the EU Directive on Product Liability provides for liability without fault, so it is not necessary to prove the negligence or fault of the producer or importer. And, as also mentioned, there is a wide definition of the term 'manufacturer', which includes those who affix or allow to be affixed their name or mark to products manufactured by someone else under their authority. In other words, licensors can also be held legally liable for defective products produced by their licensees, which cause harm to consumers. For example, this could be a particular problem where, for example, toys and novelty items for children are licensed. Thus, it is usual to include indemnity provisions in favour of the licensor in the Licence Agreement, backed by product liability insurance on the part of the licensee. It is also usual and advisable to include provisions for noting the interests

[13] Official Journal L 210 of 07.08.1985.

of the licensor on the licensee's product liability insurance policy. Likewise, provisions dealing with the handling of any corresponding litigation, including, as mentioned above, infringements of intellectual property rights, also need to be expressly included in the Licence Agreement.

### *11.1.6 Maximising Sports Licensing Revenues*

As previously mentioned, one of the most important clauses in a Licence Agreement is the 'consideration clause'—the financial provisions. To maximise the financial returns from the Licence, careful thought needs to be given to all the financial arrangements. The impact of any corresponding withholding and other taxes also needs to be taken into account. The price of the Licence can be a lump sum ("licence fee") and/or periodic payments ("royalties") based on turnover. In the latter case, the basis on which the royalties are to be calculated needs to be precisely defined. If, as is usual, they are to be charged on the 'net invoice price' of the licensed products, this needs to be carefully defined. For example, what about 'trade discounts', what about sales to 'associated companies' (which also need to be defined) of the licensee; what about defective and returned goods; and so on?

There should be provisions defining when the royalty is earned ('accrues') and when and where (specified bank account) the royalty is to be paid ('settlement') and who bears any bank costs. Likewise, there need to be provisions on sales accounting, delivery of royalty statements and the right of the licensor (or its agent) to inspect the licensee's accounting records and take copies of them. The royalty provisions can usefully be set out in one of the Schedules to the Sports Licensing and Merchandising Agreement.

In the case of International Sports Licensing and Merchandising Agreements, it will also be necessary to specify the 'currency of payment' of the licence fee and/or the royalties, as well as the corresponding exchange rate for converting from one currency to the other. Royalties may accrue and be calculated in one currency ('currency of obligation') but payable in another ('currency of payment').

Furthermore, provision will also need to be made for exchange control implications for payments from countries that limit the transfer of funds abroad, especially 'hard currency' (e.g. US dollars), and require governmental approvals of Licence Agreements, especially their financial terms (e.g. royalty rates). A supplementary provision will need to be included to cover the case of failures to obtain exchange control approvals, within a specified period of time (say three months) and their practical consequences (for example, termination of the Licence Agreement).

Again, the question of any right of *set-off* between the licensor and the licensee and the right to claim interest, and, if so, at what rate, on late payments of licence fees and/or royalties also need to be provided for in the Licence Agreement.

Finally, any tax considerations need to be factored into the Licence Agreement. For example, whether payments are to be made free or subject to any required 'withholding tax'. In other words, payable net or grossed up.

Another tax consideration is to structure the sports licensing arrangements through a no or low tax jurisdiction to eliminate or mitigate the fiscal burden, as far as is legally possible, considering the current OECD crack down on the use of so- called 'tax havens'. On the Fiscal Aspects of Sports Marketing Agreements, see Chap. 15.

### *11.1.7 Managing Sports Licensing and Merchandising Agreements*

A successful licensing/merchandising deal not only needs a carefully planned licensing strategy but a good licensing manager to implement it in practice. This is particularly true of Sports Licensing and Merchandising Agreements.

Ideally, in the experience of the Author of this Book, the person managing the project should be the same person who negotiated the deal. Having the background, this ensures continuity and also helps to avoid any misunderstandings and clarify any ambiguities or uncertainties in interpreting the Licensing and Merchandising Agreement.

The qualities needed to be a successful licensing manager include:

- product and market knowledge;
- patience;
- empathy, especially an ability to understand and get on with cultural difference in international licensing deals;
- attention to detail;
- an appreciation and understanding of the legal issues;
- an organised and systematic approach;
- foresight;
- a willingness to make things work; and, above all,
- integrity and fair mindedness.

Knowledge of the product and belief in it, as well as an understanding of the market place and the role of advertising and sales promotion, as well as retailing and distribution, are particularly crucial requirements for a successful licensing pro-gramme. Licensing and Merchandising also need trust and understanding and a close working relationship on the part of both the licensor and the licensee. The licensing/merchandising relationship is not an easy one to manage, but provides a challenging and rewarding work experience.

## 11.2 General Precedent of a Merchandising Agreement

Included in the Appendix of this chapter (11.4), the reader will find a General Precedent of a Merchandising Agreement, which provides a checklist of the scope of and the kinds of provisions that should be included in a Merchandising

Agreement generally; the Precedent will, of course, need to be adapted when drafting a Merchandising Agreement relating specifically to Sport and a particular Sports Event.

## 11.3 Concluding Remarks

As will have been seen from the above account, Sports Licensing and Merchandising is a complex matter and highly lucrative business. The guiding principle for success is paying attention to details and getting the commercial and financial terms and conditions right in the first place, and reflecting them in a clearly drafted and unambiguous Agreement, in which nothing should be assumed or implied or left to chance.

As mentioned above, all the terms and conditions should be expressly included and there should be no reliance on any pre-contract oral promises or any side-agreements. If any such exist and are relevant, they should be expressly incorporated in the Sports Licensing and Merchandising Agreement.

In the case of Sports Licensing and Merchandising Agreements involving an international dimension—as is often the case—it is most advisable to have the final draft Agreement reviewed by local legal and tax counsels to ensure its validity and effectiveness, from both a local legal and tax point of view. Likewise, it is also very important to take account of any EU Competition Law aspects, which may have a bearing on the legal enforceability of any restrictive clauses, especially any territorial licensing arrangements, which are part and parcel of the Agreement. In such cases, it is also advisable to include a so-called 'severance' clause that will eliminate or 'sever' from the Agreement any restrictions which may fall foul of EU Competition Law and thus be void, whilst, at the same time, preserving the validity and enforceability of the rest of the Agreement. See further on this in Chap. 19 on 'Boilerplate Clauses'.

See also further on the Fiscal and EU Aspects of Sports Marketing Agreements in Chaps. 15 and 16 respectively.

## 11.4 Appendix

### General Merchandising Agreement*,[1]

**This Agreement** is made the...... day of.........

**Between:**
(name of licensor) of (address) ('the Licensor') and
(name of licensee) of (address) ('the Licensee')

**It Is Agreed** as follows

**Definitions and interpretation**

1.1 In this Agreement except where a different interpretation is clear from or necessary in the context the following terms shall have the following meanings:

| | |
|---|---|
| ['Agent' | (name) of (address)] |
| 'Intellectual Property' | the copyrights trade marks and other rights listed in Schedule [1] |
| 'Minimum Guaranteed Royalty' | the sum specified in clause 6[2]. |
| 'Notice' | notice in writing served in accordance with the provisions of sub-clause 20.8 |
| 'Products' | the goods listed in Schedule [2] |
| 'Rights' | the [non- exclusive right by way of licence to use the Intellectual Property to manufacture distribute and sell the Products throughout the Territory |
| 'Royalties' | the payments to be made to the Licensor by the Licensee under clause 6 |
| 'Specifications' | the specifications set out in Schedule [3] or as may from time to time be agreed between the parties |
| 'Term' | the duration of this Agreement as set out in clause 5 |
| 'Territory' | the area designated in Schedule [4] |

2.1 In this Agreement unless the context requires otherwise:

- words and expressions that are defined in the Copyright, Designs and Patents Act 1988 or in the Trade Marks Act 1994 shall bear the same meanings in this Agreement

* Source: Lexis Nexis; reproduced with permission.

- words importing the singular number shall include the plural and vice versa
- ords importing any particular gender shall include all other genders
- references to persons shall include bodies of persons whether corporate or incorporate words importing the whole shall be treated as including a reference to any part of the whole

Any reference in this Agreement to any statute or statutory provision shall be construed as referring to that statute or statutory provision as it may from time to time be amended modified extended re-enacted or replaced (whether before or after the date of this Agreement) and including all subordinate legislation from time to time made under it

The expression 'copyright' shall include the entire copyright, design right rental right, right to authorise or prohibit lending and database right subsisting now or created at any time during the Term under the laws of the United Kingdom and all analogous rights subsisting now or created at any time during the Term under the laws of each and every other jurisdiction throughout the Territory

References in this Agreement to clauses schedules and exhibits are to clauses of and schedules and exhibits to this Agreement except where otherwise expressly stated Headings are used in this Agreement for the convenience of the parties only and shall not be incorporated into this Agreement and shall not be deemed to be any indication of the meaning of the clauses schedules or exhibits to which they relate

**Recitals**

The Licensor is the sole owner of the Intellectual Property

3.1 The Licensor has the right to grant licences of the Intellectual Property in the Territory

3.2 The Licensee has requested a licence to use the Intellectual Property in order to manufacture distribute and sell the Products

3.3 The Licensor has agreed to grant such a licence to the Licensee upon the terms set out in this Agreement

**Grant**

4.1 In consideration of and subject to the obligations undertaken by the Licensee under this Agreement the Licensor with [full or limited] title guarantee grants the Rights to the Licensee for the Term

**Reservation**

5.1 The Licensor reserves the right to grant licences of the Intellectual Property in the Territory to other licensees.

**Term**

This Agreement shall extend for an initial period of (specify period) from (date) until (date) ('the Initial Period')

6.1 If the aggregate Royalties paid by the Licensee to the Licensor during the Initial Period shall exceed £...... then this Agreement shall continue for one further period of (specify) until (date) ('the Further Period') unless either of the parties shall have given to the other notice of termination not less than 3 months before the expiry of the Initial Period

**Royalties**

In consideration of the Rights granted by the Licensor to the Licensee the Licensee shall pay to the Licensor the following sums:

7.1. upon the signing of this Agreement an advance royalty of £...... which shall not in any circumstances be repayable either wholly or partly by the Licensor but which may be set- off against the royalty payments due under sub-clause 7.2

7.2 a royalty of...% on the net selling price of each unit of the Products sold by the Licensee calculated by deducting from the price at which each unit was sold by the Licensee VAT or other governmental taxes and levies

7.3 The Minimum Guaranteed Royalty shall be £...... in respect of each year of the Initial Period and £...... in respect of each year of the Further Period

7.4 The provisions of clauses 7.1 and 7.2 shall apply to the Further Period (if any) granted in accordance with the provisions of clause 6.1 save that in sub-clause 7.1 for the words 'signing of this Agreement' there shall be substituted the words 'commencement of the Further Period'

7.5 All payments under this Agreement to the Licensor shall be made in pounds sterling. Any conversion of foreign currency into pounds sterling shall be made at the rate of exchange ruling on the date of accounting

7.6 The Licensee shall within 30 days of the expiration of each calendar quarter during the subsistence of this Agreement deliver to the Licensor a statement giving particulars of all sales of the Products effected by or on behalf of the Licensee during the quarter and showing the total royalty payable to the Licensor and at the same time deliver to the Licensor a remittance for the full amount of that royalty

7.7 When sending a statement and remittance for the final calendar quarter of any year during the Term the Licensee shall pay to the Licensor the difference (if any) between the Minimum Guaranteed Royalty and the Royalties earned by the Licensor under this Agreement for the year in question

7.8 The Licensee agrees to keep proper records and books of account relating to all dealings with the Products and to make all such entries in such records and books of account as may be necessary to calculate the Royalties payable to the Licensor and shall allow the Licensor or a firm of [chartered] accountants on the Licensor's behalf to examine such books and records in so far as they relate to the sale of the Products and to take copies and extracts of such books and records. Any such inspection shall be during normal office hours and not carried out more than twice in any calendar year and shall be at the Licensor's expense unless such inspection shall reveal an underpayment to the Licensor of more than £...... in which event the Licensee shall bear the costs of such inspection

7.9 In the event of late payment of any money due to the Licensor under the terms of this Agreement (including without limitation any moneys found on an inspection carried out under clause 6.8 to have been underpaid) the Licensee shall pay to the Licensor interest accruing from day to day calculated at the annual rate of…% above the base rate from time to time of (name of bank) on all such money overdue from the due date for payment until the actual date of payment

**Licensee's obligations as to conformity to specification and quality**

8.1 The Licensee shall manufacture and package the Products according to their respective Specifications and at all times ensure that the Products and packaging are of the highest quality attainable within such specifications

8.2 The Licensee shall deliver to the Licensor for approval free of charge true and accurate samples of each of the Products including wrappings and packaging and the Licensee shall not commence distribution of any unit of any one of the Products until it has received written approval from the Licensor of its design standard of workmanship quality of presentation and intrinsic merit

8.3 The Licensee shall ensure that all other units of the Products including their wrappings and packaging correspond to the samples approved by the Licensor in accordance with sub-clause 7.2

8.4 The Licensee shall supply to the Licensor free of charge such further samples of the Products as the Licensor may reasonably require from time to time

**Requirements contract**

9.1 The Licensee shall supply to the Licensor or to such other persons as the Licensor shall require any of the Products that the Licensor may require up to the quantities and at the prices specified in Schedule [5]

**Use and protection of Intellectual Property Copyright material**

10.1 Every unit of the Products and all packaging advertising and point of sale materials used in connection with them shall bear the following copyright identification '© (year of first publication) (name of Licensor)'[5] or any other copyright notice as the Licensor may notify to the Licensee from time to time. With the prior written consent of the Licensor an abbreviated version the terms of which must first be approved in writing by the Licensor may be used on such Products but not on the packaging or other material

10.2 The date to be placed in brackets after '©' shall be the year specified for that purpose for the particular copyright material by the Licensor or in the case of a combination design the year of first marketing by the Licensee in which case the Licensor shall be notified in writing of such year by the Licensee

10.3 No copyright material comprised in the Intellectual Property may be altered or amended by the Licensee without the prior written consent of the

Licensor but the Licensee may use a combination of such materials even where such a combination has not previously been used

10.4 No artwork other than copyright material comprised in the Intellectual Property shall be used in relation to any of the Products without the prior written consent of the Licensor

10.5 No copyright material comprised in the Intellectual Property may be used in connection with the manufacture distribution or marketing of any goods other than the Products for which the use of such material is specified

**Trade marks**

11.1 Each unit of the Products for which a trade mark comprised in the Intellectual Property is specified shall display that mark in a manner first approved by the Licensor

11.2 No other trade mark shall be affixed by the Licensee to the Products or to any associated packaging advertising or point of sale materials without the prior written consent of the Licensor

11.3 The Licensee shall not use in relation to or affix to any goods other than the Products for which such marks are specified any of the trade marks comprised in the Intellectual Property

**Provisions relating to all IP property**

12.1 The Licensee shall not use any of the Intellectual Property as part of the Licensee's name or the name of any entity associated with it without the prior written consent of the Licensor

12.2 The Licensee shall not during the subsistence of this Agreement or at any time subsequently register or use any of the Intellectual Property in its own name as proprietor

12.3 The Licensee recognises the Licensor's title to the Intellectual Property and shall not claim any right title or interest in the Intellectual Property or any part of it

12.4 The Licensee shall promptly call to the attention of the Licensor the use of any part of the Intellectual Property by any third party or any activity of any third party which might in the opinion of the Licensee amount to infringement or passing off of the Licensor's rights in the Intellectual Property

12.5 The Licensee shall not assign mortgage charge or otherwise deal with (whether wholly or in part) the benefit of this Agreement or grant any sub-licence[6] without the prior written consent of the Licensor

12.6 The Licensee shall hold all goodwill generated by its operations under this Agreement as bare trustee for the exclusive benefit of the Licensor

12.7 Any designs or other works derived by the Licensee from the Intellectual Property or any part of it shall be held by it as bare trustee for the Licensor and at the Licensor's request shall be assigned to it without compensation[7]

**Registered user**

13.1 When required by the Licensor the Licensee shall join with the Licensor at the [Licensee's or Licensor's] expense[8] to become a registered user of the Intellectual Property or any part of it in any part of the Territory and on termination of this Agreement the Licensee shall co- operate with the Licensor in securing the cancellation of any such registration

**Licensee not to use the Licensor's name**

14.1 The Licensee shall not except with the prior written consent of the Licensor make use of the name of the Licensor in any connection otherwise than is expressly permitted by this Agreement

**Licensee's obligations as to marketing**

15.1 The Licensee shall ensure that a full range of the Products shall be on sale to the public within [6] months of the date of this Agreement

15.2 The Licensee undertakes that the Products will be sold only to recognised wholesale firms for resale to retail firms or to retail firms for resale to the public or direct to the public

15.3 The Licensee shall ensure so far as it is reasonably practicable that the Products are not supplied for re-sale as an integral part of another product and shall not be supplied either directly or indirectly to other manufacturers or to hawkers pedlars street vendors and the like or to any person intending to distribute the Products gratuitously for publicity

15.4 The Licensee shall at all times during the Term use its best endeavours to promote and sell the Products throughout the Territory

15.5 The Licensee shall consult with the Licensor regarding the Licensee's proposed marketing of the Products and shall ensure that the marketing of the Products does not conflict with the image of the Intellectual Property promoted or intended to be promoted by the Licensor. No marketing materials shall be published or distributed without the prior written consent of the Licensor

**No premiums**

16.1 The Licensee shall not sell or otherwise dispose of any of the Products as premiums to any person or persons whatsoever

16.2 The right to sell any of the Products as premiums is expressly reserved by the Licensor and if the Licensee shall receive any approach for the purpose of the use or sale of the Products as premiums it shall as soon as possible notify the Licensor and furnish it with the names and full particulars of the person or persons making the approach

16.3 For the purposes of this clause 'premium' means a product or product combined with a service which is sold or supplied in association with the promotion of another product or service offered in association with the sales promotional activities of retailers wholesalers or manufacturers' associations or with incentive programmes of all kinds

**Action against third parties**

17.1 The Licensor shall have the sole right to take action against third parties in respect of any infringement of its rights in the Intellectual Property[9] and if required to do so by the Licensor the Licensee shall co-operate fully with the Licensor in any such action which shall include if the Licensor wishes being joined as a party to any such action and the Licensee's reasonable expenses incurred in doing so shall be borne by the Licensor

17.2 If the Licensor fails to take any such action against third parties or to require the Licensee to do so the Licensee may serve Notice on the Licensor and on the expiry of 30 days after the service of such Notice the Licensee shall be entitled to take such action itself and at its own expense provided that the Licensor has not served Notice within the 30 day period of its own intention to take action

17.3 The Licensee shall in no circumstances settle any claim or action against third parties without the prior written consent of the Licensor

**Termination**

18.1 The Licensor may forthwith terminate this Agreement by giving Notice upon:

- failure on the part of the Licensee to make any payment due to the Licensor under this Agreement for 21 days after such payment shall have become due or
- failure on the part of the Licensee to perform any of its other obligations under this Agreement or
- the voluntary or compulsory liquidation of the Licensee [except for the purposes of reconstruction or amalgamation while solvent]
- or he appointment of a receiver, receiver and manager administrator or administrative receiver over all or any of its assets [the bankruptcy of the Licensee or his making an arrangement or composition with his creditors]
- or if the Licensee ceases for any reason to carry on business or takes or suffers any similar action which in the opinion of the Licensor means that it is unable to pay its debts or
- any change of directors of the Licensee without the prior written approval of the Licensor or
- the Licensor ceasing to have the right to grant licences of the Intellectual PropertyTermination

**Termination consequences**

19.1 Termination for whatever reason of this Agreement shall be without prejudice to the rights and remedies of the Licensor in respect of any pre-termination breach by the Licensee of any of its obligations under this Agreement

19.2 Upon termination of this Agreement the Licensee shall forthwith pay to the Licensor the balance of any Royalties accrued up to the date of termination together with the difference (if any) between the Minimum Guaranteed Royalty and the Royalties paid to the Licensor in respect of that year of termination

19.3 Subject to the following sub-clauses upon termination of this Agreement for whatever reason the Licensee shall discontinue all use of the Intellectual Property and return forthwith to the Licensor all material bearing or based upon any of the Intellectual Property

19.4 If the Licensee shall have any remaining stocks of the Products or have Products in the course of manufacture at the time this Agreement is terminated [and if this Agreement shall have terminated by expiry of the Term and shall not have been terminated by reason of the Licensee's breach of any of its obligations under this Agreement] it may complete the manufacture of such Products within [30] days of termination and dispose of such Products and/or remaining stocks in compliance with the terms of this Agreement but not otherwise on a non- exclusive basis for a period of [4] months from the date of termination ('the Sell-Off Period') Provided that:

- the price charged by the Licensee for each Product during the Sell-Off Period is not less than the price charged by the Licensee during the 6 months prior to the termination of this Agreement; and
- all other provisions of this Agreement (including those relating to payment of Royalties) are observed by the Licensee in respect of items sold during the Sell-Off Period

**Warranties and indemnities**

20.1 The Licensee shall indemnify the Licensor against all actions claims costs damages and expenses which it may suffer or sustain as a result of the actions of the Licensee

20.2 The Licensor warrants that it is entitled to grant to the Licensee the Rights granted under this Agreement and shall keep the Licensee indemnified against all actions claims costs damages and expenses arising out of any breach of this warranty

**Inspection**

20.1 The Licensee shall permit the Licensor [and its servants or agents] at all reasonable times to inspect the Licensee's premises in order to satisfy itself that the Licensee is complying with its obligations under this Agreement

**Product liability insurance**

21.1 The Licensee shall at its own expense obtain and maintain product liability insurance in an amount of not less than £...... with both the Licensor and Licensee as beneficiaries under the policy and providing cover for claims demands and causes of action arising out of Products sold during the Term or Sell-Off Period whether such claims demands or causes of action arise or are notified during or after the Term or Sell-Off Period

**General**

22.1 **Receipt**

The receipt of money by the Licensor shall not prevent the Licensor from questioning the correctness of any statement in respect of any money

22.2 **Force majeure**

If either party is prevented from fulfilling its obligations under this Agreement by reason of any supervening event beyond its control (including but not limited to war national emergency flood earthquake strike or lockout (other than a strike or lockout induced by the party so incapacitated) or illness) the party unable to fulfil its obligations ('the incapacitated party') shall immediately give notice of this to the other party and shall do everything in its power to resume full performance of its obligations as soon as possible

22.3 The incapacitated party shall not be deemed to be in breach of its obligations under this Agreement during the period of incapacity and the other party shall continue to perform its obligations under this Agreement save only in so far as they are dependent on the prior performance by the incapacitated party of obligations which it cannot perform during the period of incapacity

22.4 If the period of incapacity exceeds [6] months then this Agreement shall automatically terminate unless the parties first agree otherwise in writing

**Whole agreement**

23.1 This Agreement contains the whole agreement between the parties and supersedes any prior written or oral agreement between them in relation to its subject matter and the parties confirm that they have not entered into this Agreement upon the basis of any representations that are not expressly incorporated into this Agreement. No oral explanation or oral information given by any party shall alter or affect the interpretation of this Agreement

**Reservation of rights**

24.1 All rights not specifically and expressly granted to the Licensee by this Agreement are reserved to the Licensor

**Joint and several**

25.1 All agreements on the part of either of the parties which comprises more than one person or entity shall be joint and several

**Proper law and jurisdiction**

26.1 This Agreement shall be governed by English law in every particular including formation and interpretation and shall be deemed to have been made in England and subject to clause 20.7 the parties agree to submit to the [non- ]exclusive jurisdiction of the English courts

**Arbitration**[11]

27.1 Any difference or dispute between the parties concerning the interpretation or validity of this Agreement or the rights and liabilities of either of the parties shall in the first instance be referred to the arbitration of two persons (one to be nominated by each party) or their mutually agreed umpire in accordance with the provisions of the Arbitration Act 1996

**Notices**

28.1 Any notice consent or the like (in this clause referred to generally as 'notice') required or permitted to be given under this Agreement shall not be binding unless in writing and may be given personally or sent to the party to be notified by pre-paid first class post or by electronic mail or facsimile transmission at its address as set out above or as otherwise notified in accordance with this clause

28.2 Notice given personally shall be deemed given at the time of its delivery

28.3 Notice sent by post in accordance with this sub-clause shall be deemed given at the commencement of business of the recipient on the second business day following its posting

28.4 Notice sent by electronic mail or facsimile transmission in accordance with this sub-clause shall be deemed given at the time of its actual transmission provided that the sender does not receive any indication that the electronic mail message or facsimile transmission has not been successfully transmitted to the intended recipient

**No modification**

29.1 This Agreement may not be modified except by an instrument in writing signed by both of the parties or their duly authorised representatives

**Waiver**

30.1 The failure by either party to enforce at any time or for any period any one or more of the terms or conditions of this Agreement shall not be a waiver of them or of the right at any time subsequently to enforce all terms and conditions of this Agreement

**Severance**

31.1 In the event that any provision of this Agreement is declared by any judicial or other competent authority to be void voidable illegal or otherwise unenforceable or indications of this are received by either of the parties from any relevant competent authority the parties shall amend that provision in such reasonable manner as achieves the intention of the parties without illegality or at the discretion of the parties it may be severed from this Agreement and in either event the remaining provisions of this Agreement shall remain in full force and effect

**Survival of terms**

32.1 The warranties and indemnities contained in this Agreement and the provisions for payment of and accounting in respect of Royalties and other moneys due to the Licensor under the terms of this Agreement shall survive the termination or expiry of this Agreement

**Agency**

33.1 The Licensor confirms that he has appointed the Agent to act on the Licensor's behalf in all matters arising out of this Agreement including the collection and receipt of all payments due to the Licensor under this Agreement and declares that the receipt of the Agent shall be a good and sufficient discharge to the Licensee in respect of such payments

33.2 Any notice served on the Agent will be deemed to have been served at the same time on the Licensor

**VAT**

34.1 All sums payable to the Licensor under this Agreement are exclusive of VAT which shall where applicable be paid in addition at the rate in force at the due time for payment subject to the Licensor either supplying a VAT invoice to the Licensee or informing the Licensee of his VAT registration number

**Rights and remedies cumulative**

35.1 All rights and remedies available to the parties under the terms of this Agreement and under the general law shall be cumulative and no exercise by either of the parties of any such right or remedy shall restrict or prejudice the exercise of any other right or remedy granted by this Agreement or otherwise available to it

**Confidentiality**

36.1 The terms [and existence] of this Agreement are confidential to the parties

36.2 Each party agrees to maintain secret and confidential all confidential information obtained by the other both pursuant to this Agreement and prior to and in contemplation of it (including but not limited to information concerning the [existence and] terms of this Agreement) and all other information that it may acquire from the other in the course of this Agreement and to respect the other's proprietary rights in such material and to use the same exclusively for the purposes of this Agreement and to disclose the same only to its professional advisers and those of its employees officers agents and representatives pursuant to this Agreement (if any) to whom and to the extent that such disclosure is reasonably necessary for the purposes of this Agreement (and which employees officers agents and representatives shall be made aware of and required to acknowledge these confidentiality arrangements in writing)

36.3 The obligation of confidentiality shall not apply to any information which:

- prior to its receipt from one party was lawfully in the possession of the other and at its free disposal; or
- is subsequently disclosed to the recipient party without any obligations of confidence by a third party who has not derived it directly or indirectly from the other party; or
- is or becomes generally available to the public through no act or default of the recipient party or its agents employees officers and representatives; or
- is required by law to be disclosed

**Binding effect**

37.1 This Agreement shall bind and enure to the benefit of the parties and their respective permitted assigns personal representatives and successors in title

**Assignment**

38.1 Neither party may assign the benefit of nor its obligations under this Agreement without the prior written consent of the other party

38.2 It shall be a condition of any assignment that the assignor shall procure that the assignee enters into a direct written covenant with the other party to this Agreement whereby the assignee undertakes to observe and perform all of the assignor's obligations under this Agreement

**No partnership**

39.1 Nothing in this Agreement shall be deemed to constitute a partnership between the parties nor the relationship of employer and employee under a contract of service nor the relationship of principal and agent

**Third parties**

40.1 This agreement does not create any right enforceable by any person not a party to it. For the avoidance of doubt the agreement does not create any right enforceable to any successor or assignee of either Party.

As Witness etc.

SCHEDULE 1
(list of copyright, trade marks and other rights)

SCHEDULE 2
(list of goods)

SCHEDULE 3
(insert relevant specifications)

SCHEDULE 4
(insert applicable territory)

SCHEDULE 5

Requirements Contract

(insert quantities and prices and details of billing arrangements)]
(signatures of (or on behalf of) the parties)

**Notes**

1 This is a merchandising licence agreement, between a party who owns certain intellectual property, which may comprise of copyrights (particularly copyright in drawings of fictional characters) and trade marks, whereby the intellectual property rights are licensed to the licensee to enable the licensee to produce products based upon and incorporating the intellectual property.
2 See Form 88 note 6 [3714] post.
3 This clause is appropriate if the grant of rights under clause 3 is of a non-exclusive licence.
4 The licensor may wish to sell the products itself through a catalogue or shop, and this clause requires the licensee to supply the goods to the licensor, or to any person nominated by the licensor, and Schedule 5 deals with details such as quantities and price. Schedule 5 could also deal with the billing arrangements as between the licensor and the licensee in respect of the goods supplied pursuant to clause 9.
5 This is the form of copyright notice prescribed by the Universal Copyright Convention (Cmnd 8912) art III(1), which provides that the notice must be placed in such manner and location as to give reasonable notice of claim of copyright. If these formalities are complied with from the time of first publication on all copies of the book published with the authority of the author or other copyright proprietor, the book will be protected by copyright in all contracting states. This is primarily required for protection in those countries which are parties to the Universal Copyright Convention but not to the Berne Convention. In addition, this form of copyright notice has now become so widely accepted, that it serves as a useful warning to potential infringers that copyright in the work is claimed, and for this reason alone it is always worth including this form of notice even if it is not strictly a legal requirement in order to obtain copyright protection.
6 The licensor may wish to prohibit the grant of sub-licences because of the fact that the terms of the head licence between the licensor and the licensee will not be enforceable against the sub-licensee by reason of the doctrine of privity of contract
7 This provision could constitute a breach of EC Treaty art 81 (and the corresponding provisions of the Competition Act 1998 (47 Halsbury's Statutes (4th Edn) TRADE AND INDUSTRY), and should be avoided if the licensing programme is likely to exceed the guidelines set out in the Notice on Agreements of Minor Importance (OJ 1986 C231/2 updated OJ 1994 C 368/20).
8 It is in the licensee's interest that the licence should be registered (e.g. under the Trade Marks Act 1994 s 25 (48 Halsbury's Statutes (4th Edn) TRADE MARKS AND TRADE NAMES)) and so the Licensee should arguably bear the costs of registration.

9 An exclusive licensee of copyright has the same rights and remedies as if the licence had been an assignment: see the Copyright, Designs and Patents Act 1988 s 101 (11 Halsbury's Statutes (4th Edn) COPYRIGHT). The effect of this contractual provision appears to be that an exclusive licensee exercising its rights under the Copyright, Designs and Patents Act 1988 s 101 would be in breach of contract.

10 See Form 88 note 13 [3715].

11 Arbitration can be time consuming and expensive. The parties may instead wish to consider including an Alternative Dispute Resolution ('ADR') clause, providing for ADR to be carried out under the auspices of a suitable body, such as the Centre for Dispute Resolution ('CEDR').

# Chapter 12
# Sports Image Rights and Endorsement Agreements

## 12.1 Introductory Remarks

We live in an age in which image rules and perception is paramount. And this is not limited to celebrities, including sports personalities, who are anxious to project their *persona*, and thus maintain their celebrity status and popularity and, in turn, their marketability. But the phenomenon also extends to companies and their products, which, if they are to be successful in our consuming and materialistic society, also need to convey a positive image in order to command the attention of customers and increase sales. This is all down to branding, whose importance nowadays cannot be over emphasised and has been likened by Peter York, the style guru, to a kind of new religion:

> "The fastest-growing, most profitable, cleverest global corporations are organised around a new philosophy, a new religion and a new way of working. For these companies their brand is their central asset—physical products are secondary—and most of their quality time is spent making and reworking the brand—its meaning, attitude and social role, its values—because it's the brand that people buy, not the products. Products, so the thinking goes, are generic, copyable, discountable, vulnerable, but brands are unique magic."[1]

This philosophy has been successfully transferred and applied by clever marketers to sport, sports events and sports persons as products competing for consumer attention.

Again, according to York:

> "Nike isn't a maker of high-priced trainers but a world voice for sport as an agency of personal growth and achievement ... The Nike swoosh logo means precisely what the crucifix meant to an earlier generation in ghettos—it promises redemption, vindication and a way out."[2]

In a nutshell, a 'brand' is a badge of identification and, as such, a powerful and valuable marketing tool! A brand is also a valuable asset and as a leading international licensing guru has rightly remarked:

---

[1] Article entitled "Branded", '*The Times*', February 10, 2001.
[2] Ibid.

I. S. Blackshaw, *Sports Marketing Agreements: Legal, Fiscal and Practical Aspects*, ASSER International Sports Law Series, DOI: 10.1007/978-90-6704-793-7_12,

> "Businesses are no longer being valued on their manufacturing ability but on the new and frequently used basis of 'intellectual capital'."[3]

Sport is now a mega global business and branding has played a significant part in this process—often referred to as the 'commodification' of sport. In fact, Sepp Blatter, the President of FIFA, the World Governing Body of football, has said that sport is now a product!

Sports events, teams and individual sports persons are now seen and treated a 'commodities' to be commercialised, bought, sold and traded.[4] Sport is now firmly part of the worldwide entertainment industry. This is particularly true of football—the world's favourite game and most lucrative sport![5]

For example, Manchester United Football Club and Team have been developed and marketed as a brand around the world. This brand is worth millions of dollars and a significant contributor to the value of the Club, in terms of earnings, shareholder dividends and capital appreciation. Manchester United is also a publicly quoted company on the London Stock Exchange and became the first football club in the world in 2000 to achieve a market capitalisation of £1 billion.[6] The club is heavily involved in several lucrative 'affinity marketing' schemes, including a branded credit card, designed to increase its customer base—it is reported to have 50 million fans around the world, but only 1 million customers. And Manchester United has also been reported to be interested in a possible commercial opportunity to go into the casino business![7]

Power brands, like Manchester United, according to Tim Heberden, UK Managing Director of Brand Finance plc, reputed to be the leading brand valuation company in Europe:

> "....have the power to influence consumer demand, trade distribution, staff loyalty, supplier terms, and investor sentiment, transforming business performance and financial returns. [And] "...return on brand investment is becoming a critical issue for the board and the finance director."[8]

Brands are also featuring more and more on company balance sheets as an asset and sophisticated methods are being developed to value brands, especially sporting

---

[3] Angela Farrugia, co-founder and joint managing director of The Licensing Company.

[4] On the phenomenon and effects of 'commodification' in sport, see 'Sports Law' by Simon Gardiner, Mark James, John O'Leary, Roger Welch, Ian Blackshaw, Simon Boyes and Andrew Caiger Third Edition, 2006, Cavendish Publishing London at pp. 53–55. And on the related topic of the 'globalisation' of sport, see Paper of Professor Paul De Knop of Brussels University presented at the TMC Asser Instituut/CMS Derks Star Busmann Round Table Conference held in Utrecht on 9 March, 2001.

[5] In Europe, football is reputed to be worth £10 billion according to the Annual Deloitte and Touche Soccer Finance Report published on 30 July, 2003.

[6] See Ian Blackshaw 'BSkyB and sport on the net' *The Times*, 25 April, 2000.

[7] See *The Times* Sport 30 July, 2003.

[8] See 'Maximising Revenue from Licensing and Merchandising' by Ardi Kolah SportBusiness Group London 2002 at p. 252.

brands. However, Weston Anston, chairman of Trademark & Licensing Associates of New York sounds a timely warning:

> "The process of valuing brands on the balance sheet is becoming standard practice and it's interesting to see how many marketing executives overestimate the value of their brands which could lead to some bad marketing decisions."[9]

Likewise, sports persons have become celebrities in their own right—with salaries to match those of Hollywood film stars—and, as such, marketing icons.[10] The image rights of leading sports personalities, especially footballers, are increasingly being used and exploited to promote the sale of consumer products[11]—especially new ones.[12] As Anne M. Wall has pointed out:

> "One of the best uses of sports celebrities' right of publicity is product endorsements. Athletes can be ambassadors for the products and services they use. Their endorsement and positive publicity can lift consumer brand awareness, enhance brand image and stimulate sales volume. Upon introduction, licensed products that carry a celebrity's name can establish instant credibility for the brand in the market place"[13]

For a striking example of this sports marketing phenomenon, take the case of Manchester United's former striker, David Beckham. He earns many more millions more off the field of play than on it through the commercialisation of his image and name, both of which are instantly recognisable, well known and marketable throughout the world.[14] In this sense, therefore, it can be said that his face

---

[9] For an interesting account of the various methodologies and formulae used for valuing sports brands, see ibid. at pp. 264–270.

[10] Indeed, according to a Survey undertaken by 'AsiaBUS' in March 2001, the cult of the 'sports star' is now much stronger than the cult of the 'pop star' in marketing terms. For example, just less than 5% voted for Michael Jackson; whereas almost 13% voted for Michael Jordan. Over 1,000 people—between the ages of 15 and 64 years old—in Hong Kong, Singapore, Indonesia, Korea, Thailand, Malaysia, Philippines, Taiwan and in three major Chinese Cities took part in the Survey. If the same Survey were conducted today, the gap between the popularity of 'sports stars' and 'pop stars' would, it is submitted, be even wider.

[11] According to John Barton, Arnaud Le Mintier and Michael Tattersall: "Image rights are any rights that a player has vested in him as an individual person. These rights have value because they can be licensed to a third party for commercial exploitation in the market place. This may take form in a variety of methods of marketing, from the player helping to advertise non-football products such as bottled water, cars or soap, to the player appearing at a corporate hospitality event." See 'International Studies in Sport Selected Essays 2000/2001' published by Editions CIES, Neuchatel Suisse—2003, at pp. 73–79.

[12] For a general overview of the commercial value and legal significance of sports image rights, see 'Cashing in on the right image' and 'Getting the image right' by Ian Blackshaw of 9 & 10 December, 2002 on the SportBusiness web site ('www.sportbusiness.com').

[13] See 'Sports marketing and the law: Protecting proprietary interests in sports entertainment events' 7 Marquette Sports Law Journal 1996 at p. 154.

[14] Not only do football 'stars' earn mega sums from the commercial exploitation of their image and personality rights, but so also do golfers, like 'Tiger' Woods, tennis players, like Anna Kournikova, and Formula 1 drivers, like Michael Schumacher, to mention but a few!

is worth more than his feet—not only to himself but also to his club. He has become a brand in his own right.[15]

Chris Britcher, editor of the SportBusiness International website,[16] has described Beckham as a "marketing man's dream" in an article entitled "The Beckham Brand".[17] In it he posed the question whether Beckham really warrants all the media attention and hype. And goes on to explain the reasons for his success as a sports brand.[18]

## 12.2 What are Sports Image Rights?

These rights are known in different jurisdictions by a variety of names, including 'rights of privacy' (UK), 'rights of publicity' (USA) and 'rights of personality' (Continental Europe), but, for the purposes of this discussion, we will refer to them collectively as 'image rights' using the expression 'image' not in its in its narrowest sense of 'likeness' but in its wider sense of 'persona' or, *a fortiori*, 'brand' to use a marketing term. Irrespective of the term used, we are concerned with the extent to which sports persons, as human beings, have the legal right to control the commercial use of their identity.

A typical 'grant of rights' clause in a sports image licensing agreement defines image rights in rather broad terms as follows:

> "Access to the services of the personality for the purpose of filming, television (both live and recorded), broadcasting (both live and recorded), audio recording; motion pictures, video and electronic pictures (including but not limited to the production of computer-generated images; still photographs; personal appearances; product endorsement and advertising in all media; as well as the right to use the personality's name, likeness, autograph, story and accomplishments (including copyright and other intellectual property rights), for promotional or commercial purposes including, but without limitation, the personality's actual or simulated likeness, voice, photograph, performances, personal characteristics and other personal identification."

Of course, in practice, these rights need to be customised to each individual sports celebrity and each particular deal as part of a predetermined licensed strategy.

---

[15] Worth around £40 m a year in terms of sponsorship and licensing deals—slightly more than Tiger Woods at around £38 m a year!

[16] 'www.sportbusiness.com'

[17] 'www.sportbusiness.com' 18 June 2003.

[18] According to Tony Gadsby Peet of IMG, who manage many leading sports personalities, including Tiger Woods, but not David Beckham (until recently he was managed by SFX), sports brands, generally speaking, are more enduring and less ephemeral and opportunistic than entertainment brands and, therefore, require a different approach for maximisation of them: "With sports brands, you are working with a property that in most cases has been around a comparatively long time. The time frame and perspective is completely different. In this case it is much more important to understand brand strategy and long term development.".

*In Proactive Sports Management Ltd v.* 1) *Wayne Rooney,* 2) *Coleen Rooney (formerly McLoughlin),* 3) *Stoneygate 48 Limited,* 4) *Speed 9849 Limited,*[19] a recent high profile English case involving the sports image rights of the Manchester United striker, Wayne Rooney, the High Court defined these rights as:

> "Image Rights means the right for any commercial or promotional purpose to use the Player's name, nickname, slogan and signatures developed from time to time, image, likeness, voice, logos, get-ups, initials, team or squad number (as may be allocated to the Player from time to time), reputation, video or film portrayal, biographical information, graphical representation, electronic, animated or computer-generated representation and/or any other representation and/or right of association and/or any other right or quasi-right anywhere in the World of the Player in relation to his name, reputation, image, promotional services, and/or his performances together with the right to apply for registration of any such rights."

It may be noted, *en passant*, that, although, in most of the Sates of the US, 'publicity rights'—as image rights are generally known—are also generally regarded as being all embracing,[20] there are, however, certain limitations as a recent US case involving Tiger Woods has demonstrated.[21]

## 12.3 Who Owns Them?

One common concern is not only what image rights are but also who owns them. This is particularly important in the case of sports persons when they participate in organised sports events or as members of a team. This issue has been the subject of a poll—not apparently a very scientific one!—conducted by 'SportBusiness International' through their web site ('www.sportbusiness.com').[22]

The major finding of this survey shows that the majority—almost 55%—of sports industry executives polled consider that sports persons themselves should have control over their image rights and their commercial exploitation.

[19] [2010] EWHC 1807 (QB), at para [187].

[20] "First, the right to publicity recognises the economic value of an individual's identity. Second, the publicity right is an incentive for creativity, encouraging the production of entertaining and intellectual works. Finally, the right prevents unjust enrichment of those who usurp the identity of another." See the case of *Cardtoons, L.C. v. Major League Baseball Players Ass'n*, 838 F. Supp 1501 (N.D. Okla. 1993).

[21] See the case of *ETW Corporation v Jireh Publishing, Inc.* (2003 U.S. App. LEXIS 12488, 20 June 2003) discussed in the August 2003 issue of 'SportBusiness International' Magazine at p. 54, in which a painting entitled 'The Masters of Augusta' commemorating Tiger Woods' 1997 victory, produced and sold by Jireh without Woods' consent, was held by the Court not to infringe his 'right of publicity'.

[22] See 'Looking After Their Image' in the July 2003 issue of *SportBusiness International* Magazine at p. 17.

21.6% thought that the rights should be jointly held by "all interested parties"; whilst 16.5% considered that the club or team whom the sports persons represent should control them.

Only 3.7% were in favour of the national sports governing body holding the rights; and only 3.4% thought that the league in which the sports person plays should have control.

A further interesting finding of this survey is the widespread lack of clarity in commercial sports marketing contracts regarding the ownership of sports image rights. The need for precise express provisions dealing with the exploitation of such valuable rights cannot be overstated. Take, for example, the detailed provisions of clause 4 of the English FA Premier League Standard Player Contract, which are quite comprehensive and state as follows:

"4. Community public relations and marketing

4.1 For the purposes of the promotional community and public relations activities of the Club and/or (at the request of the Club) of any sponsors or commercial partners of the Club and/or of the League and/or of any main sponsors of the League the Player shall attend at and participate in such events as may reasonably be required by the Club including but not limited to appearances and the granting of interviews and photographic opportunities as authorised by the Club. The Club shall give reasonable notice to the Player of the Club's requirements and the Player shall make himself available for up to six hours per week of which approximately half shall be devoted to the community and public relations activities of the Club. No photograph of the Player taken pursuant to the provisions of this clause 4.1 shall be used by the Club or any other person to imply any brand or product endorsement by the Player.

4.2 Whilst he is providing or performing the services set out in this contract (including travelling on Club business) the Player shall:

4.2.1 wear only such clothing as is approved by an authorised official of the Club; and

4.2.2 not display any badge mark logo trading name or message on any item of clothing without the written consent of an authorised official of the Club Provided that nothing in this clause shall prevent the Player wearing and/or promoting football boots and in the case of a goalkeeper gloves of his choice.

4.3 Subject in any event to clause 4.4 and except to the extent of any commitments already entered into by the Player as at the date hereof or when on international duty in relation to the Players' national football association UEFA or FIFA he shall not (without the written consent of the Club) at any time during the term of this contract do anything to promote endorse or provide promotional marketing or advertising services or exploit the Player's Image either (a) in relation to any person in respect of such person's products brand or services which conflict or compete with any of the Club's club branded or football related products (including the Strip) or any products brand or services of the Club's two main sponsors/ commercial partners or of the League's one principal sponsor or (b) for the League

4.4 The Player agrees that he will not either on his own behalf or with or through any third party undertake promotional activities in a Club Context[23] nor exploit the Player's Image in a Club Context in any manner and/ or in any Media nor grant the right to do so to any third party.

4.5 Except to the extent specifically herein provided or otherwise specifically agreed with the Player nothing in this contract shall prevent the Player from undertaking promotional activities or from exploiting the Player's Image so long as:

4.5.1 the said promotional activities or exploitation do not interfere or conflict with the Player's obligations under this contract; and

4.5.2 the Player gives reasonable advance notice to the Club of any intended promotional activities or exploitation.

4.6 The Player hereby grants to the Club the right to photograph the Player both individually and as a member of a squad and to use such photographs and the Player's Image in a Club Context in connection with the promotion of the Club and its playing activities and the promotion of the League and the manufacture sale distribution licensing advertising marketing and promotion of the Club's club branded and football related products (including the Strip) or services (including such products or services which are endorsed by or produced under licence from the Club) and in relation to the League's licensed products services and sponsors in such manner as the Club may reasonably think fit so long as:

4.6.1 the use of the Player's photograph and/or Player's Image either alone or with not more than two other players at the Club shall be limited to no greater usage than the average for all players regularly in the Club's first team;

4.6.2 the Player's photograph and/or Player's Image shall not be used to imply any brand or product endorsement by the Player; and

4.6.3 PROVIDED that all rights shall cease on termination of this contract save for the use and/or sale of any promotional materials or products as aforesaid as shall then already be manufactured or in the process of manufacture or required to satisfy any outstanding orders.

---

[23] '"Club Context" shall mean in relation to any representation of the Player and/or the Player's Image a representation in connection or combination with the name colours Strip trademarks logos or other identifying characteristics of the Club (including trademarks and logos relating to the Club and its activities which trademarks and logos are registered in the name of and/or exploited by any Associated Company) or in any manner referring to or taking advantage of any of the same.'

4.7 In its dealings with any person permitted by the Club to take photographs of the Player the Club shall use reasonable endeavours to ensure that the copyright of the photographs so taken is vested in the Club and/or that no use is made of the said photographs without the Club's consent and in accordance with the provisions of this contract.

4.8 The Player shall be entitled to make a responsible and reasonable reply or response to any media comment or published statements likely to adversely affect the Player's standing or reputation and subject as provided for in clause 3.2.5 to make contributions to the public media in a responsible manner.

4.9 In this clause 4 where the context so admits the expression "the Club" includes any Associated Company of the Club but only to the extent and in the context that such company directly or indirectly provides facilities to or undertakes commercial marketing or public relations activities for the Club and not so as to require the consent of any Associated Company when consent of the Club is required.

4.10 For the purposes of the Contracts (Rights of Third Parties) Act 1999 nothing in this clause 4 is intended to nor does it give to the League any right to enforce any of its provisions against the Club or the Player.

4.11 Nothing in this clause 4 shall prevent the Club from entering into other arrangements additional or supplemental hereto or in variance hereof in relation to advertising marketing and/or promotional services with the Player or with or for all or some of the Club's players (including the Player) from time to time. Any other such arrangements which have been agreed as at the date of the signing of this contract and any image contract or similar contract required to be set out in this contract by the League Rules are set out in Schedule 2 para 13."

The above contractual provisions are designed to avoid cases of so-called 'Conflict Marketing'.

In Norway, for example, such a potential conflict between sports persons exploiting their individual image rights by endorsing one particular brand of sports clothing and the team, to which they belong, being sponsored by a rival sports clothing manufacturer, is dealt with in a particular way. Several national sports federations, including the Norwegian Football Federation, in their agreements with players, have accepted that the players can enter into three personal sponsorship agreements, provided that such agreements do not conflict with the federation's sponsorship programme. Under this arrangement, the federation must accept the personal sponsor prior to the individual player entering into the corresponding agreement. Alternatively, a practice has grown up whereby the federation co-signs any such agreement. Either way, potential sponsorship conflicts can be identified and nipped in the bud! And potential law suits avoided.

In The Netherlands, there are also specific arrangements for resolving cases of so-called 'Conflict Sponsorship'.

This is particularly important when planning and implementing sports image rights licensing programmes and agreements, which nowadays tend to transcend national boundaries. Whilst there are a number of similarities in various countries in Europe, there are also some important differences in concept and principle, as well as particular nuances in terms of interpretation and application of the applicable rules, reflecting differences in culture and temperament and also in the nature of the legal systems and their historical development and evolution.

The sports image rights market is more developed in some countries than others. Take the Nordic countries (Denmark, Norway, Sweden and Finland) for example. Johan Thoren has analysed the situation in these countries in a fairly recent article[24] as follows:

> "If the international sport industry can be compared to a teenager on the verge of becoming an adult, the Nordic markets are the younger siblings who don't always get to hang around and play. But with some years' delay, international developments will penetrate the Nordic countries as well."

The Nordic countries host relatively few large-scale international sports events. And in Finland, the law is probably the least developed even though Helsinki will host the World Athletics Championships in 2005. Throughout the region, however, football is extremely popular and well established—indeed the Scandinavian countries (the Nordic countries minus Finland) has a scaled-down version of the UEFA Champions League, known as the 'Royal League'—and attracts sponsors and broadcasters alike.

Luxembourg is a relatively small and undeveloped sports rights market too. In the rest of Europe, the sports market is relatively well developed and established.

Thus, when planning and devising international sports image rights marketing programmes, the state of development of the individual markets needs to be taken into consideration, and this, of course, needs to be reflected in the provisions of the corresponding Sports Image Rights Agreements.

## 12.4 Protecting Sports Image Rights

### *12.4.1 The UK*

The situation in Europe varies from country to country. Generally speaking, image rights are legally better protected in Continental Europe. In the UK, it is more difficult, as there is no specific law protecting image rights *per se*. A personality can only take legal action "if the reproduction or use of [his/her] likeness results in the infringement of some recognised legal right which he/she does own."[25]

---

[24] 'Cracking The Norse Code', SportBusiness International, February 2004, at pp. 38–42.

[25] Per Mr. Justice Laddie in *Elvis Presley Trade Marks* [1997] RPC 543 at p. 548.

Famous persons, therefore, have to rely on a 'rag bag' of laws, such as Trade Mark and Copyright Law and the Common Law doctrine of 'Passing Off' and/or vague notions of breach of commercial confidentiality. As, for example, in the Catherine Zeta Jones and Michael Douglas spat with 'Hello' Magazine and their unauthorised publication of their wedding photographs.[26] But it may be added that, even though successful, only modest damages were awarded by the Court to the celebrity pair. However, earlier, in what was seen as a softening of the previous law, the F1 racing driver, Eddie Irvine, successfully sued 'TalkRadio' under the Common Law doctrine of 'Passing Off' for using, around the time of the British Grand Prix, a doctored photograph of him holding and apparently listening to a radio (in the original photograph he was holding a mobile phone!), which implied that he was promoting or endorsing their radio station. For this breach, Irvine was finally awarded £25,000 in damages after appealing against a previous award of £2,000 made by the trial judge.[27] Again, not exactly a mega sum! Despite these cases, most commentators consider they were decided on their own particular facts and circumstances and do not herald the establishment of privacy and personality rights in the UK.

A number of sports personalities have registered their names and likenesses as trade marks under the UK Trade Marks Act 1994, for example, Damon Hill, the former Formula 1 driver, has registered the image of his eyes looking out from the visor of his racing helmet as a trade mark. And other sports personalities have taken other measures to protect their images. For example, the British athlete, David Bedford, a former 10,000 m world record holder, recently won a ruling against a phone directory company, 'The Number', over its advertising of its service ('118-118') featuring two runners in 1970s running kit. The UK Communications Regulator 'OfCom' held that 'The Number' had caricatured Bedford's image—drooping moustache, shoulder length hair and running kit—without his consent contrary to rule 6.5 of the UK Advertising Standards Code.[28]

### 12.4.2 Continental Europe

However, in Continental Europe, a legal right of personality, often combined with a right to protection of one's private and family life and honour and expressly safeguarded under the Constitution of the country concerned, generally exists. Thus making it much easier to protect and enforce image rights, which are considered to be an inherent and fundamental right of every human being to control the commercial use of their identity. A few examples follow to illustrate and contrast the legal position on the Continent with that in the UK.

---

[26] *Douglas & Others v Hello Limited* [2001] 2 WLR 992.

[27] *Irvine v Talksport Ltd* [2003] EWCA Civ 423.

[28] *Bedford against The Number Ltd*: OfCom, February 2004.

In Germany, articles 1 and 2 of the Constitution protect image rights. And last year, Oliver Khan, the German national team goalie, successfully sued Electronic Arts, the electronic games manufacturer, for using his image and name in an official FIFA computer football game. EA claimed that collective consent had been obtained from the national (VdV) and international (FIFPro) football players' unions. But not, in fact, from individual players, including Khan himself! This the Hamburg District Court ruled off side![29]

Likewise, in France, article 9 of the Civil Code confers a general right of privacy as part of a package of rights protecting the person. Thus, several years ago, the infamous football player Eric Cantona was able to successfully sue the publishing company, 'Foot Edition', and obtain substantial damages for their unauthorised commercial exploitation of his name and image in a special number of their magazine 'BUT' entitled 'Special Cantona'. The French Court held that the use of the footballer's name and image was not for general news purposes, which would not have been unlawful, but purely for the commercial benefit and financial gain of the publishing company, and thus against the law.

Again, articles 2 and 3 of the Italian Constitution also provide protection to sports persons. The general legal principle is that if an image is displayed or published except when allowed by law (the exceptional circumstances are set out in Article 97 of the Italian Law on Copyright No. 633/41), or its display causes prejudice to the dignity and the reputation of the person concerned, the Courts may order the abuse to cease and award compensation. The Italian Supreme Civil Court (*Corte di Cassazione*) has established that the reproduction of the image of a famous person, created for advertising purposes without the latter's consent, constitutes an injury to an individual's exclusive rights over their own likeness (*Cassazione Civile Sez. I,* 2nd May 1991 No. 4785). Exceptionally, para 1 of article 97 of the Law on Copyright provides that the consent of the image holder is not required when reproduction is "justified by the fame or by the public office covered by the latter, for justice and police requirements, for scientific, educational or cultural purposes, when the reproduction is connected to facts, happenings and ceremonies of public interest or, in any case, conducted in public". However, para 2 of the same article provides that "the likeness cannot be displayed or put on sale, when its display or sale might cause prejudice to the honour, reputation or dignity of the person represented".

In Sweden, unauthorised use of an individual's name or picture to promote goods and services is a civil wrong—and also a criminal offence where the use is intentional or grossly negligent—under the Act on Names and Pictures in Advertising of 1979.

In Switzerland, well-known sports persons are legally protected against unfair exploitation of their persons by article 28 of the Civil Code, which provides as follows:

---

[29] *Kahn v Electronic Arts GmbH* unreported 25 April, 2003 (Germany).

> "When anyone is injured in his person by an illegal act, he can apply to the judge for his protection from any person who takes an active part in effecting the injury.
>
> An injury is illegal where it is not justified by the injured person's consent, by a predominantly private or public interest or by the law."

And finally, article 18.1 of the Spanish Constitution (supplemented by Organic Law 1/1982 of 5 May) guarantees—in equal measure—the right to honour, to personal and family privacy and to self-image.

The increasing phenomenon of exploitation of sports image rights through new media platforms, including the Internet and (eventually) 'third generation' mobile 'phones,[30] which are now coming on stream, and the commercial opportunities they present for the creative use of sports programming and information content,[31] also raise important issues of the protection of sports persons' image rights against the unauthorised use of their names, images and likenesses. Computer, electronic and video sports games similarly pose threats to image rights in cyberspace space and the realm of virtual reality. Particular reference should be made to the recent landmark Court decision in Germany in the Oliver Khan case mentioned above.

Another issue that arises in relation to the legal protection of image rights is the impact of the European Convention on Human Rights (ECHR). In the United Kingdom, for example, the possibility of protecting a sports person's personality rights by invoking the right to privacy under article 8 and the right to property under article 1 of the First Protocol of the ECHR has arisen in a number of high profile cases. However, to date, there have been no Court decisions on these matters. Indeed, the general view amongst UK media and sports lawyers is that the interest protected by image rights is not the same as the interest, which the right to privacy is designed to protect. In the former case, the right to be protected is the right of sports personalities to commercially exploit their own names and likenesses for their own benefit and the failure to do so causes them financial loss. Whereas a person's right to privacy protects that person's personal integrity and autonomy from unwanted surveillance and intrusive behaviour. Further, the right to privacy may indeed protect celebrities—including sports stars—against invasions of their privacy, but this does not constitute *per se* a separate personality right. So far, no underlying property right in the *persona* of an individual has been legally recognised in the UK. And, indeed, any legal extension of the right of privacy to a right of personality would have to be balanced against the right of freedom of expression safeguarded under article 12 of the ECHR. This point was noted in the celebrated case of *Douglas & Others v Hello Limited*.[32] The lack of a separate personality right based on the right to privacy is discussed by Sara Whalley-Coombes and Elizabeth May in their article entitled, '*Getting 'personal'*

---

[30] These 'phones will permit one to view live or near-live clips of moving sports action.

[31] As to their value and commercial exploitation as a sports marketing tool, see 'Download Now!' by Jean-Paul de la Fuente in 'Football Business International' Magazine of 9 August 2003 at p. 19.

[32] [2001] 2 WLR 992.

*in the UK—to what extent does the law offer celebrities protection?'*[33] However, recently the super model, Naomi Campbell, won her breach of privacy case against the 'Daily Mirror' newspaper in the House of Lords.[34]

### *12.4.3 The USA*

Not surprisingly, the USA being the pioneer and 'granddaddy' of sports marketing and the cult of the 'celebrity', image rights, generally speaking, are legally recognised and protected in most of the States—not least in California, the home of Hollywood and film stars and other 'celebrities'. They are known as 'publicity rights' and are generally all embracing.[35]

However, there are certain limitations as a US case involving Tiger Woods well illustrates. In this case,[36] a painting entitled 'The Masters of Augusta' commemorating Tiger Woods' 1997 victory, produced and sold by Jireh without Woods' consent, was held by the Court not to infringe his 'right of publicity'. Of course, this decision was made according to the particular circumstances of the case. Incidentally, Tiger Woods has recently been involved in two domain name disputes. One case, which he won, concerned a domain name registered by a third party in the name of his daughter; and the second case, which he lost, concerned a domain name <charlieaxelwoods.com> registered by a third party in the name of his son, who was born on February 8, 2009.[37] Woods was not able to rely on his famous name alone to win this case: the 'Woods' of the domain name does not necessarily invoke the 'Woods' of the trademarks. Personal names are protected for the purposes of the ICANN Uniform Dispute Resolution Policy of 1999, but

---

[33] April 2002, Copyright World, at pp. 16–18. See further on this subject generally, 'The Right of a Sportsperson to Exploit His/Her Own Image and Success in the United Kingdom' by Dalton Odendaal, a Paper presented at a Conference on 'Sport: The Right to Participate' held at the Law Faculty at the University of Cape Town, South Africa, on 6 and 7 February, 2003, organised by Steve Cornelius and Rochelle le Roux of the Centre for Sports Law of the Rand Afrikaanse Universiteit, Johannesburg and the Institute of Development and Labour Law of the University of Cape Town, respectively.

[34] [2004] UKHL 22.

[35] 'First, the right to publicity recognises the economic value of an individual's identity. Second, the publicity right is an incentive for creativity, encouraging the production of entertaining and intellectual works. Finally, the right prevents unjust enrichment of those who usurp the identity of another.' See the case of *Cardtoons, L.C. v. Major League Baseball Players Ass'n*, 838 F. Supp 1501 (N.D. Okla. 1993).

[36] *ETW Corporation v. Jireh Publishing, Inc.* (2003 U.S.App. LEXIS 12488, 20 June, 2003).

[37] [1] *ETW Corp. and Eldrick 'Tiger' Woods, for itself, Tiger Woods and his minor child, Miss Sam Alexis Woods v. Leonard Meng Lee*, NAF Case, Claim Number: FA0904001256681 May 29, 2009; and [2] *1ETW Corp. and Eldrick 'Tiger' Woods, for itself, Tiger Woods and his minor child, Charlie Axel Woods v. Josh Whitf*ord Claim Number: FA0905001263352, NAF Case, June 24, 2009.

only if there is evidence of the name having been "...used in connection with the *commercial offering of goods or services* or that the personal name in question has acquired a *secondary meaning* as the source of those goods or services."

The Law on the protection of image rights in the Sates is quite complex and beyond the confines of this chapter and Book—in fact, a whole Book could be devoted to the subject. For a full account of this subject, with case studies and examples, including the fascinating concept of '*post mortem*' rights (the so-called richest person in the cemetery phenomenon), please refer to Chap. 19 in the Book entitled 'Sports Image Rights in Europe' of which the author of this Book is the Lead Editor.[38]

## 12.5 Fiscal Aspects

As with any kind of business, the commercialisation of sports image rights also has a fiscal dimension that needs to be considered. However, tax is a field in which the old adage that '*circumstances alter cases*' is particularly pertinent. In other words, tax advice very much depends upon the particular facts and circumstances of each individual case—as well as the aims to be achieved through any tax mitigation scheme. Equally, a cost–benefit analysis needs to be made in each case.

In this connection, brief mention should be made here of the English case of *Sports Club plc v Inspector of Taxes,*[39] in which Arsenal Football Club succeeded in having payments made to off-shore companies in respect of the Club's commercial exploitation of the image rights of their players, David Platt and Dennis Bergkamp, classified, for tax purposes, as capital sums and, therefore, non-taxable as income. This case is not only interesting from a fiscal point of view, but also from a jurisprudential point of view, in that, for tax purposes, image rights are considered to be capital assets even though image rights *per se* are not recognised as a separate species of property under the general law in the United Kingdom.

Opportunities exist in other parts of Europe for tax sheltering the financial returns from the commercial exploitation of sports image rights—not least in The Netherlands, which has a fairly comprehensive network of double taxation treaties around the world, which can be creatively used to save tax.

Again, in Switzerland, for example, tax mitigation structures can be devised founded on tax-exempt Not-for-Profit Foundations under Swiss Law.

For more detailed comments on these topics see Chap. 15 on the Fiscal Aspects of Sports Marketing Agreements.

---

[38] See following footnote for details of the Book: Chap. 19 is at pp. 345–373.

[39] [2000] STC (SCD) 443.

## 12.6 Legal Remedies for Infringing Sports Image Rights

Under English Law, a variety of legal remedies are available to those whose sports image rights have been infringed, ranging from damages to interim and final injunctions. Where trade marks are involved, under sections 14–16 of the UK Trade Marks Act 1994, the following specific civil remedies are available:

- damages;
- an account of profits;
- injunctions both interim and final; and
- orders for delivery up of the infringing articles.

In assessing damages, in a number of Continental European jurisdictions, a 'lost licence fee' is applied. In other words, what would the offending party have to have paid had that party been granted a licence to commercially use and exploit the sports image rights concerned.[40] However, generally speaking, damages awards on the Continent tend to be lower than in Common Law jurisdictions generally and certainly in the United States. For example, in Switzerland, Courts will rarely award more than between 10,000 and 20,000 Sw.Frs. for infringement of rights.

As for injunctions, being an equitable remedy under English law, such measures are granted by the Courts on a discretionary basis and only where damages would not be an adequate remedy. It may be possible, according to the particular circumstances of the case, to obtain specialised injunctions, such as '*Quia Timet*', which aims to prevent an anticipated breach of a legal right. In Spain, for example, under Article 9.2 of the Basic law ('Ley Organica'), a Judge can adopt all required measures in order to achieve the following results:

- to stop illegal interference by third parties;
- to restore the owner's full enjoyment of their image rights; and
- to prevent future interferences.

Where copyright infringements occur, amongst other remedies, the UK Copyright Designs and Patents Act 1988 gives the aggrieved party the right, subject to complying with certain procedures, to seize and detain infringing copies.[41]

In the European Union, under Regulation No. 3295 of 1994, copyright holders can ask their Customs Authorities to stop counterfeit or 'pirated' goods from entering their country. This is a very valuable and practical tool for fighting counterfeiting on a transnational scale.

However, apart from civil remedies, criminal sanctions may result from the infringement of sports image rights. For example, under section 92 of the UK Trade Marks Act 1994, fraudulent application or use of a trade mark constitutes a criminal

---

[40] See the discussion in Germany regarding damages in the *Oliver Khan* case and also in the *Caroline of Monaco* case in the Book *Sports Image Rights in Europe* edited by Ian S. Blackshaw & Robert C.R. Siekmann, 2005, TMC Asser Press, The Hague, at pp. 126–128.

[41] See sections 96–100 of the Copyright Designs and Patents Act 1988.

offence; and the offender can be fined and/or imprisoned, if the required criminal intent ('*mens rea*') is proved. In other words, the application or use of the mark must be either with the intention of the infringer gaining, or causing loss to someone else; and, in either case, must be without the consent of the trade mark owner.

Likewise, under section 107(1) of the UK Copyright, Designs and Patents Act 1988, there are similar criminal consequences where the copyright infringer knows, or has reason to believe, that an infringement is taking place.

Before resorting to legal proceedings, however, 'cease and desist letters' are often sent to infringers. But beware: to claim trade mark rights falsely and threaten legal action can, under section 21 of the 1994 UK Act, produce a counterclaim for a declaration that the threats are unjustified; and, in turn, this can lead to claims for damages and/or injunctions.

See further on this subject generally: 'Sports Merchandising: Fighting the Fakes' by Ian Blackshaw.[42]

## 12.7 Precedents

Included in Appendices I and II to this Chapter are General Precedents of a Sports Image Rights Agreement and a Sports Endorsement Agreement. As usual, these Precedents are for general guidance and illustrative purposes only.

## 12.8 Concluding Remarks

As will be appreciated from the above account of the legal nature and protection of Sports Image Rights in various jurisdictions, the subject is a complex and detailed one. Care should, therefore, be taken when negotiating and drafting the corresponding Sports Image Rights Agreements. Attention to detail throughout is paramount and, in particular, the scope of the rights to be granted needs to be clearly defined and agreed between the parties and spelled out in the Agreement.

As an example of the kinds of legal problems and disputes that can arise under Sports Image Rights Agreements, see the recent *Wayne Rooney* case[43] referred to above. It is quite a complex case, as the judgement of 821 paragraphs and 195 pages testifies! But a general idea of the legal issues raised in this case may be gleaned from the following rather simplistic summary of the case:

The case concerned the Image Rights Agreement signed in 2003 by Wayne Rooney (Rooney), when he was 17, with his former agents, Proactive Sports Management Ltd (Proactive). Proactive were seeking unpaid commission and invoices totalling between £1–3 m against Wayne and over £200,000 against his

---

[42] The *International Sports Law Journal*, 2004/3-4, at p. 76.

[43] *Proactive Sports Management Ltd v.* 1) *Wayne Rooney,* 2) *Coleen Rooney (formerly McLoughlin)*, 3) *Stoneygate 48 Limited,* 4) *Speed 9849 Limited* [*2010*] EWHC 1807 (QB).

wife, Coleen. Rooney signed an Image Rights Representation Agreement (IRRA) with Proactive, to represent him in his commercial affairs for the next 8 years. Midway through this Agreement, when his agent, Paul Stretford, was fired from Proactive and set-up a new sports agency, the Rooney's followed him and purported to sever their links with Proactive on 18 December, 2008. Proactive sued Rooney and his wife Coleen for liquidated damages and commission that they considered continued to be owed to them on the various Sponsorship Agreements, which had been negotiated on their behalf by Proactive. Rooney and his wife successfully counter-claimed against Proactive, arguing that any contract between them was 'void, invalid, unenforceable and of no effect' as the 8 year term represented a restraint of trade.

The marathon Judgement of Judge Hegarty QC includes at the end a summary of his findings and conclusions, which throws further light on the legal issues raised in the case under the corresponding Image Rights Agreement, in the following terms:

"PART X

CONCLUSIONS

818. Despite the length of this judgment, I can summarise my conclusions quite briefly. The Image Rights Representation Agreement dated 16th January 2003 is not void for mistake but is unenforceable by Proactive as being in unreasonable restraint of trade. Proactive cannot, therefore, recover, as a matter of contract, any sums which remain unpaid but which would otherwise have fallen due to it under the terms of the agreement had it not been unenforceable. Nor can it recover any further commission in respect of income receivable in the future by Stoneygate under contracts procured by Proactive or pursue any claim for damages for breach of the Image Rights Representation Agreement. It is, however, entitled to a restitutionary remedy in respect of those services which it has provided to Stoneygate and in respect of which it has not yet received any remuneration. That must be the subject of an assessment at a later stage in respect of which I will give directions in due course.

Even if I had found that the Image Rights Representation Agreement was valid and enforceable, I would have held that Proactive's claim for commission was limited to those sums which had already fallen due at the time when the relationship between the parties broke down at the end of October 2008. In respect of the subsequent period prior to its acceptance of Stoneygate's repudiatory breach of contract on or about 24th December 2009, Proactive would have been entitled to compensation or damages to be assessed in accordance with the principles laid down in Roberts v. Elwells Engineers Ltd [1972] 2 QB 586. Thereafter, it would have been entitled to recover damages in respect of the loss sustained as a result of the premature determination of the Agreement. But on what I consider to be the true construction of this particular contract, it would have had no right to commission on sums receivable by Stoneygate from third parties after the expiration of the eight-year term; and any claim for commission in respect of sums receivable prior to that date, but after the breakdown in relations between the parties, would have formed part of its claim for compensation and damages and would have had to be taken into account in the assessment of the appropriate sums.

820. In relation to Speed I have concluded, albeit with some hesitation, that Proactive is entitled, as a matter of contract, to recover the full amount of any commission which became due and payable prior to the end of October 2008. The total amount of the commission is, by my calculation, the sum of £78,725.25. But if I had found that Proactive

was not entitled to a contractual remedy I would nonetheless have held that it would have been entitled to a restitutionary quantum meruit.

821. Despite my conclusions on the general issues raised in these proceedings, I have nonetheless had to consider various individual invoices which were the subject of dispute; and I have sought to resolve the specific issues raised in respect of each of them. In all but three instances, the resolution of these issues is immaterial to the outcome of the proceedings. But I have concluded that, in the case of both Stoneygate and Speed, there was a wholly separate agreement for the provision of accountancy services by reason of which Proactive is entitled to recover £5,000 plus value added tax from Stoneygate under Invoice 18022 and a total of £10,000 plus value added tax from Speed under Invoices 18021 and 18026."

The full Judgement in the Rooney case is well worth reading, especially for anyone who suffers from insomnia!

The detailed matters to be covered in a Players' Sports Image Rights Agreement may be seen from the provisions of the General Precedent set out in the Appendix to this chapter. Again, this Precedent is for guidancc purposes only, and will, of course, like all Precedents, need to customised and adapted to fit and reflect the particular facts and circumstances of the actual commercial deal struck between the parties.

# 12.9 Appendices

## *12.9.1 Appendix 1*

Encyclopaedia of Forms and Precedents/SPORT AND SPONSORSHIP vol 39(2) 2004/(C) Forms and Precedents/A: EMPLOYMENT AND CONTRACTS FOR SERVICES Agreement for the use and exploitation of a player's image

**Agreement for the Use and Exploitation of a Player's Image***

**This Agreement** is made the......... day of...........

**Between:**
(name) of (address) ('the Club'), which term shall include any affiliated company to which the Club assigns any of the rights and/or licences granted to the Club under this Agreement and (name) of (address) ('the Player'), a professional football player, who has separately contracted to provide certain playing and promotional services to the Club

**It Is Agreed** as follows:

**Definitions and interpretation**
In this Agreement the following expressions shall have the following meanings:

| | |
|---|---|
| "Merchandising Activities" | means (a) the manufacture, sale, advertisement, distribution, licensing, marketing and promotion of products or services, by or on behalf of the Club or any sponsor or licensee of the Club, in conjunction with the Club's marks or logo which relate in any way to the Club, (b) the promotion of the Club and/or (c) the promotion and assistance of the Club's sponsors and licensees exclusively in relation to their marketing activities that relate to the Club; |
| "Player's Image" | means the Player's name, nickname, initials, signature, endorsement, reputation, voice, shirt number, video or film portrayal, computer generated or animated portrayal, photographs, licences, biographical information, graphical representations, images or facsimile image and all other characteristics of the Player; |

* This agreement is intended for use in addition to an employment contract between a player and a professional sports club. It is intended to be an efficient division of income between playing/employment services and those related to the use of a player's name and reputation, i.e. his 'image rights'. Source: Lexis Nexis; reproduced with permission.

| | |
|---|---|
| "Rights" | means the intellectual property rights and other rights now existing or in the future arising in the Player's Image, of whatever nature including without limitation all rights in the nature of 'personality' or 'image' rights as well as any and all patents, trade marks, service marks, trade names, Internet domain names, rights in designs, copyright and moral rights, performance rights, database rights, in each case whether registered or unregistered and including applications for registration, and all rights or forms of protection having equivalent or similar effect anywhere in the world; |
| "Rights Fee" | the fee specified in clause 5; |
| "Term" | the period specified in clause 2; |
| "Territory"' | the world. |

In this Agreement the singular includes the plural and vice versa and any gender includes any other gender.
The clause headings do not form part of this Agreement and shall not be taken into account in its construction or interpretation.

**1. Term**

1.1 This Agreement shall commence as of (date) and shall continue, unless terminated earlier in accordance with clause 5 (below), until (date).

**2. Grant of Rights**

2.1 In consideration for the Club's payment of the Rights Fee, the Player grants to the Club for the Term in the Territory the Rights in relation to the Merchandising Activities. It is agreed that:

- the Player's Image and the Rights shall remain the property of the Player absolutely; and
- all rights in any products or services marketed by or on behalf of the Club that make use of the Player's Image and/or the Rights, and any goodwill arising as a result, shall remain the property of the Club absolutely.

2.2 The grant of the Rights is exclusive and the Player shall not exploit, or authorise anyone else other than the Club to exploit, the Player's Image and the Rights in relation to the Merchandising Activities; provided always that nothing in this Agreement shall prevent or prejudice the Player from licensing third parties to use the Player's Image and the Rights in connection with the marketing and promotion of products and services that do not carry the Club's marks or logo or otherwise relate to the Club.

## 3. Player's warranties and undertakings

3.1 The Player represents, warrants and undertakes to the Club that he:

- has full power and authority to enter into and perform his obligations under this Agreement and to grant to the Club all of the rights granted under this Agreement; and
- has not done and shall not do anything that would impair the Club's free and unrestricted exercise of the rights granted under this Agreement.

## 4. Consideration

4.1 In full and final consideration for the grant of the Rights the Club shall pay to the Player £... (plus VAT, if applicable), in four equal instalments, as follows:
(insert payment schedule)
following receipt of an appropriate invoice from the Player.

4.2 The Player:

- shall pay and be solely responsible for any income tax, national insurance contributions and/or any other taxes and levies of any kind due on the payments made by the Club to the Player under this Agreement; and
- shall indemnify the Club in respect of the same, including paying to the Club, within 14 days of receipt of written demand therefor, any tax, national insurance contributions or other levy that any taxing authority demands from the Club in respect of such payments.

## 5. Termination

5.1 The Club may terminate this Agreement with immediate effect by giving written notice to the Player if:

- the Player is in material breach of any of the terms of this Agreement and fails to cure such breach within 14 days of receipt of notice of the breach;
- the Player ceases to be registered with the Club; or
- the Player receives a punishment from any competent body, including any football governing body, in respect of any drugs or alcohol-related matter.

5.2 The Player may terminate this Agreement with immediate effect by giving written notice to the Club if:

- the Club is unable to pay its debts or enters into liquidation or has a receiver or administrator appointed or takes or suffers any action that, in the reasonable opinion of the Player, means that the Club is unable to pay its debts; or
- the Club is in material breach of any of the terms of this Agreement and fails to cure such breach within 14 days of receipt of notice of the breach; or
- the Player ceases to be registered with the Club.

5.3 If either (i) the Player dies or (ii) the separate employment contract between the Club and the Player dated (date) is terminated or expires, this Agreement shall automatically terminate and the Club shall pay to the Player an amount equal to the consideration remaining outstanding at that point under this Agreement (ie, £... less any amounts paid by the Club to the Player pursuant to clause 5 of this Agreement prior to the date of termination).

## 6. Infringements

6.1 The Player shall provide reasonable co-operation to the Club in combating any unauthorised use by any third party of the Player's Image or the Rights in connection with the Club; and/or defending any claim that the rights of any third party are infringed by this Agreement.

## 7. Confidentiality

7.1 The parties shall keep this Agreement confidential and shall not disclose its contents to any third party other than their professional advisors, save as agreed by the parties or as required by law or by any competent authority or in order to exercise the rights and perform the obligations arising under this Agreement. This obligation shall survive termination of the Agreement.

## 8. Notices

8.1 Notices to be given under this Agreement shall be in writing in English and left at or sent by first class registered or recorded delivery mail to the appropriate address shown at the head of this Agreement or to such other address as the party concerned shall from time to time designate hereunder.

## 9. Assignment

9.1 Either party may assign its rights and/or obligations under this Agreement without the other party's written consent, unless, in the case of the Player only:

- such assignment is made to the benefit of the Player's wholly owned company; and
- the Player accepts an express obligation to the Club, as part of the assignment, to guarantee to the Club (as principal obligor and not merely as surety) the full due and punctual performance and observance by the assignee company of all of the obligations owed to the Club under or pursuant to this Agreement, which guarantee shall remain in full force and effect until all obligations of the assignee company under this assigned Agreement have been fully satisfied.

**10. Entire agreement**

10.1 This document contains the entire agreement between the parties relating to the Player's Image and the Rights, and may not be varied or waived, in whole or in part, except by the written agreement of the parties.

**11. Benefit of agreement**

11.1 Each party undertakes with the other to do at its/his cost such things as may be reasonably required to ensure that the other receives the full benefit of this Agreement.

**12. Rights of third parties**

12.1 A person who is not a party to this Agreement may not rely upon or enforce any rights pursuant to the Contracts (Rights of Third Parties) Act 1999.

**13. Governing law**

13.1 This Agreement shall be governed by English law, without regard to English conflict of law principles. Any disputes between the parties relating to this Agreement shall be submitted to arbitration in London according to the rules of the Sports Dispute Resolution Panel within the framework of the Arbitration Act 1996. The English courts shall have exclusive jurisdiction over any challenge made to any resulting arbitration award.

As Witness etc.
(signatures of (or on behalf of) the parties)

## *12.9.2 Appendix 2*

# Sports Promotion and Endorsement Contract*

**This Agreement** is made the day of 2[ ]

**Between**

(1) [ ] of [ ] ["the Player"]
(2) [ ] [ ] whose registered office is at [ ]["the Company" which expression includes its successors in title licensees and assigns]

**Recitals**

A. The Company manufactures and markets the Company Products
B. The Company wishes to engage the Player to provide the Promotional Services upon the terms of this Agreement
C. The Player hereby grants to the Company certain rights upon the terms of this Agreement in connection with the Licensing Rights

**Operative Provisions**

**1. Definitions**

1.1 In this Agreement the following expressions shall have the following meaning

**"Company Marks"** means the [registered] [unregistered] trade marks [insert details]
**"Company Products"** means those Products which are manufactured by the Company and marketed under or in connection with the Company Marks
**"Company Products"** means any Product other than a Company Product
**"Fee"** means all amounts payable by the Company to the Player under clause [3]
**"Governing Body"** means [insert details]
**"Licensing Rights"** means the right of the Company to use reproduce and publish

(i) the Player's name likeness voice signature and biographical details
(ii) agreed quotations

* Source: Lexis Nexis; reproduced with permission.

(iii) photographs films videos sound recordings and electronic images of the Player in any medium
(iv) artistic caricature or electronic animated images of the Player in any medium
(v) the Products of Services

endorsing the Company Products or in promotional sponsorship advertising or marketing material relating to the Company Products [in each case in such form as is agreed by the Player for such purposes in accordance with the terms of this Agreement]

**"Products of Services"** means those products in the form of any photography film sound recording or other recording in any medium of any of the Promotional Services
**"Promotional Services"** means attending and participating on up to [six (6)] occasions during each year of the Term in each case at a location not further than [ ] miles travelling time from the address of the Player at the head of this Agreement and in each case for no longer than a total of [ ] working hours

(i) promotional events and public relations exercises organised by or involving the Company including but not limited to marketing press conferences product promotions signing sessions celebrity events Company functions
(ii) photographic sessions to shoot advertising promotional and marketing material endorsing Company Products including but not limited to posters brochures in store displays billboards and wall boards
(iii) photographic filming recording or broadcasting sessions for the purpose of producing advertisements and marketing material endorsing Company Products to be used on any and all applicable broadcast media in accordance with the terms of this Agreement
(iv) training sessions
(v) benevolent or charity work and
(vi) sports or media clinics

in each case endorsing Company Products and being of a nature in accordance with the terms of this Agreement [and as agreed by the Player in each respect from time to time]

**"Products"** means [insert details for example all leisurewear and footwear]
**"Term"** means the period in clause [4]
**"Territory"** means [the world]

**2. Rights**

2.1 In consideration of the Fee the Player grants to the Company the exclusive right in the Territory during the Term to use and exploit the Licensing Rights

2.2 The Player in each case insofar as the Player is the owner of the same and is able to do so

2.2.1 grants to the Company the entire copyright and neighbouring rights for [the full period of copyright (including any extensions and renewals)] [the Term] in all the Products of Services

2.2.2 waives all so called moral rights under the Copyright Designs and Patents Act 1988 sections 77–80 in and in relation to the Products of Services

2.2.3 consents to the use of his performer's non-property rights and assigns his performer's property rights [as such terms are defined in Part II of the Copyright Designs and Patents Act 1988 (as amended)] to the Company for the use of the Products of Services

2.3 If requested to do so by the Company the Player must perform the Promotional Services

**3. Payments**

3.1 Subject to the Player performing his obligations in this Agreement and in consideration of the grant of rights made to it the Company shall pay the Player the following sums during the Term

3.1.1 [£ ] for the first contract year
3.1.2 [£ ] for the second contract year and
3.1.3 [£ ] for the third contract year

3.2 The amount due in each contract year is payable in two equal instalments on 31 March and 30 September of the contract year

3.3 If during any contract year the Player

3.3.1 [is appointed captain of his full representative national side or
3.3.2 is selected to represent his full representative national side or
3.3.3 plays in a cup or league winning team or
3.3.4 scores more than [state number of goals]]

then in addition to the amounts payable under clause 3.1 the Company shall pay the
Player a one off bonus payment of [£ ] for that contract year

**4. Term**

4.1 This Agreement shall remain in force for three (3) years commencing on [date] [from the date of signature]

4.2 If the Company gives notice to the Player not later than [insert date] the Player shall enter in good faith into negotiations with the Company with a view to extending the Term on the same terms contained in this Agreement except as to clause 3 and this clause 4 for an additional twelve (12) months from the date of expiry of the Term and shall until [ ] not enter into any negotiations in respect of such an agreement in respect of the endorsement of Products with any other person. In the event that the Company and the Player have failed for any reason to agree the terms to replace clauses 3 and 4 of this Agreement (there being no obligation upon either party to reach any such agreement) as at the said date the Player shall be free to enter into negotiations and/or any agreement or arrangement with any person upon any terms without restriction

**5. Exclusivity**

5.1 Subject to clause 5.2 the Player shall not during the Term use himself or grant the right to use the Licensing Rights or the Promotional Services (or any rights or services the same as or similar to the rights or services granted to the Company under this Agreement) and/or any endorsement or advertising marketing or promotional services of the Player to any third party

5.1.1 whose principal business is the manufacture distribution or sale (not by way solely of being a general retailer not more than 10% (ten percent) of whose total sales are of Drinks) of Competing Products or

5.1.2 where the material effect of such a grant is to grant advertising marketing or promotional or sponsorship rights in connection with the Event in relation to or in connection with any Competing Products

5.2 Notwithstanding the provisions of clause 5.1 and clause 6.2 the Company recognises that representative national and club teams are sometimes required to wear apparel in connection with their representation of their national or club team which may conflict with the terms of this Agreement. The Company and the Player agree that if the Player is obliged to wear such apparel then in those circumstances only the Player is excepted from the provisions of clause 5.1 and 6.2

**6. Player's Obligations**

6.1 During the Term the Player shall

6.1.1 render the Promotional Services to the best of his ability at such time and place as the Company requires

6.1.2 in performing the Promotional Services follow all reasonable instructions made by the Company co-operate with any third parties acting on the Company's behalf conduct himself in a proper manner and maintain a tidy appearance

6.1.3 comply with all relevant rules and regulations of the Governing Body

6.1.4 use his best endeavours to maintain his physical and mental fitness so as to be fit for competition

6.1.5 wear the Company Products whilst engaged in any sporting activities or competition and whilst performing the Promotional Services

6.1.6 wherever possible wear the Company Products when promoting products of other non-competing manufacturers

6.2 The Player shall not

6.2.1 at any time whether performing the Promotional Services or otherwise commit any act or omission or make any remarks that are in any way derogatory to or concerning the Company and/or the Company Products and/or the existence or terms of this Agreement

6.2.2 wear carry or display any Products with a visible brand or logo other than the Company Products

6.2.3 when performing the Promotional Services commit any act or omission or make any remarks that are defamatory of any person obscene or constitute any breach of any rights or any third party in any part of the world

## 7. Warranties

7.1 Each party warrants to the other that

7.1.1 it is free to enter into this Agreement and grant the rights and perform the obligations undertaken by it

7.1.2 it has not entered into and shall not enter any agreements which may conflict with this Agreement

7.1.3 it will not incur any liability on behalf of the other party or represent that it has the authority to do so

7.1.4 it will keep the terms of this Agreement and any financial marketing or business information relating to the affairs of the other which has been disclosed to it by the other pursuant to the terms of this Agreement or as a result of the discharge of its obligations pursuant to this Agreement confidential except to their respective professional advisers or as required by law or (in the case of the Player) as reasonably required by any club by whom the Player is employed from time to time and/or the Governing Body

## 8. Company's Obligations

8.1 The Company shall during the Term

8.1.1 provide adequate free supplies of Company Products for the Player's use at Player's written request
8.1.2 pay the Fee
8.1.3 ensure that all Company Products are manufactured to the highest standards such that the same are fit for all purposes for which Products are generally used and comply with all relevant safety laws and regulations or such other relevant standards
8.1.4 ensure that in exercising the Licensing Rights the Company complies with all relevant laws and regulations
8.1.5 comply with the rules and regulations of the Governing Body
8.1.6 comply with clause 9 (Approvals)
8.1.7 pay all reasonable out of pocket expenses accommodation and travel costs incurred by the Player in performing the Promotional Services

8.2 The Company shall not

8.2.1 exercise the Promotional Services at any time which would unreasonably conflict with the Player's schedule of training or competition
8.2.2 timetable any single appearance of the Player in performing the Promotional Services for more than [ ] ([ ]) hours duration [exclusive of travel time]

**9. Approvals**

9.1 The Company must send the Player all material used in exploiting the Licensing Rights and/or all proposals for or in respect of the Promotional Services to be conducted for the Player's approval not less than one (1) month before the Company intends to publish the material
9.2 The Player must give his written approval of the materials and/or proposals no later than ten (10) days after receiving any such material from the Company
9.3 If the Player does not give his written approval of the materials and/or proposals the Player may indicate any suggested modifications to the materials which the Player reasonably requires. If the Company and the Player cannot agree on any suggested modifications the final decision on the subject matter thereof may in the case of materials used in the exploitation of the Licensing Rights only (and not in the case of Promotional Services) may be taken by the [Company]
9.4 If the Player does not respond within ten (10) days after receiving the material then approval is deemed to be given

**10. Limitations**

10.1 The Company has no liability under this Agreement for any claim the Player may have for loss of publicity or chance to enhance reputation

10.2 The Company is not liable to the Player for any injury or damage suffered by the Player from wearing or using the Company Products unless such injury or damage arises from the negligence of the Company

10.3 The Company may enter a similar promotion and endorsement agreement for the Company Products with any other player

**11. Suspension**

11.1 If the Player is in the reasonable opinion of the Company unable to perform the Promotional Services through reasons of injury and/or physical or mental ill health the Company may by service of notice in writing upon the Player suspend the Term. Such suspension shall remain in force until forthwith upon either

11.1.1 the Company serves upon the Player notice in writing that such suspension shall be lifted or

11.1.2 the termination of this Agreement pursuant to clause 11.2 or clause 12

11.2 During any period of suspension of the Term the Company is not obliged to pay the Fee but in all other respects both parties continue to be bound by the terms of this Agreement

11.3 The aggregate period of any suspension of the Term shall not exceed six (6) months and forthwith upon the date on which the appropriate period of suspension of the term exceeds the period of six (6) months this Agreement shall terminate forthwith

**12. Termination**

12.1 The Company may terminate this Agreement by giving notice to the Player if the Player

12.1.1 fails to perform any Promotional Services or

12.1.2 commits any act which affects the Company's reputation in an adverse manner or

12.1.3 publicly admits to or is convicted of any offence consisting of the use of any so called controlled substance or tests positive in any drug testing organised by the Governing Body or

12.1.4 is convicted of any offence involving dishonesty or violence or

12.1.5 dies retires or is permanently disabled or

12.1.6 [...]

12.1.7 endorses Competing Products or

12.1.8 unless the provisions of clause 11 apply is in breach of any term of this Agreement and (where the breach in question is capable of remedy in such period) has not remedied that breach within fifteen (15) days of service of notice specifying such breach

12.2 The Player may terminate this Agreement by giving notice to the Company if the Company

12.2.1 is in material breach of any terms of this Agreement and (where the breach in question is capable of remedy in such period) has not remedied that breach within fifteen (15) days of service of notice specifying such breach or

12.2.2 if the Company goes into liquidation (except for the purposes of amalgamation or reconstruction) receivership (including administrative receivership) has an administrator appointed or makes any arrangement or composition with its creditors

**13. Effects of Termination**

13.1 Upon termination under clause 12 or expiry of this Agreement due to effluxion of time the rights and obligations of the parties to this Agreement cease

13.2 Subject to clause 13.3 on termination the Company must immediately pay the Player any money due under clause 3 and clause 8.1.7 up to the date of termination

13.3 If this Agreement is terminated by the Company pursuant to clause 12.1 the Company may reclaim from the Player any money in excess of the amount to which the Player is entitled on the basis that the sums payable to the Player accrue day to day on a pro rata basis within the contract year. If requested by the Company the Player must pay the amount due within thirty (30) days of the termination of this Agreement

13.4 Termination of this Agreement is without prejudice to any rights or obligations of either party which may have accrued at the date of termination

**14. Notices**

14.1 Any notice to be served under this Agreement must be in writing and served upon the other party at its address set out in this Agreement (or such other address as may be notified for this purpose) either by hand or by first class post. Notices are deemed served on delivery if delivered by hand or seventy- two (72) hours after posting if sent by first class post

**15. Taxation**

15.1 The Player shall be responsible for his own tax and national insurance and shall indemnify the Company against any liability for payment of such sums

[Boilerplate Clauses]

[Execution Clauses]

# Chapter 13
# Sports TV Rights Agreements

## 13.1 Introductory Remarks

Sport is now big business globally and there is, therefore, a lot to play for, from both a sporting and a financial point of view. Indeed, as the former UK Sports Minister, Richard Caborn, who, incidentally, initiated the EU 'White Paper' on Sport during the UK Presidency of the EU in the second half of 2005, has pointed out:

> "[t]he commercialisation of sport, especially football, has moved at a pace that no one could have envisaged."

The rise of sport as a global industry is largely the result over the years of the marketing of sports, sports persons and events, originally in the United States of America (USA), and subsequently in Europe and elsewhere. This has led to the establishment of a world-wide discrete sports marketing industry, due to the vision and pioneering work of Mark McCormack in the USA, through his company, IMG (International Management Group); and in Europe, by Horst Dassler, of the German sports goods manufacturer ADIDAS, through his Swiss company ISL (International Sport Leisure and Culture), which he founded. Sadly, neither of these pioneers is alive today to see the extent to which sports marketing has grown and enjoy the full fruits of their work. Also, ISL went into bankruptcy several years ago.

Of the sports marketing mix, which includes sports sponsorship, merchandising, endorsement of products and services, and corporate hospitality, perhaps the most important and lucrative one is the sale and exploitation of sports broadcasting rights around the world, which contribute mega sums to many sports and sports events, including the Summer and Winter Olympic Games and the FIFA World Cup. Indeed, it is fair to say that, without the sums generated by sports

I. S. Blackshaw, *Sports Marketing Agreements: Legal, Fiscal and Practical Aspects*, ASSER International Sports Law Series, DOI: 10.1007/978-90-6704-793-7_13,

broadcasting, such major events—and, in fact, many others—could not take place and consequently sport—and sports fans—would be the losers.[1]

In this respect, the commercialisation of sports broadcasting rights may be considered as the 'oxygen of sport'. There is a symbiotic relationship between sport and TV broadcasting. Indeed, according to David Griffith-Jones, QC:

> "This marriage between sport and television is one made in heaven."[2]

And according to Prof Richard Parrish:

> "The broadcasting sector and sport have……revolutionised each other."[3]

And the significance of new technology—especially broadband and quicker access to the Internet—in the development and financial importance of sports broadcasting rights cannot be over emphasised as Richard Verow, Clive Lawrence and Peter McCormick rightly point out:

> "In many ways, the rise of new platforms for the dissemination of media products and the inevitable rise of sport as the global media property it now is have been intertwined. Just as the formation of the FA Premier League and the rise of satellite pay television through BSkyB seemed inextricably linked, so when new platforms, such as the proliferation of digital television channels or the exploitation for broadcast or quasi broadcast purposes of internet and mobile telephony platforms, come to the fore, their usual test bed in terms of content is in sport. It seems that only sport has the pulling power nationally and internationally to justify the sort of investments needed to bring new media platforms to market, and maybe sport is alone considered sufficiently popular for the uptake by new customers properly to reflect the potential of the medium rather count simply as a commentary on the first content offered through it."[4]

For example, the English Premier Football League, the richest and most popular in the world, has sold its principal live broadcast rights to its matches for the next three seasons, beginning in August 2010 and ending in 2013, for another record sum of US$3.1bn (£1.782bn). Again, the lion's share of these rights has been sold to the satellite broadcaster, BSkyB, and the matches will be shown as part of its Sky Sports package on a subscription basis. Incidentally, BSyB is owned by the Australian media magnate, Rupert Murdoch, through his Group News International, who considers "sports as a battering ram and a lead offering" in all his pay

[1] See Blackshaw, in Chap. 11 ('Sports Marketing, Sponsorship and Ambush Marketing') of 'Sports Law' by Simon Gardiner, Mark James, John O'Leary, Roger Welch, Ian Blackshaw, Simon Boyes and Andrew Caiger, third edition, 2006, Sydney & London, Cavendish Publishing Limited, ISBN 10: 1-85941-894-5.

[2] Griffith-Jones, D., 'Law and the Business of Sport', 1997, London, Butterworth and Co, at p. 289.

[3] Parrish, Richard, 'Sports law and policy in the European Union', 2003, Manchester and New York, Manchester University Press.

[4] Verow, Richard, Lawrence, Clive, McCormick, Peter, 'Sports Business', Second Edition, 2005, Bristol, Jordan Publishing Limited, at p. 321.

television operations around the world.[5] This again demonstrates the great value that attaches to sports broadcasting rights globally! Other broadcast rights packages to the Premier League matches, comprising overseas rights, highlights packages and mobile phone and internet rights, have been sold separately to other companies.[6]

It is interesting to note that BSkyB has held the live rights to broadcast Premiership football in England since 1992, paying at that time for the three seasons, beginning in 2003 and ending in 2006, the sum of £1.024bn. This uplift in sports TV rights fees is staggering! According to Peter Scudamore, the Chief Executive of the English Premier League, these rights are now more valuable and "…for the first time these are platform-neutral rights available for exploitation on wider technology." The current broadcast rights fees are very impressive and there will be even more TV money for the 20 English Premier League Football Clubs to share amongst themselves accordingly.

The English Football League has signed broadcast rights deals with six international agencies and broadcasters, worth £24 million over three years, beginning in 2009–2010. The new deals represent a 300 per cent increase in revenue for the rights. Again, impressive and demonstrating the value of football!

It is the first time that the English Football League has split its worldwide rights among a number of different partners. The partners are: the IMG agency, which acquired the rights worldwide, excluding Africa and the Middle East; Pitch International, in the Middle East; Hi TV, in (part of) Nigeria; Supersport, in South Africa, (part of) Sub-Saharan Africa, and (part of) Nigeria; GTV, in (part of) Sub-Saharan Africa; and Perform, which acquired live online rights for betting websites.

Football League Chairman Lord Mawhinney welcomed the "huge increase of resources for our clubs", and said they showed that the global football audience was increasingly recognising that "The Football League prides itself on producing some of the most competitive and exciting league and cup football in the world game".

It may be added that the exploitation of broadcasting rights in football have become so valuable and important that many leading football clubs, such as the English club Manchester United, now operate their own television channels for the benefit of their fans and also their commercial sponsors/partners/suppliers, made possible with the advent of digital TV.

The value of sports broadcasting rights is replicated elsewhere in the world and in relation to other major sporting events. For instance, the International Olympic Committee sold the broadcast rights for the 2008 Beijing Summer Olympic Games for stratospheric sums too! And the upward trend in the sale of broadcast rights for major world sports events, such as the FIFA World Cup, seems unstoppable.

---

[5] Address at the AGM of News Corporation on 15 October, 1996 in Adelaide, Australia.

[6] For example, Yahoo won the rights to show English Premier League highlights over the Internet in a multi million pounds deal, outbiding the current holder of these rights, Virgin Media, in a competitive auction.

For further detailed information on the legal aspects of sports TV rights, see the recently published Book, entitled: *TV Rights and Sport—Legal Aspects*.[7] Among the legal issues addressed in this Book are:

- the ownership of sports broadcasting rights, including the position of individual sports persons, teams, clubs, venue owners;
- the different methods of protecting them, including copyright;
- the different methods of exploiting them, including collective selling and buying, as well as 'pay per view' and 'free to view' arrangements;
- the so-called new media rights, including the 'streaming' of sports broadcasts on
- the Internet (so-called 'webcasts') and on the so-called 'third and fourth generation' mobile phones; and last but by no means least
- the impact of the EU and National Competition Rules on the broadcasting of sports events.

The ownership of broadcasting rights is a particularly thorny question, not least, for example, in the UK, where there is no 'property' right per se in a 'sporting spectacle'. Likewise, in the UK, a sports game is not a 'dramatic' work, and thus not entitled to copyright protection under the UK Copyright Designs and Patents Act of 1988. And, similarly, those who participate in sports events are excluded from the definition of those accorded statutory performers' rights—they are not engaged in a copyrightable performance that can be protected under the 1988 UK Act. How these intrinsic legal problems are overcome, in practice, especially through the clever use of contractual arrangements, including players' and officials' contracts of employment.

As to the impact of EU Competition Rules on sports broadcasting rights, the vexed legal questions of the collective selling and collective buying of those rights—whether on an exclusive or non-exclusive basis—arise and need to be addressed. See further on this important subject Chap. 16 on 'EU Aspects'.

The rise of new platforms for media exploitation of sports events referred to above is also an important topic in its own right and is, therefore, dealt with separately in Chap. 14 on 'Sports New Media Rights Agreements'.

## 13.2 Sports Broadcasting Agreements

In order to broadcast a sporting event, there are many parties involved with different roles, apart from the event organiser and the broadcaster, and, therefore, there are a complex array of different but interconnected ('back-to-back') Agreements, including 'down stream' TV Rights Sales Agreements, that need to

[7] Ian Blackshaw, Steve Cornelius & Robert Siekmann (Eds.), 2009 TMC Asser Press, The Hague, The Netherlands.

be negotiated, drafted and concluded to 'get the show on the road'. Of course, within the confines of this Book, it is not possible to deal with all of them. For example, the legal, technical and operational complexities of Host Broadcaster Agreements for a major global sporting event, such as the Olympics, would require an entire Book to be devoted to them in order to do justice to them.

Accordingly, we will concentrate on a basic Sports Broadcast Licence Agreement and also a Sports Broadcast Sponsorship Agreement, General Precedents of which will respectively be found in Appendix 1 (13.5.1) and Appendix 2 (13.5.2) to this chapter. Again, it should be emphasised that these Precedents are for general guidance only and will need to be adapted and customised to fit the particular facts and circumstances of each individual case. A few salient comments on each of these Agreements now follow.

### *13.2.1 Sports Broadcast Licence Agreement*

As far as the Sports Broadcast Licence Agreement is concerned, apart from, as usual the 'grant of rights' clause defining the rights granted to the Broadcaster, perhaps the most important requirement, as far as the Event Organiser is concerned is the quality of the broadcast. As will be seen in the General Precedent, the live audio visual feed signal in respect of the Sports Event concerned (as defined in the Definitions and Interpretation Clause) must meet the specified technical requirements laid down in Schedule 3 of the Agreement ('The Event Feed Technical Specification')—a sensible and practical use of Schedules in a complex Agreement of this kind to aid interpretation especially of provisions of a technical or specialised nature. Supplementing this requirement are mandatory obligations on the part of the Broadcaster to "produce the Programme to a standard of at least the same quality and have the same production standards as other sports programming currently being produced by the Broadcaster and shall comply in all respects with the Programme Guidelines." Note that 'Programme' and 'Programme Guidelines' are defined terms of the Agreement. The latter as meaning "those detailed guidelines describing the nature and content of the Programmes set out at Schedule 4" of the Agreement. Quality control is paramount in order to ensure the highest technical standards of the broadcast coverage of the Sports Event concerned and the reference to the quality of other sports programming produced by the Broadcaster is a good yardstick. After all it was on the basis of the other sports programmes produced by the Broadcaster that the Event Organiser chose that particular Broadcaster to cover its particular Sports Event.

Note also the extent/scope of the exclusive rights granted to the Broadcaster by the Event Organiser in the defined geographical territory. They are granted in respect of a defined format, referred to in the Agreement as the 'Permitted Methods' as defined in Schedule 5 of the Agreement. These are tight interlocking provisions to avoid any ambiguities and, therefore, to prevent any differences of opinion arising between the parties the Agreement.

Another important consideration and requirement for the Event Organiser is the protection of the Event Sponsors in relation to the broadcast coverage against any competitors getting in on the act. After all, the extent of the exposure of the Sponsors through the broadcast coverage, for example, through perimeter advertising in the stadium or arena where the sports event is taking place, is perhaps the most important component in any Sponsorship Rights Package. Thus, an obligation is imposed on the Broadcaster not to appoint a broadcast sponsor or grant any sponsorship rights in relation to the broadcast coverage, nor to accept any advertising intended for transmission during immediately before or after the Programme (in other words 'commercial breaks') that is, in the reasonable opinion of the Organiser, in direct competition with the Organiser or any 'Commercial Partners' as defined in the Definitions and Interpretation Clause of the Agreement. This provision is absolutely vital to prevent any so-called 'Conflict Marketing' arising out of or in relation to the broadcast coverage of the Sports Event concerned. Often, an additional clause is included in a Sports Broadcast Licence Agreement requiring the Broadcaster to grant a 'right of first refusal' to the Sports Event Organiser's Sponsors to 'commercial breaks' before during and after the broadcast of the Event. As with any 'right of first refusal', the provision needs to be carefully drafted setting out the precise conditions for its exercise, including—most importantly—the corresponding time lines.

Another important obligation to be placed on the Broadcaster is the one requiring the Broadcaster to procure that its personnel, agents and independent contractors comply with all reasonable directions given by the Organiser its employees, agents and representatives in relation to the positioning of its personnel and equipment at the Event. Again, this clause is designed to get the maximum benefit from the broadcast coverage of the Sports Event concerned.

Again, another important clause—this time as far as the Broadcaster is concerned—is the one that requires the Event Organiser to procure that the Broadcaster has access for its personnel and equipment at the Event venue at the times reasonably required by the Broadcaster and at no charge to the Broadcaster; and also to ensure that the Broadcaster has access to the power supply, car parking space for its equipment and personnel at the Event venue and such other facilities as are set out at Schedule 8 but—this time—at the expense of the Broadcaster.

The other provisions in the General Precedent of the Sports Broadcast Licence Agreement in Appendix 1 (13.5.1) of this chapter are reasonably self-explanatory do not require any particular comments other than taking note of their inclusion in the Agreement, in particular, the 'Ownership of the Rights', 'Warranties and Indemnity' 'Intellectual Property' 'Force Majeure' 'Governing Body Compliance' and 'Limitation of Liability' Clauses, the latter Clause being very important indeed, as broadcasting a major sports event can be a particularly hazardous operation, especially with all the complex equipment that must be brought on site at the venue.

### 13.2.2 Sports Television Sponsorship Agreement

We now turn to consider the General Precedent of the Sports Television Sponsorship Agreement, set out in Appendix 2 (13.5.2) of this chapter, and will draw attention to and comment on some of its more important and characteristic features and provisions. As always, this General Precedent will need to be customised to suit the circumstances of the particular case.

Apart from the 'grant of rights' and 'consideration' (price) clauses, which, as always, needs to be carefully and well drafted, perhaps the most important provision, as far as the Sports Broadcast Sponsor is concerned, is the Sponsor's Credits (a defined term in the Agreement) that will appear as part of the Broadcast of the Sports Event concerned. These need to be agreed and the cost of producing the required materials to incorporate them into the Broadcast is, of course, to be borne by the Sponsor and this cost will be included in the Sponsorship Fee.

As far as the Broadcaster is concerned, perhaps the most important provision in the Sports Television Sponsorship Agreement is the right of the Broadcaster to retain editorial control over the content and scheduling of the Broadcast, that is, the Programme and Programme Schedules respectively. Both these matters are defined in the 'Definitions' Clause of the Agreement.

In the Obligations of the Sponsor Clause, particular note should be made of the Sponsor's warranty that it is the sole owner of or controls all the intellectual property in the Sponsor's Credits and that any use by the Broadcaster of the Sponsor's Credits in accordance with the terms of the Agreement will not infringe the intellectual property rights of any third party. Notice also the usual warranty by the Sponsor that the Sponsor's Credits do not contain any obscene, blasphemous, offensive or defamatory material and will not expose the Broadcaster to any civil or criminal proceedings, as well as the requirement for the Sponsor to take out comprehensive public liability insurance.

As far as the Obligations of the Broadcaster are concerned, particular attention should be paid to the warranty in favour of the Sponsor that the Broadcaster is the sole owner of or controls all copyright and any other rights in and relating to the Programme, and also that the Broadcaster shall be solely responsible for all costs incurred (except those involved in the Sponsor's Credits) in the production, broadcast transmission, distribution and exploitation of the Programme. Notice also the important warranty of the Broadcaster that the Broadcast or the use of the Sponsor's Credits in the Broadcast does not infringe any applicable sponsorship or advertising rules, directives, or statutes. In the UK, television and radio broadcasting are regulated by Ofcom, which has issued regulations and guidelines to be followed by broadcasters.[8]

As regards the Sponsor's Credits, the parties need to agree on the timing of them and their placement within the Sports Event Broadcast and also in respect of

[8] For more information, logo onto www.ofcom.org.uk

any and all trailers for the Broadcast. See clause 6.1 and 6.2 respectively of the General Precedent of the Sports Television Sponsorship Agreement.

One final point, notice the Indemnity Clause included in the General Precedent of the TV Sports Television Sponsorship Agreement (Clause 7), which imposes obligations on the parties to indemnify each other in the event of any breach of their respective obligations under the Agreement.

## 13.3 General Precedents of a Sports Broadcast Licence Agreement and a Sports Television Programme Sponsorship Agreement

In Appendix 1 and 2 (13.5.1 and 13.5.2) respectively of this chapter, the reader will find General Precedents of a Sports Broadcast Licence Agreement and a Sports Television Programme Sponsorship Agreement, for general information and illustrative purposes only.

## 13.4 Concluding Remarks

From the above account, it is clear that, on a global scale, sports broadcasting rights, from a legal point of view and also from a commercial point of view, constitute a very important component of the sports marketing mix. The sale of television and new media rights to national and international sports events already provide a significant source of revenue to International and National Sports Federations alike, and will, no doubt, continue to do so, and the value of them will probably reach even greater stratospheric financial heights in the foreseeable future, notwithstanding the global recession. Indeed, hardly a day passes without some announcement of a major sale of TV rights having been made in respect of a particular sporting event somewhere in the world!

Despite all this economic preoccupation, sport is now a multi-billion dollar industry worldwide and will no doubt continue to be so. As such, some would argue, that perhaps sport has lost touch with its Corinthian roots and values, as well as its Olympian ideals and *raison d'être*, since nowadays it seems to be the winning rather than the taking part that motivates sports persons and counts—and there is certainly a lot to play for in sporting and in financial terms! Nevertheless, it must be said that, without the mega sums generated by the sale of television rights, sporting spectaculars like the Olympics and the FIFA World Cup could not take place—the costs of organising and staging them would be prohibitive. And, accordingly, athletes and sports fans alike throughout the world would be the losers.

Driving the importance and increasing value of sports broadcasting rights are the further advances and developments in new broadcasting technologies. Not least, the continuing growth in digital television, as many systems in many countries change from analogue to digital broadcasting methods of transmission and delivery.[9] Digital television, in fact, particularly lends itself to the broadcasting of sports events, providing, as it does, viewers with greater choice in terms of programme content; control over how and when they watch; and also raising their expectations regarding the quality of picture and sound (the advent of high definition television (HDTV)), depth and also the personalisation and enhancement of the broadcast experience, especially through the availability of interactive and view on demand facilities.[10]

The growth of new delivery platforms, including the spread of broadband, particularly for home computers, so-called 3G and 4G mobile phones, video on demand and personalised video recorders will also play a significant part in the development of the sports broadcasting market and give rise to new legal challenges and commercial opportunities. All these developments, as Andy Fry has pointed out, have "given the industry its first glimpse of a future in which the basic rules of audience engagement will be turned on their head."[11]

All this, of course, is good news for sports broadcasting rights holders, not least the leading International Sports Federations, such as the IOC and FIFA. Again, as Andy Fry has observed: "....rights holders sense an opportunity to sell their content to customers in a range of new formats across new platforms." And adds: "In terms of pay-TV politics, digital looks like a gravy train for cable and satellite platforms—but the big threat is that telecoms companies will use it as a way of muscling in on the content delivery game."[12]

The coverage of major sports, such as the Olympics and the FIFA World Cup, are not the only sports to benefit from this broadcasting technological revolution. There is also scope for the rights holders of smaller sports to cash in as well, providing their fans with video content that has not got onto television in their particular countries. For example, Premium TV has a broadband subscription service for fans of The World Rally Championship, offering them video stage highlights, in-car footage, interviews with drivers, as well as a video archive accessible on its website. Other smaller sports are exploring video streaming via broadband as well.

---

[9] In the UK, for example, the changeover from analogue to digital broadcasting is due to begin in 2008 and end in 2012, in time for the London Olympic Games.

[10] On the subject of Digital Television generally, see 'Public Television in the Digital Era: Challenges and New Strategies for Europe', 2007 London, Palgrave Macmillan, by Petros Iosifidis, one of the contributors to this Book (see the Chapter on Greece).

[11] 'Delivering Outside The Box', Andy Fry, *SportBusiness International*, June 2005, at p. 40.

[12] Ibid.

This exciting and technology-led brave new media world[13] will undoubtedly have an appreciable effect on the sporting world in general and, in particular, present further challenges to sports broadcasting rights holders, sports governing bodies, sports persons and teams and other stakeholders, as well as their professional advisors, not least their lawyers. This will lead to all kinds of conflicts that will need to be resolved by public authorities—at the national and supra-national levels—and sports bodies and administrators themselves. As Professor Stephen Weatherill, Jacques Delors Professor of EC Law at Oxford University has pertinently observed:

> "Some of the most intriguing tensions in the years to come are likely to centre on the attempts of governing bodies to satisfy the commercial aspirations of the most powerful participants while also maintaining vertical solidarity within the sport and preserving the broader integrity of the character of the event."[14]

This is a rather difficult balancing act to perform. As Professor Weatherill further points out:

> "….. the prominence of EC law's intervention in sport in recent years is above all the consequence of the 'commercialisation' of the sector, in particular as a result of its close association with the helter-skelter development of the broadcasting industry. In fact, much of the economically significant sports-related material that tumbled into the Commission's in-tray in the late 1990 s was concerned directly or indirectly with broadcasting. In some respects the Commission's recent preoccupation with sport has been driven by its need to monitor the commercially much more important broadcasting sector, in which it is profoundly anxious to forestall practices that will facilitate existing incumbents' anxiety to impede new entrants. And it is highly plausible that the pace of technological change will increasingly throw up new forms of rapid mass communication, generating intensified fragmentation in the pattern of audiovisual services. This will fuel yet more demand for rights to broadcast sports events, and bring with it yet more challenges for EC competition law."[15]

Accordingly, interesting and challenging times lie ahead for all those involved in any way and at any level in the sports broadcasting field, not least concerning the world's favorite game, football. In this respect, it will be interesting to see how the law at the national and supra-national levels and the National level develops.

As the Chinese are wont to say: '*we are living in interesting times*!'

---

[13] See Report by Market Analysts Forrester entitled, 'The Battle For The Digital Home', referred to in 'Delivering Outside The Box', Andy Fry, *SportBusiness International*, June 2005, at p. 41. In this Report, various scenarios that might arise in the so-called 'converged sports world' are suggested, including a possible "joint venture between the NFL and Fox to create an immersive experience where sports fans can choose viewer-selected camera angles and split-screen content……and Disney's acquisition of Electronic Arts. With EA's sports games, Disney/ESPN becomes the premier sports brand on PCs, TV and 13 consoles."

[14] Weatherill, Stephen, 'European Sports Law Collected Papers', 2007 The Hague, The Netherlands, TMC Asser Press, ISBN 978-90-6704-243-7, at p. 246.

[15] Ibid., at p. 296.

## 13.5 Appendices

### *13.5.1 Appendix 1*

**Sports Broadcast Licence Agreement***

**This Agreement** is made this day of 2[ ]

**Between**

(1) [ ] [ ] whose registered office is at [ ] ("the Organiser")
(2) [ ] [ ] whose registered office is at [ ] ("the Broadcaster")

**Recitals**

A. The Organiser is the organiser of the Event (as defined in this Agreement)
B. The Organiser wishes to grant Broadcaster certain rights in connection with the [live and delayed broadcast] of the Event

**Operative Provisions**

**1. Definitions And Interpretation**

1.1 In this Agreement the following terms have the following meanings
"**Broadcast Substitution**" means the ability to superimpose an electronic image onto any surface whether real or imaginary or the ability to alter any image by any means whether electronic or otherwise
"**the Commercial Partners**" means [ ]
"**the Event**" means the event which is planned to be run on the dates and at the time set out in Schedule 1
"**the Event Feed**" means the live audio visual feed signal of the Event produced by the Producer to that detailed technical specification set out at Schedule 3
"**the Event Marks**" means [insert details]
"**Excerpts**" means excerpts from the Event Feed each having a duration not exceeding thirty (30) seconds
"**Exclusive Period**" means in respect of the Event the period commencing at the beginning of the Event and termination [ ] hours following the conclusion of the Event
"**the Governing Body**" means [ ]
"**Intellectual Property**" means patents trade marks (whether registered or unregistered) rights in any designs (whether registered or unregistered) and applications for any of the foregoing trade or business names

* Source: Lexis Nexis; reproduced with permission.

copyright and rights in performances database rights goodwill and any other rights of intellectual property in any part of the world of whatever nature

"**Permitted Methods**" means any and all of those methods forms or formats of broadcast [and/or making available to the public] of audio-visual materials set out at Schedule 5 (and the phrase "Permitted Method" shall be construed accordingly) "the Pictures" means those moving pictures (together with any associated sound but excluding commentary) of and relating to the Event arising out of the Event Feed

"**the Producer**" means [insert name] or such other person as the Broadcaster appoints to produce the Event Feed

"**the Programme**" means the audio-visual programme complying in all respects with the Programme Guidelines produced by the Broadcaster pursuant to its rights granted in this Agreement based on and including the Event using the Event Feed as described in detail at Schedule 2

"**Programme Guidelines**" means those detailed guidelines describing the nature and content of the Programmes set out at Schedule 4

"**Recorded Highlights**" means an edited highlights version of or précis of the Event edited using the Event Feed having a total duration not exceeding thirty (30) minutes in total

"**the Rights**" means the right (where applicable in accordance with the Programme Guidelines) at its own cost to

(i) produce the Programme
(ii) add commentary and sound to the Event Feed in producing the Programme
(iii) insert on-screen graphics and information within the Programme
(iv) broadcast [and/or make available to the public] the Programme by means of live or delayed recorded encrypted broadcast by a Permitted Method
(v) advertise promote or publicise the Programme by broadcast of advertising materials in respect of the same approved in writing by the Organiser to its audience

"**the Term**" means the period from the date of this Agreement up to and including the date following [ ] days following the conclusion of the Event

"**the Territory**" [insert details]

**2. Licensed Rights**

2.1 Subject to and in consideration of the terms of this Agreement the Organiser grants to the Broadcaster (on an exclusive basis in accordance with the terms of and subject to the limitations set out at clause 3) the Rights in the Territory during the Term

2.2 The Organiser reserves to itself all rights in and in relation to the Event and/or the broadcast or making available to the public of any audio-visual materials depicting the Event other than the Rights

**3. Exclusivity**

3.1 The Organiser agrees that it shall not grant itself or permit any other person to grant to any person other than the Broadcaster the Rights during the Term and in the Territory

3.2 Save as set out at clause 3.1 (and subject only to clause 3.3) the Organiser gives no warranty or undertaking to the Broadcaster that no other person shall without the express grant of rights by the Organiser to do so broadcast or make available to the public any audio-visual materials depicting the Event

3.3 The Broadcaster understands and acknowledges that the Organiser shall grant to other persons the right into alia to broadcast and/or make available to the public audio-visual materials depicting the Event during the Term

3.3.1 and in the Territory by way of methods and/or forms or formats other than the Permitted Methods

3.3.2 and in the Territory by way of any method form or format by way of Excerpts and/or Recorded Highlights provided no such materials may be broadcast or made available to the public until the expiry of the Exclusive Period

3.3.3 outside the Territory by way of any method form or format in any way or manner and in the event that any such broadcast or making available to the public becomes capable of reception or access by any means and/or for any reason in the Territory as a result of any satellite "overspill" which may not practicably and economically be avoided the Organiser shall not be liable to the Broadcaster as a result thereof for any breach of any exclusivity granted to the Broadcaster pursuant to this Agreement

**4. Expenses and Fees**

4.1 Each party shall bear its own costs of complying with the terms of and undertaking its obligations under this Agreement

4.2 In consideration of the rights granted pursuant to this Agreement the Broadcaster shall pay to the Organiser the following sums on the following dates [ ]

4.3 All sums payable hereunder are exclusive of any VAT which where appropriate shall be paid by the Broadcaster in addition

**5. Obligations of the Broadcaster**

5.1 The Broadcaster shall produce the Programme to a standard of at least the same quality and have the same production standards as other sports programming currently being produced by the Broadcaster and shall comply in all respects with the Programme Guidelines

5.2 The Broadcaster shall pay its own costs of production of the Programme

5.3 The Broadcaster shall use its best endeavours to exploit the Rights licensed to it under this Agreement by procuring the broadcast of the Programme in the Territory simultaneously with the Event or at the times dates and from the locations set out in Schedule 2

5.4 If the Broadcaster is for any reason unable to transmit the Programme as required by this clause it shall do so as soon as reasonably practicable afterwards

5.5 The Broadcaster shall

5.5.1 not appoint a broadcast sponsor or grant any sponsorship rights over the Rights the Event or the Programme

5.5.2 not accept any advertising intended for transmission during immediately before or after the Programme that is in the reasonable opinion of the Organiser in direct competition with the Organiser or any Commercial Partners

5.5.3 not do anything which in the reasonable opinion of the Organiser is or might be prejudicial or defamatory to the name and image of the Organiser the Governing Body the Event or the sport of [ ]

5.5.4 comply with and observe all provisions in the Governing Bodies' rules and regulations from time to time in force

5.5.5 comply with all particular laws and regulations applicable to the exploitation of the Rights and the organisation of the Event

5.5.6 not effect any Broadcast Substitution on any signal transmitting the Programme unless specifically requested in writing by the Organiser

5.5.7 at its expense select and provide announcers commentators technical and other personnel sufficient to produce the Programme

5.5.8 not interfere with the running of the Event

5.5.9 use its best endeavours to provide two (2) hours broadcast coverage (whether live or delayed) during each day of the Event

5.5.10 arrange for and be responsible for all necessary licences clearances permissions and fees required in connection with the production and distribution of the Programme and the exercise of the Rights

5.5.11 procure that the Event Feed complies with the requirements of the specification set out at Schedule 3 and provide in accordance with the technical facilities required as set out at

Schedule 7 a clean feed of the Event Feed to the Organiser in real time during the entire duration of the Event

5.5.12 provide access to footage extracted from the Event Feed and/or the Programme for use by other broadcasters in accordance with the new Code of Practice from time to time

5.6 The Broadcaster shall procure that its personnel agents and independent contractors comply with all reasonable directions given by the Organiser its employees agents and representatives in relation to the positioning of its personnel and equipment at the Event

## 6. Approvals

6.1 In respect of any materials for which the approval of the Organiser is required for any reason pursuant to this Agreement the Broadcaster may submit such materials at any time to the Organiser for such approval and the Organiser will use reasonable endeavours to notify in writing its approval or disapproval of the same to the Broadcaster within seven (7) working days of receipt of the same. In the event that it notifies its approval the Broadcaster may make use of the same in accordance with this Agreement. If the Organiser notifies its disapproval of the same the Broadcaster shall be entitled to submit its alternative proposals at any time. In the event that the Organiser notifies neither its approval or disapproval within seven (7) working days of receipt of the said materials it shall be deemed to have approved the same and the relevant provisions of this clause 6.1 shall apply. The Organiser shall not in any event unreasonably withhold delay or condition any approval so required pursuant to this Agreement

## 7. Obligations of the Organiser

7.1 The Organiser shall use its reasonable endeavours to ensure that the Event is properly and professionally organised

7.2 The Organiser shall procure that the Broadcaster has access for its personnel and equipment at the Event at the times reasonably required by the Broadcaster and at no charge to the Broadcaster. In addition the Organiser shall ensure that the Broadcaster has access to the power supply car parking space for its equipment and personnel at the event and such other facilities as are set out at Schedule 8 and the Broadcaster agrees to bear the reasonable agreed costs of such facilities as listed at the said Schedule 8 such sums as are set out there being invoiced to the Broadcaster within seven (7) days of the date of this Agreement

7.3 The Organiser shall provide or shall procure that the Broadcaster is provided with such information as the Broadcaster may reasonably request in relation to the Event

7.4 Subject to the terms of this Agreement the Organiser grants to the Broadcaster the non-exclusive right to incorporate the Event Marks in the Programme and in exploiting the Rights

7.5 The Organiser will endeavour to make participants in the Event available to the Broadcaster for the purposes of interviews and commentary for the Programme and reasonable promotional and cross-promotional activities relating to the Programme

**8. Ownership of the Rights**

8.1 The Broadcaster with full title guarantee hereby assigns absolutely to the Organiser any and all Intellectual Property in and in relation to the Event Feed and the Pictures (by way where applicable of present assignment of future copyright and/or other future rights) to hold the same to the Organiser absolutely for its own benefit

8.2 In consideration of the payment to it of the fees referred to at clause 4.2 the Organiser hereby grants to the Broadcaster (by way where applicable of present licence of future copyright or other future rights) the right by way of non-exclusive licence to use the Event Feed and the Pictures in relation to the exercise by it of the Rights for the Term in the Territory in accordance with the terms of this Agreement

**9. Warranties and Indemnities**

9.1 Each party warrants to the other that it has the full right power and authority to enter into and perform its obligations under this Agreement

9.2 The Broadcaster shall indemnify the Organiser against any loss cost charge liability or expense the Organiser (or any employee of the Organiser or any Commercial Partner) may sustain or incur as a direct or indirect consequence of the breach by the Broadcaster of any of its obligations under this Agreement

**10. Intellectual Property**

10.1 The Broadcaster shall promptly and fully notify the Organiser of any actual threatened or suspected infringement in the Territory of any Intellectual Property of the Organiser which comes to the Broadcaster's notice and of any claim by any third party so coming to its notice and the Broadcaster shall at the request and expense of the Organiser do all such things as may be reasonably required to assist the Organiser in taking or resisting any proceedings in relation to any such infringement or claim

10.2 Nothing in this Agreement shall give the Broadcaster any rights in respect of any Intellectual Property or the Event Marks used by the Organiser in relation to the Event or of the goodwill associated therewith and the Broadcaster acknowledges that except as expressly provided in this Agreement it shall not acquire any rights in respect thereof and that all such rights and goodwill are and shall remain vested in the Organiser

10.3 The Broadcaster shall not use any trade marks or trade names so resembling the Event Marks or trade names of the Organiser or of the Governing Bodies as to be likely to cause confusion or deception

10.4 The Broadcaster shall not authorise any third party to use the Event Marks or any Intellectual Property of the Organiser or of the Governing Bodies. If any third party requires the use of the Event Marks or any Intellectual Property of the Organiser or of the Event then the Broadcaster shall inform the Organiser of such requirement. The Organiser may (in its absolute discretion and where it is able to) grant such third party the right or licence required

10.5 The Broadcaster shall at the expense of the Organiser take all such steps as the Organiser may reasonably require to assist the Organiser in mainlining the validity and enforceability of the Intellectual Property of the Organiser during the continuance of this Agreement

10.6 Without prejudice to the right of the Broadcaster or any third party to challenge the validity of any Intellectual Property of the Organiser the Broadcaster shall not do or authorise any third party to do any act which would or might invalidate or be inconsistent with the Intellectual Property of the Organiser and shall not omit or authorise any third party to omit to do any act which by its omission would have that effect or character

10.7 The Broadcaster shall take such reasonable action and steps in relation to any potential or actual infringement of its Intellectual Property in the Rights which comes to its notice as the Organiser shall at the request and expense of the Broadcaster do all such things as may be reasonably required to take or remit any proceedings in relation to such infringement of the Rights

10.8 The Broadcaster shall not grant any rights in connection with or deriving out of the Rights or otherwise share in its exploitation of the Rights or of any benefit arising out of or in connection with this Agreement with any third party save with the express written consent of the Organiser at its discretion

**11. Confidentiality**

11.1 Confidentiality

11.1.1 Subject to sub-clauses 11.2 and 11.3 each party

11.1.1.1 shall treat as strictly confidential and use solely for the purposes contemplated by this Agreement all documents materials and other information whether technical or commercial obtained or received by it as a result of entering into or performing its obligation under this Agreement and relating to the negotiations relating to or the provisions or subject matter of this Agreement ("confidential information") and

11.1.1.2 shall not accept with the prior written consent of the party from whom the confidential information was obtained publish or otherwise disclose to any person any confidential inuformation

11.2 Permitted disclosures

11.2.1 Each party may disclose confidential information which would otherwise be subject to sub-clause 11.1 if but only to the extent that it can demonstrate that

11.2.1.1 such disclosure is required by law or by any securities exchange or regulatory or governmental body or Governing Body having jurisdiction over it wherever situated (and including without limitation the London Stock Exchange the Panel on Takeovers and Mergers and the Serious Fraud Office) and whether or not the requirement has the force of law

11.2.1.2 the confidential information has come into the public domain other than through its fault or the fault of any person to whom the confidential information has been disclosed in accordance with sub-clause 11.3

11.2.1.3 the said disclosure is to its legal or other professional advisers

11.3 Persistence of restrictions

11.3.1 The restrictions contained in this clause shall survive the termination of this Agreement

## 12. Termination

12.1 Either party may terminate this Agreement forthwith upon notice in the event that the other

12.1.1 commits a material breach of any obligation under this Agreement which breach is incapable of remedy or cannot be remedied prior to commencement of the Event

12.1.2 commits a material breach of any obligation under this Agreement and if such breach is capable of remedy fails to so remedy such breach within [ ] days of receiving notice from the other requiring remedy

12.1.3 enters into a composition or arrangement with its creditors has a receiver or administrator or administrative receiver appointed or becomes insolvent or unable to pay its debts when they fall due

12.1.4 Consequences of termination

12.1.4.1 Upon termination in accordance with clause 12

12.1.4.1.1 the rights and obligations of the parties under this Agreement shall terminate and be of no future effect except that clauses 10 and 11 shall remain in full force and effect

12.1.4.1.2 any rights or obligations to which any of the parties to this Agreement may be entitled or be subject before such termination shall remain in full force and effect

12.1.4.1.3 termination shall not affect or prejudice any right to damages or other remedy which the terminating party may have in respect of the circumstances which gave rise to the termination or any other right to damages or other remedy which any party may have in respect of any breach of this Agreement which existed at or before the date of termination

12.1.5 Effect on the rights

12.1.5.1 If either party terminates this Agreement under clause 12 or this Agreement terminates otherwise for any reason during or immediately after the Event has been held that termination will not affect the assignment of all rights assigned to the Organiser pursuant to this Agreement whether pursuant to clauses 8.1 or otherwise but forthwith upon such termination the Broadcaster shall forthwith cease to have any right to enjoy or exploit the Rights

**13. Force Majeure**

13.1 Neither party to this Agreement shall be deemed to be in breach of this Agreement or otherwise liable to the other as a result of any delay or failure in the performance of its obligations under this Agreement if and to the extent that such delay or failure is caused by force majeure (as defined in sub-clause 13.2) and the time for performance of the relevant obligation(s) shall be extended accordingly

13.2 Definition of force majeure

13.2.1 For the purpose of this clause "force majeure" means any circumstances not foreseeable at the date of this Agreement and not within the reasonable control of the party in question including without limitation

13.2.1.1 any strike lockout or other industrial action or any shortage of or difficulty in obtaining labour or raw materials

13.2.1.2 any destruction temporary or permanent breakdown malfunction or damage of or to any premises plant equipment (including computer systems) or materials

13.2.1.3 any breach of contract default or insolvency by or of any third party (including an agent or sub-contractor) other than a company in the same group as the party affected by the force majeure or an employee or officer of that party or company

13.2.1.4 any action taken by government or public authority of any kind including not granting a consent exemption approval or clearance

13.2.1.5 any civil commotion or disorder riot invasion war threat of or preparation of war

13.2.1.6 any fire explosion storm flood earthquake subsidence epidemic or other natural physical disaster

13.3 Obligations of affected party

13.3.1 A party whose performance of its obligations under this Agreement is delayed or prevented by force majeure

13.3.1.1 shall forthwith notify the other party of the nature extent effect and likely duration of the circumstances constituting the force majeure

13.3.1.2 shall use all reasonable endeavours to minimise the effect of the force majeure on its performance of its obligations under this Agreement and

13.3.1.3 shall subject to sub-clause 13.4 forthwith after the cessation of the force majeure notify the other party thereof and resume full performance of its obligations under this Agreement

13.4 Termination for force majeure

13.4.1 If (where the terms of clause 14 do not apply) any force majeure delays or prevents the performance of the obligations of either party for a continuous period in excess of one (1) month the party not so affected shall then be entitled to give notice to the affected party to terminate this Agreement specifying the date (which shall not be less than seven (7) days after the date on which the notice is given) on which termination will take effect. Such a termination notice shall be irrevocable except with the consent of both parties and upon termination the provisions of clauses 12.1.4 and 12.1.5 apply

**14. Governing Body Compliance**

14.1 This Agreement is expressly subject to the rules and regulations of [the Governing Bodies] wherever relevant and nothing in this Agreement shall in any way prevent or restrict the Organiser from abiding by the said rules and regulations and/or the terms of sponsorship of any tournament league and/or event in which the Organiser at any time participates and for the avoidance of doubt in the event that any of the said rules and regulations and/or any such condition or term of sponsorship in any way conflicts with any obligation arising pursuant to this Agreement then that rule of regulation and/or condition or term of sponsorship shall prevail over the conflicting obligation arising pursuant to this Agreement and no failure by the Organiser to comply with such an obligation arising pursuant to this Agreement shall be construed as or have the effect of comprising any breach of this Agreement but rather the effect of the conflicting obligation arising pursuant to this Agreement shall be deemed to be suspended throughout any period such conflict exists

**15. Limitation of Liability**

15.1 The following provisions of clauses 15.1 to 15.5 inclusive set out the [Broadcaster's] entire liability (including any liability for the acts and omissions of its employees agents and sub-contractors) to the [Organiser] in respect of

15.1.1 any breach of its contractual obligations arising under this agreement and

15.1.2 any representation or tortious act or omission including negligence arising under or in connection with this Agreement

15.2 Any act or omission on the part of the [Broadcaster] or its employees agents or sub-contractors falling within clause 15.1 above shall for the purpose of clause 15.1 be known as an "Event of Default"

15.3 The [Broadcaster's] liability to the [Organiser] for death or injury resulting from negligence shall not be limited

15.4 Save as set out at clause 15.3 above the [Broadcaster's] entire aggregate liability howsoever arising and of whatever nature in respect of any and all Events of Default of whatever nature and howsoever arising shall be limited to the aggregate amount of the Fees actually payable by the [Broadcaster] to the [Organiser] as at the date of such liability to repay arising plus the sum of £[ ] ([ ] pounds sterling)

15.5 Subject to clause 15.3 above only the Broadcaster shall not be liable to the [Organiser] in respect of any Event of Default for loss of profits goodwill or any type of special indirect or consequential loss or pure economic loss (including loss or damage suffered by the [Organiser] as a result of an action brought by a third party) even if such loss was reasonably foreseeable or the [Broadcaster] had been advised of the possibility of the [Organiser] incurring the same

NOTE the same terms can apply with the terms "Broadcaster" and "Organiser" reversed as an additional set of provisions

## 16. Provisions Relating to this Agreement

16.1 [Boilerplate Clauses]

[Execution Clauses]

SCHEDULE 1
The Event

SCHEDULE 2
The Programme

SCHEDULE 3
The Event Feed Technical Specification

SCHEDULE 4
The Programme Guidelines

SCHEDULE 5
The Permitted Methods

SCHEDULE 6
Programme Timings and Broadcast Locations

SCHEDULE 7
Technical Facilities Event Feed

SCHEDULE 8
Facilities to be provided to Broadcaster

## *13.5.2 Appendix 2*

### Sports Television Programme Sponsorship Agreement*

**This Agreement** is made this day of 2[ ]

**Between**

(1) [ ] [ ] whose registered office is at [ ] ("the Sponsor")
(2) [ ] [ ] whose registered office is at [ ] ("the Broadcaster")

**Recitals**

A. The Sponsor is a company engaged in the business of [ ] who wish to sponsor programmes through the Broadcaster
B. The Broadcaster is the broadcaster of the programmes the Sponsor wishes to sponsor and is fully and effectively licensed to broadcast in the United Kingdom by Ofcom and/or any and all relevant authorities

**Operative Provisions**

1. **Definitions**
   1.1 In this Agreement the following expressions shall have the following meanings

   "**Broadcast**" has the meanings ascribed to it in the Copyright Design and Patents Act 1988 (as amended from time to time) (and cognate expressions shall be construed accordingly)
   "**Fee**" means £[ ] plus VAT
   "**make available to the public**" has the meanings ascribed to it in the Copyright Design and Patents Act 1988 (as amended from time to time) (and corporate expressions shall be construed accordingly)
   "**Ofcom**" means the office of Communications (Ofcom) whose principal address is at Riverside House 2A Southward Bridge Road London SE1 9HA
   "**Programme**" means the terrestrial broadcast television programmes and any associated sound recordings titled [" "] being [ ] minutes long the full nature and description of which is set out at the Schedule 3
   "**Programme Schedules**" means the provisional timetable for the broadcast and/or making available to the public of the Programmes set out in the Schedule 2 [setting out details of all channels and/or platforms by which the same are to be so broadcast or made available to the public together with times and dates]

---

* Source: Lexis Nexis; reproduced with permission.

"**Rights**"

(i) means the exclusive right for the Sponsor to sponsor the programme using the Sponsor's Credits
(ii) the additional rights set out in clause [ ] of this Agreement

"**Sponsor's Credits**" means the full range of agreed visual and/or audio-visual recorded sequences (including all permutations thereof) incorporating the logo and trade mark of the Sponsor together with associated words to be agreed between the parties as more fully described in respect of each of the relevant permutations thereof at the Schedule 4 in each case as approved by the Broadcaster from time to time such approval not to be unreasonably withheld delayed or conditioned
"**Term**" means the period commencing on the date of signature of this Agreement and expiring on [date]
"**Territory**" means the United Kingdom the Channel Islands and the Isle of Man

**2. Grant of Rights**

2.1 In consideration of the Fee and subject to the terms of this Agreement the Broadcaster grants to the Sponsor the Rights for the Term throughout the Territory
2.2 The Broadcaster undertakes that it shall not grant any third party the right to sponsor the Programme during the Term
2.3 The Broadcaster undertakes to use its reasonable endeavours to broadcast or make available to the public or procure the broadcast or making available to the public of the Programme in accordance with the Programme Schedules throughout the Territory during the Term
2.4 The Sponsor acknowledges and agrees that all copyright and all other rights of whatever nature in the Programme are the property of the Broadcaster and that this Agreement grants the Sponsor rights in or in relation to the Programme
2.5 The Broadcaster acknowledges and agrees that any copyright and any other rights in the Sponsor's Credits shall remain the sole and exclusive property of The Sponsor together with any goodwill and that the Broadcaster shall not acquire any rights in the Sponsor's Credits
2.6 The Sponsor hereby grants to the Broadcaster an exclusive licence to broadcast the Sponsor's Credits on the terms of this Agreement for the Term in the Territory
2.7 The Sponsor acknowledges the common custom and practice as with all sponsored sporting events that whilst the Sponsor remains at all times the exclusive and official sponsor of the Programme it may well be the case that the official timing and computer companies will be visible on-screen from time to time

## 3. Editorial Control And Programme Scheduling

3.1 The Sponsor acknowledges and agrees that all final editorial and creative decisions concerning the development production content and scheduling of the Programme shall be the sole responsibility of the Broadcaster
3.2 The Broadcaster shall consult the Sponsor with a view to agreeing jointly the design of the opening title sequence of the Programme incorporating The Sponsor's Credits
3.3 Without prejudice to the generality of clause 3.2 above the Broadcaster may at its sole discretion and cost make such changes deletions alterations interruptions or additions to the Programme as may be required by the scheduling requirements of the Broadcaster in line with the terms of its licence or any generally applicable relevant rule of law or by the Ofcom or any other statutory body and agrees to ensure that as far as reasonably practicable the Sponsor shall be informed in advance of any significant alterations to the Programme
3.4 Both parties acknowledge that the transmission dates and scheduling are still to be confirmed. The Broadcaster shall use its reasonable endeavours to ensure that broadcast of the Programme will be the same as or reasonably similar to Schedule 2. The Broadcaster shall supply a more detailed and accurate Programme Schedule to the Sponsor prior to broadcast

## 4. Consideration

4.1 The Sponsor shall pay to the Broadcaster in respect of the Programme the Fee as follows

4.1.1 £[ ] plus VAT upon signature of this Agreement
4.1.2 £[ ] plus VAT on delivery by the Sponsor of the Sponsor's Credit to the TV Company
4.1.3 £[ ] plus VAT on the day after the first broadcast referred to in the Programme Schedule

## 5. Obligations Of The Sponsor

5.1 The Sponsor warrants that it is the sole owner of or controls all the intellectual property in the Sponsor's Credits. The Sponsor confirms and warrants to the Broadcaster that any use by the Broadcaster of the Sponsor's Credits in accordance with this Agreement will not infringe the intellectual property of any third party
5.2 The Sponsor warrants that the Sponsor's Credits do not contain any obscene blasphemous offensive or defamatory material and will not expose the Broadcaster to any civil or criminal proceedings
5.3 The Sponsor confirms that it will obtain comprehensive public liability insurance cover which will be in force during the Sponsorship Period covering any writs claims actions or damages which may arise as a direct or indirect result of the use by the public of the specific products or

services being credited under this Agreement together with all other products or services owned or controlled by The Sponsor which the public would reasonably associate with the Sponsor's Credits. The Sponsor undertakes to provide the Broadcaster with a copy of all relevant insurance policies upon request

5.4 The Sponsor confirms that it has and will retain all rights and full authority in order to enable it to enter into this Agreement

5.5 The Sponsor acknowledges that the Broadcaster may use its sole discretion as to the manner and method to be used in the marketing promoting and advertising of the Programme irrespective of any rights granted under this Agreement and that the Broadcaster shall retain all proceeds from the exploitation of the Programme in any manner or media at any time

5.6 The Sponsor shall bear all costs of creating producing designing and the Sponsor's Credits and of supplying the Sponsor's Credit to the Broadcaster for incorporation in the Programme

5.7 The Sponsor agrees to be bound by the requirements of the Broadcaster in respect of any sponsorship or advertising rules directives or statutes which apply to the Broadcaster or have been issued by Ofcom or by any other person having the power to issue the same concerning the broadcast or transmission of the Sponsor's Credits including but not limited to its size shape colour wording and on-screen position and general nature

**6. Obligations Of The Broadcaster**

6.1 The Broadcaster agrees to use its reasonable endeavours to broadcast and make available to the public or procure such broadcast or making available to the public of the Programme as per the Programme Schedules incorporating the Sponsor's Credits in all other relevant permutations as set out at the Schedule 4 including but not limited to as follows

6.1.1 fifteen (15) seconds (maximum) opening titles—voice and visual credits

6.1.2 ten (10) seconds (maximum) break-bumpers—visual credits only

6.1.3 ten (10) seconds (maximum) closing titles-voice and visual credits

6.2 The Broadcaster undertakes to give the Sponsor a visual credit of five (5) seconds maximum on all trailers for the Programme

6.3 The Broadcaster agrees to give the Sponsor access to all the recorded footage of the Programme for its own promotional purposes only. The Sponsor may edit the footage at its own cost for such purposes and may use the same in such manner and/or such purposes as may be expressly agreed between the Broadcaster and the Sponsor in writing from time to time

6.4 The Broadcaster undertakes to use all reasonable endeavours to ensure that the Programme will not contain any material which infringes the copyright or any other rights of any third party throughout the Territory during the Term

6.5 The Broadcaster shall ensure that the broadcast or making available to the public of the Sponsor's Credits does not infringe any sponsorship or advertising rules directives or statutes which apply to the Broadcaster or have been issued by Ofcom concerning the Sponsor's Credits

6.6 The Broadcaster confirms and warrants to the Sponsor that it is the sole owner of or controls all copyright and any other rights in and in relation to the Programme

6.7 The Broadcaster confirms that it shall be solely responsible for all costs incurred (except those involved in the Sponsor's Credits) in the production broadcast transmission distribution and exploitation of the Programme and that the Sponsor shall not be liable for any such sums except as provided in clause 6.3 above and further if agreed in writing

6.8 The Broadcaster covenants and warrants to the Sponsor that the Programme shall comply with the description of the same set out at the Schedule 3 hereto throughout the Term

## 7. Mutual Indemnity

7.1 The Sponsor and the Broadcaster each undertakes to indemnify the others against all liabilities claims demands actions costs damages or loss arising out of any breach by each of them respectively of any of the terms of this Agreement

7.2 In the event of any claim dispute action writ or summons in connection with clause 7.1 above the Sponsor and the Broadcaster agree to provide full details to the other party at the earliest opportunity and shall not settle any such matter without first consulting the other party

## 8. Termination and Expiry of the Agreement

8.1 In addition to any other rights and remedies at law this Agreement may be terminated by a party giving written notice of at least four (4) weeks to the other party which has breached this Agreement or had defaulted on any of the following grounds

8.1.1 where the Sponsor has failed to account or make payments as required under this Agreement

8.1.2 where the Sponsor or the Broadcaster has committed a serious breach of its obligations under this Agreement unless such party rectifies the position as far as reasonably possible within thirty (30) days

8.1.3 where the Sponsor or the Broadcaster goes into voluntary or involuntary liquidation

8.1.4 where the Sponsor or the Broadcaster is declared insolvent either in bankruptcy proceedings or other legal proceedings

8.1.5 where an agreement with creditors has been reached by the Sponsor or the Broadcaster due to its failure or inability to pay its debts as they fall due

8.1.6 where a receiver is appointed over the whole or part of the Sponsor's or the Broadcaster's business

## 9. Provisions Relating to this Agreement

9.1 [Boilerplate Clauses]

[Execution Clauses]

SCHEDULE 1

SCHEDULE 2
The Programme Schedule

SCHEDULE 3
Designation of the Programme

SCHEDULE 4
The Sponsor's Credits

# Chapter 14
# Sports New Media Rights Agreements

## 14.1 Introductory Remarks

The inexorable rise of the Internet, the advent of Digital Television and Television 'on demand' have provided new 'platforms' for not only the dissemination of information, but also programming of various kinds, including sports events. Not only are major sports events broadcast on television and radio, but they are also transmitted 'on line' in so-called 'webcasts'. The latest generations of mobile phones have also added a new 'platform' for providing a wide range of communications, including text messaging and access to the Internet. They have also provided the possibilities of downloading programmes of various kinds from the Internet, including 'webcasts'. Likewise, video technology has advanced greatly in the last decade or so, and provided a wide range of commercial and business opportunities.

Many Sports Event Organisers and Sports Rights Holders have been quick to embrace this new advanced technology and have realised the value of these new 'platforms' not only for promoting their sports events, but also for cashing in on and deriving additional and lucrative income streams from the commercial demand for and exploitation of them.

Thus, these new media developments have opened up a new world of commercial opportunities in the sports marketing and other business sectors, and given rise to the need for the corresponding Agreements to be drawn up in order to grant and protect these new media rights.

Because this is a vast, complex and highly technical subject, with a wide range of Sports-related and Sports Marketing New Media Rights Agreements that may arise, according to the particular sport and circumstances, in this chapter, we will concentrate on only a few of the main Agreements that may need to be negotiated and drafted, and provide some general comments on them.

I. S. Blackshaw, *Sports Marketing Agreements: Legal, Fiscal and Practical Aspects*, ASSER International Sports Law Series, DOI: 10.1007/978-90-6704-793-7_14,

## 14.2 New Media Sports Rights and Marketing Agreements

In the Appendices of this chapter, we provide some General Precedents of some New Media Sports Rights and Marketing Agreements, including a Video Production and Licence Agreement[1]; a Website Design and Maintenance Agreement[2]; a Mobile Sports Content Rights Agreement[3]; an Individual Online Licence Agreement[4]; and a Video Game Licence Agreement,[5] for general information; and would make some general remarks on these Agreements as follows.

As always, it is necessary to define the rights granted including, *inter alia*, whether they are exclusive or non-exclusive, the sports event, the 'platform' and, in the case of certain of these Agreements, for example, a Video Production and Licence Agreement, the geographical territory or territories in which the rights granted may be commercially exploited.

Suitable warranties from the parties as well as their respective obligations need to be included in the Agreements, as well as, where appropriate, a well-drafted and well-defined 'Force Majeure' clause, especially in the case of Agreements subject to English Common Law.

Again, the legal and practical consequences of termination also need to be spelled out in the Agreements, especially in relation to 'sell off' periods, usually six calendar months from the date of termination, and so-called 'remaindering rights' of the licensed products.

Also, when drafting these complex and technical Agreements, use Definitions Clauses and also Schedules, especially for technical details connected with the new technology the subject of the Agreement, and also complicated royalty arrangements, using mathematical formulae or financial examples to illustrate the correct way of calculating the royalties, where possible and appropriate, instead of or in addition to complex and lengthy 'verbiage'. In the same way that, in accordance with the old adage, 'a picture is worth a thousand words', a

---

[1] Sports Videos are very popular and much in demand and provide another useful income stream for Sports Governing Bodies and other Rights Holders.

[2] In the Internet age, a website for a Sports Governing Body, especially an interactive one, is '*de rigueur*'!.

[3] Mobile Phones are another useful platform for the dissemination of sports content, information, such as results of sports events, especially football matches, and sports images.

[4] For copying and downloading, for commercial and other specified purposes, of 'licensed materials' (as defined) from a website, including a sports-related one.

[5] Sports Video Games have become very popular in the last ten years or so. The corresponding Licence Agreements are highly complex and technical documents and, when drafting them, the draftsman needs to have a good understanding of the underlying technology; and, as far as warranties and liabilities are concerned, what can go wrong and how to limit the effects and damages. These Games are also often sponsored by other Companies, who wish to be associated with the sports portrayed in them. As the *Oliver Khan* case (see Chap. 12 on Sports Image Rights and Endorsement Agreements) has shown, specific 'releases' need to be obtained from the players whose images and likenesses are shown in them, even in so-called 'fantasy' games, in which the players are recognisable.

mathematical formula or worked example, for illustrative and clarification purposes, has the same value and avoids ambiguities and, therefore, potential disputes. As always, precision is the name of the drafting game!

Furthermore, 'Dispute Resolution' clauses, especially ones providing for ADR mechanisms for settling disputes arising under, out of or in relation to or in connection with the Agreements, also need to be included, in the Agreements, as well as 'Proper Law' clauses. Do not rely on the general rules of Private International Law, as these may, according to the circumstances of the particular case, produce some surprising and perhaps unwelcome results.

Finally, use general 'boilerplate' clauses as may be necessary to supplement the specific provisions of the Agreements.

## 14.3 Concluding Remarks

New Media Rights Agreements are highly technical reflecting highly complex arrangements and need to be drafted very carefully and clearly indeed, to avoid ambiguities and misunderstandings, and, therefore, unnecessary disputes in the future.

Again, use General Precedents with circumspection and adapt them to fit the particular facts and circumstances of each individual case. And above all, understand and appreciate the underlying technology involved and its application in each particular commercial deal.

## 14.4 Appendices

### *14.4.1 Appendix 1*

Encyclopaedia of Forms and Precedents/SPORT AND SPONSORSHIP vol 39(2) 2004/(C)

Forms and Precedents/G: MEDIA RIGHTS/81 Video production and licence agreement

**Video Production and Licence Agreement***

**This Agreement** is made the ...... day of .........

**Between**:

(*name of company*)[(*company registration number*)] [of (*address*) (*or*) whose registered office is at (*address*)] ("the Company") and

(*name of distributor*) [(*company registration number*)] [of (*address*) (*or*) whose registered office is at (address)] ("the Distributor")

**Whereas:**

The Company wishes to appoint the Distributor to produce the Programme.

The Distributor will assign all rights (including copyright) throughout the Territory in the Programme to the Company.

The Company has agreed to grant to the Distributor the exclusive licence and right to exploit the Programme on the following terms and conditions.

**It Is Agreed** as follows:

**1. Definitions and interpretation**

For the purpose of this Agreement the following words shall have the meanings respectively set out below unless the context requires otherwise:

| | |
|---|---|
| "Advance" | £...; |
| "CDPA" | the Copyright, Designs and Patents Act 1988 (as amended from time to time); |
| "Delivery Date" | the latest date for delivery to the Company of the Delivery Materials; |

---

* This agreement is intended for use by an event owner who wishes to authorise a video production company to enter the event and film footage for the purposes of producing a video programme. If the event is being broadcast the event organiser will need to ensure that the terms of the broadcast agreement allow access by another camera crew to film. In addition the event organiser may wish to provide a licence of the rights in any footage produced by the event broadcaster for use by the distributor. Where VAT is payable under this agreement the following clause should be inserted: 'All fees, disbursements and expenses payable under this Agreement are subject to the addition of VAT'. As to VAT generally see Paragraph 244 [472] ante. Source: Lexis Nexis; reproduced with permission.

| | |
|---|---|
| "Delivery Materials" | the technical, publicity and documentary materials listed in Schedule 3; |
| "Event" | (insert details); |
| "Interactive Formats" | all interactive media now known or hereinafter created (including without limitation CD-I and CD-ROM) to deliver interactive programmes that is to say programmes which combine 2 or more of the following media: audio–video film motion pictures text still images graphics animation which present information to a user in a non-linear fashion using computer information storage retrieval and management techniques and which contain hidden data information or other material accessed by the user; |
| "Master(s)" | the master to be delivered together with a quality control report approving it and in the form of a (insert details) tape which shall be a running master and appropriately time coded (or such other format as the Distributor may reasonably specify) embodying the Programme fully edited and assembled main and end titled with complete soundtrack (stereo dolby) printed in perfect synchronisation with the photographic action and 2-minute black period at the beginning technically fit and ready for commercial production of Videos in the English language; |
| "Programme(s)" | the original full length footage comprising the audio–visual production of the Event tentatively entitled (name) referred to in Schedule 2; |
| "Programme Specification" | the specification agreed between the Company and the Distributor as set out in Schedule 2; |
| "Programme Unit" | the Distributor's technical facilities (including cameras, gantries, scaffolding and transport) and personnel as are necessary for producing the Programme; |
| "Related Rights" | any of the rights conferred on any person in relation to the Programmes or the Masters which are the subject matter of this Agreement pursuant to the Copyright and Related Rights Regulations 1996 in respect of the Territory; |
| "Rights" | all rights in the Programme and/or the Delivery Materials of whatever nature being the entire copyright throughout the world including all extensions and renewals and any rights in performances; |
| "Royalty" | the royalty calculated in accordance with Schedule 1 and "Royalties" shall be construed accordingly; |

| | |
|---|---|
| "Sales" | Videos of the Programme which are sold, paid for and not returned; |
| "Sell-Off Period" | 6 months from the end of the Term; |
| "Synchronisation Licences" | a signed valid and binding licence for: (i) every clip and item of footage contained in the Programme and owned by any party other than the Company; and (ii) every musical composition or medley consisting of words and/or music and every Master recording contained in the Programme; andthe Synchronisation Licences shall permit the exploitation of the Programme in videogram format in accordance with the rights granted to the Distributor hereunder; |
| "Term" | (number) years from the date of signature of this Agreement; |
| "Territory" | (specify); |
| "Trade Marks" | the Company's registered and unregistered marks listed in Schedule 4; |
| "Video(s)" | means a magnetic tape cassette, cartridge video disc or DVD copy of the Programme or any like contrivance or appliance whatsoever whether now known or hereafter invented bearing or used for reproducing an audio–visual recording intended for reproduction on copies for supply to consumers for home or private use only by means of a playback device [including, without limitation (or) excluding], Interactive Formats; and |
| "Wholesale Price" | the Distributor's Recommended Retail Price excluding VAT. |

In this Agreement the singular includes the plural and vice versa and any gender includes any other gender.
The clause headings do not form part of this Agreement and shall not be taken into account in its construction or interpretation.
References to clause(s) and schedule(s) are references to clause(s) and schedule(s) of and to this Agreement.

**2. The Distributor's obligations**

2.1 The Company appoints the Distributor (and the Distributor accepts such appointment) to produce the Programme and the Distributor shall produce the Programme at its own cost in accordance with the Programme Specification.

2.2 The Distributor shall deliver the Programme, fully edited and synchronised, to the Company on or before the Delivery Date for its approval prior to release of the Programme on Video by the Distributor. The Company shall notify the Distributor of its approval or otherwise within 10 days of receipt of the Video by the Company. If the Company indicates to the Distributor that the Video is not approved then the Distributor shall further edit the Video (at its own cost) to the satisfaction of the Company.

2.3 The Distributor warrants and represents that:

2.3.1 it is the sole owner of and controls all copyright and other rights in the Programme; and

2.3.2 it has and will retain full authority to enter into this Agreement and is not bound by any previous agreement that adversely affects this Agreement.

2.4 The Distributor shall clear all copyright and any other rights in the Programme (musical or otherwise) including any consents required under the CDPA in respect of the Rights assigned under this Agreement.

**3. Assignment of rights**

3.1 In consideration of and subject to the terms of this Agreement the Distributor assigns (by way of a present assignment of future copyright) with full title guarantee to the Company the Rights in the Programme.

3.2 In consideration of the grant of Rights in clause 3.1 the Company grants to the Distributor (by way of a present licence of future copyright) the exclusive right throughout the Territory for the Term to:

3.2.1 manufacture duplicate and reproduce the Masters embodying the Programme and Delivery Materials as supplied for reproduction in the form of Videos as the Distributor may decide;

3.2.2. sell, distribute, supply, promote, advertise, sub-license and otherwise exploit Videos through all channels now known or hereafter invented including but not limited to sales to wholesalers, traditional rental video outlets, all retail outlets and via direct response mail order and video and record clubs and including sales at mid and budget price for home use in accordance with the rights granted;

3.2.3 if reasonably necessary for the exploitation of the rights (including but not by way of limitation the legal classification or censorship reasons or other similar requirements anywhere in the Territory) to change or amend the title, adapt, edit, re-edit, dub, subtitle, cut, re-arrange and translate (if applicable) the Programme and/or the promotional material or any part thereof with the prior written consent of the Company (such consent not to be unreasonably withheld or delayed);

3.2.4 add introductory and concluding material and include on any Video or any part of any Video any other material including material in respect of other products or services manufactured or distributed or supplied by or on behalf of the Distributor or any third party;

3.2.5 use without restriction promotional material (including trailers and other excerpts of the Programme) and all its visual and audio elements in all media (including but not limited to television, radio and print) strictly for the purposes of advertising, marketing and promoting Videos; and

3.2.6 exercise any Related Rights required to be exercised by the Distributor in connection with clauses 3.2.1 to 3.2.5.

3.3 The Company reserves to itself all of the Rights not specifically granted to the Distributor.

**4. Advance and Royalties**

4.1 In full consideration of the licence and rights granted hereunder the Distributor shall pay the Company upon signature of this Agreement the non-returnable but recoupable Advance and shall pay the Royalty calculated in accordance with Schedule.

**5. Accounting**

5.1 The Distributor shall account to the Company in respect of Royalties due to the Company from Sales of Videos hereunder from the end of each calendar quarter ending 31 March, 30 June, 30 September and 31 December during the Term. If the Royalty exceeds the Advance then the Distributor shall pay any sums due per quarter to the Company within 60 days from the end of each such quarter accompanied by the relevant statement of account.

5.2 The Company may at any time in any year of the Term (but not more than once in any 12-month period) appoint a firm of recognised chartered accountants to examine the books and sales records of the Distributor during normal business hours and upon giving the Distributor reasonable prior written notice thereof but only in so far as such books and records relate to the sale of Videos. If any third party is carrying out or has arranged to carry out an audit or similar inspection of the Distributor's books and records at the same or substantially the same time as the Company's proposed audit then the Company shall defer its audit until a reasonable time after conclusion of any such prior audit or inspection.

5.3 The Company shall furnish the Distributor in advance of any audit with a written undertaking by itself its servants or agents or otherwise to keep confidential all information pertaining to such inspection save only in so far as disclosure to the Company's professional advisers is necessary. If any such examination reveals an underpayment of Royalties exceeding 10% of the sums actually found to have been due during the period examined then in addition to any appropriate payment or credit of the Royalty the Distributor shall pay all reasonable costs in respect of such examination.

5.4 The Distributor shall not pay royalty earnings due to the Company under this Agreement in any quarter when such earnings are below £[50] but shall carry forward any such earnings until such time as earnings due and payable to the Company exceed £[50].

5.5 The Distributor may establish a reasonable reserve against potential returns of Videos in any calendar quarter provided that such reserve is released no later than 3 months after the close of the calendar quarter year in which the reserve is established. The Distributor's liability to pay Royalties is limited to Sales of Videos and no Royalties shall be payable on deletions or promotional copies.

## 6. Company's warranties and undertakings

6.1 The Company warrants, undertakes and represents that:

6.1.1 It shall obtain free non-exclusive access to the Event for the Programme Unit and for such representatives of the Distributor as is reasonable for the filming of the Programme and provide such facilities as the Distributor reasonably requires to undertake its obligations in clause 7.

6.1.2 It has the full right power and authority to enter into this Agreement.

6.1.3 It shall indemnify and keep the Distributor indemnified from and against all losses, damages, costs (including legal costs) and expenses arising out of any breach of the Company's obligations, warranties, representations or undertakings in this Agreement.

6.1.4 It will endeavour to secure other licensing and promotional activities such as publishing and merchandising activities in respect of the Event to coincide with the Distributor's release of the Video.

6.2 The Company shall provide the Distributor with reasonable assistance in the promotion and distribution of Videos and shall ensure that its employees, agents, all Event personnel and participants in the Event provide all reasonable assistance to the Distributor (at the Distributor's expense and request) in performing its obligations under this Agreement.

6.3 The Company shall not grant any third party any rights to produce Videos during the Term without first offering such rights to the Distributor on identical terms to those upon which the Company offers such rights to a third party. The Distributor shall indicate its acceptance or rejection of such terms within (*number*) days of them being offered by the Company failing which the Company may offer the rights to such third party as it sees fit.

## 7. The Distributor's warranties and undertakings

7.1 The Distributor warrants, undertakes and represents that:

7.1.1 it shall attend each Event and film the Programmes using the Programme Unit to a first class technical quality suitable for the manufacture and sale of Videos;

7.1.2 it shall deliver up all footage, materials and tapes produced and/or created by it or by any person on its behalf relating to the Event to the Company;

7.1.3 it shall, pursuant to the grant of Rights in clause 3.2, produce, manufacture and promote Videos in sufficient numbers to satisfy anticipated public demand;

7.1.4 it shall commercially release, distribute and sell Videos throughout the Territory and use its best endeavours to maximise the Royalties payable to the Company pursuant to this Agreement provided that the Distributor shall not less than (*number*) months after first commercial release of the Video during the Term and Sell-Off Period have the right at its discretion to decide whether and when to commence or discontinue or recommence the exploitation of Videos and to fix and alter the prices of such Videos;

7.1.5 it shall promptly pay all and any Royalties due on Sales hereunder in accordance with the terms of this Agreement;

7.1.6 it shall classify the Video in accordance with the Video Recordings Act 1984 and, if appropriate, undertake editing of the Video (at its own cost) to obtain an appropriate classification if the Video or any part of it contravenes the Video Recordings Act 1984 and is refused a BBFC classification;

7.1.7 it shall obtain from any third party (including without limitation any party participating in or otherwise involved in the management and/or organisation of the Event) any consent or authority that may be required for any exercise whatsoever by the Distributor of any of the rights licensed to the Distributor and the obligations undertaken by the Distributor under this Agreement;

7.1.8 all costs incurred in producing the Programme and the reproduction thereof onto the Masters shall be paid in full including payments to all parties involved in the Event and incorporated on the Masters and that the Distributor is solely responsible for all and any fees payable in connection with securing the music and music publishing rights musical copyright clearances and mechanical licences in and to the soundtrack of the Programme and Video;

7.1.9 it shall pay for all releases, licences and consents (where necessary in writing) to exploit and use the rights in the Programme and its soundtrack including without limitation all such releases, licences and consents required for exploitation of the Video throughout the Territory for the Term and for any advertising, marketing and promotional use (as set out in clause 3.2.5) by the Distributor;

7.1.10 the Delivery Materials which are delivered to the Company and the rights and copyright in the Delivery Materials are free from any liens, charges or other encumbrances and will be of a high technical quality suitable for reproduction in the manner now intended by the Distributor;

7.1.11 it shall pay any mechanical copyright royalties and clearance fees in connection with exploitation of the Video under this Agreement;

7.1.12 it will not make any statement or supply any information relating to this Agreement to any third party other than to the Distributor's own or the Company's professional advisers and without prejudice to the generality of the foregoing the Distributor will not by oral or written word or deed bring the Company or the Programme into disrepute;

7.1.13 it shall indemnify and keep the Company indemnified against all losses, damages, costs, and expenses arising out of any breach by the Distributor of its obligations, warranties or undertakings in this Agreement;

7.1.14 it shall provide 10 copies of the Programme in Video format (including packaging) to the Company during each year of the Term;

7.1.15 it shall not accept any sponsorship, advertising or product placement from any third party other than a duly appointed sponsor of the Company and the Distributor shall include in the Video up to a maximum of (*number*) seconds' advertising for any sponsor nominated by the Company, along with opening and closing credits, all at the sponsor's expense, in the Video.

7.1.16 it shall accord such credits and notices as required and notified to it by the Company on all promotional and packaging material relating to the Videos.

**8. Trade marks and liability**

8.1 The Company grants the Distributor the non-exclusive right to use the Trade Marks on the Videos, in their promotion and marketing and on their packaging and for no other purpose.

8.2 The Distributor shall use the Trade Marks together with the following credit [® the Company] in exercising any of its rights under this Agreement.

8.3 The Distributor shall submit all materials featuring or otherwise using the Trade Marks to the Company for its approval and shall (without limitation) use the Trade Marks in the form required by the Company, observe any directions given by the Company on the colour, size and placing of the Trade Marks and shall not use the marks in a way which would tend to allow them to become generic or lose their distinctiveness.

8.4 The Distributor shall promptly notify the Company of any actual or suspected infringements of the Trade Marks or any intellectual property rights of the Company and shall (at the request and expense of the Company) take such action as the Company requires in taking or defending any proceedings.

8.5 The Company is not required to take or defend any proceedings in relation to the Trade Marks.

8.6 The Distributor is not entitled to bring an action for infringement of the Trade Marks under the Trade Marks Act 1994 Section 30.

8.7 The Distributor shall maintain a policy of insurance with a minimum of £3 million cover for each and every claim arising out of any breach of contract by the Distributor and (in particular but without limitation) in respect of any product liability claims arising from the sale and/or use of the Videos.

8.8 The Distributor acknowledges that it has no title or rights in the Trade Marks or intellectual property of the Company other than as set out in this Agreement. The Distributor shall hold any goodwill generated from its use of the Trade Marks on trust for the Company and shall unconditionally assign such goodwill to the Company free of charge upon the Company's request.

**9. Termination**

9.1 Without prejudice to its other legal or equitable rights or remedies either party may terminate this Agreement forthwith by written notice to the other party in any of the following circumstances:

9.1.1 if the other party fails within 28 days after receiving written notice requiring it to do so to remedy any breach (if capable of remedy) of any provision of this Agreement;

9.1.2 if the other party is in material breach of this Agreement which breach is not capable of remedy; and

9.1.3 if the other party has a receiving order made against it, or makes an assignment for the benefit of its creditors, or if a receiver or liquidator is appointed for all or substantially all of that other party's assets who is not discharged within 28 days of the date of the appointment, or in the event that the other party shall petition or consent to any relief under bankruptcy, receivership, liquidation, compromise or arrangement.

**10. Post-termination provisions**

10.1 On expiration of the Term and subject to its compliance with all terms of this Agreement, the Distributor has the non-exclusive right to sell existing stocks of Videos throughout the Territory during the Sell-Off Period. Any stock remaining at the end of the Sell-Off Period shall, at the Company's election, either be sold to the Company at the Distributor's manufacturing cost or destroyed by the Distributor who shall provide an appropriate certificate of destruction if requested.

10.2 On termination of this Agreement the Distributor shall be relieved from all future performance of its obligations and any rights or obligations to which the Distributor has become entitled or subject before termination shall remain effective provided that the Distributor may not receive any third party licensee income following any such termination if the Distributor ceases to perform its obligations and the Distributor shall direct any such licensees to remit such income direct to the Company.

## 11. Notices

11.1 Notices under this Agreement shall be in writing and delivered personally or sent by first class post to the party to be served at the party's respective address specified above. In the case of the Distributor any such notices shall be addressed FAO: The Chief Executive with a courtesy copy to the (*insert details, eg head of legal and business affairs*). Any notices sent under this Agreement shall be deemed served when actually received or within 7 working days after the date of posting.

## 12. Approvals and consents

12.1 All decisions, approvals or consents to be given by the Company under this Agreement must not be unreasonably withheld or delayed and will be deemed given if no refusal is given within 5 working days of request therefor. Any refusal or retention must be in writing together with written reasons for such refusal or retention.

## 13. Entire agreement

13.1 This Agreement sets out the entire agreement and understanding between the Company and the Distributor relating to Videos of the Programmes and no variation shall be effective unless in writing and signed by a duly authorised representative of each of the parties.

## 14. Headings

14.1 Headings in this Agreement are for guidance only and do not form part of this Agreement.

## 15. No assignment

15.1 The Company may assign the benefit of this Agreement only upon giving written notification thereof to the Distributor and provided that the Company remains primarily liable for its obligations under this Agreement notwithstanding such assignment. The Distributor may assign this Agreement only with the Company's prior written consent.

## 16. Force Majeure

16.1 Neither party shall be deemed in default of this Agreement if the performance or any part of their respective obligations under this Agreement is delayed or becomes incapable of performance for any reason beyond either party's reasonable control including but not limited to war, invasion, act of foreign enemy, hostilities whether war be declared or not, act or threatened act of terrorism, civil war or strife, rebellion, strikes, lockouts or other industrial disputes or any other cause beyond the control of the parties, act of God or failure of any technical facilities. If any of the above events occur to the extent that this Agreement cannot be enforced or performed according to its terms for a period in excess of 6 consecutive months this Agreement shall be deemed to have terminated at the end of such 6-month period.

**17. Jurisdiction**

17.1 This Agreement shall be governed by the laws of England and Wales whose courts shall be its competent courts of exclusive jurisdiction.

**18. Further assurance**

18.1 The Distributor shall execute such further documentation as is reasonably required in order to give effect to the terms of this Agreement.

**19. Rights of third parties**

19.1 A person who is not a party to this Agreement may not rely upon or enforce any rights pursuant to the Contracts (Rights of Third Parties) Act 1999.

## SCHEDULE 1

Royalties

1. In consideration of the licence and rights granted under this Agreement the Distributor shall pay in pounds sterling to the Company a Royalty on Sales based upon the Wholesale Price as follows:
2. Videos sold at Full Price: Royalty payable shall be...%;
3. Videos sold at Mid Price: Royalty payable shall be...%; and
4. Videos sold at Budget Price: Royalty payable shall be...%.
5. For the purposes of this Agreement the following definitions of the Recommended Retail Prices ('RRP') shall apply:
6. Full Price shall mean a RRP of not less than £...;
7. Mid Price shall mean a RRP of between £... and £...; and
8. Budget Price shall mean a RRP of £... or less.
9. In respect of Videos sold through mail order or so-called club sales by or through a third party the Royalty payable hereunder shall be...% of the normal Royalty rates stated above.
10. The above royalties are inclusive of all copyright royalties (if applicable) and other payments in respect of rental rights or otherwise.

## SCHEDULE 2

The Programme Specification
(*insert details*)

## SCHEDULE 3

The Delivery Materials

The Distributor agrees that it shall effect Delivery of the following:

1 the Master(s) and material(s) strictly in accordance with this Agreement and with the terms below;
2 a quality control report approving the Master(s);
3 production negatives suitable in the Distributor's opinion for the packaging, publicity and advertising of Videos;
4 samples of other promotional material available to the Distributor including a selection of at least (*number*) stills and colour transparencies from the Programme;
5 a music cue sheet for the Programme; and
6 the Synchronisation Licences.

The Distributor shall deliver the Master and materials not later than (*number*) days after the last day of the Event. If the Distributor fails to effect satisfactory Delivery as aforesaid then it will have an additional 10 days to rectify the situation before it is considered in breach of this Agreement and the Company may immediately terminate the grant of rights to the Distributor under clause 2.2 but the assignment of the Rights to the Company by the Distributor shall not be affected by such termination which is without prejudice to any other rights or remedies the Company may have under this Agreement or otherwise.

## SCHEDULE 4

The Trade Marks

(*insert details*)

(*signatures on behalf of the parties*)

## *14.4.2 Appendix 2*

Encyclopaedia of Forms and Precedents/SPORT AND SPONSORSHIP vol 39(2) 2004/(C) Forms and Precedents/G: MEDIA RIGHTS/83 Agreement for the design, development, production and maintenance of a website

**Agreement for the Design, Development, Production and Maintenance of a Website***

**This Agreement** is made the ...... day of .........

**Between**:

(*name of company*)[(*company registration number*)] [of (*address*) (*or*) whose registered office is at (*address*)] ("the Owner") and
(*name of company*)[(*company registration number*)] [of (*address*) (*or*) whose registered office is at (*address*)] ("the Company")

**Whereas**:

The Company is a company specialising in the design, development and production of web products.
The Owner wishes to utilise the services of the Company in designing, developing, producing and maintaining a dedicated site for the Owner on the World Wide Web.

**It Is Agreed** as follows:

**1. Definitions and interpretation**

In this Agreement, unless the context otherwise requires, the following words have the following meanings:

| | |
|---|---|
| "this Agreement" | this Agreement (including any schedule or annexure to it and any document in agreed form); |
| "Business Day" | a day (other than a Saturday or Sunday) on which clearing banks are open for business in the City of London; |
| "Commencement Date" | (date); |
| "Content" | any material (whether text, sound, graphics, photographs, files or otherwise) made available (or to be made available) on the Website; |
| "Customer" | any person (including all users of the Website) to whom the Owner provides access or services in whole or in part |

* This agreement is intended for use by a club, governing body or similar organisation wishing to appoint a third party to create and host a website. Care should be taken over matters such as the ownership and maintenance of all rights relating to the website, such as the URL, as well as the use of any third party materials contained on the site and the responsibility for obtaining the right to use such materials. Source: Lexis Nexis; reproduced with permission.

| | |
|---|---|
| | either dependent on or comprising the Web Services or any part thereof; |
| "Data" | all data received, processed or conveyed via or otherwise in connection with the Web Services; |
| "Date Compliant" | software, hardware, firmware and services shall be unaffected by any change in data [including without limitation the advent of (date) or any subsequent date]; |
| "Existing Rights" | all intellectual property rights in and relating to the Web Package used before and/or existing at the Commencement Date; |
| "Fees" | the fees in Schedule 2; |
| "Intellectual Property Rights" | all registered or unregistered legal and beneficial intellectual and industrial property rights (including without limitation, copyright and related rights, database rights, patents, trade mark and trade secret rights) throughout the world no matter what such rights may be known as in any particular country in the world; |
| "New Rights" | all intellectual property rights in and relating to the Web Package and the products of the Web Services used from the commencement of and during the term of this Agreement; |
| "Notice" | includes any notice, demand, consent or other communication; |
| "Owner Information and Materials" | any information or materials supplied by the Owner (or on its behalf but with its approval) to the Company for the purposes of this Agreement; |
| "Term" | the period of the Agreement as set out in clause 3; |
| "Web Package" | all software, data, databases, Content, artwork, designs and any other materials or software solutions used for or in connection with the provision of the Web Services; |
| "Web Services" | the services specified in Schedule 1 relating to the design, construction, hosting and maintenance of the Website together with any other services specified by the Owner; and |
| "Website" | World Wide Website on which Owner Information and Materials and other Content will be displayed. |

In this Agreement, unless the context otherwise requires:

- words in the singular include the plural and vice versa and words in one gender include any other gender;
- a reference to:
- any party includes its successors in title and permitted assigns,
- a 'person' includes any individual, firm, body corporate, association or partnership, government or state (whether or not having a separate legal personality), and

- clauses and schedules are to clauses and schedules of this Agreement and references to subclauses and paragraphs of the clause or schedule in which they appear; and
- the headings are for convenience only and shall not affect the interpretation of this Agreement.

**2. Appointment**

2.1 The Owner appoints the Company (and the Company accepts the appointment) to provide the Web Services on the terms of this Agreement.

**3. Duration**

3.1 This Agreement shall come into effect on the Commencement Date and shall remain in effect until (*date*) unless terminated earlier in accordance with clause 9.

**4. Representations and warranties**

4.1 The Company represents, warrants and undertakes to the Owner that:

4.1.1 it shall perform the Web Services with all due care, skill and diligence using good quality materials and the best applicable techniques;

4.1.2 it shall ensure that the Website, on completion of the Web Services, at all times meet the functionality specified by the Owner and that down time is eliminated;

4.1.3 it shall provide all personnel to perform the Web Services and all such personnel shall be its employees;

4.1.4 all personnel providing the Web Services possess such skill and experience as is necessary for the proper performance of the Web Services and that the Company shall use its best endeavours to minimise changes to personnel;

4.1.5 it will not make any changes to the Owner Information and Materials;

4.1.6 it will remain up to date with all technical developments in the Web Services during the term of this Agreement and will introduce all appropriate improvements;

4.1.7 that the Web Package does not infringe any third party Intellectual Property Rights, is not obscene or defamatory and that the Company has acquired all rights in and to such material free of incumbrances in any and all media in perpetuity.

4.1.8 it has all requisite corporate power and authority to enter into this Agreement and to carry out the services contemplated hereby.

4.1.9 it has obtained all consent, permissions and licences necessary to enable it to perform its obligations.

4.1.10 the Web Services shall be provided using only hardware, software, firmware and systems which are Date Compliant

4.1.11 the Web Services shall be provided in compliance with the Data Protection Act 1998 and so as to enable the Owner to comply with its obligations thereunder.

4.1.12 the Web Services shall be provided in compliance with any applicable EC law or EC Directive or Regulations relating to the provision of goods and services by electronic means or the rights of consumers accessing the Web Services and so as to enable the Owner to comply with its obligations thereunder;

4.1.13 all Company software and Content incorporated into the product or the services or otherwise used in connection with the Web Services will be created using reasonable skill and care and by persons who are either employees of the Company in the course of their employment or who are acting subject to a written agreement providing for the vesting of all Intellectual Property Rights in the Company;

4.1.14 it shall remedy any defects and bugs in all software;

4.1.15 it will use its best endeavours to ensure that all software supplied in connection with this Agreement is free from viruses (including, without limitation 'Trojan Horses' and worms) and that, without prejudice to the generality of the foregoing, all such software shall have been first checked for viruses using the current and fully updated versions of all commercially available virus checking software;

4.1.16 the operation, possession or use of the Website will not infringe any Intellectual Property Rights or other rights of any third party; and

4.1.17 that it is authorised to utilise and to permit the Owner and the Customer's utilisation of any Intellectual Property Rights, items or Data required for the provision by the Company of the Web Services.

4.2 The Company's obligations under subclause 4.1 shall be continuing and, in the event of breach of any of them, the Owner shall have the right to require the Company to rectify the breach at no additional charge to the Owner.

4.3 Commencing on the Commencement Date, the Company shall perform the Web Services.

4.4 In respect of each element of the Web Services, the Company shall notify the Owner of the date when the relevant element is ready for acceptance by the Owner in order to provide the required level of functionality.

4.5 If any element of the Web Services is not accepted by the Owner as not (in its reasonable opinion) providing the required level of functionality then the Company shall ensure (at its own cost) that the missing or degraded functionality is corrected as soon as practicable and in any event within one month of notice from the Owner.

4.6 The Company shall indemnify the Owner from any actions, proceedings, costs, claims and demands brought or made against it and against any loss or expenses suffered by them as a result of a failure by the Company to comply with clause 4.1.

## 5. Confidentiality, data protection and security

5.1 The Company shall ensure that any confidential information ('the Information') disclosed to it by the Owner shall not be used or disclosed save as is strictly necessary for the purposes of this Agreement and shall return to the Owner promptly on request any such Information provided by the Owner.

5.2 The restrictions contained in this clause 5 shall not apply to the extent that disclosure or use of the Information is required by law.

5.3 The Company acknowledges that the Data and all Intellectual Property Rights therein shall (as between the Company and the Owner) belong to the Owner and undertakes:

5.3.1 that the Data shall only be processed in accordance with the Owner's instructions either under this Agreement or as provided in writing by an Owner representative.

5.3.2 that the Data shall not be used or accessed by the Company or by any of its employees or sub-contractors for any purpose other than as strictly necessary to provide the Web Services to the Owner under this Agreement; and

5.3.3 that neither the Data nor any part of it shall be disclosed to any third party (which shall not include the Company's employees and sub-contractors as referred to above) by the Company not withstanding that the Data may not otherwise be capable of protection as confidential information.

## 6. Rights and Content

6.1 The Company agrees with the Owner that:

6.1.1 it assigns for £1 (receipt of which is acknowledged) to the Owner with full title guarantee all of the Existing Rights throughout the world for the full duration of such rights.

6.1.2 all copyright, trade marks and other Intellectual Property Rights in the Owner's Information and Materials supplied to the Company for the purposes of this Agreement shall remain the property of the Owner; and

6.1.3 the Owner shall (as between the Owner and the Company) be the sole legal and beneficial owner of the New Rights and the Company shall assign by way of present assignment of future rights) all such rights to the Owner with full title guarantee throughout the world for the full duration of such rights.

6.2 The Company shall supply the best Content, information and Data at its disposal and shall ensure that it is accurate and up-to-date and that the Website will not include any information or material which is illegal or the accessing, holding, transmitting or supplying of which would be a criminal offence or otherwise unlawful or in breach of any regulations or codes of practice which may apply.

6.3 The Company shall procure that all necessary licences, consents and/or waivers (including but not limited to those from all rights owners, performers and other contributors) shall be obtained and paid for by the Company such that the Owner may make the Website available to Customers without:

6.3.1 any liability to make payments to third parties; or
6.3.2 infringing any Intellectual Property Rights of any third party.

6.4 Without prejudice to its rights of termination under this Agreement and notwithstanding that the Company has complied with all its obligations under this Agreement, the Owner may reject the whole or any part of the Web Services on the grounds that it does not reasonably consider them suitable for its use.

6.5 The Company acknowledges and agrees and shall (following the Owner's request) for as long as is necessary (in the Owner's opinion) suspend or discontinue any Customer's access either to the Website or to the product of the Web Services affected, as required to put an end to the events listed below, at any time if the Website contains anything which is or may be or the showing of which is or may be:

6.5.1 illegal, defamatory, offensive, abusive, indecent, obscene or menacing;
6.5.2 likely to cause annoyance, inconvenience or needless anxiety to Customers; or
6.5.3 likely to affect adversely the quality of the Website as a whole.

6.6 The Company may not include advertisements, merchant links or any commercial messages within the Website without the Owner's prior written consent or instruction

**7. Payment**

7.1 In consideration of the provision of the Web Services, the Owner shall pay to the Company the Fees.

7.2 All payments to the Company shall be made against the Company's invoices. The invoices shall be payable as agreed by the parties within 30 days of receipt.

7.3 Where under this Agreement any party agrees to pay to any other party any sum or to furnish to any other party consideration which (in either case) is consideration for a taxable supply that sum or consideration shall be exclusive of VAT payable on it and the recipient of the supply shall pay VAT in addition to any sum or consideration on receipt of a valid VAT invoice from the relevant party.

**8. Time of the essence**

8.1 Time shall be of the essence for the performance of the Company's obligations under this Agreement.

## 9. Termination

9.1 The Owner may by notice in writing immediately terminate this Agreement if the Company:

9.1.1 commits a breach of this Agreement which in the case of a breach capable of remedy shall not have been remedied within 30 days of the receipt of a notice from the Owner identifying the breach and requiring its remedy;
9.1.2 is unable to pay its debts or enters into compulsory or voluntary liquidation (other than for the purpose of effecting a reconstruction or amalgamation in such manner that the entity resulting from such reconstruction or amalgamation if a different legal entity shall agree to be bound by and assume the obligations created by this Agreement) or compounds with or convenes a meeting of its creditors or has a receiver or manager or an administrator appointed or ceases for any reason to carry on business; or
9.1.3 suffers or undergoes a change of control.

9.2 The Owner may terminate this Agreement at any time prior to completion of the Web Services on [14] days' notice in writing. On such termination, the Owner shall pay the Company all sums accrued and properly due on or prior to the date of termination.
9.3 Upon termination or expiry for any reason (including completion of the Web Services), the Company will return to the Owner at the Company's expense all Owner Information and Materials, an electronic copy of the Existing Rights and an electronic copy of the Web Package and all other material belonging to the Owner in its possession or control, in a form specified by the Owner.
9.4 If required by the Owner the Company will provide online notices to subscribers and users of the Website informing them of the termination of the service and providing them with such other information as is reasonably required by the Owner. Such notice will remain online for a period of 6 months after termination.
9.5 Upon termination or expiry of this Agreement (for whatever reason) the Owner shall have the right, by notice in writing served within 28 days of termination or expiry, to require the Company to continue to provide the Web Services until either such time as the Owner appoints an alternative provider of the services or the date 90 days following termination or expiry, (whichever is earlier). The Owner shall continue to pay the Company the applicable Fees in respect of such continuing Web Services.

## 10. Assignment

10.1 This Agreement shall be binding on and enure for the benefit of the successors in title of the parties. The Company shall not assign any of its rights under this Agreement without the prior written consent of the Owner.

**11. Force majeure**

11.1 Neither party shall be liable to the other for any loss, damage or delay consequent upon any circumstances outside of its control.

**12. Invalidity**

12.1 To the extent that any provision of this Agreement is found by any court or competent authority to be invalid, unlawful or unenforceable in any jurisdiction, that provision shall be deemed not to be a part of this Agreement, it shall not affect the enforceability of the remainder of this Agreement nor shall it affect the validity, lawfulness or enforceability of that provision in any other jurisdiction.

**13. Variation**

13.1 No purported variation of this Agreement shall be effective unless it is in writing and signed by or on behalf of each of the parties.

**14. Entire agreement and conflicts**

14.1 This Agreement sets out the entire agreement and understanding between the parties in respect of the subject matter of this Agreement.

14.2 The parties acknowledge that they have entered into this Agreement in reliance only upon the representations, warranties, and promises specifically contained or incorporated in this Agreement and save as expressly set out in this Agreement, neither party shall have any liability in respect of any other representation, warranty or promise made prior to the date of this Agreement unless is was made fraudulently.

**15. Releases and waivers**

15.1 The rights, powers and remedies conferred on any party by this Agreement and remedies available to any party are cumulative and are additional to any right, power or remedy which it may have under general law or otherwise.

15.2 Either party may, in whole or in part, release, compound, compromise, waive or postpone, in its absolute discretion, any liability owned to it or right granted to it in this Agreement by the other party without in any way prejudicing or affecting its rights in respect of that or any other liability or right not so released, compounded, compromised, waived or postponed.

15.3 No single or partial exercise, or failure or delay in exercising any right, power or remedy by any party shall constitute a waiver by that party of, or impair or preclude any further exercise of, that or any right, power or remedy arising under this Agreement or otherwise.

**16. Notices**

16.1 Any notice to a party under this Agreement shall be in writing signed by or on behalf of the party giving it and shall, unless delivered to a party personally, be left at, or sent by pre-paid first class post, pre-paid recorded delivery or facsimile or comparable means of communication to the address of the party as set out in this Agreement or as otherwise notified in writing from time to time and marked for the attention of the responsible officer.

16.2 Except as referred to in sub-clause 16.4 a notice shall be deemed to have been served:

16.2.1 at the time of delivery personally;

16.2.2 48 hours after posting in the case of an address in the United Kingdom and 96 hours after posting for any other address; or

16.2.3 2 hours after transmission if served by facsimile or comparable means of communication on a business day prior to 3 pm or in any other case at 10 am on the business day after the date of dispatch.

16.3 If the deemed time of service is not during normal business hours in the country of receipt, the notice shall be deemed served at, or in the case of faxes 2 hours after, the opening of business on the next business day of the country.

16.4 In proving service it will be sufficient to prove:

16.4.1 in the case of personal service, that it was handed to the party or delivered to or left in an appropriate place for receipt of letters at its address;

16.4.2 in the case of a letter sent by post, that the letter was properly addressed, stamped and posted; and

16.4.3 in the case of facsimile or comparable means of communication, that it was properly addressed and dispatched to the number of the party.

16.5 A party shall not attempt to prevent or delay the service on it of a notice connected with this Agreement.

## 17. Exclusion of third party rights

17.1 No term of this Agreement is enforceable pursuant to the Contracts (Rights of Third Parties) Act 1999 by any person who is not a party to it.

## 18. Miscellaneous

18.1 The Company undertakes at the request of the Owner and at the Owner's reasonable expense to execute and deliver such further assignments and documents as the Owner may require in order to perfect its title to the rights referred to in this Agreement.

18.2 As between the parties, all Intellectual Property Rights in the Data and the Content which is processed by the Company as part of or in connection with the Web Services, as well as the data and information produced by such processing, shall belong to and remain vested in the Owner.

18.3 If during the term of this Agreement either of the parties becomes aware of any threatened or actual unauthorised use of any of the other party's Intellectual Property Rights then that party shall immediately inform the other party in writing, setting forth the facts in reasonable detail. Each party shall, at the other party's request and expense, co-operate in any action the other party shall take in respect thereof.

18.4 The Owner licenses the Company to use specific brands and marks of the Owner (and the Company shall provide the suppliers of any proposed usage to the Owner for its prior consent) strictly for the purpose of the provision of the Web Services. The Company shall comply with any brand guidelines issued by the Owner from time to time.

**19. Governing law and jurisdiction**

19.1 This Agreement shall be governed by and construed in accordance with English law.

19.2 Each of the parties irrevocably submits for all purposes in connection with this Agreement to the exclusive jurisdiction of the courts of England.

As Witness etc.

SCHEDULE 1

The Web Services

1. Site design
2. Database design and integration
3. Content integration
4. Technical services
5. Management of interactive online services and site marketing

SCHEDULE 2

Fees

(*insert details*)

### *14.4.3 Appendix 3*

Encyclopaedia of Forms and Precedents/SPORT AND SPONSORSHIP vol 39(2) 2004/(C) Forms and Precedents/G: MEDIA RIGHTS/84 Mobile rights agreement

**Mobile rights agreement***

**This Agreement** is made the ……… day of ………

**Between**:

(*name of company*)[(*company registration number*)] [of (*address*) (*or*) whose registered office is at (*address*)] ("the Rights Holder") and

(*name of company*)[(*company registration number*)] [of (*address*) (*or*) whose registered office is at (*address*)] ("the Company")

**Whereas**:

The Rights Holder holds the commercial rights to the Event including, inter alia, the right to exploit audio–visual materials derived from the Event.

The Company is a company engaged in the mobile telecommunications business in the Territory and wishes to offer certain content to users of its service.

**It Is Agreed As Follows**:

**1. Definitions and interpretation**

In this Agreement the following terms shall have the following meanings unless the context otherwise requires:

| | |
|---|---|
| "Broadcaster" | any person authorised to make audio and/or visual broadcasts of transmissions of the Event; |
| "Commercial Rights" | any and all rights of a commercial nature connected with the Event including without limitation broadcasting rights, new media rights, interactive games rights, sponsorship rights, merchandising and licensing rights, advertising rights and hospitality rights; |
| "Company Group" | the Company and each of its holding companies, subsidiaries and parent and subsidiary undertakings and the subsidiaries and subsidiary |

* This Form is intended for use by a rights holder who wishes to grant a licence of rights to a mobile telephone company to exploit certain content and materials to offer to its users. It is similar in form and structure to a traditional broadcast rights licence. Great care must be taken to ensure that any agreement with a mobile telephone company is 'back to back' with all other agreements in its commercial programme; this includes all sponsorship and licensing agreements, in particular any other agreement involving the transmission of audio–visual materials by an appointed broadcaster. The convergence of transmission methods for audio–visual materials means that the distinctions between certain technology are difficult to sustain, e.g., many mobile telephone users are able to access the Internet. Source: Lexis Nexis; reproduced with permission.

| | |
|---|---|
| | undertaking of its holding company or parent undertaking for the time being (as such terms are respectively defined in the Companies Act 1985 Sections 258, 736, and 736A as amended); |
| "Competitor" | any team or club which participates in the Event during the Term; |
| "Content" | all information and data provided by or on behalf of the Rights Holder (but not including any information or data not supplied by or on behalf of the Rights Holder) relating to the Event including without imitation literary works, text, statistics, scores, news, visual images, audio and/or audio–visual footage, promotional activities and other commercial rights which are from time to time owned and/or controlled by the Rights Holder as such Content is more particularly described in Schedule 1; |
| "Designated Account" | (insert details of bank, sort code and account number); |
| "Event" | (insert details); |
| "Event Marks" | the marks set out in Part 1 of Schedule 2; |
| "Event of Force Majeure" | any event affecting the performance of any provision of this Agreement arising from or attributable to acts, events, omissions or accidents which are beyond the reasonable control of a party (other than lack of funds on the part of the Company) including without limitation any abnormally inclement weather, fire, explosion, earthquake, subsidence, epidemic or other natural physical disaster, failure or shortage of power supplies, war (or threat thereof), military operations, riot, crowd disorder, strike, lockouts or other industrial action, act or threatened act of terrorism, civil commotion and any legislation, regulation, ruling or omissions (including failure to grant any necessary permissions) of any relevant government, court or any competent national or international authority; |
| "Feed" | the live television signal and/or tape delay of a Match provided free of charge at (insert details) by the relevant Broadcaster of a particular Match; |

| | |
|---|---|
| "Match" | any match played as part of the Event; |
| "Mobile Device" | mobile telephones [and all other personal hand-held portable devices] capable of receiving and/or sending content and which is designed or adapted to be capable of being used whilst the user is on the move but not including laptop or desktop computers, portable radio or television sets; |
| "Mobile Rights" | the rights to transmit Content by means of Mobile Wireless Technology for reception and/or viewing on a Mobile Device in accordance with Schedule 3; |
| "Mobile Wireless Technology" | any wireless technology utilised by the Company or any company within the Company Group which is or may be used during the Term with radio frequency spectrum in any band, to enable or facilitate transmission of textual material, data, voice, video or multimedia services to Mobile Devices and which includes (without limitation) wireless technology employed in General Packet Radio Services ("GPRS"), the Global System for Mobile Communications ("GSM"), Personal Communications Networks ("PCN"), I-mode, Code Division Multiple Access ("CDMA"), Time Division Multiple Access ("TDMA"), Tetra, Wireless Application Protocol ("WAP") and the Universal Mobile Telecommunications System ("UMTS") and their related or derivative systems and services or any combination of them; |
| "Official Sponsors" | the Rights Holder's commercial partners from time to time in respect of the Event as notified to the Company by the Rights Holder; |
| "Promotional Materials" | any and all items and/or samples of the Company product and/or services and/or promotional marketing or advertising materials and/or premiums produced by or on behalf of the Company which bear the Event Marks and/or the Rights Holder Marks and/or which otherwise associate the Company with the Rights Holder or the Event or either of them which shall for the avoidance of doubt include all material appearing on the Company's Website; |

| | |
|---|---|
| "Revenues" | revenues howsoever generated by the Company through exploitation of the Mobile Rights; |
| "Rights Fee" | (insert details); |
| "Rights Holder Marks" | the registered trade marks or pending applications of the Rights Holder as are set out in Part 2 of Schedule 2; |
| "Service" | the service incorporating Content offered by the Company to Users; |
| "Term" | the term of this Agreement described in clause 2; |
| "Territory" | the world; |
| "Users" | the Company's customers and customers of the Company Group and any users of Mobile Device in the Territory; and |
| "Website" | the official Internet website of the Event with the URL: (insert details). |

In this Agreement the singular includes the plural and vice versa and any gender includes any other gender.
The clause headings do not form part of this Agreement and shall not be taken into account in its construction or interpretation.
References to clause(s) and schedule(s) are references to clause(s) and schedule(s) of and to this Agreement.

**2. Term**

2.1 This Agreement shall take effect on and from the date of signature and shall continue subject to clause 11 until (date).

**3. Grant of rights**

3.1 In consideration of and subject to the payment to the Rights Holder by the Company of the Rights Fee, the Rights Holder grants to the Company the Mobile Rights in the Territory during the Term. The Mobile Rights are granted to the Company on an exclusive basis for use throughout the Territory during the Term subject to the restrictions set out in this Agreement.

3.2 All rights not expressly granted to the Company under this Agreement including but not limited to rights to offer betting and gaming via Mobile Wireless Technology are reserved to the Rights Holder.

3.3 The Company acknowledges and agrees that:

3.3.1 the Rights Holder is the owner of the Commercial Rights and of all rights in the Rights Holder Marks;

3.3.2 the Company shall not be entitled to exploit any of the Commercial Rights other than as set out in this Agreement or any other agreement executed by the parties from time to time; and

3.3.3 the Company shall have no rights under this Agreement (other than those expressly set out in this Agreement) in relation to any Competitor.

**4. Consideration**

4.1 In consideration of the grant of the Mobile Rights the Company shall pay into the Designated Account the Rights Fee on the date of this Agreement as follows: (insert details).

**5. Provision of content and content restrictions**

5.1 The Rights Holder shall consult with the Company in relation to the method of provision of Content to the Company and the terms of this Agreement.

5.2 The Company may offer Content as part of the Service as follows:

5.2.1 the Company may provide news, score flashes, live related text and other "live" information in text only form and may provide a similar service by means of short messaging service ("SMS") to Users;

5.2.2 the Company may provide not more than (specify) single frame still photographs of action from each half of a Match together with relevant audio on an "as live" basis provided that any stills used in any linear or sequential presentation remain visible for not less than 30 seconds;

5.2.3 the Company may provide live or delayed audio-only commentary and/or reports of Matches (not including any commentary from any of the Rights Holder's licensed broadcasters);

5.2.4 the Company may offer audio or audio–visual interviews from Match venues or any other venue with players and coaches following the end of a Match;] [and

5.2.5 the Company may exhibit audio–visual highlights of Matches of not more than 3 minutes duration and not more than 12 minutes in aggregate per Match at any time not less than (number) hours after the end of a Match.

5.3 The Company has the non-exclusive right to develop official mobile interactive games for Users of Mobile Devices in accordance with this Agreement.

5.4 The Company will be responsible for editing the Content in accordance with the terms of this Agreement for the Service and shall ensure that such Content is of a high standard befitting an event in the nature of the Event.

5.5 The Rights Holder acknowledges that the Company is not obliged to use the Content and nothing in this Agreement shall prevent the Company from obtaining information and data from a third party and from using such information and data or from storing, accessing or otherwise using information or data which is the same as or similar to any information or data forming part of the Content, provided always that the Company shall not include any third party branding, promotion or advertisement in the Service except as required by this Agreement and shall not offer the Service as part of any bouquet or bundle of content or services to Users without the Rights Holder's prior written consent.

5.6 As soon as reasonably practicable after the Company becomes aware of any exploitation or use of the Content by an unauthorised third party the Company shall give the Rights Holder notice in writing with all relevant particulars which are in its possession and which it is permitted to disclose to the Rights Holder and in this event (or if such an event otherwise comes to the attention of the Rights Holder) the Rights Holder shall then take all reasonable actions to enforce its rights in the Content so as to protect the Company's rights as set out in this Agreement.

5.7 If the Rights Holder reasonably believes that any Content used as part of the Service or any Content otherwise distributed by the Company to Mobile Devices as part of the Service is unsuitable, it shall notify the Company and the Company shall immediately remove such Content from the Service and shall not further distribute such Content to any Users.

5.8 The Company acknowledges and agrees that third parties may have access to and offer content the same as or similar to the Content pursuant to news access regulations and under applicable laws.

## 6. Promoting and marketing the mobile services

6.1 The Company shall actively promote the Service to its Users and the availability of Content via Mobile Wireless Technology as follows: (insert details).

6.2 The Company shall add the Rights Holder Marks and any suitable designations of the Official Sponsors as required by the Rights Holder on the Service.

## 7. Ownership of Mobile Telephone Site Content and domain name

7.1 The Company acknowledges and agrees that the domain name assigned to the Mobile Telephone Site (as defined in Schedule 3) is and shall remain the property of Rights Holder.

7.2 All intellectual property rights and other rights in the Content exhibited on the Mobile Telephone Site (other than the rights in any trade marks belonging to the Company) shall be owned by and/or vest in the Rights Holder.

## 8. Obligations and warranties of the Rights Holder

8.1 In consideration of the payment of the Rights Fee, the Rights Holder warrants and undertakes to the Company (in addition to the other obligations of the Rights Holder set out in this Agreement) as follows:

8.1.1 that the Rights Holder has and will continue to have throughout the Term full right and title and authority to enter into this Agreement and to grant the authorities and licences referred to in this Agreement and to accept and perform the obligations imposed on it under this Agreement;

8.1.2 that the Content (if any) provided by the Rights Holder is to the best of the Rights Holder's knowledge accurate, free from errors and up-to-date at the time of supply and shall not so far as the Rights Holder is reasonably aware contain any information or material which contravenes any law, regulation or guideline whatsoever;

8.1.3 that the Rights Holder will use its best endeavours to overcome interruptions, errors or other problems of whatever nature in the provision of relevant Content of which it becomes aware; and

8.1.4 that to the best of the Rights Holder's knowledge, information and belief all licences, consents and/or waivers (including but not limited to those of rights owners, performers, players and other contributors required to enable the Rights Holder to make the Content available to the Company and the members of the Company Group have been obtained by the Rights Holder and will be maintained by the Rights Holder the cost of which is included in the Rights Fee.

**9. Company's obligations**

9.1 The Company represents, warrants and undertakes that:

9.1.1 it has and will continue to have throughout the Term full right and title and authority to enter into this Agreement and to accept and perform the obligations imposed on it under this Agreement;

9.1.2 it shall exercise the Mobile Rights strictly in accordance with the terms of this Agreement and that it shall not distribute Content other than via Mobile Wireless Technology;

9.1.3 it shall observe and abide by all relevant rules, regulations, directions, codes of practice or guidelines imposed by national law or by any competent authority which are applicable to the Event or to any Match or to the activities of advertisers or sponsors in connection with the Event and/or any Match and which are notified to the Company by the Rights Holder in writing from time to time;

9.1.4 it shall promptly observe and comply with all reasonable instructions, directions or regulations issued in writing by or on behalf of the Rights Holder in relation to the exploitation of the Mobile Rights;

9.1.5 it shall take reasonable steps to ensure that neither it nor any of its directors or employees make any defamatory statements or take part in any activities or use the Mobile Rights in any manner which is, in the reasonable opinion of the Company, derogatory to, or is, in the reasonable opinion of the Company otherwise detrimental to the reputation or goodwill of the Rights Holder;

9.1.6 it will refer to the Event by such title as the Rights Holder may notify to the Company in writing from time to time; and

9.1.7 any Content it provides and displays on the Mobile Telephone Site will not violate or infringe any third party intellectual property rights or rights of privacy and that such information and data will not be obscene, libellous, blasphemous, defamatory or in any other way unlawful and will not bring the Rights Holder or the Event into disrepute.

**10. Intellectual property rights**

10.1 Each party acknowledges that, save as expressly set out in this Agreement, nothing in this Agreement shall operate to transfer the title to one party of any intellectual property rights owned by the other party. Without prejudice to any other express licence in this Agreement, no other use of the other's intellectual property rights is permitted without the prior written consent of the other party.

10.2 The Company warrants and represents that it will not infringe the copyright, privacy rights or other rights of any third party in exercising its rights under this Agreement. Without limitation, the Company undertakes to obtain the necessary consent for the use of any third party work or material used by the Company as part of a service offered to Users or otherwise in exercising its rights under this Agreement.

10.3 The Company acknowledges and agrees that the Rights Holder has not granted and will not grant to the Company any rights in relation to: (i) the names, colours or logos of any Competitors; or (ii) the names or images of any players, coaches, officials or other persons connected to the Event and accordingly the Company acknowledges and agrees that the Rights Holder is not granting to it the right to advertise, promote or sell its service in any way which creates the impression that the Service is endorsed by specific Competitors, team(s) or player(s). The Company shall ensure that it does not infringe the proprietary rights of any such persons, and, in particular, the Company shall be responsible for obtaining, at its cost, the permission of any relevant team and/or individual for any uses of any team name, colours or logo or any individual's name or image in such a manner.

10.4 The Company acknowledges that each and every use of the Rights Holder Marks requires the Rights Holder's prior written approval. Accordingly:

10.4.1 The Company shall submit to the Rights Holder for its prior written approval (not to be unreasonably withheld or delayed) final form representative samples of each proposed use of the Rights Holder Marks including without limitation on any Promotional Material, at least 10 days prior to their release to the public. If the Rights Holder does not respond within 10 days of receipt of the samples from the Company, any such proposed materials shall be deemed approved by the Rights Holder. The Company shall not release any material without the approval or deemed approval of the Rights Holder. If the Rights Holder disapproves any item submitted for approval under this clause it shall provide reasons for such disapproval. The Company may resubmit such items for approval in accordance with this clause. The Rights Holder shall not unreasonably delay the subsequent approval process.

10.4.2 The Company shall ensure that the Rights Holder Marks are used solely on or in connection with the exercise of the Mobile Rights and the advertising, promotion and sale of the same. In particular, the Company shall use the Rights Holder Marks in its advertisements, including radio and television broadcasts, point of sale materials, printed matter and the like in connection with the Mobile Rights only, excluding any other product and/or service manufactured, distributed, provided, sold or advertised by the Company. The Company shall not use any tickets to the Event or offer any premium items in any advertising or promotion.

10.4.3 The Company shall not permit any trade name, logo or any other mark, denoting or identifying any third party or any third party's product or service, to be affixed to or be a part of any Promotional Materials (except as may be required by applicable laws in which case the size of such identification shall not exceed what is strictly necessary to comply with such applicable regulations).

10.4.4 The Company shall not participate with a third party in any promotions in exercise of its rights under this Agreement.

## 11. Termination

11.1 Either party shall have the right at any time to terminate this Agreement immediately by giving written notice to the other in the event that such other party:

11.1.1 shall have committed a material breach of any of its obligations under this Agreement and shall not have remedied such breach (if the same is capable of remedy) within 20 days of being required by written notice so to do;

11.1.2 goes into liquidation whether compulsory or voluntary, or if an administrator or receiver is appointed over the whole or any part of that other party's assets, or if that other party enters into any arrangement for the benefit of, or compounds with, its creditors generally, or threatens to do any of these things, or any judgment is made against that other party, or any similar occurrence under any jurisdiction affects that other party; or

11.1.3 ceases or threatens to cease to carry on business.

## 12. Consequences of termination

12.1 The expiry or termination of this Agreement shall be without prejudice to any rights which have already accrued to either of the parties under this Agreement.

12.2 Upon expiry or termination of this Agreement:

12.2.1 all of the Mobile Rights shall forthwith terminate and automatically revert to the Rights Holder;

12.2.2 subject to the terms of any other agreement between the parties the Company shall not use or exploit its previous connection with the Rights Holder or the Event whether directly or indirectly save that the Company may continue to circulate any Promotional Materials produced prior to such expiry or termination for a period of 60 days following the date of expiry or termination;

12.2.3 the Rights Holder shall be entitled to grant all or any of the Mobile Rights to any third party;

12.2.4 the Rights Holder and the Company will promptly return to the other all of the property of the other within its possession; and

12.2.5 all intellectual property rights in any Content (other than any mobile-interactive games provided by the Company in accordance with Schedule 3) on the Mobile Telephone Site and ownership of the Mobile Telephony Site domain name will remain in or revert to the ownership of the Rights Holder.

12.3 The termination of this Agreement in its entirety for whatever reason shall not effect such of the provisions of this Agreement as are expressed or are implied to have effect after such termination.

## 13. User data

13.1 Any User data whether amalgamated or personal collected by the Company in connection with the Service shall be owned by the Company and, subject to any relevant data protection or privacy legislation, the Company shall during the Term make such User data in its possession available to the Rights Holder on the Rights Holder's reasonable request.

## 14. Force majeure

14.1 If by reason of any Event of Force Majeure either party ("the Affected Party") is delayed in or prevented from performing any of the provisions of this Agreement then such delay or non-performance shall not be deemed to be a breach of this Agreement and no loss or damage shall be claimed by the other party by reason thereof.

14.2 If the Affected Party's exercise of its rights or performance of its obligations under this Agreement is materially hampered, interrupted or interfered with by reason of any Event of Force Majeure then the obligations of the other party shall be suspended during the period of such hampering, interference or interruption consequent upon such event or events and shall be postponed for a period of time equivalent to the period or periods of suspension and the parties will use their best endeavours to minimise and reduce any period of suspension occasioned.

**15. Liability**

15.1 Nothing in this Agreement shall exclude or restrict either party's liability for death or personal injuries resulting from the negligence of that party or of its employees while acting in the course of their employment.

15.2 Neither party shall be liable to the other under this Agreement for any loss, damage, costs, expenses or other claims for compensation arising as a direct or indirect result of breach or non-performance of this Agreement due to an Event of Force Majeure.

15.3 Under no circumstances shall either party be liable for any costs, damages, claims, actual or alleged indirect loss or consequential loss howsoever arising suffered by the other including, but not limited to, loss of profits, anticipated profits, savings, business or opportunity, or loss of publicity, or loss of reputation or opportunity to enhance reputation or any other sort of economic loss.

**16. Assignment**

16.1 Neither party may assign any of its rights or obligations under this Agreement without the prior written consent of the other party such consent not to be unreasonably withheld or delayed.

**17. Confidentiality**

17.1 Neither party shall disclose to any third party other than its professional advisers or as required by law any confidential business or future plans of the other party at any time acquired during the existence of this Agreement (other than any business or future plans which are or become publicly known other than as a result of its breach of this Agreement) and no reference is to be made to the terms of this Agreement by either party in any advertising, publicity or promotional material without the prior written consent of the other party.

**18. No partnership or employment**

18.1 This Agreement shall not be deemed to create any partnership, agency or employment relationship between parties.

**19. Notices**

19.1 Any notice served under this Agreement shall be in writing. Any notice which has been sent by first class pre-paid post shall be deemed to be received 48 hours thereafter (excluding Saturdays, Sundays and public holidays).

## 20. Third party transfers

20.1 Neither party shall assign, transfer, charge or make over this Agreement or any of its rights or obligations hereunder, without the prior written consent of the other party.

## 21. Rights of third parties

21.1 A person who is not a party to this Agreement may not rely upon or enforce any rights pursuant to the Contracts (Rights of Third Parties) Act 1999.

## 22. Governing law

22.1 This Agreement shall be subject to the laws of England and Wales and the parties hereto submit to the [non-]exclusive jurisdiction of the English courts.

As Witness

## SCHEDULE 1

Content

The Content means:

1 match fixture lists;
2 news items produced by the Rights Holder and available on the Website;
3 live scores;
4 team profiles;
5 team news and line-ups;
6 results and tables;
7 score flashes/snaps including scorer and time and nature of score; and
8 audio–visual materials derived from the footage of a Match produced by or on behalf of the Rights Holder as follows:

   8.1 during a Match 4 clips of up to 30 seconds from each half of a match,
   8.2 during any period of extra time 2 clips of up to 30 seconds from each half of extra time, and
   8.3 following the Match a further total of up to 50 clips of up to 30 seconds each.

The Rights Holder shall not sell any advertisements or sponsorship in the Content whether embedded or otherwise without the prior approval in writing of the Company.

[(*include any future data/information which may be provided by Rights Holder*)]
[(*include full specification for archive and live video and audio footage*)]

Form of delivery

[(*include full specification of the feeds to be provided*)]
[Data feed—technical requirements for format of information]

The Rights Holder shall not change the format in which the Content is delivered or made available to the Company without the prior written agreement of the Company.

Means of delivery

The Content shall be hosted by (*insert details*)
[(*insert details/specification of means of delivery of Content*)]

## SCHEDULE 2

Part 1

Event Marks
(*insert details*)

Part 2

Rights Holder Marks
(*insert details*)

**[1767]**

## SCHEDULE 3

Mobile Rights

1 The right to provide means and rights of access to Content by way of sending end users text messages or SMS giving information about the Event.
2 The right to develop, create, launch and host via the Company WAP portal an official Rights Holder Event WAP site (or other mobile-centric information site accessible through Mobile Wireless Technology ('the Mobile Telephone Site') which shall be designated 'the Official WAP/Mobile Telephone Site of the Event'.
3 The right to exploit the Mobile Telephone Site for the distribution of Content to Users in accordance with the restrictions and guidelines set out in this Agreement and the Company acknowledges that these rights in no way preclude the Rights Holder from exploiting or authorising third parties to exploit the same and/or similar rights on the Internet or by any other means of delivering Content other than Mobile Wireless Technology.
4 The right to develop, market and distribute Rights Holder official mobile-centric games accessible via Mobile Wireless Technology including but not limited to fantasy league, managerial and action games and for the purposes of assisting the Company to exercise such right the Company may consult with the Rights Holder to obtain clarification of which Competitor names, logos, stadia names and images and similar information and related intellectual property rights (if any) the Company is entitled to use.

5 The right to access archive and live video and audio footage (as such footage is more particularly described in Schedule 1) for re-purposing and distribution via Mobile Wireless Technology.

6 The right to access the Feed on such terms as may be agreed between the Company and the relevant Broadcaster but which access shall usually be free of charge at the location indicated by the Rights Holder but the Company acknowledges that the technical costs of onward distribution of the Feed shall be borne by it.

7 The right to no less than (*number*) media passes for all venues at which any Match is to be played (including access to the Internet or other communication system for the purposes of delivery of SMS to Users throughout the duration of the Match being played) and for all press conferences to be held by the Rights Holder.

8 The right of access to players, managers and other relevant individuals both before and after each match [in the designated interview rooms/areas] for video and/or audio interviews to be distributed via Mobile Wireless Technology as part of the Service.

(*signatures of* (*or on behalf of*) *the parties*)

### 14.4.4 *Appendix 4*

**BMJ Publishing Group Limited: Individual Online Licence Agreement***

This individual online agreement ("the Agreement") is made between the BMJ Publishing Group Limited ("Licensor") and the individual purchasing the online subscription ("Licensee").

**1. Key Definitions**

In this Agreement, the following terms shall have the following meanings:

1.1 "Agreement" means this document including any schedules and any properly executed variations or addenda.

1.2 "Commercial Use" includes i) copying or downloading any of the Licensed Materials or linking to the Licensed Materials for further redistribution, sale or licensing, for a fee; ii) copying, downloading or posting of any of the Licensed Materials on a site or service that incorporates advertising with such content; iii) the inclusion or incorporation of any of the Licensed Materials in other works or services (other than legally permitted quotations with an appropriate citation) that is then available for sale or licensing, for a fee; iv) use of any of the Licensed materials howsoever (other than legally permitted quotations with an appropriate citation) by organisations for promotional purposes, whether for a fee or otherwise; and v) use of the Licensed Materials for the purposes of monetary reward by means of sale, resale, license, loan, hire, transfer or other form of commercial exploitation.

1.3 "Fee" means the subscription fee payable by the Licensee for the Licensed Material as set out on the Website.

1.4 "Licence" means the Licence set out in Clause 2 below.

1.5 "Licensed" means the electronic version of the Licensor's publication(s) which the Licensee subscribes to.

1.6 "Site" means the electronic site on which the Licensed Materials will be displayed.

1.7 "Start Date" means the date upon which the contract between the Licensor and Licensee comes into effect.

1.8 "Location" means one year from the Start Date, unless terminated earlier under Clause 6.

1.9 "Website" means http://journals.bmj.com and relevant subdomains.

**2. The Licence**

2.1 In consideration of receipt of the Fee, Licensor grants the Licensee a non-exclusive, non-transferable Licence to access the Licensed Materials with a password or other necessary authentication to access the Licensed Materials.

* Permission for reproduction received from BMJ Publishing Group Ltd.

2.2 Subject to clause 6.3, except with respect to, Best Health, Best Practice, BMJ Case Reports, BMJ Learning, Clinical Evidence and DTB. Licensor also hereby grants to Licensee, a non exclusive, royalty free, perpetual licence to use the Licensed Materials that were subscribed to via this Licence and published during the Term of this Agreement, and with the exception of any portion of the Licensed Materials that has been expunged from the archive, damaged or sold. For the avoidance of doubt should any back issues of any Licensed Materials be available to the Licensee and Authorised User during the Term, these shall not be part of the Licensees perpetual access rights granted herein. Such use by Licensee of any Licensed Materials for which perpetual access is granted, shall be in accordance with the provisions of this Agreement, which shall survive expiry of this Agreement. The means by which Licensee shall have access to such Licensed Materials shall be in a manner as determined by Licensor, but shall be in electronic form. Where any Licensed Materials is sold, Licensor shall use all reasonable endeavours to ensure that the purchaser can provide ongoing access to Licensee for the relevant portion of the Licensed Materials.

2.3 Licensor holds the copyright (or all necessary licences or rights of use), for all works published in the Licensed Materials, as a compilation and as to the individual articles, collectively and individually, unless otherwise expressly noted.

2.4 The Licensee shall not claim ownership of the Licensed Material, or any intellectual property rights in the Licensed Material, by reason of its use of or access to the Licensed Material.

2.5 The Licensor and via its licensors reserves the right at any time to withdraw from the Licensed Materials, any item or part of an item for which it no longer retains the rights to publish, or which it has reasonable grounds to believe infringes copyright or is defamatory, obscene, unlawful or otherwise objectionable.

**3. Permitted Uses**

3.1 All use of the Licensed Material is subject to all applicable copyright laws and fair use conventions, and reproduction of any portion of the Licensed Material (other than certain journal articles which have noted on them "Open Access Article" which have more liberal uses as set out in Clause 3.2 herein) is permitted for personal, non Commercial Use as follows:

3.1.1 Access the Site in order to search the Licensed Materials, and to view and retrieve small proportions thereof;

3.1.2 Electronically save small portions of the Licensed Materials; and

3.1.3 Print out single copies of portions of the Licensed Materials.

3.2 Notwithstanding any other provision in this Clause 3, and only for any Licensor journal articles (and not for other Licensed Materials) which expressly have stated on them "Open Access Article", Authorised Users may copy, distribute, transmit and adapt such articles subject to:

3.2.1 such use being non Commercial Use;
3.2.2 attributing such use of the article as follows:
"This article has been published in the [insert journal name] [give full reference] and can also be viewed on the journal's website at [insert link]"
3.2.3 Such use otherwise being fully governed and in accordance with the Creative Commons Attribution Non Commercial 2.0 licence as set out in Schedule 1;
3.2.4 subject to ensuring all third party rights within all images, diagrams, photographs or other illustrative material, not owned by the authors or Licensor are cleared independently and appropriately and all the Licensor or third party trademarks are removed from any derivative works; and
3.2.5 ensuring any translations, (other than for which a prior translation agreement with BMJ Group has been established), have prominently displayed on them the statement:
"This is an unofficial translation of an article that appeared in a BMJ Group publication. Neither BMJ Group or its licensors have endorsed this translation".

**4. Licensee's Obligations**

4.1 Licensee agrees that the Licence is personal to the Licensee and:

4.1.1 it will not knowingly permit anyone else to use designated passwords so to access the Licensed Materials.
4.1.2 it will, if it becomes aware of unauthorised access to the Licenced Materials, notify Licensor immediately and co-operate in locating and attempting to stop the specific individuals who are abusing the service. If the specific abuser(s) cannot be identified or stopped, Licensor has the right to withhold, suspend, or terminate access to all or any portion of the Licensed Materials, without liability; and
4.1.3 will not remove, cover, overlay, obscure, block, or change any copyright notices, legends, or terms of use which Licensor or its licensors may post on the Site in order to inform users about system features, terms of use, or copyright notices.
4.1.4 it will not systematically make printed or electronic copies of multiple portions of the Licensed Materials for any purpose or created any derivative works from the Licensed Materials.
4.1.5 create any derivative works from the Licensed Materials;
4.1.6 display or distribute any part of the Licensed Materials on any electronic network, including without limitation, an intranet, the internet and the Worldwide Web; or
4.1.7 make any Commercial Use of the Licensed Materials.

## 5. Technical Access

5.1 Licensor intends for the Site to be available 24 hours per day, 7 days per week. However, neither to the fullest extent permitted by law, Licensor nor any of its licensors will be liable for damages or refunds should the Site become unavailable or access to the Site becomes slow or incomplete due to system back-up procedures, internet traffic volume, upgrades, overload of requests to the servers, general network failures or delays, or any other cause which may from time to time make the Site inaccessible to Licensee.

## 6. Termination

6.1 Either party may terminate this Agreement:

6.1.1 where the other party commits a material or persistent breach of any term of this Agreement and fails to remedy such breach (if capable of remedy) within 30 days of notification in writing from the other party; or

6.1.2 immediately upon the other party becoming insolvent, subject to receivership, liquidation or similar external administration.

6.2 On termination of this Licence for just cause, access to the Licensed Materials by Licensee and Authorised Users shall be terminated.

## 7. Warranty and Liability

7.1 While Licensor seeks to provide updated and accurate content as part of the Licensed Materials, the Licensed Materials are supplied on an "as is" basis. Any statements made to the contrary are void. Licensee shall be responsible for notifying all Authorised Users and any other users of the Licensed Materials or Site acting under Licensee that such users must always read the full disclaimers on the relevant website for each of the Licensed Materials and that their use of the Licensed Materials shall be deemed acceptance of those terms. Licensee shall indemnify Licensor and its licensors against any claims, costs, expenses, proceeding, awards and demands made against the Licensor or its licensors by Authorised Users or any other party using the Licensed Materials or Site under Licensee. Licensor and its licensors do not warrant or guarantee its accuracy, completeness, merchantability, non-infringement or fitness for a particular purpose of the Licensed Materials or the Site and to the fullest extent permitted by law, Licensor and its licensors expressly disclaim the foregoing and all others, (other than where expressly agreed to herein) and in addition, any conditions, warranties and other terms howsoever, which might otherwise be implied by statute, common law or otherwise.

7.2 To the fullest extent permitted by Law and other than expressly provided for herein, in no circumstances is Licensor or its Licensors liable to the Licensee Authorised Users, or other users acting under Licensee for any indirect of consequential losses or expenses, however caused, including, without limitation, loss of anticipated profits or savings, goodwill, reputation, business receipts or contracts, or losses or expenses resulting from third party claims. Nothing in this Agreement seeks to exclude liability for death or personal injury caused by Licensor's negligence or fraudulent misstatement and this does not effect the Licensee's Statutory Rights.

7.3 To the fullest extent permitted by law, in the event the Licensor or its Licensor's have any liability under this Agreement, Licensor's and their Licensors aggregate liability for any content, accessibility or problems with the site or Licensed Materials will not exceed the amount of subscription fees paid for the Licensed Materials during the 12 month period preceding any claim or notice of damages.

**8. Indemnities**

8.1 Licensor shall indemnify and hold License harmless for any losses, claims, damages, awards, penalties, or injuries incurred, including reasonable attorney's fees, which arise from any claim by any third party of an alleged infringement of copyright arising out of the use of the relevant Licensed Materials (subject to that component being owned by Licensor) by Licensee or any Authorised User. No limitation of liability set forth elsewhere in this Agreement is applicable to this indemnification.

8.2 Should Licensee wish to invoke the indemnity in clause 8.1, the Licensee must promptly notify Licensor of any such claims at its own expense and not make any admission of liability and shall limit its own costs as is reasonably possible. The Licensee shall provide Licensor with all necessary assistance in investigating and defending such claims as Licensor may reasonably request and have the right to participate in the defence at its own expense, subject to following all reasonable instructions of Licensor.

**9. General**

9.1 Neither party shall be liable for failure, default or delay in performing its obligations under this Licence, caused by a Force Majeure event which shall include any act of God, war, or threatened war, act or threatened act of terrorism, riot, strike, lockout, individual action, fire, flood, drought, tempest or other event beyond the reasonable control of either party.

9.2 Licensor may assign or transfer any of its rights and obligations under this Agreement, upon written notice to Licensee. Licensee may not assign its rights or transfer its obligations herein without the prior written consent of Licensor.

9.3 Alterations to this Agreement are only valid if they are recorded in writing and signed by both parties.

9.4 In the event that any provision of this Agreement is held to be invalid, the remainder of the provisions shall continue in full force and effect.

9.5 There shall be no right whatsoever for any third party to enforce the terms and conditions of this Agreement. The Parties hereby expressly wish to exclude the operation of the Contracts (Rights of Third Parties) Act 1999.

9.6 No delay or failure by either party to exercise any of its powers, rights or remedies under this Agreement will operate as a waiver of them nor will any single or partial exercise of any such powers, rights or remedies preclude any other or further exercise of them. Any waiver, to be effective, must be in writing and signed by a duly authorised representative of each party.

9.7 Any notice under this Agreement must be hand written and may be delivered or sent by fax or first class post to the offices of the relevant party set out on the first page of Agreement (or as otherwise notified from time to time) and such notice shall be deemed to have been received upon successful transmission of faxing or 7 (seven) days from the date of posting.

9.8 To the fullest extent permitted by law, this Agreement constitutes the entire Agreement between Licensor and Licensee with respect to the Licensed Materials.

9.9 To the fullest extent permitted by law, this Licence will be governed by the laws of England and shall be governed and construed in accordance with the laws of England. Any action arising out of or relating to this agreement shall be brought in courts situated in England save where it is necessary for Licensor for enforcement to bring proceedings to bring an action in an alternative jurisdiction.

**Date of document: November 2008**

## SCHEDULE 1

### Creative Commons Legal Code

Attribution-NonCommercial 2.0

Creative commons corporation is not a Law firm and does not provide Legal services. Distribution of this License does not create an attorney-client relationship. Creative commons provides this information on an "as-is" basis. Creative commons makes no warranties regarding the information provided, and disclaims liability for damages resulting from its use.

### License

The work (as defined below) is provided under the terms of this creative commons public license ("CCPL" or "license"). The work is protected by copyright and/or other applicable Law. Any use of the work other than as authorised under this License or copyright Law is prohibited. By exercising any rights to the work provided here‘ you accept and agree to be bound by the terms of this License. The Licensor grants you the rights contained here in consideration of your acceptance of such terms and conditions.

1. **Definitions**

   a. **"Collective Work"** means a work, such as a periodical issue, anthology or encyclopedia, in which the Work in its entirety in unmodified form, along with a number of other contributions, constituting separate and independent works in themselves, are assembled into a collective whole. A work that constitutes a Collective Work will not be considered a Derivative Work
   (as defined below) for the purposes of this License.
   b. **"Derivative Work"** means a work based upon the Work or upon the Work and other pre-existing works, such as a translation, musical arrangement, dramatization, fictionalization, motion picture version, sound recording, art reproduction, abridgment, condensation, or any other form in which the Work may be recast, transformed, or adapted, except that a work that constitutes a Collective Work will not be considered a Derivative Work for the purpose of this License. For the avoidance of doubt, where the Work is a musical composition or sound recording, the synchronization of the Work in timed-relation with a moving image ("synching") will be considered a Derivative Work for the purpose of this License.
   c. **"Licensor"** means the individual or entity that offers the Work under the terms of this License.
   d. **"Original Author"** means the individual or entity who created the Work.
   e. **"Work"** means the copyrightable work of authorship offered under the terms of this License.
   f. **"You"** means an individual or entity exercising rights under this License who has not previously violated the terms of this License with respect to the Work, or who has received express permission from the Licensor to exercise rights under this License despite a previous violation.

2. **Fair Use Rights.** Nothing in this license is intended to reduce, limit, or restrict any rights arising from fair use, first sale or other limitations on the exclusive rights of the copyright owner under copyright law or other applicable laws.
3. **License Grant.** Subject to the terms and conditions of this License, Licensor hereby grants You a worldwide, royalty-free, non-exclusive, perpetual (for the duration of the applicable copyright) license to exercise the rights in the Work as stated below:

   a. to reproduce the Work, to incorporate the Work into one or more Collective Works, and to reproduce the Work as incorporated in the Collective Works;
   b. to create and reproduce Derivative Works;
   c. to distribute copies or phonorecords of, display publicly, perform publicly, and perform publicly by means of a digital audio transmission the Work including as incorporated in Collective Works;
   d. to distribute copies or phonorecords of, display publicly, perform publicly, and perform publicly by means of a digital audio transmission Derivative Works;

The above rights may be exercised in all media and formats whether now known or hereafter devised. The above rights include the right to make such modifications as are technically necessary to exercise the rights in other media and formats. All rights not expressly granted by Licensor are hereby reserved, including but not limited to the rights set forth in Sections 4(d) and 4(e).

4. **Restrictions.** The license granted in Section 3 above is expressly made subject to and limited by the following restrictions:

   a. You may distribute, publicly display, publicly perform, or publicly digitally perform the Work only under the terms of this License, and You must include a copy of, or the Uniform Resource Identifier for, this License with every copy or phonorecord of the Work You distribute, publicly display, publicly perform, or publicly digitally perform. You may not offer or impose any terms on the Work that alter or restrict the terms of this License or the recipients' exercise of the rights granted hereunder. You may not sublicense the Work. You must keep intact all notices that refer to this License and to the disclaimer of warranties. You may not distribute, publicly display, publicly perform, or publicly digitally perform the Work with any technological measures that control access or use of the Work in a manner inconsistent with the terms of this License Agreement. The above applies to the Work as incorporated in a Collective Work, but this does not require the Collective Work apart from the Work itself to be made subject to the terms of this License. If You create a Collective Work, upon notice from any Licensor You must, to the extent practicable, remove from the Collective Work any reference to such Licensor or the Original Author, as requested. If You create a Derivative Work, upon notice from any Licensor You must, to the extent practicable, remove from the Derivative Work any reference to such Licensor or the Original Author, as requested.
   b. You may not exercise any of the rights granted to You in Section 3 above in any manner that is primarily intended for or directed toward commercial advantage or private monetary compensation. The exchange of the Work for other copyrighted works by means of digital file-sharing or otherwise shall not be considered to be intended for or directed toward commercial advantage or private monetary compensation, provided there is no payment of any monetary compensation in connection with the exchange of copyrighted works.
   c. If you distribute, publicly display, publicly perform, or publicly digitally perform the Work or any Derivative Works or Collective Works, You must keep intact all copyright notices for the Work and give the Original Author credit reasonable to the medium or means You are utilizing by conveying the name (or pseudonym if applicable) of the Original Author if supplied; the title of the Work if supplied; to the extent reasonably practicable, the Uniform Resource Identifier, if any, that Licensor specifies to be associated with the Work, unless such URI does not refer to the copyright notice or licensing information for the Work; and in the case of a

Derivative Work, a credit identifying the use of the Work in the Derivative Work (e.g., "French translation of the Work by Original Author," or "Screenplay based on original Work by Original Author"). Such credit may be implemented in any reasonable manner; provided, however, that in the case of a Derivative Work or Collective Work, at a minimum such credit will appear where any other comparable authorship credit appears and in a manner at least as prominent as such other comparable authorship credit.

d. For the avoidance of doubt, where the Work is a musical composition:

   1. Performance Royalties Under Blanket Licenses. Licensor reserves the exclusive right to collect, whether individually or via a performance rights society (e.g. ASCAP, BMI, SESAC), royalties for the public performance or public digital performance (e.g. webcast) of the Work if that performance is primarily intended for or directed toward commercial advantage or private monetary compensation.
   2. Mechanical Rights and Statutory Royalties. Licensor reserves the exclusive right to collect, whether individually or via a music rights agency or designated agent (e.g. Harry Fox Agency), royalties for any phonorecord You create from the Work ("cover version") and distribute, subject to the compulsory license created by 17 USC Section 115 of the US Copyright Act (or the equivalent in other jurisdictions), if Your distribution of such cover version is primarily intended for or directed toward commercial advantage or private monetary compensation.

e. Webcasting Rights and Statutory Royalties. For the avoidance of doubt, where the Work is a sound recording, Licensor reserves the exclusive right to collect, whether individually or via a performance-rights society (e.g. SoundExchange), royalties for the public digital performance (e.g. webcast) of the Work, subject to the compulsory license created by 17 USC Section 114 of the US Copyright Act (or the equivalent in other jurisdictions), if Your public digital performance is primarily intended for or directed toward commercial advantage or private monetary compensation.

5. **Representations, Warranties and Disclaimer**
   Unless otherwise mutually agreed to by the parties in writing, Licensor offers the work as-is and makes no representations or warranties of any kind concerning the work, express, implied, statutory or otherwise, including, without limitation, warranties of title, merchantibility, fitness for a particular purpose, noninfringement, or the absence of latent or other defects, accuracy, or the presence of absence of errors, whether or not discoverable. Some jurisdictions do not allow the exclusion of implied warranties, so such exclusion may not apply to you.
6. **Limitation on Liability.**
   Except to the extent required by applicable law, in no event will Licensor be liable to you on any Legal Theory for any special, incidental, consequential,

punitive or exemplary damages arising out of this License or the use of the work, even if licensor has been advised of the possibility of such damages.

7. **Termination**

   a. This License and the rights granted hereunder will terminate automatically upon any breach by You of the terms of this License. Individuals or entities who have received Derivative Works or Collective Works from You under this License, however, will not have their licenses terminated provided such individuals or entities remain in full compliance with those licenses. Sections 1, 2, 5, 6, 7, and 8 will survive any termination of this License.
   b. Subject to the above terms and conditions, the license granted here is perpetual (for the duration of the applicable copyright in the Work). Notwithstanding the above, Licensor reserves the right to release the Work under different license terms or to stop distributing the Work at any time; provided, however that any such election will not serve to withdraw this License (or any other license that has been, or is required to be, granted under the terms of this License), and this License will continue in full force and effect unless terminated as stated above.

8. **Miscellaneous**

   a. Each time You distribute or publicly digitally perform the Work or a Collective Work, the Licensor offers to the recipient a license to the Work on the same terms and conditions as the license granted to You under this License.
   b. Each time You distribute or publicly digitally perform a Derivative Work, Licensor offers to the recipient a license to the original Work on the same terms and conditions as the license granted to You under this License.
   c. If any provision of this License is invalid or unenforceable under applicable law, it shall not affect the validity or enforceability of the remainder of the terms of this License, and without further action by the parties to this agreement, such provision shall be reformed to the minimum extent necessary to make such provision valid and enforceable.
   d. No term or provision of this License shall be deemed waived and no breach consented to unless such waiver or consent shall be in writing and signed by the party to be charged with such waiver or consent.
   e. This License constitutes the entire agreement between the parties with respect to the Work licensed here. There are no understandings, agreements or representations with respect to the Work not specified here. Licensor shall not be bound by any additional provisions that may appear in any communication from You. This License may not be modified without the mutual written agreement of the Licensor and You.

Creative Commons is not a party to this License, and makes no warranty whatsoever in connection with the Work. Creative Commons will not be liable to You or any party on any legal theory for any damages whatsoever, including without limitation any general, special, incidental or consequential damages

arising in connection to this license. Notwithstanding the foregoing two (2) sentences, if Creative Commons has expressly identified itself as the Licensor hereunder, it shall have all rights and obligations of Licensor.
Except for the limited purpose of indicating to the public that the Work is licensed under the CCPL, neither party will use the trademark "Creative Commons" or any related trademark or logo of Creative Commons without the prior written consent of Creative Commons. Any permitted use will be in compliance with Creative Commons' then-current trademark usage guidelines, as may be published on its website or otherwise made available upon request from time to time. Creative Commons may be contacted at http://creativecommons.org/.

### 14.4.5 *Appendix 5*

**Confidential Video Game License Agreement for [A] Video Game System (Western Hemisphere)***

**This Agreement** is entered into between [X] INC., a Washington corporation and [B] Inc., a California corporation ("LICENSEE").

[X] and LICENSEE acknowledge and agree as follows:

**1. Recitals**

1.1 [X] markets and sells a high-quality video game system, including hardware, software and an input controller, marketed by [X] under its trademarks "[A]" and "[B]", for playing video games.
1.2 LICENSEE desires to gain access to and rights to utilize highly proprietary programming specifications, development tools, trademarks and other valuable intellectual property rights in order to develop video game software and to purchase and sell such video game software from [X] for play on the [A] system, which system was developed by NCL and Silicon Graphics, Inc.
1.3 [X] is willing to grant a license to utilize such proprietary information and intellectual property rights and to sell video game software to LICENSEE upon the terms and conditions set forth in this Agreement.

**2. Definitions**

2.1 "Artwork" shall mean the final art and mechanical formats for the Licensed Product including the Game Cartridge box, user instruction manual with consumer precautions and warranty, Game Cartridge label and inserts.
2.2 "Competing Systems" shall mean hardware platforms, whether marketed now or in the future, designed to play interactive video games, including but without limitation: [...], and any successors or derivatives of any of the foregoing.
2.3 "Effective Date" shall mean the last date on which all parties shall have signed this Agreement.
2.4 "Exclusive Licensed Product" shall mean the audiovisual work in its current form and as hereafter developed, which is sold by LICENSEE as a Licensed Product under this Agreement.
2.5 "Finished Goods" shall mean the Game Cartridge, fully assembled with exterior labels, packaged in a plastic or polyethylene bag, placed in a high quality, custom packaging box, including all required Artwork.
2.6 "Game Cartridge(s)" shall mean interchangeable plastic cartridges adapted for use with the [B] System, housing the Game embodied in electronic memory devices or comparable medium authorized by [X] for storing and playing Games on the [B] System.

* Thomson Reuters (FindLaw); reproduced with permission.

2.7 "Game(s)" shall mean video game software compatible with the [B] System developed under this Agreement.

2.8 "Guidelines" shall mean the "[A] Packaging Guidelines" and the "[A] Development Manual" setting forth trademark, copyright and related artwork standards, as published from time to time by [X].

2.9 "Independent Contractor" shall mean any third party agent, consultant, contractor or independent programmer, other than LICENSEE.

2.10 "Licensed Copyright(s)" shall mean various copyrights in printed materials, art or logo designs, trade dress, computer software, microcode, electronic circuitry and rights in integrated circuit layout designs employed in the [B] System.

2.11 "Licensed Intellectual Properties" shall mean individually, collectively or in any combination, the Licensed Inventions, Licensed Proprietary Information, Licensed Copyrights and Licensed Trademarks.

2.12 "Licensed Invention(s)" shall mean improvements and inventions concerning the [B] System, including inventions that are or may become the subject matter of various patents or patent applications.

2.13 "Licensed Product(s)" shall mean Game Cartridges (or comparable medium authorized by [X]) for employing the Licensed Intellectual Properties and having electronic memory devices storing the Games.

2.14 "Licensed Proprietary Information" shall mean any of the following information relating to the [B] System: (a) all current or future information, know-how, techniques, methods, information, tools, emulator boards, software development specifications, and/or trade secrets, (b) any patents or patent applications, (c) any business, marketing or sales data information, and (d) any other information or data relating to development, design, operation, manufacturing, marketing or sales. "Licensed Proprietary Information" shall include information disclosed to LICENSEE by [X], [X]'s affiliated companies, [Y], and/or other third parties working with [X]. Such Licensed Proprietary Information shall include all confidential information disclosed, whether in writing, orally, visually, or in the form of drawings, technical specification, software, samples, pictures, models, recordings, or other tangible items which contain or manifest, in any form, the Licensed Proprietary Information. Licensed Proprietary Information shall not include: (a) data and information which was in the public domain prior to LICENSEE's receipt of the same hereunder, or which subsequently becomes part of the public domain by publication or otherwise, except by LICENSEE's wrongful act or omission, (b) data and information which LICENSEE can demonstrate, through written records kept in the ordinary course of business, was in its possession without restriction on use or disclosure, prior to its receipt of the same hereunder and was not acquired directly or indirectly from [X] under an obligation of confidentiality which is still in force, (c) data and information which LICENSEE can show was received by it from a third party who did not acquire the same directly or indirectly from [X] and to whom LICENSEE has no obligation of confidentiality, and (d) data and information which is required to be disclosed by an authorized governmental or judicial entity, provided that LICENSEE shall notify [X] at least thirty (30) days prior to such disclosure.

2.15 "Licensed Trademarks" shall mean registered and unregistered trademarks and trademark applications used in connection with the [B] System, including "[X]", "[A]", "[B]", "Official [X] Seal of Quality" and trade dress in the [B] System.

2.16 "Marketing Materials" shall mean marketing, advertising or promotional materials that incorporate the Licensed Intellectual Properties that are developed by or for LICENSEE to promote the sale of the Licensed Products.

2.17 "NCL" shall mean [X]'s parent company, [X] Co., Ltd. of Kyoto, Japan.

2.18 "[A] System" and "[B] System" shall mean the 64-bit [A] video game system, including the hardware, software and input controller marketed by [X] and NCL.

2.19 "Product Proposal" shall mean a written proposal that provides a detailed explanation of the Game.

2.20 "Schedule 1" shall mean the "[X] of America Inc. Price Sheet [B] Licensed Game Paks" attached to this Agreement and incorporated by reference into this Agreement.

2.21 "[Y]" shall mean [...], Inc.

2.22 "Stripped Cartridge(s)" shall mean fully assembled Game Cartridges with exterior labels shipped in a plastic or polyethylene bag, excluding the required Artwork.

2.23 "Term" shall mean three (3) years from the Effective Date.

2.24 "Territory" shall mean all countries within the Western Hemisphere, including the United States, Canada, South America, Central America, Mexico and all applicable territories and possessions.

## 3. Grant of License; Reservation of Rights by [X]

3.1 Grant.

For the Term and in the Territory, [X] hereby grants to LICENSEE, and LICENSEE hereby accepts under the terms and conditions set forth in this Agreement, a nonexclusive license to employ the Licensed Intellectual Properties solely to develop and sell video games incorporated into Game Cartridges for play on the [B] System. Except as may be permitted under a separate written authorization from [X] or NCL, LICENSEE shall not use the Licensed Intellectual Properties for any other purpose.

3.2 Reservation of Rights in the Licensed Intellectual Properties.

LICENSEE acknowledges [X] and NCL's right, title, and interest in and to the Licensed Intellectual Properties and the goodwill associated with the Licensed Trademarks. LICENSEE will not at any time do or cause to be done any act or thing which in any way impairs or is intended to impair any part of such right, title, interest or goodwill. LICENSEE shall not represent that it has any ownership in the Licensed Intellectual Properties. Use of the Licensed Intellectual Properties shall not create any right, title or interest therein in LICENSEE's favor.

3.3 Reservation of Rights of Distribution Outside the Territory.
LICENSEE shall market and sell the Licensed Products only in the Territory. LICENSEE shall not directly or indirectly export any Licensed Products from the Territory nor shall LICENSEE knowingly permit or assist any third party in doing so.

3.4 Reservation of Rights to Reverse Engineer.
LICENSEE may utilize and study the design, performance and operation of the [B] System and the Licensed Proprietary Information solely for the purpose of developing software which is compatible with the [B] System for license under this Agreement. LICENSEE shall not, directly or indirectly, reverse engineer or aid or assist in the reverse engineering of all or any part of the [B] System, including the hardware, software, input controller and/or tools. For purposes of this Agreement, "reverse engineering" shall mean: (a) the x-ray electronic scanning and/or physical or chemical stripping of semiconductor components; (b) the disassembly, decompilation, decryption, simulation, debugging or code tracing of microcode; and/or (c) the disassembly, decompilation, decryption, simulation, debugging or code tracing of object code or executable code, specifically including, but not limited to, any [X] supplied or developed libraries or microcode. The limitations set forth in this Section 3.4 shall not preclude LICENSEE from engaging in reverse engineering of any Game code which was developed solely by LICENSEE and related only to the Game and was not supplied by nor derived from any code supplied by [X].

3.5 Reservation of Rights of Electronic Transmission.
LICENSEE shall not directly or indirectly duplicate, distribute or transmit Games via electronic means or any other means now known or hereafter devised, including within limitation, wireless, cable, fiber optic means, telephone lines, satellite transmission, microwave or radio waves or over a network of interconnected computers or other devices. Notwithstanding this limitation, LICENSEE shall not be prohibited from the electronic transmission of Games during the development process for the sole purpose of facilitating development; provided, however, that no right of retransmission shall attach to any such transmission, and, provided further, that LICENSEE shall use reasonable security measures, customary within the industry, to reduce the risk of unauthorized interception or retransmission of such transmissions.

3.6 Notification Obligations.
LICENSEE shall promptly notify [X] of the loss or unauthorized use or disclosure of any Licensed Proprietary Information and shall promptly act to recover any such information and/or prevent further breach of the confidentiality obligations herein.

**4. Confidentiality**

4.1 Disclosure of Proprietary Information.
[X] has and shall during the Term provide LICENSEE with highly proprietary development information, development tools, emulation systems, programming specifications and related resources and information constituting and incorporating the Licensed Proprietary Information to enable LICENSEE to develop video games for use with the [B] System.

4.2 Confidentiality of Licensed Proprietary Information
LICENSEE shall maintain all Licensed Proprietary Information as strictly confidential and will use such Licensed Proprietary Information only in accordance with this Agreement. LICENSEE shall limit access to the Licensed Proprietary Information to LICENSEE's employees having a strict need to know and shall advise such employees of their obligation of confidentiality as provided herein. LICENSEE shall require each such employee to retain in confidence the Licensed Proprietary Information pursuant to a written non-disclosure agreement between LICENSEE and such employee. LICENSEE shall use its best efforts to ensure that its employees working with or otherwise having access to Licensed Proprietary Information shall not disclose or make unauthorized use of the Licensed Proprietary Information.

4.3 Agent/Consultant Confidentiality.
LICENSEE shall not disclose the Licensed Proprietary Information to any Independent Contractor without [X]'s prior written approval. Each approved Independent Contractor shall be required to enter into a written non-disclosure agreement with [X] prior to receiving any access to or disclosure of the Licensed Proprietary Information.

4.4 [Y] as a Third-Party Beneficiary.
LICENSEE hereby acknowledges and agrees that [Y] shall be a third-party beneficiary of LICENSEE's confidentiality obligations as set forth in this Section 4.

**5. Development; Quality Standards; Artwork; Manufacturing**

5.1 Development and Sale of the [B] System Programs.
During the Term, LICENSEE may develop Games and/or sell Licensed Products for the [B] System in accordance with this Agreement.

5.2 Exclusivity; Exclusive Licensed Product.
For the Exclusive Licensed Product, LICENSEE agrees that, commencing on the Effective Date and continuing for a period of one (1) year from [X]'s first shipment of such Exclusive Licensed Product to LICENSEE, neither the Game incorporated into such Exclusive Licensed Product nor any adaptation, translation, derivative, sequel or substantially similar game which is sold by LICENSEE as a Licensed Product under this Agreement shall be sold anywhere in the Territory by LICENSEE or by any third party for play on any Competing System. Except as provided herein with regard

to the Exclusive Licensed Product, or as may otherwise be limited by the legitimate intellectual property rights of [X] or any third party, LICENSEE shall retain all rights with regard to the adaptation of Games for development and sale in any other format, including on any Competing System.

5.3 Submission of Game Concept.

Before commencing development of a Game, LICENSEE shall submit to [X] for approval, a Product Proposal. Such Product Proposal must include a detailed explanation of the manner in which the Game will utilize and exploit: (a) the unique 3-D capabilities and high quality graphics display of the [B] System; (b) the complex, high-capacity processing speed of the [B] System; and, (c) the dynamic interfaces and touch control features of the unique [B] System controller. For that purpose, the Product Proposal shall include: (a) a description of the proposed Game; (b) the development team profile, including information regarding any Independent Contractor which LICENSEE proposes to retain to work on the Game; (c) a description of any special hardware or software requirements; and, (d) the anticipated completion date of the proposed Licensed Product. Subsequent to acceptance and approval of a Product Proposal, LICENSEE shall notify [X] in writing of any material proposed changes in the Product Proposal and/or the proposed Licensed Product. From time to time, at approximately quarterly intervals or such other reasonable times [X] may establish for purposes of ensuring utilization and exploitation of the [B] System in the manner set forth above, LICENSEE shall submit work-in-progress on the Game to [X] for further review in accordance with the criteria set forth herein. [X] shall not unreasonably withhold or delay any approval provided for herein.

5.4 Delivery of Completed Game.

Upon completion of a Game, LICENSEE shall deliver to [X] one (1) prototype of the Game in a format specified by [X], together with written user instructions and a complete screen text script. [X] shall promptly evaluate the Game with regard to: (a) its technical compatibility with and error-free operation on the [B] System; (b) the suitability of the Game content, taking into account reasonable standards set forth in the Guidelines; and, (c) whether the Game achieves the objectives set forth in LICENSEE's approved Product Proposal. LICENSEE shall have satisfied the Game content suitability criteria by providing [X] with proof that the Game has been provided with a certificate of a rating other than ADULTS ONLY (or its equivalent) from the Entertainment Software Ratings Board or comparable independent ratings body which reviews and certifies product for violent or sexual content.

5.5 Approval of Completed Game.

[X] shall, within a reasonable period of time after receipt, approve or disapprove such Game. If such Game is disapproved, [X] shall specify in writing the reasons for such disapproval and state what corrections and/or improvements are necessary. After making the necessary corrections and/or improvements, LICENSEE shall submit a revised Game for approval by

[X]. The approval of any Game by [X] shall not relieve LICENSEE of its sole responsibility for the development, quality and operation of the Game or in any way create any warranty for a Licensed Product by

5.6 Development and Quality of Artwork.
In connection with the submission of a proposed Licensed Product to [X], LICENSEE shall submit all Artwork to [X]. All Artwork shall conform to the requirements set forth in the Guidelines. Within fifteen (15) business days of receipt of the Artwork, [X] shall approve or disapprove the Artwork based upon the Guidelines. If any of the Artwork is disapproved, [X] shall specify in writing the reasons for such disapproval and state what corrections and/or improvements are necessary. After making the necessary corrections and/or improvements to the disapproved Artwork, LICENSEE shall resubmit new Artwork for approval by [X]. [X] shall not unreasonably withhold or delay its approval of any Artwork.

5.7 Appointment of NCL as Manufacturer of Licensed Product.
LICENSEE hereby appoints NCL, and [X] hereby confirms that NCL accepts such appointment, as manufacturer of the Licensed Products in the form of Finished Goods and/or Stripped Cartridges. NCL shall acquire and retain responsibility for all equipment, tooling, molds or masks used in connection with the manufacture of the Licensed Products. NCL shall have the sole responsibility for establishing and fulfilling all aspects of the manufacturing process of the Licensed Products, including selecting the location of the specifications of any manufacturing facilities, appointing suppliers and subcontractors, and managing all work-in progress.

5.8 Manufacture of Licensed Products.
Upon approval of a Game and upon receipt from LICENSEE of an order in accordance with Section 6 herein, NCL will manufacture the Licensed Products for LICENSEE. LICENSEE may, at its option, order Stripped Cartridges rather than Finished Goods and utilize an Independent Contractor to manufacture the Artwork and/or complete the final pack-out only, provided such Independent Contractor is approved in writing by [X].

5.9 Retention of Sample Licensed Products.
NCL may, at its own expense, manufacture samples of the Licensed Products, only to the extent necessary, to be used by [X] for archival purposes, legal proceedings against infringers of the Licensed Intellectual Properties, and for other lawful purposes.

**6. Purchase Price; Payment; Delivery of Completed Licensed Product**

6.1 Minimum Initial Orders.
Upon placement of an initial order, LICENSEE shall order a minimum quantity of [*] units of a Licensed Product.

6.2 Subsequent Minimum Orders.
LICENSEE may subsequently order additional Licensed Product in a minimum quantity of [*] units per title.

6.3 Purchase Price.
The purchase price to be paid by LICENSEE to [X] for the Licensed Products shall be in accordance with [X]'s pricing schedule currently set forth in the attached Schedule 1. The purchase price includes the cost of manufacturing, printing and packaging the Licensed Products and a royalty for the use of the Licensed Intellectual Properties.
Schedule 1 is subject to change by [X] at any time without notice.

6.4 Payment.
At the time an order is placed, LICENSEE shall provide to [X] an irrevocable letter of credit in favor of [X] and payable at sight, issued by a bank acceptable to [X] and confirmed, at LICENSEE's expense, if requested by [X]. The letter of credit shall be in United States dollars in an amount equal to the purchase price of the Licensed Products ordered. All associated banking charges are for LICENSEE's account.

6.5 Shipment and Delivery.
The Licensed Products shall be delivered F.O.B. Japan, with shipment at LICENSEE's direction and expense. Orders may be delivered by [X] in partial shipments, each directed to no more than two (2) destinations designated by LICENSEE in the Territory. Title to the Licensed Products shall vest in accordance with the terms of the applicable letter of credit.

## 7. Marketing, Sale And Rental Of The Licensed Products

7.1 Marketing Materials.
LICENSEE agrees that any Marketing Materials shall all be of high quality and shall comply with the Guidelines.

7.2 Submission of Proposed Marketing Materials.
Prior to actual use or distribution, LICENSEE shall submit to [X] for review and evaluation initial samples of all Marketing Materials. [X] shall, within fifteen (15) business days of receipt of such samples, approve or disapprove of the quality of such samples. If any of the samples are disapproved as to quality, [X] shall specify the reasons for such disapproval and state what corrections and/or improvements are necessary. After making the necessary corrections and/or improvements to the disapproved samples, LICENSEE may resubmit new samples for approval by [X] as to quality. No Marketing Materials shall be distributed or utilized by LICENSEE without obtaining prior written approval as to quality by [X]. [X] shall not unreasonably withhold or delay its approval of the proposed Marketing Materials. [X] reserves the right to disapprove Marketing Materials that include non-licensed accessories.

7.3 Warranty and Repair.
With respect to the Licensed Product, LICENSEE shall provide to the original consumer a minimum ninety (90) day limited warranty, comparable to that offered by [X]. LICENSEE shall also provide to the original consumer, either directly or indirectly through authorized service centers,

reasonably accessible product service, including out-of-warranty service for a period of three (3) years following sale of the Licensed Product. In the event LICENSEE is unable to obtain sufficient quantities of repair parts for service obligations from defective and/or product returns, [X] shall cooperate in providing reasonable quantities of repair parts to LICENSEE at its standard cost.

7.4 Business Facilities; Sales of Game Cartridges.
LICENSEE agrees to develop, maintain and utilize during the Term: (a) suitable office facilities within the Territory, adequately staffed to enable LICENSEE to fulfill all responsibilities under this Agreement; (b) necessary warehouse, distribution, marketing, sales, collection and credit operations to facilitate proper handling of the Licensed Product; and, (c) customer service and game counseling support, including telephone service, to adequately support the Licensed Product.

7.5 Defects; Recall.
In the event of a material programming defect in the Licensed Product, which defect in the reasonable judgment of [X] would significantly impair the ability of a consumer to play the Licensed Product, [X] may require the LICENSEE to recall the Licensed Product and undertake suitable repairs or replacements prior to sale.

7.6 Rental.
In the event LICENSEE elects to engage in the commercial rental of the Licensed Products within the Territory on such terms and conditions as LICENSEE shall determine, LICENSEE shall secure appropriate authorizations and/or assignments from the author(s) of the copyrightable elements in the computer programs for the Licensed Product. LICENSEE shall clearly provide notice on the Artwork for each Licensed Product of any rental right or reservation thereof.

7.7 [X] Promotional Materials, Publications and Events.
At its option, [X] may: (a) insert in the packaging for the Licensed Product promotional materials concerning [X] Power magazine; (b) utilize screen shots, package art and related art and information regarding the Licensed Product in [X] Power, [X] Power Source ([X]'s on-line version of [X] Power) or other media or marketing programs which promote [X] products; and (c) exercise public performance rights of the Licensed Product, related trademarks and art in [X] sponsored contests, tours and events which generally promote [X] products, provided that no other third party approvals are required.

7.8 [X] Gateway System.
LICENSEE acknowledges that [X] operates the [X] Gateway System in various non-coin activated commercial settings including, but not limited to, commercial airlines, cruise ships and hotels, whereby customers may be charged on a per use basis to play various Games on an adapted [A] and/or Super [X] Entertainment System. The purpose of the Gateway System is to promote and increase demand for [A] software in general. LICENSEE

acknowledges that [X] selects high quality [A] software for possible participation in the program and may indentify one or more of LICENSEE's Games for possible adaptation and participation. Should [X] identify one of LICENSEE's Games for possible participation, LICENSEE hereby agrees to conduct a good faith discussion with [X] about the inclusion and adaptation of such Game for the [A] Gateway System.

**8. Licensee's Copyrights and Trademarks**

8.1 Copyright and Trademark Warranties.
LICENSEE represents and warrants that, throughout the Territory, LICENSEE is either: (a) the sole owner of all right, title and interest in and to the trademarks, copyrights and Artwork used on or in association with the Licensed Products; or (b) the holder of sufficient rights to the trademarks, copyrights and Artwork which have been licensed from a third party for use in the Licensed Product.

8.2 Licensee's Indemnification.
LICENSEE shall indemnify and hold [X] and NCL harmless from any claims, losses, liabilities, damages, expenses and costs, including, without limitation, reasonable attorneys' fees and costs, which result from: (a) a breach of any of the representations or warranties provided by LICENSEE herein; (b) any claim of infringement of any third party's intellectual property rights with respect to the Licensed Product, excluding claims based solely upon [X]'s trademarks, copyrights and patents; or, (c) any claim of bodily injury (including death) or property damage arising out of, or in connection with, the development, sale and/or use of any of the Licensed Products. [X] shall give LICENSEE prompt written notice of the assertion of any such claim and provided, further, that LICENSEE shall have the right to select counsel and control the defense and/or settlement of any such claim, subject to the right of [X] to participate in any such action or proceeding at its own expense with counsel of its own choice.

8.3 Insurance

**9. Limitation of Liability**

9.1 Disclaimer of Licensed Intellectual Properties.
[X] makes no representations, guarantees or warranties concerning the scope or validity of the Licensed Intellectual Properties and does not warrant that the sale of the Licensed Products by LICENSEE will not infringe upon the patent, trade secret, copyright, mask work or trademark rights of another in the Territory. LICENSEE HEREBY ASSUMES THE RISK OF INFRINGEMENT.

9.2 Warranty Disclaimer.
[X] disclaims any and all warranties of the Licensed Products as between [X] and Licensee and as between [X] and any third party purchasers from licensee. Licensee purchases and accepts all Licensed Products from [X] on an "as is" and "where is" basis and without any warranties, express or

implied. With respect to the Licensed Products, [X] disclaims all warranties of merchantability and fitness for a general or particular purpose and shall in no event be liable for any incidental and/or consequential damages of Licensee, its retailers or customers. Licensee shall be solely responsible for providing warranty and repair/replacement services for any defective licensed products. Notwithstanding the conditions set forth in this paragraph, [X] will use its best efforts to resolve any catastrophic defect in the Licensed Products purchased by Licensee from [X]. a "catastrophic defect" is defined as a manufacturing defect rate of five percent (5%) or greater in any shipment of Licensed Products to Licensee.

**10. Infringement of Licensed Intellectual Properties and Licensee's Trademarks and Copyrights**

10.1 Reporting

In the event (a) any claim is asserted against either party alleging that any of the Licensed Intellectual Properties or a Licensed Product constitutes an infringement of another's rights; or, (b) either party discovers that any of the Licensed Intellectual Properties or LICENSEE's copyrights or trademarks used in connection with the Licensed Products have been infringed by a third party, then the party with such knowledge shall promptly notify the other party.

10.2 Licensed Intellectual Properties.

[X] shall have the sole right, at its expense, to commence and/or defend a legal action or negotiate a settlement relating to any alleged infringement by the Licensed Intellectual Properties. LICENSEE agrees to give reasonable assistance in any such legal action, but at no expense to it. [X] shall be entitled to all of the recovery or damages collected as a result of such legal action or negotiated settlement. In the event of a legal action against LICENSEE alleging an infringement by the Licensed Intellectual Properties as incorporated into LICENSEE's Licensed Products which [X] affirmatively elects in writing not to defend, LICENSEE may defend or settle such legal action, at its option and expense. [X] agrees to provide reasonable assistance in defending any such legal action. LICENSEE agrees to keep [X] fully informed with respect to developments in any such legal action and to provide [X] reasonable notice of the terms of any proposed settlement and to consider any comments by [X] before settlement is made.

10.3 Infringement of Licensed Products.

LICENSEE shall take reasonable steps to abate any infringement of LICENSEE's copyrights and trademarks in the Licensed Products. LICENSEE shall also take all reasonable and necessary steps, including legal action, to defend against any alleged infringement caused by any of LICENSEE's software programs developed under this Agreement or any Artwork, title or designation used in conjunction with any of the

Licensed Products. [X] shall give to LICENSEE reasonable assistance and cooperation in any such legal action, but at no expense to [X].

**11. Term and Termination**

11.1 Default or Breach.
In the event that either party is in default or commits a breach of this Agreement which is not cured within thirty (30) days after written notice thereof, then this Agreement shall automatically terminate on the date specified in such notice.

11.2 Bankruptcy/Insolvency.
At [X]'s option, this Agreement can be terminated immediately and without notice in the event that LICENSEE: (a) makes an assignment for the benefit of creditors; (b) becomes insolvent; (c) files a voluntary petition for bankruptcy; (d) acquiesces to any involuntary bankruptcy petition; (e) is adjudicated as a bankrupt; or (f) ceases to do business.

11.3 Termination Other Than by Breach.
Upon the expiration of this Agreement or its termination other than by LICENSEE's breach, LICENSEE shall have a period of one hundred sixty (160) days to sell any unsold Licensed Products. LICENSEE shall destroy all Licensed Products in LICENSEE's control following expiration of such sell-off period, within ten (10) days.

11.4 Termination by LICENSEE's Breach.
If this Agreement is terminated by [X] as a result of a breach of its terms and conditions by LICENSEE, LICENSEE shall immediately cease all distribution, promotion or sale of any Licensed Products. LICENSEE shall have a period of one hundred sixty (160) days to sell any unsold Licensed Products. All Licensed Products in LICENSEE's control following expiration of such sell-off period shall be destroyed by LICENSEE within ten (10) days.

11.5 Licensed Intellectual Property Rights.
Upon expiration and/or termination of this Agreement, LICENSEE will cease all use of the Licensed Intellectual Properties for any purpose, and will not disclose to third parties any Licensed Proprietary Information. LICENSEE shall also return to [X] all writings, drawings, models, data and other materials and things in LICENSEE's possession or in the possession or any past or present employee, agent or contractor receiving the information through LICENSEE, which constitute or relate to or disclose any Licensed Proprietary Information without making copies or otherwise retaining any such information.

11.6 Termination by [X]'s Breach.
If this Agreement is terminated by LICENSEE as a result of a breach of its terms or conditions by [X], LICENSEE may continue to sell the Licensed Products in the Territory until the expiration of the Term, at which time the provisions herein relating to termination other than by default of LICENSEE shall apply to any unsold Licensed Products.

## 12. General Provisions

12.1 Nonassignability/Sublicensing.

This Agreement is personal to Licensee and may not be sold, assigned, delegated, sublicensed or otherwise transferred or encumbered, in whole or in part, including without limitation, by operation of law, without the prior written consent of [X], which consent may be withheld by [X] in its sole discretion. For purposes of determining whether an assignment of this agreement by Licensee (but not by Licensor) has occurred under this Section 12.1, a merger of Licensee into another business entity or a merger of another business entity into Licensee; the sale or transfer of more than twenty percent (20%) of the stock of Licensee, Licensee's assets, or ownership interest or control of Licensee; or, the granting of any security interest or other encumbrance in this Agreement or any rights arising under this Agreement, shall be deemed an assignment requiring notice to, and the prior written consent of, [X], which consent may be withheld by [X] in its sole discretion. Upon any attempted sale, assignment, delegation, sublicense or other transfer or encumbrance in violation of the preceding sentences, this Agreement shall be deemed null and void, and of no effect, and in such event, notwithstanding anything in this Agreement to the contrary, [X] shall have the immediate, unqualified right to terminate this Agreement in addition to all other rights and remedies it may obtain due to Licensee's breach. This Agreement may be assigned by Licensor upon written notice to Licensee but without any consent, provided, however, that any such assignment shall not release the Licensor from its obligations to the Licensee under this Agreement. Subject to such restriction and to the restriction against assignment provided above, this Agreement shall be binding upon and inure to the benefit of the parties, their successors and assigns.

12.2 Force Majeure.

Neither party shall be liable for any breach of this Agreement occasioned by any cause beyond the reasonable control of such party, including governmental action, war, riot or civil commotion, fire, natural disaster, labor disputes, restraints affecting shipment or credit, delay of carriers, inadequate supply of suitable materials, or any other cause which could not with reasonable diligence be controlled or prevented by the parties. In the event of material shortages, including shortages of microcomputer chips necessary for production of the Licensed Products, [X] reserves the right to allocate essential materials among itself and its licensees.

12.3 Waiver; Severability; Integration.

The failure of any party to enforce any provision of this Agreement shall not be construed to be a waiver of such provision or of the right of such party to thereafter enforce such provision. In the event that any term, clause or provision of this Agreement shall be construed to be or adjudged invalid, void or unenforceable, such term, clause or provision shall be construed as severed from this Agreement, and the remaining terms, clauses and provisions shall remain in effect. This Agreement constitutes the entire agreement between the parties relating to the subject matter hereof, provided, however, that the Other Agreements shall remain in effect, except as may be modified by specific reference herein. All prior negotiations, representations, agreements and understandings are merged into, extinguished by and completely expressed by this Agreement. Any amendment to this Agreement shall be in writing, signed by both parties.

12.4 Governing Law; Venue.

This Agreement shall be governed by, subject to and construed under the laws of the State of Washington. Any legal actions prosecuted or instituted by [X] or by LICENSEE under this Agreement, with respect to any matters arising under or growing out of this Agreement, shall only be brought in a court of competent jurisdiction in King County, Washington and each party hereby consents to the jurisdiction and venue of such courts for such purposes.

12.5 Equitable Relief.

LICENSEE acknowledges that in the event of its breach of this Agreement, no adequate remedy at law may be available to [X] and that [X] shall be entitled to seek injunctive or other equitable relief in addition to any relief available at law.

12.6 Attorneys' Fees.

In the event it is necessary for either party of this Agreement to undertake legal action to enforce any of the terms, conditions or rights contained herein, or to defend any such action, then the prevailing party in any such action shall be entitled to recover from the other party all reasonable attorneys' fees, costs and expenses relating to such legal action.

12.7 Notices.

All notices required or permitted under this Agreement shall be sufficiently given when: (a) personally served or delivered; (b) deposited, postage prepaid, with a guaranteed air courier service, addressed as stated herein, or to such other person or address either party may designate in a notice; or, (c) by facsimile, with an original sent concurrently by first class U.S. mail. Notice shall be deemed effective upon the earlier of actual receipt or two (2) business days after transmittal.

12.8 Counterparts; Signature by Facsimile.

This Agreement may be signed in counterparts, which shall together constitute a complete Agreement. A signature transmitted by facsimile shall be considered an original for purpose of this Agreement.

12.9 Time is of the Essence.

Time if of the essence with regard to this Agreement and the performance of the parties' obligations hereunder.

IN WITNESS WHEREOF, [X] and LICENSEE have entered into this Agreement on the dates set forth below.

| | |
|---|---|
| [X]: | LICENSEE: |
| [X] INC. | [LICENSEE], INC. |
| By: | By: |
| --------------------- | --------------------- |
| Its: Executive Vice President, Administration | Its: President |
| --------------------- | --------------------- |
| Date: | Date: |
| --------------------- | --------------------- |

SCHEDULE 1
[X] OF AMERICA INC.
PRICE SHEET
[B] LICENSED GAME PAKS

| Memory Capacity | NOA Price |
|---|---|
| <S> | <C> |
| 32 Megabit | $ [*] |
| 32 Megabit + 4K bit E. ROM | $ [*] |
| 32 Megabit + 16K bit E. ROM | $ [*] |
| 32 Megabit + 256K SRAM + Battery | $ [*] |
| 64 Megabit | $ [*] |
| 64 Megabit + 4K bit E. ROM | $ [*] |
| 64 Megabit + 16K bit E. ROM | $ [*] |
| 64 Megabit + 256K SRAM + Battery | $ [*] |
| 96 Megabit | $ [*] |
| 96 Megabit + 4K bit E. ROM | $ [*] |
| 96 Megabit + 16K bit E. ROM | $ [*] |
| 96 Megabit + 256K SRAM + Battery | $ [*] |
| 128 Megabit | $ [*] |
| 128 Megabit + 4K bit E. ROM | $ [*] |
| 128 Megabit + 16K bit E. ROM | $ [*] |
| 128 Megabit + 256K SRAM + Battery | $ [*] |
| 256 Megabit | $ [*] |
| </TABLE> | |

*Confidential Portions Omitted and Filed Separately with the Commission

| | |
|---|---|
| 256 Megabit + 4K bit E. ROM | $ [*] |
| 256 Megabit + 16K bit E. ROM | $ [*] |
| 256 Megabit + 256K SRAM + Battery | $ [*] |

Price includes an instruction manual up to 40 pages. There will be an extracharge for manuals larger than 40 pages (including the front and back cover).

EXTRA PACKAGING (Must be ordered with product on a separate PO)

| | |
|---|---|
| Game Pak Box | $[*] |
| Instruction Manual | $[*] (under 40 pages) |
| Instruction Manual | $[*] (over 40 pages) |
| Game Pak Label | $[*] |
| Game Pak Poster | $[*] |
| Warranty Card | $[*] |
| Inner Carton | $[*] |
| Master Carton | $[*] |

ALL PRICES ARE SUBJECT TO CHANGE WITHOUT NOTICE

* Confidential Portions Omitted and Filed Separately with the Commission

# Chapter 15
# Fiscal Aspects

## 15.1 Introductory Remarks

When negotiating, drafting and concluding Sports Marketing Agreements, especially international ones, the fiscal implications need to be taken fully into account. The commercial and financial arrangements need to be made in the most tax efficient manner and this needs to be reflected in the contractual provisions of the Agreements. However, tax is a field in which the old adage that 'circumstances alter cases' is particularly pertinent. In other words, tax advice very much depends upon the particular facts and circumstances of each individual case—as well as the aims to be achieved through any tax mitigation scheme.

Tax mitigation not only goes to the 'bottom line' and affects the profitability of Sports Marketing ventures, but is also a perfectly sensible and legitimate exercise. Tax avoidance—organising your affairs and contractual arrangements in the best possible way tax wise—is legal, whilst tax evasion is illegal. In fact, it is a criminal offence and will attract heavy fines and penalties and, in very serious cases, even imprisonment, as Leona Helmsley, the US Hotel Operator, found to her cost when she was jailed for tax evasion in 1989. Her famous–or infamous—catch phrase was: 'only little people pay taxes!'

For example, in the case of Sports Merchandising and Licence Agreements, the Licensor should, if possible, take advantage of any no or low tax jurisdiction. It may be worth, for instance, tax sheltering the royalties through a 'Holding Company' in The Netherlands to take advantage of their favourable tax treatment of such corporate entities and also their extensive network of Double Taxation Agreements around the world. Double taxation Agreements, however, do not apply to VAT/TVA and this presents a problem in the case of Sponsorship Agreements as VAT/TVA is payable on sponsorship fees and also on Value in Kind (VIK), that is where the Sponsor provides, instead of money, certain products, services or other facilities, for example, official cars to transport sports governing body officials and their VIP guests to and from the sports events'

I. S. Blackshaw, *Sports Marketing Agreements: Legal, Fiscal and Practical Aspects*,
ASSER International Sports Law Series, DOI: 10.1007/978-90-6704-793-7_15,

venues. Thus, it is necessary to place a value on VIK and this value needs to be expressed in the corresponding Sponsorship Agreement. Of course, the relevant Tax Authorities can check this value and, if necessary, put a higher value on the VIK to reflect its actual and realistic value. The issue here is whether the cost price or the normal retail price of the VIK is the proper basis for tax assessment purposes. The treatment can vary from country to country. To mitigate or eliminate the tax burden, from the sponsored party's point of view (the rights holder), a so-called 'tax free' clause can be included in the Sports Sponsorship Agreement along the following lines:

> "All payments made and value in kind granted under this Agreement to the rights holder shall be made and granted free of all taxes, levies and imposts of any kind whatsoever, including, but not limited to, withholding, corporation, capital gains and value added taxes."

However, when contemplating any tax avoidance scheme, as legal and administrative costs will be involved, especially where it is necessary to form and maintain intermediate companies, a cost–benefit analysis should be made, in each case, to ensure that, in the final analysis and reckoning, there are overall and real financial savings to be made. Equally, you will need to be ready to pay the costs—especially legal costs which can be quite heavy—to defend your tax avoidance arrangements against challenges made by the Tax Authorities, who are always looking to claw back lost taxes, which can often amount to quite substantial sums.

One kind of Sports Marketing arrangement that has attracted and continues to attract the attention of the UK Tax Authorities [Her Majesty's Revenue and Customs (HMRC)] is the commercialisation of sports image rights by footballers, following the landmark decision in the so-called 'Sports Club' case in 2000.[1]

## 15.2 Sports Club Case

Before we take a look at this important decision, which continues to haunt HMRC, a word or two on the legal position in the UK would not be amiss as general background to the fiscal treatment of image rights in the UK.

In the UK, it is difficult to protect image rights from a general legal point of view, because there is no specific law protecting image rights *per se*.[2] A personality can only take legal action as follows:

> "if the reproduction or use of [his/her] likeness results in the infringement of some recognised legal right which he/she does own."[3]

[1] *Sports Club plc v Inspector of Taxes* [2000] STC (SCD) 443.

[2] Note that Guernsey is due to introduce a specific IP Image Right in the near future.

[3] Per Mr. Justice Laddie in *Elvis Presley Trade Marks* [1997] RPC 543 at p. 548.

Famous persons (including sports personalities), therefore, have to rely on a 'rag bag' of laws, such as Trade Mark and Copyright Law and the English Common Law doctrine of 'Passing Off' and/or vague notions of breach of commercial confidentiality. As, for example, in the Catherine Zeta Jones and Michael Douglas spat with 'Hello' Magazine and their unauthorised publication of their wedding photographs.[4] But it may be added that, even though successful, only modest damages were awarded by the Court to the celebrity pair. However, earlier, in what was seen as a softening of the previous law, the F1 racing driver, Eddie Irvine, successfully sued 'TalkRadio' under the Common Law doctrine of 'Passing Off' for using, around the time of the British Grand Prix, a doctored photograph of him holding and apparently listening to a radio (in the original photograph he was holding a mobile phone!), which implied that he was promoting or endorsing their radio station. For this breach, Irvine was finally awarded £25,000 in damages after appealing against a previous award of £2,000 made by the trial judge.[5] Again, not exactly a mega sum! Despite these cases, most commentators consider they were decided on their own particular facts and circumstances and do not herald the advent of privacy and personality rights in the UK.

For fiscal purposes, the situation is different, as image rights are recognised as a species of legal property as the Sports Club case demonstrated. In that case, Arsenal Football Club succeeded, against a legal challenge from HMRC claiming that the image rights arrangements were a sham, in having the payments made to off-shore companies in respect of the Club's commercial exploitation of the image rights of their players, David Platt and Dennis Bergkamp, classified, for tax purposes, as capital sums and, therefore, non-taxable as income. Equally, in respect of those sums, neither the Club nor the players are liable for social security contributions. Another substantial saving on the Club's costs and the players' salaries!

This case is not only interesting from a fiscal point of view, but also from a jurisprudential point of view, in that, for tax purposes, image rights are considered to be capital assets even though image rights *per se* are not recognised as a separate species of property under the general law in the United Kingdom.

Opportunities exist in other parts of Europe for tax sheltering the financial returns from the commercial exploitation of sports image rights—not least, as already mentioned, in The Netherlands, which has a fairly comprehensive network of double taxation treaties around the world, which can be creatively used to save tax.

Again, in Switzerland, for example, tax mitigation structures can be constructed founded on tax-exempt not-for-profit foundations, which is the legal structure adopted by the International Sports Federations that are headquartered in Switzerland.

---

[4] *Douglas & Others v Hello Limited* [2001] 2 WLR 992.

[5] *Irvine v Talksport Ltd* [2003] EWCA Civ 423.

As mentioned above, HMRC in the UK are having another go at staunching this haemorrhage of tax from the commercialisation of sports image rights. The subsequent and latest campaigns by HMRC, following the decision in the Sports Club case, against sports image rights arrangements and schemes are summarised by the London Sports and Media Law Firm of Charles Russell & Co[6] in the following terms:

> ".....notwithstanding that the Sports Club decision can be limited to its facts, image rights contracts multiplied, often with little regard to the commerciality of the arrangement. This can be highlighted by the revelations that Joey Barton earned £675 k p.a. from Newcastle United in respect of image rights payments and that Sol Campbell received 50% of his earnings from Portsmouth for the use of his image rights.
>
> After licking its wounds for a couple of years following the defeat in Sports Club, HMRC decided to revisit the area and, in 2006, launched a specialist unit to look into image rights payments in sport. A major crackdown on team sports was commenced with cricket, rugby union and rugby league serving as the initial targets, perhaps as a warm-up for the HMRC before taking on football. A compromise cap of 15% of remuneration payable for image right exploitation was agreed in rugby union.
>
> Football was next on the HMRC's list. During the autumn of 2009 the majority of Premier League clubs received a letter from HMRC advising them that an initial investigation was being launched into payments made to players by Premier League clubs in the financial years 2005/06, 2006/07 and 2007/08. The potential impact of the investigation was revealed by Manchester United's bond prospectus in January 2010. It revealed potential liabilities for Manchester United of approximately £5.3 million relating to employer's NIC contributions during the period 2000/01-2009/10. On that basis, in relation to Manchester United alone, there would be a potential player liabilities (in respect of unpaid PAYE and national insurance) of around £21 million before penalties and interest. Multiplying these potential liabilities across the other Premier League clubs the scale of the issue becomes clear.
>
> It is unsurprising, therefore, that the Premier League has entered into formal discussions with HMRC. "We are in discussions with HMRC", said a FAPL spokesperson. "It is legitimate to have some element of image rights, but HMRC would query the level that some have attached to them". A fixed percentage, without prejudice agreement (as in rugby union) appears unlikely to be agreed due to the vastly greater amounts in question.
>
> Following settlement of this issue with HMRC, it will be particularly interesting to see if clubs pursue their players (and former players) to contribute to the settlement amount pursuant to the indemnities that are generally included in image rights agreements.
>
> The HMRC crackdown will undoubtedly lead to a reduction in the use of image rights agreements in football. This reduction in image rights payments, taken together with the increase of the top rate of tax as of 6 April 2010 will mean a considerably higher tax bill for Premier League footballers in the future."

It will be interesting to see the final outcome of these moves by HMRC to rein in lost taxes on sports images rights in the UK. For further information on the extent and scope of the ongoing HMRC investigations and campaign against the

[6] www.charlesrussell.co.uk

English FA Premier League, its Clubs and Players, see some recent UK Press Reports in Appendix 1 (15.7.1) of this Chapter.

## 15.3 Structuring Sports Image Rights Arrangements and Agreements in the UK

So, can anything be done to beat HMRC at their own game, and, if so, what? In other words, how can one structure the image rights arrangements to fall within the existing Law and how can these arrangements be reflected in the corresponding Sports Image Rights Agreements?

The background, current situation and the measures that can be taken to mitigate the UK tax burden on payments for English FA Premier League footballers' sports image rights are well discussed and clearly explained by Stephen Woodhouse and Debbie Masterton of Deloitte's in London in their article 'United Kingdom: Image Rights' which appeared in the first issue of *Global Sports Law and Taxation Reports* published in November 2010.[7] It is attached to this Chapter as Appendix 2 (15.7.2).

To take advantage of the tax savings mentioned in this article, the corresponding Sports Image Rights Agreements need to be drafted in accordance with the general principles and ideas summarised in the article. In other words, the terms of the Agreements have to be realistic, reasonable, proportionate and justifiable, and reflect the true factual position, which can be explained and proved by documentary and other evidence.

## 15.4 Structuring Sports Image Rights Arrangements in Guernsey, Channel Islands

As mentioned above, the Channel Island of Guernsey is soon to introduce the possibility of registering an Image Right as a new species of Intellectual Property Right, which can be legally protected accordingly.[8]

The situation is summarised by Jason Romer and Brandon Doffing of the Guernsey Law Firm of Collas Day in their article 'Comparative Survey on Sports Image Rights: Guernsey Collas Day', which appeared in the first issue of *Global Sports Law and Taxation Reports* published in November 2010[9] and is attached to the Chapter as Appendix 3 (15.7.3).

---

7 GSLTR 2010/1 at pp. 41–43, published by Nolot BV, The Netherlands; website: www.nolot.nl

8 See 'The Island of Guernsey to Introduce New IP Image Right' by Ian Blackshaw, The International Sports Law Journal, ISLJ 2010/1-2, at p. 135.

9 GSLTR 2010/1 at pp. 19–26, published by Nolot BV, The Netherlands; website: www.nolot.nl

## 15.5 Structuring Sports Image Rights Arrangements in Luxembourg

Another interesting jurisdiction for tax sheltering the financial returns from the commercial exploitation of Sports Image Rights—on a world-wide basis—is Luxembourg, or, to give it its rather grand title, The Grand-Duchy of Luxembourg. The legal position and tax situation in the Grand-Duchy for the protection and marketing of Sports Image Rights is described and explained in the following article by Lars Goslings, which appeared in the first issue of *Global Sports Law and Taxation Reports* published in November 2010 and is attached to the Chapter as Appendix 4 (15.7.4).

## 15.6 Concluding Remarks

As has been demonstrated in this Chapter, the importance of getting the Sports Marketing Arrangements and the corresponding Agreements, especially Sports Image Rights Agreements—where there is much money to be made and lost- right, from a tax as well as a legal point of view, in the first place cannot be overemphasised.

The financial and commercial arrangements must be realistic, reasonable, proportionate and justifiable[10] and reflect the true factual position and must be faithfully represented and covered in the corresponding Sports Image Rights Agreements. Otherwise, they will fall foul of the applicable legal and tax rules and, therefore, be open to a successful legal challenge by the Tax Authorities, with the resulting substantial financial consequences, including the possibility of penalties, for the sports personality concerned. Tax mitigation is perfectly legal—no one wishes to work for the Revenue!

Essential to the success of any tax avoidance/mitigation scheme in relation to the commercial exploitation of sports image rights is valuing the rights being transferred and licensed and these valuations must reflect the current and the potential future value of the sports personality and this, in turn, will depend upon his/her achievements and standing in his/her sport. This, in practice, is a difficult thing to get right but it is absolutely crucial to do so!

[10] In 2009, Joey Barton, the Newcastle United midfielder, who was given a suspended jail sentence for assault, was reputedly paid £675,000 for his image rights by the club: I wonder, without casting any aspertions on the individual concerned, whether such a large payment could be justified, for tax purposes, in the particular circumstances?

## 15.7 Appendices

### *15.7.1 Appendix 1*

**Some Recent UK Press Reports on the HMRC Ongoing Investigations and Campaign against the English FA Premier League Its Clubs and Players**

**Daily Mail 13 September 2010***
**Wayne Rooney facing another crisis as taxman gets set to chase him for £1million**
**by Rob Draper**

Many of the Premier League's highest-earning players could be hit with huge tax bills as the Revenue step up their crackdown on football.

Wayne Rooney can expect to have to fork out up to £1million, with the whole Premier League liable for as much as £200m, if HMRC rule that controversial image-rights payments should be taxed the same as income tax.

Hundreds of players have image-rights deals written into contracts, which can represent up to a third of a player's earnings. Paid into a separate image-rights company, it has only been taxed at corporation tax rates of 21% rather than the old top rate of tax, which has increased from 40 to 50%. HMRC regard the arrangement as a tax dodge.

Some players have set up image-rights companies abroad in offshore accounts. But already a row is brewing as clubs and players argue over who will cough up the cash.

The potential liability incurred by Manchester United and their players since 2001, for instance, could be more than £17m. The club believe they will end up only paying £5.3m if the ruling goes against football, with players, including Rooney, expected to make up the rest.

'It would be correct to assume that the players and their companies are liable for the income tax,' said a United spokesman.

HMRC's discussion with the Premier League is an intensification of their battle with football. They are frustrated that clubs in administration, like Portsmouth, have been allowed to pay off creditors yet have their tax liabilities written off.

Several Premier League clubs, like United, are understood to have made provision for players to make up any shortfall in tax, but with a ruling expected later this year, star names and their agents are likely to be furious if they find they are liable to pay back millions of pounds.

Gordon Taylor, chief executive of the players' union, the PFA, insisted that the burden of responsibility lay with the clubs and is seeking clarification from the tax office.

'It is the clubs who draw up the contracts,' he said. 'We are trying to get a meeting with the HMRC and this is something we will add to the agenda. We

* Reproduced with permission.

know they are looking into image rights—regarding the validity of them—and it's something of which we've made our members aware.'

HMRC's investigation could potentially cost the Premier League more than £200m if United's liability, estimated by tax experts at around £17m, is replicated among the other 19 clubs.

And although top players such as Rooney might be able to convince the taxman that their image is, in fact, worth £1.52m a year, lesser-known players will have a harder time justifying their deals.

Rooney, who has appealed for privacy following the allegations of a prostitute that he paid her for sex, earns £1.52m a year in image rights and £4.68m a year in basic salary. His contract was signed in 2006, meaning he would have earned £6.08m in image rights alone over the past four years.

Taxed at 21%, that would earn the taxman £1.27m but if treated as income tax it would have brought in around £2.4m, leaving a shortfall of about £1.15m. Players have done nothing illegal, but the reclassification of earnings could cost them millions.

United conceded in their prospectus to bondholders earlier this year that they were liable for £5.3m if the ruling went against them, but that was only for national insurance contributions. They confirm that they have an indemnity with players' image-rights companies against tax claims from HMRC.

Clubs that do not have such an indemnity written into the contract may have to foot the bill.

Portsmouth have admitted that HMRC is chasing them for £18.2m in unpaid taxes over image rights. In Sol Campbell's last season at Pompey, his image rights deal was worth £1.56m a year, even though the club's entire merchandising operation generated only £7.2m.

Birmingham City also concede they may be liable for £5.024m in tax and national insurance payments if the ruling goes against football.

And those tax demands may arrive in the new year.

**The Guardian 17 March 2010***
**West Ham suspend players' image-rights payments**
**by Stuart James**
**Hammers withhold payments due to seven players**
**Revenue and Customs investigating tax status of image rights**

West Ham United have risked upsetting a number of their key players after taking the unprecedented step of freezing image–rights payments. The club have decided to withhold money due to seven of their first-team squad until Her Majesty's Revenue & Customs completes an ongoing investigation into tax due on image-rights contracts, a move that other clubs will view with interest.

The payments, which are typically free of PAYE and National Insurance, and often channelled through an offshore company, have come under increased

---

* Reproduced with permission.

scrutiny across the Premier League as HMRC seeks to recover up to £60m in unpaid taxes. It is unclear just how much individual clubs would be liable to pay back if the Revenue is able to prove that image rights contracts are a form of remuneration but West Ham are not prepared to wait and find out.

Kieron Dyer, Matthew Upson, Robert Green and Scott Parker are believed to be among those who have received letters informing them that the payments will stop. The decision could be seen as further evidence of West Ham's financial plight but David Sullivan, their chairman, maintains the move is a "logical, common-sense solution to a potential problem".

He said: "Because the Inland Revenue are saying that tax has to be deducted at source, until the people receiving the image rights have clarified things with the Inland Revenue, we are freezing payments on the basis that there has been a backlog of deductions that have not been made. Every penny they are entitled to will be paid in due course, but until it is agreed with the Inland Revenue we can't release the money.

"Until we build up the deficit for the previous payments, the payments will be held in escrow pending a settlement with the Inland Revenue. If anyone wants to sort out their particular case with the Inland Revenue, we'll abide by whatever they say. But what we can't have is a situation where a guy goes back to France and then in two years' time they [HMRC] say to us: 'You've given him £1m in image rights; we want 40% of that.'"

It is understood that the legal and financial representatives of the players have contacted West Ham to contest the decision, which they claim breaches contractual obligations. Sullivan, however, has urged them to deal directly with HMRC. "They can bring it to a head with the Revenue themselves. Their lawyers and their accountants should write to the Inland Revenue and resolve it," said Sullivan, who claimed "people are not particularly disgruntled" despite suggestions to the contrary.

Licensing payments are commonplace in the Premier League and often equate to at least 10% of a player's salary, but Sullivan believes his predecessors were too quick to approve image-rights contracts. "The previous board have been irresponsible in the way they have paid it and we are immediately reversing things in a fair and reasonable way," he said. "We are not doing anything tricky. We are just trying to limit our exposure for any punitive back-tax."

**The Sunday Times 21 February 2010***
**Taxman chases football stars for £100m**
**by Robert Watts**
**Steven Gerrard is one of several players who have received letters from HM Revenue and Customs**

They earn hundreds of thousands of pounds a week, showing off their skills in packed stadiums and in front of a worldwide audience of millions.

---

* Reproduced with permission.

Now the gilded lifestyles of Premier League footballers are under attack from a new set of opponents—a team of modestly paid civil servants based in a nondescript office block in the West Midlands.

Some 20 tax inspectors from HM Revenue & Customs' (HMRC) special civil investigations unit in Solihull are writing to top players who receive part of their income from their clubs in return for "image rights".

The arrangements have until now allowed players legally to avoid paying an estimated £100m a year in tax. The letters advise the players that their affairs are being investigated and that they may need to hand over copies of accounts, contracts, receipts and other documents to the Revenue.

Their agents have cried foul. "Many of these arrangements have been in place for years and suddenly the Revenue has got a problem with them," said one agent, who represents a player who received one of the letters shortly before Christmas.

"This is a Revenue fishing expedition—it's about raising money."

Clubs started paying many players part of their earnings as image rights during the 1990s. These payments—said to relate to any of the player's off-field earnings, such as replica shirt sales, endorsements and promotional work—are normally paid to service companies owned by the player.

The firm of the Manchester United player Michael Owen is known as Owen Promotions; that of Steven Gerrard, the Liverpool star, is called Steven Gerrard Promotions.

Other well-known players with these companies include Rio Ferdinand, Gary Neville and Joe Cole.

Because the image rights payments are made to a company rather than an individual, they are subject to corporation tax levied at 21 or 28%, rather than National Insurance and income tax—currently paid at up to 40%, but with a new top rate of 50% from April.

If the player is from overseas, his service company is based offshore, often in the Netherlands or the British Virgin Islands, allowing the star to avoid even more UK tax.

The sums paid by clubs to players in image rights can be vast. A court recently heard that Wayne Rooney, who plays for Manchester United, was paid £760,000 a year for his image rights.

Last year it emerged that Joey Barton, the Newcastle United midfielder who was given a suspended jail sentence for assault, was paid £675,000 a year for his image rights by the club.

Frank Lampard, the Chelsea midfielder, also receives images rights as part of his earnings from the club.

Last week Lampard's agent said the arrangement complied with tax rules and that all relevant documentation had been filed with the authorities. He would not discuss whether Lampard had received one of the Revenue's letters.

Earlier this year Manchester United, Britain's richest club, revealed it was in litigation with HMRC regarding image rights over £5.3m of tax, saying the Revenue's view was that "image rights may be a form of remuneration and, as such, should be taxed as income".

Vantis, an accountancy firm that acts for numerous clubs and players, said the image rights deals of all Premier League clubs were being looked at by the Revenue.

Nine days ago representatives from Premier League clubs met in London to discuss ways to respond to HMRC's assault on these pay deals. One option discussed was to limit the amount of a player's income that could be paid in this way to 15%.

Accountants and agents say that only in the past few months have HMRC officials begun writing to the players. Such investigations can last up to two years.

If the Revenue decides the image rights deal constitutes tax avoidance, either the player or the club could be liable for a huge tax bill, depending on how the contract is worded.

A senior Revenue source confirmed that all image rights deals of Premier League players would be scrutinised as part of the investigation. Those players with such arrangements who had not received a letter so far could expect one before long, he said.

### *15.7.2 Appendix 2*

**United Kingdom: Image Rights***

Stephen Woodhouse and Debby Masterton

**Background**

As Premier League players and managers become celebrities and marketable personalities in their own right, the use of image rights contracts has become more prevalent. Leading players with international reputations can command fees for personal appearances, interviews with the media and personal endorsements.

Broadly, under an image rights contract, the club negotiates the right to use or control the personality and image of the player or manager with a third party company (the "IR Company"), which legally holds the image rights of the player or manager. The image rights contract ("IR Contract") will take the form of a contract or licence between the club and the IR Company to exploit the image of the particular player or manager.

Many clubs are considering offering IR Contracts to their top players as it allows them to exploit the player's image rights to generate revenue, mainly through merchandising and other promotion. In addition, as the club will hold the licence to use the image rights the club can ensure that a player devotes his time to sporting activities and, furthermore, is able to control the use of the image rights to ensure the player does not undertake any activities which may potentially have a negative impact on the club, e.g. endorsing competitor brands. For the purposes of this Article, we have considered:

- the UK tax implications of IR Contracts;
- how best to structure the IR Contracts to achieve the intended tax treatment; and
- HM Revenue & Customs ("HMRC") current attitude towards IR Contracts.

**The Use of IR Contracts**

Since the advent of the Premier League in 1992, revenues generated by Premier League clubs have increased considerably. Between 1992 and 2008, revenues for the top 20 clubs grew at a compound annual rate of 16%, compared with 5.4% for the UK economy as a whole.

The Premier League is the richest football league in the World. In the 2010 Annual Review of Football Finance by the Sports Business Group at Deloitte, it was reported that Premier League revenues for 2008/09 were €2,326m, which was €751m above the second highest revenue generating league, the Bundesliga (Germany) with revenue of €1,575m. This remarkable growth in revenue has enabled Premier League clubs to compete with clubs from the Spanish, Italian, French and German leagues to attract the best players from around the world. However, this competition has led to record high wage bills, with the total wage bill for Premier League clubs topping €1.3bn in the 2008/09 season.

---

* First appeared in *Global Sports Law and Taxation Reports*, 2010. Reproduced with permission.

In the past three years, total wages for Premier League clubs has grown by in excess of 55% (£474m). With wages growth outpacing revenue growth in 2008/09, the Premier League's wages/revenue ratio increased to 67%—a record high. Agents regularly seek to renegotiate player contracts, with a key focus on how much the player will actually take home after tax. In a world of increasing tax rates, the cost to a club of paying a player £1 million per annum after tax is increasing (see ***Salary Comparison***).

***Salary Comparison***

Club pays a player a net salary of £1 million.

Salary comparison

| | 2011/12<br>£ | 2010/11<br>£ | 2009/10<br>£ |
|---|---|---|---|
| Salary payment to player | 2,083,333 | 2,040,816 | 1,694,915 |
| Income tax and employee NIC | 1,083,333 | 1,040,816 | 694,915 |
| Net pay | 1,000,000 | 1,000,000 | 1,000,000 |
| Employer NIC | 287,500 | 261,224 | 216,949 |
| Total employer cost | 2,370,833 | 2,302,040 | 1,911,864 |

Note: Income tax at 40% in 2009/10 and 50% in 2010/11 and 2011/12. Employee and Employer NIC of 1 and 12.8% respectively in 2009/10 and 2010/11 and 2 and 13.8% respectively in 2011/12

The following table shows the taxes incurred by clubs in the Premier League and the Football League in the 2008/09 season, showing that tax is a significant cost to Premier League clubs.

| | PAYE | | NIC | | VAT | | Crop tax | | Total | |
|---|---|---|---|---|---|---|---|---|---|---|
| | 2008/<br>09<br>£m | 2007/<br>08<br>£m | 2008/<br>09<br>£m | 2007/<br>08<br>£m | 2008/<br>09<br>£m | 2007/<br>08<br>£m | 2008/<br>09<br>£m | 2007/<br>08<br>£m | 2008/<br>09<br>£m | 2007/<br>08<br>£m |
| Premier league | 418 | 376 | 183 | 162 | 93 | 99 | 29 | 11 | 723 | 648 |
| Championship | 88 | 71 | 55 | 47 | 28 | 26 | (6) | 3 | 165 | 147 |
| League 1 | 20 | 17 | 17 | 16 | 10 | 11 | 0 | 0 | 47 | 44 |
| League 2 | 7 | 6 | 9 | 9 | 6 | 6 | 0 | 0 | 22 | 21 |
| Total | 533 | 470 | 264 | 234 | 137 | 142 | 23 | 14 | 957 | 860 |

Therefore, methods of saving income tax and National Insurance Contributions ("NIC") are of significant interest to clubs, with one such structure being the IR Contract which has become increasingly common (see *Salary plus IR Contract*). Several high profile players in the Premier League receive a payment to their IR Company for use of their image rights. The payments under IR Contracts can represent up to a third of a player's total earnings, which can, in turn, offer a 33% saving on employer's NIC for the club.

***Salary plus IR Contract***

Club pays a player a net salary of £1 million including £330,000 as a payment to an IR Company.

| Salary plus IR contract | |
|---|---|
| | 2010/11 |
| | £ |
| Salary payment to player | 1,367,347 |
| Income tax and employee NIC | (697,347) |
| Image rights payment | 330,000 |
| Net to employee | 1,000,000 |
| Employer NIC | 175,020 |
| Total payable | 1,872,367 |

Note: Income tax at 50% and Employee and Employer NIC of 1 and 12.8% respectively in 2010/11

**Structuring the IR Contract**

Assuming the player has previously transferred his image rights into a separate IR Company, the IR Company will enter into a contract with the club to exploit that player's image. The payment is therefore not connected to the employment of the player and as it is between two companies, there is no requirement to withhold income tax under Pay-As-You-Earn ("PAYE") or NIC on the payment. Depending on the jurisdiction in which the IR Company is established, there may be no corporation tax due on the payments received by the IR Company, thus allowing the payments to remain tax free until they are drawn out of the IR Company in the form of dividends or capital distributions.

However, in order to achieve the desired tax treatment, the payment must be shown to be under a contract which has independent value and is separate from the contract of employment.

Clearly, with the ability to reduce the player's income tax bill (and the club's NIC liability) the arrangements have come under the close scrutiny of HMRC, who argue that the large sums paid under IR Contracts are not commensurate with the value received by the club and consequently that the payments are a smoke-screen for additional remuneration, which is paid in a form not subject to income tax or NIC.

In fact, HMRC challenged the use of IR Contracts in the case *Sports Club & Ors vs HM Inspector of Taxes* in 2000 and were unsuccessful. The key points of the case found that the IR Contracts were:

- Genuinely commercial agreements which the parties could seek to enforce;
- Agreements which had independent value: established players are capable of earning very substantial sums each year from commercial contracts;

- Not a smokescreen for the payment of additional remuneration: the agreements were real and the parties intended activities to be performed under them in return for payments. The club took steps, including appropriate legal advice, to ensure they acquired the rights that they were paying for;
- The payments were made in return for promotional rights and were not made "in reference to" the playing of games i.e. the payments were not connected with employment.

Certain players are well established and have a strong image and therefore are capable of earning very substantial sums each year from commercial contracts. It is well known that organisations are willing to pay for the right to use the players' images in association with their products. Therefore, if properly established, valued and exploited, the payments under IR Contracts should not attract income tax or NIC in line with current case law.

HMRC do not automatically assume that payments made under an IR Contract are earnings from employment. HMRC's concern comes from the valuation of the image rights. In particular, where negotiations centre on a pay package, which cover both payments for playing and payments for image rights, HMRC do not consider an arbitrary carve up of an amount to be sufficient to prove that the image rights have been properly valued. HMRC also want to see a clearer link between the income generated through the players' image rights and payments under the IR Contract.

**Steps**

It is essential that the commercial reality is that the club wishes to purchase or manage the player's image and promotional activities, over and above the extent to which it is already provided for in his contract of employment.

In order to ensure the best chance of success when establishing an IR Contract, the club should consider the following issues:

- The Board of the club should consider its policy with regard to IR Contracts, the benefit to the club, the success of previous arrangements and the extent to which they may be improved;
- Club's are likely to benefit from agreeing a pro-forma contract which can be used as a starting point for future IR Contract negotiations;
- The club should ensure the IR Company is set up in an appropriate jurisdiction and the players have legally transferred their image rights to that company. Note that if the player is UK resident at the time of the transfer, capital gains tax would be payable on the value of the image;
- The terms of each IR Contract should be negotiated with the IR Company and the contract drafted according to the facts and circumstances of the image involved;
- When signing a player, the club should consider whether that player has an independent image that the club wishes to exploit. If so, the image rights of the player should be included as a separate component of the negotiations on which the player should take independent advice;

- A business plan should be drafted setting out:
  - o the rights to be covered;
  - o the extent to which these are to be used;
  - o the value to the club of the contract; and
  - o a plan for how the rights are to be exploited.

  The rights acquired must be over and above those provided for in the player's contract of employment and the valuation should exclude any value attributable to contractual activity;

- The club will normally assess the value of the image rights contract based on previous experience. However, it would be useful if the club could also obtain independent third party expert valuations to support its negotiations;
- Once the negotiations on the value of the image rights have concluded and been documented, the agent can then negotiate salary as a separate matter. It will be clear therefore that there are two separate arrangements which the club has entered into; one with the IR Company for the players image rights and the other with the player for his services as a football player;
- The promotional activities provided under the IR Contract should be monitored and an annual report should be prepared to demonstrate the activities performed and the value to the club of those activities. The success of the IR Contracts should be reported to the Board to inform future decisions or policy changes.

**HMRC's Preferred Structure**

As IR Contracts have become more common, agents have negotiated ever-increasing proportions of the overall player's package to take the form of payments for image rights. As a result, HMRC have sought to challenge the arrangements on the basis that payments under the IR Contracts are excessive and are essentially a smokescreen for additional remuneration.

We understand that HMRC have suggested that their preferred structure for an IR Contract is for the contract between the club and the IR Company to provide for a low fixed annual fee ("retainer") at an appropriate level plus a percentage of income generated from the player's image rights (e.g. percentage of "net revenue").

If clubs structured their IR Contracts this way, HMRC consider this structure would be robust as the value the player receives from the IR Contract would be linked directly to the value created for the club through exploitation of the player's image rights.

However, it is not necessary to structure IR Contracts this way as, provided the amounts paid for use of the image rights is commensurate with the value of those image rights, the amount can be paid as a fixed sum per annum. Clubs may choose to increase the payment made under the IR Contract if the income from exploitation of the image rights exceeds the fixed sum, however this is a point for commercial negotiation between the club and the agents.

From a commercial perspective, a fixed sum structure is often preferable for clubs than providing for a share of incomes generated to be paid under the IR Contract, for the following reasons:

- Identifying the revenue generated through exploitation of a particular player's image with such direct causality may be difficult from a practical perspective;
- The player's image may provide indirect and intangible enhancement to the value of the club's brand, which cannot be recognised simply by participation in direct income generated through exploitation of their image (e.g. revenue from sales of player named shirts);
- In granting a licence to the Club to exploit their image, a player is ceding his ability to generate income on his own behalf without any control or recourse to the Club to actually take steps to exploit that image. The player would therefore seek appropriate consideration for this;
- In addition, this structure of IR Contract does not deliver full value to the club for the benefit of being able to control the player's image such that his time and energy are used on sporting activities and not in a manner which could potentially damage the clubs brand.

**Valuing the Image Rights**
In determining the value of the rights granted under the IR Contract, the club should assess the value of the IR Contract to it. This would include an assessment of a number of factors, including:

- The player's contracted salary for playing football;
- Whether the player is already recognisable;
- How many international appearances the player has made to date;
- Whether the player is likely to appear in the first team; and
- The level of control over the activities of the player and the ability to ensure the player focuses on their sporting activities rather than commercial activities.

In addition when valuing the IR Contract, the club should consider the terms of the contract, including:

- Any carve-outs from exclusivity;
- The term of the licence;
- The ability to prevent the player from undertaking activities which have a detrimental impact on the value of the image rights to the club.

When determining the valuation of the IR contract the club will only take into account information available at the time the contract is entered into. The club may seek advice to determine what the value of the image rights is e.g. an indication of how much money players of a similar calibre have made from their image and promotional activities.

In making this assessment of the value of the IR Contract, the club should ideally complete a business plan, setting out the rights to be covered, the extent to which these are to be used and a plan for how the rights are to be exploited.

Notwithstanding this, it is understood that contract negotiations are often time pressured and therefore it may not always be possible to conduct a thorough valuation process prior to signing the player.

Therefore the IR Contract should be reviewed periodically to determine if the payments under the contract still represent good value to the club. The club should aim to maximise the value received from the exploitation of the player's image. Clearly the club should intend to recoup from the exploitation of the player's image the fees paid under the IR Contract and make a further profit, which they may wish to share with the player by allowing an additional percentage of revenues to be paid over and above the fixed annual payment under the IR Contract.

To the extent the services under the IR Contract are not being provided then the club should seek to rectify the position. The club should prepare an annual report for each IR Contract setting out the specific activities performed under the IR Contract in the year and assessing how the activities are providing value to the club with quantification.

It is understood that in certain circumstances the basis for determining the fee under the IR Contract may be valid but ultimately lead to a mismatch between the actual value created from the exploitation of the player's image rights. For example, from time to time the club may undertake an action which directly or indirectly impacts on the value of the player's image, e.g. if a promising player performs poorly and is dropped from the first team, or if the player is injured, this would reduce the marketability of the player and therefore the potential to exploit the player's image to create value. Such action should not invalidate the basis for valuing the IR Contract at the time it was entered into, nor change the nature of the payments to employment income. Information that becomes available after the IR Contract has been agreed should not be taken into account when determining the value of the IR Contract at inception.

One concern that has been expressed by HMRC is that the IR Contracts provide for a fixed fee for a number of years (usually the number of years of the employment contract) which may or may not turn out to be an appropriate valuation of the player's image. Therefore, a periodic review and adjustment should be built into the contractual terms.

**HMRC Challenges to Historic Arrangements**

HMRC are investigating the use and implementation of IR Contracts at a number of clubs and it has been reported in the press that they intend to scrutinise all image rights deals of Premier League players. If HMRC found that payments under IR Contracts should be reclassified as remuneration, the clubs could be liable for a significant amount of underpaid PAYE and NIC.

As noted above, based on existing case law payments under IR Contracts should not be considered earnings from employment where the IR Contracts are properly established and operated. However, HMRC would be in a strong position where there is a lack of evidence that the image rights have been properly valued or that any steps have been taken by the club to exploit the rights it has been granted under the IR Contract.

HMRC are likely to challenge arrangements where they do not believe there is any commercial substance. However, clubs should not simply accept HMRC's view. HMRC cannot merely ignore the existence of the commercial contract between the club and the IR Company and therefore will have to attack the arrangements on the basis of the valuation of the rights. Provided clubs can demonstrate that the value they have placed on the rights granted under the IR Contract is appropriate and that they have the intention and have tried to exploit the rights, they should have a robust starting position to defend any HMRC challenge.

**The Future for IR Contracts**

As HMRC will be looking into IR Contracts, clubs should review their existing arrangements and be ready to provide evidence to support the value of the payments made under the existing IR Contracts.

Notwithstanding HMRC scrutiny, IR Contracts can provide significant value to clubs. Therefore, entering into IR Contracts with high profile players and looking for ways to generate value from their image rights will allow clubs to grow their commercial revenue streams through a share in the income from the players' promotional activity.

### 15.7.3 *Appendix 3*

**Comparative Survey on Sports Image Rights: Guernsey Collas Day***

Jason Romer and Brandon Doffing**

**Image Rights**

The concept of an 'image right' is relatively new when compared to 'traditional' intellectual property ("IP"). Generally speaking, an 'image right' may be defined as a right intended to protect the use of an individual's name, image, likeness or other aspect of his or her distinctiveness or personality.

Some jurisdictions have accepted the concept of an image right more readily than others. However, it seems somewhat inevitable that an image right will become one of the major IP rights that high profile individuals seek to protect.

Over time, intellectual property has developed in response to the needs of business and society. When it became possible for authors to mass produce their books by way of printing processes, copyright law was introduced to protect the authors' efforts in creating a book and their right to exploit this. Similarly, inventions were recognised and protected by way of patent law to ensure the creators of such inventions were rewarded for their efforts in creating the invention. In today's modern society, where celebrity status is sought after and provides a source of revenue in itself, it is clear that individuals will wish to protect the right to their image as a 'celebrity' as far as possible. This may be seen as the basis for an image right.

Civil law jurisdictions such as France and the Netherlands have recognised the concept or potential for the concept of an image right under their laws. Article 21 of the Dutch Copyright Act provides that "if a portrait is made without having been commissioned by or on behalf of the persons portrayed, the copyright owner shall not be allowed to communicate it to the public, in so far as the person portrayed or, after his death, his relatives have a reasonable interest in opposing its communication to the public". This clearly provides an individual (or, if deceased, his relatives) with some control over the use of their image.

Certain common law jurisdictions have also made progress in recognising the right of an individual to control the use and exploitation of their image. In the US, certain States recognise a 'right of publicity', which prevents the unauthorised commercial use of an individual's name, likeness, or other recognisable aspects of their persona. It gives an individual the exclusive right to license the use of their

---

* This article first appeared in *Global Sports Law and Taxation Report*, November 2010.

** This article is a summary of the subject matter discussed and is provided for information purposes only. The authors do not purport to give specific legal, tax or other advice, and before acting, further advice should always be sought. Neither the authors nor Collas Day shall be liable for any errors, misprint or misinterpretation of any of the matters set out in this article. 

identity for commercial promotion. Alternatively, the Federal Lanham Act provides protection where a person's identity is used to falsely advertise a product or designate its origin.

The concept of an image right is clearly big business for sportspersons. The exploitation of their image may amount to a significant percentage of their overall income. Michael Jordan, the basketball player often recognised as one of the greatest sportsmen of all time, is said to have earned approximately $90 million in total salary during his active career as a player. However, he earned another $750 million from sponsors for the use of his image. Tiger Woods, considered the first sportsperson to earn more than $1 billion in his career, is a similar example. Even with the negative PR fallout from his personal issues of late, it is estimated that he receives approximately $70 million per year from endorsement fees.[1]

Regardless of the above very few jurisdictions, if any, have expressly and specifically recognised or created a basis for image rights as a separate IP right. However, their importance has no doubt been accepted in the UK legal and commercial arena. For example, in anticipation of the Olympics in 2012, the London Olympic Games and Paralympic Games Act 2006 (the "2006 **Act**") was introduced. The 2006 Act gives the London Organising Committee of the Olympic Games and Paralympic Games the exclusive right to grant its sponsors and licensees authorisation to create an association between their business, goods or services and the 2012 Olympics. The concept of 'association' is not strictly limited, but may include the use of athletic images or iconic images which 'evoke the spirit' of the 2012 games. Although this may not be a specific or even general recognition of an image right, it clearly acknowledges that certain images are important from a commercial standpoint and warrant protection from use by unauthorised parties.

In addition, even though image rights may not be expressly recognised under English law, they still form an important part of commercial agreements and individuals will seek to enforce them as far as possible. A notable recent example involves Wayne Rooney[2] and the rights to his "off-field" image, which he assigned to his management company in return for the payment of commission. Mr Rooney sought to terminate this agreement following the resignation of a key employee of the management company. Interestingly, the agreement was made for eight years (with very little possibility of termination) and found to be unenforceable by the courts on the basis of restraint of trade. The judge noted the imbalance of bargaining powers between the parties and that the agreement imposed "*significant restrictions on Wayne Rooney's freedom to exploit his talents*". It was, however, acknowledged that an agreement relating to image rights and their exploitation had become a common and accepted form of commercial agreement in such situations.

[1] Kurt Badenhausen, Forbes Blogs, 23 September 2010.

[2] *Proactive Sports Management Limited v Wayne Rooney* [*2010*] *EWHC 1807* (*QB*).

Given the above, it is clear that there is an increasing acknowledgment of image rights as a form of IP right whether by legislation, case law or commercial practice. The authors are, however, not aware of a jurisdiction that has yet to take the step of creating a registrable image right as a specific form of registered IP. The importance of an image right should not be underestimated in a sporting context. It is essential for sportspersons to consider how and where is best to register, manage and exploit such rights.

**Offshore, Image Rights and Other IP**

The effort to harmonise IP protection on a global scale indicates the fundamental importance of IP to the world economy. IP rights have become a key asset for many individuals and businesses. Although various agreements and treaties have sought to harmonise the recognition and procedural aspects of certain IP rights, IP is very much an evolving area of law and new rights will undoubtedly develop with the demands of society.

For sportspersons, sports clubs or any other individual or business associated with sport, the recognition and use of image and IP is vital in today's marketplace. Whether it is the branding of a sport betting company or the image of a well known sportsman, it is important that IP is adequately recognised, protected and commercialised where possible.

When IP forms a significant part of the assets or income of an individual or business, it is important to manage them in a way which will meet the legal and commercial objectives of the holder. While "identification", "protection" and "exploitation" are recognised as the key considerations, "location" is arguably now just as important. Moving image rights and other IP to tax neutral jurisdictions may contribute not only to their protection, but also to the flexibility of their exploitation and the reduction of the tax burden on any related income. This could have a significant impact on entities with a multitude of IP rights, such as sport clubs and famous sporting icons.

Traditionally, offshore centres, now more correctly referred to as Specialist Financial Centres ("SFCs"), have not tended to be used extensively for the management of IP. This has generally been because of the somewhat outdated legislation that has not always been conducive to the international recognition that the sporting and commercial markets require. However, Guernsey has taken steps to further develop itself as a highly regulated financial centre with IP legislation that is not only internationally recognised but that also provides some unique advantages for individuals and companies wishing to locate their IP in a tax benign environment with a robust legal framework to look after it. The relatively new IP laws in Guernsey have been designed to be flexible, modern and progressive. While they are primarily based upon UK and European laws and models, they also have the benefit of the lessons learned in those jurisdictions.

The development of IP legislation in Guernsey can benefit from case law and UK precedent but also retain flexibility from the European regime (as it is not part of the EU). This flexibility allows for Guernsey to provide protection where it would otherwise be unavailable and the ability to adjust to ever-changing markets with the recognition of new IP rights, such as image rights.

If a company is looking to locate its image rights and other IP within an SFC, the legal protection afforded by that jurisdiction is critical. This protection must be considered not only in the context of the statutory protection afforded to such IP, but also the process of enforcing those rights. The court process should be clear, swift and capable of providing an effective remedy. One must also consider whether they have multiple types of IP requiring protection. For example, a sports club may wish to hold its trade marks, copyrights, database rights and image rights in a location where they will be adequately protected both locally and internationally.

Alongside the legal considerations, there are many practical and financial factors worthy of note. Cost will play an important part of an individual or business's decision, as will the speed of registration. It is also important to take note of the tax implications, as well as local expertise and knowledge.

It is possible for an individual or business to move all of their IP into Guernsey, either by assigning existing IP to an entity in Guernsey, or registering future IP through such an entity. This will allow for ease of administration and the efficient exploitation of these rights, especially where they may currently be held by a number of entities in a variety of locations. It would then be possible to take advantage of the progressive and robust structures offered by Guernsey, as well as its tax regime. It is highly likely that any individual or business involved in or linked with sport would benefit greatly from such a move.

**Guernsey IP Legislation**

Guernsey has a comprehensive legislative structure for protecting and exploiting IP. The Intellectual Property (Enabling Provisions) Bailiwick of Guernsey Law 2004 (the "Enabling Law") created the power for the States of Guernsey (Guernsey's executive and legislative house) (the "States") to introduce separate ordinances relating to IP.

The Enabling Law also gave the States the power to establish the office of the Intellectual Property Registrar [under the Intellectual Property (Office of Registrar) (Bailiwick of Guernsey) Ordinance 2005] and bring in several ordinances that deal with specific areas of IP. The Registrar and the Intellectual Property Office are responsible for the registration and protection of IP registrations within Guernsey.

To date, Guernsey has implemented legislation in respect of a number of IP rights, including trade marks, copyright, design rights and database rights. Further legislation and IP rights, such as specific laws relating to image rights, have been proposed and are currently being progressed. However, below is a snapshot of some of Guernsey's key IP legislation which is likely to be relevant to those involved in the sporting world.

**Trade Marks**

The Trade Marks (Bailiwick of Guernsey) Law 2006 is the principal legislation governing trademarks within Guernsey, which is currently in the process of acceding to the main conventions governing trademarks.

Any sign capable of being represented graphically and which is capable of distinguishing the goods and services of one undertaking from those of other undertakings is, subject to the requirements of the Registrar of trademarks, registrable. In the world of sport, this would include such important brand items as team badges, logos and potentially even the colour of a team's kit.

Like English law, there are both absolute and relative grounds for refusal of registration and the criteria bears a resemblance to UK provisions e.g. trademarks devoid of distinctive character are not inherently registrable.

A trade mark in Guernsey is protected for a period of 10 years starting on the date of registration. On application (and payment of a fee) up to six months before or after the end of the protection period, registration of a trade mark may be renewed for an unlimited period (for 10 years per renewal). Guernsey trademarks are classified using the ninth edition of the Nice classification system, which is based on the most up to date system used by the UK and recognised by the World Intellectual Property Office. Applications for trademarks in more than one class are accepted and do not require separate applications.

The proprietor of a registered trade mark must actually make genuine use of the trade mark within the Bailiwick of Guernsey in relation to the goods or services for which it is registered. It should be noted that, where a sportsperson locates their worldwide trade marks in Guernsey as well as registering a Guernsey trade mark, failure to use such a mark in Guernsey should only impact on the Guernsey registration and not any elsewhere. Given the cosmopolitan nature of the island and its links to global finance, it is unlikely that this problem would arise.

**Copyright**

The Copyright (Bailiwick of Guernsey) Ordinance 2005 is the principal legislation governing copyright in Guernsey.

Original literary, dramatic, musical or artistic works, sound recordings, films or broadcasts, and the typographical arrangement of published editions are all protected by copyright in Guernsey. Protection lasts for varying periods of time, depending upon the type of work subject to copyright, and this scope varies widely. 'LDMA' works and films are generally protected for 70 years, sound recordings and broadcasts for 50 years and published editions for 25 years.

Copyright does not subsist in a work unless the qualification requirements of the Copyright Ordinance are satisfied. Qualification may arise by reference to the country of first publication or broadcast (i.e. copyright will be protected if first publication or broadcast is in Guernsey or in a recognised jurisdiction under Guernsey laws and regulations). As such, should a famous footballer choose to write his memoirs whilst spending the off-season in the South of France, he would be provided copyright protection for this within Guernsey.

Like English law, infringement can be both primary and secondary and the principles are largely the same. The rights of the copyright holder in relation to infringement are also similar, with copyright holders having the right to, for example, sue for damages, or be recognised as the true author of the work. Copyright can also be licensed, assigned, lent and in unpublished works can be passed under a will. This would allow the memoir-writing footballer to licence his Guernsey-based rights in this work to a publisher, or assign them to his wholly-owned Guernsey based company, allowing for the benefit to be passed through the generations by way of trust or corporate arrangements that Guernsey is so well known for.

**Database Rights**

The Database Rights (Bailiwick of Guernsey) Ordinance 2005 is the principal legislation governing database rights in Guernsey.

Whilst seeming irrelevant for sporting purposes, database rights may have relevance for those using statistical applications, such as “fantasy sports” leagues, sports-based computer games and other products reliant on player statistics. In particular, this protection will likely be very important for sport betting companies, many of which are choosing to relocate to Guernsey to take advantage of the world-leading e-gambling regime being pioneered in Alderney (one of the islands within the Bailiwick of Guernsey).

For a database right to subsist there must be a “database”, defined as a collection or collation of independent works which are arranged in a systematic or methodical way and accessible physically or electronically. There must also be “substantial investment” from the maker and publisher of the database in some form.

The Database Ordinance widens the type of investment that will qualify for the development of a database right and grants the sort of protection that many thought the EU directive on database protection was intended to afford. As such, it may be possible to obtain such a right in Guernsey when not available elsewhere.

Protection lasts for 15 years from completion of the database or, if made available to the public, 15 years from the date it was first made available. Substantial changes to the contents of the database would be considered a new investment subject to its own protection as a new database right.

**Image Rights Cases**

Law in practice in Guernsey generally follows the principles of English and Commonwealth law, meaning image rights cases in these countries will have a bearing on the approach taken by the Guernsey courts. With this said, following the proposed introduction of image rights legislation it will be more difficult to find appropriate case law as the legislation will be unique to Guernsey. English case law may still offer some guidance on certain issues, but it will be the Guernsey courts that are tasked with interpreting Guernsey’s statutory image right.

The English courts have been faced with the issue of image rights in a number of guises, whether on the basis of a trade mark, passing off, data protection, advertising standards or otherwise. Although English law has not yet established a recognisable and specific image right, some of these approaches have had varying degrees of success in protecting the use of an image. It is therefore appropriate to consider how such case law and practices may be interpreted and utilised in Guernsey.

**Trade Marks**

Trade marks are a registered IP that provide the owner with a monopoly over the use of a distinctive 'mark' or 'brand'. Although trade marks are generally recognised as protecting the identity of a business (e.g. Coca-Cola), trade mark laws have been used to protect the images of famous individuals. Given the concept behind an image right, trade marks may in fact be the best fit for protecting images in the absence of specific image right recognition. For example, Damon Hill has a registered UK trade mark for the image of his eyes looking out from his racing helmet.[3] Notably, the proprietor of this trade mark is Damon Hill Grand Prix Limited, a company incorporated and registered in the Channel Islands. This is one of many examples of individuals choosing to hold their IP in an SFC registered entity.

To be registrable, a mark must be 'distinctive' and capable of graphic representation. As such, a common approach is to register the name of a famous individual in respect of classes in which that name may be exploited. For example, Tiger Woods has a Community trade mark for his name in relation to interactive software for computer games,[4] thereby helping to protect the use of his name in the popular "Tiger Woods PGA Tour" series of games produced by EA Sports. In addition, certain sportsmen have gone even further and registered their image as a trade mark. Damon Hill has already been discussed above and Alan Shearer had also registered his image as a UK trade mark, although this has now expired.

Issues could potentially arise with such trade marks where there was no *bona fide* intention to use the mark in respect of the goods or services for which it is registered. The 'distinctive' requirement may also cause problems for sportspersons looking to register their name or image. The use of their name or image will need to be associated with the relevant goods or services for it to be 'distinctive'. Given that most sportspersons are famous for their particular sport, and not for any goods or services, this test may prove difficult to overcome.

Although it may be possible to register a sportsperson's name, or even their image, as a trade mark, the enforceability of such registrations is not yet known.

As highlighted above, Guernsey's trade mark legislation largely reflects that of the UK and other key jurisdictions. The UK has published its Registry's Manual of Trade Marks Practice and this deals with certain issues relating to the registration of celebrity names and images. Guernsey does not have such a manual, but this

---

3 UK Trade Mark Registration Number 2036489.

4 CTM Registration Number 1021795.

would likely result in the IP Registrar in Guernsey taking a discretionary view on registrability and most likely would follow the UK position.

**Data Protection**

The law governing data protection in Guernsey is the Data Protection (Bailiwick of Guernsey) Law 2001 (the "Data Law"), which was largely based on the UK's Data Protection Act 1998 (the "Data Act").

The Data Act imposes certain obligations on entities collecting and processing personal data. "Personal data" can be construed very widely and potentially covers the name or a photograph of a famous sportsperson or celebrity. As such, there have been attempts to use this as a statutory basis for creating a right over the use of an individual's image and personality.

Should this be considered "personal data", the person looking to make use of such data will need to ensure they comply with the provisions of the Data Act. In particular, should the data be used for commercial purposes without the consent of the relevant sportsperson (e.g. an image of the sportsperson used for a poster campaign), it may be that the personal data has been "processed" in contravention of the processing requirements of the Data Act.

In a case against Hello! Magazine,[5] it was considered that a photograph could be subject to "processing" for the purposes of the Data Act where automatic equipment transmitted it to printers or in the processes used in the preparation for, and in the course of, the printing. Therefore, where a photograph or representation of a famous person is considered "personal data", its use in a commercial context may very well be classed as "processing" meaning it will fall within the provisions of the Data Act. Although the case was not decided on this point in the end, the use of the Data Act in this way is intriguing.

English case law has suggested that there are limitations to the Data Act's use as a means of creating an image right. In Murray,[6] Patten J's comments imply that damages for such unlawful processing of data are limited to circumstances where the sportsperson has suffered some form of loss, such as the loss of fees that may have been received for the use. As such, the recourse against the infringer under the Data Act seems somewhat limited.

Although it is not common practice in Guernsey to use the Data Law to protect image rights, given the similarities with the Data Act there does not seem to be any reason why this could not be applied in the same way. As such, Guernsey should restrict the use of images from a data protection perspective to an equal degree as that in the UK.

---

[5] Douglas & Ors v Hello! Limited & Ors [2003] 3 All ER 996.

[6] *David Murray v (1) Express Newspapers plc (2) Big Pictures (UK) Limited* [2007] *EWHC 1908.*

**Passing Off**

In *Reddaway v Banham*[7] Lord Halsbury stated that "no-one has the right to represent his goods as the goods of somebody else". As such, the law of passing off in the UK seeks to restrict the taking of business by presenting goods or services as someone else's. For an action to succeed there must be three elements: goodwill in the relevant 'mark' or 'brand', a misrepresentation leading to confusion and damage caused.

In a case involving *Eddie Irvine,*[8] the retired British Formula 1 driver, Mr Irvine successfully sued Talksport Limited ("Talksport"), a UK radio station, for passing off. This improved the protection of image rights in the UK by recognising passing off as a potential cause of action.

Talksport used a photograph of Mr Irvine which had been doctored to show him holding a Talksport branded radio. The judge in this case highlighted the necessity for damage to goodwill before passing off may be established. At the time of the incident, Mr Irvine was an extremely well known sports figure and his image would clearly have had significant goodwill. Talksport's use of his image falsely implied the endorsement of Mr Irvine and Mr Irvine had not received any remuneration for this use. As such, Mr Irvine was awarded a sum equivalent to the royalty he would have received for such an endorsement.

Although there have been no passing off cases involving image rights in Guernsey, it is highly likely that precedents such as the *Irvine* case would be looked to for guidance.

**Advertising Standards**

A significant example of image rights enforcement in the UK was in relation to David Bedford. Mr Bedford was a well-known runner in the 1970 s and had a recognisable image due to his clothing, hairstyle and facial hair. The Number (UK) Limited (better known to us as "118 118") introduced an advertising campaign featuring two characters with appearances very similar to that of Mr Bedford.

Mr Bedford was reported as saying that "he wanted to sue, but his lawyer had told him he had no case because he had no control over the image rights".[9] That said, in 2003 Mr Bedford lodged a complaint with the Independent Television Commission. Ofcom found that 118 118 had been in breach of the UK's Television Advertising Standards Code. However, as a result of Mr Bedford's delay in taking action, the lack of any actual financial harm to Mr Bedford and the expenditure incurred by 118 118, Ofcom refused to ban the relevant advertisement.

Guernsey does not have a code similar to the UK's Television Advertising Standards Code or CAP Code. Given that these are non-statutory codes, it is unlikely that these would be applied or even considered for Guernsey based complaints. Clearly any activities in the UK (or any other jurisdiction) involving a

---

7 *Reddaway v Banham [1896] AC 199.*

8 *Edmund Irvine v Lewis A May (Produce Distributors) Limited [1947] 2 All ER.*

9 BBC News Website, 5 October 2003.

Guernsey resident individual or incorporated company would still be subject to that jurisdiction's advertising standards. Given the very limited amount of Channel Island-specific television broadcasts (Guernsey receives the vast majority of its television from the UK), the lack of an advertising code is unlikely to cause Guernsey-specific issues.

**Guernsey's Position**

Given the above, it is clear that the IP regime in Guernsey generally provides equivalent protection for sport-related IP rights to that of the UK. As such, sportspersons, sport clubs, sport related businesses and other such entities will be able to seek protection in Guernsey on a very similar basis to that in the UK. In addition, should they choose to relocate ownership of their current IP rights to Guernsey, they will still be able to enforce these rights in the relevant jurisdiction, whether in the UK or elsewhere.

**Image Rights Legislation**

One of the most interesting rights that is being considered as part of Guernsey's continuing development of IP, is a plan to define and create a legal register of image rights in Guernsey, thus allowing owners of such rights to register them and thereby create a more clearly separable and marketable asset.

As discussed in detail above, the UK does not have a recognised image right. However, cases such as that of Sports Club plc[10] have recognised image rights of famous sportsmen (in this case, Arsenal Football Club's Dennis Bergkamp and David Platt) as separate capital assets in their own right. Although this case involved image rights from a tax point of view, it does show a progression towards the recognition of image rights, at least from a fiscal perspective.

Certain other countries, such as the US, Australia, Mexico and France, have legally recognised the existence of image rights. However, these are generally based on civil law or case law and are not supported by a searchable register. Guernsey's proposed statutory image right would be the first of its kind and provide a clearly distinguishable and definable asset for the owner of the right.

The creation of such a right will clearly have significant commercial value in the sporting arena. As discussed above, although image rights are not expressly recognised as a separate right in the UK, parties still pursue various legal avenues in an attempt to restrict the use of their image. There are also many agreements and licences entered into in relation to image rights, whether it is the right of a company to associate a famous sportsman with their product, or a manager to have control over the use of their client's image. The lack of a recognised image right potentially creates confusion as to the subject matter of such agreements or licences. This lack of clarity could have an impact on their value and enforceability.

---

10 *Sports Club plc v Inspector of Taxes* [2000] *STC (SCD) 443.*

By way of comparison, the image rights regime in Guernsey is likely to be akin to that of trade marks. However, where trade marks seek to recognise and protect the distinctiveness of a brand, image rights will do so for the distinctiveness and personality of an individual.

An understandable criticism with the proposed image rights legislation in Guernsey is the limit of its territorial application. Given the current status of image rights around the world, it is clear that we are a significant way from having a harmonised approach to this IP right. Guernsey's statutory image right would go further towards protecting such rights than any other jurisdiction. Therefore, it would be very difficult to agree any reciprocal enforcement of image rights with other countries. In addition, the image rights legislation will only apply to and be able to protect the use of images within the Bailiwick of Guernsey.

While it may at first prove difficult to enforce the image right outside the Bailiwick of Guernsey, there are still significant potential benefits in registering them here. In particular, creating a Guernsey registered image right would establish a legally recognised asset. This could then be marketed, traded or charged (e.g. as security for the raising of finance) with greater certainty for all parties concerned.

The image right could also be linked to a number of other internationally recognised IP rights (such as trade marks) held by the relevant party. The IP holder would then exploit the image right in addition to these other rights.

Although the statutory image right has not yet been introduced in Guernsey, IP holders should consider Guernsey for image rights purposes now and regardless of any potential legislation. An individual could assign and transfer all of their image rights (and other relevant IP rights) to an entity in Guernsey, most likely a Guernsey incorporated company. These rights could then be licensed to third parties in return for payment (e.g. royalties) by way of a licensing agreement. The individual would likely enjoy potentially large savings on income and capital taxes. It is unlikely that they would be subject to any local taxes, provided the beneficial owner of those rights is not resident in Guernsey.

There are also many non-tax reasons for separating image rights (and other IP rights) into a separate legal entity, not least of which are for future estate planning and asset protection reasons. IP rights (including, potentially, image rights) can survive and be valuable long after the death of the individual. For example, the use of Elvis Presley's name or image in relation to a product is highly likely to increase the demand for and popularity of that product.

It should be noted that the image rights legislation remains subject to consideration and approval by the States of Deliberation in Guernsey.

With the fiscal advantages of a leading SFC, image right protection on level pegging with the UK, impending world-first image right legislation and the backing of many locally based service providers, Guernsey is a leader in the realm of image rights and other IP and is primed to continue building upon this position in the future.

**Potential Structures**

The introduction of a statutory image rights regime is not the only advantage Guernsey has to offer from an IP management perspective. It may be extremely beneficial for IP holders, particularly sporting figures and other famous individuals, to consider holding all of their IP in Guernsey.

Below is a brief explanation of some of the many ways IP rights may be held and exploited from Guernsey. Needless to say, the appropriate structure to be used will change on a case-by-case basis. It is therefore very important to seek legal and tax advice when considering restructuring IP in this way.

**IP Holding Company**

Once an individual has identified and protected their IP, whether in Guernsey or anywhere else, it is then necessary to find an effective and tax efficient way of holding and exploiting that IP. This is where the "IP Holding Company" can be utilised.

Sporting stars may have any number of IP rights registered (e.g. trade marks for their name, autograph and/or image, copyright in commissioned photographs or their autobiography). These rights may be in a wide variety of jurisdictions and subject to an array of agreements and licences. This will likely create a complex international IP portfolio. The wrong decisions in how this IP is managed may produce unwieldy structures or mean that IP is missed or its true value never fully realised. Depending on certain factors, such as the residency of the individual and their activities, there is potential for such structures to have significant tax implications.

The IP holder may choose to assign all of their rights, title and interest in their IP to the IP Holding Company. The IP holder is then able to streamline the processes for registration, licensing and monitoring this IP. They could then effectively value their IP through analysis of the IP Holding Company's income stream. In addition, incorporating the IP Holding Company in an SFC will likely have significant tax benefits.

By using an IP Holding Company registered in Guernsey, the IP holder can simplify their IP structure, streamline licensing procedures and minimise cross jurisdictional transfers of IP, whilst ensuring the continued protection afforded to it. The obvious answer would therefore seem to be that such an entity should be an essential part of any IP holder's repertoire.

**Simple Licensing Arrangement**

After an individual has successfully assigned all of their international IP rights to an IP Holding Company, it will then be appropriate to exploit this IP to its fullest commercial extent.

For example, consider a renowned football player in the English Premier League wishing to protect and benefit from the use of his image. The footballer incorporates an IP Holding Company in Guernsey and is the sole shareholder of this company. He immediately assigns all of his image rights (and other IP) to this IP Holding Company. In addition to these existing image rights, and following introduction of the legislation in Guernsey, the IP Holding Company registers the footballer's image rights in Guernsey. The IP Holding Company is then in a position to licence, assign, charge or otherwise deal with any of the image rights of the footballer.

Should the footballer wish to allow a third party to exploit his image (or other IP right), the IP Holding Company will simply enter into a licence agreement for the use of that image with the relevant third party.

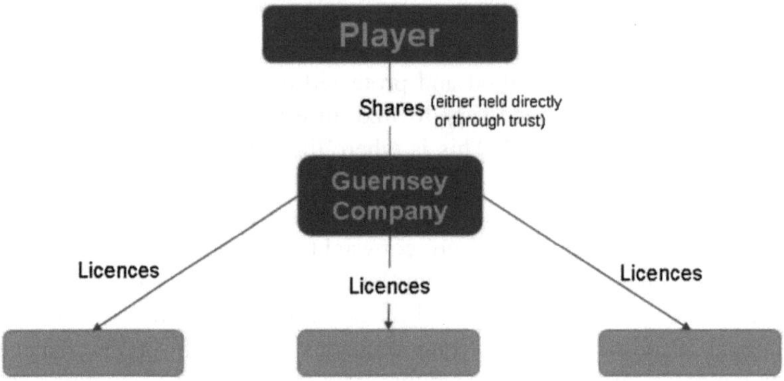


Although the Guernsey registered image right will only be enforceable in Guernsey, it will provide identifiable subject matter for the licence agreement and be supported by the other relevant IP rights (such as trade marks) for international enforcement.

Given the early stages of the Guernsey image right, it is not yet known how enforcement will work in practice. However, taking such steps as making the licence agreement subject to Guernsey law and jurisdiction and requiring the parties to comply with the use of the image as though it were being used in Guernsey may go some way to create more certainty for such licences.

The licensees would then make payments to the IP Holding Company. If structured correctly, the entire income stream under the licences would be received by the IP Holding Company (the "Guernsey Company" in the diagram) and then not be subject to taxation within Guernsey.

How the IP is licensed would obviously depend on tax advice and the overall structure may differ slightly depending on the tax residence of the IP rights holder. Used correctly such a structure can result in large savings in terms of tax on royalty payments and also a greater degree of flexibility on, for example, the sale of the IP rights (a sale of shares may not be subject to any tax at all).

The above example predominantly relates to image rights. However, as has been alluded to, once an IP holder has assigned all of their IP to the IP Holding Company, such structures could be used to exploit any IP, whether registered in Guernsey or elsewhere.

**The "Club" Structure**

A slightly more complicated structure may provide the theoretical English Premier League footballer with an even more tax efficient way to hold their image rights and other IP. The structure below would most likely suit a non-UK domiciled footballer looking to move into the UK. Prior to this move, he would set up the below.

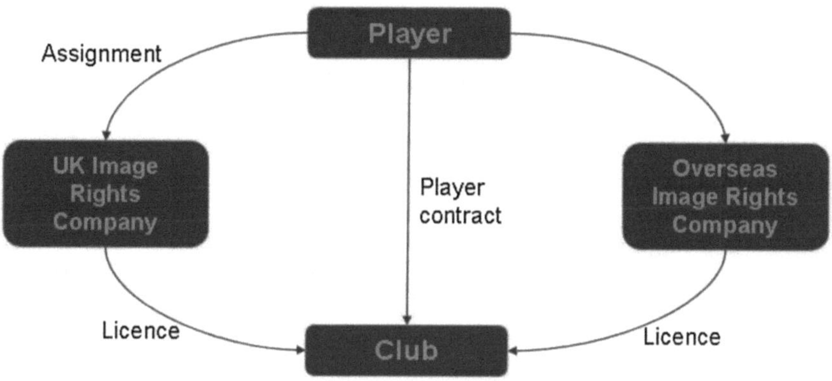


In this structure, prior to relocating to the UK the player would establish two companies intended to hold image rights (and potentially other IP): one to hold his UK based image rights and the other for all other countries. The location of the UK Image Rights Company would be subject to tax advice, but would likely be in a jurisdiction benefiting from a dual taxation treaty with the UK. The Overseas Image Rights Company would be incorporated in Guernsey.

Once the two companies had been incorporated and the footballer assigned the relevant image rights, the companies could then licence these rights to the footballer's new team as part of his contract. The royalties payable in respect of the use of his image within the UK would be paid to the UK Image Rights Company. All other royalties are paid to the Overseas Image Rights Company.

The above structure has not yet been subjected to rigorous review or testing in court and its adoption is strictly subject to legal and tax advice. However, such structures may go some way towards ensuring the proceeds of UK based image rights will be specifically definable. The Agassi[11] case found that Andre Agassi, the famous US tennis player, owed taxes in the UK on his global sponsorship income apportioned to reflect the amount applicable to the UK (for example, based on the number of UK tournaments he played in that year). Mr Agassi was taxed on his global sponsorship, even though his image rights were held by non-UK entities and payments were received from non-UK sources. It is cases such as this that

---

[11] *Agassi v Robinson (Inspector of Taxes)* [2006] *UKHL 23.*

have stopped Usain Bolt and other famous sportspersons from attending events in the UK.

Although the above structure is by no means a definitive answer to such tax practices, it may help to evidence the proportion of royalties paid in respect of UK image rights. This UK based royalty stream could potentially be used as a guide for tax purposes, rather than the much more liberal approach taken in the Agassi case.

**The PCC Model**

The concept of a protected cell company ("PCC") was a world-first when introduced in Guernsey in 1997 and has since been replicated in many other jurisdictions. This type of company is now governed by the key legislation for companies in Guernsey, the Companies (Guernsey) Law, 2008 (the "Companies Law").

A PCC is a single legal entity with a "core" and separate and distinct "cells" within it. Each cell may, but is not required, to have "cell shares". Assets and liabilities of each cell in a PCC are, by law, segregated from those of other cells and the core. Creditors of one cell will not have recourse beyond the specific cell, unless a recourse agreement has been entered into.

Although PCCs were originally used solely for investment funds and insurance purposes, they are now used for an extremely wide variety of purposes. Most notably, they are extremely useful for asset holding where the intention is to protect certain groups of assets from others. For example, where a football club or agent holds IP rights for multiple players (as set out below).

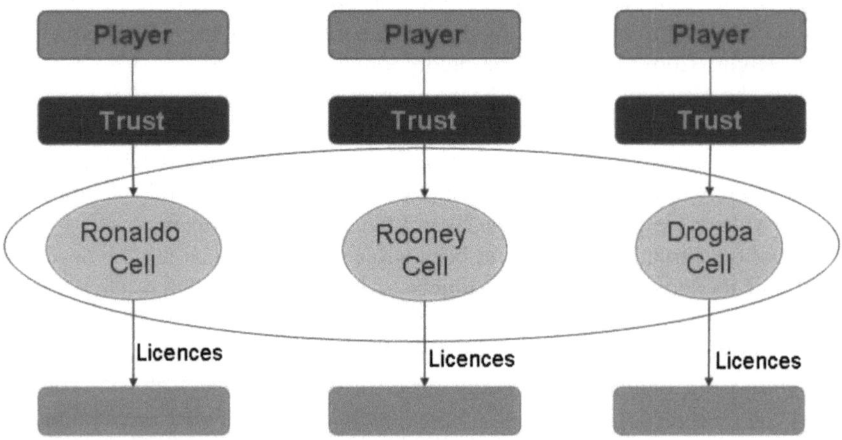


1. Player assigns image rights to cell of PCC in consideration for issuance of shares
2. Need for trust subject to tax advice

The core of the PCC would hold the IP for the club or agent (if any), with a separate cell established to hold each player's IP rights. This structure would ensure that any creditors of one player would not be able to pursue an action against any other player's or the club's IP. The club or agent would hold the core shares and the player would hold the relevant cell shares.

Otherwise the structure is very similar to the "simple licensing arrangement" described above. Each cell would licence the relevant IP rights to third parties and receive royalties and other payments in this regard. The income would then be held in the cell before being returned to the player in the most tax efficient manner.

In the event that a player transfers club or changes agent, it is not possible to transfer a cell into another PCC. It is possible to transfer the assets of a cell by way of a cell transfer order, but this will most likely require court approval. As such, the ICC Model described below may be more appropriate for such structures.

**The ICC Model**

An incorporated cell company ("ICC") is similar to a PCC in that it is a legal entity with separate "cells". However, the cells of an ICC (each an incorporated cell, or "IC") are a separate legal entity in their own right. The ICC and its ICs will share the same directors, secretary and registered office and will file one annual validation. Given the distinct legal status of the ICC and each IC, there are no issues in relation to cross liabilities.

As with a PCC, a club or agent would establish its own ICC and create an IC for each of its players. The player then assigns his IP to the IC and the shares in that IC are held by the player. Royalties are paid to the IC and subsequently returned to the player.

Although similar to a PCC, an ICC structure offers much more flexibility for the purposes of asset holding, particularly in relation to sports IP. Where a player transfers club or changes agent, it is a straightforward process requiring special resolutions of the ICC and relevant IC to simply transfer the IC to another ICC. In the example below, the Manchester United ICC Limited and Ronaldo IC could simply have approved the transfer of the Ronaldo IC to the Real Madrid ICC Limited. This allows the IP of a club or agent and all relevant players to be efficiently administered through one structure.

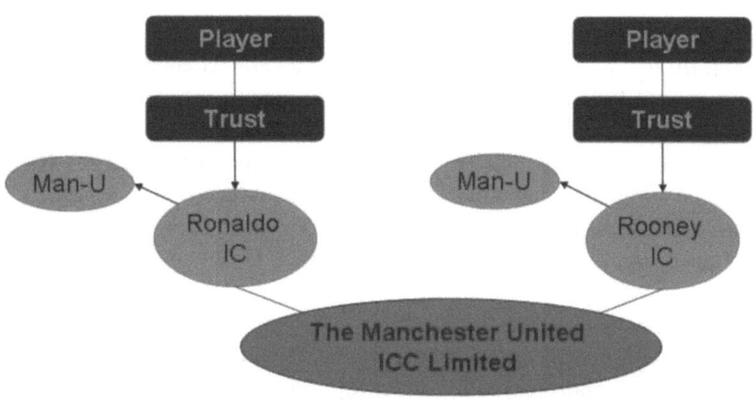

Alternatively to a transfer, and given that an IC is its own legal entity, it is also a relatively straightforward process to convert an IC into a stand-alone limited company. Structured correctly, the ICC method would be an incredibly efficient and cost-effective way to manage the IP rights of clubs or agents and the professional sportsmen they manage.

**Taxation**

When considering locating IP in an SFC, tax will always be a factor of great importance. Despite being close to the UK geographically, Guernsey's taxation system is entirely different from that of the UK. In Guernsey, there is no inheritance tax, capital gains tax, capital transfer tax or VAT. Corporate income tax is charged at a rate of 0%.

The introduction of the "Zero-10" tax regime in Guernsey brought about significant changes to the island, making it far more competitive as a jurisdiction than previously possible. While companies in Guernsey are taxed at a rate of 0%, it is the responsibility of the companies themselves to deduct tax from distributions of profits (as opposed to capital) made to its shareholders. How these profits are taxed will depend upon the shareholder's place of residence. If the shareholder is an individual resident in Guernsey, a rate of 20% (the income tax rate) is charged. If the shareholder is a company, the company standard rate of 0% applies. If the shareholder is a non-Guernsey resident, no Guernsey income tax is paid or withheld.

By way of example, a famous footballer resident in the UK for tax purposes may choose to hold his IP through an IP Holding Company similar to the "simple licensing arrangement" discussed above. Prior to creating such a structure, the footballer may, in theory, be subject to tax at a rate of 50% on the income from their IP. By creating such a structure, the footballer would be able to make a substantial difference to their net income.

It is worth noting that there have been concerns raised recently by some members of the ECOFIN Code of Conduct group as to whether the current corporate tax regimes in Guernsey and the other Crown Dependencies are strictly compliant with the spirit of the EU Code of Conduct for business taxation. Although Guernsey and the other Crown Dependencies are not part of the EU, they will generally try to comply with EU requests where possible, given the islands' close business relationship with many EU countries. Guernsey and the other Crown Dependencies have confirmed they will review their tax regimes. However, the States have confirmed that any replacement to the current "Zero-10" regime will continue to ensure that Guernsey maintains its position as one of the most competitive SFCs in the world. It has been suggested that changes may include the introduction of double-taxation treaties with other EU countries.

**Guernsey**

The Bailiwick of Guernsey incorporates the island of Guernsey as well as a number of other islands including Alderney, Sark, Herm, Jethou and Brecqhou. The official and primary language spoken is English. The islands are conveniently located in the same time zone as London and Guernsey has easy access to the UK, France and other key European countries.

As an international SFC, Guernsey's four key markets are banking, insurance, funds and fiduciary administration. As a result, Guernsey has developed modern, robust and highly regarded legal, tax and regulatory regimes. This has been highlighted in a number of ways recently, including The Banker magazine recognising Guernsey as one of the world's top five SFCs, and its early acceptance onto the OECD's 'white list' (a list of jurisdictions that have substantially implemented the internationally agreed tax standards).

Guernsey's legal system is unique. The island was historically part of Normandy (now an area of France) before becoming part of the British Isles in 1066. As a result, its legal system was originally based on the laws of Normandy, but has since followed a common law system similar to that in England. In practice, Guernsey looks to the case law of England and other Commonwealth countries for guidance where precedents have not been set in Guernsey courts. Although such decisions are not binding on Guernsey courts, they are persuasive in nature. Other than case law, the laws and practice of law in Guernsey are often very similar to that of England.

The professional services provided in Guernsey are of a world class standard. Many industry leading accountancy firms, banks, asset managers and administrators have an established presence in the island. This provides for extremely efficient provision of information and ongoing support for anyone choosing to do business within Guernsey.

The financial regulator in Guernsey is the Guernsey Financial Services Commission ("GFSC"). The GFSC's primary objective is to regulate and supervise financial services in Guernsey and help to uphold the international reputation of Guernsey as a finance centre. The GFSC is an internationally recognised regulator and ensures the financial services provided by Guernsey based companies continue to maintain the highest standard possible.

As set out above, Guernsey also has a significant amount to offer in respect of IP. There are numerous IP rights registrable in Guernsey. However, it is also possible to register (or renew) international IP rights from Guernsey. In particular, through Collas Day IP Limited (part of the Collas Day group) ("CDIP"). CDIP, along with legal advice from Collas Day, is able to offer a unique one-stop shop for international IP registration, management and protection. As the only Guernsey advocates with specific IP qualifications, Collas Day is ideally placed to provide IP legal advice with a Guernsey perspective that is second to none.

**Conclusion**

Image rights appear set to become an important part of the IP scene in the near future. Individuals and businesses with image rights and all other forms of IP are advised to think carefully about where they should hold their IP. With a high quality, robust IP regime already in place, ground-breaking IP laws in the making and the advantages of holding IP in an SFC, Guernsey is perfectly to become the home for image rights and all other IP. The structures available in Guernsey can be used to ensure the holder of any IP is able to manage and exploit this to its fullest extent.

***Collas Day***
Collas Day is a leading and highly respected Guernsey law firm with a truly global outlook. We are one of the oldest, yet most innovative, of Guernsey and Channel Islands law firms and our advocates and lawyers deliver legal solutions to businesses and private individuals in local, international, cross-border and complex multi-jurisdictional matters.

***Authors***
Jason Romer is a partner in the Commercial Department of Collas Day and a director of Collas Day IP Limited ("**CDIP**"). He has a broad corporate and commercial experience with a particular emphasis on intellectual property, utility regulation, e-commerce and IT. He has advised a wide range of Guernsey companies. Jason is the only Guernsey advocate with specialist IP post-graduate qualifications. He is a member of Guernsey's IP Specialist group and represents that group on the IP Steering Group of the Commerce and Employment department. He is the author of a number of chapters in IP publications.

Brandon Doffing is an associate in the Commercial Department of Collas Day. He is qualified as a solicitor in England & Wales and as an attorney in New York. Brandon has experience in a wide variety of corporate and commercial matters, including in relation to intellectual property. He is currently studying a Master's degree in international legal practice, which involves a specialist unit relating to the international practice of intellectual property.

***CDIP***
CDIP can register, manage and protect intellectual property. Based in Guernsey, it provides both local and international IP registration together with management of existing portfolios and IP assets. David Evans is one of the directors of CDIP. He has spent over 10 years involved in the intellectual property business, part of which as head of IP for a multinational company. David advises businesses of all sizes on their IP strategies and portfolio management. He is also qualified to register a variety of IP rights in multiple jurisdictions throughout the world.

## 15.7.4 *Appendix 4*

### The Luxembourg IP Regime, a Hole-in-one Shot for the Marketing of Sports Image Rights?*

Me Lars R. Goslings
AS AVOCATS
Luxembourg

### I. Introduction

It is an indisputable fact that the marketing of Sports Image Rights is of significant economic importance in our globalizing world, which indisputable fact is on a day-to-day basis being confirmed by the considerable sums of money being invested into the world of sports, including but not limited to the creation of sporting idols and the subsequent marketing of the relevant idols once they have been created and accepted by the public i.e. the consumer.

Despite its tiny size the Grand-Duchy of Luxembourg (hereinafter to be referred to as "Luxembourg") has generated a few remarkable sportsmen, including but not limited to the "Angel of the Mountain" Charly Gaul, the five time World Cup overall champion alpine ski racer Marc Girardelli and the country's current famous road bicycle racing brothers Fränk and Andy Schleck, which icons represent the country's proud and goal, namely to despite its tiny size play a noteworthy role in our globalizing world.

In consideration of the aforementioned, the object of the present article is to analyse whether Luxembourg can play such noteworthy role in the marketing of Sports Image Rights, more in particular the legally well-protected and tax-efficient marketing of Sports Image Rights "belonging" to international sportsmen and sportswomen (hereinafter to be jointly referred to as "Sportsmen" respectively "Sportsman").

Can Luxembourg thereby mark a Hole-in-one or does the Grand-Duchy need to satisfy with a Birdie, an Eagle or even an Albatross?

### II. The Grand-Duchy of Luxembourg

As a result of amongst others its strategic location within the European Union, the country's well-adapted legislation and the country's substantial volume of professional and multilingual service providers, Luxembourg has over the past decades succeeded in establishing itself as a major business place for important international businesses.

From an intellectual property (hereinafter to be referred to as "IP") perspective, Luxembourg has implemented all principal international agreements and treaties, including but not limited to the Agreement on Trade Related Aspects of

---

* This article was first published in *Global Sports Law and Taxation Reports,* November 2010.

Intellectual Property Rights (also known as the "TRIPS" Agreement) signed in Morocco on April 15, 1994, the Bern Convention of 1886 for the Protection of Literary and Artistic Works, the Patent Cooperation Treaty (also known as "PCT") concluded in 1970, the Paris Convention for the Protection of Industrial Property signed in France on March 20, 1883, the Patent Law Treaty (also known as "PLT") signed in Switzerland on June 1st 2000, the Madrid Agreement concerning the International Registration of Marks concluded in 1891 and the Madrid Protocol of 1989 relating to the Madrid Agreement concerning the International Registration of Marks, the memberships to which aforementioned agreements and treaties form an important basis for Luxembourg being the home of an increasing number of IP related businesses.

Another basis for the establishment of these and other businesses is constituted by the large number of Double Tax Conventions[1] concluded by Luxembourg and the benefit from European Directives such as the European Interest and Royalties Directive 2003/49/CE.

Recognizing the increasing importance of its IP related competitiveness within our globalizing world, Luxembourg has in 2007 created an IP platform by implementing a favourable tax regime to IP related businesses.

Although the Luxembourg IP regime (hereinafter to be referred to as the "IP Regime") had in first instance been created to develop Luxembourg's attractiveness for scientific companies, the IP Regime makes Luxembourg an attractive location for IP related business in the wider sense of the word, which includes but is not limited to the marketing of IP.

This logically brings to the table the question whether or not national and international Sports Image Rights could also fall within the scope of the IP Regime, as a result of which the marketing of Sports Image Rights could also benefit from the thereto related favourable tax regime?

The aforementioned question shall be analyzed by first under subsection III considering the protection of image rights under the Luxembourg law and more in particular, the protection and marketing of Sports Image Rights under the Luxembourg law.

Subsection IV shall subsequently analyse the IP Regime and the latter's application to the marketing of Sports Image Rights, the findings of which shall subsequently be summarized in the conclusion to be made under subsection V.

---

1 Luxembourg has concluded double tax treaties with the following countries:
South Africa, Albania, Germany, Argentina, Armenia, Austria, Azerbaijan, Bahrain, Barbuda, Belgium, Brazil, Bulgaria, Canada, China, Cyprus, South Korea, Denmark, United Arab Emirates, Spain, Estonia, United States of America, Finland, France, Georgia, Greece, Hong Kong, Hungary, India, Indonesia, Ireland, Iceland, Israel, Italy, Japan, Kazakhstan, Kyrgyzstan, Kuwait, Latvia, Liechtenstein, Lithuania, Malaysia, Malta, Morocco, Mauritius, Mexico, Moldavia, Monaco, Mongolia, Norway, Uzbekistan, Netherlands, Poland, Portugal, Qatar, Czech Republic, Romania, United Kingdom, Russia, San Marino, Singapore, Slovenia, Sweden, Switzerland, Thailand, Trinidad and Tobago, Tunisia, Turkey and Vietnam.

**III. Sports Image Rights Under Luxembourg Law**

The present subsection shall first under subsection III.1 give an introduction to the general protection of image rights under the Luxembourg law, which general protection consists of the protection of an individual's private life including but not limited to the protection of images taken of an individual.

Subsection III.2 shall subsequently analyze the marketing of image rights, more in particular Sports Image Rights under the Luxembourg law, including the protection of Sports Image Rights for such marketing purposes.

**III. 1 The Protection of Image Rights Under Luxembourg Law**

An individual's image rights in fact designate the relevant individual's property rights with respect to the relevant individual's personality. Consequently, the individual's image rights include the relevant individual's right to prevent the unauthorised use of its personal characteristics including but not limited to its name, likeness, voice and signature.

There is no specific Luxembourg law regulating the protection of an individual's image rights, following which the protection of image rights must be based on different Luxembourg laws.

The main relevant law is the Luxembourg law dated August 11th 1982 on the protection of a person's private life (Loi du 11 août 1982 concernant la protection de la vie privée), article 1 of which law stipulates that "Chacun a droit au respect de sa vie privée. Les juges peuvent, sans préjudice de la réparation du dommage subi, prescrire toutes mesures, telles que séquestre, saisie et autres, propres à empêcher ou faire cesser une atteinte à l'intimité de la vie privée, ces mesures peuvent, s'il y a urgence, être ordonnées en référé". Article 5 of the said law further stipulates that "Est puni des peines prévues à l'article 2,[2] celui qui a sciemment publié ou fait publier, par quelque voie que se soit, le montage réalisé avec les paroles ou les images d'une personne sans le consentement de celui-ci, s'il n'apparaît pas à l'évidence qu'il s'agit d'un montage ou s'il n'en est pas expressément fait mention"

Consequently, every individual is entitled to the respect of its private life, which private life may be protected by all legal means, including but not limited to seizures and sequestration to stop or avoid any infringement to an individual's private life, notwithstanding the damages to be additionally claimed from the relevant violator. The law further sentences the publication of a dubbing with some person's images and voices without the relevant person's consent, except if the absence of the relevant person's consent is explicitly mentioned or indisputably follows from the relevant publication.

---

[2] Est puni d'un emprisonnement de huit jours à un an et d'une amende de 251 euros à 5.000 euros, ou d'une de ces peines seulement, quiconque volontairement porté atteinte à l'intimité de la vie privé d'autrui.

Claims for damages following the violation of image rights shall be based on article 1382 and 1383 of the Luxembourg Civil Code.[3] The adjudication of such damages requires a fault, a specific damage and a correlation of cause and effect between the relevant fault and the relevant damage.

With respect to images, one can admit on the basis of Luxembourg case law that the protection of images under Luxembourg law in fact consists of each person's right to allow or reject to be photographed i.e. taken in pictures and each person's right to control the use of the relevant pictures. Following the judgement of the Civil Chamber of the District Court of Luxembourg (*Tribunal d'Arrondissement de et à Luxembourg*) dated June 2nd 1976, "any person has the exclusive right to its image and to the use of the relevant image and the relevant person may oppose the distribution of such image without its consent". Consequently, the taking and use of someone's picture in principal requires an authorisation from the to be pictured person, which authorisation, if provided, the relevant person may at any time retract.

Nevertheless, distinction should be made between images of a person shot in a private place and those shot in a public place. On the one hand, the unauthorised publication or use of an image of a person shot in a private place constitutes an infringement of the relevant person's privacy and image rights. On the other hand, if the image of the relevant person has been taken in a public place and the image diffused does not imply any invasion to the relevant person's private life, there is no infringement of the relevant person's image rights and there is a presumption of an authorisation having been granted by the relevant person.

In addition must be considered the necessity of the diffusion of the relevant images for the legitimate needs of information of the public. Consequently, the diffusion of images of a footballer playing a match at the football world cup in a TV report on the relevant sporting event does not infringe the relevant footballer's image rights, following which the relevant footballer can in principle not oppose to the diffusion of the relevant images. The relevant footballer is in fact presumed to have granted its authorisation to the relevant diffusion, which presumed authorisation stops when the footballer explicitly opposes to the diffusion of the relevant images, provided that the diffusion is not necessary for the legitimate needs of information of the public.

Consequently, Sportsmen have the exclusive right to prevent the unauthorised publication of their images, provided that the relevant publication is not made for information purposes only and that the relevant publication does violate the relevant Sportsman's private life.

---

[3] Article 1382 of the Luxembourg civil code states that: « Tout fait quelconque de l'homme, qui cause à autrui un dommage, oblige celui par la faute duquel il est arrivé, à le réparer ».
Article 1383 of the Luxembourg civil code states that: « Chacun est responsable du dommage qu'il a causé non seulement par son fait, mais encore par sa négligence ou par son imprudence ».

**III. 2 The Marketing of Sports Image Rights**

For the present piece of writing the term "Sports Image Rights" refers to the image rights of Sportsmen, which image rights include but are not limited to the relevant Sportsmen's fame, images, names, nicknames, signatures and other personal characteristics.

For the analysis of the present article, the marketing of Sports Image Rights shall be subdivided into the direct and indirect marketing of Sports Image Rights.

On the one hand, the direct marketing of Sports Image Rights refers to any and all marketing acts requiring the personal appearance of the relevant Sportsman, including but not limited to the personal appearance of the relevant Sportsman in publicities, talk shows and public and private events.

The protection mechanisms of the relevant Sports Image Rights are in fact the protection mechanisms referred to under subsection III.1. As such, the Sportsman may oppose to the marketing of his voice or images without his authorisation under the conditions referred to under subsection III.1. In the same way, the unauthorized use of a Sportsman's double for publicities, talk shows and events would constitute a violation of the relevant Sportsman's image rights, which violation the relevant Sportsman could in principle challenge by the legal means referred to under subsection III.1.

The indirect marketing of Sports Image Rights on the other hand refers to any and all marketing acts related to a Sportsman's image rights not requiring the relevant Sportsman's personal appearance. Such indirect marketing of Sports Image Rights includes but is not limited to the "branding" of the relevant Sportsman's names, nicknames, slogans, pictures and/or other characteristics on a wide selection of products and services.

Contrary to the first-mentioned direct marketing of Sports Image Rights, such indirect marketing requires an anterior protection of the relevant Sportsman's image rights, including but not limited to the relevant Sportsman's names, nicknames, images, and slogans to be used for the marketing of the relevant products and services. This need of an anterior protection results from a combination of issues, such as the non-exclusivity of non-registered names and the consequent need to have the relevant names registered and protected for their commercial use and against the potential abuse of the relevant names by third parties.

The relevant Sports Image Rights can be protected by different means, including but not limited to:

- The registration of names and/or of combinations of names and words as trademarks;
- The registration of logos, signatures, images and/or physical likenesses as trademarks; and
- The registration of domain names consisting of the relevant Sportsman's names and/or combinations of such names and other words.

## IV. The Marketing of Sports Image Rights Under the Luxembourg IP Regime

For the analysis of the applicability of the IP Regime to the marketing of Sports Image Rights, the present subsection shall first under subsection IV.1 give an analysis of the IP Regime, followed by an application of the IP Regime to the marketing of Sports Image Rights.

### IV. 1 The Luxembourg IP Regime

The attractiveness of Luxembourg with respect to the creation and commercial use of IP has significantly increased since January 1st 2008 by the introduction of the IP Regime for the tax-efficient commercial use of specific IP, which tax optimisation regime has been laid down in article 50bis of the Luxembourg Income Tax Act (*Loi de l'impôt sur le Revenu*) (hereinafter referred to as the "Tax Act").

Article 50bis of the Tax Act provides an 80% tax exemption on the net income and capital gains derived on specific IP rights. Consequently, the effective combined rate of Corporate Income Tax and Municipal Business Tax rate on the aforementioned net income and capital gains is reduced to about 5,72%, depending on the city in which the relevant subject has chosen its domicile. In addition, the relevant IP rights are fully exempted from Net Wealth Tax.

#### (a) Subjects to the Luxembourg IP Regime

The IP Regime applies to:

- fully taxable resident and non-resident individuals carrying on a business in Luxembourg;
- Luxembourg Resident Corporate Entities; and/or
- Luxembourg Local Permanent Establishments of Non-Resident Corporate Entities.

Consequently, the group of beneficiaries of the IP Regime is not restricted to Luxembourg resident individuals as in principle any foreign resident may benefit from the IP Regime by directly carrying on a business in Luxembourg or indirectly, via a Luxembourg Resident Corporate Entity or a Luxembourg Local Permanent Establishment of a Non-Resident Corporate Entity (hereinafter to be referred to as a "Luxco").

#### (b) Conditions for the Applicability of Luxembourg IP Regime

As already mentioned here above, the applicability of the IP Regime is limited to a restricted number of IP meeting the cumulative conditions determined by article 50bis of the Tax Act and further enlightened in the Circular of the Luxembourg tax authorities (*Circulaire du directeur des contributions L.I.R. no. 50bis/1 sur l'exonération partielle des revenues produits par certains droits de la propriété intellectuelle*) dated March 5th 2009 (hereinafter referred to as "Circular").

First, the IP qualifying for the IP Regime (hereinafter to be referred to as the "Qualified IP"), is limited to the following types of IP.

- Copyrights on software. Copyrights other than software copyrights are excluded from the IP Regime;
- Patents, including Luxembourg and foreign substitutes of Patents, such as "Gebrauchsmuster", "Petits Brevets", "Certificats d'Utilité", "Modèles d'Utilité" and "Certificats complémentaires de protection";
- Trademarks including but not limited to word marks, figurative marks and sound marks;
- Registered 2D and 3D Designs; and
- Domain names, which the Circular defines as a "unique, personal electronic address that locates a particular website in the virtual world, thereby allowing the owner of such a domain name to advertise its presence to other internet users and to display or market the goods and services it offers".

Consequently, the IP Regime does not apply to other IP including but not limited to plans, formulas, trade secrets and other related rights, or income derived from the leasing of industrial, commercial or scientific equipment.

In order to have the Qualified IP benefit from the IP Regime, the Qualified IP must first have been created or acquired after December 31st 2007. It is important to underline that by extending the present condition to Qualified IP having been "acquired" after December 31st 2007, the applicability of the IP Regime is not restricted to Qualified IP having been created after December 31st 2007 as Qualified IP created until the aforementioned date can benefit from the IP Regime by the accomplishment of a transfer on or following the date of January 1st 2008.

In case of the Qualified IP being held by a Luxco, the Luxco may further not have acquired the Qualified IP from a "directly associated company".

Pursuant to article 50bis para 5 of the Tax Act, a "directly associated company" of the Luxco is a:

- Direct parent company of the Luxco holding a direct participation of at least 10% of the share capital of the Luxco;
- Direct subsidiary of the Luxco, of which subsidiary the Luxco holds a direct participation of at least 10% of the share capital; or
- Direct sister company of the Luxco if a third parent company holds direct participations of each 10% of the share capitals of the sister company and the Luxco.

Whether or not a company is to be qualified as a "directly associated company" of the Luxco needs to be considered at the moment of acquisition of the Qualified IP by the relevant Luxco. In case of a contribution in kind to the Luxco by another company, the question whether or not to qualify the contributing company as a "directly associated company" needs to be considered in view of the association between both companies immediately prior to the accomplishment of the relevant contribution in kind.

It is important to point out that the aforementioned restriction only applies to the acquisition of the Qualified IP by a Luxco from a "directly" associated company. Consequently, the restriction does not apply to companies, which are only "indirectly" associated to the Luxco.

The restriction does further only apply to the "acquisition" of the Qualified IP by a Luxco, following which the restriction does not apply in case of the licensing or sale of the Qualified IP by the relevant Luxco to any of its associated companies.

Favourable to individuals including Sportsmen is the fact that the restriction does further not apply to the acquisition of Qualified IP from associated individuals, following which a Luxco can without any restriction acquire the Qualified IP from its individual shareholders, including but not limited to Sportsmen.

Last but not least, Article 50bis of the Tax Act requires the activation of Qualified IP related expenses, depreciations and deductions in connection with the creation or acquisition of the Qualified IP.

Consequently, the Qualified IP related amortizations, expenses and write-downs must be recorded on the Luxco's balance sheet and must further be included in the profits and loss allocation as from the first fiscal year for which the benefit of the IP Regime is applied, provided that for a given year the aforementioned expenses, amortizations and write-downs exceed the income in relation with the same Qualified IP.

## IV. 2 Sports Image Rights Under the Luxembourg IP Regime

### (a) Sports Image Rights as Qualified IP

In consideration of the aforementioned conditions of the IP Regime, one can conclude that Sports Image Rights can benefit from the favourable tax regime of the IP Regime, more in particular with respect to the Sports Image Rights subject to the indirect marketing referred to under subsection III.2.

As explained under subsection III.2, this indirect marketing of Sports Image Rights is constituted of the marketing of amongst others the relevant Sportsman's names, nicknames, slogans and signatures, which Sports Image Rights can fall within the scope of the Qualified IP.

As such, the relevant Sportsman's names, nicknames, slogans and signatures can and should actually be registered i.e. protected as trademarks in order to maximize the protection of the relevant image rights against any infringement by any third party. Under the condition to comply with the trademarks related conditions, even images and voices of Sportsmen are eligible for registration as trademarks and as such can fall within the scope of the IP Regime.

Simultaneously, names, nicknames and slogans can be registered as domain names, on the basis of which registration these image rights can once again qualify as Qualified IP.

In consideration of the aforementioned, Sports Image Rights registered i.e. protected by the means of trademarks and/or domain names qualify as Qualified IP (hereinafter to be referred to as the "Qualified Sports IP") and as such fall within the scope of the IP Regime benefiting from the favourable tax regime of article 50bis of the Tax Act.

**(b) Subjects to the IP Regime**

With reference to the subjects of the IP Regime, one must conclude that most Sportsmen are not in the position to personally be subject to the IP Regime as most Sportsmen generating income from their image rights shall not qualify as fully taxable resident or non-resident individuals carrying on a business in Luxembourg, which is amongst others due to the circumstances that most professional Sportsmen are not residing in Luxembourg and need to travel the world in order to practice their sports.

The aforementioned substance problem can however easily be solved by making use of a corporate entity to market the relevant Sports Image Rights. In fact, the IP Regime is very open to such corporate solutions as the IP Regime is applicable to Luxembourg resident corporate entities as well as to Luxembourg local permanent establishments of non-resident corporate entities. Luxembourg resident corporate entities are nevertheless most advisable in order to reduce the risk of potential disputes with either Luxembourg or foreign authorities on the domicile of the relevant corporate entity.

A good example of such Luxembourg resident corporate entity for the marketing of Sports Image Rights is the Luxembourg "*Société de Participations Financières*" (hereinafter to be referred to as the "SOPARFI"), a fully taxable holding company entitled to carry out commercial i.e. VAT subjected operations. As such the SOPARFI is subject to the multiple Double Tax Conventions concluded by Luxembourg and the European Interest and Royalties Directive (2003/49/EC), which conventions and directive are of great importance to minimize the effective tax burden to the income to be generated with the marketing of the Sports Image Rights, which proceeds are most likely to be of international nature.

The SOPARFI may be incorporated under the legal form of a private limited company (*Société à Responsabilité Limitée*) or public limited company (*Société Anonyme*) with a minimum issued capital to the amount of € 12.500,00 respectively € 31.000,00.

The SOPARFI must further have at least one individual or corporate shareholder. Most shareholders prefer the legal form of a public limited company as the relevant type of company allows shareholders to choose between nominative and bearer shares assuring a maximum of confidentiality to the shareholder of the SOPARFI.

Another attractive characteristic of the SOPARFI and other Luxembourg resident corporate entities is the absence of any capital duty at the incorporation of the relevant corporate entity.

It is of course understood that the SOPARFI's registered office must be in Luxembourg and that the board and shareholders meetings should also be held in Luxembourg in order to minimize potential substance disputes with Luxembourg and foreign authorities.

**(c) The Acquisition of the Qualified Sports IP by the Luxco**

A valuable characteristic of the IP Regime is the fact that the beneficiary of the IP Regime is not required to be the inventor, creator or initial applicant of the

Qualified IP, following which the Qualified Sports IP is not required to be either personally held nor marketed by the relevant Sportsman in order to be subject to the IP Regime.

Consequently, the Qualified Sports IP may be held by one of the legal entities referred to here above under subsection (b), following which Sportsmen, in order to benefit from the IP Regime without being Luxembourg professionals, should make "their" Qualified Sports IP to be held by a Luxco such as a SOPARFI.

The relevant Luxco may acquire the Qualified Sports IP by creating the relevant Qualified Sports IP and/or by acquiring the relevant Qualified Sports IP from any third party individual or legal entity.

The Luxco may on the one hand create the Qualified Sports IP by the registration of the thereto-related trademarks and/or domain names, in which case the Luxco shall have the legal and commercial ownership over the relevant Qualified Sports IP.

The Luxco may on the other hand acquire the Qualified Sports IP by acquiring the legal title over the relevant Qualified Sports IP or by acquiring the license to use the relevant Qualified Sports IP, which legal title and/or license the Luxco may acquire from the individuals and legal entities referred to under subsection IV.1, including but not limited to the relevant Sportsmen.

In case of an acquisition of the legal title, the Luxembourg tax authorities require the relevant acquisition to from a tax perspective qualify as an alienation of the relevant Qualified Sports IP at a fair market value in order to qualify for the IP Regime.

**(d) The Commercial Use of the Qualified Sports IP by the Luxco**

The Luxembourg IP Regime offers to the Luxco a considerable flexibility with respect to the marketing methods of the Qualified Sports IP and the applicability of the IP Regime to the thereto related revenues.

First the Luxco may itself produce and market goods and services based on the Qualified Sports IP, which method shall nevertheless rarely be chosen by the relevant Luxco and Sportsmen in consideration of amongst others the considerable volumes of investments and efforts required with respect to the production and marketing of the relevant goods and services. In addition, the relevant method requires a determination of the relevant income attributable to the Qualified Sports IP and an acceptation of the relevant Qualified Sports IP income by the Luxembourg tax authorities.

Consequently, the licensing of the Qualified Sports IP to third parties against the payment of royalties to the Luxco is much more attractive as in principle the relevant method requires considerably inferior volumes of investment, minimizing the financial risk related to the marketing of the relevant Qualified Sports IP.

As the Luxco may in principle license the relevant Qualified Sports IP to third and affiliated parties, the IP Regime provides the Luxco and Sportsmen with a maximum of discretion with respect to the marketing of the Qualified Sports IP and the structuring of the relevant Sportsmen's wealth and business.

The third method for the marketing of the Qualified Sports IP benefiting from the IP Regime consists of the sale of the relevant Qualified Sports IP by the Luxco. Similar to the licensing of the Qualified Sports IP, the Luxco may in principle at its discretion sell the relevant Qualified Sports IP to third and affiliated parties, providing a maximum of discretion to the structuring of the relevant Sportsmen's wealth and business.

**(e) The Luxco's Benefits From the Application of the IP Regime**

As already shortly referred to here above, the tax related benefits of the IP Regime to the commercial use of Qualified Sports IP are the following:

First, the IP Regime provides an 80% tax exemption to the positive net income originating from the Qualified Sports IP's commercial use.

As a Luxembourg resident company, the Luxco is in principle subject to a Corporate Income Tax rate of 21%, if the tax base exceeds € 15.000,00 per year, and a Municipal Business Tax on its trading profits, the rate of which Municipal Business Tax varies depending on the municipality where the Luxco is established. If the Luxco is established in Luxembourg City, the Municipal Business Tax is about 6.75% per year, following which the combined Corporate Income Tax and Municipal Business Tax rate of a Luxembourg City established Luxco is about 28.59%.

Consequently, the IP Regime, as a result of the aforementioned 80% tax exemption to the positive net income originating from the Qualified Sports IP's commercial use, provides the relevant Luxembourg City established Luxco with a combined effective rate of Corporate Income Tax and Municipal Business Tax of only 5.72%.

The positive net income consists of the difference between the gross revenue and all expenses in direct connection with the gross revenue, which expenses include amortisation and write-offs recorded in respect of each particular Qualified Sports IP and the interest deriving from the financing of the relevant Qualified Sports IP.

The IP Regime further provides the full tax deductibility of the negative income of the Qualified Sports IP, which tax loss may be offset against other types of the Luxco's income.

The negative income of the Qualified Sports IP consists of the excess of expenses in direct economic connection with the Qualified Sports IP over the revenues of the relevant Qualified Sports IP in a relevant financial year.

The IP Regime in addition makes the capital gains on the disposal of the Qualified Sports IP benefit from the aforementioned combined effective rate of Corporate Income Tax and Municipal Business Tax of only about 5.72%, which effective tax rate is again provided by the means of a 80% tax exemption to the capital gains on the disposal of the relevant Qualified Sports IP.

The IP Regime moreover excludes the Qualified Sports IP from the Luxco's tax base for the Net Worth Tax, following which the Luxco is not due any Net Worth Tax over the value of the Luxco's Qualified Sports IP, which value can of course be significant in the case of famous Sportsmen.

Of great benefit further are the multiple Double Tax Conventions concluded by Luxembourg and European Interest and Royalties Directive 2003/49/EC.

The weight of this benefit follows from the fact that the marketing of Qualified Sports IP is a global business, in which the Luxco will grant licenses to and subsequently receive royalty payments from entities established all over the world. Consequently, the applicability of Double Tax Conventions shall in most cases considerably reduce the withholding tax due over the relevant royalty payments to be made to the Luxco, following which the Luxco's relevant income shall be most efficiently optimized from a tax point of view.

Although not a particular characteristic of the IP Regime, another benefit of the commercial use of the Qualified Sports IP by the means of a Luxco, more in particular a Luxembourg resident corporate entity, constitutes the fact that the incorporation of such resident corporate entity does not require any capital duty but merely a one-off registration tax of € 75,00.

**(f) Potential Exit Strategies**

Taken into consideration that a good structure requires good potential exit strategies, the Luxembourg lawmaker has implemented a few elements providing good potential exit strategies from the IP Regime, if such exit would be considered necessary.

An important condition for those exit strategies is already provided by Luxembourg not being listed on any of the OECD's black or grey lists of uncooperative tax havens. Consequently, funds and assets transferred from Luxembourg to other countries are in principle not being considered "suspicious" by the authorities of the countries to which the relevant assets are being transferred.

The first potential exit strategy would consist of a sale of the Qualified Sports IP by the Luxco to a third or affiliated party, the proceeds of which sale would, as already mentioned here above, benefit from the IP Regime and subsequently be subject to an effective total corporate and municipal tax burden of only about 5.72%.

The disposal of the Qualified Sports IP could subsequently be followed by amongst others a disposal, migration, liquidation or different use of the relevant Luxco.

The second potential exit strategy could consist of a sale of the relevant Luxco to a third or affiliated party, which sale could under certain conditions be exempted from Luxembourg taxation.

The third potential exit strategy could consist of a migration of the Luxco to another country, which exit strategy would require a tax-efficient structuring of the relevant migration to the relevant third country.

**V. Conclusion**

In consideration of the aforementioned one must conclude that the IP Regime in fact is a perfect Hole-in-one shot for the tax-efficient indirect marketing of Sports Image Rights.

The reason therefore lies in the fact that the indirect marketing of Sports Image Rights anyway requires the registration of the relevant Sports Image Rights as trademarks and/or domain names, which registration is fundamental to the protection and the subsequent marketing of the relevant Sports Image Rights and thereto related Sportsman's rights.

This anyway needed registration makes the relevant Sports Image Rights qualify as Qualified Sports IP and as such eligible for the IP Regime provided that the IP Regime's other conditions are also being accomplished.

The accomplishment of these further conditions does however not constitute any serious obstacle to the applicability of the IP Regime as the IP Regime itself provides enough elements for the completion of the relevant conditions. A good example of these elements is the applicability of the IP Regime to Qualified Sports IP holding Luxco's, following which any Sportsman can make its relevant image rights subject to the IP Regime.

In addition, the possibility to have a Luxco market the relevant Sports Image Rights provides the relevant Sportsman with a maximum of discretion to structure the protection and marketing of the relevant image rights. Another example of these elements consists of the multiple ways by which the Luxco may acquire and/or create the relevant Sports Image Rights, again providing the Luxco and Sportsmen with a maximum of discretion with respect to the marketing and structuring of their Sports Image Rights.

Consequently and in consideration of the IP Regime's tax related benefits, one must conclude that although Luxembourg is unlikely to once take home the football world cup, the Grand-Duchy, by means of its IP Regime has definitely set the standards for the well-protected and tax-effective marketing of the relevant footballers' and other Sportsmen's image rights.

**About the Author:**
Lars Goslings is a senior associate at the Luxembourg law firm AS AVOCATS. He is a member of the Dutch and Luxembourg bar and specialises in corporate and intellectual property law, with a particular focus on international issues, with respect to which fields of expertise Lars represents and advises Luxembourg and foreign corporations and professionals.

Contact: AS AVOCATS
Me Lars R. Goslings
1, Rue Jean-Pierre Brasseur
L-1258 Luxembourg
GD Luxembourg
Tel.: (+352) 44 46 331
Fax: (+352) 45 43 03
Email: l.goslings@as-avocats.com[4]

[4] Please note that the above article is merely intended to comment on the relevant issues of Luxembourg law and is not intended to provide legal advice. Before taking action or relying on the comments and the information given, the addressees should seek specific advice on the matters which concern them.

# Chapter 16
# EU Aspects

## 16.1 Introductory Remarks

Over the last 36 years or so, The European Union (EU), through the European Commission and the Court of Justice of the European Union (CJEU) has developed a clear Policy and also a distinct body of EU Law in relation to Sport.[1]

In a thought-provoking article entitled 'Is there such a thing as EU sports law?' which appears in the first issue of 'Global Sports Law and Taxation Reports',[2] Stephen Weatherill, Jacques Delors Professor of European Law, Somerville College and the Faculty of Law, University of Oxford, answers this question in broad general terms at the beginning of his article as follows:

> "The simple answer to the question posed in the title to this paper is: yes, there is such a thing as EU sports law!
>
> But most simple answers tend to mislead, and the risk is real here too. There is such a thing as EU sports law, in the sense that since the entry into force of the Treaty of Lisbon on 1 December 2009 sport has been explicitly recognised as an area in which the EU has authority to intervene. However, this is apt to mislead in two quite different senses. First, it obscures the point that December 2009 was certainly a notable milestone in the shaping of EU sports law, but that in fact the relevant newly-introduced Treaty provisions are cautiously drafted and limited in their scope. They emphatically do not elevate the EU to the position of general 'sports regulator' in Europe. So, in short, one should not get too excited about them. Second, a focus on the Treaty reforms of 2009 obscures appreciation that for some 35 years the EU has already exerted an influence on sports governance in Europe. Beginning with its famous Walrave and Koch judgment[3] in 1974 the Court of Justice has subjected sport to the requirements of what was then EC law, and is now EU law, in so far as it constitutes an economic activity. So sport has been brought within the explicit scope

---

[1] See *The European Union and Sport: Legal and Policy Documents* by R C R Siekmann and J W Soek (Eds.), 2005 TMC Asser Press, The Hague, The Netherlands; and *European Sports Law: Collected Papers* by S. Weatherill, 2007 TMC Asser Press, The Hague, The Netherlands.

[2] 2 GSLTR, 2010/1, at pp. 10–13.

[3] Case 36/74 [1974] ECR 1405.

I. S. Blackshaw, *Sports Marketing Agreements: Legal, Fiscal and Practical Aspects*, ASSER International Sports Law Series, DOI: 10.1007/978-90-6704-793-7_16,

> of the EU Treaties only as late as December 2009 but well in advance of that date sport, though unmentioned by the Treaty, was required to comply with its rules in so far as it constituted an economic activity—which meant, most prominently, that sporting practices fell to be tested against the Treaty prohibitions against practices which are anti-competitive or which obstruct inter-State trade or which discriminate on the basis of nationality. So an EU sports law (of sorts) developed as a result of the steady accretion of decisional practice where sporting rules exerted an economic effect and interfered with the fulfilment of the EU's mission."

As far as the commercial exploitation of Sports TV rights is concerned, EU law also has a significant part to play in this field in that, as laid down by the European Court of Justice in the *Walrave and Koch* case, cited above, an economic activity is involved.

Professor Weatherill explains the intervention of EU law particularly in the field of Sports TV rights in the following terms:

> "... the prominence of EC law's intervention in sport in recent years is above all the consequence of the 'commercialisation' of the sector, in particular as a result of its close association with the helter–skelter development of the broadcasting industry. In fact, much of the economically significant sports-related material that tumbled into the Commission's in-tray in the late 1990s was concerned directly or indirectly with broadcasting. In some respects the Commission's recent preoccupation with sport has been driven by its need to monitor the commercially much more important broadcasting sector, in which it is profoundly anxious to forestall practices that will facilitate existing incumbents' anxiety to impede new entrants. And it is highly plausible that the pace of technological change will increasingly throw up new forms of rapid mass communication, generating intensified fragmentation in the pattern of audiovisual services. This will fuel yet more demand for rights to broadcast sports events, and bring with it yet more challenges for EC competition law."[4]

As will be appreciated, if only from the brief but pertinent introductory remarks above, the EU and Sport is a vast subject in its own right—not least in the field of Sports TV rights[5]—and, therefore, in this chapter, we will concentrate on just a few aspects of EU law in relation to Sports Marketing Agreements, namely:

- Collective Selling of Sports TV Rights;
- Territorial Restrictions in Sports Merchandising and Licensing Agreements; and
- Options to Renew and Rights of First Refusal in Sports Marketing Agreements Generally.

Clearly these legal principles and other aspects of EU Law, in general, and EU Competition Law, in particular, need to be taken into account when negotiating

[4] See S Weatherill, 'European Sports Law Collected Papers' 2007, TMC Asser Press, The Hague, The Netherlands, at p. 296.

[5] See 'TV Rights and Sport-Legal Aspects', Ian Blackshaw, Steve Cornelius and Robert Siekmann (Eds.), 2009 TMC Asser Press, The Hague, The Netherlands.

and drafting Sports Marketing Agreements generally, which, for one reason or another, have an EU dimension to them.[6]

## 16.2 EU Competition Rules

Before looking at the above particular EU aspects in turn, a reminder of the EU Competition Rules now enshrined in Articles 101 and 102 of the Treaty on the Functioning of the European Union (TFEU)[7] as follows:

*Article 101* (ex Article 81 TEC)

1. The following shall be prohibited as incompatible with the internal market: all agreements between undertakings, decisions by associations of undertakings and concerted practices which may affect trade between Member States and which have as their object or effect the prevention, restriction or distortion of competition within the internal market, and in particular those which:
   (a) directly or indirectly fix purchase or selling prices or any other trading conditions;
   (b) limit or control production, markets, technical development, or investment;
   (c) share markets or sources of supply;
   (d) apply dissimilar conditions to equivalent transactions with other trading parties, thereby placing them at a competitive disadvantage;
   (e) make the conclusion of contracts subject to acceptance by the other parties of supplementary obligations which, by their nature or according to commercial usage, have no connection with the subject of such contracts.
2. Any agreements or decisions prohibited pursuant to this Article shall be automatically void.
3. The provisions of para 1 may, however, be declared inapplicable in the case of:
   - any agreement or category of agreements between undertakings,
   - any decision or category of decisions by associations of undertakings,
   - any concerted practice or category of concerted practices,

[6] See, for example, the *Danish Tennis Federation* (DTF) case, OJ C 138/7, 1996. In this case, the DTF authorised three manufacturers to label their balls as 'official' and only such balls could be used in DTF tournaments. To qualify for 'official' status did not require any particular technical criteria to be satisfied: the arrangement was purely a revenue raising exercise. The Commission found the practice as being anti-competitive and ordered the DTF to allow other manufacturers of tennis balls to participate in the scheme.

[7] C 115/47 EN Official Journal of the European Union 9.5.2008.

which contributes to improving the production or distribution of goods or to promoting technical or economic progress, while allowing consumers a fair share of the resulting benefit, and which does not:

(a) impose on the undertakings concerned restrictions which are not indispensable to the attainment of these objectives;
(b) afford such undertakings the possibility of eliminating competition in respect of a substantial part of the products in question.

*Article 102* (ex Article 82 TEC)
Any abuse by one or more undertakings of a dominant position within the internal market or in a substantial part of it shall be prohibited as incompatible with the internal market in so far as it may affect trade between Member States.
Such abuse may, in particular, consist in:

(a) directly or indirectly imposing unfair purchase or selling prices or other unfair
trading conditions;
(b) limiting production, markets or technical development to the prejudice of consumers;
(c) applying dissimilar conditions to equivalent transactions with other trading parties, thereby placing them at a competitive disadvantage;
(d) making the conclusion of contracts subject to acceptance by the other parties of supplementary obligations which, by their nature or according to commercial usage, have no connection with the subject of such contracts.

We now turn to the particular EU aspects for consideration.

## 16.3 Collective Selling of Sports TV Rights

In this context, the starting point, as far EU Sports Law is concerned is the leading 2003 Decision of the Commission, which involved the collective selling of the broadcasting rights to the UEFA European Champions League.[8] This Decision has been used as kind of 'template' in subsequent sports broadcasting cases at the national level; and then there is the unresolved legal questions regarding the matter of the so-called 'organisational solidarity' in sport—considered to be legally and politically sensitive—which are of crucial importance in practice.

Following the Champions League Decision, the Commission requires the following conditions to be satisfied when offering for sale on a collective basis the TV rights to a sports event:

- An open tender;
- An 'unbundling' of the offer allowing more than a single buyer;

[8] Dec. 2003/778.

- No excessive exclusivity (a term of three years being regarded as a general norm); and
- No automatic renewal (regarded as a disguised extension of the term of the exclusivity).[9]

The Commission's aims in relation to opening up competition within the single EU market in the field of sports broadcasting rights may be summarised in the following remarks of the Competition Commissioner, Neelie Kroes, in the context of the 2005 Commission Decision in the German Bundesliga case[10]:

> "The decision benefits both football fans and the game. Fans benefit from new products and greater choice. Leagues and clubs benefit from the increased coverage of their games. Readily available premium content such as top football boosts innovation and growth in the media and information technology sectors. Moreover, open markets and access to content are an essential safeguard against media concentration."[11]

As mentioned above, the EU Commission now requires that the collective sale of sports TV rights be carried out through an open tender—in effect an auction—and the terms of the tender must comply with EU requirements on tendering. The Author of this Book requested a copy of the Form of Tender for the Sale of the TV Rights to the UEFA European Champions League, for inclusion in this Book for general information and interest purposes, but the request was denied by UEFA on the grounds that the document is confidential. So much for open tendering!

Incidentally, the same rules also apply to the collective buying of sports broadcasting rights and the European Broadcasting Union (EBU) ('Eurovision') have been involved in a number of EU Competition Law cases.[12]

Also, a brief mention should be made of the so-called 'Television without Frontiers' Directive,[13] allowing EU Member States to draw up lists of 'protected events' which must be available on live or deferred coverage on 'free to view' television, and the House of Lords decision in the English case of *R v Independent Television Commissioners ex p TV Danmark 1 Ltd.*[14] in which the Court held that the protection for certain designated sports events "was not qualified by

---

[9] Speech entitled 'Commercialising Sport: Understanding the TV Rights Debate' delivered in Barcelona by Herbert Ungerer, of the EU Competition Directorate General, on 2 October, 2003, in which, *inter alia*, Ungerer argued that "there must be a clear separation between sports regulation and the commercialisation of sport." And added: "TV is of high significance for football clubs, 30–70% of football clubs' revenue come from TV, and this explains why sometimes our efforts [the Commission] to bring joint selling into line with Competition law requirements meet a certain anxiety—even bitterness—on the side of some leagues, and are initially misunderstood."

[10] COMP/C.2/37.214.

[11] IP/05/62, 19 January, 2005.

[12] See, in particular, the Commission Decision 91/130/EEC of 19 February 1991 in *Screensport/ Members of the EBU*, OJ L63 of 9 March, 1991.

[13] Directive 89/552 as amended by Directive 97/36.

[14] [2000] 1 WLR 1604.

considerations of competition, [or] market economics." In other words, public access to listed events overrides EU Competition Law considerations.

Likewise, in the context of restrictions placed on broadcasters by the EU, mention should also be made of the Commission's Decision of 20 April, 2001 concerning UEFA's rules allowing national football associations to prohibit the broadcasting of football matches during a period of two and a half hours on a Saturday or Sunday coinciding with the holding of matches in the country concerned.[15] The *rationale* for this decision is to encourage supporters to attend the matches in person rather than watching them on television. The Commission considered that these rules were purely sporting ones and did not appreciably restrict competition, thus falling outside the EU Competition Rules (particularly, at the time of the decision, Article 81(1) of the EC Treaty; now Article 101(1) of the TFEU).

A final general comment:

Whilst the legal treatment of sports TV rights varies from country to country, in the European Union there is some degree of harmonisation. This is the consequence of the inexorable rise of EU Competition Law generally and its particular application to the sporting world, which has produced something of an overarching, unifying and harmonising factor in the field of sports broadcasting in those Countries, which are members of the EU or the European Economic Area (EEA), in which the EU Competition Rules generally apply. But it should be noted generally that, in the brave new world of Europe, there is a growing move towards competition issues in the EU being handled by the National Competition Authorities in preference to those at the EU level pursuant to the so-called '*subsidiarity*' principle.

Included in the Appendix of this Chapter (16.7) is an interesting Paper by Werner Rumphorst, at the time Director of the Legal Department of the European Broadcasting Union, Geneva, Switzerland,[16] presented as part of a Panel Discussion on 'The Collective Selling of Sports Television Broadcasting Rights' at an International Conference which took place in London on 12 October, 1999. Although the Paper is rather dated, it makes many interests points and sets out some general principles, which are still relevant today, so it is worth reproducing the Paper in full.

## 16.4 Territorial Restrictions in Sports Merchandising and Licensing Agreements

An agreement between competitors requiring each to stay out of the other's market or territory (or to refrain from selling to the other's customers) is another type of restriction which may be caught by the EU Competition Rules. As with price

[15] Comm. Dec. 2001/478.

[16] www.ebu.ch

fixing arrangements between competitors, this sort of restriction will usually attract severe penalties and will hardly ever be permissible.

However, in relation to agreements between parties operating at different levels of the supply chain (so-called 'vertical' agreements), certain forms of territorial restriction may, however, be allowed. This is because certain restrictions mean that the parties' investments in the arrangements will be protected and so the restrictions actually encourage the parties to enter into the agreement in the first place.

Although complete territorial restrictions, such as export bans, are not permitted, a supplier may be permitted to set up an exclusive distribution system. This involves the supplier allocating the exclusive right to sell into a particular territory to one distributor whilst reserving to himself or other exclusive distributors the right to sell into other territories.

If the supplier's market share is relatively modest (less than 30%), then a distribution system with territorial restrictions will be permissible, provided that all distributors within the system are permitted to make so-called 'passive' sales into the territories reserved to other distributors. 'Passive' sales are those made in response to a customer approaching the distributor without that approach having been solicited. In contrast, it is possible to restrict so-called 'active' sales. The use of the Internet to advertise or sell products is generally considered to be a form of 'passive' sale. 'Active' sales occur where the distributor actively seeks custom, for instance, through advertising designed to elicit sales in another territory, or by directly contacting customers.

If the market share threshold is exceeded, it may still be possible to include some form of territorial restrictions; however, this will require a detailed assessment of the proposed restriction to see if it gives rise to competition law concerns.

Many kinds of Sports Marketing Agreements, especially Sports Licensing and Merchandising Agreements, grant exclusive rights on a territorial basis and expressly forbid sales outside the assigned territory. As mentioned above, 'active' sales outside the territory can, generally, be prohibited; whilst 'passive' sales outside the territory cannot. These sales usually arise where the demand in one territory outstrips the supply in that territory, so it is in everyone's interests for that demand to be satisfied.

In this connection, it is worth mentioning that if the licensee is merely granted the sole right to sell the licensed products in a particular territory, then and in such a case, the licensor can sell directly in that territory. This is because the rights granted to the licensee are those of a sole licensee, which means that the licensor cannot grant any other licensee any rights in the assigned territory; but that does not, of course, preclude the licensor from selling directly in that territory, should the need arise to do so, because the rights granted to the licensee are not exclusive. The use of the term 'sole and exclusive' licensee, which crops up from time to time, is contradictory and meaningless and should be avoided. Note also that, where the rights are exclusive in a particular territory, the licensor cannot appoint another licensee for that territory and neither can the licensor sell directly in that territory—except, of course, with the consent of the exclusive licensee. Of course, where the rights granted are non-exclusive, the Licensor can appoint other non-exclusive Licensees to sell in the assigned territory and the Licensor can also sell directly into that territory. So, many commercial scenarios are possible to suit the requirements of the particular case.

Thus, the 'grant of rights' clause in a Sports Licensing and Merchandising Agreement needs to be carefully drafted accordingly to reflect the intended position. The usual clause in a Sports Licensing and Merchandising Agreement covering the above issues in the case of a grant of exclusive territorial rights in respect of the licensed products runs as follows:

> "The Licensee shall refrain outside the Territory from seeking customers for the Licensed Products and from establishing any branch or maintaining any distribution depot in connection with the Licensed Products. Nothing in this clause shall prevent the Licensee from supplying any bona fide unsolicited order or request for the Licensed Products to any person outside the Territory."

As always with all kinds of Commercial Agreements, including Sports Marketing Agreements, especially ones with an international dimension, clarity is the name of the game!

## 16.5 Options to Renew and Rights of First Refusal in Sports Marketing Agreements Generally

*Rights of first refusal and option clauses* are characteristically found in Sports Marketing Agreements, particularly Sports Licensing and Merchandising Agreements.

Options to renew need to be drafted carefully, otherwise they could become perpetual options, if worded loosely. For example:

> "The Licensee may renew this Agreement for a further period of [two years] on the same terms and conditions...".

To avoid this outcome, namely, creating a perpetual option, after the words "*terms and conditions*" include the following words:

> "with the exception of this present clause."

Again, in Sports Marketing Agreements, options to renew are often accompanied by so-called '*matching option*' clauses. Likewise these clauses need to be precisely worded to avoid ambiguity and uncertainty rendering them legally void. Also, options to renew and matching options may also raise National and EU Competition Law issues, where they are granted for long periods of time and restrict access of other possible licensees from entering the 'relevant market' for sports licensing and merchandising in relation to a particular sports event. In other words, the terms and conditions of the options to renew and matching options must be reasonable in all the circumstances of the particular case and must be proportionate, that is, go no further than is reasonably necessary to achieve their commercial and sporting aims. Otherwise, these clauses may well fall foul of National and EU Competition Rules.

The matching option clause in a Sports Licensing and Merchandising Agreement may be drafted along the following lines:

> "On the expiration of the Term of this Agreement the Licensor hereby grants the Licensee a right of first refusal to renew this Agreement for a further period of [three] years on such terms and conditions as the Licensor and Licensee may negotiate and agree within a period of thirty (30) days following the expiration of this Agreement. The Licensor and the Licensee hereby agree that they will negotiate the renewal of this Agreement in all respects in good faith and in the event of failing to agree the new terms and conditions for the renewal of this Agreement within the said period of thirty (30) days then and in such case the Licensor shall be entitled to grant a Licence to a third party for such period and on such terms and conditions as may be agreed between the Licensor and the third party. In the event of the same or less favourable terms and conditions being agreed between the Licensor and the third party compared with the terms and conditions proposed by the Licensee and rejected by the Licensor, notice of the same or less favourable terms and conditions must be given in writing by the Licensor to the Licensee within five (5) days of the same being agreed between the Licensor and the third party then and in such case the Licensee shall have the right to be exercised at its sole and uncontrolled discretion by giving notice in writing within a further period of five (5) days counting from the date of the notice of the Licensor being received by the Licensee of the agreement of the Licensee to proceed with the renewal of this Agreement for same period and on the same terms and conditions as those agreed between the Licensor and the third party. The Licensee and the Licensor hereby further agree that they will enter into the renewal of this Agreement with ten (10) days of the Licensee giving notice to the Licensor of the agreement of the Licensee to proceed with the renewal of this Agreement as aforesaid. The Licensor and the Licensee hereby also agree in good faith and in a timely manner to do any and all such acts and things and sign any and all such documents as may be necessary to give full legal and practical effect to this present clause in this Agreement. In the event of the Licensee failing to give such notice within the period aforesaid to the Licensor of the agreement of the Licensee to proceed with the renewal of this Agreement for same period and on the same terms and conditions as those agreed between the Licensor and the third party then and in such case the Licensor shall be free to conclude the agreement with the third party as aforesaid."

As with all EU Competition Law cases, whether or not this right of first refusal and matching option clause falls foul of the EU Competition Rules (or, indeed, National Competition Rules) depends upon the facts and circumstances of each individual case, including, of course, the actual terms and conditions for the renewal of the Agreement finally agreed between the Licensor and the Licensee in accordance with the terms of the right of first refusal and matching option clause.

## 16.6 Concluding Remarks

The question is often asked: what has Sport got to do with the EU and what has the EU got to do with Sport? Quite a lot, in fact, to quote Professor Stephen Weatherill again[17]:

[17] GSLTR, 2010/1, at p. 13.

> "After Lisbon there is no longer any doubt that the EU has a legitimate, if subordinate, role in the field of sport. There will be legislation (of a supporting nature): there will be a budget. And the Treaty does at last contain material capable of nourishing the Court's interpretation of the free movement and competition rules in the particular context of sport. The specific nature of sport is now written into the Treaty. One would suppose that sporting bodies would no longer waste time claiming EU law has no application to their activities and instead seek to rely on the wording of the new provisions as a basis for minimising the transformative effect of EU law on their practice."

The same point equally applies to negotiating and drafting Sports Marketing Agreements of various kinds with a European dimension. So, if you fail to take into account the EU aspects of the matter, you do so entirely at your own risk and peril, bearing in mind that breaches of the EU Competition Rules, for example, can result in heavy fines of up to 10% of the group world-wide turnover of the offending party.[18]

You have been warned!

[18] See, for example, Case T-43/92 *Dunlop Slazenger v EC Commission* [1994] ECR II-441, in which Dunlop Slazenger International were fined 5 million ECUs for applying a general ban on exports of squash and tennis balls!

## 16.7 Appendix

**European Broadcasting Union**

*Legal Department*
25.7.2001/3
DAJ/WR/mp

**Sports Broadcasting Rights and EC Competition Law***

**I. Introduction**

Applying EC (or national) competition law to the business aspects of the broadcasting of sports events is nothing new, but it remains a difficult and largely unknown issue. Let me try to give you some guidelines.

The collective exploitation of sports broadcasting rights is not, of itself, a dominantly negative factor in determining legality under competition law. The existing case law clarifies that most, if not all, objections were raised against the (additional) *conditions* of such practices, such as the excessive duration of the rights packages and, in combination with the extensive exclusivity, its blocking effect on the development of new broadcasting services.

**II. The relevant market**

One of the main unresolved questions concerns the relevant market for sports broadcasting rights (see, for example, the orientation document by the EC Commission, Broadcasting of Sports Events and Competition Law, Competition Policy Newsletter, June 1998.)

Competition law is concerned with the effects that anti-competitive agreements or practices have on the consumer. Consequently, determining relevant markets calls for inquiries into the impact that restrictive agreements have on the opposite side of the market by asking about the effect on the choices of the enterprises which are the clients of the parties to a restrictive agreement. Thus, the anti-competitive effects of restrictions of supply will be assessed in terms of whether the demand side does have reasonable supply alternatives (substitute products) to meet its needs, reasonable being defined by price and quality. Conversely, anti-competitive effects of restriction of demand (such as collective buying) will be assessed in terms of whether the supply side may reasonably turn to other enterprises or whether it may reasonably modify its offer. The two tests are different because when suppliers are faced with restrictive demand, they are normally in no real position to modify the nature of the product or service they offer.

Applying these seemingly simple tests to the markets for sports rights meets with several difficulties.

* Reproduced with permission.

Firstly, collective buying by television organizations (or any other restrictive agreement) will have effects on both sides, the up-stream market for the acquisition of sports rights and the down-stream market for the exploitation of the acquired rights. But it is primarily the latter aspect which interests antitrust authorities. They are concerned with the question of whether the collectively acquired rights unduly enhance the position of broadcasters vis-à-vis their clients or consumers, i.e. advertising agencies in the case of commercial television and television viewers in the case of pay-TV; or, in other words, whether the position of competing broadcasters vis-à-vis these same consumers is weakened.

The second problem is that the substitutability of individual broadcast offers is not what really matters. This is already obvious as far as the advertising agency is concerned, since it consumes not television broadcasts as such but television space for advertising. For the agency, the value of the broadcast offer and its substitutability (in the eyes of the audience) is of interest only as a factor—albeit a major factor—in determining the value of the television advertising space. This is frequently overlooked when television programmes are held to be too different to be substitutable. For the advertising agency, it is not the content of a programme as such that matters but only its value in terms of attractiveness to viewers. For them, therefore, all programmes are basically interchangeable if they attract the same number of viewers, whether or not the programmes involve a sports event. Consequently, very different sports events may be substitutable as a matter of guaranteeing attractive television advertising space.

Thirdly, sports broadcasting rights have certain aspects which make them unique. Each sports event is characterized by its particular "live" value, which will (almost) completely diminish as soon as the event is over. This short-lived nature has special consequences for the different forms of use in broadcasting; a weekly sports event or even a European football final cannot be exploited to the same extent as a new James Bond film. For the same reason, the live broadcasting rights to such sports events are only attractive to the broadcaster on an exclusive basis.

Fourthly, the objective of the "relevant market" test is to assess correctly existing competitive relationships. In addition to the products or services concerned, as well as the territorial limits of markets, the time factor has to be taken into consideration. Competition is a process, and services are rendered over time. Therefore, relevant time periods must be determined. There may be single events which by their nature also determine the relevant time window. But competition between broadcasters is mostly determined by programme differentiation. The broadcaster's programmes may be specialized (dedicated channels) or they may be mixed programme services. It is the mix over time which defines the service offered, and the time period defines the relevant market.

As far as the consumer of pay-TV is concerned, it can also be assumed that every sport has its own characteristics and specific financial circumstances. In particular from the point of view of the potential recipient of sports broadcasting services, the general public interested in sport as a whole, one type of sport is not likely to be a real substitute for another, and even a possible selection of the most popular sports (such as football, motor racing, tennis, rugby, skiing, boxing and ice hockey) will depend on the cultural background of that public.

From the viewpoint of broadcasters and rights marketing agencies, therefore, the differences between each sport do not create as many separate markets for the corresponding broadcasting rights. In order to accept the logic of this view, we should be prepared to admit that, under traditional competition law principles, the restraining effects on competition are usually assessed on a short-term basis, whereas the relevant market for sports broadcasting rights requires a long-term analysis; the predominant question for any broadcaster is not how to attract as many spectators as possible *for a given broadcast production* but how to achieve a (sufficiently high) audience share *for (at least) a complete broadcasting season.*

Any broadcaster, whether or not it has already established itself on the market, needs some "special offers" on a regular basis to attract the attention of the potential audience, but no broadcaster could deny that the ultimate challenge for its full programme package is to maintain a more or less permanent share of the audience as a whole.

On the other hand, it is evident that the relevant market for sports broadcasting rights cannot be determined by the actual or potential spectator, as in that case not only different types of sports, but also individual matches from the same sports competition or even within a given tournament, as well as each single match of the national team, will have varying degrees of spectator appeal. Just as the substitutability of feature films cannot be annulled by assuming that a Disney film will appeal to a different audience from a James Bond film (and even among the existing James Bond films you will find varying spectator appeal, partly because different actors have played the hero), the demarcation of the relevant market for sports broadcasting rights would be largely unpredictable, if not virtually impossible, if the emphasis were put on the potential audience.

As a result of these specific characteristics of sports events and broadcasting, there are always various "premium" sports events during a broadcasting season, such as a weekly football championship match or a tennis tournament, which are sufficiently attractive to a substantial part of the potential audience. From the broadcaster's point of view, such events within a particular type of sport (i.e. apart from the so-called "major events", which take place only once a year or even less often) are to a large extent interchangeable, as long as they can be used throughout the broadcast season to maintain the audience attention or share level.

For example, although the potential audience for football is likely to be different from that of tennis, for broadcasters and rights marketing agencies the broadcasting rights for a particular selection of tennis tournaments are regarded as a substitute for a given series of European football matches. The extent to which broadcasting rights to sports events are substitutable is even more obvious with respect to the *less popular* sports.

These consequences of the special nature of the relevant market for sports broadcasting rights imply that the demand side of this market has a certain level of choice available and, thus, there is no absolute necessity for any broadcaster or agency to acquire the live broadcasting rights to a particular batch of events of these sports.

## III. National case law on football television rights

The creation by a sports federation of a "solidarity pool" to share the income from the broadcasting rights in one way or another in order to maintain the necessary degree of competitiveness among the participating clubs cannot be regarded as generally incompatible with EC competition law. In each case, however, it remains to be seen whether the actual conditions for creating such a pool could help justify a possible exemption for the central marketing of the broadcasting rights. Most cases which were decided under national competition law involved the sale of television broadcasting rights on a collective and exclusive basis by the national football federations.

### *1. France*

The most "drastic" approach seems to have been introduced in France, where the national football federation is designated by law (Art. 17/18 of the Law No. 84-610 of 16 July 1984, as amended in 1992) as the sole authority for exploiting the broadcasting rights to the matches of the official competitions, which are organized by that authority, on a collective basis.

However, although the federation thereby enjoys a *sui generis* type of right, it should be recalled that the original basis thereof is be found in unfair competition law (Art. 1382 of the *Code Civil*).

This unique position of (in fact, all) official sports federations has been reinforced by an amendment of the law in 1992, which was confirmed by a decision of the Supreme Court in 1994 (*Fédération Française de Football ./. La Cinq*). According to that decision, the French Football Federation participates in providing the public service of sport by exercising the prerogatives of public power. Even though the existing broadcasting agreements between the Federation and the broadcasters were governed by private law, the exclusivity of these contracts was deemed not to be discriminatory. However, the law prohibits the conclusion of exclusive broadcasting agreements for more than five years.

### *2. Netherlands*

The opposite situation from that of France can probably be found in the Netherlands, where the objections to collective selling caused the collapse of the proposed football channel "Sport 7". The Dutch Football Federation wished to sell the broadcasting rights for the first national football league to a commercial channel of which the Federation would also be one of the main shareholders. However, the proposal broke down after an Appeal Court's decision that these rights belonged (at least) also to the clubs, based on their ability to control public access to the matches in their stadiums, and that the national Federation could not obtain those rights on an exclusive basis simply through a change in the statutes (Hof Amsterdam, 8 November 1996, RvdW/KG 1996, No. 448—*Feyenoord/ KNVB*).

Later, shortly before the new Competition Act entered into force, the Dutch Football Federation asked for an exemption (under the old rules) to its collective sale of the broadcasting rights with respect to "*extracts*" from the matches in the national championship (the most popular clubs had sold the rights to live broadcasts of their home matches on an individual basis to Canal+). The exclusive position of the Football Federation was limited to 24 hour after the last match of the day on which most of the matches were played; after that period, the clubs were free to sell these rights individually. The Ministry for Economic Affairs took account of the possible interests of the viewers in having all highlights shown by a single broadcaster on a fixed time, but was not convinced that such interests alone could justify the exemption, even in combination with the argument that the championship as a whole would be at risk; financial inequality among the clubs could also be reduced by creating a "solidarity fund" on the basis of collecting a certain percentage of the revenue which was generated individually. The exemption was nevertheless granted, but limited to "a reasonable time" (see also *Lugard*, Markt & Mededinging 1998/No. 1, 28).

***3. Germany***

In a judgment handed down in December 1997, the German Supreme Court confirmed two decisions of the Federal Cartel Authority that, with respect to football matches played in Germany in the UEFA Cup and the European Cup Winners' Cup, the German Football Federation is not allowed, on the basis of national competition law, to market centrally the broadcasting rights for these matches, by imposing on the associated clubs a statutory obligation to grant these exploitation rights exclusively to the Federation.

Concerning the matches played by the club teams in their home stadia, the Court considered that the respective clubs were the real organizers of these matches, since they provide the ingredients (the players) and the local infrastructure which result in the "product" in which the spectator is interested. Following on from the explanatory regulations in the UEFA competition bye-laws, the home club is not only responsible for the organization and cost of its matches in the European competitions but is also entitled to the revenue therefrom. Under these circumstances, the Court held that the clubs, at least, were entitled to exploit the broadcasting rights. The Court deemed it possible that UEFA would be entitled to share in the revenue from the rights, but since UEFA was not a party to the proceedings this question was left undecided. In contrast, with respect to the UEFA and European Cup matches involved, the activities of the German Football Federation were regarded as limited to merely a coordination role, which could provide a better, balanced exploitation of the broadcasting rights but did not actually bring about the existence of the transmissions as such.

Since the individual UEFA and European Cup matches were capable of being exploited separately, there was no compelling need to sell as a package the broadcasting rights for the matches of all the clubs which had qualified. Thus, the central marketing of the broadcasting rights by the Federation eliminated any competition over the prices or conditions that might be set by the individual clubs. An exemption for a "rationalization cartel" was also refused by the Court, because the system of central exploitation, as applied by the German Football Federation, would merely serve to increase the revenue from the broadcasting rights and would not improve any cost-benefit relationship. For the same reason, the central marketing of the rights could not be justified by the "pooling" principle based on solidarity among the clubs. Contrary to the situation in the United States, the Court considered that an exemption under competition law could not follow on from the social or political aim of retaining a sufficiently large number of clubs which are (also) financially capable of participating in the leagues. Otherwise, such a justification would seem to enable the Federation to cover all of its costs simply by increasing the broadcasting fees, and those fees would have to be financed at least partly by television viewers of the matches. However, this observation must be seen in the context of the Court's emphasis that the decision concerns only the two European Championships, the situation regarding the central marketing of national sports leagues being a quite separate issue.

After it became known last year that the revision of the German Competition Act would include an explicit exemption in favour of the collective selling of broadcasting rights by sports associations for matches organized by such associations, the European Commission stated its opposition to this development in so far as such an exemption might apply to matches in the national league but, when applied to European championships, would be subject to EU competition law. The German Football Federation was therefore forced to notify the collective selling of the television and radio broadcasting rights to the matches in the first and second national football leagues and the matches in the national cup competition for negative clearance or an exemption under EU competition law (see EC *Official Journal* of 9 January 1999, C 6, p. 10.)

***4. Spain***

In 1998, the Audiencia Nacional confirmed the decision of the Spanish Competition Authority in 1993 that the agreements between the Federation and some Spanish broadcasters on the live transmissions of the national football championship matches were unlawful, because the scope of the exclusivity was too wide. The term of the contracts was eight years and they covered world-wide broadcasting rights, including highlights and the commercial exploitation of videos, for all competitions organized by the Federation. The Federation had also agreed not to sell any rights to any other broadcaster and, in addition thereto, to extend the agreement for another term of five years if the broadcasters were prepared to match any other offer.

However, the decision of the Audiencia Nacional has been appealed to the Supreme Court,and as far as I know, the issue is still under debate.

***5. Italy (and the United Kingdom)***

During the past summer, we have been presented with new case law. On 1 July 1999, the Italian Competition Authority prohibited collective selling practices by the national football federation (Lega Calcio) with respect to live transmissions of the Serie A and Serie B championship matches, but allowed them for the making of highlights programmes while granting an exemption as regards to the "knock-out phase" of the national Cup competition.

(The decision is available at the website of the Italian Competition Authority, at http://www.agcm.it.)

In contrast, a few weeks later the Restrictive Practices Court in the United Kingdom concluded that the collective sale of broadcasting rights is generally not contrary to the public interest. The case in the United Kingdom, as decided by the Restrictive Practices Court on 28 July 1999 (available at http://www.courtservice.gov.uk), will be explained in detail by other panelists.

With respect to the Italian decision, the Authority considered that the Lega Calcio did not assume any immediate entrepreneurial risk for the specific organization of each individual match, but that its institutional task was limited to a general involvement of a technical and administrative nature. Thus, the Lega Calcio was not regarded as being entitled to ownership, or even co-ownership, of the broadcasting rights involved.

Moreover, the Authority considered that the purposes for which the Lega Calcio had been established, namely to provide mutual support for its member clubs through the promotion of financial equality and to maintain a high level of consumer interest in sports events, were not sufficient to justify the selling of all broadcasting rights on a collective basis. The Authority found that redistribution of income among the major and minor clubs, which is necessary to maintain a competitive balance among them, could also be achieved by adopting alternative mechanisms which were equally effective but less restrictive (for example, by collecting shares of the income of the individual clubs on the basis of a gradually increasing scale).

On the other hand, the centralized marketing of the broadcasting rights with respect to the *highlights* of Serie A and Serie B championship matches did not restrict competition, because it would seem to be extremely complicated to sell these rights individually. In addition, that practice could even change their characteristics altogether; for example, it would seem difficult to offer a complete review of all matches played on a given day. The rights to broadcast the highlights of these matches would thus have real value only if they were sold as a single package.

Finally, concerning the matches in the *Coppa Italia*, the Authority considered that it was technically possible to sell the broadcasting rights to these matches on an individual basis. However, it concluded that by limiting the collective sale to the matches played in the immediate elimination rounds, under the statutory changes which the Lega Calcio had introduced in March 1999, the rule was eligible for an exemption. The reasons for granting this exemption (for three years) were the high transaction costs related to the large number of clubs involved (48), the uncertainty faced by broadcasters when they wished to acquire the broadcasting rights (as it would be unknown until immediately after each match from whom rights were to be acquired), the need to ease the transition towards a system in which most of the rights will be negotiated on an individual basis, and the fact that these rights would represent only 10 to 12% of the market for premium sports broadcasting rights.

## IV. Conclusions

### *1. Main lessons*

What do we learn from this overview, other than finding a lack of uniformity which nobody would have reasonably expected? Were the specific clauses of the UK agreements so different from the circumstances which resulted in the prohibition of the collective selling arrangements in several other countries? Or are the UK authorities protecting the primary nature of football as a sport more than others (also bearing in mind the complete prohibition of the proposed merger between BSkyB and Manchester United); and if the answer is affirmative, is this because UK competition law has yet to be modernized in line with the rules of the EC Treaty? Or is it simply caused by the great cultural attachment to football that has traditionally existed in the United Kingdom, so that the outcome may be different from an investigation of similar arrangements with respect to—for example—skiing?

For the United Kingdom Court, the substance of the relevant exclusivity clauses was the obligation not to grant to any broadcaster other than Sky or the BBC "the opportunity to experience and use for its own purposes the entertainment which consists of the playing of the match", if the purpose of that attendance is the making of any broadcast intended for reception within the agreed territory. Under this approach, the broadcasting rights are based primarily on the *providing of entertainment services in the form of witnessing the playing of the match.*

This implies a different notion than the so-called "arena rights", which merely derive from the basic principle under civil law that the home club may allow or refuse anybody admission to its premises (as, for example, under Dutch case law). In the latter case, only the home club will be regarded as the possible proprietor of the broadcasting rights to its home matches, whilst the entertainment services approach presupposes significantly stronger involvement by the organizer of the national championship as a whole. This is confirmed by the United Kingdom Court's consideration that the main "production" of the League and its member clubs, i.e. the 380 matches of a Premier League season, is not limited by the exclusive position of the League to sell the broadcasting rights to these matches. Subsequently, the idea of jointly or collectively "co-producing" football entertainment services logically reduces the restrictive extent of binding rules between the federation and the clubs on the collective sale of the broadcasting rights.

The decision of the Italian Competition Authority seems to fall between these positions, as it emphasizes the right of the home club to prevent stadium access, but this is accompanied by the entitlement of the organizer of an event, under the law on unfair competition, to enjoy the fruits of the commercial exploitation thereof. In line with its purely economic approach, however, the Authority did not grant the visiting club any co-ownership rights. When a competition is based on an equal number of home and away matches, this may not be decisive or even relevant. However, the United Kingdom Court recognized more realistically that the entertainment value of a match at least depends on two clubs and that the value of the television rights in any individual Premier League match is also affected by the value of the League competition itself; thereby, it shows the necessary respect for the entitlement of visiting clubs to share in the proceeds of the rights to matches for which they have also mobilized their entertainment forces.

The different approaches to the notion of broadcasting rights also explain the decision of the German Supreme Court, since the input of the German Football Federation was not sufficient to justify any co-ownership of the broadcasting rights to the European matches between clubs of different leagues; the position of the UEFA was not a subject of that decision. However, it should be realized that such Cup competitions *on the national level*, although perhaps also involving knock-out matches in the final phase, are nevertheless different, because the value of these national Cup matches depends, to a much larger extent than at the European level, on the actual achievements of the clubs concerned within the national competitions, and thus shows more involvement by the organizer of both competitions.

Other reasons that may justify the collective sale of national Cup matches are given by the Italian Competition Authority.

According to a paper issued by the European Commission (which I referred to earlier), the determination of the notion and ownership of the broadcasting rights is only a matter of national law. Does this mean that the European Union will have to accept divergent opinions on the legitimacy of collective selling? To a certain extent, the current cases before the Commission will pave the way for the application of national competition law. On the other hand, we have come to realize that it is not the difference *between the sports* but the difference between the *types of competition* which leads to different approaches.

***2. Alternatives to collective selling?***

In view of the extraordinary increase in the value of broadcasting rights for popular sports, it is realistic to assume that in many national sports leagues a strict system of individual negotiations by the clubs will steadily jeopardize the financial situation of the less successful clubs. A certain "polarization" effect is already visible in the extent and intensity of the commercial activities of individual sports clubs: only the most popular ones are capable of generating high income. Any individual selling regime must therefore include some restrictions in order to safeguard the competitive balance among the clubs and thus maintain the competition as a whole.

Removing the right of the national federation to negotiate on a collective basis, in favour of a situation where the clubs compete with each other for broadcasting revenue, will result in shifting the balance of competition towards and among broadcasters. But that will not necessarily lead to an increase in the choice of televised sports, as the market for broadcasting is currently dominated by the sale of *exclusive rights*. Thus, another solution may be to allow collective selling only if broadcasting rights are not granted on an exclusive basis to a single broadcaster. However, the United Kingdom Court had many doubts about the feasibility of such a solution, and, moreover, it does not diminish the applicability of competition law.

***3. Alternatives to collecting and sharing the income?***
The most critical point may therefore be the *specific method for collecting and sharing the income* from the television rights by the national federation. From that point of view, a possible exemption for central marketing of broadcasting rights to the matches of the national football championship—and this can probably be extended to many other national sports competitions—will depend largely on the alternative means of maintaining the viability of that national competition. For example, the German Court clarifies that merely sharing the revenue among all participating clubs for their own financial benefit is not sufficient to justify complete restraint of the club's own marketing possibilities.

Moreover, to maintain the existing structure of national championships as such, the Italian Authority has indicated that the rules for supporting financial equality among the clubs could be placed under more scrutiny than the test applied by the United Kingdom Court. Less restrictive practices by the sports federations, such as merely requiring a (differentiated) percentage of the individually achieved revenue, in order to create a "social fund" for the less popular clubs, will be less prohibitive under competition law. For example, in 1994, the Austrian Supreme Court allowed its national skiing federation to make the exclusive nomination of local committees for the organization of international championships dependent on receiving a large share of the marketing revenue of the nominated committee (notably the advertising and sponsorship rights) but with a guarantee of financing the organizational costs.

Thus, concerning the future arrangements for the sale of the Premier League broadcasting rights, i.e. after the termination of the current agreements in 2001, it is far from certain that an investigation under the new UK Competition Act will yield the same result, even assuming that similar agreements are concluded. On publishing its White Paper on Competitiveness, prior to the enactment of the new Competition Act, the United Kingdom Government promised to use the new Act to "get tough on anti-competitive behaviour".

Nevertheless, the fundamental flaw of proposing alternative redistribution schemes is that it is still unclear how the creation of such "social funds" could function in practice: What would be a "fair" percentage to collect and how would the necessary consensus on that percentage be established among the clubs? Would it not be more realistic to assume that such a system will even increase the cost of the rights for broadcasters, since the more popular clubs would be likely to recoup the expected "loss" of income by raising the overall price for their home matches?

***4. Neglected interests***
Since public service broadcasters always take account of the interests of minorities and the public as a whole, there are a number of "players" whose interests should not be neglected—notably the less popular sports, and the viewing public.

For example, the mere possibility of a sports event forming the content of a television broadcast does not transform that event into a purely commercial product and even less does it deprive the event of its *human, social and cultural dimension*. Why should the public be forced to pay more and more for viewing sports events which are part of their own cultural environment? (It should not be overlooked that higher costs for broadcasting rights will raise the prices for the advertising customers, and these costs will thus be paid by the public consuming the advertised goods or services.) The socially integrative role of sport in each European society should not be put at risk, which implies that an investigation under national or European competition law cannot limit itself to purely economic deliberations in order to meet the desire of the most popular clubs to be more successful in financial terms.

Neither would it be socially acceptable for the general public to be obliged to pay more (whether for decoders or for pay-per-view) in order to be able to watch the same sports events that they are used to watching. At least the German Supreme Court and the United Kingdom Court seemed to have recognized—and disliked—the development whereby the increased cost of sports broadcasting rights is allocated to the potential audience. This means that practical solutions aimed at promoting the social and cultural aspects of sport and resulting in a considerable reduction in the financial burden on the audience would be a highly relevant factor with respect to a possible exemption under the rules for rationalization cartels. Further case law should therefore put more emphasis on these aspects.

Of course, the responsibility for maintaining *the interest of the public in each sport as a whole* remains, in any case, a matter for both the clubs and the federation. However, with respect to the practice of central marketing from a competition law point of view, the situation would seem to be very different, if even the successful clubs in a given sport were unable to derive sufficient income from the broadcasting rights, because of the overall lack of popularity of the sport as such. In such situations, there is a strong social reason for the collective exploitation of those rights in order to maintain the public's interest in the sport as a whole.

In view of the growing desire of the larger football clubs in several European countries to prefer the conclusion of individual contracts for pay-per-view broadcasting, it may be assumed that the rights market with respect to the *live* broadcasting of football matches will change to some extent. In fact, in all countries where collective selling is practiced, the federations have not been reluctant to involve the pay-TV market; on the contrary, the colossal increase in the cost of the broadcasting rights is at least partly caused by the attractiveness of these rights for pay-TV operators—and the willingness of the federations to grant them these rights—on an exclusive basis. However, if the attractiveness of pay-TV for the audience affects the *live attendance* of football matches and the *game* of football in general, an own goal will have been scored.

The sports federations are already aware of the risks of "over-commercialization", which are the result of the increasing control of popular clubs by media companies. For example, a new UEFA rule prohibits the control of more than one club in the same UEFA club competition. (See the Communication by the EC Commission *Official Journal* of 17.12.1999, C 363.)

However, this is only the tip of the iceberg; in my view, preserving the integrity of sport should involve the more fundamental question of placing a proper limit on *any substantial form* of ownership of a football club by a media company. In cases where such a limit cannot be set by present merger regulations, as a result of the high "thresholds" to be passed (the proposed BSkyB/Manchester United merger was an exception), this task should be taken on by the federations.

Whether these developments could have any effect on the conditions for the sale of broadcasting rights to *highlights* programmes is even less predictable. Whereas both the Italian and United Kingdom decisions allowed the central marketing thereof, partly because their sale on an individual basis would not seem to be practicable, the Dutch Ministry assumed the opposite (but without any full investigation). The UK approach is more reasonable, as it concentrated on the exclusivity of the rights and held such exclusivity to be more difficult to justify, in cases where it is possible to include time windows between such programmes.

***5. New EC Commission—new hope?***

One of the conclusions of the first European Union Conference on Sport was the consideration that "the interests of sport are best served by a system of collective sale of rights, in particular by federations". However, the contrasting results of the decisions on the collective selling of broadcasting rights by the national football federation still leave many doubts about the circumstances under which such practices are legitimate. It is to be hoped that the present cases before the new European Commission will add more transparency to the issue.

# Chapter 17
# Alternative Dispute Resolution

## 17.1 Introductory Remarks

With so much money circulating and to be made in sport at the national and global levels, it is not surprising that disputes arise from time to time, not only of a purely sporting nature, for example, eligibility issues, but also of a commercial nature, for example under Sports Marketing Agreements, the subject of this Book. Such Agreements, however well drafted, are not immune from disputes, controversies and disagreements of one kind or another; and the question that naturally arises and falls to be answered, in each case, is how best to resolve them. By traditional or modern means? In other words, through the Courts or by some form of Alternative Dispute Resolution (ADR) outside the Courts system, that is, by *extra-judicial* means?

ADR in its various forms is proving to be very popular in the sporting world for settling disputes, especially international commercial ones. Generally speaking, *extra judicial* methods of dispute resolution are quicker, more flexible, less expensive, and confidential. The sporting community, generally, prefers not '*to wash its dirty sports' linen in public*!' ADR methods also result in win–win situations, unlike the adversarial process of Court litigation, which is always, by its very nature, a win–lose situation. Also, ADR enables the parties in dispute to maintain and preserve their business relationships and to do business together in the future. This is particularly true in relation to sports disputes and the settlement of them by Mediation.[1]

Perhaps the most common and effective forms of ADR are Mediation and Arbitration. Or, even a combination of these two processes: '*Med-Arb*'. That is, Mediation to identify the issues and, if unsuccessful, Arbitration to settle them. Although it should be mentioned that, where Mediation is appropriate to settle

---

[1] See '*Sports Mediations: Preserving Sporting and Business Relationships*' by Ian Blackshaw, Association for International Arbitration (AIA), Brussels, Belgium, November 2010 Newsletter, at pp. 9 & 10.

I. S. Blackshaw, *Sports Marketing Agreements: Legal, Fiscal and Practical Aspects*, ASSER International Sports Law Series, DOI: 10.1007/978-90-6704-793-7_17,

the dispute, 85% of Mediations prove to be successful. In any case, Mediation and Arbitration are conducted by individuals with particular expertise and experience in the field of business concerned and this is a further advantage that ADR has over the Courts system, in which the Judges often lack these backgrounds and traits.

There are a number of bodies and organisations offering general ADR services for the settlement of international commercial disputes. Mention may be made of just a few of them: the American Arbitration Association (AAA), based in New York, USA, which also, it should be mentioned, deals exclusively with disputes of the US Olympic Committee (USOC); the International Chamber of Commerce (ICC), based in Paris, France; and the Centre for Effective Dispute Resolution (CEDR), based in London, United Kingdom.

There are also several Sports Bodies offering Mediation and Arbitration of international sports-related commercial disputes, such as the Court of Arbitration for Sport (CAS)[2]; the UK Sports Dispute Resolution Panel, now known as Sports Resolutions UK[3]; the FIBA (International Basketball Federation) Arbitration Tribunal (FAT),[4] which operates 'on line'; and EQUESTES in The Netherlands, which offers Expert Determination of Equestrian-related disputes, including commercial ones, for example, involving the sale of sport-horses.[5]

In this chapter, however, we will concentrate on the settlement of sports business and commercial disputes through the CAS, which is based in Lausanne, Switzerland, and has established itself over its 26 years of operations as the principal and most popular Body in its specialised field of settling sports-related disputes.

Before dealing with the CAS dispute resolution clauses to be included in Sports Marketing Agreements, some words on the CAS itself on how it is organised and how it operates would not be inappropriate.

## 17.2 The CAS

The CAS was established in 1983 with the express purpose of providing a forum outside the ordinary Courts system for the settlement of disputes related to sport 'within the family of sport', and began its operations in 1984. It was the 'brain-child' of the late Juan Antonio Samaranch, the former President of the International Olympic Committee (IOC).

---

2 See on the CAS generally, '*The Court of Arbitration for Sport 1984–2004*' I. S. Blackshaw and RCR Siekmann (eds.); and '*Sport, Mediation and Arbitration*' I. S. Blackshaw; both Books published by the TMC Asser Press, The Hague, The Netherlands in 2006 and 2009 respectively.

3 Ibid.

4 See 'The FIBA Arbitration Tribunal (FAT)' by Ian Blackshaw, The International Sports Law Journal, ISLJ 2009/1 & 2, at pp. 65–67 (both inclusive). This article includes the wording of the required written request for arbitration by the FAT.

5 See 'Equestrianism Gets Its Own Alternative Dispute Resoluion Body 'Equestes' In The Netherlands' by Ian Blackshaw, Entertainment and Sports Law Journal, ESLJ Vol. 8 No. 2, 2010.

The CAS offers Arbitration, Mediation and Advisory Opinions and has its seat in Lausanne, Switzerland. In other words, it is a Swiss Arbitral Body.

During the Olympic Games, the CAS operates an '*Ad Hoc*' Division (AHD), which was first set up on September 28, 1995, for the Centennial Atlanta Summer Games of the Modern Era in 1996, resolving disputes relating to the Games within 24 hours and free of charge.[6]

### *17.2.1 The Organisation of the CAS*

The CAS is governed by the ICAS, the International Council of Arbitration for Sport. The ICAS main function is to safeguard the independence of the CAS and the rights of the parties appearing before it.[7] Thus, it is responsible for the administration and financing of the CAS. The ICAS has 20 members, who, on appointment, must sign a declaration in which they undertake to exercise their functions in a personal capacity, with total objectivity and independence. The members comprise 5 sports persons; 5 independent persons, who are outside the Olympic Movement and sport generally; 5 persons from the IOC; 5 persons from the Association of Summer Olympics International Sports Federations (ASOIF) and the Association of Winter Olympics International Sports Federations (AIWF); and 5 persons from the Association of National Olympic Committees (ANOC). ICAS members are appointed for four-year renewable terms. ICAS, like CAS itself, is a Swiss Foundation based in Lausanne, Switzerland. The ICAS appoints the CAS arbitrators and mediators and approves the budget and the accounts of the CAS.[8]

### *17.2.2 The Funding of the CAS*

The funding of CAS is shared between the constituents of CAS as follows:

- 4/12 by the IOC;
- 3/12 by the ASOIF;
- 1/12 by the AIWF; and
- 4/12 by the ANOC.

---

[6] See Ian Blackshaw, 'A sporting decision in just 24 hours', 'The Times', 23 July, 2002.

[7] For a complete list of the functions of ICAS, see Article S6 of the CAS Code of Sports-related Arbitration, the latest version of which is the one in force as of 1 January, 2010.

[8] See generally on the ICAS Articles S4–S11, ibid.

### *17.2.3 The Legal Status of the CAS*

The CAS, also known by its French acronym TAS (*Tribunal Arbitral du Sport*)—the official languages are French and English—as mentioned above is based in Lausanne, Switzerland, but has two permanent branches in Sydney, Australia, and New York, USA, facilitating access to CAS for parties residing in Oceania and North America.[9] Because CAS is based in Switzerland, with its seat in Lausanne, the CAS is generally governed by Swiss Law.[10] It has its legal seat in Lausanne for all purposes, even when it hears cases outside Switzerland.[11] The CAS Court Office, headed by the Secretary General and assisted by several Counsel and secretaries, supervises the arbitration and mediation procedures and acts as a Registry; it also organises the '*Ad Hoc*' Divisions and deals with other administrative matters.

### *17.2.4 CAS Arbitrators*

The CAS has a minimum of 150 arbitrators, who are specialists in arbitration and sports law.[12] They are appointed for four-year renewable terms and must sign a 'letter of independence' confirming that they will act impartially. In establishing the list of CAS arbitrators, the ICAS must, in principle, respect the following distribution of candidates:

- 1/5 of the arbitrators selected from among the persons proposed by the IOC, chosen from within its membership or outside;
- 1/5 of the arbitrators selected from among the persons proposed by the IFs, chosen from within their membership or outside;
- 1/5 of the arbitrators selected from among the persons proposed by the NOCs, chosen from within their membership or outside;
- 1/5 of the arbitrators chosen, after appropriate consultations, with a view to safeguarding the interests of the athletes;
- 1/5 of the arbitrators chosen from among persons independent of the bodies responsible for proposing arbitrators in conformity with the present article.[13]

---

[9] See generally M. Reeb, 'The Role and Functions of the Court of Arbitration for Sport (CAS)', *The International Sports Law Journal* 2 (2002), 21, 23–25.

[10] For more information, log onto the CAS official website at 'www.tas-cas.org'.

[11] For the legal and practical significance of this, see the Judgement of the New South Wales Court of Appeal of 1 September, 2000 in the case of *Angela Raguz v Rebecca Sullivan* [2000] NSWCA 240. In that case, a legal challenge against a CAS arbitral award was dismissed on the ground of lack of jurisdiction because the Court upheld the choice of Lausanne, Switzerland as the seat (i.e. place) of arbitration under the CAS Code of Sports-related Arbitration.

[12] At the time of writing, there are some 300 CAS arbitrators, from 87 countries, and around 200 cases are registered with CAS each year.

[13] Article S14 of the Code of Sports-related Arbitration.

The CAS also has a permanent President, who is an Italian Lawyer, Mino Auletta, who has recently been appointed as Interim President until 2010 in succession to the previous President and Founder Member of CAS, Judge Keba Mbaye, from Senegal, who died on 11 January, 2007. Mr. Aulettta is also Acting President of ICAS until 2010.

CAS arbitrators, who sit on panels composed of one or three members, are not generally obliged to follow earlier decisions (*stare decisis*), but they usually do so in the interests of legal certainty.[14] Thus, a useful body of sports law (*lex sportiva*) is steadily being built up.[15] The extent to which this is happening continues to be the subject of academic debate.[16]

### *17.2.5 The Legal Status of CAS Awards*

Awards made by the CAS, like other international arbitral awards, are legally enforceable generally in accordance with the rules of International Private Law, and also specifically under the provisions of the New York Convention on the Recognition and Enforcement of Foreign Arbitral Awards of 10 June, 1958.

The CAS is also recognised under the European Convention on the Recognition of the Legal Personality of International Non-Governmental Organizations.

So, the CAS decisions are legally effective and can be enforced internationally. This is particularly important in the case of disputes involving intellectual property rights, especially trademarks, which are generally of a territorial nature.

### *17.2.6 Legal Challenges to CAS Awards*

The CAS awards can be legally challenged in the Swiss Federal Supreme Court, which is also based in Lausanne, by a dissatisfied party, but only in very limited circumstances, under the provisions of article 190(2) of the Swiss Federal Code on

---

[14] See Case of *UCI v J.* 7 NCB, CAS 97/176 Award of 28 August, 1998, 14.

[15] From time to time, the CAS publishes Digests of Cases, but respecting, as appropriate, the confidentiality of the parties. The latest Digest of CAS Awards Volume III covers the period the period 2001–2003 and was published in 2004 by Kluwer Law International, The Hague, The Netherlands (ISBN 90-411-2259-1). Previous Volumes I and II covered the periods 1986–1998 and 1998–2000 respectively and were published by Editions Staempfli SA Berne and Kluwer Law International/Editions Staempfli respectively.

[16] See K. Foster, 'Is There a Global Sports Law?', *Entertainment Law* 2/1 (2003), 1–18. Foster argues that the CAS as an institutional forum is not yet "globally comprehensive". And see also James A.R. Nafziger, *International Sports Law*, Second Edition, 2004, Transnational Publishers, Inc., Ardsley, New York, 48–61. Prof. Nafziger characterises the CAS *lex sportiva* as "still incipient".

Private International Law of December 18, 1987. This article reads (in English translation) as follows:

> "[The Award] can be attacked only:
>
> (a) if a sole arbitrator was designated irregularly or the arbitral tribunal was constituted irregularly;
> (b) if the arbitral tribunal erroneously held that it had or did not have jurisdiction;
> (c) if the arbitral tribunal ruled on matters beyond the claims submitted to it or failed to rule on one of the claims;
> (d) if the equality of the parties or their right to be heard in an adversarial proceeding was not respected;
> (e) if the award is incompatible with Swiss public policy."

In practice, perhaps ground (d) is the most important one, and the CAS bends over backwards in each case to ensure that the parties are properly heard and receive a fair hearing.[17]

In practice, there have been few legal challenges to CAS awards. In the latest challenge in 2003 concerning the independence of the CAS in view of its association with and partial funding by the IOC, the Swiss Federal Court held that the CAS offered all the guarantees of independence and impartiality to be regarded as a real court of arbitration, even where the IOC—as in that case—was a party in its proceedings.[18]

## 17.3 CAS Dispute Resolution Clauses

Before dealing with these Clauses, it is necessary to explain the legal rules on which the jurisdiction of the CAS in any given case is based.

The general rules on jurisdiction are as follows:

> "These Procedural Rules apply whenever the parties have agreed to refer a sports-related dispute to the CAS. Such disputes may arise out of an arbitration clause inserted in a contract or regulations or of a later arbitration agreement (ordinary arbitration proceedings) or involve an appeal against a decision rendered by a federation, association or sports-related body where the statutes or regulations of such bodies, or a specific agreement provides for an appeal to the CAS (appeal arbitration proceedings)."[19]

Furthermore, under the special provisions that apply to the CAS Ordinary Arbitration Proceedings, the party seeking CAS Arbitration of a sports-related

---

[17] See the Judgement of 22 March, 2007 in the ATP Tour Appeal case brought before the Swiss Federal Court against a CAS Award of 23 May, 2006; Reference: 4P 172/2006, which was brought under either para. (d) or para. (e) of article 190(2) of the Swiss Federal Code on Private International Law of December 18, 1987.

[18] See Judgement of 27 May, 2003 of the First Civil Division of the Swiss Federal Tribunal in the case of *A. & B. v International Olympic Committee and International Ski Federation* (4P. 267/2002; 4P. 268/2002; 4P. 269/2002; and 4P. 270/2002).

[19] Article R27 of the CAS Code of Sports-related Arbitration.

dispute is required to file a written Request for Arbitration, which shall contain, *inter alia*:

> "a copy of the contract containing the arbitration agreement or of any document providing for arbitration in accordance with these Procedural Rules."[20]

It will be seen from the above procedural requirements, that it is advisable to include express provisions in Sports Marketing Agreements, especially international ones, dealing with dispute resolution by ADR and, in particular, expressly referring disputes to Arbitration and Mediation through the auspices of the CAS. Of course, it is possible to refer disputes to the CAS for resolution at the time they arise. Such so-called 'ad hoc' references, however, as will be appreciated rely upon the agreement of the parties to the dispute. This is not always achieved, in practice: one party, for example, may be willing to go to Arbitration; whilst the other party is not!

There are some standard clauses for expressly referring sports-related commercial disputes to CAS Mediation and/or Arbitration, under the CAS Ordinary Arbitration Procedure, as well as Med-Arb references as follows:

The standard CAS Arbitration reference clause for a commercial dispute is as follows:

> "Any dispute arising from or related to the present contract will be submitted exclusively to the Court of Arbitration for Sport in Lausanne, Switzerland, and resolved definitively in accordance with the Code of Sports-related Arbitration."

The parties may—and it is advisable to do so—include in this reference clause additional provisions regarding the number of CAS arbitrators (from one to three) and the language in which the CAS proceedings will be conducted (for example, English, which, together with French, is one of the two official languages of the CAS).

The standard CAS reference clause for Mediation is as follows:

> "Any dispute, any controversy or claim arising under, out of or relating to this contract and any subsequent amendments of or in relation to this contract, including, but not limited to, its formation, validity, binding effect, interpretation, performance, breach or termination, as well as non-contractual claims, shall be submitted to mediation in accordance with the CAS Mediation Rules. The language to be used in the mediation shall be..."

The standard CAS reference clause for Mediation followed by Arbitration (Med-Arb) is as follows:

> "If, and to the extent that, any such dispute has not been settled within 90 days of the commencement of the mediation, or if, before the expiration of the said period, either party fails to participate or continue to participate in the mediation, the dispute shall, upon the filing of a Request for Arbitration by either party, be referred to and finally settled by CAS arbitration pursuant to the Code of Sports-related Arbitration. When the

---

[20] Article R38, ibid.

circumstances so require, the mediator may, at his own discretion or at the request of a party, seek an extension of the time limit from the CAS President."

For the sake of completeness, the standard CAS reference clause for an '*ad hoc*' CAS Arbitration, that is, a reference to the CAS by the parties in dispute after the dispute has arisen, is as follows:

"'AD HOC' CAS Arbitration Clause

1. [Brief description of the dispute]
2. The dispute will be submitted exclusively to the Court of Arbitration for Sport in Lausanne, Switzerland, and settled definitively in accordance with the Code of sports-related arbitration.

Alternative 1

3. The Panel set in operation by the Court of Arbitration for Sport will consist of a sole arbitrator designated by the President of the CAS Division concerned.

Alternative 2

4. The Panel set in operation by the Court of Arbitration for Sport will consist of three arbitrators. Each party designates the following arbitrator:

   - Claimant: Mr/Mrs ... [insert the name of a person included on the list of CAS arbitrators (see Annex I)];
   - Defendant: Mr/Mrs ... [insert the name of a person included on the list of CAS arbitrators (see Annex I)];

   These two arbitrators will designate the President of the Panel within 30 days following the signature of this agreement. If no agreement is reached within this time limit, the President of the Division concerned will designate the President of the Panel."

## 17.4 Expert Determination Dispute Resolution Clauses

It may be appropriate that a provision for Expert Determination should also be included, as part of the Dispute Resolution Clause. Such a provision would be especially relevant for settling quickly and finally disputes of a technical nature arising under Sports Marketing Agreements, especially Sports Merchandising and Licensing Agreements.

Under Expert Determination, the parties in dispute agree to appoint an Expert to determine their dispute and further agree to be bound by the Determination.

To avoid a deadlock occurring on the particular Expert to be appointed through failure of the parties to agree, the Expert Determination provision should also provide, in such case, for the appointment of the Expert by an independent third party, such as the President for the time being of The Law Society of England and Wales, and also the agreement of the parties to accept and abide by the appointment made by that third party. Ideally, the parties should agree on the Expert themselves, so that, as they say, they have 'ownership' in the process, which is generally considered as a *sine qua non* for the success of ADR.

For example, an Expert Determination Clause recommended by the World Intellectual Property Organization (WIPO) for the settlement of Intellectual Property related disputes is as follows:

> "We, the undersigned parties, hereby agree to submit to expert determination in accordance with the WIPO Expert Determination Rules the following matter:
> [brief description of the matter referred to expert determination]
> The determination made by the expert shall [not] be binding upon the parties. The language to be used in the expert determination shall be [specify language]."

WIPO also recommends, according to the circumstances of the dispute, the following clause providing for Mediation followed in the absence of a settlement by Expert Determination:

> "We, the undersigned parties, hereby agree to submit to mediation in accordance with the WIPO Mediation Rules the following matter:
> [brief description of the dispute or difference between the parties]
> The place of mediation shall be [specify place]. The language to be used in the mediation shall be [specify language].
> We further agree that, if, and to the extent that, any such matter has not been settled pursuant to the mediation within [60][90] days of the commencement of the mediation, it shall, upon the filing of a Request for Expert Determination by either party, be referred to expert determination in accordance with the WIPO Expert Determination Rules. Alternatively, if, before the expiration of the said period of [60][90] days, either party fails to participate or to continue to participate in the mediation, the dispute or difference shall, upon the filing of a Request for Expert Determination by the other party, be referred to expert determination in accordance with the WIPO Expert Determination Rules. The determination made by the expert shall [not] be binding upon the parties. The language to be used in the expert determination shall be [specify language]."

As with all general precedents, the wording of them needs to be customised to fit and reflect the particular facts and circumstances of the Agreement concerned.

Another form of ADR that may be appropriate—and also cost-effective—for settling disputes under Sports Licensing and Merchandising Agreements is '*expert determination*', especially for resolving disputes of a technical, quality control and financial nature. The expert's decision is final and binding on the parties. Of course, the success of this form of dispute resolution depends upon the parties finding and agreeing on a suitably qualified and independent expert, who is also experienced in these matters. In the appointment clause, it should be expressly stated that the person appointed is acting as an expert and not as an arbitrator, to ensure that the expert's decision is final and not subject to any kind of appeal or legal challenge.

Before agreeing to such a provision, however, the parties need to appreciate the legal nature of this dispute resolution procedure, and, in particular, the limited rights of appeal against the expert's findings. In three recent cases, the Courts have looked at several aspects of expert determination, and, in summary, their findings are as follows:

- once agreed expert determination clauses are binding and the parties have no recourse to the courts;
- where the expert determination clause provides that the expert shall give reasons for a decision the Court will order that they be given; and
- where a defendant refused to take part in an expert determination the claimant may recover damages if it has to issue legal proceedings.

In *Douglas Harper v Interchange Group Ltd*,[21] there has been a clear reiteration that the Courts will enforce an expert determination provision in an Agreement and that a party will be prohibited from bringing Court proceedings where the dispute falls within an expert determination provision and that provision is ignored. In this case, the Agreement contained a comprehensive expert determination procedure. The High Court found that the parties were contractually bound by this procedure, so the plaintiff was barred from issuing Court proceedings claiming commission due. He had not complied with the requirements set out in the expert determination provision.

In *Halifax Life Ltd v The Equitable Life Assurance Society*,[22] the Court provided further confirmation that expert determination procedures are binding on the parties, and although the Court may intervene to resolve issues, such as whether the expert should provide a reasoned decision or not, the actual decision of the expert will not be disturbed. Halifax had agreed to reinsure Equitable Life's unit-linked and non-profit business. This required an assessment of an initial premium for the reinsurance, which was referred to an expert to determine. Crucially the parties agreed that the expert would provide reasons for his decision. The expert made his determination, but failed to give reasons. Halifax challenged the decision claiming that it was non-binding on the ground of manifest error. The High Court said that:

> "In litigation justice will not be done if it is not apparent to the parties why one has won and the other has lost."

And, therefore, held that the appropriate course was to adjourn the hearing of Halifax's claim and to remit the matter back to the expert in order that he could state the reasons for his decision. This allowed Halifax the opportunity to understand the reasons for the decision and to decide whether to continue with its legal challenge. The Judge referred by analogy to the provisions in the UK Arbitration Act 1996 (Section 70(4) which allows the Court to order an arbitral tribunal to provide reasons or sufficient reasons for its decision) and was able to require the expert to give reasons either by way of remedy in respect of the provisions of the contract, under the court's inherent jurisdiction or under its case management powers contained in the Civil Procedure Rules. This case is a reminder that the Courts can still intervene in an expert determination, although a 'hands off' approach is generally favoured. Parties can take comfort from the fact

[21] [2007] EWHC 1834.

[22] [2007] EWHC 503.

that they can now expect a properly reasoned decision, if they have expressly agreed that reasons are to be given and they should certainly so provide in their expert determination clause.

In *Sunrock Aircraft Corporation V Scandinavian Airlines System Denmark–Norway–Sweden*,[23] the Court of Appeal upheld the validity of an expert determination clause. It considered the measure of damages to be awarded where a party had refused to participate in the expert determination, but the other party had asked the Court to award damages rather than asking for a mandatory order for expert determination. In this particular case, the Court held that nominal damages were the correct measure of the claimant's loss.

These cases indicate that an increasing number of parties are agreeing to such dispute resolution procedures in their Agreements, whether out of a desire to minimise their legal costs or implement a quicker dispute resolution procedure or both. They also underline the need for the parties to carefully consider and think through the suitability of such clauses, and also to appreciate that, once agreed, the procedure is compulsory and the expert's findings may only be legally challenged on the narrowest of grounds. In other words, the Courts will uphold Expert Determination clauses.

## 17.5 'Mixed' Dispute Resolution Clauses

Of course, a Dispute Resolution Clause may be a so-called 'mixed' clause, combining ADR with reference to the Courts in specific circumstances, for example, where interim relief is required, such as an Interlocutory Injunction. For it has been well said that ADR is not a panacea for the resolution of all disputes.[24] To use a sporting metaphor, it is always a case of 'horses for courses'. In other words, what is appropriate in the particular circumstances.

However, the drafting of a 'mixed' dispute resolution clause needs to be precise, separating out clearly those cases in which each kind of dispute resolution applies to avoid any ambiguities. This can be achieved by referring to specific clauses in the Sports Marketing Agreement concerned under which the dispute arises and indicating that the corresponding dispute resolution method provided for in the Dispute Resolution Clause applies.

---

23 [2007] EWHC Civ 882.

24 Lord Irvine of Lairg, the former UK Lord Chancellor, in the Inaugural Lecture to the Faculty of Mediation and ADR, London, 27 January, 1999.

## 17.6 Concluding Remarks

It is most advisable to include an express Dispute Resolution Clause in Sports Marketing Agreements and not to rely on an '*Ad Hoc*' one at the time a dispute arises. Advantage should be taken of using the various forms of ADR that are available for settling disputes quickly, fairly, effectively and, of course, inexpensively. In the sporting context, generally speaking, it is useful to refer disputes for settlement by the Court of Arbitration for Sport, which has proved to be—and continues to be—a very effective forum for settling all kinds of sports-related disputes, including international commercial ones arise under, out of or in relation to Sports Marketing Agreements.

Apart from Arbitration and Mediation, Expert Determination as a means of settling disputes *extra-judicially* should not be overlooked. Expert Determination is particular relevant in cases of IP-related disputes of which many arise, from time to time, in relation to the commercial side of sport.

However, as has been pointed out, ADR is not the be all and end all for settling all kinds of disputes, and, in appropriate cases, disputes should be referred to the Courts, especially where some form of interim relief is required, which ADR bodies are less able to grant and, more importantly, to enforce legally.

Whatever form of dispute resolution is decided upon, the careful and precise drafting of the corresponding Dispute Resolution Clauses in Sports Marketing Agreements is absolutely essential and cannot be overemphasised!

# Chapter 18
# 'Best Endeavours' Clauses

Meaning of the terms 'best endeavours' 'reasonable endeavours' and 'all reasonable endeavours' in Sports Marketing Agreements

## 18.1 Introductory Remarks

So-called 'best endeavours' clauses, which are generally known in the United States as 'efforts' clauses, are very popular in Commercial Agreements in general and also in Sports Marketing Agreements in particular. However, they are problematic, in practice, and should be used with care and circumspection. They should always be mutual and never unilateral.

'Best endeavours' clauses come in various guises ranging from pure and unadulterated ones requiring the party concerned to use its 'best endeavours' or in watered down variations requiring the party concerned to use either 'all reasonable endeavours' or just 'reasonable endeavours'.

When using these various versions, it is crucial to have a clear understanding of their precise meaning and legal effect. In other words, to be fully aware of the nature and extent, legally and practically speaking, of the obligations their inclusion in Sports Marketing Agreements impose upon the parties concerned.

We will now take a look in this chapter at the various forms of 'best endeavours' clauses and see what legal obligations they actually entail.

I. S. Blackshaw, *Sports Marketing Agreements: Legal, Fiscal and Practical Aspects*, ASSER International Sports Law Series, DOI: 10.1007/978-90-6704-793-7_18, 

### *18.1.1 'Best Endeavours'*

The inclusion of the term 'best endeavours' in a clause originally placed an onus on the obliged party to "broadly speaking, leave no stone unturned."[1]

This very onerous obligation has been lessened somewhat over the years in subsequent English Court cases to allow for the concept of standards of reasonableness to be introduced into its meaning. In other words:

> "'best endeavours' are something less than the efforts which go beyond the bounds of reason, but are considerably more than casual and intermittent activities."[2]

What is now required is that parties must do:

> "all that a reasonable person reasonably could do in the circumstances"[3]

They must take all the steps that a reasonable person:

> "acting in their own interest and desiring to achieve that result would take."[4]

An obligation to use 'best endeavours' probably requires a party to take all the reasonable courses he/she can. The party concerned must act honestly, reasonably and make a positive effort to perform the relevant obligation.

In the case of a company, the required standard is that of a

> "reasonable and prudent board of directors, acting properly in the interest of their company and applying their minds to their contractual obligations."[5]

In other words, a company must do all that is reasonable in the particular circumstances. This obligation does not, however, extend to a situation where a company should put itself at risk of financial ruin to fulfill its obligation.[6]

It seems clear, therefore, that a company should carry out such actions that are commercially practicable and incur any reasonable associated cost in order to fulfill its responsibilities.

What actually amounts to 'best endeavours' must be considered at the time of performance or breach of the undertaking and not at the time of the creation of the contract.[7]

---

1 See *Sheffield District Railway Co. v Great Central Railway Co.* (1911) 27 TLR 451.

2 See *Pips (Leisure Production) Ltd. v Walton* (1980) 43 P&CR 415.

3 Ibid.

4 See *IBM UK Limited v Rockware Glass Ltd.* [1980] FSR 335 (CA).

5 See *Terrell v Mabie Todd & Co. Ltd.* (1952) 69 RPC 234.

6 Ibid.

7 See *Midland Land Reclamation Ltd. and Leicestershire County Council v Warren Energy Limited* 1995 ORB No. 254.

### 18.1.2 'Reasonable Endeavours'

The obligations imposed by the term 'reasonable endeavours' are "appreciably less than (those imposed by) best endeavours" and can be satisfied by an "honest try" by the obliged party.[8]

If a company can show any practical, financial or other commercial disadvantage in proceeding with the obligation this could justify its failure to take positive action, as also could the likelihood or lack thereof of being successful.

Any disadvantage to the obliged party seems to justify a failure to take positive action. In order to ensure the enforceability of a 'reasonable endeavours' clause, parties should ensure that objective criteria are included in the contract clearly stating what the parties must do in order to meet their 'reasonable endeavours' obligations.[9]

Without such objective criteria, the clause may be unenforceable due to uncertainty, as it can be difficult to decide what is reasonable and unreasonable in an area where the parties may have differing views (the subjective test). In other words, no criteria are in place to enable a third party to determine, with certainty, whether or not the behaviour of the party concerned amounts to 'reasonable endeavours' in the particular circumstances of the case.[10]

In an important new development, the English High Court recently held that, where a clause in a contract requires a party to use 'reasonable endeavours' and the clause specifies certain steps to be taken in order to fulfill an obligation to use reasonable endeavours, those steps would need to be taken even if it involves that party sacrificing their own commercial interests.[11]

This development clearly increases the onus placed on parties who undertake an obligation to use 'reasonable endeavours'. As Mr. Justice Flaux (as he now is) put it in that case:

> "There may be a number of reasonable courses which could be taken in a given situation to achieve a particular aim. An obligation to use reasonable endeavours to achieve the aim probably only requires a party to take one reasonable course, not all of them, whereas an obligation to use best endeavours probably requires a party to take all the reasonable courses he can. In that context, it may well be that an obligation to use all reasonable endeavours equates with using best endeavours."[12]

The Court reiterated the position that 'reasonable endeavours' only requires a party to take one reasonable course, not all of them; whereas the obligation to use

---

[8] See *UBH (Mechanical Services) Ltd. v Standard Life Assurance Co.* The Times 13 November, 1986.

[9] See *RAE Lambert v HTV Cymru (Wales) Ltd.* 1998 Court of Appeal.

[10] See *Phillips Petroleum Co UK Ltd. v Enron Europe Ltd.* [1997] CLC 329.

[11] See *Rhodia International Holdings Ltd. v Huntsman International LLC* [2007] EWHC 292.

[12] Ibid.

'best endeavours' probably requires a party to take all the reasonable courses he/ she can.[13]

The principle laid down in *Rhodia* was confirmed in the case of *Yewbelle Ltd. v London Green Developments Ltd.*,[14] namely, that a party will not be required to spend a significant amount of time or money on fulfilling a 'reasonable endeavours' obligation. As to what the Court will judge to be significant will be decided on a case-by-case basis.

See also the latest case, at the time of writing, on the subject: *CPC Group Ltd. v Qatari Diar Real Estate Investment Company*,[15] in which the clause 'to use all reasonable but commercially prudent endeavours' was considered and held not to equate to a 'best endeavours' obligation, but a 'reasonable endeavours' obligation only, because of the qualifying words 'commercially prudent'. But note that such qualifying words would not extend to 'political interests' but only commercial ones. As usual, the devil is in the detail of the drafting.

### *18.1.3 'All Reasonable Endeavours'*

To take 'all reasonable endeavours' has been described as "something more than reasonable endeavours but less that best endeavours."[16]

Clearly, whilst it does not impose as onerous an obligation as 'best endeavours', an obligation to take 'all reasonable endeavours' requires the party concerned to expend more than merely minimal efforts in an attempt to fulfill its responsibility; but the party is not required to take all those steps in its power to reach the desired result.

## 18.2 Concluding Remarks

As has been seen in the above account, 'best endeavours' clauses are problematic and should be used with caution. When drafting them, the draftsman should ensure that all the parties to the Agreement, in which they are included, are fully aware of the extent of the obligations that they impose upon them.

In fact, if they can, in practice, despite their popularity, be avoided, in my opinion, it is better not to use these clauses in any shape or form! For one main reason: however well these clauses are drafted, as they are open to interpretation they involve some degree of uncertainty.

---

13 Ibid.

14 [2007] EWCA Civ 475.

15 [2010] EWHC 1535 (Ch).

16 See footnote 8, supra.

Clearly, 'endeavours' clauses do not amount to an absolute obligation as is imposed by the use of terms such as "must" or "shall" which are obviously mandatory and, incidentally, much clearer and, therefore, easier to enforce. Nevertheless, whilst 'best endeavours' does not impose an "absolute obligation",[17] a 'best endeavours' clause is still considered as an onerous obligation requiring the party concerned to do all that is prudent and reasonable in the particular circumstances of the case to fulfill its obligation.

A clause in an Agreement requiring a party to take 'reasonable endeavours' creates a lower level obligation with only minimal effort being required; but, in the absence of clear criteria as to what is considered to be reasonable in the particular circumstances, 'reasonable endeavours' clauses may be considered void for uncertainty and, therefore, unenforceable. In fact, it is usually easier to define 'unreasonable endeavours' rather than 'reasonable endeavours' in practice.

Importantly, where criteria have been included in an Agreement, minimal effort will not be considered sufficient to have fulfilled a party's obligations. If certain steps are set out, then those steps must be carried out, even though they may be detrimental to the commercial and financial interests of the party concerned.

It is settled Law that 'all reasonable endeavours' clauses impose an obligation on the party concerned midway between 'reasonable endeavours' and 'best endeavours' clauses and are to be construed and applied accordingly.[18]

All in all, to answer the question posed at the beginning of this article, 'endeavours' clauses of whatever kind are probably more of a curse than a blessing and are, therefore, best avoided, if possible! If that is not possible, they should always be mutual obligations on the parties to the Agreement and include some specific requirements on the amount of time and money to be expended on their performance, in order to add some degree of certainty into them. This is very important indeed in these present economically uncertain times!

---

[17] See footnote 7, supra.

[18] See footnote 8, supra.

# Chapter 19
# 'Boiler Plate' Clauses

## 19.1 Introductory Remarks

So-called 'Boiler Plate' Clauses[1] are standard clauses found at the end of an Agreement, which, as their name suggests, are intended to reinforce and strengthen the Agreement, and make it 'water-tight' from a legal point of view.

As with standard clauses generally, they need to be used with care and only included where it is appropriate to do so; and, in any event, they need to be customised to reflect the particular commercial facts and circumstances of the deal. In other words, they should not be used slavishly and as a matter of course.

## 19.2 Some Common 'Boiler Plate' Clauses

The most commonly used 'Boilerplate' clauses in Agreements are as follows:

### *19.2.1 Amendment Clause*

An Amendment Clause provides the means by which the parties are entitled to make changes to the Agreement. Amendments are usually to be made in writing and to be signed by or on behalf of the parties to the Agreement, with the proviso that any and all other such amendments are not legally binding on the parties to the Agreement. In other words, strict compliance with the Clause is required. Additionally, it is advisable to indicate what is meant by 'in writing'. For example, are amendments made by e-mail with encrypted digital signatures valid?

[1] Also known, in the jargon, as 'belt and braces' clauses!

I. S. Blackshaw, *Sports Marketing Agreements: Legal, Fiscal and Practical Aspects*,
ASSER International Sports Law Series, DOI: 10.1007/978-90-6704-793-7_19,

This is a useful Clause because it reflects very well Sam Goldwyn's famous aphorism that: "oral contracts are not worth the paper they are written on!"

### *19.2.2 Assignment Clause*

This Clause deals with the assignability or not, as the case may be, of the Agreement and the rights and obligations arising under it to a third party. Often Sports Marketing Agreements, especially Sports Merchandising and Licensing Agreements, contain a 'no-assignment' provision, because such Agreements are usually entered into because of the particular characteristics of the parties concerned. For example, because of the expertise, experience and reputation of the Licensee in the field of sports merchandising. They are so-called '*intuitu personae*' Agreements.

### *19.2.3 UK Contracts (Rights of Third Parties) Act 1999 Clause*

This Statute allows a third party that is a person who is not a party to the Agreement to enforce a term of the Agreement in two situations:

Firstly, if the Agreement expressly includes this right; or

Secondly, if it is apparent from its tenor that the Agreement gives a third party some kind of benefit.

In other words, the Statute overrides the normal English Common Law principle of 'privity of contract', namely, that anyone that is not a party to an Agreement cannot claim any rights or incur any obligations under the Agreement concerned.

In practice, many Agreements exclude third parties from claiming any rights under the Agreement; or, alternatively, expressly list the parties who are to have recognised rights under the Agreement.

### *19.2.4 Counterpart Agreements Clause*

This Clause makes it clear that where the Agreement is executed in two or more Counterparts that each counterpart shall be considered to be an original and the Counterparts taken together shall constitute one legal document ('instrument').

### *19.2.5 Entire Agreement Clause*

This is a very useful clause that has the effect of limiting all the parties' rights and obligations to only the provisions contained within the Agreement and any Schedules forming part of the Agreement.

This means that neither party can claim to have acted based on any statement, discussion or document not expressly contained within the Agreement. This excludes so-called 'side agreements' whether oral or in writing.

Such a Clause can have serious consequences for a party relying on a pre-contract 'understanding' as the English High Court case of *White v Bristol Rugby Club*[2] clearly demonstrtates. In view of its importance, the full text of the Judgement of Judge Havelock-Allan, QC in Appendix 1 of this Chapter (19.5.1). Incidentally, this decision has been generally criticised as being an unduly harsh one!

### *19.2.6 Force Majeure Clause*

A 'Force Majeure' Clause prevents the parties to an Agreement from being liable in the event that circumstances outside their control preclude them from being able to undertake and fulfill their obligations under the Agreement. The theory behind this lies in the legal doctrine of 'frustration' and that parties should not be penalised for the actions or fault of another which they could not reasonably have foreseen at the time the Agreement was entered into.

Under English Common Law, it is necessary to spell out in some detail the actual circumstances that would constitute a 'Force Majeure' situation relieving the parties from their obligations of fulfilling the terms of their Agreement. Thus, in the English practice, such 'Force Majeure' Clauses tend to cover several pages of text: certainly in the case of American Agreements!

Whereas, under European Continental Civil Law, the 'Force Majeure' Clause is a much shorter one as the applicable Civil or Commercial Code contains a full definition of what amounts to 'Force Majeure'.

### *19.2.7 Further Assurance Clause*

This Clause takes care of a situation that may arise, in practice, after the execution of the Agreement that requires the completion of some other formality or the execution of some other document to make the Agreement fully effective legally.

### *19.2.8 Good Faith Clause*

This is a Clause requiring the parties to an Agreement to act in good faith and in a timely manner in order to give full legal and practical effect to the Agreement.

---

[2] [2002] IRLR 204.

Of course, one difficulty in drafting this Clause is defining the concept of 'good faith' which is better known and recognised in Civil Law than at English Common Law.

### *19.2.9 Notices Clause*

This Clause is a useful one that provides the parties to an Agreement with a pre-agreed method of giving notice upon the occurrence of specific events. For example, notice of termination on breach of the Agreement.

The Clause is a very important provision, in practice, as it sets out the manner in which the parties to an Agreement should communicate with one another, and also lays down the corresponding timescales in which the notices shall be given. In this way, disputes later on may be avoided.

If the parties to the Agreement are in different countries, notices could be by electronic means, but this must be expressly reserved in the Agreement. In any case, the Notices Clause should provide for all communications between the Parties to the Agreement will only be legally effective if made in writing. As to what constitutes written notices, this should also be clearly defined in the Agreement.

Likewise, regarding timelines in which notices are to be given and expressed in days or months, the Notices Clause should expressly define the meaning of days and months—natural days or working days; lunar or calendar months. In practice, it is better, for example, to lay down these time lines in days rather than months: for example, 30 days; 90 days; 180 days.

### *19.2.10 Relationship of the Parties*

This is a useful Clause which makes it clear that the parties to the Agreement are acting as independent contractors and that the Agreement does not constitute a partnership or a joint venture, with the resulting rights and obligations, particularly the sharing of profits.

### *19.2.11 Schedules Clause*

This Clause is used to make the Schedules an integral part of the Agreement, even though they may appear in the Agreement after the signature clause.

Avoid lazy drafting by including in this Clause the further provision that, in the event of any conflicts between what is provided in the body of the Agreement and the Schedules, the provisions in the Schedules shall prevail. Ensure, in the first place, that by careful drafting and editing of the Agreement as a whole no such conflicts arise!

### *19.2.12 Set Off Clause*

This is generally a clause that prevents one party from deducting money owed from money payable to the other party, even if the transactions are unrelated. For example, if a seller owes a purchaser money, for whatever reason, the purchaser cannot deduct this from money that is used to pay the seller the purchase price under the Agreement. In other words, both debts are kept separate and dealt with under their respective terms and conditions accordingly.

This Clause, however, may be useful, from a practical and accounting point of view, under, for example, a Sports Merchandising and Licensing Agreement, where there are several accounts to be settled between the parties. Again, it is a matter of looking at the commercial and financial arrangements of the actual deal and deciding whether such a Clause would be relevant or not.

### *19.2.13 Severance and Invalidity Clauses*

If a clause in an Agreement is found to be invalid, illegal or otherwise unenforceable, the Severance Clause allows the parties to remove the offending clause/words and continue with what remains of the Agreement. Thus, if severance of the illegal or invalid clause makes the rest of the Agreement unworkable, the Agreement will be void and of no legal or practical effect.

Again, this Clause may well be useful in the case of Sports Merchandising and Licensing Agreements, which contain territorial restrictions, which may be found subsequently to fall foul of National and European Competition Rules.

### *19.2.14 Survival of Clauses*

Again, this is a useful Clause which provides that certain rights and obligations—it is necessary to specify them—continue after the Agreement has come to an end for whatever reason—expiration of the term or by reason of premature termination.

This Clause is particularly relevant in the case of confidentiality provisions, which are a particular feature of Sports Marketing Agreements.

### *19.2.15 Time of the Essence Clause*

This Clause requires deadlines provided for in the Agreement to be complied with strictly and on time; otherwise, the party, that is entitled to the benefit of the deadline in the event of the other party's failure to meet it, can terminate the Agreement.

But, be careful in using this Clause, which may operate as a two-edged sword! Because of its mutuality, on occasions, it may either work for you or against you! However, its effects may be tempered by making the right of termination a discretionary and not a mandatory one. In other words, to be exercised at the option of the party entitled to terminate the Agreement, according to the particular facts and circumstances of the case obtaining at the time.

### *19.2.16 Waiver Clause*

This Clause is a useful one, allowing flexibility in the operation of the Agreement, in that it provides that waiver by one of the parties of strict compliance by the other party on one particular occasion will not prevent that party on insisting on strict/complete performance of the same provision (that is, the one previously waived by that party) on some future occasion.

## 19.3 Some Examples of 'Boilerplate' Clauses

In Appendix 2 to this Chapter (19.5.2), the reader will find some examples of common 'Boilerplate' Clauses, for general information purposes.

## 19.4 Concluding Remarks

So-called 'Boilerplate' Clauses should be included in Sports Marketing Agreements with great care and a clear understanding of their legal nature and effects. They should never be included as a matter of course, but always with a view to their usefulness and relevance to the particular Sports Marketing deal that needs to be reflected contractually. They should also be customised to fit the particular circumstances of each case. This is particularly true in the case of 'Entire Agreement' Clauses as noted above.

As with any other Clauses in Sports Marketing Agreements they should be drafted with great care and precision to avoid any ambiguities and thus disagreements in the future regarding their meaning, application and scope.

The old drafting adage that Clauses have been included in an Agreement because they do no harm and may do some good is a dangerous one to follow in practice. Each Clause included should be carefully considered; serve a definite purpose and, therefore, be deliberately included; and not merely included on the off chance—or in the pious hope—that they may do some good!

# 19.5 Appendices

## *19.5.1 Appendix 1*

Industrial Relations Law Reports/2002/March 2002/WHITE (claimant) v. BRISTOL RUGBY LTD (defendants)—[2002] IRLR 204

**WHITE (claimant) v. BRISTOL RUGBY LTD (defendants)***

**High Court Queen's Bench Division, (HCQBD)**

*Contracts of employment*
*Terms of employment*
*Terms of employment—pay*
*Terms of employment—duty of mutual trust and confidence*
*Termination—employee repudiation*
*Termination—employer repudiation*
*Misrepresentation Act 1967 section: 3*

**The facts:**
Julian White is a professional rugby player. Until 30 June 2001, he was under contract to a London club, Saracens. However, he wished to return to the West Country and, to that end, at the beginning of 2000 he instructed his agent to start looking for clubs in the West Country who might employ him when his contract with Saracens came to an end.

As a result, his agent negotiated the terms of a three-year contract with Bristol Shoguns to run from 1 July 2001 at an annual salary of £80,000. At Mr White's request, it was agreed that he would be paid £15,000 of his salary in advance on signing the contract. A provision to that effect was included in a draft contract drawn up by Bristol's chief executive. Under that provision, "Upon signing this contract, an advance of £15,000 will be paid to the player which will be deducted out of his first year's salary. Should the player, for whatever reason, not join Bristol Rugby Club the £15,000 will of course be repayable."

At a meeting on 12 May 2000, Mr White, his agent and the club's chief executive went through the provisions of the draft contract and it was agreed that the provision relating to the £15,000 advance would be amended so that instead of the whole sum being deducted out of the salary payable in the first year, it would be repaid at the rate of £5,000 per annum over the three years of the contract term. There was also some discussion as to the circumstances in which the £15,000 would be repayable. At the end of the meeting, Mr White signed the contract. However, he did not ask for the £15,000 advance until September.

* Source: Lexis Nexis (UK Law Reports); reproduced with permission.

Mr White began to have doubts about joining Bristol and eventually, he decided that he wanted to exercise the right, which he thought he had, to opt out. He also decided to terminate his agreement with his original agent and appointed a new agent. On 31 January 2001, the new agent wrote to Bristol notifying them that Mr White would not be joining the club on 1 July 2001 and enclosing a cheque for £15,000 by way of repayment of the advance of salary. The letter alleged that the club's chief executive had represented that Mr White could walk away from the agreement at any time on repayment of the £15,000 and it was only in reliance of that representation that Mr White had agreed to sign the contract. The club returned the cheque, maintaining that no such representation was made and that the contract was valid and binding.

Subsequent attempts to resolve the dispute failed, notwithstanding an open offer from Bristol to Mr White on 11 May 2001 to improve the contract terms by increasing his salary from £80,000 to £100,000, adding a bonus of £500 for each match in which he was selected to play in the first team and giving him an option to break the contract after the first season.

At all material times since the end of January 2001, Mr White denied that he was bound by any obligation to join Bristol. Since 1 July, which was the first day of employment under the contract, he was absent from the club premises and made no attempt to make contact with the club or to proffer his services. The club in turn refused to pay him so long as he remained unwilling to make himself available to them.

Mr White began proceedings against Bristol, seeking a declaration that he was not bound by the contract. His primary case was that, by virtue of the alleged representation of the club's chief executive, the contract contained an express oral term to the effect that he could opt out of it by returning the advance of £15,000.

In the event of a finding that the contract was still binding because it contained no "opt-out" clause, a further argument was advanced to the effect that the contract had been terminated by Mr White's repudiatory breach of contract and that Bristol, by their conduct in various respects, had accepted the repudiation as bringing the contract to an end. Alternatively, it was submitted that that conduct amounted to a repudiation by Bristol which Mr White had accepted.

The High Court, Queen's Bench Division [Bristol Mercantile Court] (Judge Havelock-Allan QC) on 17 August 2001 found that the contract between the claimant and the defendants remained valid and subsisting and dismissed the claim.

**The High Court held:**

The contract between the claimant professional rugby player and the defendant rugby club could not be interpreted as containing an express oral clause allowing the claimant to opt out of the contract by returning a salary advance of £15,000.

Such an interpretation was precluded by a clause in the written contract under which the parties to the agreement acknowledged that "this agreement and its schedules together with the documents referred to in this agreement contain the whole agreement between the parties and that they have not relied upon oral or written representations made to them by other persons, its employees or agents." "Entire agreement" clauses are an increasingly common feature of sophisticated and detailed contract documents and, if clearly worded so as to do so, which the clause in the present case was, are effective to exclude claims based on collateral warranties or oral terms outside the four corners of the written document.

In the present case, therefore, the clause precluded the claimant's contention that the contract included a separate oral term not reflected in the written document or that anything said at a meeting which was not reflected in the written wording may never-theless have acquired contractual force as a contract term or collateral warranty.

It could not be accepted that the provision in the agreement that "Should the player, for whatever reason, not join Bristol Rugby Club the £15,000 will of course be repayable", when properly construed in the context of statements allegedly made, conferred a right to opt out on the claimant. The wording of that provision was not apt to create a right not to join the club; it simply addressed what was to happen if the player did not join. In any event, the evidence did not substantiate that any statement had been made which the claimant could fairly interpret as giving him the right to opt out of the contract on repayment of the salary advance.

There was nothing in the defendants' conduct which indicated that they had accepted the claimant's repudiation as bringing the contract to an end, notwithstanding their declared position that the contract was still open and the claimant was welcome to join them at any time.

An acceptance of a repudiation must be unequivocal. If a party says one thing and does another, his conduct is equivocal. Although it is possible for a party to a contract to declare that he is treating it as open for performance by the other party who is in repudiatory breach, but to be held in reality to have accepted the breach as bringing the contract to an end, that would be an unusual case and would probably only arise where there was conduct on the part of the innocent party which had effectively disabled him from entertaining further performance by the party in breach. For example, in the context of the present case, it would not have availed the defendants to announce that the claimant's contract was being kept open if at the same time they had engaged someone to replace him. It was not suggested, however, that the defendants had done anything so final.

The defendants' conduct in failing to pay the claimant his salary was not an indication of their acceptance of the claimant's repudiatory breach in refusing to make himself available to train and to play for the club. Nor was it a repudiation of the contract by them.

The claimant was not entitled to any salary because he did not do any work. Whilst it is entirely possible for a contract of employment to provide that an employee should receive his full wage even where he refuses to turn up for work through his own free choice and through no fault of the employer, the contract in the present case could not be read as containing any such provision.

It could not be accepted the defendants must be regarded as having accepted the claimant's conduct as bringing the contract to an end because the trust and confidence on which the master and servant relationship is based had been irrevocably destroyed and they could therefore have no purpose in keeping the contract alive. If the logic of that argument was accepted, it would come very close to acknowledging that an employee can, by unilaterally refusing to serve his employer, bring about the termination of the contract of employment. That was precisely the result which Vice-Chancellor Megarry declined to countenance in *Thomas Marshall Ltd v Guinle*. In any event, in the present case, the master and servant relationship had not irretrievably broken down.

**Cases referred to:**
*Deepak Fertilisers and Petrochemicals Corporation v ICI* [1999] 1 Lloyd's Rep 387 CA
*Evening Standard Co Ltd v Henderson* [1987] IRLR 64 CA
*Gillespie Bros & Co v Cheney, Eggar & Co* [1896] 2 QB 59
*Government of Zanzibar v British Aerospace Ltd* [2000] 1 WLR 2333 HC
*E Grimstead & Sons Ltd v McGarrigan* 27 October 1999 CA
*Inntrepreneur Pub Co v East Crown Ltd* [2000] 3 EGLR 31 HC
*McGrath v Shah* [1989] 57 P & CR 452
*Ross T Smyth & Co Ltd v T D Bailey Son & Co* [1940] 3 AER 60 HL
*Thomas Marshall (Exports) Ltd v Guinle* [1978] IRLR 174 HC

**Appearances:**
For the Claimant: OWEN WILLIAMS, solicitor advocate of Clarke Willmott and Clarke
For the Defendants: TIM KERR QC and TERENCE FINN, instructed by Withy King

**1** JUDGE HAVELOCK-ALLAN QC: The claimant, Julian White. is a professional rugby union player. He plays as a tight-head prop forward. He has recently been a member of the England squad on its tour of the United States and Canada. He has been described by one witness in this case as 'probably the best prop in the northern hemisphere'. Even if that may be hyperbole, there is no doubt that he is a rising star in the Allied Dunbar Premiership and that his services as a player are in great demand.

**2** In this action Mr White claims against the defendant, Bristol Rugby Ltd, who are popularly known as 'Bristol Shoguns' and whom I shall refer to simply as 'Bristol', declarations that either:

(i) the contract between himself and Bristol dated 12 May 2000 ('the contract') contained an express oral clause allowing him to bring the contract to an end by returning the advance of £15,000 and that he has exercised that opt-out; or
(ii) he was entitled to and has rescinded the contract by reason of misrepresentation; or
(iii) Bristol are estopped from asserting (a) that the contract contained an express opt-out clause, and (b) that he is bound by the contract

**3** An alternative claim made on his behalf for rectification of the contract is no longer pursued: but alternative relief is sought in the event that the court holds that the contract contained no opt-out clause and is therefore binding unless it has been terminated for breach. I will expand on that alternative case shortly.

**4** The background is that until 30 June 2001, Mr White was under contract to Saracens. He had signed a two-year contract with Saracens which expired on that date. Saracens are a London club and Mr White comes from the West Country. His parents live in Devon. Not long after he joined Saracens, Mr White decided that he would like to return to the West Country and play for one of the West of England clubs. He tried to gain release from his Saracens contract after the first six months. He was unsuccessful. The club insisted that he stay with them for the two seasons. Nevertheless he told his agent early last year to start looking for clubs in the West Country who might employ him when his contract with Saracens came to an end.

**5** His agent at the time was Mike Burton Management. Mr Burton began to look around for other clubs in the Allied Dunbar Premiership who were based in the West Country and who might be interested in signing Mr White. When Mr Burton approached Bristol, their chief executive, Mr Nick de Scossa, expressed an interest and Mr Burton entered into negotiations with him. He negotiated the terms of a three-year contract to run from 1 July 2001 at an annual salary of £80,000 per annum. When he reported this offer to Mr White, he was willing to accept it but asked if Mr Burton could get Bristol to agree to pay £15,000 of his salary in advance. Mr Burton went back to Mr de Scossa and secured from him Bristol's agreement to pay Mr White an advance of £15,000 on signing of the contract.

**6** A meeting was arranged to take place at the Bath Spa Hotel on 12 May 2000, at which Mr White would sign the contract. The meeting was attended by Mr White and Mr Burton and by Mr de Scossa. Mr de Scossa brought with him a typed copy of the contract. I have been told that the RFU has certain standard terms for players' contracts, which member clubs are recommended, but not obliged, to use. In practice, player contracts differ between clubs, even within the Premiership, but certain features are common. The draft contract which Mr de Scossa produced was based upon the RFU standard terms with adaptations. It was a formal document consisting of a frontsheet and 21 clauses, some with sub-clauses, occupying 13 pages of A4. Appended to these were four schedules of eight pages in total and a page for signatures. The contract was dated 12 May 2000.

**7** From Mr White's point of view, the essential provisions of the draft contract were the salary and that his employment would commence on 1 July 2001 and terminate at midnight on 30 June 2004. The draft contract also contained detailed provisions entitling him to be released by Bristol to play for England; but, aside from the England team, his services were to be devoted exclusively to Bristol. His salary was recorded in s.1 of Schedule 1 in the following manner (the italics are mine):

"Basic salary" means the sum of £80,000 sterling per annum, payable monthly in accor-ance with clause 4 of this agreement. Upon signing this contract, an advance of £15,000 will be paid to the player which will be deducted out of his first year's salary. *Should the player, for whatever reason, not join Bristol Rugby Club the £15,000 will of course be repayable.*'

**8** During the meeting on 12 May 2000, Mr Burton spent about 15 minutes taking Mr White through the main provisions of the draft contract because Mr White had not seen it before. Mr White accepted in evidence that he read the draft contract and understood the general effect of it. At some stage, probably when they looked at the basic salary clause quoted above, there was a discussion between the three persons present about the £15,000 advance. There is no issue that Mr de Scossa was persuaded to agree to amend the provision which stated that the advance would be deducted from the salary payable in the first year and to substitute instead a provision that it be repaid at the rate of £5,000 per annum over the three years of the contract term. Mr Burton deleted in ink the words 'out of his first year's salary' and wrote in the margin 'at the rate of £5,000pa over the period of the contract'. Both he and Mr White then initialled this change.

**9** Before the contract was signed, something was also said about other circumstances in which the £15,000 would be repayable. Here recollections differ. Mr White says that Mr de Scossa made it clear to him that even if he signed the contract he had an option not to go to Bristol: but in that event the £15,000 would have to be repaid. Mr White says in his first witness statement that Mr de Scossa said: 'If you don't come to Bristol or change your mind, £15,000 has to come back.' Mr de Scossa's recollection, and Mr Burton's as well, is that nothing of that kind was said. They both maintain that the only other remark made about the £15,000 was a remark by Mr de Scossa towards the end of the meeting that If Mr White failed a medical the £15,000 would have to be refunded. Mr White denies that this remark was made.

**10** Although the contract was not subject to any condition that Mr White should pass a medical before joining, I was told by Mr Burton and by Mr de Scossa that it is routine for rugby clubs to subject new players to a comprehensive medical test before the start of their employment, not least because, if they are found to have a pre-existing injury, this has implications for the club's medical insurance. In certain circumstances, the player would be required to bring his previous medical cover with him. All this makes perfect sense. So it is strange that the contract should not have contained a term that the start of Mr White's employment with Bristol was conditional on his passing a medical. Indeed, Mr de Scossa thought that the contract did contain such a term. His remark, however, was focused on the £15,000. If Mr White was subjected to a medical before starting his employment and failed it badly, it might be argued that the contract was frustrated, in which case it is plain that the advance of salary would have to be repaid. The issue is whether this was all that Mr de Scossa said or whether he went further and conceded that Mr White could opt out of the contract if he changed his mind.

**11** Mr White did not seek payment of the £15,000 immediately. He waited until September of last year, when he wanted to buy a house in Devon. He did not need the £15,000 in order to finalise the purchase but his financial adviser suggested that it would be a good idea to make use of it. It was paid to him on or about 19 September and used to finance the purchase. However, he was already having doubts about joining Bristol. His doubts increased to the point where he decided that he wanted to exercise the right, which he thought he had, to opt out.

**12** On 5 January 2001, Mr White parted company with Mike Burton Management. He terminated his agreement with them and wrote to Mr Burton thanking him for his support in the past. Mr White then appointed Mr Powell of Clarke Willmott & Clarke as his new agent and Mr Powell arranged for Mr White to receive advice from Mr Richard Harry of that firm as to his entitlement under the contract not to join Bristol.

**13** Mr Harry met Mr Dean Ryan, Bristol's head coach, on 23 January. Following that meeting, at which it is to be inferred that Mr Ryan indicated that Bristol regarded Mr White as bound by the contract, Mr Harry wrote to Bristol on 31 January 2001 notifying them that Mr White would not be commencing employment at the club on 1 July 2001 and enclosing a cheque for £15,000 by way of repayment of the advance of salary. Mr Harry provided in the letter the following explanation:

> '... We are instructed that our client was unwilling to sign the agreement with Bristol Rugby Club unless and until Mr do Scossa represented that our client could walk away from the agreement at any time on payment of the £15,000 that was presented at that time as consideration.
> As the document was signed by our client in reliance on this representation, it is clearly of fundamental importance, and will be construed as a term of the agreement. In the alternative our client now wishes to take advantage of that representation.'

**14** The response from Bristol's solicitors, on 12 February 2001, was to maintain that the contract was valid and binding and to deny that any such representation was made. They returned the cheque for £15,000 and the money has remained in an escrow account ever since. Subsequent attempts at resolving the dispute have failed, notwithstanding an open offer from Bristol to Mr White on 11 May 2001 to improve the contract terms by increasing his salary from £80,000 to £110,000, adding a bonus of £500 for each match in which he was selected to play in the first team and giving him an option to break the contract after the first season. The resulting impasse now threatens to deprive fans of the opportunity of seeing Julian White playing Premiership Rugby in the forthcoming season. Both parties urgently require a decision as to their respective rights. Bristol say that they still hope to persuade Mr White to play for them; but sooner or later they must make alternative arrangements if he will not do so. Mr White needs to know whether he is contractually free to look for employment as a prop forward elsewhere and whether, by reason of his refusal to play for Bristol, he is liable to that club in damages.

**15** Mr White commenced the present action on 15 May 2001. His primary case is that, by virtue of the alleged representation by Mr de Scossa, the contract contained an express oral term to the effect that he could opt out of it by returning the advance of £15,000. In the alternative he alleges that Mr de Scossa misrepresented that the contract did contain such a term and he is therefore entitled to rescind the contract, and has rescinded it, on the grounds of that misrepresentation. In essence, these contentions raise a comparatively straightforward issue, which depends on the recollection of those who attended the meeting on 12 May 2000 as to what was or was not said to persuade Mr White to sign. Mr White's alternative case is of more recent origin. Mindful of the possibility that the court might decide that the contract was still binding because it contained no 'opt-out' clause and was not liable to be rescinded on grounds of misrepresentation, those representing Mr White advance a number of further arguments to the effect that the contract has been repudiated by Mr White and that Bristol, by their conduct in various respects, have accepted the repudiation as bringing the contract to an end. Conversely, in the further alternative, it is said that the selfsame conduct amounts to a repudiation of the contract by Bristol which Mr White has accepted as bringing the contract to an end. Bristol's response is that they have kept the contract open for performance and have *not* accepted Mr White's admitted renunciation of it, nor have they repudiated it themselves.

**16** These additional arguments are somewhat complicated by the fact that, at the outset of the action, Mr White applied for, and was granted by this court on 19 May 2001, an interim injunction restraining the club:

> '(a) from effecting or seeking to effect the registration of the claimant as its player under the RFU registration rules;
> (b) interfering with or seeking to prevent any other rugby club from effecting the registration of the claimant as its player under the RFU registration rules;
> (c) seeking to prevent the claimant from playing for any other rugby club.'

**17** The court granted the injunction because it appeared that there was a serious issue to be tried as to whether the contract contained an opt-out, and that if the order was not granted Bristol could, by taking the prohibited steps, effectively preclude Mr White from seeking employment by any other club and thereby bring pressure on him to play for them against his will and even if he was not obliged to do so. The injunction was intended to leave Mr White free to seek engagement with another club at the risk, if his primary case failed at trial, that he might have to pay damages to Bristol for the privilege of doing so.

**18** In the event, the injunction has not had that effect. Under the RFU Code of Conduct, a club wishing to sign a player currently under contract to another club must pay a transfer fee equivalent to 'the maximum remuneration achievable by the player in the remaining term of that contract to the limit of 12 months'. Although it is a little-disguised secret that Bath have been keen to secure Mr White's services, it appears that neither they, nor any other club in the RFU, are willing to sign a contract with Mr White until his contractual position with Bristol, and therefore any contingent liability to pay a transfer fee, is clarified.

**19** The injunction has complicated the argument about repudiation of the contract because Bristol say that certain of the steps they have taken, or rather not taken, and which Mr White now relies upon as conduct constituting a repudiation or alternatively an acceptance of a repudiation of the contract, were steps dictated by a desire on their part not to infringe the injunction. Thus (i) Bristol did not include Mr White in their squad which toured Argentina in July 2001, (ii) Bristol have not hitherto included Mr White's name in the list of first team players on their website (although, following cross-examination of Mr White on the first day of the trial, they have now done so) and (iii) Bristol have not invited Mr White to any training sessions since 1 July 2001 and have not yet offered him any work. Mr Ryan explained in the course of his evidence that he had adopted this stance because he was instructed by his superiors that the injunction prevented him from doing otherwise. Whether or not the injunction did have that effect is a matter I will have to consider when I come to Mr White's alternative case.

**20** The fact remains that, at all material times since the end of January 2001, Mr White has denied that he is bound by any obligation to join Bristol. Since 1 July, which was the first day of his employment under the contract, Mr White has been absent from the club premises and appears to have made no attempt to make contact with the club or to proffer his services. The parties' respective positions are therefore as follows. Mr White vigorously asserts, through his legal advisers, that he is not contractually bound to play for Bristol and therefore declines to do so. But he complains, in the alternative, that Bristol should be paying his salary even though he has not made himself available for training and has obtained an injunction precluding Bristol from registering him as their player. By contrast, Bristol maintain, equally vigorously, that Mr White is contractually bound to play for them and that they want him to do so. But so long as he refuses to make himself available to the club, they are not willing to pay him. With that broad survey of the history of this dispute, I turn to Mr White's primary case.

**21** **The opt-out clause**

As already indicated, the principal argument on Mr White's primary case is that, by virtue of what was said by Mr de Scossa at the meeting on 12 May 2000, the contract contained an express oral term that he could opt out of the contract by returning the advance of £15,000. Although Mr Harry claimed in his letter of 31 January that this meant that Mr White could walk away from the contract 'at any time', I think that, if there was a right to opt out, it can only have been exercisable prior to 1 July 2001, since Mr White was due to start work at the club on that date and cancellation thereafter would have been highly disruptive to the arrangements of both parties. In the event, Mr Owen Williams, on behalf of Mr White, was content to accept this time limit.

**22** The burden is on Mr White to prove what Mr de Scossa is alleged to have said, to establish that any statement made bears the interpretation for which he contends and that it was a statement intended to have contractual effect. That burden is heavy one because, where the parties have reduced the terms of their bargain to writing, '... the implication or presumption is very strong that such contract is intended to contain all the terms of their bargain...' (per Lord Russell of Killowen CJ in *Gillespie Bros v Cheney, Eggar & Co* [1896] 2 QB 59 at 62. *Chitty on Contracts,* 28th edn at para 12-095). Mr White is inviting the court to find that the bargain struck between himself and Bristol included an oral term, notwithstanding that all of the remaining terms were incorporated into an apparently comprehensive and detailed written document. Moreover, the oral term is one which would permit him to determine that the written contract is not binding.

**23** The starting point must be to consider the oral evidence of Mr White, Mr de Scossa and Mr Burton as to what happened at the meeting. But Mr Tim Kerr QC, who appears for Bristol, says that that inquiry is unnecessary. He relies on two clauses in the written contract which are in the following terms:

> '*15. Acknowledgment*
>
> Each party to this agreement now acknowledge that this agreement and its sched-ules together with the documents referred to in this agreement contain the whole agreement between the parties and that they have not relied upon oral or written representations made to them by other persons, its employees or agents.
>
> *17. Previous agreement*
>
> All previous agreements between the club and the player are hereby can-celled with- out prejudice to any rights or obligations which shall have accrued or become due between the parties prior to the date of termination of any previous agreements.'

**24** Mr Kerr says that these clauses, in particular clause 15, are designed to preclude any factual investigation into the pre-contract history. They are fatal to the contention that the contract here was part oral and part written. I agree that the purpose of an entire agreement clause, such as clause 15, is to defeat any argument that the contract is qualified or supplemented by any oral collateral warranty or oral term existing outside the four corners of the written document. However, I am not persuaded that a clause such as clause 17 has any bearing on oral terms alleged to have been agreed simultaneously with the written contract. In the end, Mr Kerr did not press his reliance on clause 17. He did not need to, in view of the plain terms of clause 15.

**25** Entire agreement clauses are an increasingly common feature of sophisticated and detailed contract documents and, if clearly worded so as to do so, are effective to exclude claims based on collateral warranties or oral terms like Mr White's claim in the present case. In *Deepak Fertilisers and Petrochemicals*

*Corporation v ICI* [1999] 1 Lloyd's Rep 387, one of the clauses under consideration provided that: 'This contract comprises the entire agreement between the parties... and there are not any agreements, understandings, promises or conditions, oral or written, expressed or implied, concerning the subject-matter which are not merged into this contract and superseded hereby...' Rix J and the Court of Appeal (at p. 395) held that the opening phrase, in conjunction with the words 'and there are not any agreements, understandings, promises or conditions, oral or written' plainly excluded a claim based on a collateral warranty.

**26** Another example of an entire agreement clause is given in *Chitty on Contracts,* 28th edn, at para 12–102. The opening words are 'This agreement contains the entire and only agreement between the parties...' Mr Williams seized on this example to draw a distinction between a clause which said that the written contract was the entire *and only* agreement between the parties and a clause such as clause 15 which simply stated that the contract was the entire agreement and included no further exclusion of other potential agreements not reflected in the written document. In my judgment, this is a distinction without a difference so far as the effect of the clause is concerned.

**27** In *Inntrepreneur Pub Co v East Crown Ltd* [2000] 3 EGLR 31, Lightman J was confronted by an entire agreement clause in these terms:

> '14.1 Any variations of this agreement which are agreed in correspondence shall be incorporated in this agreement where that correspondence makes express reference to this clause and the parties acknowledge that this agreement (with the incorporation of any such variations) constitutes the entire agreement between the parties.
> 14.2 Before executing this agreement the tenant and guarantor have:
> 14.2.1 received independent professional advice about its terms; or
> 14.2.2 been advised of the wisdom of taking independent professional advice but have chosen not to do so and accordingly they have not relied upon any advice or statement of the company or its solicitors.'

**28** In response to the claim in that case, the defendant raised a counterclaim which was founded on an alleged collateral agreement. The claimant argued that. the defendant was precluded from doing so by the 'entire agreement' wording of clause 14.1. In holding that clause 14.1 was effective to preclude reliance on the alleged collateral agreement, Lightman J made the following observations (at p. 33A-E), with which I respectfully agree:

> 'The purpose of an entire agreement clause is to preclude a party to a written agreement from threshing through the undergrowth and finding, in the course of negotiations, some (chance) remark or statement (often long-forgotten or difficult to recall or explain) upon which to found a claim, such as the present, to the existence of a collateral warranty. The entire agreement clause obviates the occasion for any such search, and the peril to the contracting parties posed by the need that may arise in its absence to conduct such a search. For such a clause constitutes a binding agreement between the parties that the full contractual terms are to be found in the document containing the clause and not elsewhere, and that, accordingly, any promises or assurances made in the course of the negotiations (which, in the absence of such a clause, might have effect as

> a collateral warranty) shall have no contractual force, save in so far as they are reflected and given effect in that document. The operation of the clause is not to render evidence of the collateral warranty inadmissible in evidence, as is suggested in *Chitty on Contract* (28th edn) vol. 1 para 12–102; it is to denude what would otherwise constitute a collateral warranty of legal effect.
>
> Entire agreement clauses come in different forms... In this case the formula used is abbreviated to an acknowledgment by the parties that the agreement constitutes the entire agreement between them. That formula is, in my judgment, amply sufficient to constitute an agreement that the full contractual terms to which the parties have agreed to bind themselves are to be found in the agreement and nowhere else. That can be the only purpose of the provision...'

**29** It is impossible to draw any material distinction between clause 15 and the clause in the *Inntrepreneur Pub* case or, in my judgment, between clause 15 and the clause given as an example in *Chitty*. Clause 15 precludes Mr White's contention that the contract here included a separate oral term not reflected in the written document or that anything said by Mr de Scossa at the meeting on 12 May which is not reflected in the written wording may nevertheless have acquired contractual force as a contract term or collateral warranty.

**30** In *Inntrepreneur Pub Co v East Crown Ltd*, Lightman J held that clause 14 had two features. The first was the entire agreement provision in clause 14.1. The second was the wording in clause 14.2 which acknowledged that the tenant and guarantor had not relied upon any advice or statement of the company. He described the latter provision as one which set out to exclude liability for misrepresentation and breach of duty. Clause 15 contains a similar additional feature whereby the parties acknowledge that they 'have not relied upon oral or written representations made to them by other persons, its employees or agents' (it was agreed that 'its' must refer back to 'each party' at the beginning of the clause). Mr Kerr submits that this wording clearly has the effect of excluding Mr White's alternative primary claim based on misrepresentation, because it precludes him from asserting the necessary reliance. It is convenient to deal with that argument at this juncture.

**31** The argument is one which was not pleaded in the defence. It was raised for the first time in Mr Kerr's skeleton argument. No objection was taken to it by Mr Williams, either when the skeleton argument was served, or when he opened the case, or when Mr Kerr addressed it in the course of his closing submissions. But in his own closing speech Mr Williams riposted that if Mr Kerr was right that clause 15 had the additional effect of excluding the claim in misrepresentation, the clause could only do so if the exclusion satisfied the test of reasonableness in s.3 of the Misrepresentation Act 1967. Furthermore, he pointed out that the burden of proving reasonableness would lie on Bristol. At this point Mr Kerr intervened to say that he had not appreciated, from the absence hitherto of any objection to his reliance on clause 15 in this context, that Mr Williams was relying on s.3 by way of an answer. Mr Kerr said that, if Mr Williams was to be allowed to do so, Bristol would want to argue that s.3 did not apply but that, if it did, the exclusion was reasonable. On this last point Mr Kerr said that Bristol would want to call evidence.

**32** It is unfortunate that clause 15 was not pleaded: but there are mitigating circumstances. The time for preparation of the trial has been somewhat compressed. Mr Kerr was only instructed by Bristol at a comparatively late stage and the amended defence and counterclaim which he drafted, and which was only served on 3 August 2001, had to deal not only with the re-amended particulars of claim dated 13 July, but also with further draft amendments notified in letters from Mr White's solicitors dated 30 July and 1 August.

**33** The impact of s.3 on a provision in an entire agreement clause stating that the parties have not relied on any pre-contract representations was considered in *Government of Zanzibar v British Aerospace Ltd* [2000] 1 WLR 2333 (at 2344B-2347F). But in that case the clause also contained an express exclusion of 'all liabilities for and remedies in respect of any representations' and, in his judgment, Judge Jack QC focused on this part of the wording as attracting the test of reasonableness in s.3. He held that he could not decide the issue of reasonableness without hearing evidence.

**34** Clearly, if the wording in the last one-and-a-half lines of clause 15 is subject to s.3, it will not be possible to determine the effect of the clause on Mr White's claim in misrepresentation without hearing further evidence. However, there is likely to be an argument as to whether s.3 applies at all. In *McGrath v Shah* [1989] 57 P & CR 452, Mr John Chadwick QC (as he then was) held (at p. 459) that s.3 had no application to an entire agreement provision. In *Inntrepreneur Pub Co v East Crown Ltd*, Lightman J agreed with him (p. 33F). Neither case appears to have been cited to Judge Jack in *Government of Zanzibar v British Aerospace.* Nor do they appear to have been cited to the Court of Appeal in *E Grimstead & Sons Ltd v McGarrigan* (unreported) 27 October 1999; Court of Appeal (Civil Division) transcript no.1733 of 1999. That case is referred to by Judge Jack in *Government of Zanzibar v British Aerospace* at some length. It is a case in which Chadwick LJ delivered the leading judgment. He held that a clause containing an express acknowledgment by the parties that they have not relied upon any oral or written representations could exclude a claim in misrepresentation by founding an evidential estoppel. But he expressly declined to decide whether an acknowledgment of non-reliance fell within s.3. He did not have to decide that issue, because he held that the clause in that case satisfied the test of reasonableness in any event. The contract also contained an entire agreement provision, but the appellant did not seek to rely on it.

**35** None of these authorities, with the exception of the *Inntrepreneur Pub* case, were referred to at the trial for the reasons I have indicated. I have to decide how the matter should proceed from here. I am not minded to refuse permission to Mr Kerr to rely on clause 15 as a defence to the misrepresentation claim simply because it was not pleaded as a defence, any more than I am minded to refuse Mr Williams leave to respond to that defence by relying on s.3. In the light of the cases I have just referred to, it seems to me that there are arguments which both parties have not addressed to me, and might wish to address, as to whether, and if so how, clause 15 operates to exclude the claim in misrepresentation. There may also be further evidence which one or other or both parties would wish me to hear on these issues. In the end, I think it best to leave the parties to review their respective positions after reading this judgment, in particular the reasons given for the conclusion in paras 43 to 47 below that the alleged representation was not made. Unless that conclusion is to be challenged on appeal, the application of clause 15 to the misrepresentation claim is academic.

**36** Before coming to the factual issue of what was said at the meeting on 12 May 2000, I should deal with the alternative way in which the claim in contract is advanced. Mr Williams submits that, even if there was no oral term by reason of clause 15, the wording in italics in the definition of the basic salary ('*Should the player, for whatever reason, not join Bristol Rugby Club the £15,000 will of course be repayable*'), when properly construed in the context of the statements made at the 12 May meeting, confers on Mr White a right to opt out.

**37** Even accepting the premise that Mr White's version of what was said at the meeting is the correct one, I am not persuaded that the words in italics bear this interpretation. They deal with what is to happen to the advance if, 'for whatever reason', Mr White does not join the club. The wording is not apt to create a right not to join: it simply addresses what is to happen if Mr White does not. The phrase 'for whatever reason' is general. Whilst it probably does cover the present situation, where Mr White is simply refusing to join Bristol because he has changed his mind, it covers any situation regardless of the reason for not joining. The reason might be that, through no fault of Mr White, the contract had become impossible to perform by the starting date of 1 July 2001. Alternatively the reason could be that, through the fault of one or other party, Mr White was unable to join, or that one or other party had changed its mind. In these circumstances arguments might arise as to whether the party responsible for the fact that Mr White had not joined was in breach of the contract. But the agreement is that the advance of salary is to be refunded pending resolution of those arguments.

**38** If I am right that the words in italics are a contractual provision providing for what is to happen to the advance of salary in the circumstances I have described, Mr Williams says that the words are redundant unless they confer on his client a right to opt out of the contract with impunity any time prior to the starting date. The reason, he says, is that the common law would provide for restitution of the advance in any circumstance where it became impossible, through no fault of either party, for Mr White to join Bristol. I think that there are three answers to this submission. The first is that it is not at all unusual for contracts to make express provision for what is to happen in certain eventualities, notwithstanding that the common law may provide its own remedy. Force majeure clauses are classic example. The second is the point I have already mentioned, namely, that the words do not purport to absolve Mr White from the consequences of a decision not to join Bristol if the implementation of that decision would arguably be a breach of the contract. If the words were to have that effect they would have needed at least to say 'if for whatever reason, *such as the cancellation of this contract by either party*...' The third point is that if the words are to be construed as Mr Williams submits, they must confer a similar right of opt-out on Bristol. Maybe Mr Williams would concede that they do, but the only indication in the circumstances surrounding the concluding of the contract that Bristol might want an opt-out was if Mr White failed a medical. There is nothing to suggest that Bristol wanted a general right to reconsider the signing. And so far as passing a medical is concerned, I do not understand from the evidence I have heard that Bristol wanted the right to cancel the contract if Mr White failed his first medical on grounds falling short of those which might frustrate the contract. I take the reference by Mr de Scossa to 'failing a medical' to have been a reference to Mr White being found medically so unfit that it was unlikely he would be able to play for the club at all or at least for a very long time.

**39** For the above reasons, I do not consider that either way in which Mr White seeks to contend that the contract was subject to an express opt-out clause in his favour can possibly succeed.

**40** In consequence, it is strictly unnecessary for me to consider the evidence concerning the statement alleged to have been made by Mr de Scossa. But I shall do so in case I should be wrong in my conclusions thus far or in case Mr White should hereafter successfully demonstrate that, by virtue of s.3, clause 15 is not effective to preclude a claim in misrepresentation.

**41** As I have already said, I heard oral evidence from Mr White, Mr Burton and Mr de Scossa about the meeting on 12 May 2000. I also heard oral evidence from Mr Andrew Reid, Bristol's financial controller, and Mr Ryan. Mr Reid's evidence concerned his understanding of the circumstances in which the salary advance would be repayable and the mechanics of the payment of the £15,000. His understanding derived from what he was told. It is no disrespect to him to say that his evidence is of little assistance in determining what was said at the meeting on 12 May. The evidence of Dean Ryan was largely directed to matters which may be relevant to whether the contract has been terminated for breach, and is also of little assistance in determining what was said at the meeting on 12 May.

**42** I have outlined the conflict of recollection between Mr White on the one hand and Mr de Scossa and Mr Burton on the other about the statements made by Mr de Scossa in the course of the meeting. It is for Mr White to prove that Mr de Scossa made a statement or statements to the effect that he could opt out of the contract and, as I have already observed, in so far as Mr White asserts that these statements acquired contractual force as an oral term of the contract, this burden is a heavy one.

**43** I have come to the clear conclusion that that burden has not been discharged. I can summarise my reasons under three heads: (1) in the circumstances it is inherently improbable that Mr de Scossa should have granted an opt-out, (2) the terms in which the opt-out was allegedly granted are not sufficiently clear, and (3) of the three vital witnesses on this issue I find Mr de Scossa and Mr Burton the more reliable. I will expand on each of these heads in turn.

**44** A remarkable feature of the evidence is that, contrary to the instructions which Mr Harry said in his letter of 31 January he had received from his client, there was no suggestion that Mr White was unwilling to sign the contract unless he was given an opt-out. None of the witnesses said that Mr White asked for an opt-out or needed to be given one. The evidence was that he came to the meeting ready and willing to sign the contract which Mr Burton had negotiated for him. He did not need persuading. There was no hint that he hesitated or expressed himself in any way reluctant to sign the contract. It was not said by anyone that he held out for some further inducement. On Mr White's case, this was an unsolicited and unprompted concession by Mr de Scossa. There was simply no need for Mr de Scossa to give Mr White a right to cancel the contract. Since Mr de Scossa thought that Mr White was probably the best prop in the northern hemisphere and he appeared willing to sign for Bristol, it is hard to see why he would jeopardise the whole deal by telling Mr White, just before he was going to sign, that, in effect, he could tear the contract up if he had second thoughts.

**45** Mr White's evidence as to exactly what was said to give rise to this contractual opt-out was not entirely satisfactory. True, the meeting was some 15 months ago. On the other hand, he might have better cause to remember what was said at a meeting focused on his personal future than Mr Burton or Mr de Scossa, whose professional lives were concerned with the careers of many players. However, Mr White was unable in the witness box to pinpoint with any precision the words which led him to believe that he could treat himself as released. When he was cross-examined, it transpired that the words placed in quotation marks in his witness statement, namely, 'If you don't come to Bristol or change your mind, £15,000 has to come back', were not the words which he recollected Mr de Scossa as saying but merely an expression of his understanding of what was said. When pressed to say whether the quote reflected his understanding or represented the actual words, his answer was, 'That is what I thought he said'. Elsewhere in his statement Mr White says that Mr de Scossa 'made it clear to me that even if I signed the service contract, I had the option not to go to Bristol'. Yet Mr White did not suggest that Mr de Scossa said anything other than the single remark, the effect of which is summarised in the quote. In my judgment it is not self-evident that those words do confer a general right to opt out in any circumstances, including even a change of mind. At the very least one would have expected Mr White or Mr Burton to have sought clarification from Mr de Scossa that that was precisely what he meant. But there is no evidence that there was ever any discussion of the point. Certainly nothing was said by Mr White to Mr de Scossa to indicate that he understood he was being given a right to opt out and that in view of that concession was now happy to sign. I am left with the firm impression that, at best, if the remark attributed to Mr de Scossa was made, Mr White read more into it than was justified. On balance, however, I do not think that the evidence substantiates that Mr de Scossa made the statement alleged or any statement which could fairly have been interpreted as giving Mr White the right to opt out which he claims.

**46** It follows, in my view, that this is not a case where I have to decide the conflict of recollection by reference to the impression which the witnesses made in giving their evidence. Nevertheless, if I am driven to choose between them on this ground, I prefer the evidence of Mr de Scossa and Mr Burton to that of Mr White. All three witnesses gave their evidence in a clear and forthright manner and were undoubtedly trying to give as truthful a version of what happened at the meeting as they could remember. However, I consider that Mr White's recollection is the more likely to be at fault for two reasons. The first is that on two aspects of the case I do not believe that the answers Mr White gave in cross-examination were accurate. He admitted that he had discussed the Bristol contract with Mr Burton in the winter of last year, but denied that Mr Burton had told him that the deal was binding. He further said that lack of support from Mr Burton for his attempt to get out of the Bristol signing had played no part in his decision to dismiss Mr Burton as his agent early in January. Mr White also said that he was not introduced to his new agent, Mr Powell, until after he had dismissed Mr Burton. I am afraid that I find all of these answers impossible to accept. Mr Burton's evidence-in-chief, which I accept because it is inherently likely to have been the case and because Mr Burton was not challenged about it in cross-examination, is that he did indeed discuss the Bristol contract with Mr White towards the end of last year and told him that It was a binding commitment. In the circumstances it is simply not credible to suppose that Mr Burton's stance was not a factor in Mr White's decision to get rid of him in the New Year. Moreover, it is, to my mind, equally incredible that at such a critical juncture in his career Mr White should have dispensed with the services of so well-known and experienced an agent as Mr Burton, having no one in mind to replace him. I find as a fact that the overwhelming probability is that Mr White already had in mind to appoint Mr Powell as his agent when he dismissed Mr Burton, and that one reason for the change was that he believed that Mr Powell would be of greater assistance than Mr Burton in getting him out of the Bristol contract.

**47** The second reason why I find that Mr White's recollection is likely to be less reliable than that of Mr de Scossa or Mr Burton is that, in not dissimilar circumstances, Mr White misunderstood the result of the negotiations for his previous contract with Saracens. On that occasion, the evidence was that the signing was an altogether more hurried affair. Nevertheless, Mr White believed that he had been given an oral assurance by the club that he could leave at the end of 1999 if he so chose. When he tried to do so, he was told that the contract contained a break clause in favour of Saracens, which could be operated after the first six months; but no break clause in his favour. He therefore had to stay with Saracens for the full two years of his contract. As I say, the circumstances of the negotiations and signing were different: but not so different as to dispel the impression which I have that Mr White has a tendency not fully to understand the implications of remarks made in the course of negotiating a deal or the implications of signing a detailed written contract in which such remarks have not been translated into an express term. For Mr de Scossa, and certainly for Mr Burton, negotiating and concluding player contracts was second nature.

**48 Misrepresentation**

The claim in misrepresentation is advanced as an alternative case. The premise here is that the contract contained no opt-out clause. The false representation was that it did. I add in parenthesis that Mr Williams abandoned the submission that the representation was that Bristol would not enforce the contract if the advance of salary was repaid. For that statement of intent to found a misrepresentation, Mr Williams would have to contend that the Mr de Scossa did not genuinely have that intention when he made the representation, and Mr Williams very properly disclaimed any imputation of fraud or dishonesty on the part of the club.

**49** It will be plain from the findings I have already made about the 12 May meeting that I am not persuaded that any such representation was made. However, if it was made, and clause 15 does not preclude Mr White from raising it, there is no dispute that he relied on the representation in signing the contract, in other words, that it was an inducement to him to contract. The issue is whether Mr White had lost the right to rescind before he purported to exercise that right on 31 January 2001.

**50** Rescission for misrepresentation is an equitable remedy. The right to rescind a contract for innocent or negligent misrepresentation can be lost by affirmation, by the inability of the court to restore the parties to the position they were in before the contract was made (which may arise from any change of circumstance making restitution impossible, including the intervention of third party rights), and by lapse of time, if of sufficient duration that it would be unjust to allow the remedy to be exercised after so long a delay.

**51** It is common ground here that it was still possible to restore the parties to their pre-contract positions on 31 January 2001. But Mr Kerr submits that Mr White should have exercised his right, if any, to rescind the contract much earlier than the end of January. By that time, he says, Mr White had elected to affirm the contract, alternatively it was too late to rescind having regard to the prejudice to Bristol caused by the delay.

**52** It is a fundamental principle that there can be no affirmation without actual or constructive knowledge. The affirming party must be aware or ought reasonably to be aware of the right which he will forgo by his election to maintain the contract. The key question, therefore, is, 'when should Mr White reasonably have appreciated that the contract did not allow him to opt out and therefore, that a misstatement had been to him?' Mr Williams submits that that point did not arise until he tested the water by getting his new agent, Mr Powell, to meet Bristol representatives on 23 January 2001. Mr Kerr submits that Mr White was sufficiently alerted to the possibility that the contract did not permit him an opt-out when he was told so by Mr Burton some time in the winter of 2000. He was then at least on inquiry that his agent did not share his interpretation of the deal which had been struck.

**53** I think the latter view is correct. Neither Mr White nor Mr Burton could remember precisely when they discussed the contract, but it must have been some time in late November or December 2000. Mr Kerr argues that Mr White should therefore have exercised his right to rescind well before 31 January 2001, especially if the court takes the view, as I have already indicated that I do, that one reason why Mr White dismissed Mr Burton on 5 January 2001 was that he did not agree with Mr White's view that he was free to get out of the Bristol contract. If he could sack Mr Burton by 5 January, he could notify Bristol that he was rescinding the contract within the same timeframe.

**54** Whilst I recognise the force of this submission, the court must look at the whole picture. From Mr White's perspective, I do not think it was unreasonable to have waited until his new agent was engaged before purporting to rescind. From Bristol's perspective, I do not think that much changed between the end of November 2001 and the end of January 2002. According to Mr Kerr, Bristol suffered prejudice by the lapse of that interval in that they lost two valuable months in which they could have been looking for an alternative prop forward. This is true: but the disadvantage was not great. Mr Williams points to rule 6.3 of the RFU Code of Conduct which precludes member clubs from approaching players under contract to other clubs without the written consent of the other club until the last three months of that player's contract, The RFU Code of Conduct was drawn up in January 2000 and only subscribed to by Bristol on 22 December 2000. I was not told if a similar restriction had operated between Premiership clubs previously. At any rate, this is the first year in which the new Code has operated and, if rule 6.3 is loyally observed by the clubs, it would suggest that the bulk of activity in the transfer market takes place from about the beginning of April. Against that background, I do not think that the fact that Bristol were deprived of looking to recruit elsewhere between end November 2000 and end January 2001 is so significant that Mr White should be held to have lost the right to rescind.

**55** If the alleged misrepresentation was made, I would not have been inclined to hold that Mr White lost the right to rescind by not purporting to exercise that right until 31 January 2001. However, the point is immaterial, since I am satisfied that the alleged misrepresentation was not made.

**56** **Estoppel**

Mr Williams accepts that the plea in estoppel (which by rights should have appeared in a reply rather than in the particulars of claim) adds nothing to the claim in misrepresentation. Moreover, he concedes, rightly in my judgment, that any estoppel is defeated by the acknowledgment of non-reliance in clause 15. I therefore say no more about the estoppel argument.

**57** It follows that the contract of 12 May 2000 is binding on Mr White unless it has been terminated for breach.

**58** **Whether the contract has been terminated by the acceptance of a repudiatory breach**

Mr White's consistent stance since 31 January 2001 is that he does not regard himself as in any way bound to join Bristol. His position is that he renounces the contract of 12 May 2000 in its entirety. That much is common ground. It is also common ground that a repudiation by the employee does not automatically discharge a contract of employment. The employer is entitled to keep the contract open for performance even though he cannot obtain an order for specific performance of it (see Megarry V-C in *Thomas Marshall Ltd v Guinle* [1978] IRLR 174 at 180). However, if the employer wishes to enforce the contract to the extent of obtaining an injunction to restrain the employee from committing breaches of his obligations under it, the court may, in the exercise of its discretion, require him to provide the employee with all of his contractual benefits, which would include paying the employee's salary (see *Evening Standard Ltd v Henderson* [1987] IRLR 64).

**59** Mr Williams submits that, contrary to their stated position, Bristol have accepted his client's conduct as terminating the contract. By the conclusion of the evidence it was plain that he was relying on the following steps taken by Bristol as leading inevitably to this conclusion:

(i) they have tried offering Mr White a different contract containing an improved deal;
(ii) they did not include him in their squad to tour Argentina in July 2001;
(iii) they have not included his name in the list of first team players on their website (until this was rectified in the course of the trial);
(iv) they have not invited him to any training sessions since 1 July 2001 and have not offered him any work;
(v) they have not paid his salary;
(vi) they have counterclaimed against him in this action damages which include the potential loss of a transfer fee;
(vii) they have abandoned at the trial their pleaded counterclaim for an injunction restraining him from signing with another club without their prior written consent;
(viii) they have not invoked disciplinary procedures against him.

**60** An acceptance of a repudiation must be unequivocal. If a party says one thing and does another, his conduct is equivocal. It is certainly possible for a party to a contract to declare that he is treating it as open for performance by the other party who is in repudiatory breach, but to be held in reality to have accepted the breach as bringing the contract to an end. But it would be an unusual case and would probably only arise where there was conduct on the part of the innocent party which had effectively disabled him from entertaining further performance by the party in breach. Transposing this scenario into the present context, it would not have availed Bristol to announce that Mr White's contract was being kept open if at the same time they had engaged a prop forward to replace him. However, it is not suggested that Bristol have done anything quite so final.

**61** The second point, which is a concomitant of the first, is that the court must examine the whole course of the innocent party's conduct in order to ascertain whether, in truth, the repudiation has been accepted. It is not legitimate to look at certain acts in isolation. This aspect of the task is made easier in the present case because Mr Williams does not contend that any one of the above steps on its own constituted an acceptance of Mr White's repudiation. Rather, he relies on the cumulative effect of all of these steps as compelling that conclusion.

**62** Mr Williams began by drawing a distinction between the club's words and deeds. According to him, all of the evidence on which Mr Kerr relied in support of Bristol's contention that they had kept the contract alive consisted of statements and declarations of intent. Bristol's actions were very different. I cannot accept this distinction. Even if it were permissible in this situation to apply the maxim 'actions speak louder than words' (which I do not think it is), the matters on which Mr Kerr relies include actions as well as words. First and foremost, Bristol returned the cheque for £15,000 on 12 February. That was positive conduct which asserted that, so far as Bristol were concerned, the contract was still on foot. Second, they drafted the revised contract of 11 May and put it to Mr White in an endeavour to persuade him to change his mind again. The revised contract was clearly prepared without prejudice to Bristol's contention that Mr White was already under an existing commitment to join them. The significant feature of the offer is that it publicly reinforced the club's declared position that they still wanted Mr White to join them and to play for them. Viewed in its proper context, I am quite unable to interpret the offer as being inconsistent with the stance that Mr White was still bound by the contract of 12 May 2000. Third, Bristol posted on their website on 10 July what was described at the time as 'an impassioned plea' by their chairman to Mr White to think again. All the while, Bristol's declared position, in correspondence with Mr White's solicitors, in this action and even in the evidence of the head coach, Mr Ryan, has been that the contract is open and Mr White is welcome to join the club at any time.

**63** Against that background, I address the various steps relied on by Mr Williams, remembering that it is the cumulative effect of all of them which he says shows that the contract is at an end. I have already expressed my view about (i). I regard it as excessively technical to treat the offer of improved terms in this situation as somehow involving a recognition that the old terms were no longer binding. To my mind it simply shows that the old terms, although binding, are not good enough to persuade Mr White to move.

As to (ii) to (iv), Mr White knows the club's address better than the club knows Mr White's address. He has made no attempt to contact the club, let alone to visit the club's premises. He made no secret of the fact, in his oral evidence, that he was not in the least bit perturbed or disappointed at not having been selected to tour Argentina or at not being named on the website or at not being invited to training sessions. The reason is not hard to divine. He has had no intention of responding to any such invitation were it to have been made. Indeed, his legal representatives would have insisted that he reject any such overtures lest it compromise his stated position that he was under no binding commitment to the club. I am therefore quite unable to attribute to the absence of such 'window-dressing' measures on the part of Bristol an acknowledgment by them that the contract was at an end. In the light of this conclusion it is unnecessary, after all, for me to consider whether the conduct in (ii) to (iv) above is excusable in any event by reason of the injunction. Had that been a live issue, I would have been inclined to hold that it was not. If Bristol were in any quandary as to the ambit and effect of the injunction, they could and should have returned to the court for clarification.

**64** I will leave the non-payment of salary until last, and come to the counterclaim in this action. It is true that a claim for loss of a transfer fee presupposes that the contract is terminated. If it were alive, Bristol would still be entitled to exact a transfer fee from any other club wishing to sign Mr White. But the counterclaim is expressly pleaded as being subject to Bristol's principal defence that Mr White's breach has not been accepted and that the contract remains in being. The counterclaim for the potential loss of a transfer fee is not prefaced by the phrase 'if, which is denied, the contract has been terminated by reason of the claimant's breach…', but it is quite plain that it should be read in that way. The damages counterclaimed therefore give no clue as to whether the breach has been accepted. Nor, in my judgment, does the abandonment of the counterclaim for an injunction. This head of counterclaim was abandoned by Mr Kerr because he recognised that, if Bristol were to seek such relief, the court might only be willing to grant it on terms that Bristol pay Mr White's salary. Bristol is not willing to pay Mr White's salary whilst he refuses to make himself available to train and to play for the club, and so this particular counterclaim was dropped. There is nothing more to be read into it. As for disciplinary procedures, the contract provides for disciplinary procedures to apply 'If the player is in breach of any obligation in this agreement' (clause 10.1). I have my doubts whether this provision applies where the player is not in breach of a particular obligation in the contract but repudiates the entire agreement and refuses even to join the club. Assuming, however, that it does, I do not read clause 10 as imposing on Bristol an obligation to invoke disciplinary procedures whenever a player is in breach. The clause merely provides that, if a player who is in breach is to be punished or suffer any sanction, the disciplinary procedures annexed to the contract are to be applied. Bristol are free in any given situation to decide not to institute disciplinary procedures. In the present case it is rather obvious why they have decided not to do so. It would only exacerbate the situation. Moreover, disciplinary procedures conducted in the absence of Mr White, and against the background that he does not recognise the validity of the contract, would be fraught with legal problems. The fact that Bristol have not invoked disciplinary procedures against Mr White is no indication whatever that Bristol are accepting that the contract is terminated.

**65** I come, finally, to the non-payment of salary. The basic common law principle underlying the payment of salary pursuant to a contract of employment is that the salary is earned in return for the specified work. As the work is done, a debt arises, from employer to employee, for the salary due in respect of it. Aside from any express contractual provision to the contrary, if the employee does not work, eg because he goes on strike, no salary is due or payable. If he renders partial performance of his duties, the consequences probably depend on whether the employer accepted that performance. The present case is one of total non-performance. Unless Mr White can show that the contract otherwise provides, he is entitled to no salary because he has done no work.

**66** It is entirely possible for a contract of employment to provide that, even where the employee refuses to turn up for work through his own free choice and through no fault of the employer, he should receive his full wage; but I do not read the contract of 12 May 2000 as containing any such provision. Mr Williams submitted that, read as a whole, the contract entitled Mr White to be paid his salary unless either payment of it was suspended because Mr White was incapacitated by illness, injury or accident for a period of more than 26 weeks (clause 8.3), or Mr White was fined in the course of disciplinary proceedings and the fine was deducted from his salary pursuant to the set-off agreed in clause 10.2. However, Mr Williams conceded that there might be debate as to the salary entitlement of a player who was renouncing the entire contract. I agree. For my part, I am unable to accept that the contract of 12 May 2000, on its proper construction, confers any entitlement on Mr White to be paid his salary in the circumstances of this case. Mr Williams's alternative argument is that the non-payment of salary, and all the other steps enumerated above, constitute a repudiation of the contract by Bristol If they are not an acceptance of a repudiation. Ultimately he conceded, in my view rightly, that the non-payment of salary could not, on its own, amount to a repudiatory breach by the club. It is simply relied on as evidence, together with the other enumerated matters, of either a repudiation or an acceptance of a repudiation by Bristol. In my judgment it is negligible support for either, especially against the background of Bristol's declared intention that if only Mr White will join the club they will pay him his salary and, better still, will pay him at the enhanced rate in the revised contract of 11 May 2001 if he agrees to it.

**67** It only remains for me to mention one further argument which Mr Williams advances in support of his contention that Bristol has accepted Mr White's conduct as bringing the contract to an end. He submits that there are two limbs to a contract of employment: the first is the master and servant relationship and the second is the contractual engagement between the parties on the various terms agreed. The former is usually regarded as being founded on mutual trust and confidence. In the present case, Mr Williams submits that that trust and confidence has been irrevocably destroyed. All that is left is the contractual engagement. What purpose, asks Mr Williams rhetorically, can Bristol possibly have in keeping the contractual engagement alive when the master and servant relationship has been destroyed? If the logic of this argument is accepted it comes very close to acknowledging that an employee can, by unilaterally refusing to serve his employer, bring about the termination of the contract of employment. This is precisely the result which Megarry V-C declined to countenance in *Thomas Marshall Ltd v Guinle.* In any event, I would not concede that the master and servant relationship has irretrievably broken down in this case. Bristol still have a legitimate aim of building bridges with Mr White if only he will change his mind and honour the contract. Second, I would hold that, even if the master and servant relationship is destroyed and Bristol can expect nothing more than that Mr White will remain recalcitrant on the touchline, they have a legitimate interest in seeking to preserve the contractual arrangement with him, if only to secure the payment of a transfer fee when he seeks to move to another club.

**68** It will be apparent from what I have said thus far that, with no disrespect to the ingenuity of Mr Williams, I am no more impressed with his argument that all of the steps relied upon as evidencing an acceptance of a repudiation by Bristol may equally be regarded as evidence of a repudiation by them, than I am with the alleged acceptance of the repudiation. A repudiation of a contract is not to be lightly inferred (see Lord Wright in *Ross T Smyth v Bailey* [1940] 3 AER 60 at 71). If, as I find, Bristol have not accepted Mr White's repudiation of the contract as bringing it to an end, they have certainly not repudiated it themselves. In my judgment, no reasonable person, viewing the whole of Bristol's conduct since the end of January 2001, would infer that Bristol had repudiated the contract.

**69** Accordingly, I hold that the contract of 12 May 2000 remains valid and subsisting. I will hear the parties' advocates on clause 15 and s.3 and, subject to that point, on the form of order which is appropriate.

## *19.5.2 Appendix 2*

### Some Specimen 'Boilerplate' Clauses*

**'Force Majeure' Clause**

If either party is prevented from fulfilling its obligations under this Agreement by reason of any supervening event beyond its control (including but not limited to war national emergency flood earthquake strike or lockout (other than a strike or lockout induced by the party so incapacitated) or illness) the party unable to fulfil its obligations ('the incapacitated party') shall immediately give notice of this to the other party and shall do everything in its power to resume full performance of its obligations as soon as possible.

Subject to compliance with the requirements of the foregoing sub-clause the incapacitated party shall not be deemed to be in breach of its obligations under this Agreement during the period of incapacity and the other party shall continue to perform its obligations under this Agreement save only in so far as they are dependent on the prior performance by the incapacitated party of obligations which it cannot perform during the period of incapacity.

If the period of incapacity exceeds [6] months then this Agreement shall automatically terminate unless the parties first agree otherwise in writing.

**'Entire Agreement' Clause**

This Agreement contains the whole agreement between the parties and supersedes any prior written or oral agreement between them in relation to its subject matter and the parties confirm that they have not entered into this Agreement upon the basis of any representations that are not expressly incorporated into this Agreement. No oral explanation or oral information given by any party shall alter or affect the interpretation of this Agreement.

**Reservation of Rights Clause**

All rights not specifically and expressly granted to the Licensee by this Agreement are reserved to the Licensor.

**Joint and Several Clause**

All agreements on the part of either of the parties which comprises more than one person or entity shall be joint and several.

**Notices Clause**

Any notice consent or the like (in this clause referred to generally as 'notice') required or permitted to be given under this Agreement shall not be binding unless in writing and may be given personally or sent to the party to be notified by

* By I.S. Blackshaw.

pre-paid first class post or by electronic mail or facsimile transmission at its address as set out above or as otherwise notified in accordance with this clause.

Notice given personally shall be deemed given at the time of its delivery.

Notice sent by post in accordance with this sub-clause shall be deemed given at the commencement of business of the recipient on the second business day following its posting Notice sent by electronic mail or facsimile transmission in accordance with this sub-clause shall be deemed given at the time of its actual transmission provided that the sender does not receive any indication that the electronic mail message or facsimile transmission has not been successfully transmitted to the intended recipient.

**No Modification Clause**
This Agreement may not be modified except by an instrument in writing signed by both of the parties or their duly authorised representatives.

**Waiver Clause**
The failure by either party to enforce at any time or for any period any one or more of the terms or conditions of this Agreement shall not be a waiver of them or of the right at any time subsequently to enforce all terms and conditions of this Agreement.

**Severance Clause**
In the event that any provision of this Agreement is declared by any judicial or other competent authority to be void voidable illegal or otherwise unenforceable or indications of this are received by either of the parties from any relevant competent authority the parties shall amend that provision in such reasonable manner as achieves the intention of the parties without illegality or at the discretion of the parties it may be severed from this Agreement and in either event the remaining provisions of this Agreement shall remain in full force and effect.

**Schedules Clause**
The Schedules to this Agreement shall form an integral part of this Agreement and shall be construed accordingly.

**Survival of Terms Clause**
The warranties and indemnities contained in this Agreement and the provisions for payment of and accounting in respect of Royalties and other moneys due to the Licensor under the terms of this Agreement shall survive the termination or expiry of this Agreement.

**Agency Clause**
The Licensor confirms that he has appointed the Agent to act on the Licensor's behalf in all matters arising out of this Agreement including the collection and receipt of all payments due to the Licensor under this Agreement and declares that

the receipt of the Agent shall be a good and sufficient discharge to the Licensee in respect of such payments

Any notice served on the Agent will be deemed to have been served at the same time on the Licensor.

**VAT Clause**
All sums payable to the Licensor under this Agreement are exclusive of VAT which shall where applicable be paid in addition at the rate in force at the due time for payment subject to the Licensor either supplying a VAT invoice to the Licensee or informing the Licensee of his VAT registration number.

**Rights and Remedies Cumulative Clause**
All rights and remedies available to the parties under the terms of this Agreement and under the general law shall be cumulative and no exercise by either of the parties of any such right or remedy shall restrict or prejudice the exercise of any other right or remedy granted by this Agreement or otherwise available to it.

**Confidentiality and Non-Disclosure Clause**
The terms and existence of this Agreement are confidential to the parties.

Each party agrees to maintain secret and confidential all confidential information obtained by the other both pursuant to this Agreement and prior to and in contemplation of it (including but not limited to information concerning the existence and terms of this Agreement) and all other information that it may acquire from the other in the course of this Agreement and to respect the other's proprietary rights in such material and to use the same exclusively for the purposes of this Agreement and to disclose the same only to its professional advisers and those of its employees officers agents and representatives pursuant to this Agreement (if any) to whom and to the extent that such disclosure is reasonably necessary for the purposes of this Agreement (and which employees officers agents and representatives shall be made aware of and required to acknowledge these confidentiality arrangements in writing).

The obligation set out in the prior sub-clause shall not apply to any information which:

(1) prior to its receipt from one party was lawfully in the possession of the other and at its free disposal or
(2) is subsequently disclosed to the recipient party without any obligations of confidence by a third party who has not derived it directly or indirectly from the other party or
(3) is or becomes generally available to the public through no act or default of the recipient party or its agents employees officers and representatives or
(4) is required by law to be disclosed.

**Binding Effect Clause**

This Agreement shall bind and enure to the benefit of the parties and their respective permitted assigns personal representatives and successors in title.

**Assignment Clause**

Neither party may assign the benefit of nor its obligations under this Agreement without the prior written consent of the other party.

It shall be a condition of any assignment that the assignor shall procure that the assignee enters into a direct written covenant with the other party to this Agreement whereby the assignee undertakes to observe and perform all of the assignor's obligations under this Agreement.

**No Partnership Clause/Relationship of the Parties Clause**

Nothing in this Agreement shall be deemed to constitute a partnership between the parties nor the relationship of employer and employee under a contract of service nor the relationship of principal and agent.

The parties to this Agreement shall act towards one another at all times and for all purposes under this Agreement as independent contractors.

**Third Parties Clause**

This Agreement does not create any right enforceable by any person not a party to it.

For the avoidance of doubt this Agreement does not create any right enforceable to any successor or assignee of either party to this Agreement.

**'Good Faith' Clause**

The Parties to this Agreement hereby mutually agree and declare that both during and after the termination of this Agreement for whatever cause they will act at all times and for all purposes towards one another in the utmost good faith with a view to giving full legal and practical effect to the terms and conditions whether express or implied of this Agreement and any amendment or amendments thereof.

**'Covenant for Further Assurance' Clause**

The Parties to this Agreement hereby mutually agree and declare that both during and after the termination of this Agreement for whatever cause they will at their own expense and in a timely manner sign and execute any and all such further documents and deeds and do any and all such further acts and things as may be required to give full legal and practical effect to the terms and conditions whether express or implied of this Agreement and any amendment or amendments thereof.

# Chapter 20
# Concluding Remarks

The promotion, marketing and commercialisation of sport, sports events and sports personalities—collectively, in the jargon, Sports Marketing—has come a long way since the early pioneering days of Mark McCormack, of IMG, and Horst Dassler of ADIDAS and ISL fame. Indeed, Sports Marketing has developed and grown into a sophisticated, complex and discreet multi-billion US$ global 'industry'. The part played by the Law to date in these developments is quite significant and will continue to be of critical importance, in the foreseeable future, as Sports Marketing further develops and expands.

With the advent of the digital broadcasting age and the inexorable rise of the Internet, both of which provide innovative marketing and commercial platforms for sport, Sports Marketing is set to grow even further and reach stratospheric heights in terms of reach and revenues, offering new challenges not only to the creativity of sports administrators and marketers, but also placing further demands upon the technical skills and resourcefulness of their legal and other professional advisers, especially in the drafting of the corresponding Sports Broadcast and New Media Agreements, which are highly complex and technical and require particular attention.

In this process of the continuing and further development and evolution of the commercialisation of sport, often nowadays referred to as the 'commodification of sport',[1] the need for well-drawn and creative Sports Marketing Agreements of various kinds will also be of crucial importance. In particular, these Agreements will need to cope with the new and ever-widening and expanding concepts of Sports Marketing and faithfully reflect the underlying commercial, financial and technical arrangements.

---

[1] For an interesting explanation of this phenomenon, whereby sport is now a commodity to be bought, sold, traded and commercially exploited like any other goods and services, see *Sports Law* by Simon Gardiner, Mark James, John O'Leary, Roger Welsh, Ian Blackshaw, Simon Boyes and Andrew Caiger, Third Edition, 2006, Cavendish Publishing, London and Sydney, at pp. 53–55.

I. S. Blackshaw, *Sports Marketing Agreements: Legal, Fiscal and Practical Aspects*, ASSER International Sports Law Series, DOI: 10.1007/978-90-6704-793-7_20,

Sports Marketing Agreements, as has been seen in this Book, also need to include suitable provisions dealing with all kinds of unfair competition, especially, 'Ambush Marketing', which, like Sports Marketing itself, has also become more sophisticated and more widespread, not least because of the very valuable commercial opportunities riding on major sports events, in order to protect not only the integrity of the sport concerned, but also the commercial and financial interests of the sports bodies concerned, as well as other major rights holders, such as their corporate sponsors, whose financial contributions—in the form of sponsorship fees—cannot be underestimated or, indeed, taken for granted. Even the sports business is a highly competitive one in a financial and business sense.

Likewise, Sports Marketing Agreements need to take into account the Fiscal and European Union aspects, which impact—more and more—upon their validity and viability. The need, therefore, for Sports Marketing arrangements to be structured from a tax efficient point of view and appropriate Agreements entered into to reflect these aims cannot be overstated. This is especially true, as has been explained in the Book, in the case of Sports Image Rights Agreements in Chap. 15 on 'The Fiscal Aspects'. Why pay more tax than is properly due if, quite legitimately, one can arrange matters in order to significantly reduce this financial burden? As has been well said, the only certainties in life are taxes and death!

Again, Sports Marketing Agreements also need to include suitable Alternative Dispute Resolution (ADR) Clauses for the more effective, efficient and less time consuming and more economical settling *extra-judicially* of disputes arising under, out of or in relation to these Agreements, whenever and wherever it is appropriate to do so. However, as has been pointed out, ADR is not a panacea for the settlement of all disputes—in certain cases, the Courts are the appropriate forum.

As has been demonstrated in the Book when negotiating and drafting Sports Marketing Agreements, planning and precision are the essential hallmarks of this process, for it has also been well said that, if a Sports Marketing deal makes commercial and financial sense, it also makes legal sense, and, therefore, with care, it is relatively easier to draft a meaningful and legally effective corresponding Agreement. But, be very careful not to overload Sports Marketing Agreements with unnecessary clauses; only include those clauses that serve a particular purpose in relation to the deal at hand and merit inclusion. Gone are the days when lawyers were paid by the folio—the length of the documents they produced! And always edit your drafts to ensure that there are no inconsistencies in them and that they are clear and make sense.

The Author and the Publishers sincerely hope that this Book will make a useful and significant contribution to the exciting and challenging brave new world of Sports Marketing, which, despite the general economic downturn and recession, seems to be going from strength to strength, and also provide helpful guidance on the planning and drafting of a variety of Sports Marketing Agreements , especially from a legal, fiscal and practical point of view.

But, of course, the final judgement on these matters rests with you the readers and users of this Book!

# Table of Legislation



I. S. Blackshaw, *Sports Marketing Agreements: Legal, Fiscal and Practical Aspects*, ASSER International Sports Law Series, DOI: 10.1007/978-90-6704-793-7,

# Table of Cases



I. S. Blackshaw, *Sports Marketing Agreements: Legal, Fiscal and Practical Aspects*,
ASSER International Sports Law Series, DOI: 10.1007/978-90-6704-793-7,

# Index



I. S. Blackshaw, *Sports Marketing Agreements: Legal, Fiscal and Practical Aspects*, ASSER International Sports Law Series, DOI: 10.1007/978-90-6704-793-7,

MIX
Papier aus verantwortungsvollen Quellen
Paper from responsible sources
FSC® C105338

If you have any concerns about our products,
you can contact us on
**ProductSafety@springernature.com**

In case Publisher is established outside the EU,
the EU authorized representative is:
**Springer Nature Customer Service Center GmbH**
**Europaplatz 3, 69115 Heidelberg, Germany**

Printed by Libri Plureos GmbH
in Hamburg, Germany